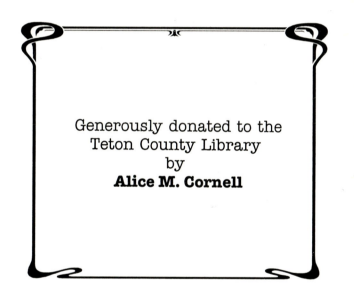

News of the
Plains and Rockies
Volume 6

NEWS

of the

PLAINS AND ROCKIES
1803-1865

Original narratives of overland travel and adventure
selected from the Wagner-Camp and Becker
bibliography of Western Americana

VOLUME 6
K: Gold Seekers, California, 1849–1856
L: Railroad Forerunners, 1850–1865

Compiled and Annotated by

David A. White

THE ARTHUR H. CLARK COMPANY
Spokane, Washington
1999

In memory of
THOMAS WINTHROP STREETER
1883-1965

Lawyer, financier, altruist, renowned book collector, authoritative
bibliographer, honorary Doctor of Literature
from Dartmouth College

Copyright 1999 by
DAVID A. WHITE

LIBRARY OF CONGRESS CATALOG CARD NUMBER 96-3726
ISBN-0-87062-231-5 (complete set)
ISBN 0-87062-256-0 (volume 6 only)

Orders and information:
THE ARTHUR H. CLARK COMPANY
P.O. Box 14707
Spokane, WA 99214

White, David A., 1927-
    News of the Plains and Rockies, 1803-1865: original narratives of overland
travel and adventure selected from the Wagner-Camp and Becker bibliography of
Western Americana / compiled and annotated by David A. White.
        p.   cm.
    Includes bibliographical references.
Contents: v. 6, K: Gold Seekers, California, 1849–1856; L: Railroad Forerunners,
1850–1865
ISBN 0-87062-231-5 (set: alk paper). —ISBN 0-87062-256-0 (v. 6: alk. paper)
    1. West (U.S.)—Description and travel—Sources.   2. West (U.S.)—
—Discovery and exploration—Sources.   3. Exploration—
—West (U.S.)—Sources.   I. Wagner, Henry Raup, 1862-1957. Plains &
the Rockies.   II. Title.
F591.W67 1996   96-3726
978'. 02—dc20   CIP

Contents

Maps, Tables, Facsimiles

Preface

This sixth of eight volumes in the series brings to light 21 short primary accounts of the courage and travels of the California gold seekers and the railroad-route explorers in the early West. Volumes 1 through 5 covered the first American explorers, the fur hunters, Santa Fe adventurers, settlers, religious pioneers, Indian observers, soldiers, scientists, artists, and later government explorers. Future volumes will deal with gold seekers of Pike's Peak and other areas, and mail carriers. Volume 8 will contain the series index.

In the 168 news reports reprinted in the whole series, the pioneers in their own words tell of adventuring in the Plains and Rockies from 1803 to 1865, from the Louisiana Purchase to the building of the Pacific Railroad. Although few of the white male authors espoused the Indian point of view, the courage and sacrifices of the First Americans, who lost homes and ways of life, are evident throughout.

The notes for each reprint provide the significance, background, biographies, itineraries, travel times, highlights, repercussions, references, and listings of the first printing and of other reprints. Present-day localities given with the itineraries appear in commonly available road atlases. The perspective for each section contains an index map and a travel-time table summarizing the Who, When, Where, and How Long of each exploration. Anything in quotes is the way it was originally. Document resettings are verbatim et literatim. I thank Robert A. Clark for his encouragement and advice. Alan Jutzi and Lisa Ann Libby of the Huntington Library, San Marino, California, kindly provided a facsimile of Thomas H. Benton's 1854 speech, L5. Todd I. Berens provided some excellent critical commentary.

REFERENCES

Simple in-text citations of authors and dates document sources. Details of these specific references consulted are listed at the end of each annotation; these entries give dates of writing or reminiscing as well as those of publication or reprinting. General bibliographic references for each reprint, as given in the heading of the annotation, are listed in detail only in this Preface. Similarly, general biographic references cited at the end of each biography are detailed only in this Preface. Any abbreviated citation—name or abbreviation only, name and page only, name and number only—should be looked for in the Preface. Government documents are identified by number of Congress/Session, House or Senate document number, and volume number in the serial set, e.g., 15/1 H197, serial 12.

GENERAL BIBLIOGRAPHIC REFERENCES

Ayer, Edward E, 1912 and 1928, Narratives of captivity among the Indians of North America: Chicago, 120 p., 339 items, and Supplement 1 by Clara A. Smith, 49 p., 143 items.

Barry, Louise, 1972, The beginning of the West: Topeka, Kansas State Historical Society, 1296 p.

Cowan, Robert E., and Robert G. Cowan, 1933 (1964 reprint), A bibliography of the history of California 1510-1930: Los Angeles, 926 p.

Crawley, Peter, and Chad J. Flake, 1984, A Mormon fifty: Provo, [36] p., 50 items.

Currey, Lloyd W., and Dennis G. Kruska, 1992, Bibliography of Yosemite, the Central and Southern Sierra, and the Big Trees 1839-1900: Los Angeles, 234 p., 411 items.

Eberstadt, Edward, 1935-56 (1965 reprint), The annotated Eberstadt catalogs of Americana, numbers 103 to 138: N.Y., 4 v.

Field, Thomas W., 1873 (1951 reprint), An essay towards an Indian bibliography: Columbus, 430 p., 1708 items.

Flake, Chad J., 1978, A Mormon bibliography 1830-1930: Salt Lake City, 825 p., 10145 items.

Gilcrease. Hargrett, Lester, 1972, The Gilcrease-Hargrett catalogue of imprints: Norman, 400 p.

Graff. Storm, Colton, 1968, A catalogue of the Everett D. Graff collection of Western Americana: Chicago, 854 p., 4801 items.

Greenwood, Robert, 1961, California imprints 1833-1862, a bibliography: Los Gatos, 524 p., 1748 items.

Haferkorn, Henry E., 1914 (1970 reprint), The war with Mexico 1846-1848: N.Y., 93 p.

Hasse, Adelaide R., 1899 (1969 reprint), Reports of explorations printed in the documents of the United States government: N.Y., 90 p.

Holliday, W. J., 1954, Western Americana: N.Y., Parke-Bernet Galleries, 266 p., 1233 items.

Howes, Wright, 1962, U.S.Iana (1650-1950): N.Y., 652 p., 11620 items.

Jones. Eames, Wilberforce, 1964, Americana collection of Herschel V. Jones: N.Y., 3 v., 1746 items.

Kurutz, Gary F., 1997, The California gold rush: San Francisco, 771 p., 706 items.

Lowther, Barbara J., 1968, A bibliography of British Columbia 1849-1899: Victoria, 328 p., 2173 items.

Mattes, Merrill J., 1988, Platte River Road narratives: Urbana, 632 p., 2082 items.

Meisel, Max, 1924 (1967 reprint), A bibliography of American natural history: N.Y., 3 v., 1700 p.

Miles, George, 1991, Go West and grow up with the country: Worcester, 45 p., 44 items.

Mintz, Lannon W., 1987, The Trail, a bibliography [of travelers to CA, OR, UT, MT] 1841-64: Albuquerque, 201 p., 627 items.

NUC. National Union Catalog, 1968-80, Pre-1956 imprints: Washington, 685 volumes and supplements.

Paher, Stanley W., 1980, Nevada, an annotated bibliography: Las Vegas, 558 p., 2544 items.

Peel, Bruce B., 1973, A bibliography of the Prairie Provinces to 1953, 2d ed.: Toronto, 780 p., 4408 items.

Phillips, P. Lee, 1901 (reprint, n.d.), A list of maps of America in the Library of Congress: N.Y., 1137 p.

Pilling, James C., 1885 (ca. 1975 reprint), Proof-sheets of a bibliography of the languages of the North American Indians: Brooklyn, 4303 entries.

Rader, Jesse L., 1947, South of Forty, the Mississippi to the Rio Grande: Norman, 336 p., 3793 items.

Rittenhouse, Jack D., 1971, The Santa Fe Trail, a historical bibliography: Albuquerque, 271 p., 718 items.

Smith. Mayhew, Isabel, 1950, Charles W. Smith's Pacific Northwest Americana, 3d ed.: Portland, 381 p., 11298 items.

Soliday. Decker, Peter, 1940-1945, A priced and descriptive checklist...of the important library (in four parts) formed by George W. Soliday: N.Y., 682 p., 5082 items.

Strathern, Gloria, 1970, Navigations, traffiques & discoveries 1774-1848, British Columbia: Victoria, 417 p., 631 items.

Streeter. Parke-Bernet Galleries, 1966-1970, The celebrated collection of Americana formed by the late Thomas Winthrop Streeter: N.Y., 8 v., 3002 p, plus indices, 4421 items.

Streeter TX. Streeter, Thomas W., 1955-1960, Bibliography of Texas 1795-1845: Cambridge, 5 v., 1661 items.

UPRR. Library Bureau of Railway Economics, 1922 (reprint, n.d.), A list of references to literature relating to the Union Pacific System: Newton MA, 299 p.

Vaughan, Alden T., 1983, Narratives of North American Indian captivity, a selective bibliography: N.Y., 363 items.

WC or Wagner-Camp. Camp, Charles L., 1953, Henry R. Wagner's The Plains and the Rockies, a bibliography of original narratives of travel and adventure 1800-1865, third edition: Columbus, 601 p., 540 items.

WCB or Wagner-Camp-Becker. Becker, Robert H., 1982, Henry R. Wagner & Charles L. Camp, The Plains & the Rockies, a critical bibliography of exploration, adventure and travel in the American West 1800-1865, fourth edition: San Francisco, 745 p., 700 items.

Warren, Gouverneur K., 1859 (1861 printing), Memoir to accompany the map of the territory of the United States from the Mississippi River to the Pacific Ocean: Washington, Reports of [Pacific Railroad] Explorations and Surveys, "36/2 S -," serial 768, v. 11, 115 p.

Wheat, Carl I., 1957-63, Mapping the Transmississippi West: San Francisco, 5 v. in 6, 1302 items.

Wheeler, George M., 1889, Memoir of explorations and surveys 1500-1880, [including reprint of Lt. Gouverneur K. Warren's memoir, 1859, for 1800-1857 surveys]: Washington, U.S. Geographical Surveys West of the One Hundredth Meridian, v. 1, Appendix F, p. 481-745.

GENERAL BIOGRAPHIC REFERENCES

ACAB, 1887-1899, Appleton's cyclopaedia of American biography: N.Y., 6 v.

Bancroft, Hubert Howe, 1882-1891, Works: San Francisco, 39 v.

Columbia. Harris, William H., and Judith S. Levey, 1975, The new Columbia encyclopedia: N.Y., 3052 p.

Congress. Jacob, Kathryn A., and Bruce A. Ragsdale, 1989, Biographical directory of the United States Congress 1774-1989: Washington, 100/2 S100-34, 2104 p., 11000 entries.

Cullum, George W., 1891 3d ed., Biographical register of the officers and graduates of the U. S. Military Academy: Boston, v. 1 nos. 1 to 1000, v. 2 nos. 1001 to 2000.

DAB, 1928-1937 (1943 reprint), Dictionary of American biography: N.Y., 20 v. plus index.

DCB, 1966-1979, Dictionary of Canadian biography: Toronto, 4 v.

DNB, 1885-1900, Dictionary of national biography: London, 63 v.

Dockstader, Frederick J., 1977, Great North American Indians: N.Y., 386 p.

Ewan, Joseph and Nesta, 1981, Biographical dictionary of Rocky Mountain naturalists: Utrecht, 253 p., 1000 entries.

Hafen, LeRoy, 1965-1972, The mountain men and the fur trade of the Far West: Glendale, 10 v., 292 biographies.

Heitman, Francis B., 1903 (1965 reprint), Historical register and dictionary of the United States Army: Urbana, 2 v., 1069 and 626 p.

Hodge Frederick Webb, 1910-1911, Handbook of American Indians north of Mexico: Washington, Bureau of American Ethnology Bull. 30, 2 v., 972 and 1221 p.

Jenson, Andrew, 1901-1920 (1971 reprint), Latter-Day Saint biographical encyclopedia: Salt Lake City, 3 v.

Lamar, Howard R., 1977, The reader's encyclopedia of the American West: N.Y., 1306 p.

McHenry, Robert, 1978 (1984 reprint), Webster's American military biographies: N.Y., 548 p. 1033 entries.

McKelvey, Susan D., 1955, Botanical exploration of the Trans-Mississippi West 1790-1850: Jamaica Plain MA, 1144 p.

Merrill, George P., 1906, Contributions to the history of American geology: Washington, Annual Report of the Smithsonian for 1904, p. 189-733.

NCAB, 1898-1941, National cyclopaedia of American biography: N.Y., 29 v. plus index.

Samuels, Peggy and Harold, 1976 (1985 reprint), Samuels' encyclopedia of artists of the American West: n.p., 549 p., 1700 entries.

Thrapp, Dan L., 1988 and 1994, Encyclopedia of frontier biography: Glendale and Spokane, 4 v., 1698 and 610 p., 5530 entries.

TX Handbook. Webb, Walter P., H. Bailey Carroll, and Eldon S. Branda, 1952 and 1976, The handbook of Texas: Austin, 3 v., 3075 p.

TX Handbook, New. Tyler, Ron, ed. in chief, 1996, New Handbook of Texas: Austin, 6 v., 6945 p.

Waldman, Carl, 1990, Who was who in Native American history: N.Y., 410 p.

SPECIAL MAP REFERENCES

Franzwa, Gregory M., 1982, Maps of the Oregon Trail: Gerald MO, 292 p., mostly maps.

Franzwa, Gregory M., 1989, Maps of the Santa Fe Trail: St. Louis, 196 p., mostly maps.

Goetzmann, William H., and Glyndwr Williams, 1992, Atlas of North American exploration: N.Y., 224 p., mostly maps.

Oregon-California Trails Association, 1991 (1993 2d ed.), Robert L. Berry, ed., Map of western emigrant trails: Independence, 1 sheet.

Section K
Gold Seekers, California, 1849–1856

Gold Seekers, California, 1849-1856
Perspective

The First News In your comfortable eastern home, you are reading the morning edition of the *New York Herald* on Saturday, August 19, 1848. You come across the headline, "Affairs in Our New Territory. Interesting Narrative of the Voyage to California, by a New York Volunteer—Commodore Stockton, General Kearny, Colonel Freemont—San Francisco—Customs—Religion—Cattle—Produce—Press—Inhabitants &c., &c." You read on, "San Francisco, Alto California, April 1, 1848. Being a subscriber to and constant reader of your invaluable paper in New York…I take the liberty of addressing you these lines." The equivalent of four large book pages later, after news of the voyage to California, its conquest, its towns, prices, the "lazy" inhabitants, their religion, the herds and crops, laws, Indians, and mere mention of "the mines of gold, silver, quicksilver, saltpetre, coal, &c., &c.," you find, "I am credibly informed that a quantity of gold, worth in value, $30, was picked up lately in the bed of a stream of the Sacramento." This is immediately followed by accounts of coal, copper, saltpeter, sulfur, asphalt, limestone, soda springs, and salt.

Then you see, "The gold mine discovered in December last [January 24, 1848, by James W. Marshall], on the south branch of the American fork, in a range of low hills forming the base of the Sierra Nevada, distant thirty miles from New Helvetia, is only three feet below the surface, in a strata of soft sand rock. From explorations south twelve miles, and north five miles, the continuance of this strata is reported, and the mineral said to be equally abundant, and from twelve to eighteen feet in thickness; so that, without allowing any golden hopes to puzzle my prophetic vision of the future, I would predict for California, a Peruvian harvest of the precious metals, as soon as a sufficiency of miners, &c., can be obtained." (This section was copied with minor changes from Dr. Victor J. Fourgeaud's account in the *California Star* of April 1.) Immediately following are lists of ship arrivals, and values of imports and exports. The concluding statement is, "We expect to be disbanded next fall, many of the regiment not relishing the country." So it's only $30, and the New York Volunteers want only to come home.

Since you also read *Niles' Register,* you know that cries of gold in California are not new. On October 8, 1842, the report was, "CALIFORNIA GOLD. A letter from California, dated May 1, says they have at last discovered gold, not far from San Fernando, and gather pieces the size of an eighth of a dollar. Those who are acquainted with these 'placeres,' as they call them, (for it is not a mine), say it will grow richer, and may lead to a mine. Gold in the amount of some thousands of dollars, has already been collected." On April 6, 1844, *Niles'* reported, "CALIFORNIA...On the 16th January a vessel arrived at Tepic, bringing about thirty ounces of the purest gold ore taken from a vein lately discovered, and said to extend upwards of thirty leagues. Some weeks ago over 300 men left for Upper California." Baron von Humboldt had observed way back in 1811, "The more imperfectly a country is known, and the farther it is removed from the best peopled European colonies, it more easily acquires a reputation for great metallic wealth...The peninsula of California was for a long time the *Dorado* of New Spain. A country abounding in pearls ought, according to the vulgar logic, also to produce gold, diamonds, and other precious stones in abundance."

The eastern papers did not directly copy the first solid California announcements of the gold discovery. The San Francisco *Californian* of March 15, 1848, stated on its last page, "GOLD MINE FOUND—In the newly made raceway of the Saw Mill recently erected by Captain Sutter, on the American Fork, gold has been found in considerable quantities. One person brought thirty dollars worth to New Helvetia, gathered there in a short time. California, no doubt, is rich in mineral wealth; great chances here for scientific capitalists. Gold has been found in almost every part of the country" (Paul 1966, Bieber 1937). Nor did the eastern press pick up on other salient comments in Fourgeaud's April 1 article in the *California Star:* "We saw a few days ago a beautiful specimen of gold from the mine newly discovered on the American Fork. From all accounts the mine is immensely rich; and already, we learn, the gold from it, collected at random and without any trouble, has become an article of trade at the upper settlements. This precious metal abounds in this country."

Publisher Samuel Brannan sent 2,000 copies of the April 1 *Star* east to Missouri via Salt Lake City, by private express leaving San Francisco April 3, according to Hafen (1954). Kit Carson brought a copy to Washington in early August, 1848 (see 5:J1 Itinerary). But no eastern paper seems to have reprinted the gold news therein. Even the August 19 *Herald* article "was deemed of such little importance that it was not copied by the rest of the press" (Bieber 1937); it was reprinted in full by Douglas C. McMurtrie in 1943, and by Peter Browning in 1995. (See K3 for more on the *Star-Californian* relations.)

The Official News   Navy Lt. Edward Fitzgerald Beale arrived in Washington, D.C., on September 16, 1848, bearing California nuggets and official dispatches of the gold discovery from the Navy and Consul Thomas O. Larkin. Beale had dashed across Mexico on horseback in 15 days, evading bandits at an average 66 miles per day (see 5:J9 Itinerary). The New Orleans *Daily Picayune* of September 12 published an August 20 report from Mexico City that "Lieutenant Beale carries with him highly interesting information in regard to the discovery of gold mines in Upper California." On September 14 the Philadelphia *North American and United States Gazette* published a July 2 letter from Navy Chaplain Walter Colton, Alcalde of Monterey: "But a recent gold discovery has thrown all others into the shade…The tract of land where the gold is found covers a hundred miles in one direction and fifty in another. It is said that ten thousand men in ten years could not exhaust it."

The Washington *Daily Union* of September 17 briefly excerpted Larkin's July 1 report to the Navy, including the statement, "I have myself seen eight men in a company average $50 each per day for two or three days." The *Union* editor had seen Beale on his arrival: "His dispatches and the accounts he himself brings confirm what is said in Mr. Larkin's letter above of this new El Dorado…We received these details last evening at too late an hour to bring them out this morning." (Bieber 1937.)

Larkin wrote letters signed "Paisano" on June 1 and July 1, 1848, that were published on September 18 and 17, respectively, by the *New York Herald*. The June 1 letter said, "We are in danger of having more gold than food…but onward goes this fever, raging strongly in the brains of all, depopulating towns, carrying off men, women, and children. A six-year-old child can gather $2 or $3 a day…Who would print *Heralds* at $3 or $4 a day, when in the Far West he could gather a cup of gold a day? I had better stop as I am, or your men will quit as it is." The *Herald* summed up on September 21: "All Washington is in a ferment with the news of the immense bed of gold, which, it is said, has been discovered in California. Nothing else is talked about." (Browning 1995.)

The Army sent its official samples and news of the gold discovery by sea with Lt. Lucien Loeser, who had to reach Panama by way of Peru. The New Orleans papers announced his arrival there on November 23. He had visited the mines himself, carried Col. Richard B. Mason's August 17 report (which reached Washington by other means November 22; see next heading), and confirmed all that Beale had said. Loeser brought 230 ounces of gold in a tea caddy to Washington on December 7. (Bieber 1937.)

The President's News   On page 10 of his annual message of December 5, 1848, President James K. Polk announced, "It was known that mines of the precious metals existed to a considerable extent in California at the time of its acquisition. Recent discoveries render it probable that these mines are more extensive and valuable than was anticipated. The accounts of the abundance of gold in that territory are of such an extraordinary character as would scarcely command belief were they not corroborated by the authentic reports of officers in the public service." Appended to this message was a folding map of the "Gold and Quicksilver District" by Lt. Edward O. C. Ord, dated July 25, 1848.

Accompanying Polk's message was a letter from U.S. Consul Thomas O. Larkin, dated June 1, 1848, from San Francisco: "I have to report to the State Department one of the most astonishing excitements and state of affairs now existing in this country, that, perhaps, has ever been brought to the notice of the government. On the American fork of the Sacramento and Feather river, another branch of the same, and the adjoining lands, there has been, within the present year, discovered a placer, a vast tract of land containing gold, in small particles." Larkin reported in his next dispatch of June 28, "I have visited a part of the gold regions, and found it all I had heard, and much more than I anticipated."

Next in Polk's message was the August 17, 1848, long report of Col. Richard B. Mason on his July visit to the placers. (Lt. William T. Sherman wrote in 1875, "I prepared with great care the letter to the adjutant-general of August 17, 1848, which Colonel Mason modified in a few particulars.") By July, San Francisco was "almost deserted." Twenty-five miles up the American River, "men were at work in the full glare of the sun washing for gold, some with tin pans, some with close woven Indian baskets, but the greater part had a rude machine known as the cradle. This is on rockers, six or eight feet long, open at the foot, and, at its head, has a coarse grate or sieve; the bottom is rounded with small cleets nailed across...the current of water washes off the earthy matter, and the gravel is gradually carried out at the foot of the machine, leaving the gold mixed with a heavy fine black sand above the first cleets. The sand and gold mixed together are then drawn off through augur holes into a pan below, are dried in the sun, and afterwards separated by blowing off the sand. A party of four men, thus employed, at the Lower Mines, averaged a hundred dollars a day...[I heard] that upwards of four thousand men were working in the gold district, of whom more than half were Indians; and that from $30,000 to $50,000 worth of gold, if not more, was daily obtained...The discovery of these vast deposits of gold has entirely changed the character of Upper California." Mason's report was quoted in many of the early guidebooks on California.

The Presidential confirmation elevated the nation's gold fever to the boiling point, excepting only a few scattered naysayers. After reprinting the message on December 7, the *New York Herald* momentarily worried: "Meantime, we should like to have some of this gold dust from California assayed and analyzed, to ascertain whether it is mica, or iron pyrites, or gold." But next day the paper published Mason's glowing report. On December 9 the *National Intelligencer* cautioned, "Adventurers are starting off for California by the dozen, the score, and the hundred, hardly allowing themselves time to pull on their boots…[but they] may find themselves in a fool's paradise at the end of their journey…All is not gold that glistens." (Browning 1995.)

On December 11, 1848, the U.S. Mint found the California gold brought by Lt. Loeser to be extraordinarily pure; samples at the War Department drew great crowds (Bieber 1937). The rush became an landslide.

The Yellow Fever of 1849   Eastern newspapers were preoccupied with reporting the gold rush throughout 1849, as ably recorded by Browning in 1995. As one further example, the following notes of enterprise and trouble come from my copy of the Massachusetts *Salem Register* of April 23, 1849:

"CALIFORNIA OUTFITS. To the Travelling Public!…It is amusing to see Oak Hall daily thronged with various groups—old men, young men, boys—rich and poor,—very few admitting where they are bound,—but the Outfit selected from the following useful Mining Articles, generally tells the story:—Feather River Overcoats—Spanish or California Cloaks, adapted to the double purpose of Cloak by day, and Blanket at night—Sutter's Long Mining Waistcoat…Oil, or India Rubber suits—Life Preservers—Isthmus Bags, for pack mules…Gold Bags…Fancy Striped Travelling Shirts—Red Flannel Shirts and Drawers…El Dorado Caps—California Hats—Bowie Knives…Mining Clothes, for laboring class…We hope that all who are going will succeed to their anticipations, but they will not unless they lay in a good supply of the above named articles."

"ROMANTIC." Parents whose daughter was too young for marriage compromised: One hour after the wedding, "the bridegroom took leave for California, thence to return in two years and claim his wife."

"BAD NEWS FROM A CALIFORNIA COMPANY…the destruction of life on the Rio Grande, by cholera, has been most fearful." Seven survivors headed back to New England after their leader, who left a wife and seven children in Marblehead, died in Brownsville.

"TWO MONTHS LATER FROM CALIFORNIA." A preacher newly arrived in San Francisco from Hawaii was setting up a church and temperance society: "We hear the excitement in the States is very great, and that, across the continent, by the Isthmus, and around the Horn, great numbers are flocking hither. But, oh! the worldliness—the moral desolation, this gold fever creates!" So he elevated the fever by adding, "New discoveries of the precious dust are constantly being made."

"A CALIFORNIA ADVENTURER MURDERED IN MEXICO." A gold seeker got halfway across Mexico, only to be killed by a guard at Irapuato over a 12-cent breakfast-bill dispute.

The Cholera The scourge of the gold rush was the cholera epidemic of 1849-54. Charles E. Rosenberg's 1962 book describes how the disease spread from India to Europe, then crossed the Atlantic in a packet ship from France to reach New York on December 1, 1848. The 300 immigrants were quarantined in the customs warehouses. Many were sick, some died, and half of them scaled the walls to spread the disease to the town. Cold winter temperatures slowed its progress, but it raged in warm New Orleans, seeded from a German ship. Gold seekers infected the continent, albeit with decreasing intensity westward. One-tenth of the people in St. Louis and in the Rio Grande Valley died.

In 1849 English physician John Snow recognized that cholera was transmitted from the excrement and vomit of its victims, via contaminated water, unwashed hands, and uncooked fruits and vegetables. But his was only one of many theories, and he could not prove it until 1855. In 1849 the clergy said that cholera was God's retribution for avarice—most particularly, gold seeking. They also blamed poverty, filth, lechery, gluttony, alcoholism, and Sabbath-breaking. Doctors were in low repute. None of their treatments worked. Their unfortunate patients were vigorously bled, purged, puked, sweated, and immersed in ice water or rubbed with whiskey; they were given calomel (mercury), laudanum (opium), pepper, mustard plasters, whiskey-soaked meal, sulfur pills, electric shocks, strychnine, and tobacco-smoke enemas. President Zachary Taylor's solution was to declare August 3 a day for national prayer and fasting. The miracle was that anybody survived.

Holliday estimated in 1981 that cholera killed 1,500 Forty-niners east of Ft. Laramie. That year it also killed at least 1,500 Pawnees, 25 percent of the whole tribe (Hodge 1910), and unknown numbers of other tribes.

Not until 1866 did New York's new Metropolitan Board of Health successfully battle an epidemic by cleaning up mountains of filth, quarantining, burning victims' bedding and clothing, disinfecting the surroundings with chloride of lime, and boiling drinking water. The responsible bacterium, *Vibrio comma*, was discovered in 1883.

The Way West Artist John Wesley Jones took eastern audiences the easy way over the trail to the California gold fields. He had sketched his own way out in 1850 and Daguerreotyped the way back in 1851. He turned these early portraits of the Plains and Rockies into a "Pantoscope" of about 35 successive panoramic paintings of the trail, plus about 25 scenes in California. These were scrolled across a stage (see Naef and Wood 1975). In the 1854 pamphlet written about Jones by journalist George Spencer Phillips, the impressed editor of the *Boston Journal* was quoted: "At the rising of the curtain we seem suddenly translated to the far Missouri River, amid all the bustle and excitement of camp life. Thence we start with the emigrant on his long journey, across the broad prairies of Nebraska...climb the Black Hills and beetling crags of the Rocky Mountains, and visit the Mormon in his polygamous home, beside the mysterious waters of Great Salt Lake...following the dreary, tortuous course of the Humboldt...and forcing the terrific defiles and perpetual snows of the Sierra Nevada Mountains...We are introduced to the miner in his home and at his labors...and after walking the streets of Sacramento...and San Francisco...we return home perfectly delighted and almost persuaded that we have actually been to California and really 'seen the elephant.'"

Jones's companions on the trail were a little racier than most, at least by the record. There was one episode of wife-swapping. Another rascal was drummed out of camp: "While the captain had been out on guard duty, the villain had invaded the sanctity of his family tent, and crawled into bed beside the captain's wife; but his actions and his voice betrayed him. A frightful scream aroused the camp."

John Hawkins Clark, 1852 overlander, wrote west of Ft. Laramie, "The sublime, the pathetic, the outrageous and the ridiculous follow each other in quick succession on this road." He had just passed the grave of a murderer "hung upon the spot." Then he saw an old lady's grandson, whose head had been run over by the wagon wheels the day before, back swinging from the wagon cover. When another 1852 train arrived in California, 17-year-old Eliza Ann McAuley wrote that the miners gathered around to get a glimpse of her, "a woman being a rare sight here. One enthusiastic miner declared he would give an ounce of gold dust for the sight of a woman's sunbonnet." Forty-niner Charles R. Parke, who had two cows, on July 4 found a snow bank and did "something no other living man ever did in this place and on this sacred day of the year, and that was to make *Ice Cream at the South Pass of the Rockies.*"

The reprints of this section include five representative 1849-53 gold-rush guidebooks for the main Oregon-California Trail, one piece of overland fiction, and one account of harrowing travel on the Southern Trail. Each of the five guides is here reprinted probably for the first time, two of them from their only known copies. Joseph H. Colton's early 1849 map had a brief text, K1, that, like most of the 1848-49 guides produced in the east, was made up of clippings from published sources pasted together with naive advice. Sidney Roberts's 1849 propaganda, K2, touted the Salt Lake route for his own personal gain. The 1850 guide of Brigham H. Young and John Eagar, K3, accurately covered two popular new trail segments, the Carson River and Salt Lake Cutoff, that Mormons had opened to wagons in 1848. The 1853 guides of Francis M. Drake and Dr. J. Tarbell, K4 and K5, were accurate in the Plains but had inflated mileages down the Humboldt. In K6 is a fictitious, mixed-up view of the Western landscape by an anonymous Englishman who never saw it. But K7 is the real-life drama of a passenger train thrown on its own in the Southwestern deserts by swindler and murderer Parker H. French.

Other 1848-49 and 1851-53 guidebooks are summarized in K1 and K4, respectively.

The itineraries, summarized in Table Ka, compare travel times and distances for various routes from the Missouri to the Sacramento, 1849-53. Table Kb gives today's mileages for most segments of the California trails. It also provides Up-Down Factors that give some idea of the topographic difficulty of each segment. But no factor system yet devised can portray the challenge of the horrendous hulk of the Sierra. When the gold seekers got over this last barrier, they had a pretty good notion of what the elephant really looked like.

The Wife Back Home   William and Sabrina Swain were married less than two years, and had a 10-month-old daughter, when William took off for California from Youngstown, New York, in April, 1849. In 1981 James S. Holliday published their poignant correspondence:

Sabrina addresses William on April 15: "I want very much to describe my feelings as near as I can, but in doing so I hope not to crucify yours. I feel as though I was alone in the world…William, if I had known that I could not be more reconciled to your absence than I am, I never could have consented to your going."

She adds on April 22, "O William, I wish you had been content to stay at home, for there is no real home for me without you…Most of the people tell me that I am a fool for letting you go away and that no man that thought anything of his family would do so…I hope we shall meet again. How can I be reconciled if we do not? Farewell, farewell, my dear. Yours affectionately, Sabrina."

William writes to his brother George from St. Louis, April 25: "Tell Sabrina that she must be happy and take her comfort. I would be glad to be wealthy and be able to travel with my family and enable them to enjoy the pleasures of an easy life; therefore I take my way to the mountains to get the rocks."

William replies to Sabrina on May 3, 5, and 10 from Independence: "We find the cholera prevalent here in virulent form. Today I have felt unwell...I solace myself with the thought that you are all at home in comfortable circumstances, and I am in the post that duty calls me to fill...tell them [those who say that I will not get home alive] that they have not soul enough to comprehend the intentions of one who would risk all for the sake of his family." On June 4 he writes from the Big Blue, "This morn I am very unwell. I am very weak, having eaten nothing to speak of for a long time, and I dare not drink much of the water."

Sabrina writes on May 27, "Here I am at home...with rather poor health for myself and the child...writing to one she has already forgotten...Not only my back, but my stomach troubles me very much; also I have a great deal of pain in my head." On June 24 and 26 she reassures William, "I hope my being unwell will not give you any uneasiness, for I think when the weather becomes cooler I shall feel better...I hope you will not keep anything back, let it be ever so bad. Nothing could make me feel worse than I do now." Finally, on July 26, "My health is poor, more so I think than our folks are aware of. Not only my back is bad, but I have a pain in my chest and left side, palpitation of the heart, and dyspepsia. But do not give yourself any uneasiness about me, for I am getting better."

William returned to Youngstown on February 6, 1851. He had left San Francisco with only $500 in gold dust and $10 in specie. "I have seen many hardships, dangers, and privations, and made nothing by it, i.e. accumulated no property; but if I arrive at home with my health, I shall ever be glad that I have taken this trip." He and Sabrina lived happily into their eighties.

The gold rush disrupted families all over America. Yet a number of women— ultimately perhaps as many as 10 percent of the total rushers—headed for California (Levy 1990).

The California Indians   The more the gold rush energized the whites, the more it desolated the natives. As some editors and others pointed out at the time, the genocide of the California Indians was the most sickening chapter in the conquest of the West. At first many Indians were in the diggings, some as virtual slaves. A letter from "A friend of the Red Race," published in the Washington *National Intelligencer*, January 24, 1849, observed that the Indians "are precisely the class of gold diggers who are likely to find most gold and realize least for it. But small as their gains may be, it is the dictate of a sound public morality that they should not be poisoned with ardent spirits, and driven from the face of the country, without an effort to reclaim them to society and industry." This voice was not heard in California, nor could the Friend have envisioned the enormity of the problem. On August 18, 1849, S. S. Osgood's letter appeared in the *Intelligencer,* telling of miners beginning to hunt down Indian men to avenge alleged murders, and enslaving the women in the mines. (Browning 1995.)

The number of California Indians dropped from probably more than 300,000 at the founding of the missions in 1769, to about 150,000 in 1845, to only some 30,000 in 1860 (Cook 1976). Starvation and disease took the greatest tolls, but whites murdered and massacred significant numbers.

Superintendent Edward F. Beale estimated that 15,000 Indians starved to death in the winter of 1851-1852 (Bonsal 1912). This number probably includes deaths from malaria, smallpox, alcoholism, and venereal disease. The Sacramento *Union* of February 3, 1855, noted a common occurrence in "the commencement of a war of extermination against the Indians…The intrusion of the white man upon the Indians' hunting grounds has driven off the game and destroyed their fisheries. The consequence is, the Indians suffer every winter for sustenance. Hunger and starvation follow them wherever they go. Is it, then, a matter of wonder that they become desperate and resort to stealing or killing?" (Heizer 1974). The California Legislature of 1850 passed an act allowing Indian indenture, a euphemism for slavery, and legalized kidnapping of Indian children. Gov. John McDougall's 1851 message stated, "a war of extermination will continue to be waged between the races until the Indian race becomes extinct" (Castillo 1978).

Among the more notable of many massacres of California Indians was the slaughter of some 200 Pomos on "bloody islands" in Clear Lake and the Russian River, May 15, and 19, 1850, by the Army. Gen. Persifor F. Smith's instructions were "to waste no time in parley, to ascertain with certainty the offenders [in the deaths of Capt. William H. Warner in Surprise Valley, and of two citizens near Clear Lake], and to strike them promptly and heavily." (Paiute or Pit River Indians, not Pomos, killed Warner.) The Pomos previously had taunted the shore-bound infantry from their island sanctuary in Clear Lake. But Capt. Nathaniel Lyon brought boats on wagons, cleared the island, and chased the survivors into the rushes "with the most gratifying results. The number killed [men, women, children] I confidently report at not less than sixty, and doubt little that it extended to a hundred and upwards…Their fire upon us was not effective, and no injury to the command occurred." Four days later Lyon surrounded another group on an island in Russian River: "as they could not escape, the island soon became a perfect slaughter pen…Their number killed I confidently report at not less than seventy-five, and have little doubt it extended to nearly double that number." Two soldiers were wounded. Gen. Smith estimated that total Indian deaths were at least 200.

The San Francisco *Daily Alta California*, May 4, 1852, recounted "the particulars of a fearful act of retributive slaughter recently committed in that district [near Weaverville]. A rancheria of 148 Indians, including women and children, was attacked [by the sheriff and 36 armed men], and nearly the whole number [excepting three prisoners] destroyed." The sheriff's men surrounded the Indians at night for a daylight surprise attack. "Each rifle marked its victim with unerring precision—the pistol and the knife competed the work of destruction and revenge." The Indians had killed a rancher and stolen his cattle. The attackers reported no casualties. (Heizer 1974.)

In August, 1852, Modocs killed about 36 emigrants at Bloody Point on Tule Lake in northern California. In September, Capt. Ben Wright's company from Yreka retaliated by slaying from 60 to 80 Modocs. (Hunt 1989.)

In about April, 1859, the notorious H. L. Hall took "a large group of settlers out along the Eel River, where for two weeks they hunted down and killed about 240 Indians [Yukis]." Hall reportedly said that "He did not want any man to go with him to hunt Indians who would not kill all he could find, because a knit would make a louse. Mr. Hall said he had run Indians out of their rancherias and put strychnine in their baskets of soup." (Carranco and Beard 1981.)

Capt. Walter S. Jarboe, head of the State's Eel River Rangers, reported in December, 1859, at the end of a five-month operation, that with 20 men "I fought them twenty-three times, killed 283 warriors [Kato and Yuki men, women, children]…I had four men severely wounded, as well as myself." Jarboe burned some Indians alive in their huts. A Sacramento editor did not notice any wounds on him that winter. Special U.S. agent J. Ross Browne wrote, "Peaceable Indians, including women and children, were cruelly slaughtered by the whites [who] ranged the hills of the Nome Cult [reservation], killing every Indian that was too weak to escape; and what is worse, they did it under a State Commission…A more cruel series of outrages…never disgraced a community of white men." (Carranco and Beard 1981.)

Army Maj. Gabriel J. Raines described the massacre of February 26, 1860, at Humboldt Bay near Eureka: "I beheld a scene of atrocity and horror unparalleled not only in our own Country, but even in history, for it was done by men self acting and without necessity, color of law, or authority—the murder of little innocent babes and women [most of the Yurok men were absent that day]…cut and hacked with axes…by these men, Volunteers, calling themselves such, from Eel

River...About 188 Indians, mostly women and children have been murdered."
(Heizer 1974.)

Along the Eel and Trinity rivers in May and June, 1861, Lts. Joseph B. Collins
and James P. Martin, leading regulars and civilian volunteers, killed 149 Indians,
mostly men, in 17 skirmishes. Arrows wounded one soldier and two civilians.
(Strobridge 1994.)

In September, 1861, Charles Bourne with 10 settlers and 50 picked Indian
allies slew from 100 to 240 Wailakis at Horse Canyon in the Eel River drainage.
(Carranco and Beard 1981.)

The federal government abandoned the California Indians to their fate. In
1851-52 three commissioners wrote out 18 treaties "of friendship and peace,"
promising reservations, beef and flour, farming tools, clothes, and teachers, in
exchange for their lands (Heizer 1972). The commissioners immediately
defrauded the Indians on the beef contracts (Beale 1853, Bancroft 24:482-86).
Then, at the urging of the California Senator William M. Gwin, the Senate
rejected the treaties and buried them in secrecy until 1905. Beale founded one
reservation, and his successor three others and two farms, but the whole system
failed from incompetence, corruption, and white squatting and slaughtering
(Castillo 1978).

The Mining Upshot   The early miners used knives to pry some of the best
gold out of crevices in bedrock at the bottom of stream channels. Forty-niner
Henry Degroot remembered in 1874 how he reasoned that the deep holes in the
rivers should likewise be full of the metal. He dove into the icy depths of the
American River in a casket-shaped contraption covered with India rubber. He
brought up "buckets consisting in every case of only barren gravel mixed with
twigs, leaves, mud, and sand." He nearly drowned in the process.

The average miner's prize dropped from perhaps 20 dollars a day in 1848, to 16
in 1849, to 5 in 1852, to about 3 in 1856-60. At the high prices in the camps, most
barely eked out a living. Even at the low 1860 returns, 100,000 miners were still
digging, a quarter of them Chinese. But many of the early, restless crowd had
rushed off after minerals to other areas, where they opened up much of the rest of
the West. (Paul 1963; Browne 1867; see 7:N and 8:P).

California gold production peaked in 1852, and the rich, accessible surface
placers in modern stream deposits were largely played out by 1864. Miners found
gold-bearing quartz lodes in bedrock in 1849, but deep underground mines
developed slowly; the last one shut down in 1965. Fifty-million-year-old Tertiary
placers, former stream deposits commonly perched on present ridges, were
washed out by strong water jets from 1852 to 1884; this hydraulic mining was a

California innovation. Dredging of low-grade modern stream deposits lasted from 1898 to 1968. The gold originally occurred in the bedrock quartz veins coming from the massive igneous granodiorites of the Sierra Nevada. Weathering and erosion of these veins formed the placers. The largest water-worn nugget was 54 pounds, and the largest bedrock lode mass was 195 pounds, discovered in 1854 and 1859, respectively. The California mines provided one-third of total U.S. gold production through 1967. (Clark 1969.)

Hydraulic mining created utter havoc. As John McPhee recounts in his elegant portrayal of the gold rush, "In a year and a half, hydraulic mining washes enough material into the Yuba River to fill the Erie Canal...Broad moonscapes of unvegetated stream-rounded rubble conceal the original land...ultimately eleven hundred and forty-six million cubic yards are added to the bays. Navigation is impaired above Carquinez Strait. The ocean is brown at the Golden Gate." Judge Lorenzo Sawyer put a stop to this devastation in 1884.

California gold founded and populated a state with whites, depopulated the Indians, financed a good bit of the Civil War for the Union, and made the Pacific railroad an urgent priority.

REFERENCES

Beale, Edward F., 1853, Condition of Indian affairs in California: Wash., 32/2 S57, serial 665, 18 p.

Bieber, Ralph P., 1937, Southern trails to California in 1849: Glendale, quotes from Californian p. 65, from California Star 65-66, on first Herald article 68, Beale in Picayune 69, Colton 71-72, Larkin in Union 76-77; on Loeser 95-99, 125-26; on Mint 127-29.

Bonsal, Stephen, 1912, Edward Fitzgerald Beale: N.Y., p. 175.

Browne, J. Ross, 1867, Report upon the mineral resources west of the Rocky Mountains: Wash., 39/2 H29, serial 1289, p. 18-21.

Browning, Peter, 1995, To the Golden Shore: Lafayette CA, 418 p.; reprint of first Herald article 10-15; Larkin quotes on gold, food 18, cup of gold 20, bed of gold 23; mica 38; fool's paradise 43; glistens 44; Friend of Red Race 110; Osgood 307-08.

Carranco, Lynwood, and Estle Beard, 1981, Genocide and vendetta, the Round Valley Wars of Northern California: Norman, 403 p.; Hall quotes 82, 63; Jarboe 95-96; Browne 97; Horse Canyon 111-12.

Castillo, Edward D., 1978, The impact of Euro-American exploration and settlement; in Robert F. Heizer, ed., California, v. 8 of Handbook of North American Indians: Wash., p. 108-12; McDougall quote 109.

Clark, John H., 1852 journal (pub. 1888, reprinted 1942), Overland to the gold fields of California in 1852; Louise Barry, ed.: Topeka, separate from Kansas Hist. Quart., quote p. 255.

Clark, William B., 1969 (1980 reprint), Gold districts of California: Sacramento, p. 1-19.

Cook, Sherburne F., 1976, The population of the California Indians 1769-1970: Berkeley, p. 43-44, 199.

Degroot, Henry, 1874, Diving for gold in '49: San Francisco, The Overland Monthly 13:273-80, quote 279.

Hafen, LeRoy and Ann W., 1954, Old Spanish Trail: Glendale, p. 338-39.

Heizer, Robert F., 1972, The eighteen unratified treaties of 1851-52 between the California Indians and the U.S. government: Berkeley, 101 p.

Heizer, Robert F., 1974 (1993 reprint), The destruction of California Indians: Lincoln, quotes on extermination p. 35-36, Weaverville Massacre 249-50, Humboldt Bay Massacre 259-60.

Hodge, Frederick W., 1910, Handbook of American Indians north of Mexico: Wash., Bureau Am. Ethnology Bull. 30, 2:216.

Holliday, James S., 1981 (1982 reprint), The world rushed in: N.Y., 559 p.; quotes on rocks 75-76, crucify 80-81, home 83, reconciled 85, cholera 96, duty 100, soul enough 104, unwell 131, stomach troubles 138-39, weather 171, feel worse 173, dyspepsia 198, hardships 423; cholera numbers 114-15.

Humboldt, Alexander von, 1811, Political essay on the Kingdom of New Spain; translated by John Black: N.Y., quote p. 221.

Hunt, Thomas H., 1989, Anatomy of a massacre, Bloody Point, 1852: Independence, Overland Journal 7/3:10.

Jones, John W., 1854, Amusing and thrilling adventures of a California artist: Boston, 92 p.; editor quotes 44; racy companions 14-16, with quote 14.

Levy, JoAnn, 1990 (1992 reprint), They saw the elephant, women in the California gold rush: Norman, 265 p.; number of women xvi-xvii.

McAuley, Eliza Ann, 1852 diary (1985 printing), Covered wagon women; Kenneth L. Holmes, ed.: Spokane, quote 4:81.

McMurtrie, Douglas C., 1943, A report in April, 1848 on the discovery of gold and other minerals in California: Evanston IL, 7 p.

McPhee, John, 1993, Assembling California: N.Y., p. 41-68; quote 66.

Naef, Weston J., and James N. Wood, 1975, Era of exploration, the rise of landscape photography in the American West 1860-85: N.Y., p. 32-33.

Niles' Register, 1842 and 1844, California gold: Baltimore, quotes on San Fernando 63:96, Tepic 66:81.

Parke, Charles R., 1849 diary (1989 printing), Dreams to dust; James E. Davis, ed.: Lincoln, quote p. 46.

Paul, Rodman W., 1963, Mining frontiers of the Far West 1848-80: N.Y., p. 35-36.

Paul, Rodman W., 1966 (1967 reprint), The California gold discovery: Georgetown CA, 237 p.; quote from Californian 70; California Star article of April 1, 77-78.

Polk, James K., 1848, Message: Wash., 30/2 H1, serial 537, December 5, 69 p.; quote on CA gold 10; Larkin quotes on discovery 51, visit 53; Mason quotes on San Francisco 56, cradle 57, Indians 60, people to mines 61.

Rosenberg, Charles E., 1962, The cholera years: Chicago, p. 101-225.

Sherman, William T., 1875 (1890 3d ed.), Personal memoirs: N.Y., quote p. 85.

Smith, Persifor F., and Capt. Nathaniel Lyon, 1850, Clear Lake Expedition: Wash., 31/2 S1, serial 587, p. 75-83; quotes of Smith 78, Lyon 82.

Strobridge, William F., 1994, Regulars in the Redwoods: Spokane, p. 240-41.

TABLE KA. TRAVEL TIMES OF CALIFORNIA GOLD SEEKERS IN DAYS*

(and in miles; the three values given for groupings of travelers are minimum-mean-
maximum times; in brackets are the mean travel rates in miles per day)

MISSOURI RIVER TO SACRAMENTO VALLEY

K1. 74 trains	1849	Soda Springs, Carson/Truckee (1860 mi.)	92-120-154	[15]
K1. 22 trains	1849	Salt L. City, Carson/Truckee (1870 mi.)	93-122-150	[15]
K1. 28 trains	1849	Soda Springs, Lassen Trail (2070 mi.)	125-145-177	[14]
K1. 10 trains	1849	Salt L. City, Lassen Trail (2080 mi.)	128-142-156	[15]
K1. 6 packers	1849	Soda/Salt L., Carson/Truckee (1865 mi.)	71-87-104	[21]
K1. Green	1849	Sublette, Ft. Hall, Carson (1730 mi.)	71	[24]

(Fastest Forty-niner; left Old Ft. Kearny, packed from Green R. to Hangtown)

K3. 65 trains	1850	Soda Springs, Carson/Truckee (1860 mi.)	73-107-149	[17]
K3. 27 trains	1850	Salt L. City, Carson/Truckee (1870 mi.)	75-114-148	[16]
K3. 12 trains	1850	Salt L. City, Hastings Cutoff (1905 mi.)	100-120-133	[16]
K3. 14 packers	1850	Soda/Salt L., Carson/Truckee (1865 mi.)	72-86-98	[22]
K3. Keller	1850	Sublette, Ft. Hall, Lassen Trail (1950 mi.)	86	[23]

(Fastest via Lassen Trail; left St. Joseph, packed from Goose L. to Lassen's Ranch)

K4. 29 trains	1852	Soda Springs, Carson/Truckee (1860 mi.)	83-107-138	[17]
K4. 16 trains	1852	Salt L. City, Carson/Truckee (1870 mi.)	88-114-144	[16]
K5. 5 trains	1853	Soda Springs, Carson/Truckee (1860 mi.)	114-125-136	[15]
K5. 12 trains	1853	Salt L. City, Carson/Truckee (1870 mi.)	97-127-148	[15]

OTHER ROUTES

K3. Eagar	1848	Open Carson Trail, Salt L. Cutoff (820 mi..)	74	[11]
K7. Miles	1850	Port Lavaca TX to San Diego (1500 mi.)	136	[11]

(About half by wagon, half by inept packing)

*Excluding long unusual stopovers, if known. Most times include 10-20 percent necessary layover days.
Overland travel involves wagons or carts unless otherwise specified.

TABLE KB. LENGTHS OF SEGMENTS OF THE CALIFORNIA TRAIL IN MILES

(Compiled from Rieck 1993-95. Segment letter designations, such as a-f, are keyed to the map. Underlined are the Up-Down Factors in feet per mile; they are the vertical elevations of the steeper ascents and descents cumulated graphically from Rieck's profiles and divided by the segment length; the factor gives a partial measure of topographic trail difficulty, a zero indicating a smooth inclined plane.)

a-f	Independence to Ft. Kearny	335	<u>11</u>
c-f	St. Joseph to Ft. Kearny	265	<u>11</u>
e-f	Council Bluffs to Ft. Kearny	195	<u>4</u>
f-g	Ft. Kearny to Ft. Laramie	340	<u>8</u>
g-h-j	Ft. Laramie to Parting of Ways, near South Pass	290	<u>30</u>
j-k	Parting of Ways to Ft. Bridger	100	<u>16</u>
k-m	Ft. Bridger to Bear R. (Sublette) Jct.	75	<u>63</u>
j-m	Parting of Ways to Bear R. Jct. via Sublette Cutoff	115	<u>100</u>
m-n	Bear R. (Sublette) Jct. to Soda Springs	70	<u>43</u>
n-p-q	Soda Springs to City of Rocks via Ft. Hall	155	<u>51</u>
n-q	Soda Springs to City of Rocks via Hudspeth Cutoff	135	<u>121</u>
k-s	Ft. Bridger to Salt L. City via Emigration Canyon	110	<u>102</u>
k-s	Ft. Bridger to Salt L. City via Golden Pass	115	<u>90</u>
s-q	Salt L. City to City of Rocks via Salt L. Cutoff	160	<u>40</u>
q-r	City of Rocks to Hastings-Humboldt Jct.	155	<u>41</u>
s-r	Salt L. City to Humboldt Jct. Via Hastings Cutoff	350	<u>28</u>
r-t	Hastings-Humboldt Jct. to Lassen Meadows	160	<u>29</u>
t-u-v	Lassen Trail from Meadows to Ranch via Goose L.	400	<u>58</u>
v-z	Lassen's Ranch to Sacramento (Sutter's Fort)	100	<u>0</u>
t-w	Lassen Meadows to Sierra base on Truckee R.	130	<u>5</u>
w-z	Sierra base at Truckee R. to Donner Pass to Sacramento	150	<u>111</u>
t-x	Lassen Meadows to Sierra base on Carson R.	140	<u>4</u>
x-z	Sierra base at Carson R. to Carson Pass to Sacramento	160	<u>114</u>

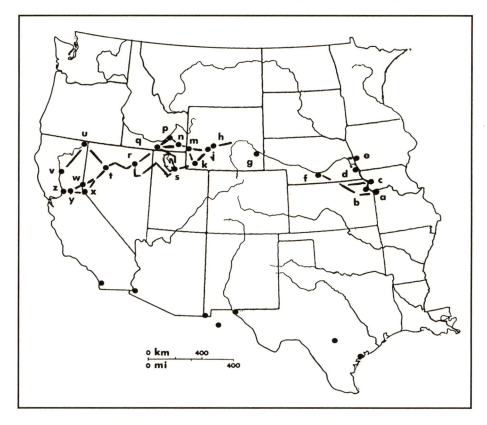

GOLD SEEKERS ON THE OREGON–CALIFORNIA TRAILS, 1848–53

a.	Independence MO	p.	Ft. Hall ID
b.	Ft. Leavenworth KS	q.	City of Rocks ID
c.	St. Joseph MO	r.	Hastings Jct. on Humboldt R. NV
d.	Old Ft. Kearny NE	s.	Salt Lake City UT
e.	Council Bluffs IA, opposite Omaha NE	s-q.	Salt Lake Cutoff UT-ID
f.	Ft. Kearny NE	s-r.	Hastings Cutoff UT-NV
g.	Ft. Laramie WY	t.	Lassen Meadows NV
h.	South Pass WY	u.	Goose L. CA
j.	Parting of Ways WY	v.	Lassen's Ranch CA
j-m.	Sublette Cutoff WY	t-u-v.	Lassen Trail NV-CA
k.	Ft. Bridger WY	w.	Truckee R. NV below Donner Pass
m.	Bear R. (Sublette) Jct. WY	x.	Carson R. NV below Carson Pass
n.	Soda Springs ID	y.	Hangtown (Placerville) CA
n-q.	Hudspeth Cutoff ID	z.	Sacramento CA

TEXAS–SOUTHERN TRAILS, 1850 (CARDINELL)

East to West: Port Lavaca TX—San Antonio—El Paso—Corralitos Chih.—Guadalupe Pass NM—Yuma CA—San Diego CA

Joseph H. Colton, 1849

Colton's Map Of The United States, Mexico &c. Showing The Gold Region In California
[Title on label on front cover]

[New York, 1849], 11 p., map. [WCB 164a; Eberstadt 127:139; Graff 835; Kurutz 149; Phillips p. 900; Streeter 2534; Wheat 3:map 591; NUC NC 0569941.] Reset verbatim from a facsimile, by courtesy of The Newberry Library, Chicago, Illinois.

Significance Colton's was the first commercial large map to highlight the gold region in order to cash in on the furor created by President Polk's message of December 5, 1848. But Colton's slipshod advice to gold seekers was typical of the early armchair guidebooks sprouting in the east. Three helpful works already on booksellers' shelves gained new luster. On December 8 the *New York Tribune* carried an ad for Maj. William H. Emory's recently published, authoritative *Military Reconnoissance to San Diego* (4:G6) under a new "Ho! For California" banner. This was immediately followed by ads for Col. John C. Fremont's *Geographical Memoir upon Upper California* with its superb map, and Edwin Bryant's excellent book, *What I Saw in California*. Fremont's map notably had "El Dorado or Gold Region" inserted on the American and Feather ("Rio d. l. Plumas") rivers. A fourth work, William Clayton's meticulous 1848 *Latter-Day Saints' Emigrants' Guide* from Council Bluffs to Great Salt Lake, published in St. Louis, was less well known in the east but was much more practical than the others.

Then in record time, on December 14, 1848, booksellers Dewitt & Davenport announced George G. Foster's *Gold Regions of California*, with a one-page map, and 80 pages of text slapped together with scissors and paste from the recently published reports. On the 17th Joyce & Co. brought our Henry I. Simpson's misleading pamphlet, *The Emigrant's Guide...Three Weeks in the Gold Mines*, with a double-page map. J. Ely Sherwood and Charles E. Kells also published similar guides at about this time, without maps.

Then on December 20, 1848, came an ad in the *Tribune* for Colton's map: "Also just published, a capital Map of California, showing the Routes of the United States Mail Steam Packets, and a plan of the Gold Region. Price in sheets, 25 cts." A related ad on the 26th stated, "This is a beautifully engraved, cheap and

reliable Map, unlike the catch-penny things called Maps, so industriously circu-
lated. For sale, wholesale and retail, by the publishers and by [booksellers]." On
January 4, 1849, booksellers Stringer & Townsend announced Fayette Robinson's
California and its Gold Regions, which carried Colton's large, folded map: "NEW
WORK ON CALIFORNIA. No catch-penny, but a reliable book—and now
ready." (The above *Tribune* ads are from Wheat 3:64-68.)

Colton's own 11-page pamphlet to accompany his map presumably was also
published early in 1849. Warren Heckrotte (1995) identified three issues of this
Colton map, all based on Fremont. The first, dated 1848, did not mention gold.
The second, copyrighted 1848 but dated 1849, mounted on linen, had "Gold
Region" and "R. de Plumas." The third, also copyrighted 1848 and dated 1849,
had "El Dorado or Gold Region" and "Feather R." The third issue was used in
both Robinson's and Colton's works. This may be the first reprint of Colton's
pamphlet. See Highlights for its errors and for discussion of Fayette Robinson's
not-so-reliable, definitely catch-penny book.

Reproduced here is only the part of Colton's map that shows the U.S. Pacific
coast and the inset of the Gold Region. The full map is 38.5 x 54 cm. (15.2 x 21.2
in.), titled "Map of the United States, the British Provinces, Mexico &c., showing
the Routes of the U.S. Mail Steam Packets to California, and a Plan of the Gold
Region. Published by J. H. Colton, 86 Cedar St. New York, 1849. Drawn &
Engraved by J. M. Atwood, New York. Entered according to Act of Congress in
the year 1848."

Author   JOSEPH HUTCHINS COLTON, New York publisher of maps. Colton's
first map was issued in 1833 (Sheets 1994). Wheat lists Western maps by J. H.
Colton from 1847 to 1864, using language such as, "the celebrated New York map
house" (3:46); "The important map publishing house" (3:74), whose 1854 map
was "one of the best and most up-to-date that appeared during this period"
(3:167); "the ever-reliable J. H. Colton" (5:99), in 1863; "Colton was inordinately
fond of the Pony Express" (5:107) and in 1864 continued to show its route long
after its demise. Wheat's 1865 Colton map was "a responsible job of cartography…Polished as we would expect a Colton map to be" (5:157), but now it was
published by G. W. and C. B. Colton.

Itineraries, 1849   The average Forty-niner travels from the MISSOURI
RIVER TO THE SACRAMENTO RIVER drainage via South Pass WY, Soda
Springs ID, and the Carson or Truckee routes over the Sierra, in 120 days.
Detouring by Salt Lake adds only 10 miles and only 2 days, even though the aver-
age layover in Salt Lake City is 5 days. But the trip by Soda Springs and the

Lassen Trail takes an average of 145 days; by Salt Lake and the Lassen Trail, the distance again is 10 miles more, but the time in the data below is a statistically insignificant 3 days *less*. The few who use pack animals instead of wagons on the Carson/Truckee route reach the diggings in only 87 days on average. Of 140 diarists studied, 35, or 25 percent, go via Salt Lake City.

The longest distance from the Missouri to Sacramento City on the regular route is from Independence via Ft. Bridger, Ft. Hall, and Carson Pass—1,980 miles. The shortest, from Omaha and using the Sublette and Hudspeth Cutoffs and the Truckee River and Donner Pass, is 1,740 miles. The average, 1,860 miles, is the same as the average from St. Joseph MO. The average using the Lassen Trail is 2,070 miles. Via Salt Lake City, each of these averages is only 10 miles more. On all trails, wagons average 15 miles per day, packers 21.

These numbers come from the compendious summaries by Dale Morgan (1959) and Merrill Mattes. Travel times are based on the appropriate 88 diaries studied in detail by Morgan, supplemented without duplication by 53 outlined with sufficient data in Mattes's *Platte River Road* bibliography. Times include all days between crossing or leaving the Missouri from various points and reaching the diggings at various points in the Sacramento drainage, with widely varying layovers and waits for river crossings. No one laying over two weeks or more in Salt Lake City is knowingly included. Averaged times are tied to averaged distances. The distances are compiled from the magnificent trail profiles published by Richard L. Rieck in 1993-95.

WAGONS VIA SODA SPRINGS, CARSON/TRUCKEE TRAILS. Average travel time is 120 days. The 74 diarists record leaving the Missouri generally in late April or May, variously from Independence MO, Ft. Leavenworth KS, St. Joseph MO, Old Ft. Kearny NE (now Nebraska City), or Omaha NE, opposite Council Bluffs IA. Their routes merge at Ft. Kearny NE on the Platte, then diverge at the Parting of the Ways just west of South Pass WY. Some go west on the Sublette Cutoff to Bear River and Soda Springs ID. Others go southwest to Ft. Bridger WY and back northwest to Bear River and Soda Springs. (Those going on from Ft. Bridger to Salt Lake City are considered under the next heading.)

From Soda Springs some take the old trail to Ft. Hall and along the Snake and Raft rivers to City of Rocks in south-central Idaho. Others take the new Hudspeth Cutoff to the City of Rocks. (Thomas Fitzpatrick outlined this cutoff in 1845; see 4:G5.) Those that leave the Humboldt at Lassen Meadows, now Humboldt NV, to take the Lassen Trail to the northwest, are considered below. Those treated here continue down the Humboldt and ascend either the Carson River or the Truckee River to the crest of the Sierra, fanning out into the gold fields of the

Sacramento drainage on their descent. Elisha Stephens took the first wagons over the Truckee route in 1844 (Graydon 1986). That same year Kit Carson and John Fremont went over Carson Pass, which an eastbound group of Mormon Battalion veterans opened for wagons in 1848 (5:J9, and K3). About half of the diarists follow the Carson Trail to Hangtown (Placerville). The other half on the Truckee generally go to Johnson's Ranch near present Wheatland CA. Many on both trails go on to Sutter's Fort at Sacramento. Most arrive in August or September.

This journey of 1,860 miles on average takes minimum-mean-maximum 92-120-154 days, at an average 15 miles per day.

WAGONS VIA SALT LAKE CITY, SALT LAKE CUTOFF, CARSON/TRUCKEE TRAILS. Average time is 122 days. The 22 diarists record much the same journey as above, except that they go from Ft. Bridger to Salt Lake City and take Samuel J. Hensley's Salt Lake Cutoff, pioneered in August, 1848, to rejoin the others near City of Rocks. This trip of 1,870 miles on average takes minimum-mean-maximum 93-122-150 days, at an average 15 miles per day. The times are not significantly different from those on the Soda Springs route.

WAGONS VIA SODA SPRINGS, LASSEN TRAIL. Average time is 145 days. The 28 diarists jump off from various points on the Missouri, mostly in May, and follow the various routes to Soda Springs and on to Lassen Meadows on the Humboldt. They all reach the Meadows after August 11, when Milton McGee's train is the first to take the 400-mile Lassen Trail northwest to Goose Lake in northeasternmost California, and thence back southwest through the Sierra to Lassen's Ranch, now Vina CA north of Chico, on the Sacramento River. Most arrive in September and October. The total journey, averaging 2,070 miles, takes minimum-mean-maximum 125-145-177 days, at an average 14 miles per day.

The Applegate Trail from Lassen Meadows to Goose Lake and on to Oregon's Willamette Valley was laid out in 1846 (5:J10). In 1848 Peter Lassen, a Dane who became a Mexican citizen and California rancher in 1844, attempted to lead some emigrants from Lassen Meadows to his ranch via Goose Lake (Hammond 1986). But, lost and worn out in the mountains southwest of Goose Lake, Lassen was saved when overtaken by Peter H. Burnett (2:D6) and his strong party of 50 wagons and 150 men. This party came from Oregon on the Applegate Trail to Goose Lake and were headed thence southwest for the California mines. Burnett's wagons were the first to go from Oregon to central California, and Burnett would become the first governor of the new state.

Burnett wrote in his 1880 book, "Peter Lassen had met the incoming immigration that fall [1848], and had induced the people belonging to ten wagons to come by his new route. This route he had not previously explored…the moment they came to heavy timber, they had not force enough to open the road…they converted their ten wagons into ten carts…One half of the party became so incensed against Lassen that his life was in great danger. The whole party had been without any bread for more than a month, and had during that time lived alone on poor beef. They were, indeed, objects of pity. I never saw people so worn down and so emaciated as these poor immigrants…We gave them plenty of provisions, and told them to follow us, and we would open the way ourselves…[At Lassen's Ranch] the old pilot was in the best of spirits, and killed for us a fat beef."

After August 11, 1849, all gold seekers agonize at Lassen Meadows about which route to take. J. Goldsborough Bruff opts for the northern route, "to avoid the long deserts, bad water at Sink of Mary's [Humboldt] river, long and heavy sand-drag beyond it, a long and very bad Cañon, and last, tho' not least, a very elevated rugged, and dangerous Pass." Also, the hordes ahead will have used up the grass on the old route, and the new route is rumored to be shorter. At the end of the dreadfully long Lassen Trail, however, Bruff sees "All, more or less, Men, women and children, are dirty and tattered—All look alike, one class of rough looking, hairy dirty, ragged, jaded men." Many have come miles wading through deep snow, hungry, fatigued, and beset with scurvy and fevers, having left behind them broken wagons, treasured possessions, dead oxen and mules, and the graves of their loved ones.

WAGONS VIA SALT LAKE CITY, LASSEN TRAIL. The 10 diarists make the 2,080-mile trip in minimum-mean-maximum 128-142-156 days, averaging 15 miles per day. The times do not differ significantly from those on the Soda Springs route.

PACKERS VIA EITHER SODA SPRINGS OR SALT LAKE CITY, AND CARSON/TRUCKEE TRAILS. The 6 diarists cover the average 1,865 miles in minimum-mean-maximum 71-87-104 days, at a fast average rate of 21 miles per day. Few Forty-niners were packers, either lacking the skills or not wishing to be without the comforts and goods conveyed by wagons; perhaps, also, fewer packers kept diaries. Half of the packer groups included here used wagons part of the way (Mattes 386, 397, 465; the others are 409?, 565, 578).

The fastest Forty-niner is Edmund Green (Mattes 465), who leaves Old Ft. Kearny May 5. At Green River he and one companion forge ahead of their wagon party with pack horses. Traveling via Ft. Hall and the Carson Trail, they reach Hangtown July 14, a record 71 days for the 1,730 miles from the Missouri, averaging 24 miles per day.

Three other diarists (Mattes 357, 644, 669) document one troubled packer group that takes the Lassen Trail. It pushes off with 70 Boston men on riding mules, leading pack mules all overloaded with galling wooden chests, and driving beef cattle. Progress is slowed by cholera and by the pilot, Joseph Thing, former sea captain and prominent member of Nathaniel Wyeth's 1834 expedition (1:B12). West of South Pass, Thing tries an abortive "shortcut" that costs them two weeks. So then the men ignore Thing's advice against taking the Lassen Trail, because a sign says "Only 110 miles to the diggings." In all they take 141 days to Lassen's Ranch—almost exactly the average for wagons. (See also Bruff 1849, and Barry p. 836.)

Highlights   In his rush to print, Colton neglected some of his homework. The prominent lines on his map are mostly Fremont's routes, except for Kearny's and Emory's 1846 track from Santa Fe to San Diego, shown in part imperfectly: Kearny left the Rio Grande 80 miles south of Socorro, not 50 miles north of it at Tome (see 4:G6). Colton's statement that Kearny's rugged pack route along the Gila "may afford facilities greater than that of Fremont, through the South Pass, or Kearney, Stockton, &c., further south," was both irresponsible and confused. The 1847 return routes of Kearny in June-August, and of Commodore Robert F. Stockton in July-October (Bancroft 22:454), followed the Truckee-Humboldt-South Pass route well north of the Gila. Colton's citing of Kearny's fast military travel times with pack animals, at 26 miles per day, could only mislead gold seekers. His claim that "the whole journey from Vera Cruz, via the city of Mexico, to Mazatlan, is performed on horseback in about 20 days" would mean covering 1,150 miles at 58 miles per day. This feat would nearly equal Edward Beale's incredible day-and-night ride carrying the news of the gold discovery (5:J9). Colton's text has "5,308" sea miles from New York to San Francisco via Panama; the map's table adds this to 5,808. Colton also takes a few liberties in quoting the President's words from the message of December 5, 1848.

Guide writer Joseph Colton quoted one of the many exciting letters about the gold discovery written by the Rev. Walter Colton, Navy chaplain and Alcalde of Monterey. Walter Colton's 1848 diary recorded the initial skepticism melting into euphoria in the first flush months of the discovery: "Monday, May 29. Our town was startled out of its quiet dreams to-day, by the announcement that gold had been discovered on the American Fork...June 12...But doubts still hovered on the minds of the great mass. They could not conceive that such a treasure could have lain there so long undiscovered. The idea seemed to convict them of stupidity...June 20. My messenger sent to the mines, has returned with specimens of the gold…Husband and wife were both packing up; the blacksmith dropped his hammer, the carpenter his plane, the mason his trowel, the farmer his sickle, the baker his loaf, and the tapster his bottle. All were off for the mines, some on horses, some on carts, and some on crutches, and one went in a litter."

The *Philadelphia Public Ledger* commented on December 19, 1848, "the accounts from the 'Gold Region," by Col. Mason, Mr. Larkin, Mr. Colton and others, we ascribe three-fourths to exaggeration, produced by excitement…Mr. Colton…has become more fanciful than ever through his inoculation with the 'yellow fever'…Make your humbugs credible, Messrs. Californians!…[Californians] want settlers, and know that a gold fever will bring them there by tens of thousands. And when they arrive, they will find that digging for gold, while paying ten dollars for a shirt, and fifty dollars for a barrel of flour, is unprofitable" (Browning 1995). These words were partly erroneous and partly prophetic. (Both Thornton 1849 and Browning 1995 reprint parts of an August 29, 1848 letter by Walter Colton, but it differs from the one of the same date reprinted here.)

Colton's maps were in two other 1849 guidebooks, one very good, the other quite bad. The good one was the initial 1849 American issue (Kurutz 95e) of Bryant's 1848 book. Edwin Bryant went overland to California in 1846 via South Pass and the infamous Hastings Cutoff (2:D7). He returned with Gen. Kearny in 1847 via Ft. Hall and South Pass (4:G6). His informative, reliable, readable, useful book came out in the east just before the first gold excitement. His book did not mention gold but contained an excellent diary and description of the trail, an accurate mileage table, and a weather record. It told gold seekers exactly what to expect. His greatest contribution, perhaps, was publicizing the torments of the Hastings Cutoff and the terrors of the Donner party—news that undoubtedly kept almost all Forty-niners from repeating such mistakes.

The bad guidebook, issued in early 1849, was by Fayette Robinson. He had been a dragoon lieutenant on the plains 1837-41, but his Western geography was still totally confused. He must never have looked at the map as he frantically copied available sources. The bulk of his 137 pages consists of quotes from newspapers, Larkin, Mason, the Mint, Emory, Kearny, T. J. Farnham, P. S. G. Cooke, Bryant, and others. He even threw in a chapter on hopes for an interoceanic canal. First he said he would, like Bryant, start for California by the "northern route" from Council Grove, Kansas, which neither Bryant nor anyone else ever did. But then, after inserting quotes about the New Mexican copper mines and the Gila, Robinson concluded of Kearny's perilous pack-path through Arizona, "This I think will long continue to be the favorite overland route to California" (cf. 4:G6; it was about the least favorite route). On his second thought, Robinson mused that Cooke's wagon-road "diversion seems important" (see 3:E6) and "is undoubtedly the best." Still, on the other hand, Robinson then allowed that he might prefer to start from Ft. Gibson, expecting to find "ripening strawber-ries...as we proceed toward the Cordilleras." He ended saying that "the great Oregon trail...is scarcely the best, or even a good one...[since it] passes round Bent's Fort, and is far too near to New Mexico to be any thing like the direct road to California." It would be hard to mix things up worse than this.

The four most useful American sources of 1848 (Bryant, Clayton, Emory, Fre-mont) were, like three 1848 European guides (Kurutz 374, 385, 562), written mainly before the gold discovery. The four 1848 commercial American guides (Foster, Kells, Sherwood, Simpson) were hastily made up of clippings glued together with bad advice. In 1849, as listed in Kurutz's splendid bibliography, some 64 American and European guidebooks were rushed to market, mostly cre-ated with scissors and paste, but including three worthy eyewitness accounts of the diggings (Kurutz 305, 363, 678) and the accurate route map of T. H. Jefferson (2:D7; Kurutz 359). See K4 Highlights for more notes on the most practical trail guides, 1848-53.

Legacy   The guidebooks were but a symptom of the raging gold fever that drove some 80,000 (Paul 1963) to 100,000 (Etter 1993) people, mostly men, to California in 1849. (Senator William M. Gwin's 1850 estimate called for 81,000, with 33,000 by sea, only about 800 of whom were women, leaving 48,000 by land, 10,000 of whom used the Southern Trail and Mexico.)

Guidebook publishers extracted the first quarters and dollars from this eager horde, most of whom would realize scant return on their investment.

REFERENCES
(See Preface for Heading references, and for Bancroft, Barry, Kurutz, Mattes, and Wheat, not listed here.)

Browning, Peter, ed., 1995, To the golden shores: Lafayette CA; Phila. Ledger quotes p. 62-63; Colton letter 57-58.

Bruff, J. Goldsborough, 1849 notes (reworked 1851, pub. 1949), Gold rush; Georgia Willis Read and Ruth Gaines, eds.: N.Y., quotes on dangerous Pass p. 140, jaded men 209; re Capt. Thing 101-02, 591-92, 625, 627.

Bryant, Edwin, 1848, What I saw in California: N.Y., 455 p.

Burnett, Peter H., 1880, Recollections and opinions of an old pioneer: N.Y., quotes p. 265, 270.

Clayton, William, 1848 (1983 reprint), The Latter-Day Saints' emigrants' guide; Stanley B. Kim-ball, ed.: St. Louis, 107 p.

Colton, Walter, 1848 diary (1850 publication), Three years in California: N.Y., quotes p. 242, 246-47.

Emory, William H., 1848, Notes of a military reconnoissance from Ft. Leavenworth MO to San Diego CA: Wash., 30/1 S7, serial 505, 416p., maps.

Etter, Patricia A., 1993, Ho! for California on the Mexican Gold Trail: Independence, Overland Journal, 11/3:2-15.

Foster, George G., 1848, The gold regions of California: N.Y., 80 p., one-page map.

Fremont, John C., 1848, Geographical memoir upon Upper California: Wash., 30/1 S148 Misc., serial 511, 67 p., map.

Graydon, Charles K., 1986, Trail of the first wagons over the High Sierra: Independence, Overland Journal 4/1:4-17.

Gwin, William M., et al., 1850, Senators and Representatives Elect from California: Wash., 31/1 H44 Misc., serial 581, p. 15-17.

Hammond, Andy, 1986, Peter Lassen and his Trail: Independence, Overland Journal 4/1:33-41.

Heckrotte, Warren, 1995, Addenda to reprint of Carl I. Wheat, The Maps of the California Gold Regions: Storrs-Mansfield CT, unpaginated Addenda following p. 148.

Jefferson, T. H., 1849 (1945 reprint), Map of the emigrant road to St. Francisco; George R. Stewart, ed.: San Francisco, [25] p., 4 map sheets; reprinted also this series 2:D7.

Kells, Charles E. ("A Traveller"), 1848, California...with a brief description of the gold region: N.Y., 32 p.

Morgan, Dale L., ed., 1959, The overland diary of James A. Pritchard: Denver; chart of 1849 diaries, in pocket.

Paul, Rodman W., 1963, Mining frontiers of the Far West 1848-1880: N.Y., p. 15.

Rieck, Richard L., 1993-95, Geography of the California trails: Independence, Overland Journal; Part 1, 1993, 11/4:12-22; Part 2, 1994, 12/1:27-32; Part 3, 1995, 13/3:25-32.

Robinson, Fayette, 1849 (1974 facsimile reprint), California and its gold regions; in The Gold Mines of California, Two Guidebooks: N.Y., 137 p.; large Colton map not reprinted; quotes 88, 96, 98-100.

Sheets, K. A., 1994, American maps 1795-1895: Ann Arbor, p. 138.

Sherwood, J. Ely, 1848, California, her wealth and resources: N.Y., 40 p.

Simpson, Henry I., 1848, The emigrant's guide to the gold mines—three weeks in the gold mines: N.Y., 30 p., double-page map.

Thornton, Jessy Quinn, 1849 (1855 reprint), Oregon and California in 1848: N.Y., Colton letter 2:291-94.

MAP OF THE
GOLD REGION.
CALIFORNIA.

PARTICULARS

OF

ROUTES, DISTANCES, FARES, &c.,

TO ACCOMPANY

Colton's Map of California

AND THE GOLD REGION.

COLLECTED FROM OFFICIAL DOCUMENTS.

The very great interest, at this time, bestowed by the Government and by the people of the United States on our recent territorial acquisitions, has induced the Publisher to compile from all the most authentic sources down to the present day, the accompanying "MAP OF THE UNITED STATES, THE BRITISH PROVINCES, MEXICO, &c.," so as to show the routes of the *United States Mail Steam Packets to California*, and to give a plan of the GOLD REGION.

The President's late message, together with official reports, confirm the daily accumulating information of the extraordinary mineral wealth of the CALIFORNIA GOLD REGION, as preceding accounts have instructed the country of its de-[p. 2] lightful climate and unrivalled fertility. It is therefore no way surprising that our enterprising people hurry to occupy and enjoy this land of promise.

Necessarily, they seek topographical information, and in a convenient form. Here, as far as possible, the geographical details are laid down as accurately as elaborately; but as it happens that the tide of emigration may require some further note of Routes, Distances, &c., than could be placed intelligibly on this, or any other map, it is here proposed to add, from the most reliable sources, such other facts as may be useful or necessary to a full geographical knowledge of the land and water routes to California.

We embody the President's own words, where, in his message, he says, "the acquisition of California and New Mexico will add more to the strength and wealth of the nation than any which have preceded them since the adoption of the Constitution, and that, great as may be the emigration to this new El Dorado, (California), the frugal and industrious will be amply repaid for their enterprise and toil." "They need only a state or territorial government for their protection," is the language of the government organ, speaking in the same spirit which [p. 3] characterises the most enthusiastic accounts which reach us from official, and from private sources, in California. It is also known that the establishment of a Mint, and speedy measures for the organization of government, in California, have been strenuously recommended to Congress by the President, and that various projects of canals, railroad routes, and steamboat lines, claim the attention of Congress, as well as compete with private enterprise. Many of these latter need, perhaps, the test of experience; it remains for the publisher, therefore, to add here such further memoranda of routes and distances, &c., as may assist the emigrant, or add to the useful information on those subjects, now being more and more developed by intelligence from abroad, and by the daily press of this country. It will be seen, from the "Tables of Distances" on the map, that the distance from New-York, via Chagres, and the Isthmus of Panama, to San Francisco, the central and nearest port of the gold region, is 5,308 miles. Other ports and intermediate distances are also detailed in the table. The following is the charge made by steam-vessels via Chagres:

From New-York to Chagres, in saloon..... $150
    "   "   "   cabin   120
  " Panama to San Francisco, saloon 250
    "   "   "   cabin   200

[p. 4] For places at a less distance, to the south of San Francisco, on the Californian coast, a proportionate reduction is made.

Some of the sailing vessels bound to Chagres charge from $75 to $50, according to the accommodations and fare on board. Persons going this way can take very little besides their luggage; the heaviest bulk will have to be sent around the Cape.

The following was formerly the charge made by the United States ships, for passage to the several ports on the Pacific, from Panama:

Panama to Realejo, 700 miles, in state rooms, $64
  "   Acapulco, 1,500 miles,   "   125
  "   San Blas ⎫ 2,000 miles, "   175
  "   Mazatlan ⎭
  "   San Diego, 3,000 miles,   "   225
  "   San Francisco, 3,500 miles.   "   250

Passage in the lower cabin at a deduction of one-fifth from the above rates.

Passage in the forward cabin from Panama to either of the above-named ports, $100.

The distance from New-York, via Cape Horn, is given as 17,000 miles, and the passage to San Francisco will occupy about five months. The price varies from $300 to $100 [400?], according to the accommodations on board the vessels; and here it may be well to add, that [p. 5]passengers via Chagres are there conveyed up the Chagres river in canoes about forty miles, when they are transferred to the backs of mules and carried twenty miles to Panama, where they take passage to

San Francisco in any vessel they can find. Chagres and Panama are proverbially unhealthy localities, yet, as commercial enterprize is sending so many vessels to these points, it is not deemed probable that any great detention will occur at Panama, but it will be seen, that, by the Isthmus route, baggage or merchandize can be carried only in very small bulk. It therefore results that, if the lesser cost, and facility of transportation in bulk, be an off-set to the more protracted voyage around Cape Horn, the latter would be preferable to those with whom time is not money; and this, perhaps, the more, that starting at this season, the voyage thus happens to occupy the period of time when the rainy season sets in in California, and the gold workings must stop.

An overland journey from Vera Cruz to Mazatlan has been suggested as affording quick and economical means of transportation—this, however, is for mere passengers unencumbered with baggage or merchandise in bulk. The passage to Vera Cruz is $80, made in about 18 days, and the whole journey from Vera Cruz, [p. 6] via the city of Mexico, to Mazatlan, is performed on horseback in about 20 days, at a cost of about $125. When at Mazatlan the traveller is 2000 miles north of Panama, and thence to San Francisco the charge by the Mail Steamers is $75, making the cost by this route to San Francisco $275, and the time occupied about 45 days. A little variation of this route, if it is wished, may strike Acapulco, but with like variation of cost and time.

The principal land routes are marked by the *blue* lines on the Map.

The southern trace being that of General Kearney, makes the distance from Fort Leavenworth, on the Missouri, to San Diego on the Pacific, via Santa Fe, New-Mexico, the Rio Grande and Rio Gila, 1916 miles, the further distance from San Diego to San Francisco 500.

The blue trace from San Francisco to Fort Leavenworth, Missouri, marks the route taken by General Kearney and party on his return in May, June and July, 1847—their progress was laborious and hazardous, yet the party was only 66 days from the settlements of California to Fort Leavenworth, and made not a day's stop—averaging for the last 57 days 31 miles per day: whole distance nearly 2000 miles.

Another route up the valley of the Rio [p. 7] Grande, and thence to start at Tome, and follow General Kearney's route to San Diego, may afford facilities greater than that of Fremont, through the South Pass, or Kearney, Stockton, &c., further south: yet of all these, it must be remembered, that their speedy and successful execution is mainly dependent upon the season of the year when undertaken.

In fact, the land routes should be undertaken in parties of considerable numbers, prepared to encounter toilsome travel, and some danger from predatory Indians, swollen streams, and snow capped mountains, giving place to arid and uninhabited wastes; until the Sierra Nevada shall have been surmounted, and the descent into the valley of the Sacramento, or of the San Joaquin, shall reward the emigrant with their golden treasure.

As abundantly descriptive of these gold regions, the publisher annexes the following letter, dated Monterey, Aug. 29, 1848, addressed to the Editors of the Philadelphia American, by the Rev. Walter Colton, Chaplain of the United States Navy, who has for some time been filling the office of Alcalde of Monterey.

"Messrs Editors:—New and important discoveries are made every day in the gold region. Instead of being confined to one stream, as was [p. 8] at first supposed, it has already been found on the banks of five, and in many dry ravines, where the water flows only during the rainy season. These streams take their rise in the chain of mountains which runs North and South through California, and the tributaries of the Sacramento. The discoveries extend already 200 miles North and South, and some 70 East and West. The strong probability is, that the entire chain—at least 500 miles of it—is richly impregnated with gold. The ore has been found in the deepest valleys and on the highest hills—at the bottom of meadow streams and on mountain cliffs, where only the eagle has been accustomed to pay his visits. It is inexhaustible. As an evidence of this, one fact will be sufficient. Seven men, with their Indians, working on Feather river, took from a space measuring 200 yards by 20, 275 pounds of gold.

"It is difficult to ascertain with much precision what the gold hunters average a day per man. But I can state this fact. I have met a great many of them, and not with one whose daily average was as low as $20; and some, it is well known, have averaged, for a week or month, over $100 a day, and this without employing any Indians or engaging in traffic. When a man finds he is gathering only his $18 or $20 a [p. 9]day, he changes his locality and looks up a richer spot. From all the facts I can gather on the subject, I must believe that the white men now at work in the mines average each about $40 a day.

"The gold diggers generally work in small companies of six or eight. They have a tent, provisions, cattle and horses. Each takes his turn in cooking and keeping camp. Four or five are engaged in getting out gold, and one or two in what they call prospecting—that is, hunting for some richer vein or deposite.

"It is impossible to procure labor at any price. The offer of ten dollars a day would not detain any one from the mines. The consequence is, our fields are without farmers, our shops without mechanics, our forts without sailors. The pay of a soldier, exclusive of his provisions and clothes, is about eight dollars a month.

One of them got a furlough for twenty days from Col. Mason, went to the mines, spent six days in going and as many in returning, leaving eight for work there, and brought back with him $800, just about what he would make in eight years soldiering it. Is it to be wondered at then that they desert? I doubt if there will be, by the time this letter reaches you, 50 soldiers at all our military posts in California. They will [p. 10] be in the mines, and if you send the few that remain to bring them back, they will themselves go to digging gold.

"Nor does the Navy fare a whit better.

"There are now about three thousand persons at work in the mines. They average, at the very lowest computation, an ounce per day each man. This makes an aggregate of more than a million a month, and this quantity will be doubled in three months. This gold now goes to Mazatlan, Peru, and Chili, where it is coined, and becomes a part of the currency of those countries. It is lost to us as the metallic basis of our circulating medium."

Extract of an official document received recently.

"Within the past six months, deposits of placer gold have been found at various points throughout a region of country in California, about six hundred miles in extent, which are believed to be equal in richness to any similar ones in the world. All that section of country lying upon the eastern side of the Sacramento river, and drained by its tributaries, from its head waters to its mouth, is known to contain rich deposits of gold. Gold is also known to exist upon some of the tributaries of the San Joaquin river, and in the various localities in the chain of mountains separating the waters of that river from [p. 11] those which run into the Pacific ocean, as far south as Ciudad de los Angelos.

"At this moment, the largest portion of the people of California are engaged in working these mines. Intelligent men from all parts of the gold regions, state that there are at least three thousand persons, whites and Indians, now employed in collecting the precious metal in California, and the least average amount obtained by each man, taking the year together, will be eight dollars per day."

TO EMIGRANTS TO THE GOLD REGION.

A TREATISE,

SHOWING THE BEST WAY TO CALIFORNIA,

WITH

MANY SERIOUS OBJECTIONS TO GOING BY SEA,

DOUBLING THE CAPE, OR CROSSING THE ISTHMUS,

WITH THE

CONSTITUTION AND ARTICLES OF AGREEMENT,

OF THE

Joint Stock Mutual Insurance Merchandizing Company.

By SIDNEY ROBERTS,

OF IOWA CITY, IOWA,

TRAVELING AGENT FOR THE COMPANY.

NEW HAVEN, JANUARY 1, 1849.

Sidney Roberts, 1849

To Emigrants To The Gold Region.
A Treatise, Showing The Best Way To California

New Haven, 1849, 12 p. [WC and WCB 172a; Cowan p. 535-36; Flake 7384;
Howes R346; Kurutz 538; Mintz 396; NUC NR 0322554.] Reset verbatim from a
facsimile, by courtesy of the Rare Books and Manuscripts Division, The New York
Public Library, The Astor, Lenox, and Tilden Foundations.

Significance   This propaganda for the overland route through Salt Lake City
was probably not authorized by the Mormon Church, but rather was Roberts's
personal attempt to make money in a merchandising venture. The last two pages
are proposed articles of agreement for a company that would buy goods in the east
and sell them to gold seekers in Council Bluffs, on the trail, or in California.
Roberts minimized the difficulties by land and exaggerated those by sea. His distances and times to Salt Lake City were very accurate, but he foreshortened the
distance to the gold fields beyond, and he threw in an extra 1,000 miles for the sea
route by faulty addition. His articles of agreement called for the four company officers and their wives to go West at company expense, with a Band of Music to cheer
them on. I have no record of what happened, if anything, or of any prior reprint.

Author   SIDNEY ROBERTS, Mormon tract writer. Flanders (1965) tells of
"the case in 1840 of an Elder Sydney Roberts of New York who commanded a
brother by the word of revelation to give him a fine suit and a gold watch. He was
also given to 'saluting the sisters with what he calls a holy kiss.' 'Much good counsel' was given Elder Roberts [by Joseph Smith] to convince him of his error, but to
no avail. So he was excommunicated and asked to give up his elder's license,
which he refused to do." Roberts was soon reinstated by the Church.

In December, 1848, there appeared a 9-page tract, "Great distress and loss of
the lives of American citizens. An appeal to the citizens of the United States for
and in behalf of suffering humanity, in the western state of Iowa, and in the
Indian territory. By Sidney Roberts of Iowa City, Iowa" (Flake 7383). This was an
appeal to help the Mormons at Kanesville (Council Bluffs), and at Winter Quar-

ters. It had a plate entitled "A Partial View of the Massacre of the Mormons," taken from a pre-Revolutionary picture of the Boston Massacre, showing red-coats blasting away at a group presumably including Joseph Smith (Bunker and Bitton 1983). Roberts expanded this to a 32-page pamphlet that was issued in January, 1849, together with the 12-page treatise reprinted here; the pamphlet was titled, "To emigrants to the gold region. An appeal to citizens of the U.S., the martyrdom of the two prophets, Joseph and Hiram [Hyrum] Smith—doctrines of the Latter day saints—on the Melchizedek priesthood—the materiality of the soul" (Cowan p. 535-36; Howes R346).

Roberts was back in trouble in October, 1849. In "Iowa City, Sidney Roberts was disfellowshipped for the unauthorized performance of 'the spiritual wife doctrine in such a way as to amount to adultery'" (Bennett 1987). Yet in Salt Lake City in 1851, "Church leaders named Sidney Roberts, apparently with some experience in building sawmills, to assist [Thomas] Howard in erecting the [papermaking] plant;" these two advertised for "ropes made of hemp, or flax, or paper hangings, or waste paper of all descriptions, and rags of all colors, of every name and denomination, either cotton, linen or woolen" (Ashton 1950). The project did not succeed.

Itinerary, 1849   Roberts's estimated distance and time from Council Bluffs to Salt Lake City, 1,033 miles and 70-80 days, from Clayton 1848, are quite accurate for non-family parties (cf. 3:E6); but Mormon settlers to Salt Lake in 1849 travel 116 days on average (3:E8). Roberts's "four hundred miles or so" from Salt Lake to the diggings fall far short of the actual 775 miles to Sacramento via Carson Pass. As shown in K1, the Forty-niners did not lose time by traveling via Salt Lake City, a route only 10 miles longer than the more northern one.

Highlights   Brigham Young at first welcomed the passing gold seekers, although he admonished his own people not to join them. In his 1849 Second Epistle (3:E8) he stated, "Thousands of emigrants from the States to the Gold Mines have passed through our city this season, leaving large quantities of domestic clothing, waggons, &c., in exchange for horses and mules, which exchange has been a mutual blessing to both parties...[but] Saints can be better employed in raising grain, and building houses in this vicinity, than digging for gold in the Sacramento."

The gain of all sorts of goods from overloaded gold seekers was indeed a boon to the struggling Mormons, who also sent parties out to pick up items abandoned on the trails. The emigrants in turn had the chance to get fresh provisions, to fix outfits, to rest, to recruit animals, to obtain medical help, to settle journey disputes (e.g., property divisions, estate settlements, breaches of contract, questionable animal sales, thefts, assaults), or to get a job during a winter layover if necessary.

Many emigrants were well pleased with their dealings with the Mormons, while others were not (Unruh 1979, Madsen 1983). Lt. John W. Gunnison, who was making a government survey of the Great Salt Lake area in 1849-50, declared in his 1852 book that "there was every appearance of impartiality and strict justice done to all parties...provisions were sold at very reasonable prices, and their [the Mormons'] many deeds of charity to the sick and broken-down gold-seekers, all speak loudly in their favor."

But emigrants who spent the winter of 1850-51 in Salt Lake City vehemently disagreed. In an 1851 report signed by 115 emigrants, Nelson Slater charged, with specific examples, that emigrants were "not being paid even the nominal values of their labor...have not a fair chance to obtain justice by legal process when their opponent is a mormon...liberty of speech is greatly abridged...'Danites' [are] murderous...treasonable sentiments [are] frequently express[ed]...taxing California emigrants [is] arbitrary, illegal, and unjust...letters of emigrants...are generally opened and examined by the mormons...and many of them totally destroyed." The Rev. J. W. Goodell's 1852 articles in the Portland *Oregonian* offered many more examples of alleged harassment and concluded "that the Mormons believed, or pretended to believe, that many of us were concerned in driving them from Missouri, and now they were determined to have revenge."

Unruh surmised, "The truth lay somewhere in between."

Legacy According to Unruh's probably very conservative figures, useful mainly in a relative sense, the 25,000 overlanders bound for California in 1849 swelled to 44,000 in 1850, dropped to 1,100 in 1851, rebounded to 50,000 in 1852, and tailed off to 20,000 in 1853 and to 4,000 in 1857. Perhaps from 25 to 40 percent of all these travelers came by way of Great Salt Lake. In 1857 Mormon-emigrant relations sank to their nadir in the horrific Mountain Meadows Massacre (4:G9).

REFERENCES

(See Preface for Heading references such as Cowan, Flake, and Howes, not listed here.)

Ashton, Wendell J., 1950, Voice in the West: N.Y., quote p. 54.

Bennett, Richard E., 1987, Mormons at the Missouri 1846-1852: Norman, quote p. 198.

Bunker, Gary L., and Davis Bitton, 1983, The Mormon graphic image 1834-1914: Salt L. City, p. 14.

Clayton, William, 1848 (1983 reprint), The Latter-Day Saints' emigrants' guide; Stanley B. Kimball, ed.: St. Louis, 107 p.

Flanders, Robert R., 1965 (1975 reprint), Nauvoo, kingdom on the Mississippi: Urbana, quote p. 254.

Goodell, Rev. J. W., 1852, The Mormons: Portland, The Oregonian, Apr. 3, v. 2, n. 18; Apr. 10, n. 19; May 1, n. 22; May 8, n. 23; May "13" [15], n. 24; May 22, n. 25; Jun. 12, n. 28; and Jun. 26, n. 30 (quoted).

Gunnison, Lt. John W., 1852, The Mormons: Phila., quote p. 65.

Madsen, Brigham D., 1983, Gold rush sojourners in Great Salt Lake City 1849 and 1850: Salt L. City, 178 p.

Slater, Nelson, 1851, Fruits of Mormonism: Coloma CA, 94 p., quotes 90-92.

Unruh, John D., Jr., 1979, The plains across: Urbana, p. 302-37, quote 337; figures 120.

THE BEST AND SAFEST ROUTE
TO
CALIFORNIA AND THE GOLD REGIONS.

AT a time like the present, when the public mind is turned with intense interest towards a region of land whence treasures, adequate to the wants and open for the appropriation of all, are presented, any intelligence which puts those who feel interested to avail themselves of the golden advantages which nature is so richly developing, in possession of the most available means of securing them, can not but possess the character of a public benefaction. And since the existence of an El Dorado, capable of enriching to their heart's content, all to whom its golden sands are accessible, is no longer a problem. It is especially grateful to those contemplating migrating thither, to be advised of a *safe, feasible* and *expeditious* route, by which they can reach this land of promise. And since any of the various routes hitherto traveled is fraught with perils of sea, of climate, of robbers, of savages, or all combined,—to be advised of a passage which at once is expeditious, and exempt from those evils, is a desideratum devoutly to be wished by all.

Such a passage exists in the track which the Latter Day Saints or Mormons have made, and may be described as follows:—First, proceed to St. Louis, Missouri, by any route that may be preferred. My own choice would be, (supposing myself east of the Hudson river,) to proceed to New York; thence to Philadelphia, whence I should go by rail road and canal to Pittsburg, Pa.; thence by steam boat to St. Louis. This city is on the west of the Mississippi Missouri. From St. Louis, the emigrant will proceed to Council Bluffs, in lat. 41° 30 N., and lon. 96° 40 W. The distance from St. Louis to Council Bluffs is about 600 miles. The next march is to Salt Lake in the Rocky Mountains. The distance from Council Bluffs to the great Salt Lakes is 1033 miles. From [p. 2] Salt Lake to the mountains of Sierra Nevada, on the west side of which lies the Gold regions, is 300—the gold being found at from four to six hundred miles from Salt Lake.

Having shown the route taken by the Mormons, I proceed next to describe the superlative advantages which render it incomparably preferable to any other. Any course requires a fitting out of wagons and provisions before reaching the gold regions; for if a passage by sea around Cape Horn be taken, the point nearest to the gold country, at which we can land, is San Francisco, which is not less than from 150 to 300 miles from the gold lands—which will be about six months passage. Now both St. Louis and Council Bluffs, especially the former, afford all desirable facilities for this purpose,—the latter more especially for horses and oxen, which about that region can be obtained for from $35 to $50, competent to perform the journey. Wagons, suitable for transports, proportionally cheap.

Second. This route lies within a range of two degrees of latitude, and hence no peril of a change of climate is to be encountered. Besides, the route selected by the Mormons was the most salubrious that could be taken, and is as healthy as any other region of country of the same extent. In fact, there is no disease incident to the climate in which their route lies.

Third. The Mormons have made a feasible road, which being continually traversed by them, is in good condition. And then, at Council Bluffs and Salt Lake, settlements, in which there are from eight to twenty thousands collected together, afford valuable facilities for recruiting provisions and transports, while the many wells which they have dug on the way, are of incalculable value in supplying the necessary beverage of life.

Fourth. Instead of meeting savages and cannibals, you will find yourself among not only civilized, enlightened and hospitable friends, but your own fellow-citizens, and in many instances your intimate acquaintances and near relations. These are a people who are and have been sojourning for the sake of religious faith, and are contending for as great a principle as our puritan fathers,—and they will extend towards [p. 3] travelers who come among them, that hospitality which oppression is so well calculated to induce.

Fifth. By this route, we not only enjoy the aid of the Mormon settlements, which is so necessary, but we may have their society and protection if we desire it. As companies of from one thousand to four are frequently passing and repassing between Council Bluffs and the Salt Lake, from April to June, the depredations of the Indians upon the cattle and horses are in companies of such entirely prevented,—the number of their wagons being sufficient to form an enclosure in which the beasts can feed at night. Indeed, it is not safe to travel, except in a company of not less than five hundred, on account of the pilfering of beasts by the Indians,—their disposition being only to plunder.

Sixth. Arrived at Salt Lake, you can remain at the Mormon rendezvous there, which contains from ten to twelve thousand, and recruit provisions, &c., and wait your own time to proceed the remaining four hundred miles or so. Companies of Mormons, with whom you can travel, are frequently passing back and forth from Salt Lake to the gold country, in such numbers as to insure complete safety. And what is most agreeable of all, they are your former neighbors, friends and kinsmen, and you can trust them with implicit confidence, and if injured, get redress without delays or costs, as their laws are more liberal than any other people.

Seventh. The company who go to dig gold must be provided with wagons, to transport their provisions, tents, &c. while pursuing after the gold,—to remove the sick, if in an unhealthy portion of the country, or remove from place to place to dig gold, &c. And at Council Bluffs, these can be procured to as good advantage as in any of the Atlantic States. Whereas, whatever other route is taken, these are to be procured after arrival near the ground, at from five to fifteen times their cost at Council Bluffs, and likely all will be so much absorbed in digging gold, that they can not be had at any price. The general market prices for provisions at Council Bluffs are at the rate of $3 50 per barrel for flour, $2 a hundred for beef, $2 for pork, and other articles of their own productions at the same ratio. Published catalogues of the provisions necessary for a person for one year, are fur-[p. 4]nished at Council Bluffs, which catalogues are founded on the experience of those who have performed the same journey which is without exaggeration.

Eighth. The soil of the country is exceedingly fertile, producing spontaneously, oats and flax, as well as fruits of various kinds. The climate is so mild, that two crops a year can usually be raised. It will be wise to carry every kind of seed that can be conveniently taken. Lastly,

The above description is a true representation of the character and advantages of the Mormon route, given as the result of my own best information, by experience, and from those who have traversed the Western Californias, to guide those who may be about to embark in an enterprise which is just and laudable, and for which there is now so great an inducement. It needs no comment to give it force, as I am persuaded that the simple statement of facts will at once render its superiority apparent to all.

And it would seem as if Providence designs to humble the pride of man, by bringing within the reach of all, the article whose unequal distribution hitherto has been the cause of lifting one man above another.

SIDNEY ROBERTS.

[p. 5] MANY REASONABLE OBJECTIONS
FOR NOT GOING BY SEA, OR ACROSS THE ISTHMUS OF DARIEN, TO CALIFORNIA

IN another section, I have given many advantages of emigrating by the Mormon route, by the way of Council Bluffs, Salt Lakes, &c.; and although in treating of the many inducements which this route offers, I have incidentally compared its advantages with those of other prominent ones, yet in the casual allusion which I have made to them, I have not attempted to describe all their advantages in comparison with the one I recommended. I have therefore thought proper, through the solicitations of many of my friends, to devote a section to the drawing of a parallel between the two southern routes and the Mormon's road, showing the evils unavoidably incident to the former, which are avoided by taking the latter.

First. Suppose a company of one hundred, say, purchase a vessel and go by Cape Horn. Their vessel will undoubtedly cost from fifteen to thirty thousand dollars, which must of course be advanced, and towards which each must contribute his share. At fifteen thousand dollars, which is the minimum, each one's share is one hundred and fifty dollars, and this will be increased as the cost of the vessel becomes greater. The services of the captain and crew for the voyage can not be less than ten thousand dollars more, as they must be employed for not less than fifteen months, in order to go and return with them,—and they must be paid sufficient to induce them to return in the service of the company.

Next comes the outfit in respect to provisions; and whatever this may cost, certain it is that the expense will be at least two or three times as much as to furnish provisions for the northern route. Besides, in furnishing supplies for an expedition by sea, no growth of vegetables can be hoped for, and whatever green things they can have, they must carry with them, at great expense and sacrifice; whereas by the land route, they can not only have, at least as far [p. 6] as Council Bluffs, any dish they wish, and that too at one third or one half the cost of it at sea, but being all the time in a vegetable producing country, and can have any of recent growth that may be desired, and also of every kind. This is a great item of advantage, and one which can not be too highly valued, when we consider that in a long voyage at sea, the health of the crew of a vessel is greatly jeoparded by the necessary use of salt and stale provisions,—and this danger is immensely greater to those who are not accustomed to the sea.

Furthermore, the country from Council Bluffs abounds in wild game, buffaloes, deer, wild turkeys, prairie chickens, &c.; and the streams teem with numerous fresh food in exhaustless abundance, which can at all times be obtained.

Second. The company, on arriving at San Francisco, or other ports from whence they proceed to the gold region, must be provided with baggage wagons, spoken of in a former section—and these must be carried from the port of departure, because they can not well, if at all, be obtained in California. These can be obtained at St. Louis, or at Council Bluffs, on as good terms, perhaps, as in the New England States, and employed as transports on the road,—thus being made to work their passage, instead of being a useless incumbrance. Although the horses can be procured in California much cheaper, yet they are not as thoroughly domesticated as are our horses, and will not serve with that efficiency as the eastern animals. Hence, if the company wish for good domesticated animals for immediate use, they must transport them at immense expense and hazard, both to the animal and the people of the vessel. Horses, as has been before observed, can be had at Council Bluffs, for half their value here, and oxen for less than half—and in journeying over the mountains, they become accustomed and inured to the service of traveling, and are therefore much more serviceable at the gold regions.

Another advantage, which may appear paradoxical, is, that the health of the emigrants will increase as they advance towards the mountains, and the animals will be in as good condition as they were when they started. Although this may seem strange, it is nevertheless true, for their daily journeys vary from fifteen to twenty miles, which does not burden them, and their passage is through a coun- [p. 7] try that abounds with luxurious grass, with which they have abundant time to fill themselves as often as they need, besides resting from their service.

Third. Each one that goes by sea must pay his share, and he that is not able to do this has no opportunity to commute for it by any kind of service, or in any other way paying his fare on the voyage. But in going by the Mormon route, and especially in company with the Mormons, the management of the teams, making and repairing different articles on the road, and other modes of service, will give numbers a chance to work their passage, whose means would not enable them to go otherwise. Besides, although provisions are much cheaper at Council Bluffs than in New England, there are articles which cost immensely more there than at the East, which a yankee can take as venture upon which to speculate. Among these are articles of clothing and materials for the same, hats, boots and shoes, and other articles of merchandize, which afford a net profit of paying your expenses from here there; so that your transportation across the mountains will be but a mere trifle in comparison with even living in the Eastern States. Besides, there are many opportunities of trading small articles with the Indians, in exchange for meat and fish, at great advantages of speculation of exchange.

Fourth. The passage around the Cape involves a total change of climate, as it lies in all latitudes, from nothing to fifty-six degrees or more South, back across the equator, under a burning sun, to forty degrees North,—making a range of about one hundred degrees of latitude; while the land route is all the way between the parallels of New York, and most of it is in the same latitude as Connecticut. But as the climate of the Mormon route has been spoken of in another place, I need not dwell long on it here.

It should be remembered, moreover, that the water you can have at sea is meted out in prudent allowances while the wells that the Mormons have dug, and the crystal streams that flow through the country, afford abundant supplies of pure water, both for the emigrants and their beasts.

To this may be added the dangers of the sea, which, although the same God watches over us in all places, all must agree are immensely greater than the perils of the land. Furthermore, if any of the company are sick at [p. 8] sea, they must unavoidably suffer all the clamor and agitation which must needs be on board a vessel, and enjoy only the miserable nursing which can be given in case of a storm. Whereas, by emigrating the Council Bluffs way, you can have comfortable conveyance for those who are indisposed; and if unable to travel, a company can halt with the sick until the issue of their disease. They can at the same time enjoy the refreshing breezes of a salubrious climate, and medical aid, and female attendance, which renders their situation incomparably more comfortable than it can be made at sea. However, the superlative healthfulness of the country through which they pass, has hitherto almost entirely exempted them from disease,—and I recollect but very few cases after leaving Council Bluffs. There are, in addition, numerous places on the coasts, which are infested with fevers and ague, yellow and bilious and other diseases incident to the country,—and at some of these places the mariner must needs stop either before or after he reaches the coast of California; so that it is hardly possible to avoid those diseases; and a resident of the New England or Middle States is most liable to their influence.

Again, the restrictions which the officers of the vessel must needs impose upon the company, bring them into an artificial stiffness, which illy contrasts with the freedom enjoyed in a company who travel by land, in the company of friends, and with the scope of action which the traversing of the prairies affords. Every thing has the appearance of domestic enterprise, and sociability, and friendly equality, which gives to the company more the aspect of the puritan fathers, bound together by a common principle, and cemented together by brotherly affection, than a company of adventurers, seeking a mine of wealth. One almost forgets that he is away from his family and friends, in consequence of his place being made so much like home.

Another thing must be kept in mind; there is no retraction from the enterprise, when once begun by sea. Should you repent your effort, as many do who are not accustomed to a life at sea, and which many undoubtedly will, there is no alternative but to proceed. You are enlisted for a voyage of from one to two years, and must take its fate. It can not be, in the nature of things, that all who engage in this laudable enterprise will retain their zeal, or desire [p. 9] to pursue their undertaking to the end, by whichever route they may commence their expedition; and the land route will admit of your giving it up, whenever you may repent your undertaking—and that without loss or sacrifice, but with actual advantage. If you stop in the country this side of the Rocky Mountains, except the places between Council Bluffs and the Rocky Mountains, you are in the garden of Eden—in a country whose climate is mild and salubrious, and whose soil produces spontaneously many of the fruits and grains of tropical and temperate regions, and is susceptible of being made to yield larger crops of useful vegetables than any of the organized States. But suppose you are not discouraged, and desire not to return prematurely. Is it not desirable to hear from home and friends at as short intervals as possible? And should the family or domestic affairs of any one assume an aspect which would indicate a return, no intelligence can be communicated by sea in less time than five or six months, and a return will occupy as much longer. But from any portion of the country this side of the Salt Lake, opportunities of communicating with any part of the United States, through Council Bluffs, are frequently occurring,—and the time required for it does not exceed eighty days, and often it is accomplished sooner.

Here I am brought to a comparison of the times occupied by the two routes. It is well known that the time required for a passage by sea can not be less than five months, and it is seldom accomplished in less than six; whereas the utmost time required for a passage from New York to Salt Lakes, by way of Council Bluffs, is from seventy to eighty days, and it is often made in sixty days. Hence, a company starting from Council Bluffs about the first of April, to the first of June, (which is the season at which the roads become settled,) can go over the mountains without any interference of snow-drifts, or any other obstacles, and reach the gold regions at a suitable time of the year to be healthy, hale and vigorous; and if disposed, you can return in the spring following, to the bosom of your family in New England, after an absence of from ten to twelve months; whereas the distance by sea is eighteen thousand miles, while the distance by land is but four thousand.

Most of the objections that I have urged against the pas-[p. 10] sage by Cape Horn, apply with full force to the route by Chagres and Panama, across the Isthmus of Darien, with others that are peculiar to this latter route. The distance from New York to Chagres is 2308 miles; from Chagres to Panama, 50 miles—30 of which is by water, and 20 by land; and from Panama to San Francisco, 3500 miles, making in the aggregate, 6908 miles, to be traveled by water in some manner. It can be performed in the Government mail steamer, at an expense of about $150. It will be perceived that this route will require repeated shipments, and a transportation of baggage by land 20 miles, which, because of the difficulty of the pass, all luggages have to be packed upon the backs of mules, which is with great difficulty, and enormously expensive. So that nothing is gained by taking this route, over that by the Cape, except the saving of a little time, say two months. But this is not only a difficult, but a dangerous and unhealthy route, as the Isthmus is infested with robbers, and both Chagres and Panama are the seats of fever and ague, and yellow fever, from which a northern man can hardly hope to escape.

In conclusion, it must be observed, that a company of a hundred is as large as will be healthy to go by sea, or as can be well furnished with provisions for such a voyage; but those who go by the way of Council Bluffs, enjoy the free air of heaven, whether they be few or many,—and the larger the company, the more invulnerable and secure they are, while the country through which they pass will yield them an inexhaustible supply of provisions to carry over the mountains with them, besides procuring a fresh supply at the Salt Lakes, where an abundance can be procured at reasonable rates.

These reflections I have suggested, for the consideration of my friends, and they have emanated from the purest and best motives, to give them such necessary information as might be desirable. Therefore, you will be governed by these motives, with a favorable conclusion. If requested, I will wait upon you with all necessary intelligence, to make a full equivalent outfit for the expedition, and will also extend that magnanimity to all classes of people, to Jew or Gentile, bond or free, that will put them in possession of a sublime country, and a salubrious climate, and the most fertile and richest mines in the world.

SIDNEY ROBERTS, *Traveling Agent.*

[p. 11] CONSTITUTION AND ARTICLES OF AGREEMENT
ARTICLES OF AGREEMENT
OF THE
CALIFORNIA
Joint Stock Mutual Insurance Merchandizing Company.
SIDNEY ROBERTS, Traveling Agent.

THIS Company is to be called and constituted, "The California Joint Stock Mutual Insurance Merchandizing Company," to form an association of immunities and privileges for the benefit of all, of every name and denomination, who shall conform to the articles of agreement below specified.

ARTICLE I.   We, the undersigned, do mutually and severally agree to appropriate each one share, which is hereby constituted and denominated one hundred dollars each, for the specific purpose of making a purchase of goods for the California trade. Each share to be paid in advance, or at the purchase of the goods in the city of New York, or elsewhere.

ART. II.   Any one can become a member of this association, by paying five dollors [*sic*] for the benefit of the agency of this Company, in collecting its members, and incidental expenditures and advertisements,—which must be paid on receiving a receipt of membership.

ART. III.   This Company shall have the privilege of increasing the funds, from one thousand to one hundred thousand dollars.

ART. IV.   All articles of goods shall be purchased by the Agent, and the Company shall not be responsible for the amount purchased, (the money being its equivalent,) and not to be sold until reaching Council Bluffs or California, by direction and disposition of the Company.

ART. V.   All goods and merchandize are to be insured from fire, and to their safe conveyance to the place of destination, and the duty of the Agent shall be to see that it is done upon the receipt of purchases.

ART. VI.   Any member shall have the privilege of examining into all the arrangements of sales, and to have a voice in the disposition of how and when to be sold, after arriving at Council Bluffs, or in California.

ART. VII.   Dividends to be made every week after the sales commence, and each member to receive his proportion of dividends, according to the sales, which shall be governed by a vote of two thirds, in all cases.

ART. VIII.   No sales to be made without cash in hand, or its equivalent in some other articles in exchange, denominated by the members of the association.

ART. IX.   Any member wishing to leave, shall have the privilege of leaving the Company, to be paid in full for all capital invested, with six per cent. interest, after the sales of the goods.

ART. X.   The Company shall appoint a Clerk, Salesman, and Treasurer, to be hired according to the counsel and advice of the Company, after arriving at the destined point.

ART. XI.   All goods must be purchased before the 20th of March, 1849, and boxed or packed ready for transportation, and insured according to article V.

ART. XII.   This Company will receive none but enterprising and [p. 12] moral men, of good character and respectability in society, without respect to name or denomination; and all shall enjoy their religious opinions, without reproach or interference by any member.

ART. XIII.   Any one can have shares in this Company, through an Agent, which is to be safely deposited in some safe Bank, to be and remain until after the purchases of the goods,—and will share his proportion in the dividends, and none exempt.

ART. XIV.   This Company is to go and return once in twelve months, or as soon as the practicability of the enterprise shall justify; and the Agent's duty shall be, to see that all are amply provided with good wagons and teams, after arriving at Council Bluffs, and a place of rendezvous for a fit-out.

ART. XV.   Any member can take his family, and can share the advantages of traveling in the Company; and it shall be the duty of every member to carry with him a good rifle or gaming gun, and equipments for the same. Each member shall have the privilege of shipping goods on his own responsibility, independent of membership.

ART. XVI.   This Company will receive members until the 20th of March, 1849, and will rally at the beat of the drum, at a place designated by a Committee of Arrangements, appointed to transact the business of the Company,—and it shall be the duty of the Agent to choose this Committee to facilitate the expedition, to be sanctioned by the Company; and said Committee, with their wives, shall go free of charge, or at the expense of the Company.

ARV. XVII.   If any member shall become refractory and contentious, the duty of the Agent shall be to cross his name from the list, and pay him his money, according to article IX, out of the funds of the Company, by the advice of a majority.

ART. XVIII.   The Company shall have the privilege of a Band of Music, organized according to the wishes of the Company, to cheer up their spirits and gladden their hearts in passing and repassing, as their wishes may be. No intoxi-cating liquors shall be used as a beverage.

ART. XIX.   The Company shall have the privilege of borrowing cash capital for its accommodation, which shall be done through a committee, appointed by the Company, according to article XVI.

ART. XX.   All business transactions shall be signed by the Agent, and coun-tersigned by the Committee of Arrangements—which Committee shall consist of four, chosen and appointed according to article XVI, and two shall have the privilege of transacting business of an especial kind, to be signed by the Agent,— and the said Committee shall call a meeting of the members every week, or as often as they may deem expedient, for transacting necessary business, at a place selected by them; and said meetings shall be opened with prayer by some person selected by the Committee; and no spectators shall be admitted.

ART. XXI.   No clergyman to receive any salary from the Company.

ART. XXII.   Of all moneys borrowed for and in behalf of the Company or traveling purposes, each member may receive of the same in proportion to his investment of capital, which shall be as security to the Company until paid.

ART. XXIII.   These articles to be and remain inviolate, until changed by a two-thirds vote of all the members who have an interest of at least one share,— and to be in force from this date, January 1, 1849.

Brigham H. Young and John Eagar, 1850

Emigrant's Guide...From Great Salt Lake City To San Francisco

[Salt Lake City, 1850], Second Edition, 8 p. [WCB 193b; Flake 10077; Kurutz 706; NUC NY 0024445.] Reset verbatim from a facsimile, by courtesy of the Yale Collection of Western Americana, Beinecke Rare Book and Manuscript Library, New Haven, Connecticut.

Significance   This momentous little guide is the first printed one to outline two new trail segments that became major arteries of the gold rush—the Salt Lake Cutoff north of the Lake, and the Carson Trail over the Sierra to Placerville. It also gave for several years the most accurate information on the Humboldt River trek. Eastbound veterans of the Mormon Battalion opened both segments to wagons in 1848. These men, including five who worked at Sutter's Mill at the time of the gold discovery (Henry W. Bigler, James S. Brown, William J. Johnstun, Azariah Smith, and Alexander Stephens), carried pouches full of nuggets but were bent on rejoining their families in Salt Lake City. With them were Ira J. Willes and also John Eagar, author of this 1850 guide. The only fully documented 1849 Mormon guide was a hand-written one by Willes. J. Goldsborough Bruff bought a copy on August 29 at City of Rocks: "one of them [a Mormon] took out of his pocket a sort of Guide book, formed of a sheet of paper folded small, miserably written, and worse spelling, which he said was the last he had, & I might take it for 50¢, but that he had sold a number, to the emigrants for $1 each." Brigham H. Young, the first printer in Utah, had not been west of Salt Lake City when he issued Eagar's guide.

Reprinted here, possibly for the first time, is the only known copy of Eagar's guide, styled "Second Edition," undated but noticed (generally unfavorably) by several 1850 emigrants. Eagar obviously had updated his 1848 observations to include 1849 conditions. Charles L. Camp speculated in 1972 that an 1850 manuscript copy by Morris Sleight of part of the guide may have been taken from the otherwise unknown first edition, because all mileages cumulated from Salt Lake are shorter by five miles. Mattes 964 noted that "Sleight has a low opinion of guidebooks. For the emigrant, 'the track is the guide. There is not a plainer or better road in America.'" Camp also found that Hugh A. Skinner, who passed through Salt Lake City July 15-19, copied Eagar's text into his 1850 diary. Unruh (1979) recorded that "Silas Newcomb, who purchased a copy of this guidebook in Salt Lake City on July 17, 1850, was unimpressed with its validity and within two weeks had pronounced it 'a poor thing.'"

Franklin Langworthy's 1855 book mentioned in the entry for May 5, 1850, in Council Bluffs, that "Every traveler is made to believe that a Mormon 'guide book' and a pair of goggles are indispensable requisites for the road. The guide book is a pamphlet of five or six leaves, and might have cost the proprietor three cents per copy. Thousands of these are sold, at prices ranging from fifty cents to two dollars each; and the goggles, in still greater numbers, are sold at fifty cents per pair, and neither of these articles were of the least service in crossing the plains." The identity of this guidebook is unknown.

Despite bad reviews, Eagar's brief guide had accurate mileages and descriptions. Many gold seekers little appreciated the heroic efforts spent in opening the trails for them.

Authors   BRIGHAM HAMILTON YOUNG, 1824-1898, Utah's first printer. A New York native and nephew of Brigham Young, B. H. Young arrived at Salt Lake in late 1847. He was "a short, stocky youth…with light brown hair, blue-gray eyes, and fair, clean-shaven skin." A year before, he was released by a mob near Nauvoo after being poisoned but before being shot while propped up against a tree. On January 22, 1849, he and Thomas Bullock set type for printing 50-cent bills on a handmade press. A Ramage press arrived at Salt Lake City on August 7, 1849; on October 20, B. H. Young used it to print the *Second General Epistle*, 3:E8, the first pamphlet made in Utah. He as pressman and Bullock as proofreader helped produce the first issue of the *Deseret News* on June 15, 1850. Young also was the printer of the 1852 *Acts* of Utah's first Territorial Legislative Assembly.

B. H. Young was a skilled craftsman who made the first shoes and harnesses in Salt Lake City. He planted the first trees and operated the first amusement park. In 1852 he led a soon-abandoned attempt to build a bridge and start a settlement at the Oregon Trail's Green River crossing (Gardiner 1900). He joined a handcart company on his 1857 return from a mission to England. Indians later attacked and burned his merchandise train on the plains; the government failed to reimburse him. He became a leader in mining and industrial affairs. He spent his later years in California. (Ashton 1950; McMurtrie 1933.)

JOHN EAGAR, printer, editor, teacher. A New Yorker, Eagar sailed in the *Brooklyn* in 1846 from New York around Cape Horn to San Francisco with Samuel Brannan and 236 other Mormons. Eagar became an associate editor of the *California Star*, published by Brannan and edited by Elbert P. Jones. The first regular issue of January 9, 1847, was greeted with civility by the existing Monterey *Californian*. But on February 20, Jones in the *Star* called the *Californian* "a dim, dirty, little paper printed in Monterey on the worn out materials of one of the old California war presses. It is published and edited by Walter Calton [Colton] and Robert Semple, the one a whining sycophant, and the other an overgrown lickspittle." (According to Lt. William T. Sherman 1875, Semple was about seven feet tall, and the *Californian* "was a curiosity in its line, using two *v*'s for a *w*, and other combinations of letters, made necessary by want of type.") When Brannan went to Salt Lake in April, 1847, he left Edward C. Kemble and Eagar to try to tone down Jones's vituperative editorials. Jones quit in a rage within a week, and Kemble edited the now more peaceful, prosperous *Star* for the rest of 1847 (Howell 1970).

A month or so after the *Star's* April 1, 1848, announcement of the gold discovery (see Perspective K), Kemble suspended publication and took off for the mines. (When he returned, he bought both the *Star* and the *Californian* and issued the first combined edition on November 18.) In July, 1848, his job gone and ignoring the diggings, Eagar headed for Salt Lake City with a group mainly composed of Mormon Battalion veterans (see Itinerary). He buddied up with Addison Pratt, a former whaler and returning missionary from Polynesia. Pratt wrote in his journal, "neither John or myself were teamsters, as I was reared at sea and he in a printing office…while in camp, we found a young man who was a teamster and with him we agreed to drive our teams." Eagar taught school after his arrival in Salt Lake City, and he later settled in Arizona. (Bagley 1991.)

Itinerary, 1848 EAGAR, MORMON OPENING OF CARSON TRAIL AND SALT LAKE CUTOFF. July 15—From "Gold Valley" about 50 miles east of Sutter's Fort, near future Placerville, one woman and 45 men, including military leader Samuel Thompson, editor John Eagar, returning missionary Addison Pratt, and diarists Henry W. Bigler, Ephraim Green, Jonathan H. Holmes (the elected President), Samuel H. Rogers, and Azariah Smith, head east over the Sierra. They have 17 wagons, two small Russian cannons purchased from Capt. John A Sutter, and some 400 horses, mules, oxen, cows, and calves. Most are Mormon Battalion veterans (3:E6) who are turning their backs on the new gold discoveries in order to rejoin their families in Salt Lake City. Their dislike of the Truckee route and its many stream crossings prompts them to forge a new road over Carson Pass (5:J1). They have sent ahead three scouts, Ezra Allen, Daniel Browett, and Henderson Cox. The one woman, Melissa Coray, wife of Sgt. William Coray, has been with the Battalion on its entire march from Council Bluffs.

July 19—At Tragedy Springs, 13 miles west of Carson Pass on today's State Highway 88, they find in a shallow grave the naked, battered bodies of the three scouts, killed by Indians on June 27. They find Allen's pouch of gold and later deliver it to his widow. That night they fire off a cannon to impress any lurking Indians, but the blast stampedes a third of their stock. They spend the next day reburying the dead and rounding up the animals. July 29—At Carson Pass, Azariah Smith records that "the wagons are crossing the back bone, and going down the Mountain on the other side which is very steep, and the men have to hold the wagons [with block and tackle] to keep them from tiping over." Progress is slowed also by clearing trail and by fixing broken wagons with new wooden parts, or with iron ones welded on an improvised forge.

July 31 to August 4—At about a mile a day, it takes five days to carve a road through the Canyon of the West Fork of Carson River. The men build repeated fires on some rocks to spall them down. The Guide says, "the road is very rough and the [three] crossings bad." On the 7th, Ephraim Green reports, "the Indians [Paiutes] stold my horse in company with three others one mule and one ox[.] we folerd them five or six milds on the trale and found there was a bout twenty in number[.] we had no guns and returnd." The next day 10 men go ahead with 14 packers who have caught up with them. August 12—The wagons leave the Carson ("Pilot") River near present Silver Springs NV and go out of their way north to the regular California Trail on the Truckee River at today's Wadsworth. The Guide, however, takes the shortcut between Carson River and Humboldt Sink.

August 15—They reach the Sink of the Humboldt ("Mary's") River after crossing the Forty-Mile Desert. Here is mountain man James Clyman, who will be the first to pass westward over the brand new Carson Trail with his 16 wagons. The Mormons meet four more California-bound parties along the Humboldt. All are elated to hear of the gold discovery and to see the dust and nuggets. A party with 25 wagons passes by on the 16th and also takes the Carson route. After continued trouble with Indians, the Mormons greet 10 wagons on the 26th that may be the ones that Peter Lassen is taking on his roundabout northern loop to his ranch (K1 Itinerary). On the 27th, packer Samuel Hensley gives them a map and directions for the Cutoff that he has just pioneered around the north end of Great Salt Lake. On August 30 the Mormons encounter the 48 wagons of veteran overlander Joseph B. Chiles and famed mountain man Joseph Rutherford Walker. Green writes that, of "mr waker we had to in quire about the rout and giv directions about ours." Walker and Chiles go on west to open the shortcut from Humboldt Sink to Carson River. August 31—The Mormons are at the junction with the Hastings Cutoff near modern Elko NV.

September 6—The party leaves the Humboldt about 10 miles west of present Wells NV and ascends Bishop Creek ("Kanyon Creek" in the Guide) to its head. Looking in vain for a shortcut mentioned by Chiles, they travel east 7 miles on the 8th but return to the head of Bishop Creek on the 9th. Thence they follow the California Trail northeast through Thousand Springs Valley to Goose Creek and down it by Nevada's northeast corner and east across Granite Pass to City of Rocks near today's Almo ID.

September 15—Bigler writes, "on our left were two towering rocks near each other which Mr. A. Pratt named the Twin Sisters." Eagar calls them "Steeple Rocks." Here at the City of Rocks, they leave the California/Ft. Hall Trail and start making a new wagon road east on Hensley's pack trace along Raft River ("Casus Creek"). They curve southeast and south around the north end of Great Salt Lake, passing Deep Creek near present Snowville UT, the Hansel Mountains (misnamed on modern maps for Hensley), Blue Springs ("Warm and Cold Springs," near today's Howell, September 21), Malad River ("Mud Creek"), Bear River Crossing (which next year is a ferry, near what is now Honeyville), and future Brigham City (near "Box Elder Creek"), and Ogden ("Brownsville") and Farmington ("Blooming Grove"). September 28—Salt Lake City.

This trip of about 820 estimated miles takes 74 rugged days, excluding 14 miles and 2 days searching for Chiles's shortcut, but still including 9 layover days and 7 in road work, at an overall average of 11 miles per day. These values come from Will Bagley's superb 1991 folding chart summarizing five diaries, with a few interpolations for blanks. Other excellent sources for the itinerary are Roderick Korns 1951, David Bigler 1990, and Norma Ricketts 1996. The 820-mile distance compares to 762 in the Eagar Guide and to about 725 in today's survey of the final trail (Perspective Table Kb). These mileages probably reflect quite well the progressive shortcuttings that evolve during a trail's history.

Itineraries, 1850   The average 1850 wagon travels from the MISSOURI TO THE SACRAMENTO via South Pass WY, Soda Springs ID, and the Carson or Truckee routes over the Sierra, in 107 days. This is 13 days faster than the average for the same route in 1849 (K1). Detouring by Salt Lake City in 1850 adds 10 miles and 7 days, presumably owing to longer layovers there. Those going from Salt Lake City over the more arduous Hastings Cutoff (see 2:D7), rather than the 35-mile shorter Salt Lake Cutoff, average 120 days for the whole trip. This is still pretty good time. The fewer packers average 86 days, at 22 miles per day, compared to 16 or 17 miles per day for wagon trains. Of 118 diarists studied, 47, or 40 percent, go via Salt Lake City.

These travel times come from Mattes's 118 bibliographic entries that have usable dates, checked against the 36 diarists studied by Becker in 1969. Times include all travel as well as layover days from the Missouri, although no diary with a two-week-or-more time in Salt Lake City is knowingly used. Distances are summed from Rieck's 1993-95 definitive trail profiles (Perspective Table Kb).

A few 1850 gold seekers take the Lassen Trail. Dr. George Keller's 1851 guide tells of his remarkable 1850 trip. He leaves the Missouri opposite St. Joseph on April 10 in a party outfitted with light mule wagons and too little flour. After South Pass, the Sublette Cutoff, and Ft. Hall, by mistake they take the Lassen Trail from Lassen Meadows on the Humboldt. Near Goose Lake they convert their wagons into packsaddles. After being robbed by Indians, they reach Lassen's Ranch on July 4, "worn out by hunger, thirst, and fatigue." They cover 1,950 miles in 86 days at an impressive 23 miles per day.

WAGONS VIA SODA SPRINGS, CARSON/TRUCKEE TRAILS. Average travel time of 65 diarists is 107 days. They leave various points along the Missouri in April or May and reach various diggings in July, August, or September; a few arrive later. Some go by Ft. Bridger and/or Ft. Hall; others take the Sublette and/or Hudspeth cutoffs (see K1 for route variations). The trip of 1,860 miles on average takes minimum-mean-maximum 73-107-149 days, at an average 17 miles per day.

WAGONS VIA SALT LAKE CITY, SALT LAKE CUTOFF, CARSON/TRUCKEE TRAILS. Travel times of 27 diarists using the Salt Lake Cutoff are minimum-mean-maximum 75-114-148 days. They cover the average distance of 1,870 miles at 16 miles per day.

WAGONS VIA SALT LAKE CITY, HASTINGS CUTOFF, CARSON/TRUCKEE TRAILS. Travel times of 12 diarists using the Hastings Cutoff are minimum-mean-maximum 100-120-133 days. Average distance of 1,905 miles is traversed at 16 miles per day.

PACKERS VIA EITHER SODA SPRINGS OR SALT LAKE CITY, AND CARSON/TRUCKEE TRAILS. Travel times of 14 diarists range 72-86-98 days, covering an average 1,865 miles at 22 miles per day. Ten diarists use light wagons on the earlier, easier stretches; half of these convert to packing on the North Platte, and the rest either at South Pass/Green River or Salt Lake City.

Highlights   In 1850 Lorenzo Sawyer made use of Eagar's Guide from City of Rocks westward: "we had no little difficulty for a time in determining which was Steeple Rock. The last two rocks, however, as we passed out of the valley, seemed pre-eminently entitled to the appellation…There is a creek running through Thousand Spring valley, but I saw but few springs…Eleven [plus 3] miles further we struck Cold Water creek…[twenty-three] miles brought us to the creek, a tributary of the Humboldt, called by the Mormons Canon [Bishop] creek. Here the road forks, the one described in the Mormon guide takes to the right, following the creek down and passing through a canon…the other crosses the creek and passes on the left…to several deep holes in a wet marshy valley [the Humboldt Wells at present Wells NV]."

The Humboldt, much higher in 1850 than in the past, made the old road along the bottoms impassable and forced the emigrants into detours much more lengthy than the guidebook indicated. "Wading in the filthy alkaline mire and water [to cut grass] produces nausea in our men, and sometimes vomiting, yet this is the only means we have of procuring a particle of food for our animals." At places the road was blocked with dead animals and abandoned wagons. "It is a pitiable sight, but still more harassing to our feelings to be constantly beset by travelers who are out of provisions." In Carson Canyon, "The road defies all powers of description for roughness. Rocks of all dimensions and shapes lay wedged in every conceivable form."

At Carson Pass Sawyer wrote, "The man who first attempted to pass this mountain with a wagon must have possessed a spirit worthy of Napoleon. The passage of the Alps could scarcely be more difficult." Yet ragged men hobbled by, merrily singing and asking if anybody had "seen the elephant pass that way." The Second Summit, still higher, lay ahead.

Legacy   Lorenzo Sawyer wrote from California on September 13, 1850, "The emigration for this year is sadly disappointed. Great numbers would go home immediately if they had the means of returning." The way West was harsh, the mines overcrowded, the best spots taken, the labor horrendous, the cost of living outrageous, and "Thousands are not more than paying for expenses." According to Mattes (p. 3), the 5,000 trail deaths of 1850 set a record. For all these reasons, the flood of 1850 gold seekers became a trickle in 1851. Joseph Cain and Arieh C. Brower produced for the limited 1851 market the new "Mormon Way-Bill to the Gold Mines," a comprehensive guide to all the trails west and southwest from South Pass.

REFERENCES

(See Preface for Heading references, and for Mattes, not listed here.)

Ashton, Wendell J., 1950, Voice in the West: N.Y., quote on B. H. Young p. 23, biog. 368.

Bagley, Will, 1991, A road from El Dorado, the 1848 trail journal of Ephraim Green: Salt Lake City; quote from Pratt p. 10 (taken from S. George Ellsworth, ed., 1990, The journals of Addison Pratt: Salt Lake City, p. 343); Green quotes on stold horse 26, mr waker 32; folding chart of 5 diarists at end.

Becker, Robert H., ed., 1969, Thomas Christy's road across the plains 1850: Denver, p. 15-23.

Bigler, David L., ed., 1990, The gold discovery journal of Azariah Smith: Salt Lake City, p. 121-46; quote on back bone 132-33.

Bigler, Henry W.: See Gudde, Erwin G.

Bruff, J. Goldsborough, 1849 notes (reworked 1851, pub. 1949), Gold rush; Georgia Willis Read and Ruth Gaines, eds.: N.Y., quote p. 117; see also 630-31.

Cain, Joseph, and Arieh C. Brower, 1851 (ca. 1968 facsimile reprint), The famous Mormon waybill to the gold fields of California: Salt Lake City, 32 p.

Camp, Charles L., 1972, one of 20 proofs for a never published Fourth Edition Revised and Enlarged of The Plains and the Rockies: Berkeley, p. 419-22.

Gardiner, Frederick, ca. 1900 reminiscences (1993 printing), A Mormon rebel, the life and travels of F. Gardiner; Hugh Garner, ed.: Salt Lake City, p. 62-64; see also 113.

Green, Ephraim: see Bagley, Will.

Gudde, Erwin G., 1962, [Henry W.] Bigler's chronicle of the West: Berkeley, p. 112-30; quote on Twin Sisters 126-27.

Howell, John, 1970, Early Newspapers: San Francisco, Cat. 39, quote p. ii, 5.

Keller, George, 1851 (1955 reprint), A trip across the plains: Oakland, 44 p.; quote 23.

Korns, Roderick J., 1951, West from Ft. Bridger: Salt Lake City, Utah Hist. Quart. 19:248-68.

Langworthy, Franklin, 1855, Scenery of the plains, mountains, and mines: Ogdensburgh NY, p. 19.

McMurtrie, Douglas C., 1933, Pioneer printing in Utah: Springfield IL, 4 p.

Ricketts, Norma Baldwin, 1996, The Mormon Battalion: Logan UT, p. 205-22.

Rieck, Richard L., 1993-95, Geography of the California trails: Independence, Overland Journal; Part 1, 1993, 11/4:12-22; Part 2, 1994, 12/1:27-52; Part 3, 1995, 13/3:25-32.

Sawyer, Lorenzo, 1850 journal and letters (1926 printing), Way sketches containing incidents of travel across the plains from St. Joseph to California in 1850: N.Y., quotes on Steeple Rock p. 67, Thousand Springs 69, Cold Water 70, Mormon guide 71, nausea 81, harassing 85, roughness 95, Napoleon 96, elephant 97, disappointed 112.

Sherman, William T., 1875 (1890 3d ed.), Personal memoirs: N.Y., quote p. 83.

Smith, Azariah: see Bigler, David L.

Unruh, John D., Jr., 1979, The plains across: Urbana, p. 498.

EMIGRANT'S GUIDE.

BEING A

TABLE OF DISTANCES

SHOWING THE

SPRINGS, CREEKS, RIVERS, MOUNTAINS, HILLS,
AND ALL OTHER NOTABLE PLACES,

FROM

GREAT SALT LAKE CITY

TO

SAN FRANCISCO.

SECOND EDITION.

BY B. H. YOUNG AND J. EAGAR.

In the following table, the first column of figures shows the distance from point to point; and the second column of figures the total distance of each point to the Great Salt Lake City.

The Streams are all very good to cross in the dry season, except the Casus, which banks are high; but in the wet season the streams are high, and also the snow remains on the California mountains until late in June.

The Desert is perfectly destitute of feed and water.

[p. 2] To Hot Springs; a plenty of good feed beyond, but not much wood; you will keep the second left hand road after you pass the Hot Springs;	4	
To Blooming Grove; around by the bluff of the mountain; good campings at the grove.	17	21
About the 24th. of July, you can go direct to Blooming Grove across a clay flat, by keeping the first left hand road from the hot springs, and save three or four miles.		
To Second creek beyond; good camping.	4	25
To Brownsville, on Weber River; before reaching Brownsville you will descend a small ridge; good campings.	15	40
To Box Elder Creek; there are several creeks between, good for camping at; good campings at Box Elder creek.	20	60
To Bear River Ferry; there are several springs near and along the road between; feed and water good, the wood is sage and willow.	20	80
To Mud Creek; (going west) there is no wood at this creek, feed good, the water clayish.	3	83

To Warm Springs; there is good feed, but no water for use, the
wood is sage and rather scarce.   6   89

To Warm and Cold Springs; these springs issue from the ground
not more [p. 3] than a rod apart and run together a few rods below,
forming quite a stream; feed and water is good, but the sage brush is
scarce.   14   103

To Sink Creek; rather a rough, crooked road, passing over some
hills into another valley; feed and water good, and you can obtain
cedar wood at the distance of a mile or two on the mountain side. 12   115

To Deep Creek crossing; you will go round the point of a mountain, then follow the creek a little way; feed and water good, the fuel
is sage brush.   6   121

To Deep Creek sink; a little above the sink the stream is narrow,
deep and swift, it then spreads out upon a sand flat and sinks; the feed
is not very thick, and the water is a little brackish, the wood is sage. 6   127

To Pilot Springs; you travel over a sand plain, and at the springs
there is no feed, but good water, the fuel is sage.   9   136

To the Sink of some creeks, on the mountain side; the first part of
the road is sandy, until you come to the bench land at the foot of the
mountain; you will find some wood on your road and would do well
to gather some for camp use, feed and water is good at this place, but
you may have to follow the creeks up some ways for water, unless the
season is wet.   7   143

[p. 4] Thence along the bench of the mountain to Casus Creek;
you will find intermediate campings along the bench that are good;
you leave the bench before reaching the creek; feed and water are
good along this creek, the principal wood is willow.   19   162

Across and up Casus Creek, to the bench land of another mountain; feed, wood and water are good.   11   173

To the Old Fort Hall road, up the side of the mountain; you will
have a steep hill to ascend, and quite rough; at the junction of these
roads there is no camping place; upon the right of this place is the
noted Steeple Rocks, in which the road to Fort Hall passes between,
which is just wide enough to admit a wagon; this is the end of the
cut-off at this end of the rout [*sic*] from G. S. L. City.   5   178

To Steep Creek on the top of the mountains; up hill nearly all the
way, camping good.   5   183

To Goose Creek: some feed and water between: the road is quite steep and sidling in places, good campings on Goose creek.   7   190

Up Goose Creek: good campings all along the creek,   18   208

To Thousand Springs Valley: the road is quite hilly and rough, their [*sic*] is no water at the entrance of the valley, there-[p. 5] fore you will continue down the valley for feed and water, the fuel is sage:—there are numerous natural wells or springs in this valley, which are from three to five feet wide and from five to twelve feet deep: some of them are not fit for use, as they are impregnated with minerals, and some contain good water.   13   221

To Cold water Creek: there are also some hot springs in this valley, and the road passes near, by them: the feed and water are good, the wood is sage.   14   235

To the end of the valley; feed wood and water good.   13   248

To Kanyon Creek, a tributary of Mary's River: you will travel over a hilly road a portion of the way, good feed, wood and water at the head of the creek; there are some springs two or three miles this side of where the stream meets the road, and form, in a degree the head of the stream, and is a good place for camping.   10   258

Down Kanyon Creek; crossing it nine times; and so down two miles beyond the kanyon for feed and water, the fuel is sage; the crossings are not bad or deep.   5   263

To the head of Mary's River: there is good feed and water between if you choose to camp; particularly in the rainy season, but in the dry season it apparently sinks and again rises and forms the [p. 6] head of Mary's River which lays in sloughs; feed, wood and water good.   18   281

Down Mary's River; there are good campings all along this distance, and the most of the way down the river.   30   311

Thence down the river; a portion of the road is a little rough. I might mention shorter distances, but it is not necessary as there is good feed, wood and water all along this river until you near the sink.   18   329

Thence down the river, crossing it three times; the crossings are good, and the banks are not high or the water deep.   14   343

Thence, leaving and returning again to the river; passing over a range of hills, in which you will find a little spring water.   17   360

Thence along the river; feed, wood and water good.   17   377

Thence a portion of the road over salaeratus ground which is bad and dusty in the dry season.   18   395

Thence, crossing the river and around the point of a mountain, the road a little rough and stony. 14 409

Thence down the river; good camping all along. 25 434

Thence down the river to a sand plain or bench of the mountain, there is good feed wood and water all along. 31 465

Thence across the sand plain leaving [p. 7] and returning again to the river. 14 479

To the last crossing of Mary's River; campings good. 14 493

Thence down the river; campings good. 30 523

To the sink of the river; feed growing thinner and the water clayish, and no wood of any account; at the sink the water lays in sloughs, and is not very good; you will have to use manure for fuel. The last slough of the river lays between two small bluffs, after which the river course turns to the left, and from this place the road leads across the Desert. 25 548

To Pilot [Carson] or Salmon Trout River across the Desert—on the left hand road—The most of the road you will find good except the last end which is very sandy. 40 588

Thence to the junction of the road that leads from Truckey's River, and thence two miles further to the [Carson] river again; you will find good campings all along this river; this days travel is up a gradual slope, and down again to the river. 20 608

Thence leaving and returning again to the river, crossing a sand plain. 13 621

Thence along the river crossing it twice, the crossings not bad. 20 641

Thence good campings all along and an abundance of timber from here to Sacramento. 20 661

To the mouth of a large Kanyon; good campings between. 24 685

[p. 8] Through the Kanyon, crossing the stream three times; the road is very rough and the crossings bad. 4 689

To Red Lake; at the foot of the dividing ridge of the California mountains travelling over hills and through woods. 10 699

Over the ridge and so down to another lake at the foot of another mountain; a rough, steep and sidling road, particularly at the beginning. 5 704

Up the side of the mountain and thence over and down to Rock Valley; a rough and sidling road up and down the mountain. 10 714

To Tragedy Springs on the main ridge leading to the mines; this

road also is rough and through woods, but not as bad as the last; good
campings in the mountains on your left.   6   720

    To Leek Springs Valley; you will pass down Iron Hill, quite a
steep pitch.   12   732

    To Deep Valley at a small river; the road is good.   8   740

    To Gold Valley down the ridge: road and campings good.   22   762

    To Sacramento City; the road is good most of the way, and a
plenty of campings.   46   808

    To San Francisco by water.   150   958

Francis M. Drake, 1853

The Emigrant's Overland Guide To California

Ft. Madison, Iowa, Printed at the Evangelist Book and Job Office, 1853, 16 p. and back wrapper. [WCB 222b; Kurutz 204; Mintz 129.] Reset verbatim from a facsimile, by courtesy of the Yale Collection of Western Americana, Beinecke Rare Book and Manuscript Library, New Haven, Connecticut.

Significance   Drake's slim guide had very accurate mileages on the Soda Springs route to the City of Rocks but overblown ones beyond. His 1852 route started at Council Bluffs and followed the north side of the Platte. West of South Pass he took the Hams Fork and Hudspeth cutoffs and the Humboldt-Carson route to Sacramento. His distances west of City of Rocks were 150 miles greater than those measured today and 115 greater than those of the authoritative Young and Eagar 1850 (K3). The Hams Fork Cutoff was an old fur-hunters' packer route that probably was first used in 1825 by Zacharias Ham, discoverer of the Fork (Hafen 9:193). It tied into the Sublette Cutoff opened to wagons in 1844. See Highlights for the Kinney Cutoff, also mentioned by Drake. Almost two-thirds of potential users of this guide, the 1853 diarists listed by Mattes, started from Council Bluffs.

This appears to be the first reprint of the only known copy, which lacks the front wrapper.

Author   FRANCIS MARION DRAKE, merchant, overlander, guide writer. Drake ran a general store in Drakesville IA. He advertised his business as Drake & Son, purveyors of dry goods, groceries, and hardware, wholesale and retail, outfitters to Western emigrants. Drakesville lay on the Mormon route between Nauvoo and Council Bluffs (Kanesville). Drake's recommended (p. 2) "best route" across Iowa, on the divide south of the Des Moines River, took his readers, of course, right through Drakesville.

Itineraries, 1852   The average 1852 wagon travels from the MISSOURI TO THE SACRAMENTO via Soda Springs in 107 days, and via Salt Lake City in 114 days. These both are exactly the same averages achieved in 1850 (K3). Of the 45 diarists taken from Mattes's compilation, 16, or 36 percent, go via Salt Lake City. Times and distances are figured as outlined in the K3 Itineraries. Data are too few to cover packers or any other routes in 1852, or any of the migration of 1851.

WAGONS VIA SODA SPRINGS, CARSON/TRUCKEE TRAILS. Travel times of 29 diarists are minimum-mean-maximum 83-107-138 days. They cover the average distance of 1,860 miles at 17 miles per day.

WAGONS VIA SALT LAKE CITY, SALT LAKE CUTOFF, CARSON/TRUCKEE TRAILS. Travel times of 16 diarists are minimum-mean-maximum 88-114-144 days. They cover the average distance of 1,870 miles at 16 miles per day.

Highlights   The most practical trail guides for the gold rushers included William Clayton's superb 1848 road log to Salt Lake City (see 3:E6); the marvelously accurate 1849 maps of Charles Preuss and of T. H. Jefferson (2:D7), and Joseph E. Ware's rudimentary 1849 armchair synthesis; Brigham H. Young and John Eagar's pioneering 1850 guide west from Salt Lake City; Joseph Cain and Arieh C. Brower's 1851 waybill west from South Pass, and Franklin Street's 1851 table of distances from St. Joseph; 1852 guides by Andrew Child, by Hosea B. Horn, and by Philip L. Platt and Nelson Slater; and the 1853 guides by Francis M. Drake, via Soda Springs, and Dr. J. Tarbell (K5), via Salt Lake City.

The chief problem with many of these guides was the overestimated distance west from City of Rocks down the Humboldt and across the Sierra. The best two guides for this last leg were Jefferson, and Young and Eagar. Their mileages from City of Rocks (Hastings Junction for Jefferson) to Sacramento were only 35 miles greater than today's measure of 595, and the trail probably was longer in their day. The other guides were farther off the mark, by from 90 (Tarbell) to 205 (Horn) miles. Horn's guide, the farthest off despite its fancy map, was published by J. H. Colton. A very accurate measure of the entire Oregon-California Trail, based on Fremont, was published by railroad engineer William L. Dearborn in 1850 (L1).

Ware's was the only one of these guides not based on personal travel. He relied heavily on Fremont and Clayton. Although his descriptions and many mileages were sketchy, it was still a notable achievement (Caughey 1948). His most complete success was renaming the Greenwood Cutoff for Solomon Sublette: "We acknowledge our obligations to Mr. S. Sublette, for useful aid in the enterprize...you save nearly five days travel by following what I have taken the liberty to call Sublette's Cut Off." Tradition has it that 81-year-old Caleb Greenwood first guided California-bound Elisha Stephens over this cutoff in 1844 (Hafen 9:190). Stewart (1962), however, credited 64-year-old Isaac Hitchcock, rather than Greenwood, with promoting this cutoff, which followed Capt. B. L. E. Bonneville's 1832 track. Ashley's men used the cutoff as early as 1826 (Hafen 8:373).

The several branches of the Kinney Cutoff ran from Green River to the Sublette Cutoff, eliminating the latter's long desert drive. Either old mountain man Charles Kinney, or a Green River ferryman of that name, made these improvements in about 1852 (Hafen 4:171).

The Beckwourth Trail across the Sierra was opened in 1851. The Nobles, Henness Pass, Johnson Cutoff, and Walker River-Sonora trails were opened over the Sierra in 1852 (5:J9).

After studying 240 diaries, Mattes (1167) concluded from all the quarrels, jockeyings for position, abandonments, murders, and hangings, that "the 1852 migration was an ill-tempered one."

Legacy   In 1852 when Drake journeyed, almost all trail segments and cutoffs to California were in place, excepting the Central Overland Trail (5:J10). The gold rush was all but over. The resurgent number of emigrants aimed to settle, and more families came with more sheep and cattle (Stewart 1962). Drake ends his recital, "hoping that you have enjoyed a pleasant trip, and seen the 'Elephant' *tamed.*"

REFERENCES
(See Preface for Heading references, and for Hafen and Mattes, not listed here.)

Cain, Joseph, and Arieh C. Brower, 1851 (ca. 1968 facsimile reprint), The famous Mormon waybill to the gold fields of California: Salt Lake City, 32 p.

Caughey, John W., 1948, Gold is the cornerstone: Berkeley, p. 53-54.

Child, Andrew, 1852 (1946 reprint), Overland route to California; Lyle H. Wright, ed.: Los Angeles, 60 p.

Clayton, William, 1848 (1983 reprint), The Latter-Day Saints' emigrants' guide; Stanley B. Kimball, ed.: St. Louis, 107 p.

Horn, Hosea B., 1852, Horn's overland guide: N.Y., 81 p., map.

Jefferson, T. H., 1849 (1945 reprint), Map of the emigrant road...to St. Francisco; George R. Stewart, ed.: San Francisco, [25] p., 4 map sheets; reprinted also this series 2:D7.

Platt, Philip L., and Nelson Slater, 1852 (1963 reprint), Travelers' guide across the plains upon the overland route to California: San Francisco, 59 p., map.

Preuss, Charles, 1849, Topographical map of the road from Missouri to Oregon, in 7 sections; in John A. Rockwell, Canal or Railroad Between the Atlantic and Pacific Oceans: Wash., 30/2 H145 Report, serial 546, 678 p., 16 maps.

Stewart, George R., 1962 (1983 reprint), The California Trail: Lincoln, p. 307.

Street, Franklin, 1851 (1974 reprint), California in 1850; in The Gold Mines of California, Two Guidebooks: N.Y., 88 p.

Ware, Joseph E., 1849 (1932 reprint), The emigrants' guide to California; John Caughey, ed.: Princeton, 63 p., map; quotes on Sublette xxiii, 26.

THE

EMIGRANT'S

OVERLAND GUIDE

TO

CALIFORNIA

By F. M. DRAKE
OF IOWA.

FORT MADISON, IOWA.

PRINTED AT THE EVANGELIST BOOK AND JOB OFFICE

. . . .

1853

[p. 1] PREFATORY REMARKS

It is not the purpose of the author, in presenting this brief work to the public, to make it a scheme of speculation; but it is done through the belief that it may be of some benefit to the adventurous emigrant to California.

It is not prepared from memory, after his return, and after the incidents connected with the journey are partially obliterated from the mind, but from a Journal kept by him while performing the journey, in the Spring and Summer of 1852; in which every important thing was carefully noted down, at the time.

Aware of the many difficulties the emigrant has to encounter, owing to numerous stretches, void of either timber, grass, or water, these notes were taken for the benefit of himself and friends, with the view of crossing again the present year. Believing, therefore, that much of the suffering heretofore experienced in crossing the plains might be avoided, did the emigrant know each day where to pitch his tent the following evening, so as to have the most eligible situation to procure the articles his wants demanded—know where he is, and the progress made each day. These, and other reasons of a similar character, are deemed a sufficient apology, for laying this little work before the public.

Numerous "Guides" of a like purport have been issued from the press, many of which are quite imperfect, although most of them have been found to be of great utility to the emigrant. To B. B. [H. B.] HORN'S, of Iowa, and Andrew CHILD'S, of Wisconsin, [p. 2] I would refer, as having been of intrinsic worth to the last year's emigrants. But as material changes have been made in the route since their issue, the author of this work, believing that a Guide of more recent date than those alluded to, would better suit the wants of future emigration, feels warranted in offering it to the public for what it is worth, making COUNCIL BLUFF CITY, on the Missouri river, the *starting point*. He would also apprise all emigrants crossing the Mississippi river above Quincy, that the natural road on the South side of the Des Moines river, is on a fine ridge, extending quite to the Missouri river, and is consequently the best route. Those crossing at Keokuk, Montrose, Fort Madison, and Burlington, will find it to their advantage to cross the Des Moines River on the *Bridge at Farmington,* and intersect the divide road at *Harmony Inn.*

The author has deemed it unnecessary to encumber his work with a super-abundance of words, discussing the advantages and disadvantages of the different routes. He has marked the one he deems most eligible, and the one he would travel, were he to perform the journey again. Neither has he attempted to gloss his work with rhetorical flourishes, for the purpose of "astonishing the natives." His object is to *benefit* the emigrant rather than excite his admiration of things not serviceable to him on the route.

THE AUTHOR.

Drakesville, Iowa, February, 1853. [p. 3]

OUTFIT

I will say, in the commencement, that although the character of the trip may be greatly modified, yet it is a long and arduous journey, and one that requires a large amout [*sic*] of patience and perseverance to be "laid in" at the start. No fears need be entertained of laying in too much, as a good supply of both will be found to be indispensable *articles.*

As to the manner of outfitting, in other respects, much difference of opinion prevails.

In regard to stock, take none but No. 1, of mature age, whether horses, mules or oxen. Either, with proper attention, will perform the trip. Cattle, though generally conceded to be slower, will perform the trip in about 90 days. They are safer and easier taken care of, and pay a better interest on the money invested in them—after arriving in California—than any other other [*sic*] kind of stock.

My plan of outfitting is as follows, with the supposed cost of each article annexed. The wagon should be what is called a *two-horse-wagon,* well ironed, with a bed about ten feet in length, supplied with good bows and a double-drill or osnaburg cover. Four yoke of good oxen, from 5 to 8 years old. Such a team is sufficient for the transportation of four persons, with the following additional outfit, with which to leave the Missouri [p. 4] river. Time of leaving, 1st of May, or as soon as supplies for teams can be procured.

Supposed cost of Wagon and Team,	.	.	.	$400 00
400 pounds good Flour, in sacks,	.	.	.	10 00
250 " " Ham and Side Bacon,	.	.	20 00
200 " " Corn Meal,	.	.	.	2 00
100 " " Hard Biscuit or Boston Crackers,	7 00
100 " " Crushed Sugar, .	.	.	10 00
30 " " Rio Coffee,	.	.	.	4 00
30 " " Rice,	.	.	2 00
30 " " White Beans,	.	.	.	75
20 " " L. B. Salt,	.	.	25
75 " " Dried Apples or Peaches,	7 50
100 " " Vinegar Pickles, Pepper & sundries	10 00
100 " " Cooking Utensils, &c.,	.	.	25 00
100 " " Arms, Amunition and Clothing,	.	100 00
1535 "			$598 50

The above is a competent outfit for four persons. As little clothing should be taken as will be deemed absolutely necessary for the trip. The object should be to burden teams with nothing but what is indispensable. Fire arms may be found neces-[sary] for defense against the Indians, and a sufficient supply of amunition [*sic*] should be laid in, as it will be needed in case of an attack. The journey should be pursued steadily, laying by only when immediate necessity requires. If horses, are taken, they should be kept well shod. Take also some extra shoes, nails, shoeing hammer and rasp. Although not absolutely necessary, a few ox shoes may be found useful. Turpentine is good to remove soreness from their hoofs, as well as to harden them. Take—say, 1-2 gallon. An axe, saw, two or three augers, and a mowing scythe are tools sufficient. Have as little communication with Mr. Indian as possible. When you do encounter him, manifest the spirit of the true American, and you have nothing to fear.

We now proceed to give the distance from point to point, beginning, as above remarked, at Council Bluff City, interspersing the same with suitable remarks. [p. 5]

DISTANCES   MILES

	MILES	
From the upper, or old Mormon crossing, on the Missouri river, course North-west to Pappia creek,	16	
Elk Horn river, a tributary of the Platte. This stream is about 3 rods wide, with steep banks. We ferried it at $2 per wagon and team,	12	28
Bridge creek, a very miry and difficult stream to cross,	1	29
Platte river. Good timber and grass is found here,	12	41
4 miles further is a small lake, where good grass is found,	4	45
Platte river again,	8	53
The road here leaves the river and joins it again in about [8 mi.]. Before leaving this point the old Pawnee Village will be observed on the South side of the river,	8	61
Shell creek. Here the Pawnees are usually troublesome. The creek is bridged, and in the bend on the West side is good camping ground,	2	63
The road here is good in dry weather, and good camping ground at intervals to South Fork. This is a very rapid stream, 100 rods wide, with quicksand bottom, and though often forded at low water, it is prudent to ferry. Ferriage, $3,00 per wagon. Road now runs parallel with Loup Fork some distance,	25	88
To Sandy Bluffs,	25	113
Pass over these and good feed and several ponds and lakes are found in,	1	114
To Sandy Bluffs again. It is best to camp before reaching them,	25	139
Across these Bluffs to rolling, sandy land,	6	145
Extent of the same, about [14 mi.]. Tolerable camping ground is found here, but no timber [p. 6],	14	159
Prairie creek. There is good feed and water here,	8	167
Dry creek,	2	169
Wood river, where plenty of wood, water and grass are found. This stream is about 4 rods wide and very deep,	11	180
Road now runs along a ridge some distance, dividing Wood river and Beaver creek, which stream it follows. Good feed, water and timber are found here,	12	192
Prairie-dog-town and Swamp,	8	200
Good camping ground on slough, further on, say,	3	203
Road here runs in sight of the river to two deep ravines,	12	215

To a creek where there is grass and willows for fuel,	4	219
Dry creek—usually bad to cross,	6	225
Elm creek—tolerable camping ground—bad to cross,	3	228
Buffalo creek,	9	237
Platte river bend, where there is tolerable camping ground,	15	252
Small lake to the left of the road,	7	259
River again, where camping may be done,	12	271
River again, 5 miles, last 2 heavy sand,	5	276
Skunk creek,	6	282
Large cold spring, situate a few rods from road, South side. The bluffs here rise to a considerable height on each side of the river,	7	289
Wide creek,	5	294
River again. To the right of the road, near the head of Wide creek, is good feed,	5	299
Another creek. You now have to travel over 200 miles without timber, except one large cedar tree,	3	302
North Bluff Fork of Platte river. The river here is about 6 rods wide and 18 inches deep—good ford. You here strike sandy bluffs, and are tormented with gnats,	18	320
Road heavy sand,	6	326
Low land then with good grass,	4	330
Thence across sandy bluffs to Bluff creek, where there is good grass and water [p. 7],	3	333
Heavy roads then to a good spring and creek, where there is fine grass,	8	341
Camp creek, a good place to camp,	23	364
Wolf creek, 4 rods wide,	6	370
Lone Cedar Tree,	9	379
Sand Hill creek,	12	391
It would be advisable to camp here, as the roads are heavy sand most of the way to Shoal creek,	22	413
Pond, or lake, and spring, where there is good camping,	2	415
Over sand and gravel bluffs to where the road joins the river again,	20	435
To Single Slough, where is good grass,	4	439
River opposite Chimney Rock. Here camping may be done,	23	462
River opposite Scott's Bluff,	17	479
Cold creek. Up this creek for several miles there is good camping,	4	483
To a point of timber,	22	505

Small creek to South of road, where there is good camping,	20	525
River opposite Fort Laramie. Fort Laramie is beautifully situated on the Laramie Fork of Platte river, over which is a toll-bridge. At the Fort there is a good general store and several bakeries,	10	535
Dry creek. You now have the Black Hills to contend with—so called because of the dark appearance they present to the eye of the traveler, being covered with black pine trees. Road very heavy, and hard on cattle,	4	539
From Dry creek, after crossing several *small* creeks, you come to Deep creek. Camping may be done here. If the creek is not fordable it may be headed by going over the ridge to the right half a mile,	16	555
To Alder Clump and creek. This is a good place to camp,	9	564
Devil creek, where there is some grass,	5	569
Over hills to where the road joins the river. Good camping here,	8	577
River again [p. 8],	4	581
4 miles further the road nears the river, where is good feed,	4	585
10 miles from this you encounter a steep and difficult ascent. Pass over to the right. Between the hills, is good feed,	10	595
River again, and some feed here,	6	601
Old Ferry Landing. Road heavy at this place—sand nearing the river every few miles,	16	617
Upper crossing on Platte river,	24	641
A few miles before reaching here, there is good grass, on a slough, which we used before taking the stretch from Platte river to Willow Spring—distant,	26	667
This we performed without water, except alkali. The road here is firm and good—ascends about 13 miles to Alkali Lake, and then descends gradually to Willow Srings [*sic*]. Here are several springs of good water, but feed is scarce.		
Sage Spring creek,	10	677
Fish Run. Good grazing all along this creek, and water fine,	6	683
Lake Alkali,	7	690
Saleratus Lake,	3	693
Independence Rock—a few rods to the left of the road. This name was given to the rock by some emigrants who arrived here on the 4th of July. It is quite a natural curiosity—about 2000 feet in length, 120 feet high, and varying in width from 200 to 500 feet—composed of solid granite,	4	697

First ford on Sweet Water river, usually deep,	1	698
Devil's Gate. A few rods to the right of the road, there is perhaps the greatest curiosity on the route—a great cannon in the Rocky Mountains, through which Sweet Water river tumbles with amazing velocity. It is about 50 rods long and 120 feet wide. The walls on either side rise to the height of 400 feet,	7	705
To a creek—good camping ground all along the river, but look out for alkali,	2	707
Sage creek,	13	720
River opposite a huge rock on the left of the road—good feed on the opposite bank of the river. The mountains rise here to the height of 1000 feet, and [p. 8] upon the highest peaks may be found several natural curiosities, viz: Franklin's Pool. This is a spring of very cold water, about 2 feet deep and ten feet across, in the form of a circle. Also, Burns' Cliff of Rocks, and King David's Coffin. These are curiosities well worthy the traveler's notice,	3	723
To a small stream,	2	725
Bitter Cottonwood creek,	4	729
Second ford of Sweet Water,	7	736
Here the road forks. The right crossing Sweet Water three times in half a mile, and the left bearing round the bluffs over a heavy road to the river again,	8	744
To the river again—no water on the way,	20	764
After traveling 4 miles further there is a marsh, where it is said ice may be obtained by digging 2 or 3 feet down. The road continues good through this marsh, three miles, to sand and gravel bluffs, which extend to the river, where you ford again,	20	784
To Rocky Bluffs,	10	794
Road rough and stony to a marsh, where are some springs,	4	798
Three Mile creek,	4	802
Strawberry creek,	2	804
Aspen Spring,	1	805
Branch of Sweet Water. Good camping ground here,	4	809
To a ford of Sweet Water. This is the last you see of Sweet Water,	4	813
To South Pass between the Rocky Mountains. Here is the dividing ridge between the Atlantic and Pacific,	10	823
You now descend gradually to Pacific Springs and creek,	3	826
Ford about 2 miles—some grass here,	2	828

Dry Sandy,	8	836
Junction of roads—Salt Lake road to the left. *The Kinney Cut Off* also takes this road to where the road again forks, where you take the left hand—thus avoiding the desert between Big Sandy and Green river—a barren waste of 50 miles, without water or vegetation, except sage,	6	842
We took the old road to Big Sandy, distant [p. 9],	6	848
Here was some little feed, which we used before taking the desert.		
To Green River. The last end of this road is quite stony, with some very long and steep descents. Along the river are numerous ponds of strong alkali, which should be avoided. Green River is a very cold and rapid stream, and is considered the most dangerous on the whole route. There are several good ferries in operation. Ferriage $6 per wagon. We swam our stock from a small island about 3-4 of a mile above the ferry,	50	898
To a branch of Green River. Good grass here, but numerous sloughs of alkali,	10	908
Ford of branch,	2	910
Aspen Grove and creek,	10	920
Here ascend a long hill to Mountain Spring,	2	922
Alkali Spring. A short distance further is some good water and grass,	8	930
To the forks of the road. We took the left hand, which avoids several long hills, is better watered and abundance of grass,	5	935
To Ham's fork of Green River. Before reaching the ford, there are several miry sloughs, bad to cross. River about 2 rods wide—ford good. Good camping ground here,	7	942
Road now ascends a mountain to its summit,	3	945
Aspen Grove,	7	952
Balsam Fir Grove,	3	955
This is a fine shady grove—road passes through it, gradually ascending a long hill to its summit,	2	957
Road now descends (hill steep and stony) to some rivulets. Here is some feed—the water a short distance below the road is said to be poisonous,	3	960
Ascend again to another spring. Here the traveler encounters several long and difficult ascents and descents,	1	961
Bear River Valley,	5	966

Bear River crossings. The river is here crossed 3 times in a few rods; after [p. 11] which the road is very rocky and hard on wagons for half a mile along the foot of Craggy Mount; on the top of which a beautiful view of the surrounding country may be had. Good camping ground here. Eight miles [not in tally] farther the road forks. Take the left, which saves 6 miles travel, and crosses Thomas' fork on a bridge, — 4 — 970

From forks of road to bridge. Toll 50 cts. a wagon—good place to camp, — 2 — 972

Over mountain to the river again, — 6 — 978

Sallee's creek—good grass here, — 7 — 985

Another creek, — 4 — 989

Willow creek, — 1 — 990

Ashlie's creek—good place to camp, — 6 — 996

Muddy creek, — 10 — 1006

Willow Spring, — 6 — 1012

Soda Springs. These are observed by the large white mounds formed by the mineral water running over the surface. Along here for several miles, the earth is filled with this mineral water, which, with the addition of a little acid and sugar, makes a fine beverage. Here is a good place to camp, — 6 — 1018

Steam Boat Spring, a few miles to the left of the road, in the bend of Bear River, — 1 — 1019

Junction of roads, — 5 — 1024

The right hand here is the old Fort Hall and Oregon road. We took the left to a cold stream of water, called Mountain Willow creek. Feed may be obtained here in the mountain valleys, — 14 — 1038

Road continues mountainous to Pannock River, — 4 — 1042

Fall creek—a good place to camp, — 2 — 1044

Road ascends the mountain to its summit, — 7 — 1051

Hence down to a spring on the left, — 2 — 1053

To foot of mountain, where is a creek and good grazing, — 1 — 1054

Muddy Willow creek. Down the creek is good grazing, — 7 — 1061

Gravel, or Spring creek. Water clear and cold—no more for 25 miles, — 8 — 1069

Over mountain to a valley where is grass and wild rye, — 9 — 1078

Summit of the next mountain [p. 12], — 10 — 1088

A small creek, — 6 — 1094

A Spring—some feed up ravine,	8	1102
Another spring—head waters of Raft River. Some grass among the mountains,	3	1105
A muddy creek—bad to cross,	6	1111
Another of the same class—good grass and timber here,	3	1114
East branch of Raft River, where is good grass. Along the valley the soil bears strong evidence of inundation, and produces large crops of wild sage,	6	1120
To Raft River. This is a very miry and difficult stream to cross,	11	1131
To west branch. Water clear and ford good—good grass at either crossing. Here the old road from Fort Hall intersects,	5	1136
Road runs along this stream to another ford, and good grass,	5	1141
Rock Spring creek—which is the next water on the road. Good grass here,	10	1151
Isinglass creek,	3	1154
White creek—a good place to camp,	2	1156
Muddy creek. Here may be seen Steeple Rocks, which are numerous, and at a distant view resemble a fine city,	3	1159
To where road *via* Salt Lake City intersects,	2	1161
Little dry creek,	2	1163
Another creek. You here commence ascending Goose creek range of mountains to an elevation of 7000 feet above the level of the sea. Several long and difficult descents—hard on wagon and team, but safe with care,	4	1167
To a brook, which crosses the road through a grove of trees,	3	1170
Over a rugged mountain to a branch of Goose creek,	4	1174
Goose creek. Here are seen some beautiful table mountains—a good place to camp,	3	1177
Through Goose creek valley to a marshy creek,	8	1185
Another of the same class,	2	1187
Forks of Goose creek,	7	1194
Road continues up South fork to a pass between mountains,	2	1196
Road rough and crooked to ford [p. 13],	1	1197
Second ford—miry and bad to cross,	1	1198
Spring valley. Road now hilly and stony, with no water till getting through, where, to the left of the road, under a cliff of rocks, there is a good spring, which forms a brook where stock can drink. Not much feed here.	12	1210
6 miles further is an abundance of wild rye, but no water,	6	1216

Hot Spring valley—some good grass here,	7	1223
To a creek, near and parallel with the road. The water of this stream will do to use, but is considerably impregnated with alkali,	3	1226
To a number of springs or natural wells. Plenty of grass here, also,	7	1233
Hot creek,	4	1237
Hot Springs. The water sulphurous—temperature about 180 deg.,	4	1241
To a spring of good water,	7	1248
You now leave the valley, through a pass, and enter another, where there are some springs,	12	1260
To a number of springs in another valley. The road passes over gravel bluffs for several miles before reaching these springs; most of which are alkali water,	8	1268
Two miles further on, to the left of the road, in a valley, is a good spring and a small meadow of grass. Water stock near the spring, as the water a short distance below is impregnated with alkali,	2	1270
Deep Grass creek,	7	1277
Cross it near its head, and travel down it where there is plenty of fine grass,	6	1283
First ford of Humbolt—good ford and place to camp,	3	1286
Thence down Humbolt, on a moderate road, to the crossing of North Branch. Emigrants should guard well against alkali and Indians all the way down Humbolt river, as they are "the principal products of the country,"	21	1307
Next crossing of Humbolt,	22	1329
In eight miles cross four times. In common stage of water, crossing not bad; between [p. 14] the third and fourth, for several rods, the road is crowded quite into the river, by the steep bluffs,	8	1337
Cold creek,	4	1341
Thence through Sage plains and over mountains to a spring,	10	1351
You now descend a cannon to the river again. Road stony and hard on team,	10	1361
Here ford and travel on South side to river again,	5	1366
From here down Humbolt the road passes mostly over barren sage land, nearing the river at intervals of from 3 to 27 miles—road dusty, intermingled with alkali. The last hundred miles before reaching the Meadow, feed is usually very hard to obtain, on account of the narrow river bottoms. The banks are also deep and rugged. From the last mentioned point of river to Big Meadow,	200	1566

This is a fine meadow, which nature has furnished to recruit
  domestic animals, after their hard service over the long and barren stretches of the terrific Humbolt, preparatory to taking the
  Desert—a barren, sandy waste, 40 miles across, without water.
  The emigrants should here lay in a supply of hay for 2 or 3 feeds,
  and as the water is quite brackish, fill your vessels near the head
  of the Meadow, it being much stronger lower down.

From Head of Meadow to Sink of Humbolt,	30	1596
From Sink across the Desert to Carson river. On a slough, before entering the Desert, is some feed, mostly herd-grass. In crossing the Desert you pass several trading posts—the last twelve miles heavy sand. Grass may be found a few miles up Carson river,	42	1638
To where the road leaves the river,	9	1647
River again—road Hilly and stony. Here is a good place to camp,	14	1661
Road now follows the river. Then leave the river, traveling through heavy sand,	3	1664
To the river again, where there is good grass,	10	1674
Road now follows the river to a valley of good grass,	10	1684
Road still continues along it to point of timber and some grass,	16	1700
Gold Cannon. Here you rise a steep bluff, where a railway, for mining purposes, is built from Gold Cannon to the river [p. 15],	4	1704
To river again, over a rough road,	10	1714
Here is a fine valley and trading post—road follows river,	2	1716
Leaves it again for Carson Valley. There is good grass here, and a creek of good water,	8	1724
To Mormon Station. Here is a settlement of Mormons, and a good general store. A spring-branch crosses the road, where teams can be watered and rest under the Fir trees,	10	1734
Road continues through this valley, occasionally crossing brooks of excellent cold water, to the Cannon of Siera Nevada,	21	1755
You now have to pass over large granite rocks for 6 miles,	6	1761
Then cross Carson river 3 times to a valley where there is good grass,	1	1762
Black Salt Lake,	8	1770
Foot of the mountain,	1	1771
To Valley Lake, where there is good feed. The great *Back-Bone* of the Siera Nevada now stands before you, seemingly defying an attempt to reach the gold placers of Sacramento Valley,	8	1779

To main summit, generally covered with snow. About half a mile
farther is a lake, with some grass about the margin,   4   1783

From summit to a small creek,   7   1790

Rock Valley and Lake,   4   1794

Tragedy Springs. Here three of the first explorers of this route were
killed by Indians; their graves are to be seen at the foot of the hill,
near the spring. About 2 miles from this spring, north of the
road, is a fine clover pasture. A path turns right, before descending the hill to the spring, which leads to it,   3   1797

Lick Springs. Here wild onions and some grass may be found down
the ravine. Road forks—the right hand is the old Hangtown
road. We took the left, which is some the farthest, on account of
some feed on the route,   7   1804

Cosumne river, where there is some feed,   14   1818

Grizzly Flat. A mining town had just sprung up here, where considerable mining is done [p. 16],   14   1832

Wisconsin Bar. Here is a saw-mill, tavern, and several stores,   12   1844

Diamond Springs. This place and Mud Springs are in close proximity, and form quite a town,   15   1859

Sacramento City. Fine farms and good hotels along the last mentioned distance,   47   1906

You have now reached the great emporium of California; and hoping that you have enjoyed a pleasant trip, and seen the "Elephant" *tamed*, I bid you adieu.

F. M. DRAKE

REFER TO

The following gentlemen, as competent to judge of the Author's veracity, and
the worth of his work:

> ROBERT SEAMON, Keosauqua, Iowa.
> Dr. A. H. BALDWIN, Sacramento City, California.
> MILES WALTERS, Placerville.
> H. B. HORN, Bloomfield, Iowa.
> Dr. C. W. PHELPS, "   "
> A. W. RANKIN, Drakesville, Iowa.
> MOSES GREENE, Esq., "   "

[back wrapper]

DRAKE & SON,

DRAKESVILLE, IOWA,

South-East cor. Public Square, in a large Brick Building,

WHOLESALE AND RETAIL

MERCHANTS,

Keep constantly on hand a large and complete assortment of

STAPLE AND FANCY

DRYGOODS,

GROCERIES.

HARD-WARE, TIN-WARE, IRON, NAILS, MECHANICS'
TOOLS, BOOTS AND SHOES, AMUNITION,
FLOUR, BACON, GRAIN, &c., &c.

In short, they are in every way prepared to

OUTFIT AND ASSIST THE WESTERN EMIGRANT,

Upon most reasonable terms, and in direct competition with
river prices. Please give them a call, and see the above statements verified.

March 1st, 1853.

J. Tarbell, 1853

The Emigrant's Guide To California

Keokuk, Printed at the Whig Book and Job Office, 1853, 18 p. [WC 232a; WCB 233; Graff 4068; Kurutz 617; Mintz 455; Streeter 3175; NUC NT 0038096.] Reset verbatim from a facsimile, by courtesy of The Newberry Library, Chicago, Illinois.

Significance   Guides like this tell the gritty overland story of grass, water, wood, alkali, dust, and jaded animals and humans. Tarbell's guide had very accurate mileages on the Salt Lake route to the City of Rocks and not seriously overstated ones beyond. His route started at Council Bluffs and followed the north side of the Platte. West of South Pass he went by Ft. Bridger and Salt Lake City, thence taking the Salt Lake Cutoff and the Humboldt-Carson route to Sacramento. His distances west of City of Rocks were 90 miles greater than those measured today and only 55 greater than those of the authoritative Young and Eagar 1850 guide (K3). Streeter (3175) observed, "Dr. Tarbell makes the distance to Sacramento City 1873 miles, while his predecessor, Horn, who published a guide in 1852, made the distance 2011 miles over more or less the same route." As explained in K4 Highlights, this discrepancy is mostly related to poor estimates on the Humboldt-Carson leg, and Horn's was the farthest off of any of the major guides.

This appears to be the first reprint. Graff (4068) pointed out that all of the four known copies came from the closet of the widow of Horace H. Ayer of Keokuk, who may have known Tarbell. The originals had printed blue paper wrappers and sold for 35 cents (WC 232a).

Author   J. Tarbell, physician, overlander, guide writer. Tarbell made his overland crossing from Iowa in 146 days, in an unspecified year. He preferred horses to oxen or mules for the trip. He advised that, west of the Sierra summit, "Your main dependence now for food [forage] to the Sacramento valley, will be oak leaves." Wagner-Camp noted that "He was back in Keokuk in Nov., 1855."

Itineraries, 1853   The average 1853 wagon travels from the MISSOURI TO THE SACRAMENTO via Soda Springs in 125 days, and via Salt Lake City in

127 days. These travel times are longer than those of 1849-52. Of the 17 diarists taken from Mattes's compilation, 12, or 70 percent, go via Salt Lake City. Times and distances are figured as outlined in the K3 Itineraries.

WAGONS VIA SODA SPRINGS, CARSON/TRUCKEE TRAILS. Travel times of 5 diarists are minimum-mean-maximum 114-125-136 days. They cover the average distance of 1,860 miles at 15 miles per day.

WAGONS VIA SALT LAKE CITY, SALT LAKE CUTOFF, CARSON/TRUCKEE TRAILS. Travel times of 12 diarists are minimum-mean-maximum 97-127-148 days. They cover the average distance of 1,870 miles at 15 miles per day.

Legacy   Gary Kurutz, in his definitive bibliography, took 1853 to be the last year of importance in the California Gold Rush.

REFERENCES
(See Preface for Graff, Kurutz, Mattes, NUC, Streeter, Wagner-Camp, WC, WCB.)
Horn, Hosea B., 1852, Horn's overland guide: N.Y., 81 p., map.

THE

EMIGRANT'S GUIDE

TO

CALIFORNIA;

GIVING A DESCRIPTION

OF THE

OVERLAND ROUTE,

FROM THE COUNCIL BLUFFS, ON THE MISSOURI RIVER,
BY THE SOUTH PASS, TO SACRAMENTO CITY;
—INCLUDING—
A TABLE OF DISTANCES
FROM POINT TO POINT.

—ALSO—

Pointing out the Mineral Water so much to be dreaded
by the Emigrant.

BY DR. J. TARBELL

KEOKUK:
PRINTED AT THE WHIG BOOK AND JOB OFFICE

1853

[p. 3]

STARTING POINT:
COUNCIL BLUFFS, ON THE MISSOURI RIVER.

Here the emigrant can procure all the outfit necessary
for the journey, such as teams, provisions, etc.

MILES

From Council Bluffs cross the River and follow down the bottom,	1	
Ascend a high bluff and travel over rolling prairie to Pappia Creek, good grass and timber,	18	19
To Elk Horn, here you will have to ferry over your wagons but your stock can ford it,	9	28
To Platte River, plenty of grass and timber,	8	36
To Circular Lake,	4	40
To where road returns to the river,	10	50
You now leave the river and follow up the bottom, passing several small lakes to Loup Fork, good place to camp,	24	74
Looking Glass Creek, good camping,	10	84
Beaver River, 20 feet wide, 2 feet deep, a good place to camp,	6	90
Ford of Loup Fork, 1/4 mile wide, 3 feet deep,	10	100
Cedar Creek, 8 rods wide, 2 feet deep,	2	102
Road leaves the river and follows up a ravine and over a bluff to a small creek, bad crossing no timber,	7	109
Upper Ford of Loup Fork,	6	115
Over Sandy Bluffs [p.4],	5	120
Prairie Creek, bad crossing, no timber,	18	138
Small Creek, good camping,	2	140
Wood Creek, good grass, plenty timber,	10	150
Platte River,	2	152

The road now runs up the bottom, sometimes leaving the river from 1 2 to [sic] miles, passing several small lakes and crossing small creeks with good campings to the head of

Grand Island,	40	192
Elm Creek, plenty of timber, but little water,	3	195
Road leaves the river,	8	203
Crossing of Buffalo Creek,	3	206
Willow Lake, no wood, plenty grass,	20	226
Flat Lake, good camping,	8	234
Deep Dry Creek,	2	236
Low Sandy Bluff, extending to the river,	14	250
Skunk Creek, 6 feet wide, bad crossing,	5	255
Up Skunk Creek,	5	260
Marsh or Lake, south of the road,	1	261
Spring of cold water at the foot of the Bluffs, north of the road,	5	266
Opposite the junction of North and South Fork, roads hilly and sandy,	1	267

Canyon Creek, good grass but no timber,	4	271
Last timber on the north side of Platte. You will find no more timber for two hundred miles, except one lone tree,	8	279
North Bluff Fork, good water, not much grass,	11	290
Bluff Creek,	11	301
Goose Creek,	15	316
You now pass a very sandy bluff to		
Small Spring Creek,	2	318
Duck Weed Creek, good cold water,	2	320
Rattlesnake Creek, 20 feet wide, 1 foot deep,	6	326
Small Creek, land sandy, but little grass in this vicinity,	6	332
[p. 5] Camp Creek, 8 feet wide,	5	337
Small Creek, 3 feet wide,	4	341
Wolf Creek, 20 feet wide,	13	354
Watch Creek, 8 feet wide,	5	359
Lone Tree,	4	363
Castle Creek, 6 rods wide, swift current,	6	369
You will cross no more creeks with water in them, unless it is a wet time, until you arrive at		
Crab Creek, good roads,	30	399
Small Lake, south side of the road, good place to camp,	1	400
Cross three dry creeks to the foot of Cobble Hills,	5	405
Over steep sandy bluffs to the bottom,	2	407
Up the bottom to another range of sandy Bluffs, roads smooth, but little grass,	18	425
Across the Bluffs to the bottom,	1	426
Opposite Chimney Rock, grass poor,	15	441
Along the bank of the River to Scott's Bluffs,	19	460
Spring Creek, south of the road,	4	464
Small Creek, 200 yards south of the road. By ascending the highest Bluff, you have a view of Laramie Peak in the Black Hills, timber north side of the river. Roads very sandy balance of the way to Fort Laramie,	17	481
Raw-Hide Creek, one rod wide,	6	487
Fort Laramie,	12	499

This is a small Military Post situated on the north bank of the Laramie River, about one mile from its junction with the Platte River. Here the emigrants have crossed the Platte River and gone up the south side and recrossed near the mouth of the Sweetwater, but the best way is to keep up the north side of the Platte [p. 6] River. By so doing you will avoid two ferries and have better roads. The roads now become hilly, leaving the river several times, passing through valleys of good grass and timber to the last crossing of

Platte River,	125	624

From here the road leaves the River, you will now travel over a barren hilly country to Mineral Springs. The water is clear, but poisonous, — 13 — 637

Alkali Swamps. Here is some grass, but it is not safe to let your cattle go to it for fear of the poisonous water, — 9 — 646

Small Creek, left of the road, water has a bad taste but not poisonous, — 4 — 650

Willow Springs, right of the road, — 3 — 653

> You will find a good valley of grass over the hill to the right of the road about one mile, this is a small spring of good water, no fuel but wild sage, timber now becomes scarce, you will see but little timber until you come to the Green River.

Over a long hill to a Slough, Very muddy and bad to cross, — 4 — 657

Over rough roads to Greesewood [sic] Creek. Poor grass but plenty of sage for fuel, — 6 — 663

Alkali Spring. Some grass here, but dangerous to let the cattle on to it, the ground is covered with a crust of Salaratus [sic], — 6 — 669

Independence Rock, — 5 — 674

Ford of Sweetwater, 8 rods wide, 3 feet deep, — 7 — 681

> There are many pools along this river which are impregnated with Alkali, avoid them all as they are poisonous, [p. 7] do not let your stock drink any water that is not in a running stream.

Devil's Gate, — 4 — 685

Up the River. Crossing several creeks that are difficult to cross, grass and fuel scarce, — 12 — 697

Road leaves the river and passes over a very sandy country to the River, — 7 — 704

Bitter Cottonwood Creek, here are a few trees, but little grass, — 5 — 709

Road returns to the River, — 6 — 715

> By crossing the river here you will save some rough sandy road, but will have to cross the river three times after this, before you get back to the main road, but the crossings are not difficult.

Junction with the old Road,	8	723

The road here leaves the river, and you will find no good water for seventeen miles. About six from the junction, are several acres of low, swampy land, about one foot below the surface of which is a bed of ice about two inches thick.

Road returns to the River,	17	740
Cross over some points of Bluffs to the river again,	5	745
Up the River,	5	750

Over a succession of high rocky hills to a

Soft Swamp and a Small Creek,	8	758

You are now in a hilly, barren country, with only small patches of grass, you will find small valleys of good grass by turning off from the road and driving over the Bluffs to the right.

Strawberry Creek, plenty of willow for fuel and small patches of grass,	4	762
Quakingasp Grove, this is a small grove of trees south of the road [p. 8],	1	763
North Fork of Sweetwater, plenty of fuel but no grass,	3	766
Willow Creek,	2	768
Sweetwater, last crossing,	5	773

By going up the Sweetwater one mile you will find good grass. You will find no good grass westward from here, until you come to Big Sandy, the country is barren and destitute of vegetation except wild sage.

Up a long step [sic] hill over banks of snow to the Summit of the South Pass,	9	782
Pacific Springs. Here is a clear cold spring of good water, but the ground around it is so swampy that it is dangerous for cattle to go near it,	3	785
Dry Sandy. Water brackish, plenty of wild sage for fuel but no grass,	11	796
Fork of the Salt Lake and Sublet's Route. We will follow the road by the Salt Lake,	6	802
Little Sandy, the roads are heavy sand,	8	810
Big Sandy,	8	818

By driving up to the right of the road you will find good grass and some Cottonwood trees for fuel, here you cross the river, and travel over rough sandy roads without water or grass to

Big Sandy again,	17	835

Here the ground is covered with Alkali and several small pools of Alkali water, you had better drive your cattle to the creek and let them drink, then drive to the Bluffs to camp, there are small patches of bunch grass and wild oats on the bluffs,

Green River [p. 9]. You will have to ferry this river, there are several good ferries. Plenty of timber but little grass,	10	845
Down the River,	6	851

By swimming your cattle on to a small Island there is good grass, plenty of good timber for fuel. You now leave the river and travel over a rough barren road without grass or water to

Black's Fork, good camping,	15	866
Hams Fork,	5	871
Black's Fork second time, good grass and fuel,	12	883
Small Creek, no grass or fuel,	4	887

Over a rough barren country, without grass or water to

Fort Bridger,	20	907

This is a small Trading Post established for the purpose of trading with the Indians, it is situated in a beautiful valley, well watered with an abundance of good grass and fuel, from here you will have no scarcity of grass, fuel or water until you leave the Salt Lake valley,

Muddy Creek, difficult crossing,	13	920
Copperas Spring, to the left of the road at the foot of a hill,	4	924
Over a steep rough hill to a valley,	3	927
Down a ravine,	[5	932]

Over several steep, high mountains, the roads very rough and some places miry, the ascent and descent in many places difficult, crossing several small streams, to

Bear River,	8	940

This is a very rapid stream with a rocky bottom, about sixty yards wide, it is fed by melting snows, the snows mel-[p. 10]ting while the sun shines and freezing at night causes the river to ebb and flow daily. If you come to the river in the morning you will find it too deep to ford, but it will fall so that you can ford it in the afternoon, there is but little grass in this valley, but plenty of timber.

Up the valley to good grass and water,	3	943
Yellow Creek, bad crossing,	7	950

Over a mountain and down a ravine to Echo Creek,	6	956

About one fourth of a mile to the right of the road at the first crossing, there is a large cave in the side of the bluff, you will travel down this creek twenty-five miles, crossing it nineteen times, some of the crossings very miry, with steep banks to [sic]

To Weber River,	25	981
Down Weber River to the Ford. This stream is not fordable until		
late in the season, there is a ferry kept by the Mormons,	4	985
Up a deep ravine to the summit of a Mountain,	6	991
The descent is rough and sideling to a small Creek,	2	993
Canyan Creek,	3	996
Up Canyan Creek,	8	1004

Crossing it eleven times, many places steep banks and miry.

Turn to the right and ascend a high mountain,	4	1008

The ascent of this mountain is very rough and many places steep, it is covered with a heavy growth of timber and on the north side, banks of snow. From the summit you have a [p. 11] view of the south end of the Salt Lake valley.

Foot of the mountain, descent very steep and rough,	2	1010
Down the Creek,	4	1014
Over a high steep Mountain to last Creek,	6	1020
Down the Creek, crossing it 7 times,	5	1025

When you leave the creek you rise a gentle hill from the top of which you have a view of the Salt Lake, its valleys, surrounding mountains and the Mormon city.

City of the great Salt Lake,	5	1030

From the city the road turns north and keeps near the foot of the mountain for about eighty miles, the first fifty miles you will travel in thick settlements, where you will have a good opportunity to trade your teams for fresh ones, also procure provisions such as Beef, Flour, Chickens, Eggs, Butter, Cheese, etc.

To Boiling Spring,	2	1032

From here you will have good grass for the first fifty miles, then barren to Bear River.

Willow Spring,	6	1038
Clear Creek,	8	1046
Beaver River, 4 rods wide, 3 feet deep,	21	1067
Ogden River,	3	1070

Bitter Cottonwood Creek,	18	1088
Box Alder Creek,	4	1092
Large Pool, 20 rods to the left of the road,	10	1102
Bear River Ferry, grass poor, no fuel	10	1112

From here you will find no good water for thirty-two miles.

Muddy Creek, water not good,	2	1114
Salt Springs, brackish water, but not poisonous [p. 12],	20	1134
Sink Creek, good grass, no fuel,	10	1144
Deep Creek,	6	1150
Keep up the creek to the Sink. No water after this for ten miles,	6	1156
Pilot Springs,	10	1166

You now travel along the foot of the mountain to a

Spring in a ravine to the left of the road,	6	1172

You will now travel along the foot of the mountain, crossing several streams fed by melting snow.

To Cassus Creek,	8	1180
Up Cassus Creek,	2	1182

No water after leaving Cassus Creek for 8 miles,

Junction of Salt Lake and Sublett's Route,	5	1187

You will gradually descend into a large valley, well watered and abundance of good grass and timber.

Summit of a Mountain,	7	1194

From here the road is descending for five miles, many places rough, steep and sideling.

Small Creek at the foot of the Mountain,	5	1199
Goose Creek,	2	1201
Up Goose Creek to the mouth of a ravine,	18	1219

Travel up this ravine three miles and then cross it, after this you will find but little grass and no water for fifteen miles, roads rough and hilly,

Thousand Spring Valley,	18	1237

This valley is thirty-five miles long, well watered and in many places good grass, there are several hot springs and some alkali water which will injure your cattle.

Head of the Valley,	35	1272
Over several hills to a small Creek,	10	1282
Valley Spring [p. 13],	8	1290
Prairie Creek, abundance of grass,	10	1300

Canyon Creek, a tributary of the Humbolt,	4	[*sic*]
Humbolt River,	6	1306

You will follow down this river to the Sink, the roads are the most of the way heavy sand, and many places rough and hilly. You will have to ford this river many times, the fordings are difficult, owing to the banks being steep and miry. There are many pools of standing water that is impregnated with alkali that will make it necessary to be careful of your stock, also the Indians are thieveish [*sic*] along this river, grass is good for the first one hundred miles. There is no fuel but willow and sage,

North Fork of Humbolt, good fording,	20	1326
Over the point of three bluffs to the river,	7	1333
Down the river bottom to the foot of a bluff,	20	1353

Ascend and travel over a succession of barren bluffs, destitute of grass or water to

Small Creek,	12	1365
Small Creek, good water [mileages thus],	4	1379

You will travel over a succession of barren hills to the River [mileages thus],

[mileages thus],	12	1381
Cross a high bluff and travel down the bottom to the River,	10	1391
Small Creek, good grass,	9	1400
Point of the Bluffs,	7	1407

The country now becomes very barren, the roads heavy and sandy, the water in the river begins to taste of Alkali, grass is only found in patches, the sun pours down its intense heat, the dust forms a heavy cloud, the cattle becomes so jaded that they require constant urging to keep them moving, [p. 14] and the murmur is often heard to escape the lips of the toil worn traveler, "Had I realized what I now see before me I would [have] remained satisfied in my peaceful home."

The road now follows down the river, crossing several sandy deserts, leaving and returning to the river at intervals until you come to the great meadow or

Grazing Ground,	170	1577

Here are several thousand acres of good grass. Emigrants resort here to recruit their cattle and cut hay for the desert, there being but little grass for seventy miles. If you should happen here in a dry time, take in a supply of water, for the water at the Sink becomes brackish, when the river gets low. You will now follow down the river with sandy roads to the

Sink of the Humbolt,   23   1600

Let your cattle drink but little water at the sink, as it will weaken them so much that they will not be able to perform the journey across the desert, you will find the water more pure in the middle of the lake where there is a current. The first thirty miles across the desert the roads are level and smooth but the last twelve miles is extremely sandy.

Carson River,   42   1642

No grass on this for five miles, you will then find good grass and timber,

Road leaves the River, rough hilly country, destitute of grass or water.

Road returns to the River,   7   1649

Here the road leaves the river again [p. 15] and you will find no grass or water for twenty-five miles. The whole distance the roads are rough and heavy sand.

Road returns to the River,   25   1674

No grass when you come to the river, but by going up two miles you will find tall grass and timber.

You now follow up the River,   10   1684

Cross the River. Here you leave the river and ascend a high steep bluff and travel over a barren country with rough roads and no water.

Road returns to the River,   12   1696

Drive up the river two miles to good grass. You are now in Carson valley, it is forty miles long, the road keeps along the foot of the mountain. These mountains are covered with a heavy growth of tall pines. You will cross a number of small streams and on your left there is a heavy growth of grass. The first thirty miles the roads are good, the rest of the way to the Canyon, hilly and rough.

Mouth of Big Canyon,   40   1736

You will now have eight miles of the worst road on the journey. It is enclosed on both sides by high rocky cliffs, the stream comes rushing down from the mountains, roaring like a cataract. The road is so very rocky that it is difficult in many places to get along with a wagon.

Head of the Canyon, good grass and fuel,	8	1744

You will now find grass scarce to Sacramento City.

Foot of the first ridge of the Sierra Nevada [p. 16],	12	1756

You now ascend a steep rough mountain which is about one mile to the summit, the descent sideling and rough to a valley at the

Foot of the Second Ridge,	6	1762

You now have a very sideling ascent, and many places very rocky, near the summit there are immense banks of snow.

Summit,	4	1766

You will now find rough hilly roads, with good water but little grass to

Leek Springs, good grass down the valley,	23	1789

Your main dependence now for food to the Sacramento valley, will be oak leaves, you will have plenty of good water, roads growing better to

Placerville, here you enter the mines,	34	1823

Over rough hills to

Diamond Springs, no grass, good water,	4	1827
Sacramento City, good roads but little grass,	46	1873

ROUTE BY SUBLETT'S AND GREENWOOD CUT OFF.

Little Sandy, good place to camp,	5	
Big Sandy, good grass but no fuel,	6	11

From here no water and but little grass for fifty miles, good road.

Green River,	50	61

From here to the junction of the Salt Lake road you will find grass plenty.

Bear Creek, road hilly,	4	65
Ford of Bear Creek,	6	71
Deep Ravine,	4	75
Branch of Colerado, roads very hilly,	18	93

You will cross several streams in this distance. [p. 17]

Poplar Grove,	7	100
Bear River, roads hilly,	14	114

Thulick's Fork,	14	128
Bear River Valley,	10	138
Small Creek,	8	146
Small Creek,	13	159
Small Creek,	4	163
Small Creek,	33	196
You will cross several small streams in this distance.		
Soda Spring,	3	199
You now have a good road, with good camping to		
Junction of Salt Lake Road,	110	309

REMARKS—TEAM AND OTHER OUTFIT.

One hundred and forty-six days experience in crossing the Plains, with an ox team, gave the Author an opportunity to form a correct opinion of what kind of a team is most suitable for the journey and also what other outfit is necessary to take. In the first place, I consider ox teams the most safe, being better adapted to the feed found on the journey.

A Mule team is considered more hardy, consequently better able to stand the journey than Horses, but a horse team with care in selecting good sound horses of the largest size, with a careful driver, will perform the trip, and is a much more pleasant team than oxen or mules.

The great difficulty is overloading and overdriving at the start. If you start several hundred miles east of the Missouri River, it is advisable to only start with sufficient provision to last to Council Bluffs, as at that or any other point of crossing of the Missouri, the merchants have a large supply of provisions that can be obtained on reasonable terms, for as you are under the necessity of starting at a time when the roads are muddy, you are liable to break down your teams at the [p. 18] start, and all such will most certainly fail to perform the journey.

Take light wagons, and whether you take oxen, Mules or Horses, the largest are the best. Load light. Three men are as many as should go with one team. Have your horses or mules well shod, and take one set of shoes and nails with you. Oxen, if you keep up the north side of the Platte, do not need shoeing.

I will now give what I consider an outfit for three men, with an ox team.

> One Light Two Horse Wagon,
> Four Yoke of Oxen,

	POUNDS
Flour and Meal, per man, 150 lbs.,	450
Hard Bread, per man, 50 lbs.,	150
Bacon, this should be Sides,	300
Dried Apples,	50
Sugar,	100
Coffee,	25
Rice,	15
Beans,	25
Tea,	1
One Rifle, (large bore)	20
Six Mackinaw Blankets,	35
Fine Salt,	4
Saleratus,	5
One Sheetiron Cooking Stove, with plates,	
tin cups, knives and forks, etc.	50
	1230

If you go with horses or mules you should have two to each man. As mules or horses will perform the trip in twenty or twenty-five days less time than oxen, one sixth less provisions will be sufficient. The time of starting will depend on the season, make it a point to leave the Missouri as soon as there is grass for your teams. Drive slow; the old adage is applicable, "haste makes waste." Keep cool and let your moderation be the predominating principle, and you are ensured a safe but tedious journey.

Anonymous [Englishman], 1855

Journey From New Orleans To California [Fiction]

London, W. and R. Chambers, *Chambers's Journal of Popular Literature Science and Arts*, Vol. 4, in five chapters on December 1, 8, 15, 22, and 29, 1855, at p. 337-41, 364-68, 371-75, 397-400, and 408-11, respectively. [WC and WCB 257; Eberstadt 115:1087; Holliday 314; Mattes 322.] Reset from compiler's original, omitting many passages and all of the last two chapters.

Significance This bit of malarkey reveals one wordy Englishman's cockeyed views of overland trails and peoples he never saw. Apparently without having read it, Henry R. Wagner in his 1920, 1921, and 1937 editions of *The Plains and the Rockies* said, "This seems to be an entirely veracious narrative of a journey by persons with fictitious names from New Orleans via St. Louis, Kansas City and the overland trail to California in the summer of 1849." Charles L. Camp in the 1953 edition compounded the problem by asserting, "This seems to be L. Dow's veracious narrative...printed originally in the *New York Tribune,* according to the Platt Guide." However, Dale Morgan, in his 1963 introduction to the 1852 guide by Philip L. Platt and Nelson Slater, pointed out that Lorenzo Dow went to California by sea in 1850, not by land in 1849; Dow's article in the *Tribune* was only a short letter about Beckwourth Pass. Finally, Robert H. Becker got it right in the 1982 edition of *The Plains and the Rockies:* "The entire account is hardly worthy of a traveler's notice." Mattes concluded that the author's "coyness and other literary affectations, anachronisms, and geographical inconsistencies place a strain on creditability."

This must be the first reprint. Being unwilling to give it more than a few pages, I have cut it drastically, retaining mainly the misconceptions about lands and Indians. The last two chapters on life in California are eliminated entirely, although they may be the only true parts.

Author Although this anonymous English writer never saw the Plains or the Rockies, he may have visited California by sea. In the last two chapters he described his hero Edwardson's visits to San Francisco, Benicia, and Napa. After being very sick, and without visiting or even mentioning the gold fields, "On the 2d of February [1850], Mr. Edwardson embarked in the steamer *Panama,* bound for the town of that name…Opposite Edwardson sat Judge [Edwin] Bryant, who has written a work called *California as I Saw It,* and who has made several trips over the Rocky Mountains, on one occasion performing that arduous journey with General Kearney in only sixty days [see 4:G6]. Judge Bryant is a very amiable person, and his manners being particularly affable and intelligent, his society was a great acquisition on board [pages 399, 408]." Thomas D. Clark, in his 1985 introduction to Bryant's 1848 *What I Saw in California,* confirmed that *"The Louisville Daily Journal,* on March 22, 1850, announced that he [Bryant] had returned home via the Isthmus of Panama and New Orleans."

Highlights   The Englishman's worst mistakes were finding an 1849 Rendezvous in progress, when the last one was held in 1840; and running successively into South Pass and Independence Rock *west* of Green River, in the reverse of their actual order. The reprint calls up many lesser blunders.

Legacy   The only impact seems to have been the befuddlement of eminent bibliographers.

REFERENCES
(See Preface for Heading references not listed here.)

Bryant, Edwin, 1848 (1985 reprint), What I saw in California; Introduction by Thomas D. Clark: Lincoln, p. xviii.

Platt, Philip L., and Nelson Slater, 1852 (1963 reprint), Travelers' guide across the plains upon the overland route to California; Introduction by Dale Morgan: San Francisco, p. xi; Dow's letter 57-58.

Wagner, Henry R., 1920, The Plains and the Rockies: San Francisco, no. 214, p. 105; only 20 copies survived from this suppressed first edition.

Wagner, Henry R., 1921, The Plains and the Rockies: San Francisco, no. 214, p. 117; the nominal first edition in 325 copies.

Wagner, Henry R., revised by Charles L. Camp, 1937, The Plains and the Rockies: San Francisco, no. 257, p. 170-71; second edition.

Wagner, Henry R., revised by Charles L. Camp, 1953, The Plains and the Rockies: San Francisco, no. 257, p. 325; third edition.

Wagner, Henry R., and Charles L. Camp, revised by Robert H. Becker, 1982, The Plains & the Rockies: San Francisco, no. 257, p. 458; fourth edition.

CHAMBERS'S JOURNAL

OF

POPULAR LITERATURE SCIENCE AND ARTS

CONDUCTED BY

WILLIAM AND ROBERT CHAMBERS

EDITORS OF 'CHAMBERS'S EDUCATIONAL COURSE' 'INFORMATION FOR THE PEOPLE' &c

VOLUME IV

Nos. 79-104. JULY—DECEMBER 1855.

LONDON
W. AND R. CHAMBERS 47 PATERNOSTER ROW
AND HIGH STREET EDINBURGH

MDCCCLVI

CHAMBERS'S JOURNAL OF POPULAR LITERATURE
Science and Arts.
Conducted by William and Robert Chambers.

| No. 100 | Saturday, December 1, 1855. | Price 1 1/2 d. |

JOURNEY FROM NEW ORLEANS TO CALIFORNIA
In Five Chapters.—Chap. I

(This is the first of a brief series of papers descriptive of the journey, and its adventures, through the American wilderness to California. The heroes of the narrative are real persons, and actually performed their extraordinary pilgrimage to the temple of the golden idol, the route of which is by this time marked out with human bones and human graves.)

In our dear island-home of Britain, nature is on a scale so circumscribed that we can hardly realise suitable ideas of the interminable prairies, stupendous mountains, and sea-like lakes of the New World. *There* are trackless wastes awaiting the culturing hand of man; boundless forests, of which buffalo and deer are the aborigines; and majestic lakes and rivers, to which the largest of our own are but as brooks and millponds. To these boundless regions, inviting the swarming population of an older country, the philanthropist rejoices to see many of the hardy sons of toil bending their way, with energies newly braced, and resolutions bravely formed, to secure for themselves a home of plenty, and for their posterity, influence and independence...

There was in 1849 an amiable, well-educated, and delicately nurtured young gentleman, a native of the aristocratic state of South Carolina, who had been settled as a merchant for three years in the noble city of New Orleans. All the world was pressing thither, as the starting-point for California...One singular feature of this *omnium gatherum* was the general absence of the female sex...Men are glad to leave their gentle ones safe at home, when they bend themselves to such rugged tasks, fit for the stalwart strength of manhood alone...Among the throng that came to New Orleans were many persons with whom the young gentleman we have alluded to, and whom we shall call Tom Edwardson, had been acquainted...Mr. Edwardson and three friends, with views similar to his own, engaged a passage to St. Louis in a steam-boat...[p. 338]

In this city [St. Louis], emigrants furnish themselves with the necessary clothing, provisions, and arms...[and] suitable travelling-companions...Each individual contributed as his quota 300 dollars (£.60). And these preliminaries being settled, the party met in solemn conclave to draw up rules for their government and to make out lists of the articles required for their outfit...Two wagons were then purchased, two tents, and a coil of strong hempen rope. Each man was provided with a pair of blankets, a buffalo-robe, several pair of waterproof boots, reaching above the knee, besides the ordinary changes of clothes and linen…[p. 339]

Our travellers at length embarked on the Missouri for Independence, about 450 miles distant, at which place the land-journey would commence. On this second voyage, cholera still pursued them, with a repetition of heart-rending scenes similar to those they had already witnessed…[They stopped only] at one little German village, where excellent wine is produced…The four days' voyage terminated at 'Wayne's City,' [Upper Independence Landing], a collection of board and log huts…They then set out on foot for Independence, which is situated three miles from the river. It was first settled and named by the Mormons, after they had been expelled from Nauvoo by the citizens of the state of Illinois—only to be in like manner, after a short sojourn, driven forth from Independence [garbled history]…They endeavored to purchase draught-animals for their wagons, without which their goods could not be transported even from Wayne's City, where they had left them…

After these various delays, they at last started on the 1st of May…The appearance of the gentlemen was rendered picturesque by a blouse of red cloth, girt round the waist with a stout leathern-belt, in which were stuck the [p. 340] bowie-knife and revolver; while over the shoulders were slung the rifle and ammunition pouches. Broad-brimmed hats and wading-boots completed the equipment… [Soon] Mr. Edwardson was found to have taken cholera…[but] after a patient delay of three days, the young man recovered sufficiently to proceed…

The settlement or village of Kansas is inhabited by a half-civilised tribe of Indians, called the Pottawattimies. They were originally from Illinois, where the United States government bought their lands, and was at the expense of transporting them hither, and also of protecting and pensioning them. The pension consists of yearly presents, over and above liberal and punctual payments for their furs, skins, and other commodities…You may see a dark warrior pacing proudly about, in inexpressibles of English cloth…Anon, you perceive the stealing step of a copper-coloured black-eyed beauty, her whole person enveloped in a lady's shawl of bright colours and gay pattern…As they [some horsemen] drew near, they screamed: 'Whisky! whisky!' but the strangers were cognizant of the law, which prohibits giving the Indians any alcohol, except what is, in a regulated quantity, supplied to them by the government agent at the station…[p. 341]

Often they journeyed for days without seeing another human being, except at a time when a mounted Indian would cross the path, sweeping by like a whirlwind…[Chap. II, p. 364] Edwardson observed, with a curious and amused eye, the proceedings of the singular animal called the 'prairie dog'…[He] shot one or two of them, and they were pronounced very tolerable eating…Our emigrants had been warned strongly to be on their guard against these savages [the Pawnees], as some of them are continually in ambush, watching opportunity to carry off cattle or horses by night. Such attacks of the Indians are called 'stampedes'…[p. 365]

[At Ft. 'Kearney'] are about 100 troops, mostly mounted, and such is the moral force of the government, that this handful of men keep in thorough check many thousand savages…From 1500 to 2000 emigrants were encamped on the plain, their tents and wagons clustering round the fort…[with] 'the stars and stripes' floating from the battlements…In consequence of a rather formidable and successful stampede the Pawnees had made on a party lately arrived…the emigrants…[organized] a band of volunteers to go in pursuit of the robbers…Ten dragoons from the fort were to accompany them…[p. 366] It was the second day of hard riding…they found a party of Indians…As soon as the soldier took part in the conference—which it was not his object to do till other means failed—the enemy was at once overawed, or, as we should say, completely cowed. Their grandfather's uniform brought them to terms in a moment…The officer engaged for an amnesty, on condition that they should pay for the animals they had slaughtered, restore the remainder, and leave three of their braves as hostages, till the demands were complied with. This was humbly assented to…

Our little party had never shrunk from any personal hardship or useful labour, washing even their own linens…[p. 367] Slowly and droopingly they traversed the burning waste [west of Chimney Rock], where not a blade of grass was to be seen for hours together…At Laramie…the mild yet firm administration of the commandant has taught the Sioux to venerate their white allies too much to require any stringent measures of intimidation…Their manners are courteous and confiding, generally displaying perfect faith in the integrity and friendship of their white 'brothers.' It is a singular fact, perhaps not usually known, but well authenticated by Mr. Edwardson, that cholera hardly ever attacks the red man…

In the tent, the day they left Laramie, the thermometer was at 120 degrees…For ten days, the way was monotonous and cheerless in the extreme, and they then came to the bed of a dried-up river…called the Big Sandy…A forced march over thirty miles of sandy desert…lay between them and the next clearly defined place of encampment at Green River…[p. 368]

While resting by Green River, our energetic young friend, accompanied by some other of the wayfarers, paid a visit to an Indian [Snake] village hard by…The wigwams were very irregularly erected, composed chiefly of skins, stretched over a few sapling stems, drawn together to a point overhead. The inte-

rior was very filthy and disorderly, men, women, and children herding promiscuously, but, except at night, the families appeared to live almost entirely in the open
air; under the trees and by the river's bank they clustered in blissful idleness or
dreamy childish play. Inside and outside, the huts were covered, in festoons, with
dried venison and buffalo-meat; and Mr. Edwardson procured from an elderly
squaw, for an old shirt, several pair of deer-skin moccasins and as much venison as
he could carry. Moreover, the white visitors smoked with the chief men of the settlement the pipe of peace, which gave them the *entrée* of all the dwellings...

In the immediate vicinage of this Indian village...our travellers witnessed a
still more novel and stirring scene. It was the usual yearly meeting of the traders
from the States with the trappers who frequent these wilds, and who are under
engagement to the former to meet with them and dispose of their peltry...It was
an extensive encampment, not unlike an English fair...When Mr. Edwardson
visited this singular fair, and saw the piles of rich furs arid skins, so valuable in
commerce; the rough half-wild men who procure them; the shy dark women, and
dirty half-bred children—he could perceive no good, but evil, in this mode of
life...There was a table for gaming among the other booths...Intemperence was
also there in debasing forms, and the visitor-emigrants were at length glad to
retire from the scene...[Chap. III, p. 371]

From this point on Green River...Mr. Edwardson and his friends chose the
less frequented, though more direct course, gone over by the celebrated explorer
of those regions, Kit Carson...Our travellers now, outstripping some larger caravans, with the compass only for their guide, kept steadily on for what is called the
South Pass, being that ridge of the Rocky Mountains from which the streams
begin to flow westward into the Pacific...The Green River, which our travellers
had last crossed, is a fork or tributary of the Nebraska [Platte]...Three weeks they
floundered through this cold and hilly region...[p.372] Trunks, and almost all
their clothing, the greater part of their provisions, and the tent...were all, not
without a severe struggle, left on the mountains...Packs were then made out of
the canvas-covering of the tent...

On the banks of Bear River...a gigantic Indian of the Utah tribe stalked up to
the camping-place...He looked at those of the whites who were of less stature
with an air of superb disdain, measuring them with his eye, and uttering a con-
temptuous 'ugh.' This at length attracted the notice of an emigrant lying on the
ground, who slowly rose, and towering above the savage, looked down in turn
upon him, patting him on the head with a low expressive laugh. On this, the red
man slunk away, quite crest-fallen...They reached what is generally known as
Sweet Water River...At a short distance from the river, they found a very singular

rock, bare of any soil, and precipitously towering to a great height; it is called Independence, from its having been first discovered on the 4th of July…They journeyed by the brink of Sweet Water River till the route diverged. Crossing a steep and wooded hill, they found a barren level; after traversing which, they suddenly came to a gorge or cañon, the path through which was strewn with loose rocks and trunks of fallen trees…

On emerging from the savage gorge, our travellers found themselves in another extensive valley…one of the haunts of the Digger Indians. This tribe is the lowest in the scale of humanity…They wear no clothing whatever; they neither sow, nor reap, nor hunt…[p. 373] Knowing the cowardly and treacherous character of these Digger Indians, our emigrants thereafter took care to bivouac in open spots, where surprise was impossible…After crossing another eminence, they encamped in an extensive plain, studded with lakes, at the foot of a lofty mountain. The plain was thronged with emigrants, recruiting their teams before attempting the arduous ascent…[to] about 10,000 feet in altitude…On the summit, there was snow falling, and lying thick on the ground…Mr. Edwardson and his friends bought while they could; they then begged, to satisfy the cravings of nature; but no man gave to them. The strong men were becoming emaciated and weak…in the descent of the mountain…[p. 374] They were not now above 100 miles from the nearest settlement of the Diggings…

At length, on issuing from a thicket, they were cheered with the sight of a tent with a sign-board, bearing the interesting legend 'Wisky for sail'…Mr. Edwardson produced his last coin, and called for a drink to each…They were told they were only forty miles from Sacramento city!…They fairly lost their way amongst rocks and underwood, through the latter of which they had often to cut a passage with their bowie-knives—the compass indicating the direction of their route. At last they reached the settlement called Weaver Town [Weberville, two miles south of what became Placerville in 1850].

Charles Cardinell, 1856

Adventures On The Plains [In 1850]

San Francisco *Daily California Chronicle,* January 21, February 5 and 16, 1856. [WC 202 note; WCB 272c; Cowan p. 104; Eberstadt 115:1042, 134:171; Graff 582; Holliday 171; Kurutz 117; Mintz 526; Soliday 1:548.] Reset verbatim from compiler's copy of a 15-page separate reprint from the Quarterly of the California Historical Society for July, 1922, by courtesy of the California Historical Society, San Francisco; the *Chronicle* editor's introductory comments are taken from WCB.

Significance   Cardinell recounted a tale of greenhorn horror on a passenger expedition from Texas to San Diego promoted by swindler and murderer Parker H. French. About 230 eastern men paid French for wagon seats on an advertised 60-day Pleasure Trip to the gold fields. At El Paso they were cast adrift to wander across the Sonora and Arizona deserts, some being attacked and two murdered by French himself, but most miraculously surviving. Cardinell, alone and lost, was annoyed by the Indians, but only their presence let him live to tell his story. The year was 1850, not 1849 as he stated. This probably is the first reprint since the 1922 one of only 150 copies.

The southern routes to the gold fields, used by thousands of gold seekers, are summarized by Bieber 1937, Egan 1970, and Etter 1995.

Author   CHARLES CARDINELL, 1822-1907, adventurer, architect. Born in Ontario, Canada, Cardinell was educated in architecture at Belleville and married Jane Blaind there in 1845. Catching gold fever, he was an enlisted employee on Parker H. French's disastrous 1850 expedition to California. After arrival he made and lost money in the mines, turning then to erecting buildings in Tuolumne County. In 1867 he moved his family to Portland, Oregon, and continued his career as an architect. He was partially paralyzed after 1875 but courageously continued to supervise his buildings and his finances. (Introduction to 1922 reprint.)

Participant   PARKER H. FRENCH, scoundrel. The two main accounts of French by McGowan 1879 and Baldridge 1895 are conflicting, and both depend much on hearsay. McGowan wrote that French was born in Kentucky, was soon orphaned, and in his youth served five years as a cabin boy and powder monkey on a British Man-of-War. He became a trader in St. Louis. In 1849 he supposedly started to build a ship to sail to California but quit, leaving unpaid debts.

According to Baldridge, French in 1850 was about 24 years old, had a wife and one child, hailed from St. Louis, once worked for a steamship company, and was "rather below medium height and weight; his compact build suggested more than average physical power, while his physiognomy indicated great executive ability." After cheating the paid passengers on his promoted "Pleasure Trip" to California, and leaving them destitute half way there, he attacked and murdered some of them in Corralitos (see Itinerary). In the gun battle, French's right arm was shattered from hand to elbow. One story is that he went 200 miles to Chihuahua, with his arm packed in pulverized charcoal, for an amputation. Another is that he was still conscious, after huge doses of mescal, Spirits of Nitre, and chloroform, while his arm was taken off in Corralitos (Egan 1970).

Such was French's charisma that, after catching up with another group of his former passengers in Mazatlan, he succeeded in cheating them again. Baldridge wrote that he there robbed a silver train, was captured, then released to bring in Apache scalps, then reimprisoned when some of the scalps turned out to be Mexican. He escaped after inducing a Mexican lady to bribe the guard. McGowan had him robbing a mail coach near Durango and going through his imprisonments and scalp hunting there.

Later in California French embezzled school funds and served in the State Legislature. He joined William Walker's filibuster in Nicaragua, was its Minister to Washington for a short time, was a Confederate spy until arrested and converted into a Union spy, and was an army sutler when last heard from. (Baldridge 1895.)

McGowan stated that French was district attorney in San Luis Obispo in 1851, was elected to the California Legislature in 1854, sold some cattle not his, was in Nicaragua and Washington 1855-56, published a paper in San Jose in 1857, was arrested in New England in 1861 for outfitting a Confederate privateer, defrauded his partners in a ginseng speculation after the war, and was last heard from in 1876-77 pursuing a claim against Mexico for being "robbed" in El Paso and "unlawfully jailed" in Durango.

Itinerary, 1850   WILLIAM MILES, PORT LAVACA TO SAN DIEGO. June 17— Capt. Parker H. French's expedition leaves Port Lavaca TX for Victoria, Goliad, and San Antonio. Chronicler William Miles's 1851 journal names 49 enlisted men and 131 paid passengers, but the total grows to about 230 later. They sail from New York on May 13 via Havana, New Orleans, and Galveston. French breaks out 150 bottles of champagne on shipboard, and he puts the men up in good hotels in New Orleans. They bring with them freshly painted spring wagons with high-sounding names, each carrying a tent, camping equipment, 12 passengers, and a driver. Instead of the promised broken mules at Port Lavaca, however, they have to wait for wild ones that are soon breaking harnesses and wagons. Mosquitoes are insufferable, and rations and tempers are short. In his 1895 reminiscences, Michael Baldridge bemoans the greenhorn cooks, but "a good appetite compelled us to eat what was set before us, asking no questions…'hard tack,' although old enough to have died a natural death, was full of life…and all our previous notions of a 'pleasure trip' must be reconstructed."

July 15—After a 9-day layover, the expedition sets out on the Lower Road (5:J4) from San Antonio to El Paso. A man dies, another is shot and killed by accident, and still another is crushed by a wagon. Indians repeatedly steal horses, mules, and cattle. Prairie fires, long drives without water, broken wagons, rattlesnakes, extreme heat, and a near-empty larder bedevil the travelers. After crossing the Pecos on a government bridge, they follow instructions and bury the planks to keep them from the Indians. September 18 through about 26—Near El Paso. Soon after arrival, an officer from San Antonio catches up with them to arrest French. All of French's letters of credit and government papers are forged, and he has been defrauding merchants all along the way. French escapes to safety in Mexico. The men distribute most of the company's goods and animals amongst themselves, as needed to pursue the trip by packing, and sell the rest. In all they realize about 20 cents on the dollar invested. The company breaks up and scatters. Baldridge goes south toward Mazatlan, experiencing terrible thirst. Miles and Cardinell, in a party of about 20 inept packers, strike southwest for Corralitos and Janos.

October 7—At Corralitos French, with a recruited band of cutthroats, descends on Miles's party, "determined to wash his hands in the blood of the officers of the 'distribution,'" and to retake the company's property. French and his men kill two and seriously wound two, but the battle ends when French's arm is shattered. Joined now by some 40 other company men, the party moves northwest through Janos to Guadalupe Pass near the present southwest corner of New Mexico. Thence they go west along the modern U.S.-Mexican border, for a while on Cooke's Wagon Road (3:E6); but they keep on to Santa Cruz, Sonora, 25 miles east of today's Nogales, on Maj. Lawrence P. Graham's 1848 route (5:J7). October 19—Tubac (AZ).

From Tubac they wander northwest to the vicinity of Santa Rosa, rather than north to Tucson. Miles records daily agonizing searches for water; with Indian help he and some 80 others find the Gila and descend it to reach the Colorado about November 1. Two days from Tubac, Cardinell is separated from his mule and his companions and is completely lost. His story is one of lonely panic, aimless meandering, thirst and hunger, and help and hindrance from the Pimas. He reaches the Colorado November 18, near present Yuma AZ.

November 16—Miles reaches San Diego. Cardinell straggles in on December 5, having also taken the usual route across the Colorado Desert and on by way of "Williams" (Warner?) Ranch. Miles covers about 1,500 miles, not counting wasted wanderings, in 136 tortured days, not counting 17 at San Antonio and El Paso. Average rate is 11 miles per day.

Legacy   Michael Baldridge concluded in 1895, "Sometime ago I heard a lady giving a glowing account of what she termed a 'pleasure trip' from New York to San Francisco in seven days in a palace sleeping car, and as I listened I yielded to the influence which moved me [years ago]." Perhaps he then reflected silently on human nature's latent desires for riches at little cost, desires that fanned the gold-rush flames and that were readily ignited and exploited by charismatic villains like Parker H. French.

REFERENCES
(See Preface for Heading references not listed here.)

Baldridge, Michael, 1895 memoirs (1959 publication), A reminiscence of the Parker H. French Expedition through Texas & Mexico to California in the spring of 1850; introduction by John B. Goodman III: Los Angeles, 52 p.; quotes on French 2, appetite 8, lady 50.

Bieber, Ralph P., 1937, Southern trails to California in 1849: Glendale, 386 p.

Egan, Ferol, 1970, The El Dorado Trail: N.Y., 313 p.; French 137.

Etter, Patricia A., 1995, To California on the Southern Route 1849: Independence, Overland Journal 13/3:2-12.

McGowan, Edward, 1879 (1958 reprint), The strange eventful history of Parker H. French; Kenneth M. Johnson, ed.: Los Angeles, 63 p.

Miles, William, 1851 (1916 reprint), Journal of the sufferings and hardships of Capt. Parker H. French's overland expedition to California 1850: N.Y., 26 p.; quote 20.

ADVENTURES ON THE PLAINS

No. I.

The following are extracts from a Journal kept by Charles Cardinell, who formed one of the notorious Parker H. French Express California Train which started from Texas in the year 1849, [1850] across the Plains for this country. It makes an interesting narrative of travel.

Left New York on the 13th of May, 1849 [1850], for Port Lavaco, Texas. We arrived at El Paso near the end of September, after a long and tedious journey. Here our company of about 250 was broken up. The passengers becoming tired of so much delay took possession of the train and sold it. The amount of money taken for wagons, mules, harness, etc., would pay but twenty per cent on the demands against French. My demands being at this time $200 gave me according to the percentage allowed, $40, for which I drew a mule, valued at $45, and paid the five dollars difference. I also bought another mule from a private individual, and supplied myself with plenty of provisions and clothing.

I now joined a dozen of the old company, and we made our way to Corlitao, a Mexican town about 130 miles west of El Paso. Having arrived there, we unpacked our animals, led them to water and were engaged in washing their backs which were already becoming sore from the effect of the packs. But now a sudden yell or war-whoop of many voices broke upon our ears, and soon there appeared, to our surprise, French at the head of men, all mounted and well armed, each having a six-shooter in his right hand, and on his left shoulder a rifle. On they came, charging upon us at full speed, whooping and yelling like so many savages.

They fired upon us, and the balls were whistling about our [p. 4 of 1922 reprint] heads in every direction. My companions were falling to the earth on every side of me, with awful groans, in the last agonies of death. This lasted but a short time. French received a ball in the wrist, which passed out near the elbow, shattering his arm to pieces. One of our party, by the name of Wright, was shot through the neck. He died instantly. Another one, named Nelson, while in the act of stooping to lift a comrade from the ground, was shot through the back. He died in a few hours. Another, named Cooper, was shot through the thigh; and another, an old man, also of our party, by the name of Holmes, had both arms shot off. The groans of the wounded and dying were most affecting. There was no surgeon. French robbed us of our animals, and left us destitute. Graves were dug and our departed comrades were rolled in their blankets, and buried side by side on the spot where their blood was shed.

We remained at this place three days, in consequence of not having animals to proceed. In the meantime, the Alcalde becoming alarmed at the company's proceedings, fearing lest they would take the town, sent a dispatch to Janos for a company of Mexican Lancers. A portion of these, when they arrived, he placed at the entrance of the town to prevent other parties from coming in until ours had departed.

At length, after much entreaty, together with the Alcalde's influence, I obtained again one of my animals. Some others of the party also obtained theirs. I packed my animal with as much as he was able to bear; the remainder of my property I was obliged to carry myself. With this burden I traveled all day, the distance of 25 miles to Janos, where I was so fortunate as to obtain a horse. We now proceeded on our journey to Santa Cruz, a distance of 200 miles, arriving there just late enough to escape trouble, as 300 Apaches had just left after committing depredations of every savage nature upon the place and its inhabitants, shooting some of the males and taking some of the females prisoners. They also took away their horses, cattle, sheep, &c.

After leaving Santa Cruz and following Cook's route, we came to a deserted town named Tubac on the 19th of October, where we remained until Monday morning to recruit ourselves and our animals. On Monday we made a march of 30 miles to a watering place, where we encamped for the night. During our journey, being scantily supplied with water, we suf-[p. 5]fered very much. I offered a dollar for a pint, but was unable to obtain it. On Tuesday morning we again started, and after traveling a few miles, I and two or three others had some difficulty with our animals in consequence of the packs becoming loose, and we were left some distance behind the company, when we met a large party of Pimo Indians, who kindly offered to conduct us to water, which offer we gladly accepted. After following them a long distance up a mountain, we at last came to a spring, where the Indians left us. We remained there until near night, cooking and eating our supper. The sun was about two hours high when we left and proceeded on our journey. Following the trail in our winding way we passed through a deep valley, and after traveling a short distance we came upon several trails leading in several directions. We followed the one which we thought the company in advance of us had taken, for two hours after dark, when we encamped for the night. I was apprehensive at this time that we might be on the wrong trail, as I had noticed what appeared to me a much larger one breaking off to the left.

The next morning, at dawn of day, I arose, and awakening one of my companions, we held a short consultation, when I concluded to take a short cut across the prairie and examine the trail between us and the mountain, which I had noticed

the previous evening. So, shouldering my gun, I left my comrades with my animals and baggage, and directed my steps in a south-southeast direction. After
walking about five miles I came upon the trail that I was in quest of, but found it
was the wrong one, as the foot-marks on it were in an easterly direction. I then
endeavored to retrace my steps, but after traveling two or three hours, I found I
had lost my way. I instantly became so excited that I hardly knew what I was
about. I began calling my companions' names at the top of my voice, hoping they
would hear me, but in vain. I continued running in every direction, and calling till
my throat was so sore that I could call no more; and then I discharged the load in
my gun. I continued running all day, under the scorching rays of an almost vertical
sun. About sunset I struck a trail, which I followed nearly all night, when I came
to a deep hole in the bed of a river, which I examined for water. I descended to the
bottom, though it was eight or nine feet deep. After digging in the quicksand
with my hands for a while, I found water, [p. 6] which I dipped up with my powder pouch, holding a half pint. I drank it full fourteen times, and thought it the
sweetest water I had ever tasted. After quenching my thirst I lay down to rest, but
my mind was laboring under such intense excitement that I was unable to sleep.

No. II

In about two hours day began to dawn, when I arose, filled my gun barrel with
water and continued following the trail. About noon I came to a Pimo Indian village. I asked for bread and was presented with a water-melon. I asked for corn,
and he gave me two or three small ears, for which I gave a pair of stockings which
I happened to have in my pockets. I related to the Indians, as well as I was able by
signs, my troubles, and offered my coat, pants, shirt and boots, to any one that
would go with me and look after my animals and baggage. But no one would go. I
then agreed to give a mule in case we should find them. To this an Indian agreed,
and taking his bows and arrows, a dozen small ears of corn and a gourd of water,
he was equipped for the journey.

We started back on the same trail we came in on. Before proceeding far he told
me I had better leave my gun, as it would be useless to me. He hid it in some
bushes. We then marched forward till dark, when we came upon the water holes
in the bed of the river. Here we ate the corn, and slept about two hours. Then we
arose and followed the trail until daylight, when we came to the place where I
supposed my animals might be near. We examined one trail after another till 2
o'clock, in vain. The Indian becoming tired and hungry, muttered and expressed
his unwillingness to search any further. I told him to lend me his gourd and I
would go up a mountain which he had pointed out to me, for water, and he might

go home, while I remained until night searching for my animals. He then wanted four dollars for his trouble. I offered him two dollars, but he would not accept that sum. I being wholly in the savage's power, was obliged to give him what he asked. I had still one dollar remaining, and had only about a thousand miles to travel before I could reach the land of gold. The scoundrel would not lend me his gourd, but he would give it to [p. 7] me for the dollar which I had left, or for my coat. I refused his generous offer, and went off, leaving him sitting on the ground in ill humor.

I then walked about three miles up the mountain for water, quenched my thirst, and taking off one of my boots, filled it to carry with me, and resumed the search. But in a short time my foot became wounded and sore, lamed by walking among the sharp rocks, showing prints of blood at every step. I bound it with my neck-kerchief, and searched in vain till night. Becoming discouraged I gave up the search, and hungry and faint, I once more started for the village. It was late in the night when I again came to the old water places, where I slept until daylight.

In the morning I started again, but before walking an hour was overtaken by my Indian guide, who came upon me like a mad dog, saying he had been searching all night until his moccasins were worn through, with nothing to eat. He wanted my other dollar. I refused to give it, and attempted to leave him—when springing upon me like a tiger, he laid hold of me and demanded the dollar. I begged of him not to take it, as it was all I had, and I wanted to buy bread with it. I told him I had nothing to eat, no clothes, no animals, was far from any white man, and had a long way to go. But my entreaties were all in vain. I again attempted to leave him, when he placed his bow and arrow in a position to shoot me, and I was obliged to give it up to him. He still appeared dissatisfied, and taking hold of me again took my neck-kerchief from my neck by force. After examining it, growling about the blood upon it and the holes worn through it, he tied it about his waist, and let me go.

The Indian then went towards the village, I keeping about twenty yards behind him. On coming to the bushes where my gun was hid, I found that it had been taken away. I said nothing until we came to the village; but when I asked him for it he only laughed at me. Several elderly Indians stood by looking at me, as if I had been a wild beast or a complete menagerie. To them I made complaint respecting the loss of my gun. After talking with each other for a long time, they finally brought it from a wigwam, broken. I offered to sell it to them for bread or penoles. No one seemed to care for it. I then offered it for my hat full of corn, but could not get it. [p. 8] They would give me corn, penole or musquite bread, for my coat, pants or boots. But these I could not part with, owing to the severe cold and the snow. I examined my pockets for something to sell them for bread, but found they had been picked of everything—comb, glass, gloves, and several trinkets that I had. I then resorted to my pants, and taking out my purse to sell them, on examining it to show them the quality, I fortunately found ten gold dollars, which being so small I had hitherto overlooked. At the sight of these my heart leaped for joy, and I again felt rich. One of these I offered for my hat full of corn; but no, they would give it to me for my coat, and insisted upon it. Finding I still refused, they turned up their noses, and went off each one to his wigwam, leaving me standing like a sign-post, almost dead with hunger.

It was already four days since I had eaten anything except the few small ears of corn and the water melon before mentioned. I stood motionless for a while considering what to do. I saw no alternative but to direct my steps toward San Diego. But a distance of five hundred miles lay before me before I could expect to see the face of a white man or anything that pertained to civilization; and how was I to proceed with nothing to eat? Starvation stared me in the face. I stepped forward to a wigwam where I saw an Indian drying corn and offered a dollar for my hat full, but he refused. I then fell upon my knees to him, holding the hat in one hand and the dollar in the other, begging of him to give me corn, but he still refused. In this posture I remained for fifteen or twenty minutes, continuing my supplications and imploring his mercy. He at last filled my hat with the corn, and took the money, telling me to go on and in a little while I should come to another town where I could get much corn. I was not aware of another village being near or I should not have humbled myself as I did. Taking off my coat and turning the corn into one of the sleeves, I proceeded on my way, and after traveling about six miles, I came to South Pass about ten o'clock in the evening. I told the Indians of my loss, and described to them the place. I then prepared my supper of parched corn, and lay down on the ground to sleep, but could not, in consequence of the powwow that was kept up in a wigwam near me. I also suffered severely from the cold nights, having on nothing [p. 9] but a cotton shirt and a thin pair of pants. My coat sleeves being occupied as corn sacks, I could only enjoy the skirts.

In the morning I arose, eat a handful of mashed corn, and endeavored to sell my gun. I exchanged it for a small blanket, thin enough to shake beans through, and gave my knife for a gourd to carry water in. I was kindly invited by an Indian, who was enjoying a dish of boiled squash, to breakfast with him. Sitting down near him, I laid down my coat and commenced eating, when the Indian took my coat and put it under him. Seeing his intention, I pushed the dish from me, and endeavored to get the coat. But he shoved back the dish and insisted upon having the coat. I told him no; I could not give my coat for a breakfast. Laying hold of it I pulled with all my might, expecting every moment to rend it in pieces, determined to have some of it. After struggling awhile I succeeded in getting it, and hurried away.

Feeling reluctant to leave without giving another search for my animals, I inquired of an Indian the trail they had followed, and went on it eight miles, when I came to another Indian village. I there related my story and while I was resting a little they proceeded in the search. I had not walked over two miles when an Indian came up in great haste, telling me I was on the wrong trail. Pointing towards a mountain some thirty miles off to the right, he said that it was towards that mountain that the white men had lately passed, and offered if I would give him my coat to take me to the right trail. Being by this time pretty well acquainted with the Indian character I knew he lied, only desiring to get me on the wrong trail that he might get the prize. I told him I wanted neither his assistance nor his company. He then wanted a dollar, still insisting that I should go with him. Leaving him and walking on I soon met about twenty Indians, some mounted and others on foot running and whooping apparently in great joy. I then had but little hope of recovering my property, as I mistrusted some of them were the same to whom I had explained my circumstances the evening previous at Santa Rosa. However, I continued following the trail until night came on, when I lay down to sleep.

During the night another Indian came up in great haste, telling me to go with him for water. I replied that I was tired and would not go. He then lay down near me.

In the morning I started and soon arrived at the watering [p. 10] place, the Indian keeping with me. Here I rested, and having eaten a handful of corn, proceeded again. I had not gone far when the Indian abruptly asked me for a dollar. I told him I had none; and when he asked me where I was going, I told him I was hunting for my horse and mule. He said he would give me a horse for ten dollars. But after trying this and several other plans in vain, to find out whether I had any money about me, he said he would go no further with me unless I would give him my coat or shirt, and pointing in every direction, made signs of many trails and left me; and I was very glad of it. By this time, my water-gourd becoming empty, I began to be very thirsty. I still proceeded over the prairie under a scorching sun. When near night my eyes rested upon the spot where I had left my animals and baggage. Nothing was left but a string which I had used for tying my blankets, and the stake to which my animals had been tied. The grass, as far as their halters would reach, was plucked up, and the ground was pawed by the poor hungry creatures. The Indians' tracks were fresh and plainly to be seen, indicating that they had not long been gone.

I then directed my steps towards the mountain where a few days before I had obtained water. My fevered palate was already swelling in my throat with burning thirst. It was late in the evening when I came to the mountain. After searching some time in vain for the path to the water, I endeavored to climb the mountain where I was; but while climbing up a steep cliff I fell and cut my leg. Still wandering about in the dark, endeavoring to find the path, I struck a trail leading towards another mountain. This I followed for the distance of several miles without success, nearly dead for water. Then I commenced retracing my steps, and walked all night; but in the morning I found myself far from the watering place. Towards this I again turned, but it was near noon when I came to the foot of the mountain. Again I attempted to climb it, where I supposed the water might be found; but becoming weak and faint I fell, wholly unable to go further. Thus I lay nearly an hour, expecting every breath would be my last. A light refreshing breeze springing up, I began to revive, and with great exertion I succeeded in divesting myself of my boots and the little clothes I had on, in order that I might feel the air. After sufficiently recovering my strength to stand, I again [p. 11] put on my clothes and crawled to the spot where I supposed the water to be. It was not the place I expected to find, but a ravine in the mountain about nine feet wide and fifty feet deep. At the head of this ravine I could see the water trickling down the rocks into a basin at the bottom. Rejoicing at this discovery, I crept down the sides of the mountain, and following up the ravine I drank my fill, and feasted on corn until near night, when with reluctance I left this beautiful fountain to search for the trail leading to the village. I walked two or three hours after dark, not finding it. So I lay down to sleep.

In the morning I directed my steps across the plain, toward a mountain, near which I knew a trail led to the village, which, when I found it, I again followed until I came to the water hole in the river bed. There I found some friendly Pimos, one of whom let me ride on his horse, behind him, for four or five miles, to rest myself; and so I reached another village which I had not before visited. Next morning I arrived at the other village, where I remained during the forenoon, in consequence of a heavy shower of rain. I obtained shelter in a wigwam. When the rain was over I proceeded five miles further, to the next village, which was the one I had first come to. It was four o'clock in the afternoon of Thursday, the 31st of October, when I left there, following the trail direct north, seventy-five miles.

No. III

(Here there is an evident omission in the diary.)
One Indian was smoking tobacco through a piece of reed, blowing the smoke

with all possible force through his nostrils upon the bare back of the sick Indian, at the same time pressing it with a cloth as if to smother the smoke upon his back to prevent its escape. He continued this process from one end of the body to the other for about fifteen minutes, when another Indian took his place, going through the same process. During this time all except the one engaged in smoking, were singing at the top of their voices a song to the tune I had heard at Santa Rosa. The performance was kept up all night. I could not sleep for the noise until daylight, when they all dispersed except two or three, who lay down to sleep. I then obtained a [p. 12] few hours repose. I was very sleepy, having traveled day and night for the last seventy-five miles. When I awoke I started again, following Cook's wagon route five miles, when I came to another village. Here it commenced raining, and I got shelter in a wigwam, where I remained until next morning. I bought my hat full of mesquite bread, for which I gave my last gold dollar. Tying it in my coat, I proceeded through deep mud six miles to another village. Here I was conducted by an Indian to the "captain," and told that he was a kind-hearted man, and would assist me to anything I needed. At this news I was much pleased, but on coming to the chief's wigwam, I found a fool of a fellow sitting on the ground with some three or four others playing cards, who did not seem inclined even to speak to me. I asked for something to eat, and they gave me mesquite bread, of which I already had plenty. But although it was little better than saw-dust, my craving appetite compelled me to eat it. I waited for him to get through his game of cards, thinking that he might be induced to give me some provisions for my journey. In the meantime they handed me a package of papers or recommendations to read, that had been given to him by leaders or captains of companies who had passed. He felt very proud of them, although he could not read a word. One or two of them recommended him to Americans that should happen to pass through there, as a good interpreter and an accommodating fellow; while the rest made game of him, saying he was accommodating as long as he was well paid. After waiting about two hours, and becoming completely disgusted, I left and proceeded on my way towards San Diego, which was still 400 miles distant.

The weather now began to grow much colder, with occasionally a heavy fall of rain. The nights were extremely cold, with very hard frost. A lonely traveler, I would walk all day until dark, and then being very tired, would lie down and fall asleep. Perhaps in an hour I would wake up, shivering with cold. I would then rise, throw my coat over my shoulder, travel until I became warm and tired, and again lie down to sleep till I could endure the cold no longer. Again I would rise, and walk on; and in this way continue traveling day and night, suffering with cold and hunger.

My clothes consisted of a thin cotton shirt, and pair of [p. 13] pants which had become so rotten and torn that I had to tie strings about my body and legs in several places to keep them together. In my coat I still used to carry my parched corn and musquite bread. Frequently at night when I lay down to sleep the prairie wolves would come prowling about me, and I would be obliged to get up and throw stones at them to drive them away.

It was about 12 o'clock, when becoming very thirsty I left the road to go to the river Gila for water, when passing through some bushes I suddenly came upon a drove of sheep. I was overjoyed at the sight, as I had been informed by some Indians at Moracopas that white men with a drove of sheep had lately passed that way. Concluding that I must be near their camp, I called out at the top of my voice, "Americans! Americans!" and continued calling, but received no answer. I went further towards the river, thinking the camp could not be far off, and continued calling as before, but in vain. I began to think the Indians had killed the owners of the sheep. I then lay down till morning. At daylight I arose, and after searching an hour in vain for the camp, drove the sheep to the road and continued on my way, driving the flock of sixty sheep before me. Having traveled about two hours I stopped, and after sawing on the throat of a sheep with a sort of knife about three inches long, that I had picked up, succeeded in killing it. I could not stop for a fire, and had no means of procuring one; but falling on my knees, I laid hold of the raw flesh about the neck with my teeth, like a dog, and satisfied my hunger to some extent before it had fairly done kicking. After tearing and pulling, not having a knife that I could cut with, I at last opened the carcass and tore out the entrails. I ate up the kidneys, and shouldering the carcass, took the heart and liver in my hand to eat as I walked along.

Continuing on my journey, I drove the rest before me. I was just eating the last of the heart when I came up to the camp of white men, and found that they were the owners of the sheep. They had three thousand, which they were driving to California, and were very thankful to me for bringing up the rest of the drove. They gave me good bread and meat, which I ate till I nearly killed myself, as I had been living fifteen days on very small quantities of parched corn. Then I gathered sheepskins and sewed them together, and made me a [p. 14] comfortable covering. Mr. Devoe, the leader and owner of the sheep, gave me a good mule to ride as long as I chose to remain with him, and twenty dollars in gold, with plenty to eat. We lay still four days, to recruit the animals, this being the first grass they had found since leaving the Pimo Indian village.

We arrived at the Colorado, Monday, November 18th. On Tuesday, the 19th, with three or four others, I went to a deserted Indian rancho, and gathered a quantity of beans. It was eight miles from our camp. Five of Mr. Devoe's party getting tired of so much delay and slow traveling, and anxious to get through to the journey's end, were now preparing to leave the company and go ahead. I purchased an old horse from a Mexican; one man gave me a pair of pants, another a shirt and another a bag to carry my provisions in. Mr. Devoe gave me a camp kettle, about thirty pounds of corn meal, and a sheep—two-thirds of which I gave to some of my party.

On the 22nd we left the ferry, traveled sixteen miles, and encamped at another place on the Colorado. Next day we drove sixteen miles more, to some wells. As a forty-five mile desert now lay before us, we started at 11 o'clock, but my horse broke his lariat and got away. The rest left me. I searched for my horse till daylight in rain [vain]. So leaving behind me my saddle, sheepskins, and other things, I started on the Sandy Desert with a pack of eight pounds weight on my back. This pack soon became an enormous weight. The sand being knee-deep, I had to rest every fifteen minutes. So I continued on until noon, when, becoming so fatigued that I could not lift my pack to my shoulder, I was obliged to throw away half of my corn meal, half my beans, half of my meat, all my parched corn, and musquite bread and a shirt. In the afternoon the wind blew almost a hurricane, driving the sand in my eyes, and almost blinding me. At times I was obliged to lie down and cover myself with my blanket to keep from suffocating. The whole road on the desert seemed almost covered with the carcasses of dead animals, the stench from which was terrible. Late in the evening I came to a camp of soldiers, bound for the Colorado. They gave me supper, and expressed astonishment at my pack. After resting two or three hours, I again started, and by morning arrived at another camp of soldiers, also bound for the Colorado. In a short time the rest of the [p. 15] company came in that had left me on the other side of the desert. I must have passed them in the night. The Captain gave each of us two days' rations of hard bread and pork, and also to me, a letter to his family in San Diego.

Next morning I shouldered my pack, and marched, with the rest of the company, twenty miles to water. The next day we traveled thirty miles to water, and the day following twenty miles. Then we left the main road and took a trail over the mountain, twenty-two miles to Williams' ranch. In this valley we remained one day and two nights. The mountain tops were covered with snow, and it was so cold that we had to get up and walk about till morning in order to keep from freezing. Thence we followed a trail to a Mexican ranch, twenty miles; to Don McGillo's ranch, twelve miles; to the Mission, twelve miles; and to San Diego, six miles. I reached San Diego on Thursday, December 5th, seven months from the time I left home.

Section L
Railroad Forerunners,
1850–1865

Railroad Forerunners, 1850–1865

PERSPECTIVE

The Idea   Within 40 years after the first running of a steam passenger train in the United States, a railroad spanned the continent. On August 28, 1830, the little homemade *Tom Thumb* locomotive pushed a small car with 24 passengers at 10 miles per hour over the first 13 miles of iron-shod wooden rails of the Baltimore and Ohio Railroad (Dunbar 1915). Visionaries quickly saw the full possibilities, and the idea of a Pacific railroad was in the air. Hezekiah Niles was one of the first in print. In *Niles' Register* of June 18, 1831 (40:285) he wrote, "associations are forming for settlements in the *Oregon Territory*, on the shores of the Pacific!…a rail road across the Rocky Mountains may soon enter into the speculations of some of the enterprising people of the 'far west.' A journey of a couple of thousand miles in our country, is reducing down into a mere excursion."

Judge S. W. Dexter was more specific in the February 6, 1832 issue of his Ann Arbor *Emigrant*. He thought that the railroad could "cross the Missouri about the mouth of the Platte, and thence to the Rocky Mountains near the source of the last named river, thence on by the most convenient route to the Oregon [Columbia], by the valley of the south branch [Snake] of that stream" (Dunbar 1915; Galloway 1950). On August 10, 1835, the Rev. Samuel Parker stood in South Pass and declared, "There would be no difficulty in the way of constructing a rail road from the Atlantic to the Pacific ocean" (3:E3 Itinerary). John Plumbe, Jr., who had surveyed for a railroad in 1831, promoted the Pacific railroad in Iowa in 1836, held meetings and memorialized Congress about it in 1838, and advocated it in his 1839 book. Many others in the 1830s commented on the project in the newspapers. Only Congress, which did nothing, seemed fazed by the fact that the U.S. did not then own any of the Pacific coast.

Interest in the Oregon takeover in the mid-1840s intensified the promotion of a Pacific railroad. New York merchant Asa Whitney was the first to mount a concerted campaign and to make specific explorations. He sent his first memorial to Congress in 1845, asking it to finance construction with a 60-mile-wide strip of land from Lake Michigan to the Pacific Ocean. Such a grant would have been twice the size of all New England. That summer he made a reconnaissance from

Milwaukee to Prairie du Chien to present Sioux City to the mouth of White River on the Missouri in what is now South Dakota. In the brief review of this trip in his memorial of 1846, all his localities, distances, and latitudes verify this end point. After boating down to St. Louis, he concluded that the Missouri could only be bridged at present Sioux City or above. His preferred route thence to the west went through South Pass and on by an unspecified line to the mouth of the Columbia. He claimed that he got the idea for the Pacific railroad while riding a train in England in 1830. He had made a fortune from trading in China 1842-44. Several congressional committees acted favorably on his memorials through 1850, but opposition grew, Congress did not act, and Whitney gave up in 1851 (Wheat 3:176-89; Galloway 1950).

In 1846 engineer Robert Mills proposed to Congress the building of a rock-paved road on which steam carriages could operate more cheaply than on a railroad. He claimed that he had proposed the Pacific railroad back in 1819, but his own quotes show that he advocated a highway, not a railway. Another frustrated claimant for first honors was Dr. Hartwell Carver of New York. In his 1847 proposal he included affidavits that he had written newspaper articles about the Pacific railroad in 1837-38; he remembered conceiving the idea while crossing the Alps in 1832.

The acquisition of California and its gold rush made the Pacific railroad imperative, and dozens of new proposals soon surfaced. The most elaborate of these was put forth by John Loughborough, St. Louis attorney and surveyor-general. His 80-page document, with a map by Julius Hutawa, was prepared for a national convention on the Pacific railroad at St. Louis, October 15, 1849. Loughborough's favored "new" route went from Independence via the south side of the Platte to South Pass, to the Sublette and Hudspeth cutoffs, and to the Humboldt and Truckee rivers. This was almost exactly what the Forty-niners were doing at the moment (Perspective K). He passed quickly over the difficulties for a railroad over the cutoffs and the Sierra. But he labored long and hard to point out deficiencies in the competing route proposals of: 1) Navy Lt. Matthew F. Maury, from Memphis to Ft. Smith, to Santa Fe via the Canadian, to El Paso, to the Gila, to Los Angeles and Monterey; 2) Sen. Thomas H. Benton, from Independence to Pueblo on the Arkansas, via the Kansas and Smoky Hill rivers, to Cochetopa Pass, to the south of Great Salt Lake, to the Humboldt and Truckee rivers; and 3) Asa Whitney, whose newly modified route went from Council Bluffs, via the north side of the Platte, to South Pass, to Fts. Bridger, Hall, Boise, and Walla Walla, and on to Puget Sound.

In 1850, broker Peter P. F. Degrand and engineer William L. Dearborn matured another plan whose route was almost identical to Loughborough's. Dearborn's report is reprinted in L1.

The Pacific Railroad of Missouri, later the Missouri Pacific, was the first to operate west of the Mississippi. The company was chartered by the state of Missouri in March, 1849. Its Chief Engineer, James P. Kirkwood, issued his account of preliminary surveys with the *First Annual Report* of 1851. Kirkwood counted on "various resources within the State, to sustain, when developed, your railroad, independent of any business which may hereafter accrue to it in connection with a railroad across the continent." Ground was broken on July 4, 1851, and the first train triumphantly steamed five miles out of St. Louis on December 23, 1852. But after only 125 miles were completed, the panic of 1857, bankruptcy, and the Civil War delayed the continuation, which reached Kansas City in 1865; neither the Mississippi nor the Missouri were even then yet bridged. (Riegel 1926.)

Preliminary Government Surveys for the Pacific Railroad On March 3, 1853, Congress authorized Secretary of War Jefferson Davis "to make such explorations and surveys as he may deem advisable, to ascertain the most practicable and economical route for a railroad from the Mississippi River to the Pacific Ocean" (Albright 1921). This was a last-ditch attempt to break a hopeless intersectional deadlock by picking a route on a supposedly scientific basis. Southerners wanted a southern starting point, Northerners a northern one, and middle Atlantic coastal states wanted no Pacific railroad at all. California Senator William Gwin, L3, was a prime mover in getting the matter brought to this vote. But Congress ordered that the surveys be completed within only 11 months, which of course made them scientifically inconclusive.

Davis sent topographical engineers and others out to explore four routes in 1853-54. Isaac I. Stevens, the new governor of Washington Territory, examined the northern route from St. Paul to Olympia via passes in Montana. Capt. John W. Gunnison explored the central route from Kansas City to the Great Salt Lake area via Cochetopa Pass in Colorado; when Gunnison was killed by Indians in Utah, Lt. Edward G. Beckwith carried the survey on from Salt Lake City to Ft. Reading in northern California. Lt. Amiel W. Whipple covered the south-central route from Ft. Smith to Los Angeles via Albuquerque, New Mexico. Lt. John G. Parke and Capt. John Pope surveyed the southern route eastward from San Diego to the lower Gila to Apache Pass in Arizona to the Rio Grande to the Red River at Preston, Texas. In addition, Lt. Robert S. Williamson mapped Sierra and Coast Range passes in California. These explorations are summarized in L3, except that Stevens's is reviewed in 2:D10. See also Goetzmann 1959 and 1966.

Notably missing was a survey of the Oregon-California Trail through the South Pass in Wyoming, or the promising alternative proposed in 1850 by Capt. Howard Stansbury using Lodgepole Creek and Bridger Pass (5:J3). Nor was the Donner-Truckee Pass in the Sierra considered. Beckwith, trying to break new ground, wandered off on some very devious paths in Nevada and California. The classic routes of the mountain man and emigrant were supposedly too well known to warrant further investigation. The result was that they were left out of Davis's calculations. Yet they comprised the main elements finally chosen for the first transcontinental railway.

Davis, in the first of the massive 13 quarto volumes of the Pacific railroad reports that so illuminated the West's lands and natural history, concluded that the southern route was the best and cheapest. This conclusion was backed by the analysis of Capt. Andrew A. Humphreys, and Col. John J. Abert had in 1849 advocated a Gila route. But since Davis was a Southerner, the problem was not at all solved. Senator Gwin found himself in 1858 still hoping that "sectionalism and jealousy will cease their wranglings and heart-burnings, and be stilled." He declared, "Commerce is power and empire…to California, and to the other great States arising on the Pacific, it [the railroad] is a question of life or death." But talk and pleading availed nothing until the Civil War removed the South from the railroad equation.

Robert Taft wrote in 1953 about the Pacific railroad reports: "These volumes, published by the Federal Government between 1855 and 1861, constitute probably the most important single contemporary source of knowledge on Western geography and history, and their value is greatly enhanced by the inclusion of many beautiful plates in color of scenery, native inhabitants, fauna and flora of the Western country. Ironically enough, the publication of this monumental work cost the government over $1,000,000; the surveys themselves $455,000."

Young California engineer Theodore D. Judah's 1857 pamphlet, *A Practical Plan for Building the Pacific Railroad*, pointed out the deficiencies in the government surveys: "When a Boston capitalist is invited to invest in a railroad project, it is not considered sufficient to tell him that somebody has rode over the ground on horseback and pronounced it practicable. He does not care to be informed that there are 999 different varieties and species of plants and herbs, or that grass is abundant at this point, or buffalo scarce at that. His inquiries are somewhat more to the point. He wishes to know the length of your road. He says, let me see your map and profile, that I may judge of its alignment and grades. How many cubic yards of the various kinds of excavation and embankment have you and upon what sections? Have you any tunnels, and what are their circumstances? How much masonry and where are your stones? How many bridges, river crossings, culverts, and what kind of foundations? How about timber and fuel? Where is the estimate of the cost of your road, and let me see its details?" The government men actually tried to answer these questions, but the vast ground and short time rendered the results inadequate.

Two reprints, L9 and L11, deal with proposed railroads through Sonora to ports on the Gulf of California. Both authors, Capt. Thomas J. Cram in 1858, and Maj. David Fergusson in 1863, espoused purchasing Sonora and adding it to the United States. Cram's motives for advocating such a spur from a California-bound southern Pacific railroad are obscure. Both the southern route and the acquisition of Sonora were championed by Southerners for extending slavery into the territories. But Cram was a Northerner and later a Union general who, during the Civil War, roundly condemned Jefferson Davis's earlier selection of the southern route. Fergusson, following orders of Union Gen. James H. Carleton, examined the Sonoran route for supplying the California Column. Fergusson's first experience as an explorer produced a highly informative report.

Preliminary Private Surveys for the Pacific Railroad Private enterprise also came up with some railroad explorations. We have seen that Asa Whitney on his own scouted out the Missouri River crossings into South Dakota in 1845. Trader Francois X. Aubry, L2, went from California in 1853 to Albuquerque, where he gave some good advice to Lt. Whipple, who was headed west to map the same route.

The most bizarre twists in the political knots of the railroad controversy were John C. Fremont's disastrous private explorations of a preconceived fantasy, the "Central Route to the Pacific." Fremont and his father-in-law, Senator Thomas H. Benton of Missouri, deemed it politically expedient that St. Louis and San Francisco be connected by a smooth, straight-line road. So Fremont went out in the winters of 1848-49 and 1853-54 to prove that an easy route was there, and that snow would be no problem. Nature dictated otherwise. On the first try, during the worst winter in memory, Fremont foolishly proceeded against the advice of the mountain men and of his guide, Old Bill Williams. Fremont shunned Colorado's Cochetopa Pass as being too far north of his straight line. Instead he insisted on looking for a pass up the Rio Grande Canyon into the icy, deadly jaws of the San Juan Mountains. Old Bill finally diverted him toward another pass, but it was too late. The expedition bogged down in the bitter cold and deep snow of the towering mountains. The mules all died. Fremont's mismanagement of the retreat, by stubbornly refusing to give up and then by trying to save the baggage, caused the deaths of ten men by starvation and freezing. Fremont went on from Taos to California by the southern route, accomplishing nothing of significance.

In his 1853-54 attempt, Fremont embraced the Cochetopa Pass as the center-piece of his central route. But that winter he followed a few months behind Capt. Gunnison's official survey, and Gunnison found the pass impracticable for a rail-road. Fremont forged ahead anyway over the rugged country on his vaunted straight line. This time his party nearly perished from starvation and cold in the Wasatch Mountains. One man died before they found succor in the Mormon settlements. Fremont then went straight west, only to butt into the impenetrable Sierra Nevada and to be forced into a huge detour south. Again he accomplished nothing useful, but that did not dim his boasts of total success. Fremont's itineraries, with coverage of the controversies about his routes, are given in L6. Benton's outrageous conclu-sions are in L5: "the Rocky mountains may be passed without crossing a hill…at all seasons of the year…[over] this line for a road, the longest and straightest in the world." Benton somehow also wrested a statement from respected mountaineer Antoine Leroux blaming Old Bill Williams for Fremont's 1848-49 disaster (L4). Within a year, Leroux privately repudiated this charge (L6 Highlights).

Frederick W. Lander, from his experience as an engineer on Isaac Stevens's 1853 railroad survey, felt that the northern route was unsuitable. So he returned eastward via the Columbia River to evaluate the South Pass route in 1854, almost alone and at his own expense. He managed to get his report published in the offi-cial Pacific railroad survey volumes, thus at least nominally filling one gap in Jef-ferson Davis's plans. Lander wrote another 1854 tract, reprinted in L7, favoring quick construction of a temporary trunk railroad from South Pass through Salt Lake City to California, with a branch to Puget Sound via the Columbia. In 1858 he renewed his plea for a preliminary railroad, reprinted in L8, but changed the location to his new Lander Cutoff going northwest from South Pass. Lander effectively directed the greatest of all federal wagon-road projects, going from Ft. Kearny through South Pass to Honey Lake, California, in 1857-60. All his itiner-aries are summarized in L8. But his suggestions on location and mode of con-struction of the Pacific railroad were ignored.

Minnesotan Bradley B. Meeker's 1860 pamphlet, L10, advocated building three Pacific railroads simultaneously, in order to secure the northern line from St. Paul. The tract was a prime example of sectional boosterism.

Preliminary Congressional Route Recommendation   In 1860 Representa-tive Samuel R. Curtis and the majority of his Select Committee on the Pacific Railroad came up with a route very close to the final one of the Central and Union Pacific. The Committee ignored virtually all of the official and private surveys made expressly for the railroad. Their report admitted the "question of route to be the most difficult and exciting obstacle in the determination of congressional action…every section of the republic desires and earnestly insists on that line which will best subserve its local convenience." They proposed a middle road, with many branches at each end. They "regretted that no *continuous* railroad survey on the central route has been made by government." They argued that only this middle route could have reasonable branches to Oregon and southern California. Only the middle route could best serve the great California emporium and population center at San Francisco, as well as the new Pike's Peak and Washoe mines, and the 40,000 Mormons.

Curtis favored the route "up the Platte, and following the South Fork and Lodge-pole creek as proposed by Captain Stansbury [5:J3] and Lieutenant Bryan [5:J11]." (Of course, Stansbury and Bryan both got their ideas from old Jim Bridger.) Curtis's report highlighted Bryan's conclusion that "in point of diminished distance, easy grades, freedom from serious obstacles, and convenience and abundant supply of materials for construction, the line [of Lodgepole Creek is]…decidedly preferable [to that through South Pass]." Curtis then advocated a route through Salt Lake City and down the Humboldt River to the Sierra. There, "With silver on one side and gold on the other, the Sierra Nevada mountain is now, summer and winter, traversed by thousands; and the necessity of a railroad is, therefore, greatest where the difficulties are most formidable." Curtis was drafting a Pacific Railroad Bill that would be strongly influenced by Theodore D. Judah.

Central Pacific Company Surveys   The defining document for the final Central and Union Pacific location was Theodore D. Judah's report of November 1, 1860. Judah's inspired engineering proved the practicality of the Donner Pass route and led to the foundation of the Central Pacific Railroad Company of California. He wrote, "I have devoted the past few months to an exploration of several routes and passes through Central California, resulting in the discovery of a practicable route from the city of Sacramento, upon the divide between Bear river and the North Fork of the American, *via* Illinoistown, Dutch Flat, and Summit Valley to the Truckee river; which gives nearly a direct line to Washoe, with maximum grades of one hundred feet per mile." Judah added, "it is proposed to organize a company, for the purpose of constructing a road through the State upon this route, in anticipation of the passage of this [the Pacific Railroad] bill; to procure the recognition of this as the line of the Pacific Railroad through California; to procure the appropriations appertaining to this end of the route." Furthermore, "Mr. Curtis, Chairman of the Pacific Railroad Committee in Congress…[has] been fully posted up with regard to this movement."

The Central Pacific Railroad Company was incorporated on June 28, 1861. The originating forces were Director and Chief Engineer Judah, and Director

Dr. Daniel W. Strong, a Dutch Flat druggist who first brought the Donner route to Judah's attention. But the "Big Four" Directors who provided the money and the business acumen to get the job done were Leland Stanford, Collis P. Huntington, Mark Hopkins, and Charles Crocker. Judah completed his surveys that summer and declared in his report of October 1, 1861, that his route "Overcomes the greatest difficulties of the Pacific railroad." His key technical discovery was, "The line of top or crest of ridge being far from uniform, of course the lowest points or gaps in ridge become commanding points, and it was found necessary to carry the line from gap to gap, passing around the intervening hills upon their side slopes." Judah underestimated the impact of snow, however. He concluded "that the greatest depths of undisturbed snow is 13 feet at the summit." In the 1867-68 winter, 44 feet of snow fell, and 37 miles of snowsheds and galleries had to be built (Galloway 1950). After crossing the Sierra, Judah favored the line up the Humboldt. He went to Washington and was appointed secretary of both the Senate and House committees that were drafting the Pacific railroad bill.

In the absence of Southern opposition, President Lincoln signed the Pacific Railroad Act into law on July 1, 1862. It established the Union Pacific Railroad Company and called for land grants, rights of way, bonds, a telegraph line, a construction time table, and "the most direct, central, and practicable route" from the Platte Valley westward "to meet and connect with the line of the Central Pacific Railroad Company of California." The Act also declared that "The track upon the entire line of railroad and branches shall be of uniform width, to be determined by the President of the United States, so that when completed, cars can be run from the Missouri river to the Pacific coast." Lincoln called a Cabinet meeting and opted for California's gauge of five feet, but the decision was not accepted. Congress finally settled on the standard gauge of four feet eight and one-half inches that was commonly used in England and the eastern states. The Central Pacific had to modify its locomotives and its first 31 miles of track (Williams 1988).

Judah's obsession became a reality with the Act of 1862. He had the technical brilliance to solve the knottiest route problem, the organizational capacity to found an effective company, and the political prowess to gain all government approvals. Construction started at Sacramento on January 8, 1863. But later that year Theodore Judah died of Panama fever contracted on a trip east (Galloway 1950).

Union Pacific Company Surveys   Young Grenville M. Dodge, future Chief Engineer of the Union Pacific, cut his teeth in 1853 on the first railroad survey across Iowa to Council Bluffs. He also then surveyed west of the Missouri to the Elkhorn River at the Platte. Dodge's work was under Peter A. Dey, Chief Engineer for the Mississippi and Missouri Railroad; that project, later led by Thomas

C. Durant, failed financially in the panic of 1857. Durant and Dodge continued to promote the Pacific railroad and to evaluate routes. In 1862 Union Pacific Vice President Durant sent Dey on a reconnaissance to Salt Lake City. This was while the Company was still being organized, and while Dodge was busy fighting in the Civil War as a Union general. Dey considered three routes emanating from the South Platte—Lodgepole Creek west from Julesburg, the Cache la Poudre from Greeley, and Clear Creek from Denver to the difficult Berthoud Pass (Dix 1864). In 1863 civil engineer B. B. Brayton, hampered by the onset of winter, examined the head of Lodgepole Creek and went on to Bridger Pass. Joseph A. Young, son of Brigham Young, surveyed the Provo Canyon access to Great Salt Lake Valley. These reconnaissances set up the more detailed 1864 surveys of James A. Evans, Francis M. Case, and Samuel B. Reed that are reprinted in L12, L13, and L14.

Evans, Case, and Reed got down to the nuts and bolts of selecting the best line for distance, grade, alignment, cut and fill, tunneling, bridging, timber, and coal. They did it in the 1864 summer of great Indian uprisings (see 4: G11 and 12).

James Evans's 1864 survey pointed the general way for the ultimate Union Pacific line across Wyoming from Lodgepole Creek to Bitter Creek and the Green River. Old Jim Bridger in 1850 had led Capt. Howard Stansbury over this route and across the finally chosen "Evans Pass" in the Laramie Mountains. Francis Case in 1864 found that all the possible passes directly west from Denver, including Berthoud Pass, were too difficult. Jim Bridger had guided Edward L. Berthoud through Berthoud Pass in 1861 (L13 Itinerary). Samuel Reed in 1864 established the superiority of the Echo and Weber canyons as the way for the Union Pacific to enter the Great Salt Lake Valley at Ogden. The next year Reed concluded that the line should continue west on the north rather than on the south side of Great Salt Lake. The final path of the Union Pacific was set. It would meet the Central Pacific on line with the route up the Humboldt.

Construction   Laying the first transcontinental track was the heroic engineering feat of the century. The work fell mainly on the backs of Chinese laborers carrying the Central Pacific east, and Irish laborers driving the Union Pacific west. Wood-choppers and tie-gatherers cleared the way where there were trees. Graders commonly used a wagon road ahead of the track. They moved earth with picks, shovels, wheelbarrows, and horse-drawn dump carts. Other men built bridges, trestles, tunnels, culverts, drainage ditches, embankments, and buildings. Still others laid the ballast, ties, and track. A UPRR promotional pamphlet described the 1867 track laying. Each two-horse supply truck "takes a load of rails, about forty…On each side of these trucks are rollers to facilitate running off the iron…One [man] in the rear throws a rail upon the rollers, three in advance seize it, and run out with it to the proper distance…and the chief of the squad calls out 'Down'…Every thirty seconds there came that brave 'Down,' 'Down,' on either side the track."

The engineers solved most of the staggering logistical problems of supply and labor in timely fashion. The financiers ultimately got the needed money, but not without delay and scandal. The Central Pacific completed its first 31 miles of road out of Sacramento on June 6, 1864 (Stanford 1865). But it took another full year to make the next 12 miles, and the company had to fight rivals who belatedly advocated the Placerville-Carson River route (Nevada Legislature 1865). The Union Pacific was plagued by money problems, route disputes west from Omaha, and no rail connection or Missouri River bridge from the east until 1867. It did not get government approval for its first 40 miles until January 24, 1866; but within a year it had built 305 miles across the plains (UPRR 1867; Riegel 1926).

The racing Central Pacific and Union Pacific crews, after grading wasteful overlapping lines across Utah, drove the golden spike that joined their rails at Promontory, north of Great Salt Lake, on May 10, 1869. According to Thomas and Hayden (1872), the Central Pacific had come 692 miles from Sacramento, and the Union Pacific 1,084 from Omaha, for a total of 1,776 miles. Adding the 138 miles from Sacramento to San Francisco via Stockton and San Jose, the whole distance was 1,914 miles. Summit elevations were 8,262 feet over the Laramie Mountains, 7,030 at the Continental Divide west of Rawlins, 7,835 at the Wasatch, and 7,042 at the Sierra Nevada.

In 1870 geologist Ferdinand V. Hayden published *Sun Pictures of Rocky Mountain Scenery,* a stunning portrayal of the route: "The construction of the Pacific Railroad led to the production of a large number of fine photographic views, taken by Mr. A. J. Russell, of New York, who spent more than two years along the line of the road in the employ of the Union Pacific Railroad Company. Thirty views have been chosen…which illustrate some peculiar feature in the geology or geography." Hayden also described some key engineering features, e.g.: "The tunnel at the head of Echo Canyon…is 770 feet in length, and is the longest [of four] on the Union Pacific Road. After passing through it the trains move slowly over the piers of trestle work, which creak and tremble beneath their load." An 8-mile temporary track had to be laid around the tunnel, which was not quite finished when the rails joined at Promontory.

Completion of the railroad caused a quantum jump in the speed of overland transport. Early regular connections from Omaha to Sacramento took about 5 days at 355 miles per day. In a special excursion in early June of 1876, a train went over the 1,914 miles from Omaha to San Francisco in 48 hours and 28 minutes, including stops (Poor 1879). That was 948 miles per day. A good ox-wagon might have taken 128 days at 15 miles per day. As Hezekiah Niles had put it correctly in 1831, "A journey of a couple of thousand miles in our country, is reducing down into a mere excursion."

Epilog   By the mid-1880s all sections of the country had the Pacific access about which they had squabbled so long. Sea-to-sea railroads crisscrossed the continent. The Atchison Topeka and Santa Fe, which had reached Santa Fe on a stub from the main line in 1880, linked to San Francisco with the eastward-building Southern Pacific, an arm of the Central Pacific, at Deming, New Mexico, in 1881. The Southern Pacific tied in with the Texas and Pacific at El Paso in 1882 and extended its own line to Galveston in 1883. The Santa Fe built to the Colorado River in 1883 and joined another branch of the Southern Pacific already at Needles, after exerting leverage from a connection to the Gulf of California at Guaymas on the Sonora Railway in 1882. The Denver and Rio Grande Western reached Ogden and the Central Pacific line in 1883. The Northern Pacific arrived at Portland also in 1883, followed there by the Union Pacific in 1884. The Canadian Pacific drove its last spike enroute to Vancouver on November 7, 1885, at Craigellachie, B.C. The Great Northern finished a through line in 1893 to Seattle, which the Northern Pacific had entered in 1887. (Riegel 1926.)

REFERENCES

Abert, John J., 1849, Correspondence [on Pacific railroad], in John A. Rockwell, Canal or Railroad between the Atlantic and Pacific Oceans: Wash., 30/2 H145, serial 546, p. 639-49.

Albright, George L., 1921, Official explorations for Pacific railroads 1853-55: Berkeley, 187 p.; quote from survey bill 38.

Carver, Hartwell, 1847 (1987 reprint), Memorial for a private charter: Fairfield WA, 65 p.

Curtis, Samuel R., 1860 (June 19 reprint with map), Reports of the majority and minority of the Select Committee on the Pacific Railroad: Wash., 36/1 H428 Report, serial 1069, quotes on question 5, regretted 7, Platte 9, diminished 11, Sierra 12.

Davis, Jefferson, et al., 1855-61, Reports of explorations and surveys to ascertain the most practicable and economical route for a railroad from the Mississippi River to the Pacific Ocean: Wash., 33/2 S78, serials 758-68, or 33/2 H91, serials 791-801, 11 vols.; plus 35/2 S46, serial 992, or 36/1 H56, serials 1054-55, 2 vols.; 13 vols. in all, totaling 7,477 p., 54 maps, 599 plates, 255 woodcuts; Davis report 1:1-33.

Dix, John A., 1864, Report of the organization and proceedings of the Union Pacific Railroad Co.: N.Y., early reconnaissances in Appendices 1, 1a, 1b, 2, and 3 (8, 8, 14, 20, and 4 p., respectively).

Dunbar, Seymour, 1915 (1937 reprint), A history of travel in America: N.Y., B&O p. 952, Dexter 1321.

Galloway, John D., 1950 (1989 reprint), The first transcontinental railroad: N.Y., quote on Dexter p. 28, Whitney 32-35; Judah biography 52-67; Central Pacific construction 136-54; snow 149-50.

Goetzmann, William H., 1959, Army exploration in the American West 1803-63: New Haven, p. 262-304.

Goetzmann, William H., 1966, Exploration and empire: N.Y., p. 265-302.

Gwin, William M., 1858, Speeches on the Pacific Railroad Bill: Wash., Globe Office, 22 p.; quotes on sectionalism 18, commerce 21-22.

Hayden, Ferdinand V., 1870, Sun pictures of Rocky Mountain scenery: N.Y., 150 p., 30 photos; quotes on Russell vii, Echo tunnel 11.

Judah, Theodore D., 1857, A practical plan for building the Pacific railroad: Wash., 31 p.; quote from Jane Eliot, 1985, The History of the Western Railroads, N.Y., p. 23.

Judah, Theodore D., 1860, Central Pacific Railroad of California: San Francisco, 18 p., profile; quotes on exploration 3, company 4, Curtis 5.

Judah, Theodore D., 1861, Memorial of the Central Pacific Railroad Company of California: Wash., 37/2 H12 Misc., serial 1141, 33 p.; quote on overcomes 2, ridge gaps 9, snow 23.

Kirkwood, James P., 1851, First annual report of the Board of Directors of the Pacific Railroad, and the report of the Chief Engineer: St. Louis, 70 p.; quote 63.

Lincoln, Abraham, 1862, An act to aid in the construction of a railroad and telegraph line from the Missouri river to the Pacific ocean: Wash., 37/2 S108 Misc., serial 1124, quotes on Central Pacific p. 6, gauge 9.

Loughborough, John, 1849, The Pacific telegraph and railway: St. Louis, 80 p., 2 maps.

Mills, Robert, 1846, Memorial, submitting a new plan of roadway: Wash., 29/1 H173, serial 485, 27 p., map.

Nevada Legislature, Committee on Rail Roads, 1865, Evidence concerning projected railways across the Sierra Nevada Mountains: Carson City, 256 p.

Plumbe, John, Jr., 1839 (1948 reprint), Sketches of Iowa and Wisconsin; Intro. by William J. Peterson: Iowa City, p. iv-vii, 78-79.

Poor, Henry V., 1879 (June), The Pacific Railroad: N.Y., The North American Review, n. 271, p. 671.

Riegel, Robert E., 1926 (1964 reprint), The story of the Western railroads: Lincoln; Missouri Pacific p. 1, 20-22, 106; sea-to-sea 86, 183-213.

Stanford, Leland, 1865, Office of the Central Pacific, Sacramento, October 10 letter: Wash., in Report of Lt. Col. James H. Simpson on the Union Pacific, Central Pacific, etc., in Report of the Secretary of Interior, 39/1, p. 871-1007; Stanford 988-92.

Taft, Robert, 1953, Artists and illustrators of the Old West 1850-1900: N.Y., quote p. 5.

Thomas, Cyrus, and Ferdinand V. Hayden, 1872, Lists of elevations and distances west of the Mississippi River: Wash., GPO, Unclassified Hayden report, p. 15-18.

UPRR, 1867, Union Pacific Rail Road across the continent: N.Y., 24 p.; progress 7, tracks down 11.

Whitney, Asa, 1845, Memorial, railroad to Pacific: Wash., 28/2 S69, serial 451, 4 p.; 28/2 H72, Jan. 28, serial 464, 4 p.

Whitney, Asa, 1846, Memorial, railroad to Pacific: Wash., 29/1 S161, serial 473, 10 p., map.

Williams, John H., 1988, A great and shining road: N.Y., p. 63.

TABLE L. TRAVEL TIMES OF RAILROAD FOREFUNNERS IN DAYS*

(and in miles; in brackets are the mean travel rates in miles per day)

L1. Aubry	1853	Tejon Pass CA to Albuquerque (990 mi.)	62	[16]
(Pack train with many sick and wounded men)				
L3. Gunnison	1853	Kansas City to Salt L. City (1568 mi.)	139	[11]
L3. Beckwith	1854	Salt L. City to Ft. Reading CA (950 mi.)	68	[14]
L3. Whipple	1853-54	Ft. Smith AR to Los Angeles (1649 mi.)	181	[9]
L3. Parke	1854	San Diego to Doña Ana NM (753 mi.)	48	[16]
L3. Pope	1854	Doña Ana to Preston TX (840 mi.)	63	[13]
L6. Fremont 4th	1848	Kansas City to Hardscrabble CO (725 mi.)	35	[21]
(Pack train)				
L6. Fremont 4th	1848	Hardscrabble to San Juan Mts. (170 mi.)	22	[8]
(On foot, with pack animals in snow)				
L6. Fremont 4th	1848-49	San Juan Mts. to Taos (150 mi.)	28	[5]
(On foot, starving and freezing)				
L6. Fremont 4th	1849	Taos to San Bernardino CA (1250 mi.)	67	[19]
(Pack train)				
L6. Fremont 5th	1853-54	Kansas City to San Francisco (2050 mi.)	174	[12]
(Pack train, partly on foot starving and freezing)				
L7. Lander	1854	Seattle to Council Bluffs via S. Pass (2295 mi.)	114	[20]
(Pack horses)				
L8. Lander	1857	Independence to South Pass (950 mi.)	31	[31]
L8. Lander	1858	Independence to South Pass (950 mi.)	44	[22]
L8. Lander	1858	South Pass to City of Rocks ID (346 mi.)	90	[4]
(Constructing Lander Cutoff)				
L8. Wagner	1859	Troy KS to South Pass (880 mi.)	28	[31]
L8. Wagner	1859	South Pass to City of Rocks (320 mi.)	23	[14]
(Surveying and improving Hudspeth Cutoff)				
L8. Lander	1860	Honey L. to Humboldt R. and back (270 mi.)	54	[5]
(Grading Nobles Trail, digging wells, etc.)				
L8. Moore	1860	S. Pass to Ft. Hall via Lander Cutoff (252 mi.)	19	[13]
L11. Fergusson	1862	Tucson to Puerto Libertad, Son. (225 mi.)	11	[20]
L11. Fergusson	1862	Puerto Lobos, Son., to Tucson (215 mi.)	11	[20]
L12. Evans	1864	Omaha to Laramie Mts. (575 mi.)	31	[19]
L12. Evans	1864	Laramie Mts. to Green R. (270 mi.)	70	[4]
(Surveying for Union Pacific Railroad)				
L13. Berthoud	1861	Denver to Provo (500 mi.)	28	[18]
(Pack horses)				
L14. Reed	1864	Salt L. City to Rock Springs WY (233 mi.)	–	–
UPRR	1869	Omaha to Sacramento (1776 mi.)	5	[355]
(Standard train schedule)				
UPRR	1876	Omaha to San Francisco (1914 mi.)	2.02	[948]
(Special excursion train)				

*Excluding long unusual stopovers, if known. Most times include 10-20 percent necessary layover days. Overland travel involves wagons or carts unless otherwise specified.

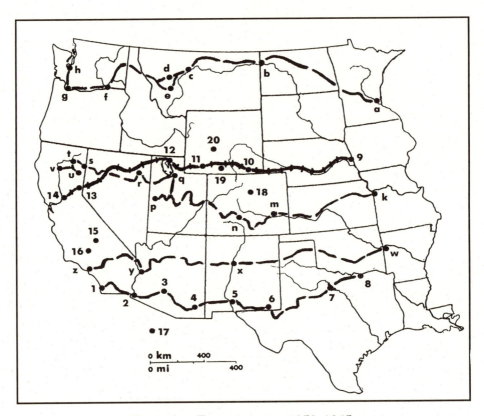

RAILROAD FORERUNNERS, 1850–1865

Stevens
a. St. Paul MN
b. Ft. Union ND
c. Ft. Benton MT
d. Cadotte Pass MT
e. Mullan Pass MT
f. Ft. Walla Walla WA
g. Ft. Vancouver WA
h. Olympia WA

Gunnison
k. Westport MO
    (Kansas City)
m. Bent's Fort CO
n. Cochetopa Pass CO
p. Sevier Lake UT

Beckwith
q. Salt Lake City UT
r. Secret Pass NV

s. Madeline Pass CA
t. Pit R.-Fall R. CA
u. Nobles Pass-Honey L. CA
v. Ft. Reading CA

Whipple
w. Ft. Smith AR
x. Albuquerque NM
y. Mouth Bill Williams R.
    (at Colorado R.)
z. Los Angeles CA

Parke-Pope
1. San Diego CA
2. Ft. Yuma CA
3. Pima Villages AZ
4. Apache Pass AZ
5. Doña Ana NM
6. Mouth Delaware R. NM

7. Ft. Belknap TX
8. Preston TX

Union-Central Pacific RR
9. Omaha NE
10. Evans Pass WY (near
    head Lodgepole Cr.)
11. Rock Springs WY
12. Promontory UT
13. Donner Pass CA
14. Sacramento CA

Miscellaneous
15. Walker Pass CA
16. Tejon Pass CA
17. Puerto Lobos, Son.
18. Berthoud Pass CO
19. Bridger Pass WY
20. South Pass WY

William L. Dearborn, 1850

Description Of A Rail Road Route
From St. Louis To San Francisco

Boston, Dutton and Wentworth, Printers, 1850, 16 p., map. [WCB 181a:1; Cowan
p. 161-62; UPRR p. 18; NUC ND 0098482.] Reset verbatim from a facsimile, by
courtesy of The Bancroft Library, University of California, Berkeley. Map is from
Wheat, Mapping the Transmississippi West, 3:192, map 602.

Significance   Dearborn's route study, although gleaned from the literature
and based on the regular emigrant trail, was the most thorough and accurate produced by the various private promoters of the Pacific railroad. Dearborn reported
his results to promoter Peter P. F. Degrand, whose petition for a government
chartered and aided company was not acted upon at the time.

An 1850 second edition of Dearborn's report was also issued. Wheat (3:190-
92) quoted extensively from Dearborn's work. The present reprint appears to be
the first modern, complete one.

Author   WILLIAM LEE DEARBORN, 1812-1875, civil engineer. A Massachusetts native, Dearborn worked for a railroad and on harbor fortifications after he
completed his engineering education. As the chief engineer of Maine he surveyed
railroad routes, as well as the Northeast Boundary in 1840. For the federal government he built breakwaters and beacons. Late in 1849 he made this literature
survey of the Pacific railroad route for P. P. F. Degrand. He married in 1860. From
1861 he directed water works, aqueducts, and bridge improvements in New York
City. In 1870 he built some of the tracks into Grand Central Station. (NCAB.)

Participant   PETER P. F. DEGRAND, ca. 1780-1855, merchant, broker, Pacific
railroad promoter. My own copy of Dearborn's report is inscribed by Degrand
and contains an unidentified newspaper clipping of his obituary, which is in full:
"DEGRAND, PETER P. F., a broker, died in Boston Dec. 23, 1855, aged about
75. A native of Marseilles, in order to escape conscription in the army he came to
Boston in 1803. He commenced business as a merchant in 1809. From 1819 to

1830 he published a useful commercial paper, the Weekly Report. In 1835 he devoted himself to the business of a stock-broker. Though an adherent of Jefferson and Madison, he aided the election of J. Q. Adams, and from that time was a Whig. As a man of business he was skilful, energetic, decisive, upright, and honorable. He acquired much property. The railroad and other enterprises he earnestly promoted. Once, in 1840, he in his folly was engaged in a duel, in which no life was lost, but he was wounded. He was never married."

Hall Jackson Kelley, Oregon booster, claimed that he projected the Pacific railroad in 1830, and that he and Degrand promoted the project in 1836. Kelley's 1830 tract mentions the need to "open communications from the Mississippi valley, and from the gulf of Mexico to the Pacific Ocean," but the word "railroad" was not used. In 1847 Degrand signed a testimonial to Kelley, urging Congress to grant him a tract of land in Oregon.

Route   Dearborn's proposed tracks simply follow the Oregon-California Trail that is in heavy use in 1849-50 by the gold rushers (Perspective K map and tables). The route passes by Independence, goes up the Big and Little Blue rivers, and continues along the south side of the Platte until crossing to the Sweetwater and South Pass. Thence he advocates using the Sublette and Hudspeth cutoffs, obviously having no idea of their real difficulties (see Table Kb). He minimizes the timber problems along the Humboldt, and the ascent of the Sierra on the Truckee. His concepts of agriculture and climate in the Far West are a bit rosy. His information comes chiefly from John Fremont 1845 and 1848, Edwin Bryant 1848, and John Loughborough. Dearborn's proposed railroad route is almost identical to Loughborough's. Dearborn notes that he did not see Loughborough's article in the St. Louis *Western Journal* until the end of his study, and he apparently did not know of Loughborough's more elaborate work issued in October, 1849.

Dearborn's estimate of 1,956 miles between the mouths of the Kansas and Sacramento rivers, based on Fremont and summarized on Dearborn's page 15, is very accurate. (Adding the segments on Table Kb from Independence to Sacramento City, plus 55 miles to the mouth of the Sacramento River, gives 1,935 miles by today's measure.) His route ends at Suisun ("Suisoon") Bay, which is connected to San Francisco Bay by the Carquinez ("Karquin") Strait and San Pablo ("St. Paul") Bay. Inexplicably, Dearborn's opening estimates (p. 3) add up to 2,170 miles.

Dearborn's last sentence states, "we must await the reports of the parties sent by General [Persifor F.] Smith," for definitive data in the Sierra. This refers to the expedition of Capt. William H. Warner, who was killed by Indians in Surprise

Valley in September, 1849. For the Benton-Fremont competing route mentioned by Dearborn, see L4, L5, and L6.

Highlights   On January 15, 1850, the Senate published Miscellaneous Document 28, the "Petition of P. P. F. Degrand and others, Praying a charter for the purpose of constructing a railroad and establishing a line of telegraph from St. Louis to San Francisco." The 1,508 listed petitioners were to put up 2 million dollars, be authorized to borrow 98 million from the government, and be granted a 10-mile-wide strip of land on the north side of the road, as well as the right to take all building materials from the public lands. The content of this petition stemmed largely from Degrand's "meeting of the friends of a railroad to California," held in Boston, April 19, 1849, predating Dearborn's route work. Degrand originally thought that the length of his railroad would be only 1,600 miles, based apparently on Fremont's central route.

Degrand argued, "Let this company be bound to carry the mail, and to carry troops and munitions of war, on very reasonable terms…and let the company be bound to build the road with *American iron* and other materials exclusively of domestic origin…when built, its very existence will defend our possessions on the Pacific. It will avert all danger of Indian wars, north and south of this line. Upon its bed, a telegraphic wire will enable the government to issue its order to California and to Oregon with the rapidity of lightning…The cost of this railroad will be more than repaid by the additional value it will impart to the public lands west of Missouri…The plan now proposed will finish the road in the short space of five years." He concluded, "The existence of this railroad will render our union with our fellow citizens in California and Oregon indissoluble."

My copy of Dearborn's report has bound with it three other reports: (1) "Railroad from St. Louis to San Francisco (From the Missouri Republican, St. Louis, Jan. 9, 1850.);" this contains the petition and a list of 116 petitioners; 6 pages; (2) "To the People of California and Oregon;" iv pages; and (3) "Rail Road to San Francisco;" a summary of the April 19, 1849, meeting, with Appendices A through E, 24 pages. With some rearrangement and the expanded list of petitioners, this material makes up Degrand's contemporaneous Senate Miscellaneous Document 28.

Legacy   Degrand's 1850 petition to Congress did not include or recognize Dearborn's good work. Instead, Degrand used his original erroneous estimate of 1,600 miles for the length of his Pacific railroad. The road ultimately constructed followed the Platte at one end and the Humboldt-Truckee at the other, but in the middle it went via the South Platte and Great Salt Lake, rather than the North Platte and South Pass. The final terms of the Pacific Railroad Act of 1862 contained some elements of Degrand's proposals.

REFERENCES

(See Preface for Heading and Author references, and for Wheat, not listed below.)

Bryant, Edwin, 1848, What I saw in California: N.Y., 455 p.

Degrand, Peter P. F., and others, 1850, Petition for constructing a railroad from St. Louis to San Francisco: Wash., 31/1 S28 Misc., serial 563, 35 p.; quotes 20-21, conclusion 29.

Fremont, John C., 1845, Report of exploring expeditions, 1842 and 1843-44: Wash., 28/2 S174, serial 461, 693 p., maps.

Fremont, John C., 1848, Geographical memoir upon Upper California: Wash., 30/1 S148, serial 511, 67 p., map.

Kelley, Hall J., 1830 etc. (1932 reprint), Hall J. Kelley on Oregon; Fred W. Powell, ed.: Princeton; quote from 1830 tract p. 65-66; Degrand's testimonial 112; Kelley's claims 198.

Loughborough, John, 1849, The Pacific telegraph and railway: St. Louis, 80 p., 2 maps.

DESCRIPTION

OF

A RAIL ROAD ROUTE,

FROM

ST. LOUIS TO SAN FRANCISCO,

IN

LETTERS TO P. P. F. DEGRAND

FROM

W. L. DEARBORN,

CIVIL ENGINEER.

1849.

WITH MAP AND PROFILE.

BOSTON:

DUTTON AND WENTWORTH, PRINTERS,

1850.

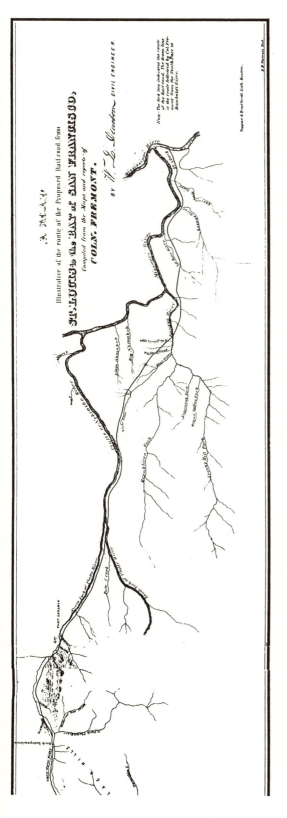

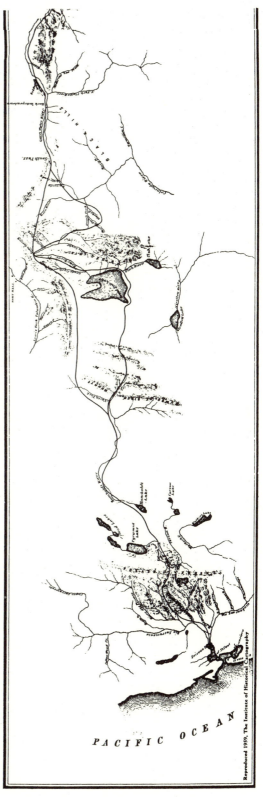

SAN FRANCISCO RAIL ROAD.

GENERAL DESCRIPTION OF THE ROUTE.

P.P.F. DEGRAND, Esq.
BOSTON

Boston, Nov. 16, 1849.

DEAR SIR,—I herewith transmit the result of the investigation, which I promised you I would make, in relation to a rail road route, for connecting the Mississippi River and the Pacific Ocean, which I beg you to accept, with a most ardent desire for, and a full belief in seeing it soon opened for travel.

From the Kansas River to the South Pass of the Rocky Mountains, a distance of 952 miles, is a gradually ascending plain, with an average rise of a little more than 7 feet per mile, and for a line of equal length, I know of no part of the world where one could be traced (except perhaps over the Pampas of South America, the Steppes of Russia, or the Plateaux of Central Asia), whose physical features would compare with it in regularity.

From the South Pass to the Sierra Nevada, 709 miles by the *red* line route, are points, on from 100 to 200 miles of it, which present obstacles to be overcome, as difficult, but not, I think, more so, than on some portions of the Western Rail Road of Massachusetts. The remaining 509 miles are very level, and well adapted to the easy construction of a rail road.

Humboldt River and Bear River Mountains are flanked and their summits avoided by the *red* line route, from the South Pass to Humboldt's River, called Sublette's Cut-off, and the distance thereby decreased so much, as to render it shorter, by a hundred miles, than any other line of travel.

The perfect practicability of the route, from St. Louis to the Sierra Nevada, may be considered as well established, and the obstacle which that mountain-range seems to present, is not by [p. 4]any means to be considered as insurmountable; for I am fully convinced, that when more thorough examinations of it have been made, that barrier will comparatively disappear, as have those of the Menai Straits and Alps, before the science, skill and enterprise of the age.

Very respectfully your obedient servant,

W.L. DEARBORN, *Civil Engineer.*

AGRICULTURAL CAPABILITIES AND CLIMATE.

P.P.F. DEGRAND, Esq.,
    BOSTON.

Roxbury, Mass., November 17, 1849.

DEAR SIR,—There are two points in relation to the country through which the proposed rail road route passes, from St. Louis to San Francisco, that have not been treated of in the statement submitted, and which I have since thought to be of such importance as to merit some attention, THEY ARE THE AGRICULTURAL CAPABILITIES AND THE CLIMATE OF THAT REGION.

From St. Louis to the Kansas River is a very fertile district, with an abundance of timber; and from the last named point to the head waters of the Little Blue Rivers, 275 miles, the soil cannot be surpassed in the United States, as is indicated by the luxuriance of the forest trees and native flora. So beautiful was it considered by Bryant, that he calls it *"the future Eden of America."* By referring to the map, it will be seen that it is traversed by numerous streams and rivers, some of which have good mill sites upon them.

The immense plain, situated between the Platte or Nebraska River on the north, the Arkansas River on the south, the Black Hills on the west, and the Kansas River on the east—embracing several degrees of latitude and longitude—has a good soil, and is capable of supporting a large agricultural population. These prairies are the pastures which nature has furnished for the support of the countless herds of buffalo that have for ages, and now range over them; which, of itself, is evincive of their fertility. The trees are here generally confined to the valleys of the streams; but there would be no difficulty in [p. 5]covering tracts, of any extent, with forest trees; and with much less labor than has been expended in planting the moors of England and Scotland, by gentlemen owning them; and this too for profit, and the result has more than equalled their expectation, in the sale of the timber obtained for mechanical purposes.

The Nebraska or Platte River is studded with beautiful islands, and some of them are of great extent—as Grand Island, which is 22 miles long, with an average width of about two miles. It has a rich soil, and is well wooded. This point has been designated, by an officer of engineers, as a favorable site for a military post.

From Laramie River to the eastern edge of the Great Basin, there are some sterile spots; but this is compensated for by many excellent tracts of land, even among the mountains.

The large valley of Bear River, north of the Great Salt Lake, is of surpassing beauty and fertility, as are portions of the valleys of the north Platte and Sweet Water Rivers, besides several others of less extent. These mountains and valleys are capable of supplying an immense quantity of timber.

The Great Basin, which extends west from the Rocky Mountains to the Sierra Nevada, is a succession of mountains and plains, having a system of Rivers and Lakes of its own;—the plains are generally sandy and sterile, but the mountains are bordered by rich belts of alluvium, and some of the valleys, particularly that near Utah Lake, on which the New Jerusalem of the Mormons has been located, and that of Humboldt River, are exceedingly rich in soil. The latter is about 300 miles long, and the river is bordered by trees; but the wood is principally confined to the mountains.

The slopes of the Sierra Nevada present many desirable localities for the agriculturist, and the valleys of the Sacramento and San Joaquin Rivers, and the territory surrounding the Bay of San Francisco and extending far north and south of it, are capable of growing many of the tropical trees, fruits and plants. Upper California is the only portion of North America where the choicest varieties of edible and wine grapes have been, as yet, successfully cultivated. Several varieties of forest trees are to be found here, which attain an enormous size. [p. 6]

In conclusion, I may safely say, that the route passes through a far better tract of country than that of Massachusetts, taken as a whole.

The climate, from the Mississippi River to the Pacific Ocean, is much milder than in the same latitude, east of the Alleghany Mountains; and that of the Great Basin, Sierra Nevada and Rocky Mountains is much less severe than could be expected, from their great elevation—*and is not more rigorous than that of the valleys of the Kennebec and Penobscot Rivers of Maine, or the upper portions of the Connecticut and Hudson.*

Very respectfully,

Your obedient servant,

W.L. DEARBORN, *Civil Engineer.*

MAP, PROFILE AND DETAILS.

P.P.F. DEGRAND, ESQ.,
BOSTON, MASS.

Roxbury, Mass., Nov. 15th, 1849.

DEAR SIR,—As the project for a Rail Road, from some point on the Mississippi River to the Bay of San Francisco, on the Pacific Ocean, is attracting so much attention, and the character of the country traversed by the routes, not being generally well known, I thought it might be gratifying to you, as one of the ardent friends of the undertaking, and interesting to the public, to have a succinct statement of the physical features and geological character of the region, on one of the proposed lines, as well as the variety of trees indigenous to the country, and characteristics of the principal rivers, followed or crossed by the route, as far as our present knowledge extends, as well as a skeleton map and profile of the line.

The one selected for this purpose is that, commencing at St. Louis, and passing up the Kansas, Platte, or Nebraska, and Sweet Water Rivers, to the South Pass of the Rocky Mountains; thence to Bear River, north of the Great Salt Lake, and by Humboldt's and Salmon Trout Rivers, crossing the summit of the Sierra Nevada near the head of the latter River, [p. 7] into the valley of the Sacramento River, and by this valley to the head of Suisoon Bay, near the mouths of the Sacramento and San Joaquin Rivers.

This route was selected for description after a careful examination of all, as far as that is now possible, by the reports and maps of the various scientific expeditions, and others that have explored the country lying west of the Mississippi River, and north of North latitude 33°, as presenting the fewest obstacles to be overcome, as well as for passing through a region, a large portion of which, is adapted to cultivation, and grazing, and would subserve the interests of the public equally as well as either of the others.

I of course do not mean to designate the exact line to be adopted for location, as that would require careful and extensive reconnoisances and surveys, before being determined upon, this being merely the general route.

The authorities consulted were—

Notes of Military Reconnoisance, from Fort Leavenworth in Missouri, to San Diego in California, including parts of the Arkansas, Del Norte, and Gila Rivers, in 1846. By Major Emory, U.S.T.E.C.

Account of an Expedition to the Rocky Mountains in 1819. By Major Long, U.S.T.E.C.

Report of Major Swords U.S.A., of a Journey from California by the South Pass to Fort Leavenworth, in 1847.

Reports of Exploring Expeditions to the Rocky Mountains, California and Oregon, in 1842, '3, '4, '5, '6 and 1847. By Capt. Fremont, U.S.T.E.C.

Narrative of a Tour to the Rocky Mountains and California, in 1832-3. By Capt. Bonneville, U.S.A.

Report of Lieut. Abert, U.S.T.E.C., of an examination of New Mexico, in 1846 and 7.

Report of J.N. Nicollet, member of the French Institute, of a Scientific Tour in the Basin of the Upper Mississippi, in 1838-9.

Memoir of a Tour in Northern Mexico, connected with Col. Doniphan's Expedition, in 1846-7. By A. Wislizenus, M.D.

Narrative of a Tour from St. Louis to California. By Edwin Bryant, in 1846. [p. 8]

History of the Expedition of Captains Lewis and Clark, to the Rocky Mountains and Oregon, in 1805-6.

Works of Baron Von Humboldt.

Reports of G.W. Featherstonhaugh, U.S. Geologist.

Reports of various Congressional Committees. By Travellers; and an article in the Western Journal. By J. Loughborough, Esq., of St. Louis.

The latter I did not see until I had collected a large portion of the facts for this paper.

Profile No. 1 is an enlargement of Col. Fremont's, for about 170 miles of the distance, the remainder was calculated and made up from his meteorological observations and notes by myself.

In giving the formation of the country and trees indigenous to it, I have generally confined the description within narrow limits, on either side of the route.

For the better elucidation of the subject, I have divided the line into sections.

SECTION No. 1.

From St. Louis, long. 90°, 15', 39"; lat. 38°, 37', 28", to a point 10 miles above the mouth of the Kansas River, distance about 275 miles.

ELEVATION of the Garden of the Cathedral at St. Louis 382 feet above the Gulf of Mexico, the base to which all the levels are referred.

SURFACE OF SECTION, undulating, rising into ridges and hills at some points, at others, formed of high plains.

FORMATION. Sand, Gravel, Alluvium, Carboniferous Limestone, Flint, and Bituminous Coal. The great Iron Mountain of Missouri, the largest mass of iron in the world, is situated about 60 miles south of this line.

TREES. Oak, Black Walnut, Hickory, Elm, Buttonwood, *(Platonis occidentalis)*, and Cotton Wood, &c.

RIVERS followed and crossed. The Missouri, the great river of the West, needs no description here, its character [p. 9] being so well known; the route touches it, near the Big Bonhomme, a large creek, crossing this and keeping near the south bank of the Missouri, and passing the Gasconade River 100 miles, from the mouth of the Missouri; the former is 157 yards wide, and 19 feet deep at its mouth; thence 27 miles to the Osage River, 397 yards wide at its mouth; the Missouri here is 875 yards wide; passing up the banks of the latter, to the La Mine

River, which is 70 yards wide at its mouth, and navigable for boats 80 or 90 miles; banks rather low; keeping up this River to Davis's Fork and crossing from thence several small streams to the Kansas River. From St. Louis to the La Mine, this route crosses 27 streams of an average width of 100 feet, besides the Gasconade and Osage. At Boonville, near the La Mine, the elevation of the Missouri Bank is 602 feet.

There is not sufficient data for a Profile of this section, as it was examined apparently without instruments by Mr. W.R. Singleton, of St. Louis.

SECTION No. 2.

From the Kansas River, long. 94°, 39' 31", lat. 39°, 6', elevation 700 feet, to the South Branch of the Platte River. Distance, 426 miles.

SURFACE of Section very level.

FORMATION. Sand, Clay, Gravel, Alluvium; the upper prairies are immense deposits of sand and gravel, covered with a good and very generally rich soil. Siliceous and yellow compact carboniferous limestone, large boulders of red sandstone, granite, flint, and ferruginous sandstone. There is a bed of Bituminous Coal on a branch of the Wak Karrussi.

TREES. Oak, Burr-Oak, Chestnut-Oak, and Black-Oak; there are in the eastern part of the section, Black-Walnut, Buckeye, Buttonwood, Hickory, Hackberry, Basswood or Linden, Beech, Pitch Pine, Red Cedar, American Elm, Sumach, Willow, and Poplar.

RIVERS followed or crossed: Keeping up the Kansas for [p. 10] 88 miles, valley 3 to 10 miles wide, river shoal except in freshets, when it is much swollen and rapid; crossing it where it is 690 feet wide, and the Big and Little Vermillion Rivers, small tributaries of the Kansas, to the Big Blue River, 76 miles; this is a rapid stream 120 feet wide; keeping up its valley 26 miles, to little Blue River, crossing several small streams, and passing up the valley of the latter for 85 miles; thence 23 miles to the Nebraska, or Main Platte River, 20 miles below Grand Island, in long. 99°, 17', 47", lat. 40°, 41', 3"; elevation here 1970 feet; passing up the right bank of this river, about 108 miles to the Forks. The main river here is 5,350 feet wide; north branch 2,250 feet; bed, sand and gravel; water 3 feet deep when very low; south branch, 450 feet wide; bed, quick sand; water 18 or 20 inches deep when lowest.

The banks of the Platte are 7 or 8 feet high; valley generally 4 miles broad; river shallow, as its name denotes, having many islands in it; does not inundate its banks much, as it is rapid, and very wide from bank to bank, and is thus able to convey the large volume of water, which it discharges in the spring, into the Missouri.

SECTION No. 3.

From the South Branch of Platte River, long. 101°, 22', lat. 41°, 5', 22". Elevation, 2,700 feet to the South Pass of the Rocky Mountains. Distance 526 miles.

SURFACE OF SECTION. From the Forks of Platte River to Laramie River, is quite level; west of this point, to where the road to Oregon and California crosses the north branch of the Platte, 144 miles, the face of the country cannot be called hilly, but is a succession of long ridges, made by the numerous streams, which come down from the neighboring mountain range; the ridges have an undulating surface, like the waves of the ocean. For 64 miles beyond to the Sweet Water, and thence to the South Pass, it is a regular and gradually ascending plain, for a large portion of the distance. To the north and south of this line, west of the Laramie, it is mountainous. [p. 11]

The South Pass of the Rocky Mountains is about 20 miles wide, having Table Mountain on the south, and the Wind River Mountains on the north.

FORMATION. Marl, Sand, Alluvium, Earthy Limestone, and Granitic Sandstone to Laramie River; west of this river, Sand, Alluvium, White Clay, Clay; compact Fossilliferous and Micacious Limestone, Granite, Gneiss, Calcarious [sic] Limestone, compact Calcarious Sandstone, Argillaceous Sandstone, Fine White, Reddish White, Gray, and Red Sandstones, Mica Slate, Gypsum, Quartz, Siliceous Pudding-stone, and magnetic Iron Ore. On the Sweet Water, the formation changes from secondary to primitive. There are beds of Bituminous Coal on the Platte, above the Sweet Water.

TREES. Ash, Ash-leaved Maple, (or Box Elder,) Beech, Pine, Cedar, Birch, Cherry, Willow, Poplar, Cotton Wood and Aspen.

RIVERS followed or crossed. From the forks of Platte River up the north branch to Laramie River, 206 miles, crossing Horse Shoe Creek, 70 yards wide. The character of this branch of the Platte, to the Laramie, is similar to the Main Platte; valley from 4 to 6 miles wide; crossing Laramie River, 90 feet wide, having here an elevation of 4,470 feet, and keeping up the Platte; crossing Deer Creek, Warm Spring Creek, Bitter Creek, Horse Creek, River La Bonte, River a la Prele, and the La Fouche Boisee; the first is the largest tributary of the Platte, west of the Laramie, and is, at a very low stage of water, 20 feet wide, but subject, like all the streams of this section, to high freshets; passing west to the point where the Oregon and California Road crosses the north branch of Platte, about 144 miles; this portion of the river varies from 800 to 1,500 feet in width; the surface of the water, at a very low stage, is from 200 to 300 feet wide; bed, rock and gravel; current swift, sometimes broken by rapids; at the gorge of the Black Hills, a short distance from Fort Laramie, it breaks through a ridge of red sand and clay, from

200 to 400 feet high; here its character is changed, from a river of the plains to a mountain stream; at the Red Buttes, it passes through a high ridge of Argillacious Sandstone, and at Hot Spring Gate, [p. 12] through one of white Calcarious Sandstone, 360 feet high; passing from the Platte, and crossing to the Sweet Water, 64 miles, to Rock Independence, and keeping up the valley of the latter to near South Pass. The valley is, for a part of the way, 4 or 5 miles broad; bordered by mountains; at some point it is rather more contracted; this river is rapid and cuts through a granite ridge 900 feet long and 400 feet high, at the Devil's Gate; its breadth here is 105 feet; thence to the South Pass 112 miles.

SECTION No. 4

From the South Pass of the Rocky Mountains, latitude 42°, 24', 32", long. 109°, 26'; elevation 7,490 feet, to Humboldt's River, near the Forks; distance 400 miles.

SURFACE OF SECTION. From the South Pass, to Soda Spring, on Bear River, 175 miles, it is very regular and even, being almost an uninterrupted plain; thence to Humboldt's River is undulating, and there are some ridges, but no very difficult obstacles to be overcome.

FORMATION. Alluvium, Clay, White Clay, Indurated Clay, with fossils, Sand, Granitic Sand, Gravel, White Limestone, Argillaceous Limestone, Fossilliferous Limestone, Scoriated Basalt, Calcarious Tufa, Blue Limestone, Granitic Gneiss, Scienitic Gneiss, Feldspathic Granite, Granular Quartz, Scienitic Feldspar, Trap, Oolitic Limestone, Gray Siliceous Limestone, Blueish Grey Slaty Limestone, Conglomerates, Brown Limestone, Yellow Quartz, Purple Red and Yellow Clayey Rocks, Ash-colored Limestone, Lava, Coal.

TREES. Oak, Ash-leaved Maple, Birch, Cherry, White Pine, White Spruce, Fir, Cotton Wood, Aspen, Willow, Cedar, Poplar.

RIVERS crossed or followed. Crossing the Little Sandy, Big Sandy, New Forks, and Green River, or Colorado,—the three former are small tributaries of the Colorado,—which, at the point of crossing, is quite a large stream; they are rapid, with sandy beds, and subject to freshets. Thence, crossing [p. 13] Tullies Fork of Bear River, a small stream, to Soda Springs on the latter, latitude 42°, 39', 57", long. 111°, 46', elevation 5,843 feet. Following Bear River, for a short distance, which has here an open valley, bordered by mountains; this river is, at some point, 200 feet wide, rapid, and passes between perpendicular walls of Basalt 1400 feet high, at Sheep Rocks, near where this line leaves it; thence passing on to the head waters of Rosseaux River, a large tributary of Bear River, crossing it, and into the Great Basin, over the dividing range; between the River and Basin, elevation of ridge about 6,300 feet; thence along the base of the dividing range, between the waters of the Pacific Ocean and the Great Basin, on the north; keeping north of Humboldt's River mountains, to Humboldt's River, near the Forks.

SECTION No. 5.

From the crossing of Humboldt's River, near the Forks, about latitude 40°, 40', long. 116°, 30'. Elevation 4,700 feet, to the head of Suisoon Bay, near the mouth of the Sacramento River, in about lat. 38°, 15', long. 121°, 40'; distance 604 miles.

SURFACE OF SECTION. From the crossing of Humboldt River, to Salmon Trout River, 309 miles, it is quite level; thence, crossing the Sierra Nevada, 205 miles, to the Bear River settlement, in the valley of the Sacramento; the route presents the usual mountain features: the western slope is quite regular, the eastern more broken and uneven; but taking into consideration the vast range of mountains passed, is remarkably favorable.

This route is the line of the Emigrant Road, over which the teams for California now travel; but a better one can possibly be found for a rail road, over the Sierra, either north or south of this, when more thorough reconnoisances shall have been made. Thence for 95 miles down the valley of the Sacramento to its mouth, it is very level.

FORMATION.Gravel, Sand, Alluvium, Red and Blue Clay, Volcanic Gravel and Ashes, Lava, Columnar Basalt, Trap, [p. 14] Slate, Conglomerates, Granite, Flint, Red Sandstone, Gold, Silver, and Quicksilver.

TREES. White, Black, Evergreen, and other varieties of Oaks, Spruce, White Spruce, White, Yellow, and Turf Pine, Red and White Cedar, Cotton Wood, Willow, Aspen, and Button-wood.

RIVERS followed and crossed. Humboldt River is followed 269 miles, to a marshy Lake, called the Sink, elevation 4,200 feet; valley from a few miles to twenty broad, bordered by mountains; river from two to six feet deep, and 40 feet wide, at a low stage of water; is subject to freshets in the spring, banks perpendicular, and passes through cannons at some points, at others is confined by sand hills; current sluggish; course sinuous, and has no affluents. Crossing the desert 40 miles, to Salmon Trout River, keeping up its valley to Truckee Lake, its source, 94 miles; this stream is rapid, passing through several cannons, and at points is 50 feet wide, and two feet deep, at low stages of water, but much swollen in the spring; bed rocky; valley confined by mountains, and narrow in parts of its course, at others open and broad; course tortuous.

One mile west of Truckee Lake, is the summit level of the Sierra Nevada, lat. 39°, 17', 12", long. 120°, 15', 20". Elevation above eastern base 3,200 feet, and above the Gulf of Mexico, 7,200 feet, being 290 feet less than the elevation of the

South Pass of the Rocky Mountains. Thence to Bear River settlements, 110 miles; this river is a considerable tributary of the Rio de Plumes, the largest afflu-ent of the Sacramento; thence 35 miles to the Rio des los Americanos, near New Helvetia. The Sacramento opposite this point is 300 yards wide, and has a depth of several fathoms of water in its channel; crossing the Americanos, which is about 100 yards wide, and shallow, except in time of freshets, and following down the left bank of the Sacramento 55 miles, to its mouth, at the head of Suisoon Bay, which communicates by the Straits of Karquin, with the Bay of St. Paul, and by the latter with the Bay of San Francisco. [p. 15]

General designation of the route, which is indicated on the map by the RED LINE.

From St. Louis to the Missouri, at a point just above the Big Bonhomme Bottom up the Missouri to the La Mine River, up the latter river to Davis's Forks, thence to the Kansas River, at a point 10 miles above its mouth, distance about 275 miles; passing up the right bank of the Kansas for 88 miles, and crossing to Big Blue River 76 miles, up the left bank of this river, and the Little Blue 131 miles, and over the dividing ridge 23 miles, to the Platte or Nebraska River, and on the right bank of this river, to the Forks 108 miles; crossing the south branch of the Platte, and passing up the right bank of the North Branch; crossing Laramie River to the point at which the Oregon and California road crosses the Platte 350 miles; crossing this river, and thence to the Sweet Water, 64 miles, up this river to within a short distance of the South Pass; and thence to the South Pass of the Rocky Mountains, 112 miles, and to Soda Springs on Bear River, 175 miles, about 50 miles south of Fort Hall, on Lewis's Fork of the Columbia River, keep-ing north of the Great Salt Lake, and passing near the head of Rousseau River, into the Great Basin; and across the Basin to Humboldt's River, near the Forks, 225 miles; following down the latter river to Humboldt Lake, 269 miles; crossing over the desert 40 miles to Salmon Trout River, at the base of the Sierra Nevada, and up this river to the summit of the Sierra, 95 miles; thence to Bear River Set-tlements, 110 miles, and New Helvetia, 35 miles, and down the Sacramento Val-ley, on the left bank of the river, to the head of Suisoon Bay, near the mouths of the Sacramento and San Joaquin Rivers, 55 miles.

Recapitulation of distances.

Section	No. 1,	275 miles
"	" 2,	426 "
"	" 3,	526 "
"	" 4,	400 "
"	" 5,	604 "
Total,		2,231 miles.

[p. 16] This probably, can be much decreased, when a definite location of the rail road is made.

I have said nothing, either of the cost, or grades, and curves, which would be required, in constructing the road, for the reason, that statements of this nature must necessarily be very imperfect, until further surveys are made.

Profile No. 2, was enlarged from one made by Col. Fremont. That portion of it, from the South Pass to E on Humboldt's River, near the Forks, is not that of the route here described; the line upon which it was based, is traced in green, on the accompanying map.

From Humboldt River to the Bay of St. Francisco, Col. Fremont's route is nearly identical with the RED LINE.

No profile could be given of the red line, from C to E, as but few barometrical observations have been made on it. For its description, I am mainly indebted to I. Loughborough, Esq. of St. Louis. It is not travelled by emigrants, on account of the scarcity of water, but, in every other respect, it is much superior to Col. Fremont's route, as it flanks the mountains, *a a*, is shorter and much more direct.

After this account was completed, I saw an extract of a letter from Col. Fremont to the Hon. Thos. H. Benton, in which he states, that *he thinks there may be found a better route than any now known,* for crossing the mountains. The one alluded to by him, is that passing between the head waters of the Rio del Norte and Arkansas River, thence to Humboldt River, and into the Sacramento, near the head of its lower valley.

As facts in relation to the elevation of some important points, as well as the physical and other features of a portion of this route are required, before a definite opinion can be formed, as to its practicability, we must await the reports of the parties sent by General Smith for its examination.

With great respect

I remain, Sir,

Your most obedient servant,

W.L. DEARBORN, *Civil Engineer.*

Francois X. Aubry, 1853

Aubry's Journey From California To New Mexico. Notes.

Santa Fe Weekly Gazette, September 24, 1853. [WC 223 note; WCB 220a; Holliday 31.] Reset verbatim from compiler's original of the reprint in the St. Louis *Western Journal and Civilian*, vol. 11, no. 2, November, 1853, Article 2, p. 84-96; this was Wagner's no. 197 in his 1920 and 1921 editions of *The Plains and the Rockies*.

Significance   Aubry's 1853 exploration from Tejon Pass to Albuquerque was an adventurous example of private promotion of a railroad route, but it added little that was new to the final analysis. Capt. Lorenzo Sitgreaves had come west over much the same ground in 1851 (5:J6). His 1853 government map and report portrayed the lay of the land much more accurately than Aubry's words, but much less enthusiastically: "almost the entire country traversed being barren, and without general interest," wrote Sitgreaves. Mountaineer Joseph Rutherford Walker, who had first reached California overland in 1833, made a private exploration with 7 men in early 1851. He went east from Walker Pass to the Mojave River to the Virgin mouth to the San Francisco Mountains to the Hopi villages to Albuquerque (Gilbert 1983). In an 1853 report to the California Senate, Walker advocated this route, except that his railroad would go through Zuni rather than the Hopi villages. The Sitgreaves, Walker, and Aubry proposed routes through Arizona were all very similar.

In October, 1853, in Albuquerque on his way back to California, Aubry met Lt. Amiel W. Whipple's government party heading west to explore for the Pacific railroad. Whipple wrote that Aubry was "cautioning us to avoid his trail as being unsuitable for our operations." This probably referred only to the part of Aubry's track along the Mogollon Rim, where he had to stick close to the mountains for water (see Itinerary). Whipple's topographer and artist, H. Balduin Mollhausen, wrote in his diary, "The only man who appeared to possess any well-founded information was a certain Aubrey, who had been with flocks of sheep to California, and had several times come into serious collision with the Club Indians. His account was not very encouraging for our journey; but at all events it was such as gave reason to anticipate interesting experiences and exciting adventures."

Aubry's journal was reprinted in the San Francisco *Herald,* December 5 and 6, 1853; in William Gwin's 1853 speech; and as a separate from the *Railroad Record,* 1866 (Graff 108). Gwin's speech is reprinted as L3 in this volume, except that Aubry's notes, given here in L2, are not duplicated. Gwin's version has some minor differences that are ignored, but it has four additional sentences which have been included in brackets in this L2 printing. Modern reprints have been provided by Wyman 1932 and Bieber 1938.

Author FRANCOIS XAVIER AUBRY, 1824-1854, trader, explorer, fastest endurance horseman on record. A Quebec farm boy, Aubry had a few years' education and worked for a merchant. He went to St. Louis in 1843 and sent most of his clerk's wages home to his destitute mother. In 1846 he became a Santa Fe trader, moving out ahead of the Army of the West, and returning with a neat profit. He made two successful trading trips to Santa Fe in 1847, racing back in 14 days on the last one. He carried mail and published accounts of his exploits in Missouri newspapers. It was dangerous work. Indians killed 47 Americans on the Trail that year.

Aubry became rich and famous from his three fast 1848 trading trips to Santa Fe. On the first trip, he left Independence in March; he returned in May in 8 days and 10 hours, having had to hike 30 miles of the way. On the second, his wagons were on the Trail in July. On September 12 he left Santa Fe for the return on his mare, Dolly. Six broken horses later, after flying through rain, mud, and swollen streams, sleeping only two and a half hours not tied to his horse, eating only six meals, walking 20 miles, and bloodying his saddle, Aubry reached Independence. It took 5 days and 16 hours to cover 780 miles, at 138 miles per day, a record never to be approached (2:C Perspective). He pushed his luck too far on the third trip in October to December, and he lost many mules and much merchandise in Raton Pass. He wintered in Santa Fe and Chihuahua, then made one trip to Missouri and back in 1849.

In 1850 Aubry went to Victoria, Texas, then to Chihuahua, to Santa Fe and Missouri, back to Santa Fe, San Antonio, Chihuahua, and Santa Fe again. Col. George A. McCall (5:J6) reported Aubry's famous interview with Apache Chief Marco. Disillusioned with the Texas-Chihuahua trade, in 1851 Aubry made three round trips between Missouri and Santa Fe, pioneering the Aubry Cutoff west of the Cimarron route. He made three more round trips in 1852, becoming rich but bored. So on November 16, 1852, he left Santa Fe for California with 60 men, 10 wagons, 200 horses and mules, and 3,500 to 5,000 sheep. The sheep were to pay for his private explorations for a railroad route. He went from the Rio

Grande via the Apache Pass Trail directly west to Tucson and then followed Cooke's Gila road to Ft. Yuma, and on to Los Angeles and San Francisco. He returned in 1853 on the shorter route due east from Tejon Pass through present Hoover Dam and Flagstaff, to Zuni and Albuquerque (see Itinerary).

Aubry's last expedition took him back to California with 50,000 sheep, from October, 1853, to February, 1854. He reached Santa Fe again on August 18, 1854, having followed nearly his 1853 return route. That afternoon in a bar he met a rival, Mexican War Maj. Richard H. Weightman, lawyer, and editor of a newspaper that had just died. The two headstrong men disagreed about railroad routes and other matters. Aubry said that Weightman's lying paper deserved to die. Weightman threw his drink in Aubry's face, then stood back, hand on belt. Aubry drew his Colt, which misfired into the ceiling. Weightman closed in with his bowie knife, stabbing Aubry in the stomach. Aubry was dead in ten minutes. Weightman pled self defense and was acquitted. (Chaput 1975; Bieber 1938; Thrapp.)

Marion Sloan Russell was seven years old when she traveled to Santa Fe with Aubry's train in 1852: "I remember his young piercing eyes and his boundless energy. He was a virile man, with a deep voice that was as resonant as a fog horn…Captain Aubry gave a lesson each day on the unpredictability of the Indian race. 'Have eyes in the back of your head,' he once stated, 'and keep all your eyes open at night and day'…My heart swells with pride when I think of Captain Aubry. He was my friend. He led mighty caravans across the prairies and in his heart was the lure of dim trails."

Lt. George D. Brewerton in 1856 recalled meeting "Little Aubrey" on the Arkansas in 1848: "In person, Aubrey was a small but very active man, all bone and muscle, just the figure for such an expedition [endurance ride]—for who doesn't know that there's no telling what a *little man* cannot do when he tries?"

Col. George A. McCall in 1850 met Aubry, "a dashing, gallant fellow," after both had traveled the Lower Road across Texas. Aubry had been caught in a mule-killing "wet Norther." McCall recorded, "the idea occurred to him that his mules might be saved by giving those who seemed to be the most likely to succumb, as much whisky as they would take from a bucket set before them. He told me these mules took from a pint to a quart, and many of them that he had regarded as lost, recovered." One mule drank a gallon, however, and died.

Itinerary, 1853   AUBRY, TEJON PASS TO ALBUQUERQUE. July 11—Aubry heads east from Tejon Pass at present Gorman CA, which is on Interstate 5 about 70 miles north of Los Angeles. He has come from San Francisco. His pack-train party includes his black servant Pompey, 6 Mexicans, 12 Americans, and 2 adventurers, Abner E. Adair, a printer's apprentice from Independence, and Pinckney R. Tulley, a young Santa Fe lawyer. They have 30 mules and horses. Aubry has talked with Fremont's former guide Alexis Godey on Kern River but still knows little of the route ahead. They strike the Mojave River 10 miles north of today's Victorville and leave it about 40 miles east of modern Barstow.

July 23 through 26—They spend four days crossing the Colorado below present Hoover Dam (Boulder City NV). Mohave Indians threaten, provisions are damaged, rattlesnakes abound, beaver cut the raft ropes at night, a Mexican muleteer discovers gold, and the animals have nothing to eat but sagebrush (*artemisia*, or "chamezo"). They go 10 miles east on the 27th but must return to the river on the 28th, to lay over on the 29th, because of sick men. Again going east, they camp probably near Hualapai Wash, which Aubry mistakes for Walker's "Little Red River," which is the Little Colorado, or Colorado Chiquita, much farther east. August 3—Probably east of what is now Peach Springs AZ, Indians shower them with arrows for two days, wounding Aubry's famous mare, Dolly. An arrow goes through Richard M. Williams's collar. One man shoots himself in the knee. They go nearly three days without water.

August 14—Near modern Flagstaff, about 250 Yuma ("Garrotero," or Club Indian) men and women attack the party with clubs, rocks, and arrows. Some Indians try to hold each man while others beat him; "but some of us having disengaged ourselves, we shot them down so fast with our Colt's revolvers, that we soon produced confusion among them, and put them to flight. We owe our lives to these firearms, the best ever were invented." Twelve of the men are wounded, several severely. Adair's skull is fractured. Twenty five Indians lie dead and scalped. Several Indian babes, cast into a brushy gully by their fleeing mothers, may also be dead. The Indians continue to shoot arrows as the party moves east with lame mules. Some men are afoot. Dolly gives out from her wounds, and Aubry must eat her flesh to survive. J. Frank Dobie (Hillerman 1991) notes that on the 1848 stupendous ride, Dolly carried Aubry "two hundred miles in twenty-six hours. So far as I know, this is the world's record for one horse in one day and night, plus two hours, of galloping." Aubry was offered $800 for the mare in San Francisco.

August 27—Perhaps on the Mogollon Rim, say, south of present Heber AZ, Aubry meets some "Belenios" (Pinaleño Apaches?), who have gold bullets for their guns. These probably are close allies with the Tonto Apaches met three days before. The party apparently travels southeast from Flagstaff and San Francisco ("Garrotero") Mountain, then east along the Mogollon Rim to near the White

Mountains ("Sierra Blanca") on September 2, then northeast across the Little Colorado River to reach Zuni (NM) on September 6. Aubry sticks close to the mountains for water. He recognizes that the railroad route obviously lies farther north in the flatter country. They survive on berries and herbs.

September 10—Albuquerque. Aubry's mileages sum to about 990, covered in 62 days, including 7 layover and river-crossing days, at 16 miles per day. This is determined travel for these sick and wounded men, not one of whom is lost. Itinerary is from Aubry's journal, augmented by the notes of Bieber 1938 and Chaput 1975.

Highlights   Editor James L. Collins, in the September 24, 1853 issue of the *Santa Fe Weekly Gazette,* introduced Aubry's diary in part as follows: "The belief which has long existed in the public mind of New Mexico, in regard to the existence of an excellent route for a wagon or railroad from the central part of the Territory to California, has received ample confirmation from this exploring expedition of Mr. Aubry. From this enterprise of noble daring, the most interesting and useful information is furnished to the world, on a subject, which at this time, engrosses the attention of statesmen and capitalists to a degree perhaps unknown in any former period of our history. This information too, although unofficial, is not the less authentic or the less worthy of credence on that account. To those who know Mr. Aubry it would be superfluous for us to say a word in behalf of his veracity and good judgment. His friends all know him to be a man absolutely without a parallel in physical qualities, and unsurpassed in all the noble traits of human character." (Bieber 1938.)

Legacy   The Santa Fe Railroad was built in the 1880s across Arizona, roughly on the Sitgreaves (and Walker-Aubry-Whipple) route. In California, one branch went west through Tehachapi Pass to modern Bakersfield, the other south through Cajon Pass to San Bernardino. In his official 1855 report of explorations for a railroad crossing the southern Sierra, Lt. Robert S. Williamson rightly declared, "Walker's Pass is badly situated, and impracticable...the position and grades [of Tehachapi Pass] eventually proved to be more favorable than those of any other in the Sierra...[and] I think the difficulties presented by the grades, taken in connexion with the tunnel that would be required, render this [Tejon] pass unfit for railroad purposes." No railroads were built through the Walker and Tejon passes.

Aubry's exploits may well have inspired the Pony Express (Chaput 1975).

REFERENCES

(See Preface for Heading references, and for Graff and Thrapp, not listed here.)

Bieber, Ralph P., 1938, Exploring Southwestern trails 1846-54: Glendale, Aubry biography p. 38-62; Aubry reprint 353-77; Collins quote 353.

Brewerton, George D., 1856, The war in Kansas: N.Y., quote p. 124.

Chaput, Donald, 1975, Francois X. Aubry: Glendale, 249 p.; 1853 journey 123-36; Pony Express 171-73.

Gilbert, Bil, 1983, Westering man, the life of Joseph Walker: N.Y., p. 236-43.

Hillerman, Tony, 1991, The best of the West: N.Y., Dobie quote p. 377.

McCall, George A., 1850 (1974 reprint of 1868 ed.), Letters from the frontiers; intro. by John K. Mahon: Gainesville FL, quote p. 491.

Mollhausen, Baldwin, 1853 (1858 pub.), Diary of a journey from the Mississippi to the coasts of the Pacific: London, quote 2:23.

Russell, Marion ("Marian") Sloan, 1936 memoirs (1989 printing), Land of Enchantment: Albuquerque; quotes on energy p. 12; Indian race 23; dim trails 30.

Sitgreaves, Lorenzo, 1853, Report of an expedition down the Zuni and Colorado rivers: Wash., 32/2 S59, serial 668, 198 p., map; quote 5.

Walker, Joseph R., 1853 (1965 reprint), Walker's R.R. routes, 1853, by Pat Adler and Walt Wheelock: Glendale, 64 p.; Walker report 29-34.

Whipple, Amiel W., 1853 journal (1856 publication), Route near 35th Parallel, in Reports of Explorations and Surveys: Wash., 33/2 S78, serial 760, 3:48.

Williamson, Robert S., 1855 report (1856 publication), Routes in California, in Reports of Explorations and Surveys: Wash., 33/2 H91, serial 795, 5:7-43; quotes on Walker Pass 16, Tehachapi 19, Tejon 25.

Wyman, Walker D., 1932, F. X. Aubry, Santa Fe freighter, pathfinder and explorer: Santa Fe, New Mexico Hist. Review 7:1-31; Aubry reprint 11-26.

THE

WESTERN JOURNAL
and Civilian,

| VOL. XI. | November, 1853. | No. II. |

ARTICLE II.
Aubry's Journey from California to New Mexico.*

NOTES.—BY F.X. AUBRY.

[In brackets are four additional sentences from Gwin's 1853 version, L3.]

TEJON PASS, *July* 10*th*, 1853.—As the country between this point and San Francisco is well known, I have kept no minutes of my journey thus far. We crossed the Sierra Nevada at the Tejon Pass, which is in about the 35th parallel of latitude, and about 50 miles south of Walker's pass. From this point we travel east until we reach the Rio Grande at Albuquerque, New Mexico. It is well to remark that, unfortunately, there is no one with us who knows anything of the country through which we must pass, and we could not obtain any information in regard to it. *My* party consists of eighteen men—twelve Americans and six Mexicans. Messrs. Tully, of Santa Fe, and Adair, of Independence, have joined us for a pleasure trip. We use pack animals entirely, having neither wagon nor carriage.

July 11*th*.—Left the Pass, and made twelve miles east over a level, gravelly and sandy soil, and found a spring of good water.

July 12*th*.—Traveled twenty miles eastward, the country similar to that of yesterday. We met with no timber, but found several springs of fresh water. There is timber in the mountains about the Tejon pass, but none on the eastern side of them.

July 14*th*. [13*th*.]—Travelled to-day 35 miles east, and struck the Mohave river, where we found plenty of good water. This river sometimes disappears in its course, whilst at others it contains as much as two feet of water. There is a little cotton-wood timber upon its banks, and canebrakes in great abundance. The cane is not of the large species.

---

*The following account of a trip made by F.X. Aubry from California to New Mexico, through an unexplored region, is full of interest, especially at the present time; and is highly worthy of being preserved in American history on account of the heroism displayed by the author and his comrades.—*Editor.*

The Mohave takes its rise in the San Bernardino mountains, which lie to the south of us, and after pursuing a northern course to a point a little north of our present camp, turns suddenly east, and soon south of east to empty into the great Colorado. Found good grass for our animals.

July 14th.—Made 20 miles east along the Mohave, and found water, timber and grass abundant.

July 15th.—Continued along the river about 18 miles further, in a direction nearly east, then leaving the Mohave to our right, we traveled 15 miles north-east.

Met with an abundance of grass, a little timber, and a few miles of fertile land along the river. There is no water in the bed of [page 85] the stream; but it may be had by digging a few feet. Found wild game from time to time. Encamped without water, grass or wood.

July 16th.—Still pursuing a north-eastern course—we traveled to-day 35 miles over a level, gravelly soil. We have deviated from our due east course in order to avoid a region of sand hills that lie to our right, and directly between us and the Great Colorado. The weather is very hot, and no rain has fallen since we left the Pass. So far we have met with neither Indians nor game of any kind. We obtained a little water about half-way in our day's journey; but saw no timber or grass.

July 17th.—Made 33 miles north-east, over a level, gravelly country; about half way obtained a little very bad water. No grass or timber in sight during the day; but at night we obtained good water, grass and wild game. Prairie mountains lie on both sides of the trail.

July 18th.—Traveled 20 miles, still north-east, over a level country. Saw but little good land, and no timber. After traveling about 5 miles, we found good spring water, but encamped without any.

July 19th.—Course still north-east, distance 32 miles, country level, soil inferior, grass and water, but no timber.

July 20th.—Made 20 miles north east over a level, gravelly country, and obtained good spring water and grass. Saw no timber.

July 21st.—Were detained in camp all day by the sickness of one of the men.

July 22d.—Traveled 20 miles east-south-east, most of the distance through a little canon, where we found good grass, water and game in abundance, and struck the great Colorado of the West. The river at this place is over 300 yards in width, and has from 10 to 15 feet water in the channel. Its banks are entirely destitute of timber and grass; in fact, no vegetation is met with except a small shrub, called *chamezo* by the Mexicans, and I believe *artemesia* by botanists. We were very fortunate in striking the river at this point, where there are neither canons nor mountains, although the country appears very rough and mountainous both to the north and south of us. To the north, the rocks are black and irregular, and seem to be volcanic: whilst the cliffs to the south are of red sandstone. The banks at the crossing are low, rocky and unchanging, and the current exceedingly rapid.

We followed the river up for 5 miles, and selected a crossing where it was some 200 yards wide and 20 or 25 feet deep. We succeeded in finding a little drift wood, of which we made a raft. Four men took charge of it, and it was carried some 3 miles with the current before it could be landed. The hights [sic] were covered with Indians, in readiness to shoot us down. I started down with four men to follow the raft and protect the men who were upon it, having ordered the camp to move down in haste. Having unloaded [page 86] the raft upon the eastern bank, the men recrossed the river, and we selected a camp opposite the place where the baggage was deposited, and during the night kept up a constant fire with our rifles across the river, and in this manner protected it from the Indians.

The animals were taken to the crossing I had first selected, to swim the river. I took them up with three men on the west bank, and four men received them on the opposite side. This detained us half a day, and altogether we were detained five days in crossing the river.

The driftwood of which we constructed our little raft, appeared to have been cut by beavers. These animals must be exceedingly abundant, as they destroyed during the first night the ropes with which our raft was bound together, and carried off the timber. The loss of the ropes was a great inconvenience to us. We set a guard afterwards at night over our second raft, to protect it from a similar fate.

The river showed signs of having been some fifteen feet higher than when we crossed it. It is here a grand and magnificent stream, swift like the Mississippi, and apparently as well adapted to navigation.

The place of our crossing is well suited to bridging, or ferriage by steam or otherwise.

We saw no water-fowl about the river, and only a few antelope and black-tailed deer. East of the river we encountered a great many rattlesnakes of an uncommonly large size. They seem to be a new species, as their tails are covered, for some six inches from the point, with alternate white and black rings of hair or bristles, about a quarter of an inch long.

According to my observations the Colorado of the west is set down upon the maps greatly too far to the east, perhaps as much as 150 miles.

The Indians were constantly in sight, and watching our movements. They could not be induced to approach us; but assured us, across the river, that they were Mohaves.

On one occasion, whilst at rest for a few minutes in a deep gulley, about a mile from the crossing on the west side of the river, a Mexican mule-boy discovered something glistening upon the ground, which on examination proved to be gold. We at once commenced washing sand in our tin cups and in every one discovered particles of gold. This gold was discovered in a dark, coarse sand, and a black heavy sand was found in the cup after washing away the gravel. The sandy soil was so compact that we could not dig it up with our fingers. The Indians being still on the hights [*sic*] near us, and our party being separated by the river, the danger was so great that we could not remain longer at this spot. I intended to return again, but the Indians became so numerous that it was impossible to do so. This gulley is on the right bank of [page 87] the river, and the head of it is in a very rough and rugged mountain.

July 27th.—We washed sand on the east side of the river, and found gold in greater abundance than on any previous occasion. [I myself washed a tin-cup full of yellow clay, and found about twenty five cents' worth of pure metal.] A Mexican boy, on washing a frying-panfull of coarse sand, found from forty to fifty particles of pure gold, some of which were as large as the head of a pin. We took the clay and sand from the top of the ground without digging. The appearance of the country also indicated gold. I made no further examination, as our animals had subsisted for five days upon the *chamezo,* without a blade of grass, and our provisions had been damaged in the Colorado, which must cause us to travel several days without anything to eat.

To-day we made 10 miles east. The country is without wood, water or grass.

July 28th.—Two of our men being sick, we were compelled to return to the river on their account.

Struck it some 15 miles below the crossing, and found that from near that point it makes a considerable bend towards the east. The country here does not indicate gold, nor could we find any on washing the sands.

July 29th.—The condition of our sick men obliged us to remain in camp all day. Our animals were in a starving condition, as there is not a particle of grass on or near the river.

July 30th.—Left the river and traveled 15 miles east, and 5 north-east. A sick Mexican was so much exhausted that we were compelled to make for a mountain north of us, which indicated water; but we found neither water, timber nor grass.

July 31st.—Traveled 8 miles, north-east, and struck a large stream, but much smaller than the Colorado, coming from the east-south-east, and running west-north-west. This stream may be what the Mexicans designate as the Rio Grande de los Apaches, and what the Americans have recently called the Little Red River.

One of our Mexicans followed this stream a few miles, and says it empties into the Colorado, 7 or 8 miles below camp, and that there is below us a valley of good soil, and grass in abundance. Where we struck this stream there is neither timber nor grass.

In the evening, we traveled 5 miles south, to avoid mountains, and as many east.

The country was level, but without grass or timber.

The mountains, or perhaps more properly hills that we have thus far met with, are nothing more than elevations of various forms and dimensions, dispersed in a detached and irregular manner over a vast and otherwise uninterrupted plateau. Hence, I have constantly termed the country level, and very properly, as it may be traversed in all directions among the solitary and detached elevations or mountains, without the necessity of crossing them. [page 88]

August 1st.—Traveled 20 miles east, and found a spring of good water; the grass was abundant, and cedar trees were seen on the highlands. The country is level, and the soil inferior.

August 2d.—Made 10 miles east, crossing a mountain or ridge, where we found a fine pass, grass and timber (cedar and pinon,) abundant.

August 3d.—Traveled 20 miles south of east, over a country somewhat broken: timber and grass abundant. Indians were around us in numbers, all day, shooting arrows every moment. They wounded some of our mules, and my famous mare Dolly, who has so often rescued me from danger, by her speed and capacity of endurance.

August 4th.—We moved 10 miles south, to avoid mountains, and struck a valley which we left a few days since, and which extends to the Colorado. The mountains which we left are covered with timber. Grass and water were found in plenty.

The Indians commenced firing on us at sunrise, and continued until we reached camp. Arrows passed through the clothes of the men, and three passed through my own clothes, and I was slightly wounded by two others in different places. An arrow passed through the collar of Dick Williams. We killed several of the Indians and wounded more. Peter Prudon accidentally shot himself in the right knee.

August 5th.—Traveled 10 miles south-east in a valley. No water; grass and timber in abundance on all the mountains.

August 6th.—Continued 10 miles south-east in the same valley in which we traveled yesterday; found no water, but good grass and plenty of timber on and below the mountains. As our sick men are unable to travel, we are suffering for water, having been nearly 3 days without any; and indications are not now favorable. Indians still around us.

August 7th.—Traveled 10 miles south-east, half the distance in the same valley, and then went to a mountain, and found good water, grass and timber. All the mountains in this country are covered with cedar, pine and pinon The grass is good in all the prairies, but none of them have any water. The soil is sandy and full of particles of mica. Indians are numerous, and continue to fire upon us.

August 8th.—Made 15 miles east-south-east, crossing a little chain of mountains, where we found a level pass, and timber, grass and water in abundance. Crossed a stream running from north-east to south-west, which I think goes to the Colorado. After crossing the mountains, we passed through a fine valley, with an abundance of good spring water, and timber near it. The Indians attacked the camp several times last night, but without success, and continued fighting us during the day, but with less boldness and resolution. [page 89]

August 9th.—After proceeding 8 miles east, we found ourselves surrounded by canons, apparently from one to four thousand feet deep; at least we sometimes could not see the bottom. We were compelled to return to the same camp. The country is high and level, and well supplied with timber, grass and water.

August 10th.—Moved 10 miles south-east over a somewhat broken country. Crossed a stream of good water, (with timber along its course,) which is evidently a tributary of the Gila. The country indicates gold in abundance. We crossed a little chain of mountains, where we found a great quantity of silver ore in flint rocks.

August 11th.—Traveled south-east over a country a little broken, but well supplied with water, grass and timber. Indications of gold still exist.

August 12th.—Made 15 miles south-east, crossing the bed of a large stream now dry, with plenty of timber along it. Struck the valley which we left some five or six days ago, having crossed a few days ago the head water of a stream which passes through it. This valley will be of the utmost importance in the making of a wagon or rail road.

To-day, for the first time on this trip, we ate a dinner of mule meat. It was a new dish to most of our men, and made some of them sick. To me it was an old acquaintance, and I feel well. It only served to remind me of hard times on other journeys. The quality of the meat depends on the appetite of the man. Several of us are now on foot.

August 13th.—Marched 20 miles east, leaving to our right the great valley so often mentioned, and which extends to the Colorado. Passed through a little valley between two mountains, where we found timber, grass and water in abundance. The soil was excellent.

We here met Indians, who professed to be very friendly, with papers of rec-ommendation from the commanding officer of Fort Yuma, on the Gila trail.

August 14*th*.—We left early, and after traveling 5 miles in an eastern direction, stopped to breakfast near an Indian Camp of Garroteros. They professed friend-ship, but having no faith in their professions, I selected a camp on the top of a small hill, which would give us advantage in case of a fight. All went on well until our mules were saddled, and we were ready to start, when, at a given signal, some forty or fifty Indians, apparently unarmed, and accompanied by their squaws, children and babies, (tied to boards,) in their arms, very suddenly charged upon us, and attempted to destroy the whole party with clubs and rocks. The signal of attack was the taking of my hand in farewell by a chief, which he held with all his strength. So soon as these first Indians commenced the fight about two hundred more rushed from behind a hill and brush, and charged upon us with clubs, bows [page 90] and arrows. I thought, for a few minutes, that our party must necessarily be destroyed; but some of us having disengaged ourselves, we shot them down so fast with our Colt's revolvers, that we soon produced confusion among them, and put them to flight. We owe our lives to these firearms, the best ever were invented, and now brought, by successive improvements, to a state of perfection.

Mr. Hendry, an American, and Francisco Guzman, a New Mexican, greatly distinguished themselves.

Twelve of us, just two-thirds of our party, were severely wounded. I, among the rest, was wounded in six places. Abner Adair, I fear, is dangerously injured. It was a very great satisfaction to me to find that none of my men were killed, nor any of the animals lost. We bled very much from our numerous wounds; but the blood and bodies of the Indians covered the ground for many yards around us. We killed over twenty-five, and wounded more. The bows and arrows that we cap-tured and destroyed, would have more than filled a large wagon.

Before the attack commenced, the squaws kept the clubs, which were from 18 to 24 inches long, concealed in deer skins about their children. When put to flight, they threw their babes down into a deep, brushy gulley, near at hand, by which many of them must have been killed. This is the first time I ever met with a war party of Indians accompanied by their wives and children. The presence of the latter was evidently to remove from our minds all suspicion of foul play on their part. I was never before in so perilous a condition with a party in all my life. On this occasion, which will be the last, I imprudently gave my right hand, in parting, to the Indian chief. The left must answer for leave taking hereafter.

We have thus far had so much ill-luck to encounter, that our arrival at our destination must be much delayed. First, our men fell sick, then our provisions were damaged in the Colorado; latterly, a man shot himself through the knee; our mules' feet, for want of shoes, are worn out; and, to crown all, to-day two-thirds of the party are badly wounded, and all have barely escaped with their lives. We are now subsisting entirely on mule meat, and do not get as much of that as we want. We are without salt and pepper, and, in their absence, it requires a stout stomach to digest our fare. But nobody complains, and the possibility of not doing what we have set out to do, has never entered the minds of my party.

We traveled 5 miles this afternoon, with the Indians at our heels, shooting arrows at us every moment.

August 15*th*.—Traveled 10 miles east among the mountains, where we found water, grass and timber in abundance. Indians around us all day shooting arrows. I omitted, in the proper place, to say that I brought away from the mountains we passed through on the [page 91] 10th, a little black sand, less than a cupful, and found in it, on washing, twelve or fifteen particles of pure gold.

August 16*th*.—Made 10 miles east and found no water; plenty of grass and timber seen on the mountains north of us. Indians still numerous and troublesome. To-day met with copper in very great quantities. A vein of the pure native metal, about an inch and a half in diameter, was seen sticking out from a rock, which must have worn away by time and left the copper exposed. I think there is gold in the ore, but am not certain.

Our condition at present is bad enough. I have eight wounds upon me, five of which cause me much suffering: and at the same time, my mule having given out, I have to walk the whole distance. Thirteen of us are now wounded, and one is sick, so that we have only four men in good health. We are unable to travel faster on account of Adair's condition.

Our canteens, &c., having been broken or destroyed in our fight with the Indians, we cannot carry water enough for more than half a day. This loss caused us to suffer more than can be imagined. Our animals are broken down by this traveling, which could not be avoided. We would come across an abundance of water every day if we could march some twenty-five or thirty miles, but our condition is such that it requires three days to make that small distance. In addition to all this, we are now on half rations of horse meat; and I have the misfortune to know that it is the flesh of my inestimable mare *Dolly*, who has so often, by her speed, saved me from death at the hands of the Indians. Being wounded some days ago by the Garroteros, she gave out, and we are now subsisting upon her flesh.

August 17*th*.—Moved to-day about 10 miles east, over a country rather rough. Suffering much for want of water. In crossing mountains we have to select the highest places instead of the regular passes, as when caught in canons or gullies we are not strong enough to fight the Indians. To-day, from the top of a little mountain, I saw the great valley, so often mentioned, extending to the Colorado, not over twenty miles south of us, and it now seems to turn more to the east. I intend to make for it. I entertain fears that Adair and Baskerville are in danger from their wounds; all the others are getting better.

August 18*th*.—Moved only 5 miles south of east. Found water, grass and some timber.

August 19*th*.—Went 5 miles to-day in the same direction as yesterday, and came to the great valley that extends to the Colorado. Encamped on a creek of good water and grass. Adair being sometimes unable to travel, we are waiting on him. Indians around us shooting arrows. We never return their fire without being certain of our shots.

August 20*th*.—Traveled 20 miles east, over a level, gravelly country; crossed a creek; found good grass; no timber in sight. [page 92]

August 21*st*.—Moved 10 miles east over a level, gravelly country, and struck a large stream which is, no doubt, a branch of the Gila. The mountains to the north of us are very rough, and without timber.

There is no grass on the stream, which is 30 yards wide, with three feet of water in the channel. Its course is from north to south.

August 22*d*.—Made 10 miles south-east to a mountain. Country level, and without grass or timber.

August 23*d*.—Moved about the same distance and in the same direction, over a low, gravelly country. Struck a stream of good water, but without grass or timber.

August 24*th*.—Went about 8 miles north-east, and emcamped [*sic*] in the mountains, where we met with the Apaches Tontos. No timber seen to-day.

August 25*th*.—Crossed the mountains where the Apaches Tontos live, and found water, timber and grass in abundance. Traveled 15 miles northeast from the top of this mountain, from which we saw the Sierra Blanca Mountains, which are near the Puebla [*sic*] of Zuni.

Saw a prairie extending from the east end of the Garrotero Mountain to the upper end of the Sierra Blanca. I saw this prairie when we were at the east end of the Garrotero Mountain, but we were not in a condition to examine it. Fifty miles is nothing with good animals; but ours were broken down, and our wounded men were unable to travel over ten miles a day. But I saw the country sufficiently well to convince me that there will be no obstacle whatever to the making of a rail or wagon road. The mountains which we crossed to-day are impracticable for either. I should like to return to the east end of the Garrotero Mountain and pursue the route I indicate; but it is utterly impossible to do so, as we are now living on berries and herbs. We would rejoice to have mule meat, but we have so few animals, and so many wounded men, that it would be unsafe to kill any more. I have the good fortune of having true men with me, otherwise it would be uncertain that the party could get through; but I have confidence in my men, and I feel positively certain that we will make the trip.

It will take us some ten or twelve days to reach Zuni, where we expect to procure provisions. I shall travel near the mountains, as heretofore, on account of the certainty and facility of getting water, but shall remain in sight of the prairie extending from the Garrotero to the Sierra Blanca mountain.

August 26th.—Moved 10 miles east-north-east, most of the way along a creek, where we found grass in plenty, and some timber. The Apaches Tontos are numerous and troublesome.

August 27th.—Made 15 miles east, crossing two streams which are branches of the Gila. We met Indians to-day, who, I think, are not Apaches Tontos, as they do not speak any Spanish, and [page 93] refuse to answer our questions. We obtained from them over fifteen hundred dollars worth of gold for a few old articles of clothing. The Indians use gold bullets for their guns. They are of different sizes and each Indian has a pouch of them. We saw an Indian load his gun with one large and three small bullets to shoot a rabbit. They proposed exchanging them for the lead, but I preferred trading other articles. Whether the Indians made these balls themselves, or whether they were obtained by the murder of miners in California or Sonora, I am unable to say.

August 28th.—Traveled 10 miles east, over a good country, met with more Indians and traded for some horse-meat, by giving articles of clothing in exchange. We traded also for a few hundred dollars worth of gold. To-day a mule broke down, and an Indian gave me for it a lump of gold weighing a pound and a half less one ounce.

The Indians are so numerous they would destroy the party if we allowed them the least chance. But we are very vigilant, and select camps on elevated places, consequently we are unable to make any examinations for gold in the sands of the country. The Indians call themselves Belenios.

August 29th.—Traveled some twenty miles in an eastern direction; the country quite level, and the land good, with plenty of grass and water.

[*August* 30.—Traveled to-day about fifteen miles east, over a country a little broken. Water and grass abundant.]

August 30*th* [31*st*].—Moved about twelve miles north of east, over a country similar to that of yesterday. Found water, grass and pine timber.

September 1*st*.—Traveled fifteen miles over a country a little broken, and well supplied with water, grass and timber. [The soil was good.]

September 2*d*.—Traveled the same distance north-east to the Sierra Blanca. Followed Indian trails all day, and found grass, water and pine timber in great abundance; and most of the soil is of a superior quality.

September 3*d*.—Pursuing the same course, we traveled some fifteen miles among the same mountains. To-day we passed through valleys of good soil, and we found the pine timber in greater abundance than yesterday. The trees are generally from two and a half to five feet in diameter, and over two hundred feet high. We have seen timber enough to-day to make a railroad from the Eastern States to the Pacific. The passes through this mountain are level, and can be traveled by wagons without any difficulty whatever.

September 4*th*.—Made 25 miles north-east, crossing the Colorado Chiquito after traveling two miles. The land is level and good, and water and wood are plenty.

September 5*th*.—Made 20 miles north-east, and got out of the mountains after traveling five miles; struck the prairie, where we found good soil, grass and water. [page 94]

September 6*th*.—Continuing north-east over a good and level country for 25 miles, we reached the Indian town or pueblo of Zuni, where we met with a hospitable and civilized population, from whom we obtained an abundance of good provisions, over which we greatly rejoiced.

We have subsisted for a month on mule and horse flesh, and for the most part of that time on half or quarter rations. But as I have reached this place with all my men, I feel satisfied. I shall take no notes of the country from this town to Albuquerque on the Rio Grande, as a level and much traveled wagon road exists between the two places, and is familiar to the people of New Mexico. It has been described by others, and is well known to present no difficulties to the construction of a railroad.

September 10*th*.—At Albuquerque, New Mexico. Before laying aside my pencil, for the use of which I have no fancy, I shall set down a few ideas that are now prominent in my recollection

I set out, in the first place, upon this journey, simply to gratify my own curiosity, as to the practicability of one of the much talked of routes for the contemplated Atlantic and Pacific Railroad. Having previously traveled the southern or Gila route, I felt anxious to compare it with the Albuquerque or middle route. Although

I conceive the former to be every way practicable, I now give it as my opinion that the latter is equally so, whilst it has the additional advantage of being more central and serviceable to the Union. I believe the route I traveled is far enough south to be certainly free from the danger of obstruction by snows in winter.

The route, in all its length, may be said to pass over a high plateau, or generally level country, for the most part thickly studded with prairie mountains, or detached elevations, seldom so linked together as to deserve to be called a chain of mountains. Numerous mountains were at all times in sight; but being for the most part isolated peaks, a detour of a few miles would always supersede the necessity of crossing them. To the south of our route from the Great Colorado to Zuni, the country was more level than on the north, and for the greater part of the distance a valley extends nearly due east and west to the Colorado. The existence of so many mountains along the way must be considered, in reference to a railroad, as a very fortunate circumstance instead of a disadvantage, as it is the mountains alone which furnish the timber and never failing water. The plains are only deserts and barren spots, if they are to be called so after the fashion of the day, which exist in all that vast region of country which lies between the Gila on the south and the British Possessions on the north, and the Rio Grande on the east, and the Sierra Nevada of California on the west. The plateau, or table lands, must of course furnish the track upon which the road is to be laid; but the mountains adjacent must furnish the timber to make it, and the water [page 95] for the use of men and animals employed in its construction, and for the use of the depots afterwards.

It is well for the country over which I passed that these mountains exist, as without them it would be in reality one vast and repulsive desert. It would be a disadvantage for a railroad to have to cross them, as, although not difficult to cross, it would much increase the expense. But I saw nothing that rendered it at all probable that they would have to be crossed. On the contrary, I am satisfied that a railroad may be run almost mathematically direct from Zuni to the Colorado, and from thence to the Tejon Pass in California. The section from the Pass to San Francisco should leave the Tular[e] Lake to the west, and should pass through the Coast Range of mountains, say in the neighborhood of San Juan, and thence to San Francisco, and by a branch to Stockton.

The west side of Tular[e] Lake is unfit for a road on account of its miry nature. The section of the route from Zuni to Albuquerque is plain sailing. That from Albuquerque to Independence to St. Louis, or Memphis, is equally plain, by two or three well known passes through the Sandia Mountains, which lie east of the Rio Grande.

Certain slight deviations from the track which I pursued would improve the route. For instance, it would be better to leave my trail to the north, at a point say 180 miles east of the Sierra Nevada, and intersect it again some fifteen miles west of the Colorado. On the east side of the Colorado the road should pursue a directly eastern course for 75 miles, and thence take an east-south-east course for nearly 200 miles, at the foot and on the south side of the mountain inhabited by the Garrotero Indians. Thence north-east for 15 miles, in a prairie between those mountains and a range of mountains which seem to extend to the Gila. From this point, the road should run easterly to the Colorado Chiquito river, and thence north-east to Zuni. The distance from the east end of the Garrotero mountain to Zuni is about 200 miles. This route, as I indicate it, will pass at all times in sight of my trail, and through as practicable a country as any railroad route of the same distance in the United States.

The proposed route by the Sangre de Cristo, north of Taos, I take, if practicable at all, to be very objectionable on account of the vast elevations the road must ascend to and the large quantities of snow which fall and remain there so long during the winter months. This route has also the additional disadvantage of crossing two rivers, the Grand and the Green, either of which would be as costly to bridge as the Colorado.

A route has been somewhat spoken of just north of the Gila, with the view of having a route wholly on American ground. This, I am satisfied, is altogether out of the question, on account of mountains alone, if no other objection existed. The Gila route proper, passing in part through Sonora, is objectionable on sev-[page 96] eral accounts, besides its situation. In the first place, there is no timber upon the plains, nor upon the volcanic mountains that are along the way. A considerable part of the route, too, lies over a country destitute of vegetation, which, when dry, is a white powder, resembling flour, in which the feet of men and animals sink several inches. This same clay, when wet, is the most treacherous of quagmires. Some parts of the road are also very sandy. Don Ambrosio Armijo, who took sheep to California last year, lost as many as eleven hundred among the sand-hills west of Colorado, by sinking in the sand, and being run over by those behind. Another serious objection to the Gila route is the great desert which lies west of the Colorado, and has an extent of 100 miles without wood or water.

I have no interest in recommending one of these routes more than another. I took sheep and wagons to California last year by the Gila route, and I am about to return that way to California again with sheep. Upon the route which I have just traveled, I encountered many hardships and dangers, and met with serious pecuniary loss; yet I say it is the best for a railroad, and would be excellent for ordinary traveling but for the Indians. A large portion of the trail over which I passed—say some 250 miles west from the Rio Grande—is, for the most part, admirably adapted to farming and stock raising.

William M. Gwin, 1853 [+ Gunnison, Beckwith, Whipple, Parke, Pope]

Speeches...On The National Railroad Bill [+ Pacific Railroad Surveys, 1853-54]

Washington, Printed at the Congressional Globe Office, December 12, 1853, 13 p. [WC and WCB 223; Graff 1697; NUC NG 0619615.] Reset from a facsimile, with omission of the Aubry journal given in L2, and of some legislative details; reproduced by permission of The Huntington Library, San Marino, California.

Significance   Senator Gwin from California here embraced the idea that the Pacific railroad should be built from both ends. This paved the political way for the California-incorporated Central Pacific Railroad that was finally adopted in Lincoln's Act of 1862. Gwin initially proposed that the State of California, using land grants, would build branches from San Francisco either north or south, and then east, "to afford a connection with any route that may cross the continent to the Pacific ocean." Gwin wisely did not try to specify the exact route. This may be the first reprint.

In December, 1852, Gwin had offered his first bill, which specified construction of a railroad from San Francisco through Walker Pass to Albuquerque and on to Texas and the Red River. Trying to satisfy all proponents, he projected a western branch to Oregon from the trunk line, and eastern branches to Council Bluffs, St. Louis, Memphis, New Orleans, and Austin. But agreement within the Senate on any specific route was impossible. Congress and President Pierce did, however, on March 3, 1853, authorize Secretary of War Jefferson Davis to make explorations to determine the best route scientifically, and to report back in February, 1854. (Albright 1921.)

Davis sent Gov. Isaac I. Stevens on the northern route from St. Paul to Olympia via passes in Montana; Capt. John W. Gunnison on the central route from Kansas City to Salt Lake City via Colorado's Cochetopa Pass, later extended by Lt. Edward G. Beckwith to northern California; Lt. Amiel W. Whipple on the south-central route from Ft. Smith to Los Angeles via Albuquerque; and Lt. John G. Parke and Capt. John Pope on the southern route from San Diego to Preston, Texas, on Red River, via the lower Gila and Arizona's Apache Pass. Davis also sent Lt. Robert S. Williamson to examine Sierra and Coast Range passes in southern California; these surveys later were extended north through Oregon. No party was sent over the well known north-central route on the Old Oregon Trail via Wyoming's South Pass. See Perspective L, with map.

Capt. Gunnison was killed in Utah by Indians, most likely without any Mormon involvement. Lt. Beckwith made the first detailed surveys of Madeline and Nobles passes in California. Lt. Whipple mapped Bill Williams River in Arizona for the first time. Lt. Parke was the first to map the Apache Pass Trail in southern Arizona and New Mexico. See the Itineraries.

Gwin included in this speech of December 12, 1853, Lt. Williamson's very first report. It contained the bad news that Walker Pass was "almost out of the question." In his 1854 report, Williamson noted that on July 31, 1853, near King's River, "We had the pleasure of meeting on the road Mr. Senator Gwin, returning from a trip to Tejon Pass, where he had been to examine personally the adaptation of the country for a railroad." Gwin's speech also contained a rambling report by Lt. George Stoneman, commander of Williamson's escort, who strongly protested the cruel treatment of the Indians and condemned the white liquor runners and horse thieves. Maj. George Andrews's contribution described a reconnaissance along the Mexican border from San Diego to the mouth of the Gila. Gwin also reprinted Aubry's journal from Tejon Pass to Albuquerque; because this is already given in L2, it is omitted here. Omitted in addition are Gwin's details of his Homestead, Imports, Expense, and Steam Line bills.

Author and Participants WILLIAM MCKENDREE GWIN, 1805-1885, physician, first full-term U. S. Senator from California. Born in Tennessee, Gwin earned an M.D. and was trained in law. After his first wife died, he married the accomplished Mary Bell Logan in 1837. He served as a U.S. marshal and as a U.S. Representative for one term, supervised construction of a custom house in New Orleans, and, because of financial problems, went to California in 1849 for the express purpose of becoming a U.S. Senator. He was a leader in the constitutional convention, voting for a free state in spite of his pro-slavery leanings, and he was indeed elected to the Senate. There he served 1850-55 and 1857-61, the hiatus being caused by political intrigue and infighting in the State Legislature. While in Congress he obtained many federal benefits for California, including a mint, coastal survey, shipyard, lighthouses, Indian agents, a judiciary, and land reforms. He led the successful fight to bury the humanitarian Indian treaties of 1851-52 (see Perspective K). He was a key advocate of the Pacific railroad and the Pony Express. During all this time he still owned slaves on his Mississippi plantation.

At the outbreak of Civil War, Gwin was arrested in Panama as a Southern sympathizer and briefly imprisoned in New York in late 1861. In 1863 he went to France, where he interested Napoleon III in a scheme to settle Sonora with Southerners and to exploit its mines. He wrote his brother in 1864, "I intend to reverse my action in California. I went there determined not to make money, but to devote all my energies to obtaining and maintaining political power. Now I go for money, and shall let power alone." Gwin went twice from France to Mexico, but the intrigues of Napoleon and Maximilian doomed the project. Upon his return to the States, Gwin was arrested again and imprisoned for eight months. Released, he spent two years of exile in France and then returned to California to recoup his fortune in deep gold mining. He was in New York, promoting a railroad across Panama, when he died of pneumonia. (Steele 1969 with quote; Stanley 1971; DAB; NCAB; ACAB; Thrapp; Congress; Bancroft 24:284-85; Lamar.)

JOHN WILLIAMS GUNNISON, 1812-1853, topographical engineer. A New Hampshire farm boy, school teacher, and 1837 graduate of West Point, Gunnison served twice in the Seminole Wars and helped remove the Cherokees to Indian Territory. He married Martha A. Delony in 1841. As a topographical engineer he made surveys in Georgia and around the Great Lakes. In 1849-50 he explored the Great Salt Lake with Capt. Howard Stansbury (5:J3) and wrote his book on the Mormons. After working again near the Great Lakes, in 1853 he led the railroad survey on the central route to Sevier Lake, Utah, where he was killed by Indians. (DAB; NCAB; ACAB; Thrapp; McHenry; Mumey 1955; Ewan; Heitman; Cullum 892; see Itinerary.)

EDWARD GRIFFIN BECKWITH, 1818-1881, soldier, Civil War general. A New York native and 1842 graduate of West Point, Beckwith served in the artillery in the Mexican War, escorted the customs collector overland to San Francisco in 1849, and during 1853-54 surveyed the central route for the Pacific railroad. In the Civil War he was chief of commissariat for Union campaigns in Virginia and Louisiana, and he commanded the defenses of New Orleans for a time. He was brevetted a brigadier general. After the war he was in the subsistence department. (ACAB; Ewan; Heitman; Cullum 1123; see Itinerary.)

JOHN GRUBB PARKE, 1827-1900, topographical engineer, Civil War general. Born in Pennsylvania and graduated from West Point in 1849, Parke surveyed the Iowa-Minnesota boundary, the Little Colorado (now the Red) River of northern

New Mexico, and the southern route for the Pacific railroad. Before and after the Civil War, he was chief surveyor in marking the northwest U.S. boundary with Canada. During the war he served with distinction in many battles in North Carolina, Maryland, Virginia, Kentucky, Tennessee, and Mississippi. He received the brevet of major general. Later he was in the corps of engineers, and he superintended the Military Academy before his retirement in 1889. (NCAB; ACAB; Heitman; Cullum 1408; see Itinerary.)

JOHN POPE, 1822-1892, topographical engineer, Civil War general. Originally from Kentucky, Pope was appointed from Illinois to the West Point class of 1842. As a topographical engineer he soon exasperated Col. John J. Abert by pulling political strings in attempts to get preferred posts. He went on leave to recover from syphilis. After surveying in Florida and Maine, he fought with coolness at Monterrey and Buena Vista. He did not get along with his commander on the 1849 expedition to the Red River of the North. Abraham Lincoln gave the eulogy when Pope's father died in 1850. Pope surveyed in New Mexico 1851-53, writing reports criticizing his superiors. "Pope, as usual, held a magnifying glass to his own achievements and a minifying glass to those of others."

After his 1854 railroad reconnaissance on the southern route, Pope experimented inconclusively with drilling artesian wells on the Llano Estacado. In 1859 he married Clara Horton and worked on Great Lakes lighthouses. In early 1861 he was one of the escort on Lincoln's train to Washington. In late 1861 he won a small battle in Missouri, and in early 1862 he brilliantly opened the Mississippi around New Madrid. After other successful actions, as a major general he was decisively defeated at Second Bull Run, August 27-30, 1862. With some justification he blamed the disaster on lack of timely support from Gen. George B. McClellan and others. Pope was banished to Minnesota to fight Indians, which he did with mixed results. Initially he was for extermination, but as commander of various departments after the war he tried to reduce the bloodshed and promote assimilation. Few of his proposed reforms were carried into effect. He retired in 1886. (Schutz and Trenerry 1990 with quote; Ellis 1970; DAB; NCAB; ACAB; McHenry; Thrapp; Lamar; Heitman; Cullum 1127; see Itinerary.)

ROBERT STOCKTON WILLIAMSON, 1824-1882, topographical engineer. A New York native and 1848 graduate of West Point, Williamson engaged in railroad surveys near the Pacific coast. He was with Capt. William H. Warner, who was killed in northeast California in 1849. He examined routes and passes in California and Oregon and made weather observations on the coast during the 1850s. In the Civil

War he was chief topographical engineer for Union operations in North Carolina, the Army of the Potomac, and the Department of the Pacific. Afterward he worked on Pacific harbor, river, and fort projects. He retired as a lieutenant colonel shortly before his death. (ACAB; Ewan; Heitman; Cullum 1373.)

GEORGE STONEMAN, 1822-1894, cavalryman, Civil War general, governor of California. Stoneman was born in New York and graduated from West Point in 1846. He went to California as quartermaster for the Mormon Battalion, scouted and skirmished with Indians 1848-52, and escorted the Pacific railroad surveys of Williamson and Parke. After 1854 he was on frontier duty in Texas. He refused to surrender to a seceding superior at the outbreak of the Civil War, seized a steamer, and escaped to the North with most of his men. During the war he saw extensive action commanding cavalry units and making daring raids behind enemy lines; near Atlanta, while leading the rear guard protecting the return of his troops, he was captured and paroled. Brevetted a major general, after the war he married Mary Hardisty and commanded Richmond and then the Department of Arizona until his disability retirement in 1871. He had a fine estate near Los Angeles, served as railway commissioner, and became governor 1883-87. (DAB; NCAB; ACAB; McHenry; Thrapp; Heitman; Cullum 1304.)

GEORGE PEARCE ANDREWS, ca. 1821-1887, soldier. From Connecticut, Andrews went into the artillery after graduating from West Point in 1845. He was brevetted a major for gallantry in action at Mexico City in 1847. He was in California 1848-53 and 1856-59, and in Indian Territory 1854-55. He was with the expedition against the Snake Indians in 1860 (5:J17). During the Civil War he served in the defense of Washington, D. C., and in California. Afterward he commanded artillery at posts in the South and in New England until his retirement as a colonel in 1885. (Heitman; Cullum 1245.)

Itinerary, 1853   STEVENS, ST. PAUL TO OLYMPIA, VIA CADOTTE AND MULLAN PASSES MT (48TH PARALLEL). Isaac I. Stevens with a party of 111 leaves St. Paul MN June 6 and reaches Olympia WA November 25. Excluding 46 days in long layovers, he travels 1,840 miles at 14 miles per day in 127 days, which still include about 15 percent rest days. Details are in 2:D10.

Itinerary, 1853   EMIGRANTS, MISSOURI RIVER TO SACRAMENTO, VIA SOUTH PASS WY (42ND PARALLEL). Although considered to be too well known for an official railroad survey, this prime route, which is the closest of any to the final Union Pacific path, is included here for comparison. Emigrants cover the 1,870 miles via Salt Lake City at 15 miles per day in 127 days. See K5 for these numbers.

Itinerary, 1853   GUNNISON–BECKWITH, KANSAS CITY TO SALT LAKE CITY, VIA COCHETOPA PASS CO (38TH PARALLEL). June 23—Capt. John W. Gunnison leads the party out of Westport (Kansas City). Lt. Edward G. Beckwith is second in command; Richard H. Kern, topographer; Sheppard Homans, astronomer; Dr. Jacob H. Schiel, surgeon and geologist; Frederick Creutzfeldt, botanist; James A. Snyder, assistant topographer; and John Bellows, personal servant to Gunnison. Capt. Robert M. Morris and Lt. Laurence S. Baker command the escort of 30 Mounted Riflemen. Civilian teamsters and employees manage the 16 wagons, instrument carriage, ambulance, and animals. Gunnison mutters, "such a muss as fifty Jackasses of brutes and a dozen of asses of men can make" (Hine 1962). The party divides for awhile, Beckwith following the Santa Fe Trail, while Gunnison goes through Ft. Riley on a parallel track 30 miles to the north. July 13—Reunited, they leave present Great Bend KS to ascend the Arkansas. Schiel bemoans "a national plague here in the mosquitoes…the little bloodthirsty monsters always found some opening through which they could reach their victims;" he finds poison ivy to be "a plague of a more serious character," which almost incapacitates young Homans.

July 16 through 18—They stop at Ft. Atkinson, built of sod near today's Dodge City. After a buffalo hunt, Schiel remarks that "Future generations will know the buffalo only from museum examples." He finds that "The meat of the prairie dog has a loathsome taste." July 29—They pass the ruins of Bent's Old Fort. Farther up the Arkansas, Schiel picks four scorpions out of his bedroll with a long pincers. A soldier finds a coiled rattlesnake under his saddle-pillow in the morning. August 13—After ascending the Apishapa and Huerfano rivers, they cross between the Culebra and Sangre de Cristo ranges at what is now called North La Veta Pass. It takes four days to chop a way through 12 miles of willow thickets on Sangre de Cristo Creek. Gunnison thinks the pass is practicable for a railroad, but Kern privately disagrees. August 19 through 22—They pause at Ft. Massachusetts, established the year before 6 miles north of present Ft. Garland CO, until Beckwith returns from a side trip to Taos to fetch a competent guide, Antoine Leroux. Beckwith acknowledges "the necessity of profiting by the practical lessons in geography gained in the school of the trapper and hunter."

September 2—North Cochetopa Pass. The expedition has come north by the Great Sand Dunes, then west across San Luis Creek and up Saguache Creek. Beckwith thinks that a railroad "will require a tunnel…of not less than two miles in length." Gunnison's barometer indicates that the "height of the summit itself is 10,032 feet," only 117 feet low. The party descends West Pass, Cochetopa, Razor, and Tomichi creeks to reach the Gunnison River at present Gunnison CO on the 6th. They skirt the south side of the Gunnison and its monumental Black Canyon. Beckwith quotes Gunnison as judging the country "the roughest, most hilly, and most 'cut up,' he had ever seen." Schiel records, "The wagons had to be dragged up steep mountains and to be let down the steeper slopes with ropes; rocky roads had to be cut through, ravines gone around, and strong mountain streams crossed…During the whole time an unusual cheerfulness engendered by the pure mountain air reigned among the men and was expressed in loud, vigorous laughing." They hit the Uncompahgre near modern Montrose, descend it to today's Delta, and thence go down the Gunnison to cross the Colorado at what is now Grand Junction, September 19. Leroux leaves on the 25th to return to Taos to join Whipple's expedition.

September 30—Gunnison reaches Green River near the present town of Green River UT, having left the north bank of the Colorado near the mouth of Westwater Creek to follow the base of the Book Cliffs. From Green River he starts on the Old Spanish Trail but soon leaves it to loop north almost to present Wellington, and then back southwest to rejoin the Old Spanish Trail south of today's Castle Dale, October 10. On the 8th Gunnison learns from an Indian that the Utes are at war with the Mormons. The route continues southwest and then winds west through the Wasatch Plateau, first along the Old Spanish Trail and modern Interstate 70, then south of these, to reach the Sevier River near Salina on the 17th. In terms of present landmarks, they follow the Sevier north through Gunnison to Interstate 15, turn southwest on it to Holden, and then turn northwest to intersect the Sevier again near Delta on the 24th.

On the way on October 9 Gunnison goes off to Manti, which is forted up against the Utes in the Walker War, and picks up two Mormon guides, George G. and William Potter. Gunnison writes his wife, "There is a war between the Mormons & the Indians & parties of less than a dozen do not dare to travel. We did not know what a risk we have lately been running until coming here, for I have been riding carelessly in the mountains hunting roads ahead and other curious capers…May the favor of Heaven attend us until the work is accomplished" (Mumey 1955). On the 22d Gunnison makes another side trip to Fillmore. Beckwith reports later that Gunnison returns from this visit with "an unusual feeling of security" about the Indians known to be near. He apparently feels safe with a dozen men. He will bet his life on this number.

October 25—Gunnison splits the party. He leads 11 men 11 miles southwest down the Sevier, intending to survey Sevier Lake. He makes camp about 6 miles west of present Deseret. The men are Kern, Creutzfeldt, Mormon guide William Potter, John Bellows, and a corporal and six privates from the escort. Beckwith's report quotes Gunnison's journal, "we met with sloughs alive with geese, ducks, brant, pelicans and gulls. A few hawks were careering in the high wind, and the black-eared and black-tailed rabbits were very numerous in the large artemisia." (Fur hunter Daniel Potts, 1:B7, was here in 1827 and called the Sevier "Rabbit River.") Beckwith and the rest of the party head northeast up the Sevier to map its canyon.

October 26—In spite of the night guard, about 30 Utes closely surround Gunnison's camp and attack at daybreak. Gunnison is hit with 15 arrows, his body disemboweled, and his left arm severed at the elbow. Kern has one bullet through the heart. Creutzfeldt is shot and beheaded. The bodies of Potter, Bellows, and three privates are stripped, mutilated, and later partly devoured by wolves. Four soldiers escape to alert Beckwith and Morris. It is about 10 days before Mormons bury what is left of the bodies and recover most of the papers and instruments.

Beckwith heads north on November 1 through Nephi, Payson, and Provo to reach Salt Lake City on the 8th. The party has traveled 1,568 miles in 139 days, surveying and road building, averaging 11 miles per day. They have spent about 30 layover days in camp. Itinerary is from Beckwith 1854, Schiel 1859, Mumey 1955, Weber 1985, and Fielding 1993. Edward F. Beale and Gwinn H. Heap are from one to three months ahead of Gunnison on the central route to Utah (5:J9). Some California emigrants with wagons have followed a week or two behind Gunnison.

COMMENT. Gunnison had written in his 1852 book on the Mormons, "from the descriptions given me by them [mountaineers], the best [railroad] route from Utah lies through the passes to Seveir [Sevier] Lake, and south-west to the depression in the Sierra Nevada north of Los Angeles, where the Tulare valleys are entered, and from which a port is to be selected on the Pacific…This wonderfully level track across the country strikes the mind with surprise…while the immense mountains are ever before and around him." Gunnison's original orders from Secretary of War Jefferson Davis were to explore through Cochetopa Pass to Mountain Meadows, thence north to Utah Lake, thence back east to Ft. Laramie.

It seems likely that only Indians perpetrated the Gunnison Massacre near Sevier Lake. The Indians confessed and did not implicate Mormons, except as later alleged by the unreliable Judge W. W. Drummond. A Mormon guide died at Gunnison's side. Had Mormons been involved, their guilt would doubtless have surfaced immediately, as it did after the Mountain Meadows Massacre. (See 4:G9; Ute Chief Kanosh steadfastly refused to join the Mormons in that attack.

Fielding in 1993 delved deeply into the records, raised many questions, but found no smoking gun; in the process he did, however, unearth stunning evidence against the Mormons at Mountain Meadows.) Beckwith, though uncertain at first, because the Mormons and Utes seemed so friendly, finally concluded that the newspaper charges that Mormons abetted the Indians against Gunnison were "entirely false." He reported that Chief Kanosh "deeply regretted the tragedy; that it was done without authority, by the young men." To be sure, Mormon reports at Fillmore of a new peace agreement may have helped to lull an uncautious Gunnison into a false sense of security. And, apparently to maintain that peace, the Mormons obstructed punishment of the guilty (5:J10 Highlights).

The day after he arrived at Salt Lake City, Beckwith prepared a very accurate account of the Massacre that was first published in the *Deseret News* of November 12, 1853. Editor Willard Richards in that issue bore "tribute to the memory of Captain Gunnison, as a gentleman of high and fine toned feeling." In a claim still debated, Richards said that the Massacre "was entirely unconnected with the late Indian difficulties, but was the direct result of the foolish, and reckless conduct of a party of emigrants" who killed a Ute.

Itinerary, 1854 BECKWITH, SALT LAKE CITY TO FT. READING CA, VIA MADELINE AND NOBLES PASSES (41ST PARALLEL). May 6—Lt. Edward G. Beckwith's party leaves the Jordan River at Salt Lake City. He has with him those left after the Gunnison Massacre, including Sheppard Homans, Jacob H. Schiel, James A. Snyder, and Capt. Robert M. Morris and Lt. Laurence S. Baker of the escort. Also along is the excellent topographer, Baron Friedrich W. Egloffstein, who has been recuperating in Salt Lake City from Fremont's Fifth Expedition (L6). Before this departure to the west, Beckwith in April has explored eastward to Ft. Bridger, going via the Weber River and returning via the Provo ("Timpanogos") River.

May 18—They go by Goshute Lake NV, having passed present Grantsville, the south end of Great Salt Lake at the Stansbury Mountains, Granite Peak in the Great Salt Lake Desert, and Ochre Mountain, all in Utah. Beckwith finds the Gosiute Indians, "Diggers" of Shoshone stock, starving after the long winter, when "their supply of rats and bugs fail…they are doubtless among the lowest of the human race in intelligence and humanity." Beckwith next takes a long detour northwest to explore Secret Pass at the north end of the Ruby Mountains on the 23d. Not being able to take the wagons through, he turns back south along the base of the Rubys, crossing them on the 28th by the Overland Pass of the Hastings Cutoff (2:D7). Thence he threads his way northwest through the ranges, parallel to and about 30 miles south of the great bend of the Humboldt, until he cuts north to that river at modern Mill City NV on June 8.

June 10—Lassen's Meadows, now the Rye Patch Reservoir. From here they go southwest to the south end of the Seven Troughs Range, thence northwest to the Mud Lakes west of present Gerlach NV, June 16. Here Smoke Creek issues from the foot of Madeline Pass at the base of the Sierra. In his discovery of Madeline Pass, Beckwith actually circles around from the north to descend Smoke Creek, then ascends it back through the pass to Observation Peak and today's Ravendale CA. He continues northwest across the Madeline Plains to the second part of Madeline Pass south of modern Adin. Then he curves west and southwest, crossing the Lassen Trail, and following the Pit River northwest to the mouth of Fall River (present Fall River Mills), June 29. The route ahead down Pit River is rough, and he plans to come at it later from the opposite direction. So to check out Nobles Pass (5:J8) he heads south-southeast on the Lassen Trail to join Nobles Trail, now California Highway 44, which leads east through the pass to where Isaac N. Roop is building a cabin that is the beginning of Susanville. Beckwith proceeds on east to the shore of Honey Lake at modern Wendel, July 5. He then goes back west past Roop's and follows Nobles Trail (Highway 44) through today's Old Station and Viola, and on to Shingletown. From here he travels due west to Ft. Reading on Cow Creek near the Sacramento River, about 10 miles southeast of the center of modern Redding CA, July 12.

On this intricate path, Beckwith explores a minimum of 950 miles in 68 days, averaging 14 miles per day. His time includes about 10 layover days, during which he usually is making further explorations. Itinerary is from Beckwith's 41st Parallel Report of 1854.

Itinerary, 1853-54 WHIPPLE, FT. SMITH TO LOS ANGELES, VIA ALBUQUERQUE (35TH PARALLEL). July 15, 1853—Lt. Amiel Whipple leaves Ft. Smith AR. With him are John M. Bigelow, surgeon and botanist; Jules Marcou, geologist; Albert H. Campbell, engineer; Heinrich Balduin Mollhausen, topographer and artist; seven scientific assistants; and 12 six-mule wagons with the necessary teamsters and helpers. Lt. Joseph C. Ives and Dr. Caleb B. R. Kennerly start earlier from San Antonio to set up an astronomical station, but they reach Albuquerque after Whipple does. The main party closely follows the 1849 track of Simpson and Marcy (5:J5), which will also be Beale's 1858 route (5:J18).

July 26—They leave present Spiro OK, having waited 8 of the first 11 days for equipment and for the escort of 70 soldiers under Lt. John M. Jones. Their route parallels the Canadian River, 10 to 15 miles to its south, through modern

McAlester, Atwood, and Ada to Byers, then called Beaversville. Here the celebrated Delaware guide, Chief Black Beaver, lives on the Canadian. Mollhausen records Black Beaver's speech: "Seven times have I seen the Pacific ocean at various points; I have accompanied the Americans in three wars, and I have brought home more scalps from my hunting expeditions than one of you could lift. I should like to see the salt water for the eighth time; but I am sick…if I die, I should like to be buried by my own people." The expedition stays in Beaversville August 17 through 21 but cannot procure a guide.

September 21—They camp near today's Tucumcari NM. They have traveled along and south of the Canadian, in terms of present towns from Purcell to Weatherford to Durham OK, and on past Canadian, Borger, and Amarillo TX. They proceed on west from Tucumcari to Anton Chico. Mollhausen describes the inevitable fandango: "We danced, and sang, and laughed, and drank, and did not go home till morning, but then, happily, without the mirth having been interrupted by any quarrels, or broken heads, which was the more praiseworthy, as waggoners and soldiers (among the latter specimens from all the nations of Europe) had thought proper to join in the revels, and that moreover with unsteady feet and cloudy brains."

October 3—The main body passes around the south end of the Sandia Mountains into Albuquerque. They have traveled 769 miles at 11 miles per day in 69 days, including 10 layovers but excluding 8 days waiting for the escort and 4 looking for guides in Beaversville. While awaiting supplies in Albuquerque, Whipple compiles data on the route ahead from the expeditions of Lorenzo Sitgreaves in 1851 (5:J6), Joseph R. Walker in 1851 (L2 note), and Francois X. Aubry in 1853 (L2); Beale, 5:J18, will in 1857 follow much of Whipple's path. Mollhausen soon makes friends with the dragoons stationed in Albuquerque: "In the Far West, acquaintances are very quickly made; questions, explanations, stories of adventures, are interchanged, as if they would never come to an end…We obtained on the very first day…the names of the streets, which certainly were not very numerous, as well as of the still fewer persons of distinction, and above all, of every handsome señorita."

November 9—Part of the group leaves the west bank of the Rio Grande opposite Albuquerque for Isleta and Laguna. The whole command will soon amount to 114 or 116, with the addition of 25 dragoons under Lt. John Tidball, more teamsters for the 16 wagons, and guide Antoine Leroux. Mollhausen observes about Leroux, "the confidence which he inspired,—a confidence that had been gained by thirty years' toil in primeval wildernesses—made us all rejoice not a little at having secured his services." They also have 50 pack animals, a flock of sheep, and some oxen and cows for subsistence. November 18—They camp at El Morro, or Inscription Rock, where Mollhausen writes, "There is a strange and even solemn feeling in standing thus before these mouldering and half-illegible, but still venerable, relics of past times." November 20 through 27—They are near Zuni, whose people are being ravaged by smallpox. During this time Campbell scouts out a good route to the north, which will be used by the Santa Fe Railroad through Grants and Gallup NM to Holbrook AZ.

November 28—They head west from Zuni, strike the Puerco River near modern Pinta AZ, and follow what is now Interstate 40 and the Santa Fe Railroad through Petrified Forest National Park, Holbrook, and Winslow. They continue northwest down the Little Colorado to today's Leupp, then cross west to Leroux Springs near Flagstaff, where they camp and reconnoiter from December 27, 1853, through about January 4, 1854. Enroute, Mollhausen records that nine men have smallpox, and word comes that the Hopis are devastated by this disease: "An adverse fate certainly seems to pursue the original inhabitants of the American continent in every way." The explorers marvel at the giant petrified trees; they find anthills full of small garnets; the mules stampede; they see impressive ruins and go three days without water; they enjoy Christmas punch in the snow near the foot of the San Francisco Mountains; and they heat blocks of lava in the fire and then roll them into their tents for warmth at night.

January 31, 1854—Whipple is at the north end of the Aquarius Mountains on modern Interstate 40, about 23 miles due south of Peach Springs AZ. His track goes west from present Flagstaff through Williams to Ash Fork, thence southwest to cross the Juniper Mountains 28 miles south of Seligman, thence northwest to the Aquarius location. Here they lighten the loads. To find a more gradual descent to the Colorado, Whipple turns south down Big Sandy River on the west flank of the Aquarius Mountains through present Wickieup and Signal, then west on Bill Williams River, after a delay of 6 days. Mollhausen says, "Not a day went by without our having to shoot, or leave behind, some of them [cattle]; and one waggon after another was abandoned...our flocks of sheep were diminishing rapidly...the rations of flour had been diminished one half." After the hard going in narrow canyons, only two wagons remain when they reach the Colorado on February 20, and these are left two days later. They now have only a small spring carriage for the odometer and other instruments as they ascend the east bank of the Colorado.

February 27—They cross the Colorado just below today's Needles CA, using an inflatable canvas boat brought along for this purpose. On the way they meet Chemehuevis and Mohaves. Mollhausen notes, "whenever one of us bearded fellows rode past them, the women burst into a fit of laughter, and put their hands before their mouths, as if the sight of us rather tended to make them sick." With Mohave guides Cairook and Ireteba, the expedition proceeds west, parallel to and about 20 miles north of Interstate 40, past Hackberry Mountain and Kelso Peak. They go on south of Soda Lake to intersect the Old Spanish Trail on the Mojave River about 20 miles east of modern Barstow, March 13. Mollhausen remarks that the few "springs were so hidden in the mountains, that had it not been for our guides were should certainly have passed them, and our doing so would in all probability have led to our destruction." Members of the party keep giving the guides clothes in thanks, all of which are donned, "so that they now looked like wandering bundles of old clothes." The guides here return home.

March 16—Cajon Pass, north of San Bernardino, in the rain. March 21—Los Angeles, where they auction off the expedition property. From Albuquerque they go 880 miles at 8 miles per day in 112 days, excluding 7 extra days at Zuni and 8 at Leroux Springs and 6 on Bill Williams River, but still including 19 layover days. From Ft. Smith they go 1,649 miles at 9 miles per day in 181 days, including 29 layovers, but excluding 33 waiting days. Itinerary is from Whipple 1855, Mollhausen 1853-54, Sherburne 1853-54, and Foreman 1941. In addition to his itinerary, Whipple writes an extensive report on the Indian tribes.

Itinerary, 1854   PARKE, SAN DIEGO TO DONA ANA (32D PARALLEL). January 24—Lt. John G. Parke leaves San Diego with 55 others, including Henry Custer, topographer; Dr. A. L. Heermann, physician and naturalist; Lt. George Stoneman and 28 dragoons; 18 teamsters and helpers; 5 scientific assistants; and one other. They take the usual Southern Emigrant Trail through Warner's Ranch and Ft. Yuma (see 5:J7) to camp February 15 on the Gila about 10 miles east of the Pima Villages, which are near present Sacaton AZ southeast of Phoenix. Distance to this point is 390 miles, traveled without doing any surveying. From here on, Parke's orders are to move fast, getting barometric heights for a profile, but mapping with only compass and odometer. February 16—Parke leaves the vicinity of the Pima Villages on Cooke's Wagon Road (the Southern Trail, 3:E6) and on the 20th reaches Tucson, where the commandant shows him two large meteorites used as anvils.

February 22—Parke leaves Tucson east on the Apache Pass Trail, which coincides with Cooke's Road as far as modern Benson on the San Pedro River. After passing south of Wilcox Playa, on March 2 they reach Apache Pass, where Ft. Bowie will be built in 1862 between the Chiricahua and Dos Cabezas mountains. They head east into New Mexico, cross the Peloncillo Mountains, and turn northeast to rejoin Cooke's Road at the gentle Continental Divide 30 miles due east of today's Lordsburg, March 6. "A joking teamster remarked, 'Here is your country for a railroad.'" March 8 through 9—At the crossing of the Mimbres near what is now City of Rocks State Park, Parke learns that the buildings at Ft. Webster, 20 miles north, have just been burned by the Indians. He does not know that the Army abandoned the fort on December 20, 1853; "This whole affair is wrapped in uncertainty." March 10—Cooke's Peak.

March 12—After coming east-southeast from Cooke's Peak, they strike the Rio Grande about opposite Doña Ana, which is 6 miles north of the center of modern Las Cruces NM. Parke in this dry season has found only 9 permanent sources of water from Tucson on. From San Diego, he has traveled 753 miles at 16 miles per day in 48 days, which include about 15 percent layover days. Itinerary is from Parke 1854.

COMMENT. Parke's original orders from Jefferson Davis, illustrated by a sketch, were from the "Pima village" to "follow the line by Tucson, thence by the blue line marked Nugent's wagon trail." Parke observed in his report, "While in San Francisco I had the good fortune to meet Mr. [John] Nugent, and am much indebted to him for a copy of his notes made during a trip across this country." Nugent's trip of 1849 was led by Texas Ranger Col. John Coffee Hays, then an Indian agent, who pioneered the Apache Pass Trail westward with 150 argonauts using wagons. Nugent later wrote that guide Antoine Leroux in 1846 had warned Lt. Col. Philip St. George Cooke and the Mormon Battalion (3:E6) that "water was not to be had on a due west course." Nugent said simply, "We took a risk, however, and followed a due west course." Nugent added his opinion of the label *Nugent's Wagon Road:* "I was not at all entitled to the credit, Hays being the leader of the party and having all the responsibility resting on him." (Greer 1952.)

On his map published in 1848 with Emory's *Military Reconnoissance,* Cooke had dotted the Apache Pass Trail across a blank area and labeled it, "Believed by Mr. Leroux to be an open prairie & a good route, if water is found sufficient."

Itinerary, 1854   POPE, DONA ANA TO PRESTON TX ON RED RIVER (32D PARALLEL). February 12—Capt. John Pope, engineer Lt. Kenner Garrard, Lt. Louis H. Marshall with the escort of 25 infantry soldiers, mineralogist and former Captain Charles L. Taplin, surgeon and naturalist Dr. W. S. Diffendorfer, computer John H. Byrne, and teamsters and herders, 75 in all, head east from Doña Ana NM. They have 8 six-mule wagons, 16 beeves, and 70 sheep. The diary of Byrne states, "The party found it impossible to obtain a guide, or to collect any information in reference to our route." This is a very surprising statement, because they know that Capt. Randolph B. Marcy was over almost all of the route in 1849 (5:J5), and Lts. Francis T. Bryan and Nathaniel Michler (5:J4) traversed parts of it that year, and all published their reports and maps in 1850. Many an emigrant also passed this way. Pope's party follows in Marcy's footsteps through San Augustin Pass at the north end of the Organ Mountains, thence going southeast to the Hueco Tanks in Texas. They stay at the Tanks, natural reservoirs in granite, February 17 through 21, waiting on wagon wheels sent to El Paso for repair.

February 22—The party moves eastward from Hueco Tanks, back into New Mexico through the Cornudas Mountains, then again into Texas to Guadalupe Pass south of the Guadalupe Mountains, March 1. They follow Delaware Creek to the Pecos, just back into New Mexico, March 8. They camp here through March 18, while Taplin explores east across the Llano Estacado, Garrard backtracks to check for other passes near the Guadalupe, and Marshall goes north up the Pecos. Meanwhile, Indians set the prairie afire upwind from base camp; the party successfully counters with a backfire. March 24—After descending the Pecos, they go over it at Marcy's Emigrant Crossing about 10 miles east of today's town of Pecos TX. They follow Marcy's track northeast through the sand hills and past modern Monaghans, Odessa, and Midland to Big Spring, March 31. Enroute, wolves stampede and carry off the remaining 32 sheep.

April 2 through 11—They lay over to reconnoiter at Sulphur Springs near present Lamesa, having left Marcy's track at Big Spring to come 40 miles northwest. They proceed east past future Snyder to rejoin Marcy's route near today's Rotan on the 17th. Thence they go on past what are now Hamlin and Stamford, add a skunk to their natural history collections, meet some California emigrants, and pause at Ft. Belknap near present Newcastle on April 27th. They march on past today's Olney and Shannon (where they regroup April 29 through May 6), Bowie, and Gainesville, and pass through the Cross Timbers to reach Preston (north of Sherman) on May 15. "In anticipation of our speedy arrival at Preston, our razors were brought into active requisition; beards of the most patriarchal cut were trimmed down to ordinary dimensions, or totally demolished, and the cherished moustache disappeared beneath the ruthless hand of the barber. These operations caused much pain and many an expression of regret." They have traveled about 840 miles at 13 miles per day in 63 days, including 4 layovers but excluding the 30 days in the long stopovers of 4, 10, 9, and 7 days. Itinerary is from Pope 1854.

Miscellany   In his letter in Gwin's speech, Williamson's Cañada de las Uvas ("Uras") is today's Grapevine Creek leading to Lebec, Tejon Pass, Gorman, and Gorman Creek, about 70 miles north of Los Angeles on Interstate 5. On his map, what he calls "Tejon Pass" is between Tejon and Cottonwood creeks, 22 miles east-northeast of what is now called Tejon Pass. Ft. Tejon was established in 1854 in the Cañada de las Uvas near today's Lebec. Williamson's "Cañada de San Arminio" is now San Emigdio Creek 10 miles west of Grapevine Creek. His "Depot Camp" was on Poso ("Pose") Creek 10 miles north of present Bakersfield.

Stoneman's Tulare Valley is the southern extension of the San Joaquin Valley. Ft. Miller was established in 1851 on the San Joaquin River at modern Millerton Lake north of Fresno. Southward, Stoneman mentioned Kings River, Tule ("Tula") River, Kern River at today's Bakersfield, and Kern and Buena Vista lakes ("Tula lakes"). Williamson did not map Stoneman's "passes of San Francisco and Walker's" through the Coast Range west of Tejon; this different Walker's Pass was named for Ute Chief Walker from the Sevier ("Severn") River in Utah. Chief Walker was an expert horse thief, and rancher Isaac Williams, among others, paid him tribute. Jurupa was a small Mormon town near present Riverside.

Andrews's journey went from San Diego pretty much along the border with Mexico, through Tecate and Jacumba ("Jacum"), which still exist, to the mouth of the Gila, an estimated 165 miles. This compares to the 148-mile direct distance (Andrews misremembered it as 141) from the Pacific along the boundary as surveyed by Lt. Edmund L. F. Hardcastle in 1849; the usual route via Warner's Ranch is closer to 217 miles long (5:J7).

Legacy   The Pacific railroad surveys were scientifically and politically indecisive. Although they were backed by previous explorations and the discoveries of fur hunters and emigrants, and they at least mentioned the more viable options, their evaluation was incomplete and injudicious. Beckwith's 41st-parallel recommendation in part came close to the ultimate Central and Union Pacific route. Although he explored too far north in California, he advocated the line along the Humboldt past Salt Lake City to Ft. Bridger; "This route is intended to connect, in the vicinity of Fort Bridger…with that explored thence eastward by Bridger's Pass to the Plains, by Captain Stansbury [5:J3]…by descending Lodge Pole creek, the South fork, and main Platte, to the Missouri." In California, Beckwith made the mistake of trying to break new ground rather than following the established emigrant trail. Similarly, his actual path through Nevada was much more tortuous than the Humboldt road.

Stevens's party found Mullan Pass, used later by the Northern Pacific. Whipple and his predecessors blazed part of the way for the Santa Fe Railway. Parke surveyed much of the future Southern Pacific route. Williamson did a good job in southern California. The three passes that he liked best—San Gorgonio, Soledad, and Tehachapi—all now have railroads through them. His next favored passes were the Cajon, which now carries a railroad, and the Tejon ("Cañada de las Uvas"), which has an Interstate highway. The passes that he condemned, including Walker, are not now the major thoroughfares.

Jefferson Davis's first 1854 report was incomplete. His 1855 summary report revealed the strengths and weaknesses of his survey plans. He declared the southern or 32d-parallel route to be the shortest and cheapest, with the best roadbed and climate, and with the fewest tunnels and ups and downs. He did acknowledge the scarcity of water, timber, and fuel, however. He properly declared the central route and its Cochetopa Pass to be wholly "impracticable." But he summarily dismissed the future path of the Union Pacific, simply because he had not ordered it surveyed: "Another route, by the South fork [of the Platte] and a tributary called Lodge Pole creek, has been suggested by Capt. Stansbury as shorter and less expensive [than the route via South Pass]; but the information respecting it is not sufficiently full to make further mention of it necessary." Nor did his surveyors have the perceptions of a Theodore D. Judah to see the suitability of the Truckee River and Donner Pass, long since heralded by emigrants.

Northerners were not about to accept a southern route, so all the work ended in continued impasse until the Civil War removed the influence of the South. See Perspective L.

REFERENCES
(See Preface for Heading and Author references not listed here.)

Albright, George L., 1921, Official explorations for Pacific railroads 1853-55: Berkeley, p. 29-43.

Beckwith, Edward G., 1854 (1855 pub.), Explorations for a route for the Pacific railroad near the 38th and 39th parallels, in Reports of Explorations and Surveys: Wash., 33/2 ("33/3") H91, serial 792, 2:1-128, quotes on trapper 39, height 47, tunnel 48, roughest 51, rabbits 72, security 73, false 74, Kanosh 75-76; mileage table 94-107; Exploration on 41st parallel, 2:1-95, quote on rats and bugs 24, Stansbury 59; mileage table 67-69; maps in v. 11.

Davis, Jefferson, 1853, Report of the Secretary of War: Wash., 33/1 H1, serial 691, Gunnison orders p. 57-58; quote from Parke orders 62.

Davis, Jefferson, 1854, Report of the Secretary of War; copies of all reports...for a railroad...that have been received at the department: Wash., 33/1 S29, serial 695, 118 p., 3 maps.

Davis, Jefferson, 1855, Report of the Secretary of War, in Reports of Explorations and Surveys: Wash., 32/2 H91, serial 791, 1:1-33, quotes on Stansbury 12, impracticable 31.

Ellis, Richard N., 1970, General Pope and U.S. Indian policy: Albuquerque, 287 p.

Emory, William H., 1848, Notes of a military reconnoissance: Wash., 30/1 H41, serial 517, map with Cooke's report p. 549-63.

Fielding, Robert K., 1993, The unsolicited chronicler, an account of the Gunnison Massacre: Brookline MA, 474 p.; Massacre 145-67.

Foreman, Grant, ed., 1941, A pathfinder in the Southwest, the itinerary of Lt. A. W. Whipple: Norman, 298 p.

Greer, James K., 1952, Colonel Jack Hays: N.Y., p. 239-52; quotes on water 245, credit 252.

Gunnison, John W., 1852 (1972 reprint), The Mormons: Freeport NY, p. 152.

Hine, Robert V., 1962, Edward Kern and American expansion: New Haven, p. 96.

Lincoln, Abraham, 1862, An act to aid in the construction of a railroad and telegraph line from the Missouri river to the Pacific ocean: Wash., 37/2 S108 Misc., serial 1124, 12 p.

Mollhausen, Baldwin, 1853-54 (1858 pub.), Diary of a journey from the Mississippi to the coasts of the Pacific: London, 2 v. 352 and 397 p.; quotes on Black Beaver 1:93, fandango 1:315, acquaintances 2:2, Leroux 2:25, El Morro 2:69, adverse fate 2:123, waggons abandoned 2:222, beards 2:263, guides 2:284, bundles 2:290.

Mumey, Nolie, 1955, John Williams Gunnison: Denver, 189 p.; biog. 7-30; quote to wife 52; Schiel translation by Maria Williams 55-111.

Parke, John G., 1854 (1855 pub.), Explorations for a route for the Pacific railroad near the 32d parallel between Doña Ana and Pimas villages, in Reports of Explorations and Surveys: Wash., 32/2 ("33/3") H91, serial 792, 2:1-28, quotes on Nugent 5, teamster 12, uncertainty 13; the final map in quarto v. 11 does not show the camps and the route is hard to follow; much better is the preliminary map in the 1854 octavo edition, 33/1 H129, serial 739.

Pope, John, 1854 (1855 pub.), Explorations for a route for the Pacific railroad near the 32d parallel, from Red River to the Rio Grande, in Reports of Explorations and Surveys: Wash., 32/2 ("33/3") H91, serial 792, 2:1-99; diary 51-93; quotes on information 52, beards 92; mileage table 98-99 does not reflect actual travel, which must be cumulated from the diary, with a few gaps filled in from the map in v. 11.

Schiel, Jacob H., 1959 (1959 translation), Journey through the Rocky Mountains and the Humboldt Mountains to the Pacific Ocean; Thomas N. Bonner, ed. and trans.: Norman, 114 p.; quotes on mosquitoes 15, buffalo 21, prairie dog 24, steep mountains 45; another Schiel translation is in Mumey 1955.

Schutz, Wallace J., and Walter N. Trenerry, 1990, Abandoned by Lincoln, a military biography of General John Pope: Urbana, 243 p., quote 38.

Sherburne, John P., 1853-54 (1988 printing), Through Indian country to California, John P. Sherburne's diary of the Whipple expedition; Mary M. Gordon, ed.: Stanford, 285 p.

Stanley, Gerald, 1971, Senator William Gwin, moderate or racist: San Francisco, Calif. Hist. Quart. 50:243-55.

Steele, Robert V. ("Lately Thomas"), 1969, Between two empires, the life story of William McKendree Gwin: Boston, 399 p.; quote 306.

Weber, David J., 1985, Richard H. Kern: Albuquerque, 355 p.; with Gunnison 215-43.

Whipple, Amiel W., 1855 (1856 pub.), Explorations for a route for the Pacific railroad near the 35th parallel, in Reports of Explorations and Surveys: Wash., 33/2 S78, serial 760, Itinerary 3:1-135; Indian Tribes 3:1-128; from 33/2 H91, serial 794, mileage table in Appendix, 4:70-74; maps in v. 11.

Williamson, Robert S., 1854 (1856 pub.), Routes in California, in Reports of Explorations and Surveys: Wash., 33/2 H91, serial 795, 5:1-43, quote on Gwin 13.

SPEECHES

OF

MR. GWIN, OF CALIFORNIA,

ON THE

NATIONAL RAILROAD BILL—HOMESTEAD BILL—CIVIL FUND BILL—CALIFOR-
NIA INDIAN WAR DEBT—APPOINTMENT OF JUDGE FOR THE NORTHERN
DISTRICT OF CALIFORNIA—AND THE BILL TO CREATE A LINE OF STEAM-
SHIPS FROM CALIFORNIA, VIA THE SANDWICH ISLANDS, TO CHINA.

DELIVERED

IN THE SENATE OF THE UNITED STATES, DEC. 12, 1853.

WASHINGTON:
PRINTED AT THE CONGRESSIONAL GLOBE OFFICE.
1853.

SPEECHES.

Mr. GWIN said: Mr. President, I move that the Senate take up, with the view to its reference to the Committee on the Public Lands, the following bill introduced by me on the second day of this session:

A BILL to make a donation of the public lands to the State of California for the purpose of constructing a railroad and telegraphic line from the city of San Francisco to the Colorado river, or southeastern boundary of said State, with a branch passing through the valley of the Sacramento river to the boundary line between said State and the Territory of Oregon.

Be it enacted by the Senate and House of Representatives of the United States of America in Congress assembled, That, for the purpose of constructing a railroad and telegraphic line from the city of San Francisco to the southeastern boundary of the State of California, with a branch of said railroad and telegraphic line passing through the valley of the Sacramento river to the Oregon Territory, or the northeastern boundary of California, at such point of termination as may be designated by the Legislature of said State, a quantity of land equal to the alternate sections for the width of forty miles on each side of said railroad and branch, to be selected from the sections which shall be designated on the public surveys of said lands by odd numbers, is hereby set apart, appropriated, and granted to the State of California, to aid in the construction of said railroad and branch thereof, and telegraphic lines, in the manner and subject to the terms, conditions, and restrictions hereinafter mentioned: *Provided,* That the terminus of said railroad and telegraphic line on the southeastern boundary of California shall lie on the line of direction of the route of any railroad that may be located to connect the Mississippi river with the Pacific ocean; and that no more or greater distance of the railroad herein provided for shall be located than may be constructed in a line which, from necessity, would be common or unavoidable to any railroad that might be constructed from the middle or southern portion of the Mississippi valley, until the location of such railroad be determined upon and will intersect the eastern or southeastern boundary of California, when the location of said railroad from San Francisco in that direction shall be completed to the said point of intersection.

SEC. 2. *And be it further enacted,* That in all cases where the United States may have disposed of any lands herein designated for selection by said State, or where, from any cause, the United States shall be unable to convey a title to the same, the deficiency may be made up by selections to be made, under the authority of the Legislature of the State of California, from any unoccupied and unappropriated lands belonging to the United States within that State, or from any such land as may have been occupied, with the consent of the occupant, and designated on the plats of public surveys by odd numbers, and which shall be nearest to said railroads and telegraphic lines, respectively, within said State; and that for the purpose of facilitating the said selections, and the construction of the said works, the President of the United States shall cause the public lands, for the width on each side of said railroads and telegraphic lines as stated in the first section of this act, to be surveyed and marked in advance of the same as the work progresses.

SEC. 3. *And be it further enacted,* That the grant of land made by this act shall be on the condition that the State of California commence the said railroads and telegraphic lines within one year succeeding the first session of the Legislature thereof after the date of this act, and complete the same within ten years thereafter; and that, when completed, all troops, seamen, arms, munitions of war, military and naval stores, and funds, and other property whatsoever belonging to the United States, and all persons in the employment of the United States, being on official business, shall at all times be conveyed and transported, with their baggage and over said railroads free of any charge or expense to them or to the Government; and, also, all telegraphic dispatches within that State on Government business: but, should cases of emergency arise in the public service, requiring an extraordinary quantity or amount of transportation, so as to affect the interest, income, or profits of said railroads, to such a degree as to operate oppressively, or to prevent the reception of fair and reasonable dividends or interest upon the amount of the costs and expenses of the said railroads, to be judged of by the President of the United States, he shall determine the amount of compensation which shall be just and reasonable for such extraordinary service; and should the same be deemed inadequate by the State of California, or those acting under its authority, the matter shall be submitted to Congress for a final determination. And the United States mail shall at all times be transported on said railroads, under the direction of the Post Office Department, at such rate of compensation as Congress may by law provide.

SEC. 4. *And be it further enacted,* That the rates of charge for the conveyance of passengers and transportation of goods, wares, and merchandise, and all kinds of freight, on the said railroads, shall be such that, with a careful and economical management of the same, the net income or profits thereon may not be reduced below the rate of eight per cent. per annum upon the amount of the costs and expenses of the said railroads; and that Congress may by law, at any time hereafter, fix, alter, and regulate the aforesaid rates of charge, so as to limit or restrict the same to any rate above that specified in this section that may be deemed proper.

SEC. 5. *And be it further enacted,* That the said road shall be constructed throughout in a thorough, substantial, workmanlike manner, with all necessary drains, culverts, bridges, viaducts, crossings, turnouts, sidings, stations, watering places, and all other appurtenants, including the complete equipment of locomotives, of sufficient speed and capacity, commodious and comfortable passenger cars, and freight cars, adapted to the business to be done; and the obli-[p. 4] gation hereby imposed upon the State of California shall so cover, in detail, all of these provisions, as to secure the construction, maintenance, and equipment of roads at all times equal, in both respects, to a road of the first class, when thoroughly organized for business; and shall also provide for the constant supervision of a sufficient number of competent, skillful engineers; the gauge of said roads to be uniform throughout, and the rails of the best quality, weighing not less than sixty-four pounds to the yard.

SEC. 6. *And be it further enacted,* That the lands hereby granted to said State of California shall be subject to the disposal of the Legislature thereof for the purposes specified in this act; and should the aforesaid railroads, or branch, not be completed within the ten years, as limited in this act, the said State shall be bound to pay to the United States the net amount which may have been received from the sales of any part of said lands by the said State, the title to remain valid in the purchasers under said sales, and the title to the residue of such land remaining unsold shall reinvest in or revert to the United States, and be held as other public land, in the same manner as if this act had never passed.

The provisions of the bill are familiar to the members of this body who served in the last Congress. It differs in some respects from the form of the bills granting donations from the public lands for the purpose of aiding in the construction of railroads in the several States, which, after elaborate discussion, passed the Senate by a large majority. It differs in the quantity of land asked for, which I will be able, I hope, to satisfy the Senate and country is not exorbitant. It also differs in not raising the price of the alternate sections reserved to the Government to two dollars and fifty cents per acre. My object in leaving out this feature of bills that have met with the approval of the Senate, will be explained by reference to the homestead bill introduced by me, and which, before I take my seat, I shall ask to be referred to the Committee on Public Lands. The policy I intend to advocate on this floor is to grant alternate sections of the public lands to the States in which they lie, to aid such roads as, with proper restrictions, they may charter, and open the whole of the residue of the public domain to actual settlers, citizens of the United States, or having signified their intention to become such; who, after three years' occupation, shall have a fee-simple title to a quarter section for each settler, being the head of a family. My reasons for favoring the policy of thus disposing of the public domain I will explain more at large when these measures are acted on by the Committee on Public Lands and reported back to the Senate.

This bill, Mr. President, is intended to be the basis of the great railroad from the Pacific to the Mississippi. The point of commencement is San Francisco, the great center of commerce, wealth, and population on our Pacific coast, running thence to the southeastern boundary of the State, there to meet such route as may be determined upon by Congress, passing through the territories of the United States to the States on the Mississippi river. From this main track the bill provides for a branch, running north to the Oregon line, or to the northeastern boundary of the State. The object of establishing this branch is to connect with the route, if one should be discovered practicable, passing the Sierra Nevada at Noble's pass, and running east through the South pass to the waters of the Missouri river, or to connect at the Oregon line with the route surveyed by Governor Stevens, if it should be discovered practicable. My object in framing this bill, Mr. President, is to afford a connection with any route that may cross the continent to the Pacific ocean.

The quantity of land asked for is large, but the proposition is not new to the Senate. The distinguished Senator from Illinois (Mr. DOUGLAS) reported, from the Committee on the Territories, during the last Congress, a bill granting the same amount of land to California, to enable that State to construct the portion of the great national railroad located within its borders. That bill was matured in the Committee on the Territories, of which I was at the time a member, after the most elaborate examination of the subject, and the committee were unanimously of opinion that the quantity of land asked for in this bill should be granted to California to enable that State to complete its portion of this great work.

During the last Congress I introduced a bill embodying, as this does, the main features of the one I have referred to as emanating from the Committee on Territories. It was elaborately discussed during that session, but not finally acted upon. I bring the measure forward at the commencement of the session, with an earnest hope that it will be acted upon at an early day.

I confine my efforts, Mr. President, in favor of this measure, to the boundaries of my own State. The bill avoids all constitutional difficulties in the construction of this great national highway. It asks for a grant of the public domain to the State to aid in its construction. The President, in his annual message, favors this policy. Congress has heretofore adopted it in several of the States, to wit: Illinois, Mississippi, Alabama, Missouri, and Arkansas. The policy of thus disposing of a portion of the public domain in these States, has been eminently successful, and it will prove to be so in all the States and Territories, if a wise precaution governs our legislation, making the grant to such works as will undoubtedly develop the resources of the country. I know this bill will meet with opposition, from the quantity of land that it proposes to donate to the State of California.

I anticipated this difficulty, and am prepared to meet it. I have documents before me which I will read to the Senate, in order that they may thus reach the Committee on Public Lands, to aid them in their deliberations on this bill, which show the vast difficulties that must be overcome in California in the construction of this great national highway. I have, during the past summer, traveled over a great portion of the route in California, and can corroborate the statements I will now read to the Senate:

DEPÔT CAMP, POSE CR., *August* 30, 1853.

DEAR SIR: During our short interview on the Dry Creek, (where, unfortunately, I was too unwell to talk to you as much as I wished,) you requested me to write to you before you left for Washington, to give you such information as I could concerning our railroad. As I have an opportunity of sending to Fort Miller to-morrow, and may not have another, I write now, earlier than I intended.

After we left you we came direct to this creek, where we made our depôt camp, (there being no grass on Kern river,) and after remaining two or three days for astronomical observations, I left with a small surveying party for Walker's Pass, and thence followed along the backbone of the Sierra Nevada to the southward, examining every depression on the ridge till I came to the Tejon. I then went through the Cañada de los Uras, entered the basin to the northeast of the Sierra, crossed the plains to the eastern end of the Tejon pass, (wagon road,) and went through this pass, thus again getting into the Tejon, by which I mean the portion of the valley nearly inclosed by the hills. After- [p. 5] wards I went some twenty-five miles to the westward, examined the Cañada de San Arminio, and finally reached here last night, having been absent twenty days.

I have had a very satisfactory trip, as I have obtained a thorough knowledge of the mountains from Walker's Pass on the north to the coast range. I am satisfied that there is no pass or depression on the mountains that has not been *examined,* and now I am prepared to go to work, understandingly, surveying. I am, however, much disappointed in the mountains themselves, as they are much higher and steeper than I expected to find them. It is difficult, in merely riding over a mountain, to judge correctly of the altitude gained, and the slope; and what appears a fine gently ascending valley, may, upon calculation, prove to be an ascent of three hundred or four hundred feet to the mile. The Tejon Pass, for instance, which you ascended, has its summit about four thousand five hundred feet above Kern Lake, and nearly all this ascent is to be gained in ten miles, or must be reduced by tunneling. The Cañada de los Uras is the lowest point of the sierra, and is three thousand one hundred feet above this place. These numbers are approximations from rough calculations.

We shall move camp at once from here to the Tejon, and I shall then commence surveying with a level, compass, and chain, through the Tejon Pass, the Cañada, &c., and you may rest assured that I shall not leave these mountains till I have data from which to make a report, based upon numbers and calculations which no one can dispute.

From what I have said, you will see that the difficulty of crossing the mountains is greater than we supposed. The extent of the difficulty, I am not, as present, able to state; and will not be till I have made a survey. As to the *practicability* of crossing, I have no doubt, and am inclined to think, the best point will be one of the passes leading into the Tejon. I conceive Walker's Pass to be almost out of the question; and if it were as good as the others, to be badly situated.

   *   *   *   *   *   *   *   *

  Truly and respectfully yours,

             R. S. WILLIAMSON,
           Lieut. U. S. Topographical Engineers.

Hon. WM. M. GWIN,
  San Francisco, California.

DEPÔT CAMP, CALIFORNIA, *(on Pose Creek,)*
August 23, 1853.

MAJOR: Since our arrival, and on the way here, I have had something of an opportunity of obtaining considerable information which is both new and interesting to me; and hoping it may be so to others, I will give it for what it is worth. I find that the character of the great Tulare Valley is very different from what most people have generally supposed. Although I had seen both ends of it several years ago, I had formed a wrong opinion of its value and advantages. At the southern extremity, I saw a very pretty, arable spot, and had formed the idea that it was much larger in extent than is really the case, and that there were other and similar locations. But to be more particular, I will begin at the northern extremity and come south, describing it as I go.

On the eastern side.—The valley, by the way of the wagon road, from the San Joaquin river to the Tejon pass, is about one hundred and ninety-seven miles in length, say in a strait [*sic*] line one hundred and fifty miles, and on an average, about fifty miles in width, or in area seven thousand five hundred square miles. From the San Joaquin to King's river it is a dry and arid plain. On King's river there is a narrow bottom averaging about half a mile wide by twenty-five long; twelve and one-third square miles. From King's river to the first of Four Creeks is a dry plain. Here is one of the most beautiful and fertile spots in California. In extent it is about twenty-five miles by ten, and about one half of it is at present susceptible of cultivation, the other half will require a great expenditure of labor in draining to make a portion of it inhabitable—say two hundred square miles in all. From the Four Creeks to Tula river is a dry, arid plain, little or no arable land on it. Tula to Kern, a barren plain. On Kern river there may possibly be twenty square miles of inhabitable land. From Kern river to Tejon pass, a sand plain. At this point there may possibly be one hundred and fifty miles of tolerably good land though in some portions it is very handsome, and the soil of most excellent quality. Through the whole length of this valley runs a tula marsh, which expands in some places into lakes. These lakes are, during most of the time, connected by a sluggish stream of water, and bordered by marshes of tula, but during very dry seasons, these canals or channels are dry, and the lakes are nearly or quite so. A Mr. Anderson tells me he crossed the valley from east to west, to about the middle, in 1844, and found the whole valley dry, with no water from mountain to mountain. The average distance from the Sierra Nevada, on the east to this marsh, is about twice as great as the distance from the marsh to the coast range of mountains on the west. As there are no streams making down from the coast range into this marsh, except in very wet weather, the whole of that portion west of the Tula lakes is worthless in the extreme.

The proportion, then, of this immense valley which can possibly be looked upon as inhabitable is small indeed—in all not more than three hundred and seventy-five square miles, or one twentieth part. With the exception of the places above-mentioned, there is little or no timber throughout the length and breadth of the whole valley. The Indians throughout this valley (and the same may be said of those in all this part of California) appear to have no particular name for any of their lakes, rivers, plains, or mountains, but call that one, or that portion of either occupied by them, after the name of the particular tribe or rancheria living there. The names thus derived of those portions of the above-mentioned Great Tulare marsh, where it expands into lakes, are commencing at the north, Tache, Clin-tache, Cho-lám, Tu-lum-ne or Kern, and Tu-lá-ris (commonly called Buena Vista) lakes. Kern river, near where it expands into Kern lake, is called, by the Indians, Po-sín-cu-la; higher up, the La-ha-lien; and in the mountains, Chi-ma-wee-ya. Pose creek is called How-che, or Haughch-che. It is a great pity that the Indian names of the different natural features of the country could not be preserved, instead of replacing them by those of psuedo discoverers, who take this means of gratifying a prurient desire for fame, at a great expenditure of good taste, common sense, and common justice. In a few years more these Indian names will be all that remains of a once powerful but rapidly decreasing people, victims of cruelty, injustice, and the various diseases which follow in the wake of civilization. The Indians that live in this valley, reside, for the most part of the time, along the base of the mountains. They have no permanent residences down in the plains, on account of the great annoyance which they experience from the mosquitoes, ants, and other insects. They come down, however, at the proper seasons to fish and gather the roots of the tula, wild rice, and grass seeds, for food. Upon these, together with the acorns on the mountains, and a little game which they contrive to kill, they manage to eke out a most miserable existence; but when very hard off for food, they are compelled to resort to theft. They have the reputation of being most accomplished thieves; but I know, from the best authority, that a great deal of the credit they have obtained for this kind of rascality is justly due to a class of Americans stopping on the Four creeks, King's river, and at some other points as far north as Stockton—particularly as to the stealing of horses, mules, and cattle. Among those to whom the most credit should be given, are two men, partners in business, *(what business* deponent saith not,) by the name of Dick Boatrights and J.S. Hawkins. These two men live on the Merced river, below Snelling's rancho. They make, as do many others of the same stamp, a periodical visit to the vicinity of the Tejon pass, bring down a few goods, and a quantity of liquors, and always go back with a number of horses and mules which they *say* they have purchased from the Indians, but that *some one* has stolen them is shown by the fact of none having been visited with the brand of the owner. However, after they get further north, they manage to get an *iron,* which serves the purpose of a vent; a piece of common hoop iron can be very easily bent so as to answer the purpose desired.

Before I proceed any further, I am going to ask myself several questions. What is the necessity or use of Fort Miller as a garrison post? What are the objects to be accomplished by having troops there? As they are at present located, can those objects be accomplished? If not, what more advantageous position can be selected? I say I ask myself these questions, because I have formed my own ideas upon the different points, or rather have presumed that such and such was the case.

I would say that as to actual necessity, there is none; and their only use is, to act as a sort of nucleus for about a hundred lazy, shiftless vagabonds, who constitute "Mugginsville," or "Millerstown." The Indians in that vicinity—and I am surprised at their paucity—are very peaceable, (in fact they are too much diseased to be otherwise,) and were they not, the white men more than equal the Indians in numbers, men, women, and children.

Some of the objects to be accomplished are, I presume, to protect the Indians from the white man's abuse, and the whites from the Indians retaliation, commonly called outrages or depredations. To prevent the Indians from the mountains from stealing from the inhabitants on the plains, [p. 6] or any other section of country, or to keep peace amongst the different tribes or Rancherias.

As to the possibility of accomplishing these objects, I, of course, cannot say; but I can say that they are not accomplished, nor do I think it possible for the troops at Fort Miller to accomplish them. I will explain: There is no business carried on in California more successfully than that of horse stealing by Indians and white horse thieves in this section of country, and no section, so long as it is occupied by those whose business it should be to check it as much as possible, presents more advantages for the business.

The Indian thieves live along the east side of the coast range, from the Cajon pass up as far as the Tejon pass, and along the east side of the Sierra Nevada as far north as the head waters of the Merced and Tuolumne rivers. These Indians are all connected together; but the largest and worst band live just north of the head waters of Kern river, and in the vicinity of a large lake, probably the one put down on Frémont's map (Frémont never was there, though a portion of his party was) as Owens's lake. They are called the Sey-pan-te-se tribe, and in the Indian language the Mez-tene-os, (or bad Indians.) Now imagine yourself in Tejon pass, to the north you have the great Tular and San Joaquin valleys, to the east the eastern slope of the Sierra Nevada, to the south the eastern slope of the coast range, and to the southwest and west, the passes of San Francisco and Walker's pass, leading to Los Angeles, and Santa Barbara respectively. (This last pass is named after an Indian chief called Walke-ra, and by Americans perverted into Walker's; and is the Walker's pass of the coast range, not of the Sierra Nevada. He is from the river Severn, and the most expert horse-thief in all California. He is a Eutaw chief, speaks Spanish, and has a large band with him; and several of the Rancheros, amongst whom is Williams, pay him tribute or black mail.) From this point you can go with wagons in each of the directions mentioned, except to Santa Barbara. Bear in mind the fact, that the mountain Indians are those who steal and commit all the depredations, (though those in the plains may be cognizant of the act,) and also that they live on the east side of the mountain range. They go to the southern country, steal animals, run them out of the Cajon or San Francisco passes, bring them north, run some of them into the Tulare valley, through the Tejon pass, dispose of them to *traders,* (many of whom are deserters from the army,) and take the rest on north and cache them near the head waters of the Merced and Tuolumne rivers, and then at their leisure dispose of them to these or other Americans and Californians. A large proportion of the animals stolen are killed for food, or used by the Indians as saddle animals. Among these horse thieves are a great many Indians who were brought up on the missions; they speak the Spanish language, and are commonly great rascals. Now, the nearest practicable way to get at any of these Indians, starting from Fort Miller, is to go by this point: fifty miles from the Tejon pass. (It is said, with what truth I know not, that horses are stolen from the north, and taken to the south by the same routes.) In fact, for all movements against these Indians living between the Cajon pass on the south, and Carson valley on the north, the Tejon, or Walker's pass, (though I think the former by far the preferable location,) appears to be the two best points from which to start; and as the great sand plain on the east, and coast range on the west, necessarily force all travelers by land between the above-mentioned limits, to go by *this point* it is most admirably adapted for all the purposes of a frontier post. There is an amount of good land sufficient for raising a supply of grain, or supporting a number of animals adequate for all practicable purposes. The distance from San Pedro, to Los Angeles, is twenty-seven miles, and from Los Angeles, to the Tejon pass, but eighty-five, and all but a few miles a most excellent and level wagon road, with plenty of grass, water, and wood: it being at an elevation of several hundred feet above the valley, the wind blowing fresh most of the year, and no marshes in the vicinity, nothing should prevent it from being one of the most healthy spots in the healthiest country in the world. From what I have already said, you can readily imagine what would be my answer to the last question. Another idea has struck me very forcibly, this point—the Tejon pass—is right in the midst of the very Indians who go to Jurupa, (a post garrisoned by fifteen or twenty soldiers, and within rifle shot of a settlement of five hundred stalwart, two-fisted Mormons,) and steal animals almost every moon. Thus, then, stands the case: The Indians which the troops stationed at Fort Miller will hereafter have to watch over, live to their east and south, and those under the charge of those stationed at Jurupa, come from their north. How would it work to bring those from the former place one hundred and seventy-five miles south, and those from the latter place one hundred and twenty five miles north, where they would be joined in one body, and furnished with supplies from San Pedro by wagons, one hundred and twelve miles, or from Santa Barbara by pack mules, about eighty-five miles, or from *Memphis, by railroad,* distance unknown? Each would then be in the very best position to accomplish the objects most necessary, and to perform the duties which will hereafter devolve upon them.

Between Walker's pass and the Tejon pass, and about thirty miles distant from each, there is plenty of pine timber for building purposes; and although it is in the mountains, is accessible. I am thoroughly convinced, that could the General form his ideas from actual observation, he would agree with me in most of the views I have advanced above; and I have not the slightest doubt but that the posts of Fort Miller and Jurupa will be broken up within a year from this time.

Lieutenant Williamson is getting along remarkably well with his survey. He has completed his reconnoissance of all that portion of the Sierra Nevada from the head of Kern river to the coast range, and a most thorough one he has made. Walker's pass is of no account at all. He will proceed, as soon as the wagons arrive from Fort Miller with the subsistence, stores, (and what detains them I cannot contrive, for they are now due six days,) to run several lines of levels through the different passes in the vicinity of the Tejon. Nothing as yet has been heard from Beal. The body of the man who strayed from Lieutenant McLean's party, was found on the plains between Kern river and the Tejon. The weather is quite warm, varying from 98° to 105° at mid-day, and in the cool shade, and from 46° to 60° at sunrise in the morning. Although the difference of temperature during twelve hours has been as great as 50°, yet this great change is hardly felt. It has been raining for the last ten days, or a fortnight, over in the basin or plain beyond the mountains, some days quite hard. We had considerable of a shower here on the 17th instant, lasting about three hours, and wetting the ground an inch or more in depth. Please excuse my prosiness and freedom of speech; and should the communication contain any ideas you may consider worthy of attention, you can make what use of them you may think proper.

I remain, very truly and respectfully,

GEORGE STONEMAN,

First Lieut. Dragoons.

Major O. CROSS, *Quartermaster U.S. Army.*

I have, in addition to these interesting statements, notes of Mr. Aubrey's expedition from the Tejon pass to the Rio del Norte, at Albuquerque, which I will read to the Senate: Notes by F. X. Aubrey

[See L2 for Aubry's full text, which is omitted here]

[p. 10] Mr. Aubrey has forwarded to me, with these notes, an interesting diagram of his route, which I shall present to the Senate to be referred to the Committee on Public Lands with this bill.

I have also received from Lieutenant Hamilton and Major Andrews, of the United States Army, notes of their explorations from San Diego to the mouth of the Gila river, and for some distance up the Colorado, with a diagram of their route, which I also present to the Senate:

Legend to accompany map of routes from San Diego to the mouth of the Gila.

It is believed that the San Diego and the mouth of the Gila are on the same parallel of latitude. The initial monument is taken thirteen miles south of the San Diego, which varies little from the truth. The distance between the initial monument and the mouth of the Gila is assumed to be one hundred and forty-one miles, which I think I remember aright. In the Indian names I adopt the Spanish sound of the vowels and the English sound of the consonants, except where they have been so long used as to render them Mexican, in which case I adopt the Mexican orthography. Carriage roads now in use are marked thus = Proposed routes of railroads, thus ——— (a red line.) Summit of mountain ranges - - - - (red dots.) Indian villages, thus (a pyramid.) Paths, thus ———. Old unusual trails or water unknown, thus ....

Commencing at San Diego, a road would run to the rancho of Tijuan along the level nearly of the sea—distance twenty-three miles, or nineteen three fourths as marked, from *New* San Diego. Hence, with but slight ascent and good road, we reach the spring of San Pedro y San Pablo, which is on the hill at a distance of fifteen miles from Tijuan. This eminance will be easily gained, or could be avoided altogether by going through Carrizita rancho and the Baja California road as indicated. Hence to Tecate is only a regular rise of water. Plenty of water at La Punta, Tijuan Creek, all the way to the last point of leaving it, spring of San Pedro and San Pablo, Carrizita, and through eight miles of Tecate Valley to

San José, on Cartouch's rancho. Tecate is forty-three three fourth miles from New San Diego. And the house is in Baja, California, by a few yards. There is plenty of wood in Tijuan Creek—cotton-wood and willow. Oak in abundance in all the other valleys as far as Jacum. From Tecate through you pass into other valleys, yet the ridges between them are hardly perceptible. At San José, four miles further, plenty of wood and water; at Valentine's rancho, three miles further, plenty of wood and water. At Milcuatai, four miles further, plenty of wood and water. This Milcuatai is a beautiful valley, long, well timbered on the edges, excellent pasture in the center, in form of a crescent, and has a pass out of it in a direct line to San Diego, now used by the Government express from the Gila. The pass is called Struck's Pass, from the first mail rider who went through it. This route I consider, from the reports I have had of it from express men, as less practicable by far, than the indicated route. The creek, as seen in the map, starting near the summit runs past Santiago, and Juan Pedro's rancho, and exhausts itself in Milcuatai valley. From first, water in Milcuatai valley to the summit between Deseret and Sea is twelve miles—to said summit by road traveled, sixty-seven miles. Thus far all is of easy ascent. An easy descent for ten miles to Jacum valley now takes place; the ground supplying wood and water. Total distance, by present wagon road, seventy and one half miles from New San Diego. To reach the desert, it is now necessary to descend, and for this purpose the present express route appears best calculated. At first sight it would require a stationary engine for an inclined plane of say four hundred feet; but the other advantages of this route being so weighty would justify a thorough examination of all the passes in this vicinity for the purpose of avoiding said plane. Don Santiago Arguella, a gentleman who will soon be in your city, informed me that a gentle slope can be found down to the desert on the eastern side. If this exists, I will insure an easy approach to the summit. I believe this to be from twenty-five to thirty miles south of Jacum, and near a place called among the Indians and old Californians "El Matadero," where a battle was once fought between the settlers and Indians, and which is common property between the Mountain Indians of this side and the Cocopas of the Colorado.

After arriving on the plain of the desert no inconveniences are found; and the whole distance, from the mouth of the Gila to San Diego, would not exceed one hundred and sixty five miles—the air-rhumb being one hundred and forty-one miles.

No difficulties are to be met with in the Vallecitos route, [p. 11] except that, by this route, it will be about one hundred and sixty miles from Camp Yuma to San José del Valle, or Warner rancho, and from thence forty-five miles to San Luis Rey—a point considered in some of the speculations on the road. This route is in every way practicable, as well as a route from San Luis to San Diego, and from San Luis to Los Angeles.

Again, arriving at San José del Valle, an excellent route lies direct through Temecula to Los Angeles. On this I have been as far as Temecula; and, I am told, the rest of the route is equally good. In fact, I believe a good route can be obtained in either of the passes mentioned; and, I might add, that an ascent from the desert can be made by the Coyotes, via Juan Bautistas, Buena Vista rancho, and thence to Temecula.

At the request of Lieutenant Hamilton, I have added to the map above described that of the country between Jacum pass and Colorado river. The whole distance is a level, or so nearly so as to rise and fall imperceptibly. Hardly any grading would be required for a rail-road, and that little only where some dry anoyo [arroyo] of, say ten feet wide, occurs. To reach Colorado river at a suitable crossing place, I think it would be necessary, after pass-ing either north or south of Pilot Mountain, to bear northeast to the point marked on the map. From this crossing is also the most favorable direction for gaining the valley of the Gila, which would be reached over the level desert fifteen miles east of the Colorado. The soil of this country is barren, save in the bottoms, where a growth of mezquit occurs. Near the Colorado the cotton-wood and willow mingle with mesquit. There is no building stone, after leaving Jacum, until reaching a point eighty miles up the Gila. The chief advantages of this line are its directness and level ground. The Colorado is navigable for steamers of good power, and five feet draught to Lighthouse Rock, about two hundred and ten miles, by the stream, from its mouth. The current in summer is three and a quarter miles, and during the June flood six and a quarter miles an hour. I have sounded from the mouth to Lighthouse Rock, and never found less than six feet six inches water. These soundings were taken below the Gila in March, 1852, and above the Gila in October, 1852, both months of low water.

Respectfully submitted,   GEO. P. ANDREWS.

Brevet Major U.S. Army.

I will here observe, Mr. President, that I have so worded this bill, that if it is ascertained that the only practicable route of the great national railroad should be by the Gila river, the State of California can provide for the appropriation of the land granted for the construction of a road passing down the valleys of the coast range of mountains to San Diego, and thence to the mouth of the Gila. I have applied to the Secretary of War for orders to Lieutenant Williamson, who has charge of the exploring party on the Pacific coast, to extend his explorations, pur-suing the course of the coast range of mountains, and the valley of the Sacramento river, to Noble's Pass, through the Sierra Nevada mountains, and to give that pass a thorough examination. The Secretary has expressed his willingness to grant my request, provided Congress would make the necessary appropriation, which, I hope, will be done at an early day.

Mr. President, I am an ardent advocate of the great Pacific railroad. I believe it is the duty of the General Government to contribute liberally in land and money to aid in the construction of this work. The national railroad is a national neces-sity. Without it, we cannot preserve the integrity of the Union, in time of war. There are members of this body who have constitutional scruples in using the national treasure in aiding in the construction of this great work; I have none. I look to the obligations of the Constitution as well as its restrictions. Among the powers conferred by the Constitution upon Congress we find prominent the obligation to provide for the "common defense" of the country. This great national highway is absolutely necessary to defend the Pacific coast of the United

States in time of war. Without it, we will be severed from the rest of the Union; with it, this Government is impregnable, and can defy all the nations of the earth. The bill was then referred to the Committee on Public Lands.

THE HOMESTEAD BILL.

Mr. GWIN. Mr. President, I move that the bill offered by me a few days ago, commonly known as the *homestead bill*, now lying on the Secretary's table, be taken up with a view to its reference to the Committee on Public Lands.

A bill to encourage agriculture, commerce, manufactures, and all other branches of industry, by granting to every man, who is at the head of a family, and a citizen of the United States, a homestead of one hundred and sixty acres of land out of the public domain, upon condition of occupancy and cultivation of the same for the period herein specified: [Details omitted]

[p. 12] COLLECTIONS FROM IMPORTS.

Mr. GWIN. Mr. President, some days ago I introduced a bill providing for the payment to the State of California of all moneys collected from imports within the borders of said State, from the date of the treaty of peace with Mexico up to the date of its admission into the Union. I move that the Senate now proceed to the consideration of that bill, that I may have it referred to the Committee on Finance.

A bill to authorize and direct the payment of certain moneys into the treasury of the State of California, which were collected in the ports of said State as a revenue upon imports, since the ratification of the treaty of peace between the United States and the Republic of Mexico, and prior to the admission of said State into the Union. [Details omitted]

[p. 13] EXPENSE OF SUPPRESSING INDIAN HOSTILITES.

MR. GWIN. Mr. President, I move that the Senate proceed to the consideration of the bill which I offered some days ago, to refund to California the expenses incurred by that State in suppressing Indian hostilities within its borders, that it may be referred to the Committee on Military Affairs.

A bill to refund to the State of California the expenses incurred in suppressing Indian aggressions in that State. [Details omitted]

THURSDAY, *December* 15, 1853.
CALIFORNIA STEAM LINES.

Mr. GWIN introduced the following bill:

A bill to establish a line of steamships from San Francisco, via the Sandwich Islands, to Shanghai, in China. [For transport of U.S. mails; details omitted]

Antoine Leroux, 1853

Slopes And Valleys Of The Rocky Mountains

[St. Louis] *The Western Journal and Civilian*, April, 1853, vol. 10, n. 1, p. 1-11; pages
6-8 contain extracts from an 1853 Leroux letter. [WC and WCB 225.]
Reset verbatim from a facsimile, by courtesy of the Missouri
Historical Society Library, St. Louis.

Significance   Seasoned mountaineer and guide Antoine Leroux here lent his
influential support to the ill conceived and ill fated Fremont-Benton central route
for the Pacific railroad through Cochetopa Pass, Colorado. In a matter so
beclouded with politics and personal gain, it is hard to tell what anybody really
thought. The *Santa Fe Gazette* of October 8, 1853, quoted another seasoned
trader, Ceran St. Vrain, as saying that "the idea of locating a railroad through the
country mentioned in Leroux's letter to Col. Benton was ridiculous and absurd"
(Bancroft 24:509). Leroux seemed to be further politically influenced by Benton
in stating that "Col. Fremont was looking for the Coo-cha-tope Pass in the winter of 1848-49…when his guide led him off into the mountains, instead of keeping up the dry valley, which he wished to do." Within a year, Leroux completely
contradicted this apologia for Fremont's disaster and acknowledged that the
Pathfinder was purposefully headed up the Rio Grande to a different pass (Mollhausen 1854). The full significance of this matter is discussed in the L6 Itinerary
and Highlights.

   This probably is the first reprint of this whole article, which promoted the
value of the sheep and wool industry of the Plains and Rockies in supporting a
Pacific railroad. The author was M. Tarver, the senior editor of the *Western Journal
and Civilian*. Leroux's quote is from the *Letter from Col. Benton to the People of
Missouri*, Washington, March 4, 1853 (WCB 221). The first four paragraphs of
Leroux's letter therein, dated Washington City, March 1, 1853, which were omitted by the *Western Journal* editor, are here supplied in the Highlights. The Hafens
reprinted Benton's and Leroux's letters completely in 1957, with excellent notes.
Parkhill reprinted parts of Leroux's letter in 1965.

   The article also quotes one of the early rosy writings of Western promoter

William Gilpin. Gilpin led the campaign against the concept of the Great American Desert—an "imaginary desert" according to the editor of the *Western Journal*. The editor did admit, however, that Gilpin might be exaggerating slightly.

Authors ANTOINE LEROUX, ca. 1801-1861, fur hunter, guide, rancher. Son of a French merchant, Leroux was born in St. Louis and educated in the public schools. He went up the Missouri with William H. Ashley and Andrew Henry in 1822 (1:B2). He reached Taos in 1824, hunted furs in the Southwest, and married Juana Valdez de Vigil in 1833. From his base at his wife's land-grant ranch north of Taos, he trapped the Gila, Colorado, Virgin, Bill Williams, and other rivers. In 1846-47 he guided Philip St. George Cooke and the Mormon Battalion to San Diego (3:E6). He became a sheep rancher and trader but took time out in 1848-49 to guide military expeditions against the Navahos, Apaches (under Maj. Benjamin L. Beall), and Utes, and to be a delegate to the convention organizing the Territory of New Mexico. In late 1849 he and Kit Carson guided the failed effort to rescue Mrs. Ann Dunn White from the Apaches (5:J2 Highlights).

Leroux was severely wounded by Havasupais in 1851 while guiding Capt. Lorenzo Sitgreaves across Arizona (5:J6). On his return from San Diego in 1852, he guided Boundary Commissioner John R. Bartlett. Leroux was in Washington in early 1853, where he gave his information on the central route to Benton. Later in 1853 on the Pacific railroad surveys, he guided Capt. John W. Gunnison across the Colorado Rockies, returned to Taos, and guided Lt. Amiel W. Whipple to Los Angeles, reaching there in 1854 (L3). In 1858 he was one of the guides on the march of Capt. Randolph B. Marcy and Col. William W. Loring from Ft. Union, New Mexico, to Ft. Bridger, Wyoming, to relieve the Utah Expedition (4:G8). His last scout was on an 1860 punitive expedition that found no Comanches or Kiowas. He died of "asthma complicated by spear wounds." Buried in a parish church that was bulldozed and replaced a century later, his forgotten bones were merged with those of the priests. (Parkhill 1965; Hafen *Mountain Men* 4:173-83; Thrapp.)

WILLIAM GILPIN, 1815-1894, soldier, first territorial governor of Colorado, author, visionary Western promoter. Probably a Pennsylvania native, Gilpin was educated as a boy in England, graduated from the University of Pennsylvania in 1833, and spent one term at West Point. President Jackson, a friend of the family, commissioned him a second lieutenant in the Seminole War of 1836. He resigned to edit a St. Louis paper and to practice law there and in Independence. He went to Oregon with Fremont in 1843 (5:J1), stayed the winter, and returned overland on his own through Ft. Bridger and Cochetopa Pass. In early 1846 he issued his first lengthy Western manifesto in testimony for Congress on Oregon. In the Mexican War he served with distinction as a major in Doniphan's campaign to Chihuahua. In 1847-48 he fought frustrating skirmishes with the resilient tribes of the Santa Fe Trail. He nearly died of malaria and then of cholera. Back in Independence, he planned a suburb, promoted the Pacific railroad (through South Pass, not the Cochetopa), and dabbled in politics.

Gilpin helped organize the Republican Party in Missouri in 1859, published his philosophy about the West in his book, *The Central Gold Region,* in 1860, and was made the first governor of the Territory of Colorado in 1861. Legend has it that future Major General Francis P. Blair told Lincoln, "Billy Gilpin has done more for that section of the country than any man now living. Why, Mr. President, Billy Gilpin built Pike's Peak." Lincoln said, "If I knew that to be true I think I should appoint him. Can you furnish any proof of it?" "Yes, sir," said Blair, "I saw him do it" (Karnes 1970). Gilpin established the Colorado judiciary, legislature, counties, and schools. He recruited troops that saved Colorado and New Mexico for the Union, but the federal government delayed honoring his drafts long enough to drive him from office in 1862. He lived in Denver the rest of his life, making a fortune in land in the San Luis Valley, writing three more books, and marrying Mrs. Julia Pratte Dickerson in 1874 for a troubled union. (Karnes 1970; DAB; Thrapp; Lamar; Heitman.)

Highlights   Following are the first four paragraphs of Leroux's letter, from Benton 1853, that were omitted from the *Western Journal* article. Many of the notes in brackets, and at the end, are condensed from the Hafens 1957:

"STATEMENT OF MR. LEROUX. At the request of Col. Benton, I, Antoine Leroux, native of St. Louis of Missouri, and now an inhabitant of Taos, in New Mexico, do make the following statement in relation to the Pass at the head of the valley of the Del Norte [Rio Grande], and of the country on each side of that Pass; and also as the best road from Missouri to California. And first tell how I got acquainted with the country:

"In the year 1820 [1822], when I was in my nineteenth [21st] year, I joined Gen. Ashley and Major Henry in an expedition of hunting and trapping to the Upper Missouri and Rocky Mountains; and after two years in that part I went to Taos, in New Mexico, and afterwards married there, and have made it my home ever since; and from that place I carried on the business of a beaver trapper for about fifteen years, generally on the waters of the Great Colorado of the West; and have trapped the whole country, every river, creek, and branch from the Gila

to the head of the Grand River fork of the Upper Colorado, and out to the Great
Salt Lake, and on the waters of the Wah-Satch Mountain, and out to the Virgen
[Virgin] River, and have been four times to California, and guide to a great many
American officers employed in Mexico, and know the country from New Mexico
to California.

"I will now describe the Pass.

"At the head of the valley of the Del Norte there is a broad Pass about eight
miles wide [long], called by the Utah Indians, *Coo-cha-tope,* and by the Mexican
Spaniards *El Puerto,* and which signifies in both languages *The Gap,* or the *Gate;*
and has been known to the Spaniards ever since they settled in New Mexico, and
by the Indians always. It is made by the *Sierra San Juan* [San Juan Mountains],
which comes up from the South on the west side of the Del Norte, *and gives out
there;* and by the *Sierra Blanca* [Sawatch Mountains], which comes in from the
east like it was going to join the San Juan, but turns off north round the head of
the Arkansas and towards the Three Parks [North, Middle, South] and is eight
miles wide. Here between these two mountains is the Pass which goes out level
from the valley of the Del Norte, (and looking like a continuation of it,) which
leads to the upper waters of the Great Colorado of the West. The Del Norte does
not head in this Pass, but in the San Juan Mountain, a little south of the Pass,
where there is also a summer Pass, but none for the winter on account of the snow
in it. There is a small creek in the Pass called by the same name, Coo-cha-tope,
which comes out from the end of the San Juan and goes about eight miles east
towards the Del Norte, but stops in a small lake, out of which a little stream gets
to the Del Norte—which shows how level the country is. [From the Pass, today's
Cochetopa Creek flows north to theTomichi and Gunnison, and a branch of
Saguache Creek flows southeast to San Luis Creek, which sinks before reaching
the Rio Grande.] The Pass is heavily timbered with large pine trees, and with
piñon; and there may be some small oaks, but I am not certain. There is not much
snow in this Pass [cf. Marcy's 1857-58 winter experience, 4:G8], and people go
through it all the winter; and when there is much snow in the mountains on the
Abiquiu route, (which is the old SpanishTrail to California,) the people ofTaos go
round this way, and get into that trail in the forks of Grand and Green rivers.
There are trails through it, but after you get through there are many trails, some
going to the Abiquiu road, and some up or down the country. This Pass is laid
down on a map I saw in the War Office, made by Lieut. Parke and Mr. R. H.
Kern, and is there named after me, because I gave Lieut. Parke information about
it. It is the only map I have seen that shows that Pass, and the best one I have seen
of that part of the country, and with a little correction would be perfect. [Parke's

1851 map actually labels the Cochetopa as "Robidoux Pass;" the map's "Leroux Pass" is 45 miles farther west—today, 25 miles southwest; see L6 Highlights and map.]

"As for the country on each side of the Pass…[see reprint]"

In the succeeding paragraphs of the reprint, Leroux's "Little Colorado" is a Rio Grande tributary now called Red River, located in northern New Mexico. Ft. Massachusetts was established in 1852 about 6 miles north of present Ft. Garland, Colorado. Leroux includes the Sangre de Cristos in his "Sierra Blanca" (Sawatch Mountains). His "Cuebadas" is the Cucharas River flowing through present Walsenburg. "Col. Beale" was Benjamin L. Beall. The "Las Vegas de Santa Clara" were the Mountain Meadows of southeast Utah. Leroux reported that William Pope and Isaac Slover, who had gone to California in 1828 with James Ohio Pattie, in 1837 took their New Mexican families with wagons from Taos over Cochetopa Pass to the Colorado, thence on the Old Spanish Trail to California. The Hardscrabble settlement was on the Arkansas near present Portland, Colorado, west of Pueblo. The "Greenhorn Pueblo on the San Carlos [Graneros?] creek" was 25 miles south-southwest of Pueblo. Williams's ("Witham's") fishery was at today's Twin Lakes about 15 miles south of Leadville. Lucien B. Maxwell was a prominent citizen of Taos. The "Ojo San Jose" is St. Joseph Spring near Parowan, Utah. The "Nicollet" is the Sevier River. Leroux's "Salinas route" to California apparently went via the Salt Fork of the Gila. See 2:C6 for the Old Spanish Trail ("Abiquiu route").

Legacy   No railroad was built through Cochetopa Pass. It was the only route of the Pacific railroad surveys declared to be "impracticable" (L3; see also L5 and L6).

REFERENCES

(See Preface for Heading and Author references, and for Bancroft, not listed here.)

Benton, Thomas H., 1853, Letter from Col. Benton to the people of Missouri, central national highway from the Mississippi River to the Pacific: Wash., 24 p., Leroux letter 2-5.

Gilpin, William, 1860, The central gold region: Phila., 194 p., maps.

Hafen, LeRoy and Ann, 1957, Central route to the Pacific: Glendale, Leroux letter reprint 28-35.

Karnes, Thomas L., 1970, William Gilpin, Western nationalist: Austin, 383 p.

Mollhausen, Baldwin, 1854 (1858 pub.), Diary of a journey from the Mississippi to the coasts of the Pacific: London, 2:182-84.

Parkhill, Forbes, 1965, The blazed trail of Antoine Leroux: Los Angeles, 235 p.; Leroux letter reprint 127-28 and 162-64.

THE
WESTERN JOURNAL
and Civilian,

| VOL. X. | April, 1853. | No. I. |

ARTICLE I.
Slopes and Valleys of the Rocky Mountains.

In reviewing what we have written and published touching the vast and varied resources of the United States, we discover that we have omitted to discuss one great element of individual and national wealth: the wool growing capacity of the slopes and vallies [sic] of the Rocky Mountains. Nor has this topic been treated in connection with the future wealth and grandeur of the American republic in any work which has come within the range of our observation.

From the adaptation of the Southern States to the production of cotton, in connection with the nature of their civil and domestic institutions, is derived the most important staple of American commerce at home and abroad. Hitherto, cotton and Indian corn have been regarded as agricultural staples, which could never be rivalled by any other branch of rural industry, on our part of this continent. There is, indeed, a peculiar adaptation of climate, soil and seasons to the growth of these plants in certain districts of the U.S., which does not exist perhaps in any other country; but we believe, it may be safely affirmed that the slopes and valleys of the mountain ranges dividing the waters of the two great oceans which bound our continent, are not less happily adapted to the production of wool, than are the Southern and Middle States to the growth of cotton and Indian corn, and that sheep growing will, in time, become a source of national wealth, equal at least to either of those great staples.

The entire region lying west of Missouri, extending to the Pacific ocean, and from the Gulf of Mexico to our northern boundary, may be described as decidedly pastoral in its character. It [p. 2] is true, this region embraces extensive deserts, and it also contains large tracts highly favorable to pursuits strictly agricultural; but the former constitute only a small proportion of its entire area, while the latter is admirably adapted to the pursuits of the herdsman as well as those of the farmer and planter.

We are led to conclude from accounts given by various individuals that sheep are more prolific in portions of this region than in any other country of which we have any knowledge. Captain Wilkes, in his account of the exploring expedition, says, in Oregon "the sheep have lambs twice a year. Those of the California breed yield a very inferior kind of wool, which is inclined to be hairy near the hide, and is much matted. This breed has been crossed with the Leicester, and other breeds, which has much improved it. The fleeces of the mixed breed are very heavy, weighing generally eight pounds, and some as much as twelve."

New Mexico, and indeed every part of this extensive region, where sheep have been introduced, has been found exceedingly favorable to their growth. In the valley of the Rio del Norte, in California and Oregon, they subsist upon the natural pastures, in good condition, throughout the winter, requiring no care beyond that which is necessary to protect them against the depredations of the Indians and beasts of prey.

None but those who have seen the immense herds of Buffalo, which subsist upon the plains, can imagine the number of sheep that this extensive region is capable of supporting. It is scarcely assuming too much to affirm that it can supply the markets of the world with one of the most important commodities of commerce and human comfort. And yet, with the exception of a few small districts, this great region is generally, nay almost universally, regarded as a desert. It is important, in many respects, that this ignorance of the true value of such a large part of our own country should be removed. The opinion, that Missouri is separated from California by a desert of two thousand miles, leads to the conclusion that it must forever remain a border State, and weakens the confidence of her own citizens as well as of capitalists, in the value of her works of internal improvement. This imaginary desert operates as a real, substantial impediment to the construction of a railway from the Mississippi river to the Pacific ocean; for, besides the imaginary difficulties to be encountered in constructing and keeping in repair a railroad across a desert of two thou-[p. 3] sand miles, no calculation is made upon any business which the country will afford along the line between Missouri and California.

We remember when, in common with others, we likewise regarded this vast region as a waste, a feature in the physical geography of the continent, calculated to detract from the political power and moral influences of the American people, by separating the inhabitants of the valley of the Mississippi from those on the Pacific coast, at a distance so great that there could be neither social intercourse nor sympathy between them; at least in a degree sufficient to bind them together as constituents of one general government. But subsequent researches into the published accounts of travellers, and information derived from intelligent and experienced individuals who have not only travelled but spent much time in different parts of the country, have lead us to a different conclusion.

All travellers agree that from the western boundary of Missouri through a district of from one hundred to one hundred and twenty miles, the soil is exceedingly fertile, the country well watered and beautifully diversified by groves and undulating prairies. This is generally regarded as one of the most desirable agricultural districts in the basin of the Mississippi. But proceeding westward, beyond this point, the timber fails, except, perhaps, near some of the principal streams; and though the soil changes in character, it is still productive of excellent pasturage to the base of the Rocky Mountains. The following is a description of the valley of the Kanzas, from the pen of Col. W. Gilpin, a highly intelligent gentleman, who has travelled extensively over mountain and plain. We extract from the "Missouri Democrat:"

"Beyond the western line of Missouri is a delicious country of immense extent, through the centre of which flow the waters of the Kansas river. Many rivulets, having their sources under the roots of the Sierra Madre, (Rocky Mountains,) issue from the bottom of the Piedmont or slope that smoothes the fading of the mountain base into the Great Prairie. These converging, some into a bunch to the left, and some to the right, form, the first the Republican river, and the second, the Smoky Hill river. These two rivers meander in channels guttered out of the plains, generally parallel but a few miles asunder, only the first arching out in its middle course towards the Platte, and the latter similarly towards the Arkansas. They receive many small affluents by both banks, and uniting one hundred and twenty miles due west of Independence, form together the Kansas river. This then flows by a nearly [p. 4] straight line due east, entering the Missouri river at the point of the elbow, where it is crossed by the western boundary line of the State of Missouri. The basin of the Kansas, in shape, resembles the open hand laid upon a table, the finger-points touching the foot of the mountains, and the wrist, above the joints, reaching the Missouri river. The length of this basin along the line traversing it east and west, is about six hundred miles—its width from south to north about two hundred—it is therefore oval in form, and the rim which surrounds it has only a gentle prairie swell. Its area is 120,000 square miles. It lies entirely within the plains, and has no contact with, nor does it receive any waters from the mountains.

The Basin of the Kansas is entirely enveloped by those of the rivers Platte and Arkansas. These two rivers have their sources in Pike's Peak, the loftiest point in the chain of the Rocky Mountains within our territory, and capped with perpetual snow. The Platte issues from the north flank; the Arkansas from the south flank of Pike's Peak. This snowy mass is due west from, and opposite to the head of the Kansas basin. These two great rivers diverge rapidly. The Platte, after a course of one thousand miles, joins the Missouri river near Council Bluff, three hundred miles north of Kansas; the Arkansas, of equal length, enters the State of Arkansas at Fort Smith, three hundred miles south of Kansas.

The characteristics of the country embraced in the Kansas Basin are novel to a great majority of the American people—but so were those of Kentucky and all other portions of the Mississippi Valley, when first visited and seen by the seaboard people. Nevertheless, these novelties are entirely in its favor, and invest it with attractions of the very highest order. It is everywhere of limestone formation, but in the upper part there is plaster, or the sulphate of lime: the surface is everywhere an uniformly undulating prairie, having the greatest depth of rich, diluvial soil; this soil is a natural compost of the carbonate and sulphate of lime, having a lustrous mulatto tint. As far as intrinsic principles of fertility and comparison are capable of settling such a question, the productive capacity of the Kansas Basin is greater and more uniform than any other equal sized patch of the earth's surface. Being entirely beyond the timbered region of the continent, and rising towards the West with the gentlest slope, its surface has the appearance of being formed by the deposit of an ocean of still water, and smoothed by its pressure. Its undulations are rounded, graceful, and everywhere rising to the most perfect picturesque beauty. Luxuriant grasses cover it in incalculable variety, and successive crops of flowers everywhere succeed one another from the vernal until long after the autumnal equinox. Meandering streams lace it with their small ravines, irrigate it and che-quer it with romantic groves. Stratified limestone and coal underlie its [p. 5] whole expanse. Beds of the latter, ignited and presenting the phenomena of pseudo-vol-canoes, have suggested the name of the *Smoky-hill* fork.

The western extremity of this basin penetrates into the great *pastoral* belt of the continent. Here the streams become attenuated, and the irrigation from the clouds greatly diminished. Without much change in the elements of fertility, the mellowness of the soil decreases, the surface grows compact, and the grasses cover the ground like a delicate velvet moss. This is the wonderful *buffalo-grass*, which, growing during the evaporations from the rivers in the hot months, cures into hay when that ceases, and furnishes winter pasture for millions of these *aboriginal* cat-tle, for the wild horse, for the antelope, and for venison. The absence of timber is no drawback—it is a supreme advantage. For fuel there is coal—for buildings the healthy *adobie* house is here dictated by the climate; the *adobie* fence combines economy and permanence. Of *Indians* there are only a few hundred in this vast territory, and they largely self-trained to habits of pastoral and arable culture. We speak of this country from the most thorough familiarity and examination. Far from exaggerating, we repress down to the coldest moderation, the wonder and admiration with which all who traverse it are inspired.

But the Kansas basin *ought* to rise to an exalted position in the favor of the whole American people. Sublimely formed by nature to fit its position, it is the GEOGRAPHICAL CENTRE of their country. If from the forks of the Kansas river as a centre, a circle be described, it will touch New Orleans and Galveston upon the Gulf frontier—the same circle will touch the 49th degree on the North, as a tangent. If, again, a circle of larger radius be described from the same centre, it will pass through the cities of San Francisco, in California, and Vancouver, on the Columbia, in Oregon; it will cut the seaport cities of Quebec and Boston, upon the Atlantic; Havana in the Gulf; Vera Cruz and the City of Mexico. It is wonderfully the centre of our territory, both present and prospective. Here is the exact geographical *centre* of the continent, of the Union, of the Valley of the Mississippi, to the North and South, and East and West."

It is possible that the enthusiasm of the writer may have infused a brilliancy of colouring into his description of the Kansas valley, which might not be recognized by the common observer, but in its principal features it is doubtless correct. Col. Gilpin says: "stratified limestone and coal underlie its whole expanse." We do not remember to have seen this fact in respect to coal stated in as strong terms by any other traveller. But the writer is a man of much learning, a close observer of natural phenomena, and well acquainted with the region which he has undertaken to describe. [p. 6]

Pursuing the same parallels of latitude occupied by the Kansas Valley, we cross the head waters of the Arkansas and Rio del Norte, and thence to the valley of Grand river, which is described by travellers as a fertile region of unrivalled beauty, abounding in streams of pure water, and possessing a climate delicious and salubrious.

In a letter from Antoine Laroux [*sic*], which recently appeared in the Missouri Democrat and other public prints, in connection with Col. Benton's letter to the people of Missouri, we find the following description of the country from the sources of the Arkansas to Las Vegas de Santa Clara, in longitude about 113° west. After describing the *Coo-cha-tope* pass, at the head of the valley of the Del Norte, Mr. Leroux says:

"As for the country on each side of the Pass, I will describe it, and on the east side first.

There is a large valley to the east about 50 or 60 miles wide, and near 100 miles long, reaching from the Coo-cha-tope to the Taos settlements, at the Little Colorado. The Del Norte runs through this valley, which is the widest and best valley in all New Mexico, and can hold more people, than all N. Mexico besides.

It is all prairie except on the creeks, and on the river, and on the mountain sides, which are well wooded. It is a rich soil and covered with good grass, and wooded on all the streams. The Spaniards called it El Valle de San Luis, and it was formerly famous for wild horses and buffalo; and ever since Taos was settled by the Spaniards, the inhabitants drove their sheep and cattle there to winter. Before the Utah Indians became so bad, the stock, as many as 50,000 or 60,000 head of sheep and cattle, have been driven there to winter, which they did well, feeding on the grass during the day, and sheltering in the woods about the shepherd's camp at night. Most of the winter there is no snow along the foot of the mountain on the north side of this valley, being sheltered from the north and open to the sun to the south. The United States have established a military post in this valley, not far from the Pass of El Sangre de Christo [sic], and about two hundred families have gone there to live, chiefly near the Fort, and raised crops there last year; and now that they have protection, the valley will soon be all settled, and will be the biggest and best part of New Mexico. About three hundred families more were preparing to move there. The post is called Fort Massachusetts.

This valley has several passes through the Sierra Blanca into the prairie country on the Upper Arkansas, and Kanzas, the best of which is called El Sangre de Christo, at the head of the little streams called Cuebadas, which fall into the Huerfano, a small river falling into the Arkansas, not far from Bent's Fort. It is a [p. 7] good pass, and Bent and St. Vrain's wagons have passed through it, and it is passable the worst of winters; for Col. Beale's dragoons passed through it the same winter, and nearly the same time, that Col. Fremont went through another Pass further West. The distance through these Passes is not more than five miles. This is the description of the country on the east side of the Coo-cha-tope Pass.

On the west side of the Pass, the country opens out broad and good for settlements and for roads, and is the best watered country I ever saw out to the Wah-satch Mountains and to Las Vegas de Santa Clara. After that the water and grass become scarce, and the land poor, and it is called a desert, though travellers find camping grounds every night; and the great cavalcades of many thousand head of horses from California to New Mexico annually passed along it. After you go through the Pass at the head of the Del Norte, there are many trails bearing southwest towards the great Spanish trail by Abiquiu, which they join in the forks of the Grand river and Green river, (forks of the Great Colorado of the West,) where it is a great beaten road, easy to follow day or night. The country is wooded on the streams with prairies between, and streams every three or five miles, as the great Colorado here gathers it head waters from the Wah-satch and Rocky Mountain ranges, which covered all over with snow in the winter, and have snow upon their tops in the summer, which sends down so much water, and cool, clear and good. And this is the case generally out to the Wah-satch Mountains and Las Vegas de Santa Clara—a distance of nearly five hundred miles from the head of the Del Norte. Wagons can now travel this route to California, and have done it. In the year 1837, two families named Sloover and Pope, went from Taos that way.

Col. Fremont was looking for the Coo-cha-tope Pass in the winter of 1848-49, and was near enough to have seen it, if it had not been hid by the lapping of the mountains, when his guide led him off into the mountains, instead of keeping up the dry valley, which he wished to do, and which would have taken him through easy. It was the worst winter for snow, but we could travel all the time in the valleys and passes. I was below him on the waters of the Arkansas at the same time, acting as guide to Col. Beale, who was out after the Apache Indians with a detachment of dragoons, and we heard of him at the Pueblo's. He went as high as Hard Scrabble and got corn before he crossed into the valley of San Luis, and we got corn at the Greenhorn Pueblo on the San Carlos creek, and about fifty or sixty miles below him; and heard that he had passed along, and supposed that he had gone through, and knew no better till he had got back to Taos, when I told him how near he had been to the place he was looking for. We passed with the dragoons through the Pass El Sangre de Christo, (Blood [p. 8] of Christ,) and got through easy; and that was the dead of winter, and greatest snow we ever had.

There is a way also up the Arkansas to get to the waters of the Great Colorado. It is by Bent's Fort, by the Pueblo's and Hard Scrabble, (at all which places corn and vegetables are raised,) and Withams' fishery, and at the head of the river, leaving the Three Parks to the north. Horsemen and stock can go that way. Maxwell, of Taos, drove out between four and five thousand head of sheep and cattle last summer, intending to take them to California, but went to the Great Salt Lake, and sold them there.

A waggon can now go from Missouri to California through the Coo-cha-tope Pass without crossing any mountain but the Sierra Blanca, (and there have the choice of three good passes,) and without crossing any swamp or large river, and nearly on a straight line all the way, only bearing a little south. And supplies of grain and cattle can be had from the Pueblo's on the Upper Arkansas, and also from the Mexicans at OJO SAN JOSE, and at their settlement on the Nicollet river, and at Las Vegas de Santa Clara.

I have been from New Mexico to California four times, viz: the way I guided Col. Cooke, the way I guided Capt. Sitgreaves, and the Salinas route, and the Abiquiu route; and of the four the one I guided Capt. Sitgreaves is, as I informed Mr. Seward, the best and shortest from Santa Fe or Albuquerque: but from places further north, and especially from Missouri, the Coo-cha-tope Pass is best and shortest; and had most water, grass, wood, and good land on it; and has most snow, but not enough to prevent winter travelling; so that when there is much snow in the trail by Abiquiu, people from Taos go that way, as I have already said. The snow in that country is dry, and the mocassins [moccasins] that we wear do not get damp or wet.

And being asked by Col. Benton to state the best way from Missouri to California, I answer: Start as the people now do, going to N. Mexico, from the frontier of the State at Kansas or Independence, and for *summer* travelling go through the prairies up towards Bent's Fort, and up the Huerfano to the Pass El Sangre de Christo; then out by the Coo-cha-tope Pass, following a trail to the great Spanish trail. The *winter* travel would be to start from the same point, but follow the Kansas river valley for the sake of the wood, and when that gives out cross to the Arkansas, which is not far off, and level between, and follow that up for wood. The prairies is the way in the *summer*, but *winter* travelling must have the protection of woods and timber against snow storms. And every thing that I tell I can show, and would undertake to guide a party safe through with wagons now."

So far from being a desert, it is obvious from these accounts that a large portion of the country from the western boundary of Missouri to Las Vegas de Santa Clara, a distance of more than [p. 9] one thousand miles, is highly favorable to pursuits strictly agricultural, and that every part of it affords rich pasturage for stock. This belt, lying between thirty-seven and forty and a half degrees of north latitude, ranges with the valley of the Ohio, and would be capable, were it settled and its resources developed, of supporting a railroad running through its center, with profit to stockholders even without the commerce and travel between the Mississippi and the Pacific. But at present the rich and beautiful valleys of the Kansas and Colorado are forbidden ground: American citizens have no right to cultivate the soil or pasture their flocks on their green meadows.

Nothing but ignorance in respect to the value of the country, could for so long a time have prevented the American people from urging the General Government to extinguish the Indian claim to the valley of the Kansas, and to organize one or more territorial governments between the Western States and the Rocky Mountains. Many thousands emigrate annually to the shores of the Pacific, leaving a country behind them far more to be desired than California with all its golden sands: a country where the rewards of labor would be more certain, and the temptations of vice far less dangerous. Besides, we need a pastoral population, possessing the honest simplicity, patience and patriotism, which have always distinguished its character in all countries, since the days of the patriarchs. Such a population occupying the central portion of the Union, would tend to modify that restless spirit which urges our people to sacrifice physical and social comforts in the pursuit of wealth. It would operate as a check to the disorganizing schemes of designing men, and give consistency and permanency to our institutions.

We rejoice that Congress, at the close of its last session, made an appropriation for the purpose of procuring the relinquishment of the Indian claim to the country west of Missouri and Iowa: a measure which entitles that body to the thanks of the nation; and if carried out in good faith and with promptness by the Executive Department, we trust another year will not elapse before the rich and beautiful valley of the Kansas will be opened to the settlement of a race hitherto excluded from its enjoyment.

The establishment of one or more territorial governments on the eastern slope of the Rocky Mountains, a modification of the laws relating to the disposition of the public domain, and the construc-[p. 10] tion of a railway from the Mississippi to the Pacific ocean, are kindred measures deeply involving the interests and prosperity of every part of the Union. By the border States, these measures should be regarded as paramount to all others which are likely to come before the next Congress. We have a new administration. There are before us several months of vacation to be followed by the long session of Congress. The time is highly auspicious for the discussion of public measures, and we trust that the press and the people will not permit it to pass without improvement.

Much has already been achieved for Western States, and it affords us a high degree of pleasure to record the fact that the thirty-second Congress evinced a disposition more favorable to western measures than has been manifested by the National Legislature for many years. The appropriation for the improvement of western rivers, the grants of land to Missouri and Arkansas to aid in the construction of railroads, and the appropriations for the extinguishment of the Indian claim to the country west of Missouri and Iowa, and for exploring the country in search of a railroad route to the Pacific ocean, authorize the hope that the people of the West will have less cause hereafter to complain of partial legislation in favor of the Eastern States. But it is to be observed that the initiatory step only has been taken in respect to these important measures: the policy which they indicate may yet be abandoned, unless, as in the last Congress, the western delegation, prompted and sustained by their constituents, stand firm and united in support of western interests.

The last democratic administration was signalized by the acquisition of California and New Mexico: during its term these extensive territories were *annexed* to the United States; but the more glorious achievment of uniting them by the means of a railroad and continuous chain of settlements was reserved for the present dynasty. The party in power will stultify itself and be compelled to yield its authority to other hands, if, appalled by the grandeur of this brilliant enterprise, it fails to undertake or accomplish a work so necessary to the convenience and welfare of the nation.

A railroad from the Mississippi to the Pacific will be the means of establishing a branch of industry in the great central region of the continent, which will add more to the wealth and happiness of the American people than all the boasted commerce of the East added to the gold of California. [p. 11]

But besides being the most extensive sheep walk upon the globe, there are portions of this region which rival, and perhaps excel the most favored districts of Europe or Asia in the production of the grape: an important element of national wealth and individual comfort.

Were this extensive country inhabited by a civilized race, and its natural resources improved, the people of the great cities of the Mississippi valley, travelling by railroad, might reach, in one day, a region highly conducive to health and longevity—a land of flocks and vineyards, of herdsmen and vine-dressers, diversified by snow-capped mountains, blooming vallies and sky-bound meadows—enlivened by the flocks of a thousand folds. A land where man will attain his full stature, and his mind receiving impressions from the beauty and grandeur of the scenery, he will rise to the highest degree in the scale of humanity.

Thomas H. Benton, 1854

Western Geography...And The Construction Of A Railroad

"Discourse...Delivered at Baltimore, Tuesday evening, December 5, 1854," 16 p. No
printer or place given, but the imprint of the second issue for delivery in Boston,
December 20, 1854, reads "Washington: Printed by J. T., and Lem. Towers. 1854."
[WC 237 note; WCB 237:1; Eberstadt 121:49 and 137:23; Graff 273 note; Howes
B366; UPRR p. 25; NUC NB 0325434.] Reset verbatim from a facsimile, and repro-
duced by permission of The Huntington Library, San Marino, California.

Significance   Thomas H. Benton defied nature and reality by fantasizing that
St. Louis and San Francisco were connected by a smooth, straight line. Acting on
this politically inspired fantasy, John C. Fremont, who should have known better,
lost 10 men in the snows of the towering San Juans in 1848-49 (L6). On his next
try in the winter of 1853-54, Fremont barely made it through the mountains via
Cochetopa Pass, where Randolph Marcy also would nearly perish in 1857-58
(4:G8). But in this late 1854 speech (p. 13-14) Benton still insisted that Cochetopa
Pass was the *Gate of the Buffaloes*, "those best of engineers, whose instincts never
commit mistakes, and which in their migrations for pasture, shelter, and salt, never
fail to find the lowest levels in the mountains...This is enough to show that the
Rocky mountains may be passed without crossing a hill—that loaded wagons may
cross it at all seasons of the year...Not a tunnel to be made—a mountain to be
climbed—a hill to be crossed—a swamp to be seen—or desert, or moveable sand to
be encountered, in the whole distance...this line for a road, the longest and
straightest in the world, is also over the smoothest and most equal surface."

After representing Missouri for 30 years in the Senate, Benton's antislavery,
pro-Union leanings defeated him in 1851. He was back for one term in the
House when he gave this railroad speech in 1854. The other Missouri Senator,
proslavery David R. Atchison, feared that the Pacific railroad would make the
Western territories free. Of Benton and the railroad he declared, "of all the humbugs the old sinner has ever mounted, of all the lame, blind, wind-broken and
spavined hobbies the old villain ever bestrode, he has now mounted the most
shabby" (Chambers 1956).

Reprinted here is the first issue of the last of Benton's 75 separately printed speeches. In it he quoted from Fremont's 1854 letter to the *National Intelligencer* (L6), and from Gwinn H. Heap's 1854 book on the *Central Route to the Pacific*, which recounted Heap's 1853 trip with Edward F. Beale (5:J9). After this 16-page address in Baltimore, Benton padded the speech to 24 pages for delivery in Boston, Providence, Hartford, and Philadelphia. He added a warm introduction, a quote from Leroux, a description of Mountain Meadows, the testimony of stock dealers driving sheep to California, acknowledgment that Humboldt first recognized the buffalo as the best of civil engineers, and a call for enlightened capitalists to step forward and build the road. He delivered the final version in Congress in January, 1855 (WCB 237:3). By this time he included attacks on the northern or "Canadian" route and the southern or "Mexican" route. This last version was reprinted in full by Charles W. Dana in 1856, and in large part by John C. VanTramp in 1858. I know of no modern reprint of any of these issues.

AUTHOR   THOMAS H. BENTON, 1782-1858, senator, lawyer, soldier, editor, promoter of the West. See 1:B3 for biography.

Highlights   From 1818 Benton had steadfastly favored using the Missouri and Columbia rivers for U.S. trade access to the Pacific (see Smith 1846). It was not until 1849 that he introduced his first railroad bill in the Senate. The termini of his Central National Road would be San Francisco and St. Louis. The line would be as straight as possible, with branches right and left to satisfy all sections. It would be iron rails where practicable, or planks or macadam or sleigh paths where not. It would be surveyed and built by the government, financed by the sale of public lands, and protected by military posts. The Indians would get $100,000 for their lands on the line. (Hafens 1960.)

Benton's foes said he was a Johnny-come-lately. William M. Hall of New York charged in 1853 that Benton was "a neophyte among the advocates of a Pacific Railroad, and a hindrance to the early commencement of that great work." John F. Darby in 1880 stated, "Col. Benton, for more than ten years after the first agitation [in 1838] on the subject of railroads in Missouri, opposed them…Col. Benton did attend the [1849 railroad] convention, and made a splendid speech, for which he [ironically] had a statue erected to him." John Loughborough's 1849 report for that St. Louis railroad convention observed, "Our gratification was enhanced by the consideration, that to support this great [Pacific railroad] measure, Col. Benton had not only to abandon a long and deeply cherished [river] system, but to adopt another [the railroad] which was in direct conflict with his feelings, personal and political."

Army humorist Capt. George H. Derby's 1856 book contained a spoof about mighty explorations for the Central Route up Kearny Street in San Francisco: "The beautiful idea, originated by Col. Benton, that buffaloes and other wild animals are the pioneer engineers, and that subsequent explorations can discover no better roads than those selected by them, would appear to apply admirably to the Central Route. Many pigs, singly and in droves, met and passed me continually; and as the pig is unquestionably a more sagacious animal than the buffalo, their preference for this route is a most significant fact."

In his speech Benton proposed the creation of five new states along his central route. He advanced the old chestnut that forests would spring from the plains as soon as the Indians stopped burning the grass every year. He did not know that Edwin James climbed Pike's Peak in 1820 (2:D1). His many named mountains, rivers, and passes, largely from Fremont and Heap, are covered in L4 and L6. With his usual flourish, Benton announced, "Westward the torrents of emigration direct their course."

Legacy   Benton's and Fremont's politically motivated geographic fantasies led to tragedy and frustration (L6).

REFERENCES
(See Preface for Heading and other references not listed here.)

Chambers, William N., 1956, Old Bullion Benton, Senator from the New West: Boston, Atchison quote p. 398; Benton's last printed speech 410-11.

Dana, Charles W., 1856 (1857 reprint), The great West, or the garden of the world: Boston, Benton speech reprint p. 358-92.

Darby, John F., 1880, Personal recollections: St. Louis, quotes on agitation p. 181, convention 183.

Derby, George H., 1856, Phoenixiana, or sketches and burlesques by John Phoenix: N.Y., quote p. 27-28.

Hafen, LeRoy R. and Ann W., 1960, Fremont's Fourth Expedition: Glendale, Benton's 1849 speech and bill p. 49-73.

Hall, William M., 1853, Speech in favor of a national rail road to the Pacific: N.Y., 68 p.; quote 68.

Heap, Gwinn H., 1854, Central Route to the Pacific: Phila., 136 p.

Loughborough, John, 1849, The Pacific telegraph and railway: St. Louis, quote p. 21.

Smith, Robert, 1846, Railroad to the Pacific Ocean: Wash., 29/1 H773 Report, serial 491, 48 p.; Benton's 1846 views 6-8, 25-33; his 1818 views 8-17.

VanTramp, John C., 1858 (ca. 1864 ed.), Prairie and Rocky Mountain adventures: Columbus, Benton speech reprint p. 284-313.

DISCOURSE

OF

MR. BENTON, OF MISSOURI,

BEFORE

THE MARYLAND INSTITUTE,

*On the physical geography of the country between Missouri and
California, with a view to show its adaptation to settlement,
and the construction of a Railroad. Delivered at
Baltimore, Tuesday evening, December 5, 1854.*

Mr. President, Gentlemen of the Institute, and Ladies:

We live in an age when utility and progress are the order of the day, and when
all propositions of the statesman and lawgiver, as well as of the philosopher and
mechanician, are brought to the touchstone of use and practice, and dismissed
from the public mind as unworthy of attention, if found unable to stand that test.
I profess to belong to that school, and come here to-night, upon your kind invitation, to discourse upon a subject which will bear that test—one which has already
much engaged the public mind, and on which practical views, and not speculative
opinions, are wanted. I speak of the country beyond the Mississippi—between
Missouri and California—its physical geography, and its adaptation to settlement
and cultivation, and to the construction of a railroad to the Pacific ocean. I have
paid some attention to this geography, induced by a local position and some turn
for geographical inquiry; and, in a period of more than thirty years, have collected
whatever information was to be obtained from the reading of books, the reports
of travellers, and the conversation of hunters and traders; and all with a view to a
practical application. I have studied the country with a view to results, and feel
authorized to believe from all that I have learned that this vast region is capable of
sustaining populous communities, and exalting them to wealth and power—that
the line of great states which now stretch half way across our continent in the
same latitudes—(Pennsylvania, Ohio, Indiana, Illinois, Missouri,)—may be
matched by an equal number of states, equally great, between Missouri and California; and that the country is perfectly adapted to the construction of a railroad,
and all sorts of roads, traversable in all seasons. This is my opinion, and I proceed
to verify it: and first, of the five states, their diagrams and relative positions; and
then their capabilities.

The present Territory of Kansas, extending seven hundred miles in length upon two hundred in breadth, and containing above one hundred thousand square miles, would form two states of above fifty thousand square miles each. A section of the Rocky mountains, embracing the Three Parks, and the head waters of the South Platte, the Arkansas, Del Norte, and the eastern branches of the Great Colorado of the West, would form another state, larger in the opinion of Frémont than all the Swiss cantons put together; and presenting every thing grand and beautiful that is to be found in Switzerland without its drawback of avalanches and glaciers. The valley of the Upper Colorado, from [p. 2] the western base of the Rocky mountains to the eastern base of the Wahsatch and Anterria ranges, 200 miles wide by 200 long, and now a part of Utah, might form the fourth—and the remainder of Utah, from the Wahsatch to California, would form the fifth—of which the part this way covering the Santa Clara meadows, and Wahsatch and Anterria ranges, would be the brightest part. Here then are five diagrams of territory, sufficient in extent, as any map will show, to form five states of the first magnitude. That much is demonstrated: now for their capabilities to sustain populous communities, and their adaptation to the construction of a railroad.

We begin with the Territory of Kanzas, and find its length above three times its breadth, and naturally divisible into two states by a north and south line, half way to the mountains. The eastern half is beginning to be known from the reports of emigrants and explorers; but to understand its whole interior the general outline of the whole Territory must first be traced—in the mind's eye, or, upon a map. Maps are not convenient in so large an assemblage; so the mind's eye must be put in requisition, and made to follow the lines as indicated—thus: Beginning on the western boundary of Missouri, in the latitude of 37 degrees, and following that parrallel [sic] west, to the eastern boundary of New Mexico; then a deflection of one degree north to the parrallel of 38; and on that parrallel to the summit of the Rocky Mountains; then northwardly along that summit to the parrallel of 40 degrees; then east with that parrallel to the Missouri line; and south with that line to the beginning. This is the outline: now for the interior: and for the sake of distinctness, we will examine that by sections, conformable to the natural divisions of the country.

We commence with the Kanzas river, on the north side of the Territory, and its four long forks—of which the Smoky Hill, the Saline, Solomon's, and the Republican—of which the Smoky Hill is the most considerable, and in the best place for the advantage of the Territory. All these forks flow in the right direction—from west to east—and are beautifully parrallel to each other, without mountains or ridges between to interrupt their communications, and making, after their junction, near two hundred miles of steam boat navigation before their united waters reach the great Missouri river. All the land drained by these streams constitute the Valley of Kanzas—if the term valley can be applied to a region which has but little perceptible depression below the general level of the country. We will consider the term applicable to all the territory drained by all the Kanzas forks and all their tributaries. One general description applies to the whole—the soil rich like Egypt! and tempting as Egypt would be if raised above the slimy flood, waved into gentle undulations, variegated with groves and meadows, sprinkled with springs, coursed by streams; and warmed by a sun which warms without burning, and blest with the alteration of seasons which give vigor to the mind and body. Egypt thus raised up, and changed, might stand for Kanzas: as she is, the only point of comparison is in the soil. For this valley is high and clean, diversified with wood and prairie, watered by springs and streams, grassy and flowery—its bosom filled with stone for building, coal for fuel, and iron for the home supply of that first of metals. This is the Kanzas of the northern, or Kanzas river side, where Fré-mont says, (and he has a right to know,) a continuous corn field two hundred miles in length, might be made;—so rich and level is the country. But of this part it is not necessary to say much, as the crowds of emigrants are directing shem-selves [*sic*] upon it, and vieing with each other in the glowing descriptions which they give of its beauty, salubrity, and fertility.

I turn to the south side of the Territory, of which little has been said, and much is to be told, and all profitable to be known. In the first place, this [p. 3]south side includes the whole body of the Arkanzas river, from near the Missouri line to its head-most spring in the Rocky mountains—a length of above seven hundred miles on a straight line, and near double that length in the meanders of the stream. This gives to the Territory a second large river, and in the right place, and flowing in the right direction—and parallel to the other, as if its twin sister; and so near together as to be seldom more than a degree, and somtimes [*sic*] not half a degree, from each other: and no mountains or high grounds between them. This, of itself, is a great advantage to the Territory: for the Arkansas, like all rivers in the prairie country, brings fertile borders, and groves of wood, and rich grass; and makes an attractive line for settlement and travel. In the next place, it gives a suc-cession of tributaries on each side—each giving lines of wood and water—the only thing wanted for settlement and cultivation. Some of these tributaries are of good length, and drain wide areas—as the Neosho, drawing its expanded head-waters from the centre of the Territory, two hundred miles long, and becoming navigable before it reaches the Arkansas river. The Verdigris is but little less than the Neosho, and next above it, and of the same characteristics; and both adapted to cultivation and pasturage. On the opposite side, coming in from the south, is the Salt fork of the Arkansas, the lower part of it within the limits of Kanzas, with its salt plains, and rock salt—impregnating the river, and rendering its waters undrinkable in the dry season. I have seen parcels of this rock salt at St. Louis, cut off with hatchets by the Indians, and of the blown salt, swept up by the squaws with turkey-wing fans when the autumnal sun had evaporated the briny waters of the saline marshes—all so useless now in the hands of the Indians, and to become so valuable in the hands of the whites.—Ascending the river, there is a continued succession of affluents from each side, all exercising their fertilizing powers upon bordering lines of wood, soil and grass; and becoming better to the very base of the mountains. So that the river advantages on the north side of the Territory are rivalled by similar advantages on the south side.

I have spoken of the two sides of the Territory: now for the centre—and that is soon dispatched: an expanded prairie, level to the view, rich in soil, scant (but not destitute) of water, green with grass, and enlivened in the proper season with myriads of buffaloes—spreads illimitably before the eyes of the traveller. Some springs, many small streams, numerous pools, peculiar to these plains, (reservoirs of the rains invaluable for stock,) furnish the present supply, to be helped out by wells as soon as settled. The annual autumnal devastating fires being stopped, the indigenous forest growth will immediately come forth, accompanied by the exotics which the thrifty farmer will lose no time to introduce. Coal will furnish fuel, so that the whole central plain will receive settlers from the begining, and especially on the line of road actually travelled, and where the railroad may be expected to be. In the mean time the settler has an attraction—superior with many, and profitable as well as pleasant in itself—to draw him into this vast plain. It is the pastoral pursuit: for this is the bucolic region of our America—now the resort of wild animals—and soon to become the home of the domestic. A short sweet grass, equally nutritions [*sic*] in the green or dried state, (for it dries of itself on the ground,) covers the face of the earth, inviting all ruminating animals to take their food upon it, without measure and without stint;—a great pastoral region, in which the ox will not know his master's crib, nor the ass the hand that feedeth him; but, in which the dumb, unconscious beast, without knowing it, will feel the bounty of the hand which is the giver of all good.

This is the description of the first Kansas—the one which will go half way to the mountains—equal in territorial extent to the firt [*sic*] class states, exceeded in [p. 4] productive capacity by none—and soon to become one of the great states of the Union. I will call it East Kansas.

The second state would occupy the remainder of the territory to the base of the

Rocky Mountains; and, like the first half will have the natural division into three parts, and with the same characteristics; but with a reversal of their localities. The Arkansas river side will be far the most valuable—both intrinsically and in its locality: but the Kansas side will still have its value and attraction. Frémont says of it; "the soil of all this country, (upper Kansas and base of the mountains,) is excellent—admirably adapted to agricultural purposes, and would support a large agricultural and pastoral population."—He says it is watered by many streams, but without wood, except on their borders—that grass abounds, and among its varieties the *esparcette*, a species of clover so valuable for the pasturage of swine— cultivated for that purpose in Germany, but indigenous in all this base of the mountains.

But the valley of the Upper Arkansas would form the pride and strength of the Upper State—West Kanzas, as I will call it, including as the Territory does, a part of the superb valley of San Luis, and the beautiful Sahwatch, which forms a continuation of it, and which leads to the famous Coochatope Pass, and the Pass itself. Frémont thus speaks of this upper part of the Arkansas, as seen by him in his various expeditions, and especially in the one of the last winter.

"The immediate valley of the Upper Arkansas, for about two hundred miles, as you approach the mountains, is continuously well adapted to settlements as well as to roads. Numerous well-watered and fertile valleys, broad and level, open up among the mountains, which present themselves in detached blocks, (outliers,) gradually closing in around the heads of the streams, but leaving open approaches to the central ridges. The whole of the inter-mountain region is abundant in grasses, wood, coal, and fertile soil. The *pueblos* above Bent's fort prove it to be well adapted to the grains and vegetables common to the latitude, including Indian corn, which ripens well, and to the support of healthy stock, which increase well and take care of themselves summer and winter."

Of the climate, and winter season in this elevated region, he thus speaks:

"The climate is mild and the winters short, the autumn usually having its full length of bright open weather, without snow, which in winter falls rarely and passes off quickly. In this belt of country lying along the mountains the snow falls more early and much more thinly, than in the open plains to the eastward; the storms congregate about the high mountains, and leave the valleys free. In the beginning of December we found yet no snow on the *Huerfano* river, and were informed by an old resident, then engaged in establishing a farm at the mouth of this stream, that snow seldom fell there, and that cattle were left in the range all the winter through."

This was the first of December. Eight days later, and when advanced an hundred miles further, and standing in the Sand Hill pass of the Sierra Blanca, which looks both into the head valleys of the Del Norte and of the Arkansas, he still writes:

"On the 8th of December we found this whole country free from snow, and Daguerre views, taken at this time, show the grass entirely uncovered in the passes."

This is the winter view of this country and its climate, and certainly no mountain region could present any thing more desirable for man or beast. A summer view of it is give by *Messrs.* Beale and Heap, in their central route journey to California, in 1853:

"Upon reaching the summit of the *buttes,* a magnificent and extensive panorama opened to our view. The horizon was bounded to the north by Pike's Peak—to the west and north west by the Sierra Mohada, (Wet mountain,) Sangre de Christo mountains, and the Spanish Peaks; to the south and east extended the prairie—lost in the hazy distance. On the gently undulating plains reaching to the foot of the Rocky mountains, could be traced, by their lines of timber, the course of the Arkansas river, and its various tributaries—among them the Huerfano, (Orphan river,) easily distinguished from the remote point (nearly due west,) where it issued from the Sierra Blanca, to its junction with the [p. 5] Arkansas, except at short intervals where it passed through canyons in the plain. Pike's Peak was a prominent object in the landscape, its head capped with eternal snow, soaring high above all the neighbouring summits. The river (Huerfano,) bottom was broad and thickly wooded with willows and cotton wood, interlaced with wild rose and grape vines, and carpetted with soft grass—a sylvan paradise. The scenery as we approached the country between the Spanish Peaks and the Sierra Mohada, was picturesque and beautiful. Mountains towered high above us, the summits of some covered with snow, (July,) while the dense forests of dark pines which clothed their sides, contrasted well with the glittering white at the top, and the light green of the soft grass at their base. The humidity of the Sierra Mohada gives great fertility to this region; and the country bordering on the sides of the mountains, as well as the valleys in their recesses, are unequaled in loveliness and richness of vegetation. To the settler they offer every inducement; and I have no doubt in a few years this tract of country will vie with California or Australia, in the number of emigrants it will invite. It is by far the most beautiful part of New Mexico, (now a part of Kansas;) and a remarkably level country connects it with the western part of the Atlantic States. As soon as this is thrown open to settlement, a continuous line of farms will be established, by which the agricultural and mineral wealth of the country will be developed."

Mr. Charles McClanahan, a Virginia emigrant to California, and a large dealer in stock to that country, writing back to me from the valley of San Luis in August, 1853, says:

"On this route almost the entire way may be settled, as all the land from Missouri to Bent's Fort is rich and very fertile, equal to the best lands of Missouri and Illinois; and no land can beat the Sierra Blanca for grass. Even to the very summit it stands as thick as the best meadows, and many acres would mow at least four tons to the acre. Then comes the large and beautiful valley of San Luis, said to be one of the most fertile in New Mexico. Indeed fine land is upon the whole route, and the climate is such that stock can live out all the winter upon the grass. On this route there is an abundance of grass and water, so much so that stock will travel and keep fat. A very large majority of our sheep are as fat mutton as any in the Philadelphia or Baltimore market; and a very large number of Mr. Barnwell's cattle are fine beef, and I have never seen any stock, after travelling so far look half so well."

This is the western, or Upper Kanzas, and will make another great state; and both will quickly be ripe for admission into the Union—East Kanzas in 1855, and the western in 1856. They will both be settled with unexampled rapidity. In agriculture and grazing alone they present irresistible attractions to the settler. But it is not agricultural and pastoral advantages alone, great as they are, which are to attract people to this region: other causes are to add their inducements to the same attractions, and render them invincible. At the head of these other causes stands the pre-emption law, now engrafted as a permanent feature in the federal land system, and made applicable to all the public lands in the Territory. By virtue of this law the laboring man, without a dollar in his pocket, is put ahead of the speculator with his thousands. He may chuse for himself out of the wide domain—mark out his choice—take possession—work it: and raise enough out of it, or on it, to pay the government price by the time the pay is demandable—with the good prospect to see it rise to ten or twenty times as much as it cost within a few years. This is a chance for a freehold, and of provision for a family, which the wise and industrious tiller of the earth will not neglect. Then come the political advantages. The act of Congress creating the Territory gives great political rights to unnaturalized settlers coming into it. It gives the elective franchise, and eligibility to office, upon the simple declaration of an intention to become a citizen of the United States, and taking the requisite oaths. This is an advantage which the foreign emigrant will know how to appreciate, and to appropriate. Then comes an advantage of a different kind still, novel but energetic, and already in full operation—the competition for excess of settlers between the free and the slave states. That competition, though deplorable in its political and social aspect, must have one good effect upon the Territory—that of rapidly filling it with [p. 6] people—the only point of view in which I refer to it. Finally comes a fourth cause in this extra list for attracting settlers—one that must have its effect upon all who can reason from cause to effect—who can look ahead and see what is to happen by seeing what exists—who can estimate the force of natural causes, which are self-acting and irresistible, and which work out their results without the directing and helping hand of government. It is the Pacific railroad!—Kanzas has the charter from nature for that road, and will use it. She has the smooth way on which to place it—the straight way on which to run it—the material with which to build it—the soil and people to support it—and the salubrious climate to give it exemption from disease: and she has in her south-west quarter, precisely where the straight line requires them to be, the multiplied gates which open the mountains to the Pacific—the Coochatope, the Carnero, the San Juan, the Poonche, the Medio, the Mosca, the Sangre de Christo, the Utah. These passes, and the rich, grand, and beautiful country in which they lie, command a road—and will have it; and the pre-emptioner who acquires a quarter section on its line, may consider his fortune made.

Now I think I have provided for two of the five states which I have promised, and that within the brief space of one and two years, and each upon a larger population than has ever yet been required from other new states. Now let us proceed to the other three, and let us dispatch them in less time than these two have required.

We take a section of the Rocky mountains, from 37 to 41 degrees—near 300 miles north and south—and go down to the base on each side, say an hundred miles or more each way—making an area of 60,000 square miles, while all the Swiss cantons have not 20,000. Here, then, is territory enough for a great mountain state. Now let us look to its contents and capabilities. First, there are the Three Parks, first described by Frémont, and since laid down on all the maps—large, beautiful mountain coves, two of them of thirty miles diameter each, the other of sixty—at a great elevation, delightful in summer, and tempered in winter, from the concentration of the sun's rays; and sheltered by the lofty rim of mountains, forever crowned with snow, which wall them in, and break off the outside storms. The name is not fanciful, nor bestowed capriciously by travellers, but a real description, translated from the Indian name of these parks, which signifies "cow lodge;" and not without reason, for the buffaloes not only feed, but lodge there, and make them the places of their immense congregation; attended by all the minor animals—elk, deer, antelopes, bears. Then the innumerable little valleys in which rise the myriad of young streams which, collecting into creeks, go off to start upon their long courses in the mighty rivers which, there rising together, go off in opposite directions, some to the rising—some to the setting sun: the South Platte, the Arkansas, the Del Norte on one side; and the Great Colorado of the West on the other—all four born so near together, to run so far apart: a point of similitude to Switzerland which the instructed mind will not fail to perceive; and also to discover another similitude in Pike's Peak, grand in its elevation, forever luminous in snow—the Mont Blanc of the Rocky mountains, which no adventurous Packard, or De Saussure, has ever yet climbed. Then an endless labyrinth of little valleys and coves, where wild animals luxuriate in summer, and shelter in winter; and where the Indians pursue their game in all seasons without impediment from cold or snow; and where their horses do well on the grass, retaining much of its moisture and nutriment. Frémont thus describes the general winter condition of these valleys:

"Our progress in this mountainous region was necessarily slow; and during ten days which it occupied us to pass through about one hundred miles of the mountainous country bordering the eastern side of the Upper Colorado valley, the greatest depth of the [p. 7] snow was (among the pines and aspens on the ridges) about two and a half feet, and in the valleys about six inches. The atmosphere is too cold and dry for much snow; and the valleys, protected by the mountains, are comparatively free from it, and warm. We here found villages of Utah Indians in their wintering ground, in little valleys along the foot of the higher mountains, and bordering the more open country of the Colorado valley. Snow was here (December 25) only a few inches deep—the grass generally appearing above it; and there being none under trees and on southern hill sides. The horses of the *Utahs* were living on the range, and notwithstanding that they were used in hunting were in excellent condition. One which we had occasion to kill for food had on it about two inches of fat, being in as good order as any buffalo we had killed in November on the eastern plains. Over this valley country—about one hundred and fifty miles across the Indians informed us that snow falls only a few inches in depth; such as we saw it at the time."

This is the winter condition of these little valleys, very comfortable for man and beast, even in their wild state, and to become more comfortable under the hand of cultivation. The summer view, as presented by *Messrs*. Beale and Heap, is absolutely enchanting—a perfect labyrinth of valleys, with their cool water and sweet grass; some wide, some narrow; some bounded by perpendicular walls of rock, like streets in a city; others by softly rounded hills; some studded with small circular mountains, called by the hunters "round mountains,"—fertile on the sides, level and rich on the top, diversified with wood and prairie, and refreshed with clear streams, and beautified with deep, limpid miniature lakes. These descriptions are charming, but too numerous for quotation; and I can only give a specimen of each:

"The trail led over low hills and down a succession of beautiful slopes, running mostly in a southern direction, until we entered a narrow winding valley, two miles and a half in length, by one and two hundred yards in breadth. It was shut in on each side by perpendicular walls of rock, rising from fifty to seventy-five feet above the level of the valley, whose surface was flat and carpetted with tender grass. A stream of clear water meandered through its centre, and the grade was so slight that the stream overflowing in many places, moistened the whole surface. As we descended this beatiful and singular valley, we occasionly passed others of a similar character. It ends in Sahwatch valley, which we entered about one hour before sunset." "The valleys down which we travelled, and which opened into each other with the regularity of streets, grew gradually broader as we descended. We finally entered one watered by Carnero, (Sheep) creek, which joins the Garita, (Gate creeek) [sic] in San Luis valley; and at noon encamped a short distance above a gate, or gap, through which the stream passes; (and whence it derives its name.) Half a mile below this gap there is another; and a quarter of a mile further a third. The passage through them is level, while the trail around them is steep and stony. In the afternoon, we went through the first gap, made a circuit around the second, as it was much obstructed with trees and bushes; and, leaving the third on our left, rode over some low hills; and five miles from camp, crossed the Garita. We were once more in San Luis valley, and all before us was a perfect level, as far the sight could reach." "Our way for a mile or two led over a barren plain, thickly covered with grice wood, but we soon struck the base of the mountain, where firm, rich mountain grass swept our saddle girths as we cantered over it. We crossed a considerable mountain covered with timber and grass, and near the summit of which was quite a cluster of small, but very clear, and apparently deep lakes. They were not more than an acre or two in size, and some not even that, but surrounded by luxurient grass, and perched away upon the mountain, with fine timber quite near them. It was the most beautiful scenery in the world. It formed quite a hunters paradise; for deer and elk bounded off from us as we approached; and then stood within rifle shot, looking back in astonishment. A few hours ride brought us to the Indian camp; and I wish I here could describe the beauty of the charming valley in which they camped. It was small, probably not more than five miles wide by fifteen long, but surrounded on all sides by the boldest mountaains [sic], covered to their summits with alternate patches of timber and grass, giving it the appearance of having been regularly laid off in small farms. Through the centre a fine bold stream, three feet deep by forty wide, watered the meadow land, and gave the last touch which the valley required to make it the most beautiful I had ever seen." "Hundreds of horses and goats were feeding on the meadows and hill-side: and the Indian lodges, with the women and children standing in front of them to look at the approaching stranger, strongly reminded me of old patriarchal times, when flocks and [p. 8] herds made the wealth and hppiness [*sic*] of the people, and a hut was as good as a palace. I was conducted to the lodge of the chief—an old and infirm man, who welcomed me kindly, and told me his young men told him that I had given of my small store to them, and to *"Sit in peace."* In about fifteen minutes a squaw brought in two large wooden platters containing, some very fat deer meat and some boiled corn, to which I did ample justice; and when about to leave, found a large bag of dried meat and a peck of corn put up for me to take to my people."—"This morning I explored the mountain lying to the south of our camp, forming a picturesque portion of our front view. After ascending the mountain and reaching the summit, I found it a vast plateau of rolling prairie land, covered with the most beautiful grass, and heavily timbered. At some places the growth of timber would be so dense as to render riding through it impossible without great difficulty; while at others it would break into beautiful open glades, leaving spots of an hundred acres, or more, of open prairie, with groups of trees, looking precisely as if some wealthy planter had amused himself by planting them expressly to beautify his grounds. Springs were abundant, and small streams intersected the whole plateau. In fact, it was an immense natural park, already stocked with deer and elk, and only requiring a fence to make it an estate for a king. Directly opposite, to the south, another mountain, in every respect similar; and a valley, more beautiful to me than either, lies between them."

Enough for a sample; and if any thing more is wanted to establish the character of this mountain region for fertility of soil and attraction for man, it is found in its character of *hunting*, and of *war* ground. Frémont says he found it the most variously and numerously stocked with game, and the most dangerous war ground, which he had seen in all the extent of the Rocky mountains—both indexes to a fertile country. The country sought for by animals, and fought for by men, is always a good country. Western men will understand this, and remember how Kentucky was called the *"Bloody Ground,"* because Indians came there to hunt the numerous game, feeding on the rich grass, product of her rich soil; and to fight for its possession. By this test, and it is one which never fails, our mountain state will be one of eminent fertility.

We Americans are in the habit of referring to Europe for a point of comparison for everything we wish to praise in our own country, although our own may be far superior: therefore, I compare this mountain state to Switzerland, although it is disparaged in the comparison. Its valleys are more numerous and beautiful—its mountains less rugged, and more fertile—its surface more inhabitable—its climate more mild, and equally salubrious—more accessible by roads; the mule anywhere sure of its feet, the carriage of its wheel; and the hunter at liberty to pursue his game without fear of slipping into a bottomless icy chasm, betrayed by a treacherous covering of snow. Its little round mountains, with their grassy sides, and rich level tops, and natural parks, and miniature lakes, and sweet flowing waters—have no parrellel [sic] in Switzerland, or in any other part of the world. And upon this view of their relative advantages, I am ready to adopt the opinion of Frémont, and to go beyond it, and to celebrate this mountain state as being as much superior to Switzerland in adaptation to settlement as it would be in extent—and, to crown its recommendations, just half way to the Pacific, and on the straight line.

The valley of the Upper Colorado would furnish the territory for the fourth state—150 miles wide from the western base of the Rocky mountains to the eastern base of the Wahsatch and Anterria ranges—and 3 or 400 in length, up and down the river. The face of the country is high and rolling, with alternations of woodland and prairie; and open to roads and settlement in any direction. The soil, like much of that on the Rio Del Norte and in southern California, is peculiar and deceptious—looking thin and sandy to the eye, but having an element of fertility in it which water impregnates, and enables to send forth a vigorous vegetation. All it wants, and that only in places, is irrigation; and for this purpose, and for all purposes, there is water enough; for this valley is probably the best watered region in the world, and is obliged to be so from [p. 9] the configuration and structure of the country. The valley is formed by the lofty ranges of the Rocky and Wahsatch mountains; which, wide apart at its lower end, converge as they go north, and unite above latitude 42—giving to the long and broad valley they enclose the form of the greek letter delta ($\wedge$), or of our V inverted. The summits of these mountains are covered with eternal snows—their sides with annual winter snows; and these latter beginning to melt early in the spring, and continuing till mid summer, fill the earth with moisture, and give rise to myriads of springs, creeks, and small rivers, which collect into the two forks of the Colorado, called by the hunters Green and Grand rivers; and, in their junction, constitute the great river itself: for the country below, being sterile and arid, contributes but little to swell the volume of the great river which traverses it. The climate in this valley is mild—the month of January being

like autumn to us. We owe this knowledge to the last winter expedition of Frémont, who says: *"The immediate valley of the Upper Colorado, for about* 100 *miles in
breadth, and from the* 7th *to the* 21st *of January, was entirely bare of snow, and the
weather resembled autumn with us."* This would be the fourth state—equal in extent
to any, inferior in soil, superior in wood and water, softer in climate, better in due
alternations of woodland and prairie: and being part of the Utah Territory, it is now
under the dominion of law and government, and open to immediate settlement:
which in fact is now going on.

The fifth state would consist of the remainder of the Utah Territory, beginning
at the eastern base of the Wahsatch and Anterria ranges, and extending 300 miles
to the California line—upon whatever breadth might be desired. It would include
(towards its eastern border,) the Little Salt Lake, which is 260 miles south of the
Great Salt Lake; and which designates a country as much superior to that of the
Great Salt Lake as itself is inferior to that large and marvelous body of salt water.
It would be a magnificent state, its eastern limit, there the rim of the Great Basin,
would embrace the broad expanse of the Wahsatch and Anterria ranges, or rather
blocks, as they are cut up into short sections—probably the richest mountain
region in the world, where nature has crowded and accumulated into an hundred
miles square, as into a vast magazine, a profusion, of her most valuable gifts to
man. Soil, water, grass, wood, timber, rock-salt, coal, stone: a due alternation of
mountain and valley—the former cut into blocks, white on the top with snow,
dark on the sides with forests, and their bosoms filled with ores; the valleys green
with grass, fresh with cool water, opening into each other by narrow level gaps, or
defiles: the climate so soft that animals live out all the winter, and February (so
frosty and frozen with us,) the usual month there for starting the plough: I say
starting the plough; for the Mormons, since several years, have seen the beauty of
this region; and have come upon it. We owe to Frémonts' last winter expedition
the revelation to public view of this magnificent region, more valuable than all the
gold mines of California and Australia put together. He had seen these ranges in
his previous expeditions, and given them a page in his journal, and a place in his
map; but it was not until his last expedition that he penetrated their recesses, and
saw their hidden treasures. He was fourteen days in them—from the 24th of January to the 7th of February—and thus speaks of what he saw:

"They lie between the Colorado valley and the Great Basin, and at their western base are established the Mormon settlements of Parowan and Cedar city.
They are what are called fertile mountains, abundant in water, wood, and grass,
and fertile valleys, offering inducements to settlement and facilities for making a
road. These mountains are a great storehouse of materials—timber, iron, coal—

which would be of indispensable use in the construction and maintenance of the road, and are solid foundations to build up the future prosperity of the rapidly-increasing Utah State. Salt is abundant on the eastern border; mountains—as the *Sierra de Sal*—being named from it. In the [p. 10] ranges lying behind the Mormon settlements, among the mountains through which the line passes, are accumulated a great wealth of iron and coal, and extensive forests of heavy timber. These forests are the largest I am acquainted with in the Rocky mountains, being, in some places, twenty miles in depth, of continuous forest; the general growth lofty and large, frequently over three feet in diameter, and sometimes reaching five feet, the red spruce and yellow pine predominating. At the actual southern extremity of the Mormon settlements, consisting of the two enclosed towns of Parowan and Cedar city, near to which our line passed, a coal mine has been opened for about eighty yards, and iron works already established. Iron here occurs in extraordinary masses, in some parts accumulated into mountains, which comb out in crests of solid iron, thirty feet thick and a hundred yards long."

Frémont brought home specimens of this coal and iron, of which Professor Baird, of the Smithsonian Institute, has made the analysis; and which I give in his own words: *"Magnectic* [sic] *oxide of iron: Paroan. Seems a very pure ore of iron, and suitable for manufacturing purposes. May be estimated to contain about 70 or 71 per centum of metalic* [sic] *iron, somewhat similar to the ore in the great beds of northern New York, but more solid than is usual there. Probably very well adapted to the manufacture of steel.* THE COAL *appears to be of excellent quality—semi-bituminous—somewhat in appearance like the transition coal of the Susquehannah mines in Pennsylvania."*

I must ask the pardon of some of my auditors for supposing that they may not be better acquainted with the language of geology than I was myself, when I supposed that this "combing out of the solid iron into crests," was mere descriptive language, suggested by the taste of the writer. I found it was not so, but the technical language which the geological science required to be used, and which, being used, conveyed an exact meaning—that of a mineral showing itself above the surface, and crowning the top of the hill or mountain, as a crest does the helmet, and the comb the head of the cock. In this view of its meaning the language here used by Frémont, and which seems to have been the suggestion of an excited imagination, becomes the subdued expression of science and technicality. And what a picture he presents. Here are, in fact, the elements of a great state—enough of themselves to build up a rich and populous state; but appurtenant to it, and interlaced with it, or bordering upon it, is a great extent of valley country—that of the Little Salt lake, of the Santa Clara Meadows, of the Nicollets river, and its tributaries; and a multitude of other coves and valleys, all stretching along the western base of the Wahsatch, and within the rim of the Great Basin; that Basin as remarkable here for beauty and fertility as in most other parts for sterility and deformity. The Mormon settlements of Paragoona, Paroan, and Cedar city are along the edge of this rich mountain region; and the well trod Mormon road from the Great Salt lake to Southern California, relieved with bridges and marked with mile-stones, pass by these towns; all announcing to the traveller that in the depths of the unknown wilderness he had encountered the comforts of civilization. *Messrs.* Beale and Heap passed these settlements at mid-summer, and speak in terms of enchantment, not only of the beauty of the country, but of the improvements and cultivation. Pretty towns, built to a pattern, each a square, the sides formed by lines of *adobe* houses, all facing inwards, with flower and kitchen gardens in front, and a large common field in the rear, crowded with growing grain— and all watered, both fields and gardens, and the front and rear of every house, with clear cool streams, brought down from the mountain sides, and from under a seeming canopy of snow. Grist and saw mills at work: forges smelting the iron ore: colliers digging the coal: blacksmiths hammering the red hot iron into farming implements, or shoes for the horses—assisted by dextrous Indian boys: cattle roaming in rich pastures: people quarrying, and the cattle licking, the rock-salt. Emigrants obtain supplies here—beef and flour at moderate [p. 11] prices:—and it was here that Frémont was refitted after his seventy days of living upon his mules which died from exhaustion. The number and beauty of these valleys and fertile mountains, seen by Beale and Heap in exuberance, their ripe rich dress of mid-summer, excite their wonder, and call forth enchanting descriptions. Broad valleys, connected by narrow ones—a continued succession of these valleys going from one to another, not by climbing ridges, but through level openings—grass, flowers and water in each. The mountains cut into blocks, some with fertile flat tops, rich in vegetation—some with peaks, white with snow—and all dark with forests on their sides. It is impossible to read their descriptions without being reminded of central Persia, and of that valley of Shiraz, celebrated as incomparable by the poets, but matched and surpassed in the recesses of the Wahsatch and the Anterria; and the climate delicious in summer, and soft in winter. From the 24th January to the 8th February that Frémont explored this region, he found in the valleys either no snow at all, or a thin covering only; and, in the first week of February, the Mormons told him they had usually commenced ploughing, and preparing the ground for the spring seeds. And yet all this would be but a corner of a state, which may spread west and north some hundred miles to the California line, and into the Great Basin—chiefly characterized as desert, but which has its *oases*—vegas, as the Spaniards call them—meadows refreshed with water, green with grass, and arable land—and with a structure of country, narrow valleys between snowy mountains—which give assurance of the artesian wells which can extend the area of fertility, and multiply the points of settlement. So that this fifth state may be as extensive, as populous, and as rich as any public interest could require.

Mr. President, and Gentlemen: I commenced this discourse with undertaking to establish two propositions—*first*, That the country between Missouri and California, in the latitude in which we now stand, is well adapted to settlement and cultivation, and capable of forming five great States: *secondly*, That it is well adapted to the construction of a railway. I believe I have made good the first of these propositions, and that we may now assume that the line of great states which now extend nearly half way across this continent, and through the centre of this Union—Pennsylvania, Ohio, Indiana, Illinois and Missouri—may be continued, and matched, by an equal number of states, equally great, between Missouri and California. I consider that proposition established, and say no more about it. The establishment of the second proposition results from the establishment of the first one, as all that has been shown in favor of the country for settlement and cultivation is equally in favor of it for the road. But I have some direct and positive testimony on this head which the importance of the subject, and the value of the testimony itself, requires to be produced. I speak of the last expedition of Col. Frémont—his winter expedition of 1853-'54—and of the success which attended it, and of the value of the information which it afforded. He chose the dead of winter for his exploration, that he might see the worst—see the real difficulties, and determine whether they could be vanquished. He believed in the practicability of the road, and that his miscarriage in 1848-'49, was the fault of his guide, not of the country; and he was determined to solve those questions by the test of actual experiment.

With these views he sat out, taking the winter for his time, the west for his course, a straight line his object, the mouth of the Kanzas for his point of departure, St. Louis and San Francisco the points to be connected. The parrallels of 38 and 39, covered his course, and between these he continued to move west until he reached the Little Salt Lake—within three hundred miles of the California line: after that upon a slight deflection to the south, between the [p. 12] parallels 37 and 38, until he entered California. This may be called a straight line; and so fulfills a primary condition of every kind of road, and especially of a railroad, where a speed of an hundred miles an hour may be as easily attained, and as safely run, as the third of that velocity in a road of crooks and curvatures.

Snow was the next consideration, and of that he found none, on any part of the route, to impede any kind of travelling. On the Kanzas, the Upper Arkansas, and the Huerfano, he found none at all: in the Sand Hill pass of the Sierra Blanca, none: in the valleys of San Luis, and the Sahwatch, none: in the Coochatope Pass, four inches! and none if he had crossed the day before; and that was the 14th of December, corresponding with the time, and almost in view of the place, where he had been buried in the snows five years before. This solved the question of snow in the passes of the mountains, and showed that his miscarriage had been the mistake of the guide, and not the fault of the country. After that—after crossing the Rocky Mountains—the climate changes. A great amelioration takes place, which he knew before, and then fully experienced. The remainder of the route, as has been shown in the view of the country, may be said to have been found free from snow—an hundred miles at a time in one place without finding any; and when found at all, both thin and transient. And that this was the common winter state of the Pass, and not an occasional exception, has been shown by Mr. Antoine Leroux, and others, and corresponded with his own theory of snow in the passes. Mr. Leroux, in his published letter to me, said: *"There is not much snow in this Pass, (the Coochatope,) and people go through it all the winter. And when there is much snow on the mountains on the Abiquiu route, (which in [is] the old Spanish trail from Santa Fe to California,) the people of Taos go round this way, and get into that trail in the forks of Grand, and Green rivers."* And Messrs. Beale and Heap, in their journal say of it.: *"Coochatope Pass, is travelled at all seasons, and some of our men had repeatedly gone through it in the middle of winter, without meeting any serious obstruction from snows."* And this was the theory of Frémont, that the passes in these mountains were nearly free from snow, and comparatively warm; while in the open plains, or on the mountain summits, deep snows would prevail, and a killing cold, which no animal life could stand. This frees the Rocky mountains from that objection. The next range of mountains, (for all the valleys have been shown to be free,) is the Anterria and Wahstach; and there again the passes are free. Frémont says of them:

"In passing through this bed of mountains about fourteen days had been occupied, from January 24 to February 7: the deepest snows we here encountered being about up to the saddle skirts, or four feet; this occurring only in occasional drifts in the passes on northern exposures, and in the small mountain flats hemmed in by woods and hills. In the valley it was sometimes a few inches deep, and as often none at all. On our arrival at the Mormon settlements, February 8th, we found it a few inches deep, and were there informed that the winter had been unusually long-continued and severe, the thermometer having been as low as 17°

below zero, and more snow having fallen than in all the previous winters together since the establishment of the colony. At this season their farmers had usually been occupied with their ploughs, preparing the land for seed."

The Sierra Nevada was the last range of mountain; and there not a particle of snow was found in the pass which he traversed, while the mountain itself was deeply covered. And this disposes of the objection of snow on this route, so formidable in the view of those who have nothing but an imaginary view of it.

Smoothness of surface, or freedom from abrupt inequalities in the ground, is the next consideration: and here the reality exceeded the expectation, and even hopes, and challenges incredulity. Let Frémont speak. He says:

"Standing immediately at the mouth of the *Sand Hill Pass*—one of the most practicable in the *Sierra Blanca*, and above those usually travelled—at one of the remotest [p. 13] head-springs of the *Huerfano* river, the eye of the traveller follows down, without obstruction or abrupt descent, along the gradual slope of the valley to the great plains which reach the Missouri. The straight river and the open valley, form, with the plains beyond, one great slope, without a hill to break the line of sight, or obstruct the course of the road. On either side of this line, hills slope easily to the river, with lines of timber and yellow autumnal grass; and the water which flows smoothly between is not interrupted by a fall in its course to the ocean."

Here is a section of the route above seven hundred miles long—being more than half the distance to California—in which there is no elevation to arrest the vision—in which you might look down the wide distance, (if the eye sight was long enough) and see the frontier of Missouri from the mouth of the first pass in the first mountain—being more than half the length of the road. This would do for a start. It would satisfy the call for a fair surface at the commencement. This first pass is called the Sand Hill, or Roubidoux, through which Frémont entered the valley of San Luis; and the way so low and level as to be seen through. And through that valley and its continuation, (the Sahwatch,) to the Coochatope the ground is so smooth as to present no exception to its level but the natural curvature of the earth. Meeting a man on horseback in this long level of more than a hundred and twenty miles, (counting the entire valleys of San Luis and the Sahwatch,) is like meeting a ship at sea: you see his head first, then his body, then his horse; and at last, the ground. The Pass itself, as well as the approaches to it, is perfect. Frémont calls it *"an open easy wagon way."* Beale and Heap say it was a question whether they had passed the dividing point between the eastern and western waters—which could only be answered by referring to the water itself. The Pass itself, of which they made a drawing, was grand and beautiful. They say of it:

"Lofty mountains, their summits covered with eternal snows, lifted their heads to the clouds; while in our immediate vicinity were softly rounded hills, clothed with grass and flowers, with rich meadows between; through which numerous rills trickled to join their waters to the Coochatope creek." But why multiply words to induce conviction when facts are at hand to command it. Facts enough abound to show the facility of this Pass, even in a state of nature. More than forty loaded wagons went through it in the summer of 1853, twenty of them guided by Leroux for Captain Gunnison—the rest by emigrant families, without guides. But more than that: the buffaloes have travelled it always—those best of engineers, whose instinct never commits mistakes, and which in their migrations for pasture, shelter, and salt, never fail to find the lowest levels in the mountains, the shallowest fords in the rivers, the richest grass, the best salt licks, the most permanent water; and always take the shortest and best routes between all these points of attraction. These instinctive explorers traverse this Pass, and gave it their name—Coochatope in the Utah language; *Puerto del Cibolos* in the Spanish—which being rendered into English signifies the Gate of the Buffaloes. And their bones and horns, strewing the ground, attest their former numerous presence in this locality, before the fire-arms of modern invention had come to their destruction at such a crowded point of rendezvous. This is enough to show that the Rocky mountains may be passed without crossing a hill—that loaded wagons may cross it at all seasons of the year. This applies to the Coochatope Pass, but there are many others, and all good; and it is curious to detect the latin language in many of their names, put upon them in the Spanish translation of the original Indian. Thus, we see *porta* in *puerto;* (a gate) constantly recurring, as *Puerto del Cibolos—Puerto del mosca:* in which latter, besides the *porta* we detect the latin *musca* (fly;) *anglice,* The Fly Gate; from the unusual number of those insects which the Indians found in it—*Puerto del Medio,* (medium) Middle Gate, &c., &c. [p. 14]

In a word, there is no difficulty about passes: the only bother is to choose out of so many, all so good, both in themselves, and in their approaches. This is enough for the passes: with respect to the whole mountain region, and the facility of going through it, and upon different lines, we have also the evidence of facts which dispense with speculation and assertion. That region was three times traversed, and on different routes, by *Messrs.* Beale and Heap in the summer of 1853. It happened thus: when they had reached the east fork of the Great Colorado of the West, and were crossing it, they lost, by the accident of an overturned canoe, their supply of munitions, both for the gun and the mouth; and were forced to send back to the nearest settlement for a further supply. That nearest settlement was Taos, in New Mexico, distant three hundred and thirty miles; and that distance to be made upon mules, finding their own food, which had already travelled, on the same condition, one thousand miles from the frontier of Missouri; and these mules, (thus already travelled long and hard, without other food than the grass afforded,) now made the double distance at the rate of forty miles a day—still finding their own food; and, on the return, bringing packs on their backs. This performance must stand for a proof that the whole mountain region between the Upper Colorado and the valley of the Upper Del Norte is well adapted to travelling; and that in a state of nature; and also well supplied with nutritious grass; and this clears us of the Rocky mountains, from which to the Little Salt Lake it is all an open practicable way, not limited to a track, but traversable on any line. Loaded wagons travel it in a state of nature. The valley of the Colorado is either level or rolling; the Wahsatch and Anterria ranges are perforated by incessant valleys; and from the Little Salt Lake to the Great Sierra Nevada, as explored by Frémont last winter, the way is nearly level—a succession of valleys between the mountains—and terminated by a superb pass, debouching into the valley of San Joaquin. Frémont, referring to previous Indian information, says of it:

"When the Point was reached I found the Indian information fully verified: the mountain suddenly terminated, and broke down into lower grounds, barely above the level of the country, and making numerous openings into the valley of the San Joaquin. I entered into the first which offered, (taking no time to search, as we were entirely out of provisions and living upon horses,) which led us by an open and almost level hollow thirteen miles long to an upland, not steep enough to be called a hill, over into the valley of a small affluent to Kern river; the hollow and the valley making together a way where a wagon would not find any obstruction for forty miles."

The discovery of this Pass was the *"crowning mercy"* of this adventurous winter expedition. It was the cherished desideratum of the central route. It fulfilled its last condition. And this completes all that is necessary to be shown in favor of the smoothness of the way—its equality of surface, throughout the whole line; although it attains a great elevation—and lands you in California, in the rich and settled valley of San Joaquin, proximate to the southern end of the gold mines. Not a tunnel to be made—a mountain to be climbed—a hill to be crossed—a swamp to be seen—or desert, or moveable sand to be encountered, in the whole distance: and all this equality of surface barometrically determined by Frémont as well as visibly seen by his eye: so that this line for a road, the longest and straightest in the world, is also over the smoothest and most equal surface. For, although, a great elevation is attained, it is on a long line, and gradually and imperceptibly—the mere rise of an inclined plane.

Rivers to be passed are obstructions to roads, to be overcome by large applications of skill and means: and here again the central route is most favorable. The entire line is only crossed in its course by the streams in the valley of the Upper Colorado, and those of inconsiderable width, with solid banks and stone for bridges. On this side of the Rocky mountains the course of the rivers is [p. 15] parallel to that of the road—the Kanzas, the Arkansas, and the Huerfano, being all in its line. Beyond the valley of the Colorado, no river at all—only small streams.

In this description of the country I have relied chiefly on Frémont, whose exploration, directed by no authority, connected with no company, swayed by no interest—wholly guided by himself and solely directed to the public good, would be entitled to credit upon his own report, unsupported by subsidiary evi-evidence [*sic*]; but he has not left the credit of his report to his word alone. He has done, besides, what no other explorer had done: he has made the country report itself. Besides determining elevations barometrically, and fixing positions astronomically, and measuring objects with a practised eye—besides all that, he has applied the daguerreotype art to the face of the wild domain, and made it speak for itself. Three hundred of these views illustrate the path of his exploration, and compel every object to stand forth, and show itself as it is, or was: mountain—gap—plain—rock—forest—grass—snow, (where there is any,) and naked ground where there is not—all exhibit themselves as they are. For daguerre has no power to conceal what is visible, or to exhibit what is non-existent. He uses no pencil to substitute fiction for fact, or fancy for memory. He is a machine that works to a pattern, and that pattern the object before him: and in this way has Frémont reproduced the country from the Mississippi to the Pacific, and made it become the reflex of its own features, and the exhibiter of its own face, present and viewable to every beholder: and that nothing may be wanting to complete the information on a subject of such magnitude, he has now gone back to give the finishing look at the west end of the line, which thirty thousand miles of wilderness explorations in the last twelve years, (all at his own suggestion, and the last half at his own cost,) authorize him to believe is the true, and good, route for the road which is to unite the Atlantic and the Pacific, and to give a new channel to the commerce of Asia.

All the other requisites for the construction and maintenance of a road, and to give it employment when done, has been shown in the view of the country. Wood, water, stone, coal, iron; rich soil to build up settlements and cities, to give local business and travel all along its course, as well as at the great terminating points—and to protect it without government troops. Add to this, picturesque scenery, and an entire region of unsurpassed salubrity. The whole route for the road between the States of Missouri and California is good—not only good, but supremely excellent; and it is helped out at each end by water lines of transportation, now actually existing, and by railways, projected, or in progress. At the Missouri end there is a railway in construction to the line of the State, and steamboat navigation to the mouth of the Kanzas, and up that river some hundred miles: at the California end there is the like navigation, up the bay of San Francisco, and the San Joaquin river, and a railway projected. And thus, this central route would be helped out at once by some three hundred miles at each end, connecting it with the great business populations of California and Missouri—at which latter point it would be in central communication with the great business population of the Union.

And now I hold it to be in order of human events—in the regular progression of human affairs—that the road will be built, and that soon; not by public, but private means—by a company of solid men, asking nothing of Congress but the right of way through the public lands; and buying the way if not granted. Such an enterprize would be worthy of enlightened capitalists, who know how to combine private advantage with public good; and who would feel a laudable desire to connect their names with a monumental enterprize, more useful than the pursuits of political ambition, more glorious than the conquest of nations, more durable than the pyramids; and which being finished, is to change the face of the commercial world—and all to the advantage of our America. [p. 16]

The road will be made, and soon, and by individual enterprize. The age is progressive, and utilitarian. It abounds with talent, seeking employment, and with capital, seeking investment. The temptation is irresistible. To reach the golden California—to put the populations of the Atlantic, the Pacific, and the Mississippi Valley, into direct communication—to connect Europe and Asia through our America—and to own a road of our own to the East Indies: such is the grandeur of the enterprize! and the time was arrived to begin it. The country is open to settlement, and inviting it, and receiving it. The world is in motion, following the track of the sun to its dip in the western ocean. Westward the torrents of emigration direct their course; and soon the country between Missouri and California is to show the most rapid expansion of the human race that the ages of man have ever beheld. It will all be settled up. Settlements will promote the road; the road will aggrandize the settlements. Soon it will be a line of towns, cities, villages and farms; and rich will be the man that may own some quarter section on its track, and some squares in the cities which are to grow up upon it.

But the road beyond the Mississippi is only the half of the whole; the other half is on this side, and either in progress or completed. Behold your own extended iron way! departing from this City, to reach the Ohio—crossing it to join the western trunk through Cincinnati, Vincennes, St. Louis—there to find the Pacific road in progress to the western limit of Missouri. Behold the lateral roads from Pennsylvania, New York, New England, all pointing to the west, and converging to the same central track. And behold the diagonal central road of Virginia to traverse the state from its southeast to its northwest corner, already finished beyond the Blue Ridge, and its advanced pioneers descending the Alleghany, to arrive at the mouth of Big Sandy, in the very latitude of St. Louis, San Francisco, and Baltimore: and there to join the same great central western trunk. And the Blue Ridge road of South Carolina, bound upon the same destination; and the roads of Georgia, pointing and advancing, to the north west. What is the destiny of all these atlantic roads, thus pointing to the west and converging upon the central track, the whole course of which lies through the centre of our Union, and through the centre of its population, wealth and power—and one end of which points to Canton and Jeddo—the other to London and Paris: what will those lateral roads become, in addition to their original destination? They will become parts of a system, bringing our Atlantic cities nearer to the Pacific coast than they were to the Blue Ridge in the time of canals and turnpikes. And what then? The great idea of Columbus will be realized—though in a different, and a more beneficial form. Eastern Asia is reached, by going west, and by a road of which we hold the key! and the channel of Asiatic commerce which has been shifting its bed from the time of Solomon, and raising up cities and kingdoms wherever it went—(to perish when it left them)—changing its channel for the last time—to become fixed upon its shortest, safest, best, and quickest route, through the heart of our America—and to revive along its course the Tyres and Sidons, the Balbecs, Palmyras, and Alexandrias, once the seat of commerce and empire; and the ruins of which still attest their former magnificence, and excite the wonder of the oriental traveller.

John C. Fremont, 1854

Exploration Of The Central Railroad Route To The Pacific

Washington, 33/1 S67 Misc., serial 705, June 15, 1854, 7 p., from a letter to the editors of the *National Intelligencer*, June 13, 1854; also 33/2 H8 Misc., serial 807, December 27, 1854. [WC 239; WCB 239:1; Cowan p. 222; Eberstadt 15:1076, 137:196; Graff 1430; Holliday 403; Rittenhouse 226; UPRR p. 25; NUC NF 0368219.] Reset verbatim from compiler's original.

Significance   This letter still stands as Fremont's own chief record of his fifth expedition, since he never got around to writing a formal report. He nearly repeated the wintry calamity of his fourth expedition. Both of these vain attempts to find a straight railroad route between St. Louis and San Francisco are reviewed here. Fremont's letter was reprinted by Bigelow in 1856 and by Spence in 1984.

The charge that the death and disaster of Fremont's 1848-49 fourth expedition was caused by the incompetence of his guide, Old Bill Williams, is not supported by the primary documents. This charge was created by Fremont to hide his own culpability. It was so much publicized by his supporters that it has become the standard stuff of "history." The conclusion here is that Old Bill made a bad choice of route, but it was the lesser of two evils forced upon him by his obsessed leader. It was the choice of possible survival over sure death.

Against all advice, in the worst winter of memory, and rejecting the better Cochetopa Pass to the north, Fremont was leading the expedition on his predetermined "central" path up the Rio Grande Canyon into the towering San Juan Mountains. The mules were already belly-deep in snow, 15 miles up the canyon. Fremont was determined to go 30 miles farther to the Leroux Pass reported by the mountain men. That looked like sure death to Old Bill. He knew exactly where he was, and he insisted on turning right and assaulting the immense jagged wall. He was thus heading directly north for Carnero Pass, near the Cochetopa. The only trouble was, the Carnero was on the second chain behind this first monstrous barrier. Old Bill must have hoped that any reasonable leader would soon see the mortal peril and retreat. Fremont was not a reasonable leader. His failure to admit defeat, even after all his mules were dead, and his total mismanagement of the belated retreat, caused 10 deaths by starvation and freezing. Old Bill's insistence, and the heroic rescue by Alexis Godey while Fremont sipped hot chocolate in Taos, deserve credit for the 24 lives saved, including Fremont's.

Because of recent controversy, special care is taken in the Itinerary and High-lights to verify Fremont's above stated intentions, as well as his route into and out of the San Juans by the Rio Grande itself. This route is precisely shown on Fre-mont's own 1887 map; it is also shown clearly though less actually on Richard H. Kern's contribution to Lt. John G. Parke's 1851 map (see Abel 1915). Kern, an expedition member, drew also from Old Bill's knowledge.

In the 1853-54 fifth expedition, Fremont forced himself into another futile mid-winter thrust into his fancied central route. Beale and Heap (5:J9) and Gun-nison's official railroad survey (L3) had just that summer gone through Cochetopa Pass, the centerpiece of the central route. Fremont's only hope for glory was to show its suitability in winter. Sickness delayed him a month. He got through the pass all right but bogged down in the snow and bitter cold of the rugged country beyond. One man died of starvation and freezing in the awesome Wasatch Plateau. Revived at the Mormon settlement of Parowan, Fremont went more or less centrally straight west until he butted into the impassable Sierra Nevada and had to take a huge detour south. Most of his wandering ways, from the Arkansas River to the Sierra, were either impracticable or undesirable for a railroad.

Author JOHN CHARLES FREMONT, 1813-1890, explorer, senator and presi-dential candidate, general. See 5:J1.

Participant WILLIAM SHERLEY ("OLD BILL") WILLIAMS, 1787-1849, mountain man. Born in North Carolina but raised and home-educated in Mis-souri, young Bill started living with the Osage Indians about 1803 and ranged widely with them, possibly to the Rockies. He stayed with the Osages until 1824, taking a year out to scout for the Mounted Rangers in the War of 1812. He also served as official interpreter for posts and missionaries, compiled an Osage dic-tionary, traded, and took three wives. In 1824-25 he trapped the upper Columbia with William H. Ashley's men. About this time the tall, sinewy, stooped, pock-marked redhead with a squeaky voice became known as Old Bill. He was back in 1825 to guide George C. Sibley's survey of the Santa Fe Trail and to interpret for the Osage treaty at Council Grove (2:C7).

Williams's incredible travels during the next 20 years took him trapping forth and back, and up and down, all over the West. In quick succession, usually visiting Taos in between each foray, he was hunting at Great Salt Lake, being left naked near the Gila by the Apaches and later rescued by the Zunis, trapping on the upper Green River, living with the Utes in the Colorado Parks, searching vainly for beaver on the Brazos in Texas, again touring the Green River, going off to the Grand Canyon 1834-35, traveling along the Yellowstone, exploring Bill Williams Fork in Arizona, pausing to rendezvous on Wind River, living with the Utes again, stealing horses in California on an 1840 raid, visiting relatives in eastern Missouri, trading pelts at Ft. Bridger and Brown's Hole, junketing to the Dalles of the Columbia, and fighting Modocs in the Klamath country. Williams, with Kit Carson, guided Fremont's 1845 third expedition from Pueblo to Great Salt Lake (5:J1); Old Bill quit after a dispute with Fremont about the desert road ahead. Bill ushered a supply train down the Santa Fe Trail in the Mexican War. In 1848 his arm was shattered in a fight with Utes in northern New Mexico. He reluctantly joined Fremont's fourth expedition, which led to his death, as given in the Itinerary. (Frederic E. Voelker in Hafen, *Mountain Men*, 8:365-94; Thrapp; Lamar; DAB; Favour 1936.)

Itinerary, 1848-49 FREMONT'S FOURTH EXPEDITION, KANSAS CITY TO THE SAN JUAN MOUNTAINS AND CALIFORNIA. October 20, 1848—Fremont's pack party leaves Westport (Kansas City). By modern landmarks he goes west up the Kansas River past Topeka to Salina on the Smoky Hill, October 29. He continues west on present Interstate 70, returning to the Smoky Hill, which he leaves south of Hayes, November 3. He heads south and west through Bazine and then south to Dodge City on the Arkansas, November 7. Thence west the route follows the Mountain Branch of the Santa Fe Trail up the Arkansas to Bent's Old Fort west of Las Animas CO.

November 15 through 17—From Bent's Fort, before he meets Bill Williams, Fremont writes Senator Benton: "We will ascend the Del Norte [Rio Grande] to its head [and]…descend on to the Colorado." He meets Thomas Fitzpatrick, who writes Fremont's wife Jessie on January 3, 1849, "Col. Fremont will fall immediately on the Rio del Norte…I believe it is his intention to steer directly for California, leaving the two hitherto traveled routes, one north [Cochetopa] and the other south [the Old Spanish Trail] of him, and passing midway between the two; and which, if he is able to find a practicable route, will be much more direct and shorter than any hitherto traveled." November 21—Farther up the Arkansas at Pueblo, Fremont hires experienced Old Bill Williams, age 61, as guide. Lancaster P. Lupton writes Senator Benton from Pueblo on November 28, 1848, "He (Col. Fremont) intends to go to the Pacific by a new route, and thereby complete all his surveys across the continent, and be able to decide the best way for the railroad…The snow is unusually deep in the mountains, and many old mountainmen here have expressed a doubt whether he can get over with so large a cavalcade." November 23 through 24—At Hardscrabble settlement between present Portland and Wetmore CO, from Pueblo about 30 miles up the Arkansas and then 5 miles up Hardscrabble Creek (Lecompte 1978), Fremont packs 130 bushels of corn and dismounts the men.

From Westport to Hardscrabble Fremont travels about 720 miles in 35 days, including only the two layover days at Bent's, averaging 21 miles per day. Dates and distances are from the diaries of the Kern brothers, Benjamin, Richard, and Edward, given by the Hafens in 1960. The Hafens also provide all the other quotes above. Further documentation of Fremont's intentions is in the Highlights.

November 25—The final party of 34 men leaves Hardscrabble afoot in the snow, leading about 120 packed mules. The men include the intrepid mountaineer Alexis Godey, his 14-year-old nephew Theodore McNabb, and Jackson Saunders, Fremont's ex-slave servant; the 3 Kern brothers, Benjamin a physician, Dick and Ned artists; Charles Preuss, topographer; Frederick Creutzfeldt, botanist; 16 veterans of former Fremont expeditions; 3 California Indians; 5 assorted adventurers; and Fremont and Old Bill. They follow Hardscrabble Creek south and cross the Wet Mountains (Sierra Mohada) on today's State Highway 96. Preuss in his diary complains of "Bill's vacillations" as guide, but nobody else does. They continue south and cut west through the Sangre de Cristos via Mosca Pass into the south end of what is now Great Sand Dunes National Monument, December 3. They circle north around the dunes, looking into Medano or Sand Hills Pass (probably the "Medio" of Benton, L5), which strikes toward the middle of the Monument. Neither pass is suitable for a railroad.

December 6—On the great dunes, Benjamin Kern writes, "very cold & clear so that each hair of mule & man was covered with frost & icicles hung down from moustache below the chin—a fine view of the [San Luis] valley & the [San Juan] mountains of the opposite side about 35 miles off." Far to the north-northwest at the head of San Luis Creek is Poncha ("Poonche, Poow-che") Pass to the upper Arkansas River. To the northwest is the wide entrance by Saguache Creek to Cochetopa Pass on the Continental Divide. Directly west is the narrow entrance by Carnero Creek to upper Saguache Creek and Carnero Pass, on the Divide 8 miles southwest of the Cochetopa. Three miles south of Carnero Creek, La Garita Creek issues from the San Juans into the San Luis Valley. To the southwest the Rio Grande flows eastward out of these mountains from a major canyon and turns south through the broad continuation of the flat San Luis Valley toward Taos.

At this view point Fremont can see all his options. Capt. James H. Simpson in Santa Fe on July 23, 1849, hears indirectly from Fremont's man John Scott that "when Lt. Col. Fremont got over to where he could see in the distance the mountain chain through which he was to pass, enquired of Williams where the pass was through which he was to go—that Williams pointed him a passage bearing to the

North [presumably the Cochetopa]. That Fremont then told him pass was too far to the North, that he wanted to go a more direct course, and that that passage— pointing to one further south, must therefore be the one [up the Rio Grande]; that thereupon Williams told him he could not by any possibility (go through) by that pass, the more southern one, and that even as it regarded the more northern one, it was a matter of doubt—that they all [mountaineers?] opposed taking the pass he proposed" [Hafens 1960]. Fremont heads purposefully southwest to the Rio Grande. This is verified explicitly by the mileages and descriptions of the Kern journals. It is proved by Fremont's 1887 map.

December 8—The party strikes the timbered Rio Grande near present Monte Vista and turns west 15 miles to the mouth of its canyon at modern Del Norte. Up the canyon 15 miles at what must be Alder Creek opposite today's town of South Fork on the 11th, Benjamin Kern observes, "snow sometimes to the mules belly—a hard day." Bill Williams must see sure death in continuing Fremont's course west 20 miles on up the Rio Grande and then 10 miles more up Willow Creek past present Creede to Leroux's Pass (Summer Pass, or Pass of the Del Norte) on the Continental Divide (see map). Williams proposes turning north up Alder Creek, which is in a direct line to Carnero Pass. Unfortunately, this line is also 30 miles long and leads first up over the towering La Garita crest and then down one branch of Saguache Creek and up another to the Divide. The La Garita crest is 1,500 feet higher than Carnero Pass. But if they get stuck, they are closer to Taos, a life-saving consideration. Did Old Bill hope that Fremont would soon see the fatal folly of it all and turn back?

In his 1856 defense of Fremont, Godey says, "scarcely a night passed without a consultation took place between the Colonel, myself, Williams, and others." Godey states that Fremont did not want to consider "Carnero Pass" and was "strongly averse to taking it in our course." On "the 12th inst. [December], when Williams and myself being ahead [up Alder Creek], were overtaken by Fremont, who rode up and halted us, and the entire party stopped in the middle of the day." Fremont still wanted to go through "a pass some thirty miles to the left [west];" this could only be Leroux Pass, although Godey, like all Fremont supporters, called it "the Cochetopy;" it does actually cross over near a branch of Cochetopa Creek. On the 12th Benjamin Kern tells of the "canon [of Alder Creek] a horrid place," with "mules falling down the rocks." The first mule gives out.

In the agonizing climb up Alder Creek, Benjamin Kern notes on December 15 that they "lost 7 mules today & 8 yesterday." December 16—Benjamin records, "when we reached the top it was so cold & windy that none could see ahead & the drifting & falling snow obscured every thing[;] in danger of all being frozen we took the back trail...Several [mules] died thro' the night from cold & hunger—

blankets ropes & comfortables were eaten by them & my light over coat had one sleeve eaten off…It was a day that tried the stoutest hearts & the whole party came very near to total destruction[.] Many had their noses &c. frozen & some became stupid from the cold." Death and doom hover at 12,000 feet in subzero temperatures and high winds. More mountains lie ahead. Now is the obvious time to call a full retreat, before all the mules are gone. Fremont does not. Why? Can he not face the total defeat of his cherished plans? He orders an advance.

From Hardscrabble to the La Garita crest near Mesa Mountain the party has trudged about 170 miles in 22 days at 8 miles per day. This part of the itinerary is based also on material compiled by the Hafens in 1960.

December 17 through 23—With unbelievable labor the men beat a mile-long path with mauls through the snow across the ridge and camp on Wanamaker Creek in the Saguache Creek drainage. Benjamin calls these "days of horror desolation despair & almost continued heavy winds intense cold & snow storms." The mules eat each others' manes and tails. On the 20th, 59 of them are still alive.

December 24 through 27—Finally they retreat 3 miles back across the ridge to make Christmas Camp at the head of Embargo Creek. Nearly all the mules are dead and covered in the snow. On the 26th, instead of ordering a full retreat and leading all his men to safety, Fremont sends Henry King, Frederick Creutzfeldt, Thomas E. Breckenridge, and Old Bill down Embargo Creek and the Rio Grande to Taos to bring back help. Why? Is he just trying to save the baggage? Why does he not send his best man, his second in command, the heroic Godey, on this crucial mission? The men in different small groups move camp at least three times, covering in all only 8 or 10 zigzag miles down Embargo Creek. (Breckenridge in his 1896 reminiscence names this creek specifically, although he thinks it is the one they ascended.) They spend all their time shuttling back and forth, moving the extensive baggage.

January 2, 1849—Fremont's lead group moves the remaining 7 miles down to the Rio Grande. The rest of the men are still above, hauling baggage. January 9— Raphael Proue is the first man to die, frozen on the trail between camps. January 11—After frittering away 26 days since he first should have retreated on December 17, Fremont takes off for Taos with Godey, Preuss, Saunders, and young Theodore McNabb. He leaves the miserable remnant of his expedition all at risk. He leaves them with an unfit Lorenzo D. Vincenthaler in charge, with orders to relay all the baggage down to the river before they move out. That order wastes 4 more precious days. Why did he not leave Godey to lead them all out, to meet him bringing back aid? With callous disregard for the lives of his men, Fremont already knows that he himself is not coming back and that Godey will have to be the rescuer.

Micajah McGehee later spells it out: "He left an order that we scarce knew how to interpret, to the effect that we must finish packing the baggage to the river and hasten down as speedily as possible…and that if we wished to see him we must be in a hurry as he was going on to California" (Hafens 1960).

February 12—As the tragedy unfolds, the last of the 24 survivors reaches Taos, leaving 10 bodies scattered along the Rio Grande. Fremont and his rescue group meet some Indians downriver and get some horses on January 15. The next day they catch up with the utterly devastated Williams, Creutzfeldt, and Breckenridge. A suspicion persists that these three starving men fed on the body of Henry King, who gave out and never got up. Fremont with these survivors reaches the Red River settlement of northern New Mexico, future Questa, on the 20th. After gathering supplies and 30 mules in Taos, the incomparable Godey sets out back up the Rio Grande on the 23d. Fremont asks him to pick up some of the precious baggage. Fremont rests at the home of Kit Carson.

Meanwhile, the main group under Vincenthaler starts downriver on January 16th, by now destitute of provisions. Near present Monte Vista on the 19th, a deer is killed. The meat is unfairly divided. Richard Kern charges that "Mr. L. D. Vinsonhaler…[intended] to have said nothing about the deer but to have taken it and the strong men & pushed on…and left the rest of us to perish." Three days later and 20 miles farther down, Vincenthaler declares that it is every man for himself and takes off with the stronger men. Thomas S. Martin later confesses that he and the stronger ones "crept out of camp" at midnight. The weak ones stay in camp, dying off, but scrupulously dividing what little food they can scavenge. Godey rescues the survivors here on the 28th and checks back all the way to Embargo Creek. There he picks up one living California Indian and Fremont's trunk. Not including Proue and King, eight men die between January 17 and 28. Fremont could have saved them all with a more timely retreat.

The first rescue party takes about 28 days to cover some 150 agonizing miles from Christmas Camp to Taos. The rate is 5 miles per day.

February 13—Fremont departs Taos for California. Amazingly, his party of 25 contains 17, including himself, of the 24 emaciated survivors of the San Juans. Only the 3 Kerns, Old Bill, and 3 others are left behind. Taos resident Antoine Leroux accompanies Fremont as far as Albuquerque. By modern towns, Fremont leaves the Rio Grande at Truth and Consequences and goes to Lake Valley and then southwest to the Arizona border near Rodeo. He is 10 to 15 miles north of Cooke's route (3:E6). From near Douglas AZ he is on the Southern Emigrant Trail in Mexico west to Santa Cruz and Nogales, Sonora. He proceeds north to reach Tucson on March 23. He takes the usual route to the Gila and Pima Villages, crosses the Colorado April 8, and goes to Isaac Williams's ranch near San

Bernardino CA by an unmapped route, probably via Warner Springs and Temecula. He disbands at San Bernardino on April 20.

Adjusted from Cooke's mileages, Fremont probably travels about 1,250 miles from Taos to San Bernardino. For 67 days he averages 19 miles per day. Itinerary is from Fremont's 1887 *Memoirs* map and Spence 1984. In all, Fremont goes about 2,290 miles from Westport to San Bernardino.

COMMENT. Old Bill Williams and Benjamin Kern went back to the San Juans for their baggage and were killed about March 21, 1849, by Utes or the Mexican muleteers. William T. Hamilton wrote in 1905 that the Utes did it by mistake, but he had the wrong place. Jessie Fremont was delayed two months in Panama in 1849 by the gold rushers. She sailed "up the coast fearing the news I might meet of Mr. Fremont's winter journey overland. Its cruel sufferings when he was midway I learned at Panama, but kept my way refusing to give up even in my own mind to the doubts almost every one had of his getting through. At the first California port, San Diego, we met the news that he *had* arrived and hurried on to San Francisco." Botanist John Torrey wrote in 1850 that even on this disastrous expedition, Fremont "gleaned a few plants, which, with all his other botanical collections, he kindly placed at my disposal."

1848-49 Highlights   The early documentary record clearly indicates that Fremont always intended to ascend the Rio Grande itself in 1848, and not the San Luis Creek tributaries to Cochetopa Pass, as afterwards claimed by his apologists. The testimony of Fitzpatrick, Lupton, Scott, Godey, and Fremont himself, given in the Itinerary, all confirm this. Benton acknowledged in his Senate speech of February 7, 1849, before he knew the tragic outcome, that Fremont "has now gone as far south as the head of the Rio Grande del Norte, to explore the passes at the head of that river." The Hafens compiled all these quotes in 1960 and fully recognized their significance.

The early documentary record also clearly indicates that Fremont actually ascended the Rio Grande. He followed it about 15 miles through the plain and then from present Del Norte 15 miles west along its canyon before turning north (right) to disaster in the high mountains. All this was carefully outlined by Brandon in 1955 and by the Hafens in 1960. This matter bears scrutiny, because Spence (1984) and Weber (1985) have adopted the opinion of Patricia J. Richmond (1990), based on extensive field work, that Fremont entered the mountains farther north. Specifically, Richmond postulates that he started west up Carnero Creek from the flat San Luis Valley (see maps). Richmond also has the main party exiting east on La Garita Creek rather than southeast directly to the Rio Grande via Embargo Creek.

A close reading of the early journals completely supports the earlier interpretations. The distances, directions, names, topography, and Fremont's intentions perfectly match entry and exit by the canyon of the Rio Grande. These factors do not match movements along Carnero and La Garita creeks. Richmond's notable find of "1848" inscribed in a rock shelter about 5 miles from Christmas Camp is within a likely range of a small reconnaissance party. Her map, given by both Spence and Weber, does show that the "Rescue Party" exited by Embargo Creek. But Preuss's diary proves that Fremont followed the line of campfires of the rescue party, and all other diarists followed Fremont's tracks. Preuss wrote, "It took us [Fremont's group] four days to reach the river, and to our surprise we found that King [of the rescue party] must have soon lost his zeal. For he, too, had, as we could tell by campfires which we came across, needed four or even five days to cover a distance of ten or eleven miles. We decided to go to the main camp at the river and wait there until everybody and everything arrived." Not a soul would go down La Garita Creek, Richmond's postulated route, when relief was expected from a rescue party returning up the Rio Grande. When the journalists said Rio Grande or River, that is what they meant, not various associated creeks. If a clincher is needed, Fremont's folding map in his 1887 *Memoirs* traces the path of the expedition into and out of the Rio Grande canyon on its south side; the line leads north up into the mountains right where Alder and Embargo creeks are. The Pathfinder may not have found many of his paths, but he almost always knew exactly where he had been.

In January, 1854, Antoine Leroux corroborated the above points about Fremont's intent and route. Leroux's account, related by Heinrich Balduin Mollhausen, contradicted Leroux's own testimony to Benton (L4) nearly a year earlier; then he had claimed that "Col. Fremont was looking for the Coo-chatope Pass in the winter of 1848-49…when his guide led him off into the mountains, instead of keeping up the dry valley, which he wished to do, and which would have taken him through easy." Quite to the contrary, Mollhausen wrote on January 18, 1854, while on Whipple's railroad survey (L3): "On this evening I was lying near Leroux, when he was talking of Colonel Fremont's fourth expedition…the survivors from which Leroux had seen enter the town of Taos, where he lived. In October, 1848, Colonel Fremont had set out on this enterprise, intending to proceed to the upper part of the Rio Grande; partly because the route to the Pacific had never been explored, and also because some mountain hunters had assured him of the existence of a good pass through the Rocky Mountains in that direction, and he desired to verify the assertion…Fremont reached the northern side of the Rio del Norte ravine, where tower up the wildest and most inaccessible masses of the Rocky Mountains chain. Bill Williams pushed on, however, and the party gradually approached the watershed."

The above statement adds credence to the gist of the controversial Leroux letter of August 22, 1850 (Hafens 1960, Brandon 1955). In it Leroux stated, "There are but two practicable & travelled roads over said mountain [San Juan], one which bears the name of [Antoine] Robidoux [the Cochetopa], the other which was discovered and first travelled by myself [Leroux Pass up Willow Creek from today's Creede]." Leroux's letter concludes that Leroux Pass "is well known to most of the hunters and trappers—& Bill Williams has himself travelled it several times in company with me. His knowledge of this part of the country was perfect." These passes with these names, together with Fremont's route up the Rio Grande, are unequivocally shown on Lt. John G. Parke's 1851 *Map of the Territory of New Mexico*, reprinted by Abel in 1915. In his credits compiler Parke stated, "assisted by Mr. Richard H. Kern...The Rio del Norte, from its head to Taos, Sierras de S. Juan and Chow Atch [Sawatch], and the region as far as the mouth of the Huerfano—are from a map by 'Old Bill Williams,' and from additional data furnished by Dr. H.[orace] R. Wirtz U.S.A., Messrs. R. H. and E. M. Kern, San [Ceran St.] Vrain, Le Roux, [John L.] Hatcher, and others." Here is further proof, from Old Bill and the Kerns themselves, of Fremont's intentions and routes, and of Old Bill's "perfect" knowledge of the country. Brandon placed this map on the endpapers of his 1955 book.

An even better pass, the Slumgullion, lies 15 miles west of Leroux Pass; it carries today's State Highway 149 to Lake City. For further notes on the Cochetopa and Carnero passes, see the 1853-54 Itinerary.

Fremont put all the blame on Old Bill and the men. While his men were still dying on the Rio Grande, Fremont wrote Jessie from Taos on January 27, 1849: "I write you from the house of our good friend Carson. This morning a cup of chocolate was brought to me, while yet in bed...The error of our expedition was committed in engaging this man [Old Bill]. He proved never to have known, or entirely to have forgotten, the whole country through which we were to pass...I determined to send in a party to the Spanish settlements of New Mexico for provisions, and for mules to transport our baggage...The courage of some of the men began to fail [Bigelow's 1856 political campaign version adds, 'in fact, I have never seen men so soon discouraged by misfortune as we were on this occasion; but, as you know, the party was not constituted like the former ones']...I remain here with these old comrades, while Godey goes back; because it was not necessary for me to go with him, and it was necessary for me to remain, and prepare the means of resuming the expedition to California as soon as he returns with the men left behind [this passage not in Bigelow]...*The survey has been uninterrupted up to this point, and I shall carry it on consecutively*...I am absolutely astonished at this persistence of misfortune—this succession of calamities which no care or vigilance of mine could foresee or prevent." (Spence 1984.)

Fremont's apologists—e.g., Jessie Fremont, Benton, Heap, Godey, Leroux at one time, the 1856 campaign biographies by Bigelow and Upham—heaped criticism on Old Bill in a vain attempt to cover up Fremont's four deadly blunders. First, in spite of many warnings, he went deep into high mountain country in the worst winter imaginable; even if they got through the first challenge, endless snowy peaks lay ahead. Second, after finding himself in a hopeless situation, he doggedly stayed on 26 crucial days, waiting for a weak relief party to come back for the baggage. Third, he then pushed to safety himself, leaving his wretched men under incompetent leadership, with orders to keep moving baggage; this order cost them 4 more days at their mortal peril. Fourth, he did not go back himself to rescue the others, because he was too busy setting up his forward journey to meet his wife in California. Fremont's obsession with his goal and his baggage killed ten men.

Itinerary, 1853-54 FREMONT'S FIFTH EXPEDITION, KANSAS CITY TO COCHETOPA PASS TO CALIFORNIA. September 19, 1853—Fremont and 22 others, as finally constituted, leave Westport with pack animals. The others are black servant Alexander (or Albert) Lea, 4 Wyandots, 10 Delawares, a Mexican, topographer Friedrich W. Egloffstein, daguerreotypist Solomon N. Carvalho, and adventurers William H. Palmer, Oliver Fuller, James F. Milligan, and Max Strobel, a member of Isaac Stevens's recent railroad exploration. They proceed up the Kansas River on Fremont's 1848 route. But on the 22d Fremont has to return to St. Louis for treatment of sciatica, inflamed hip nerves. Milligan broods, "This unlooked for delay forbodes no good to the success of the expedition and I feel exceedingly depressed" (Stegmaier and Miller 1988). Fremont has hoped to be ahead of winter's worst in the mountains. Now his party, after passing brand new Ft. Riley, must wait for him on the Saline River near present Salina, October 5 through 31. Here in the buffalo country they will not have to use up precious provisions. Milligan writes on the 16th, "All hands out of patience waiting on Colonel Fremont. The Indians getting exceedingly dissatisfied, having great fear of cold weather."

For much of the way to Utah, Fremont this year is following the tracks of Beale and Heap (5:J9), who left Westport May 15, and Gunnison's railroad surveyors (L3), who left June 23. Fremont's intent is to add winter data and to pursue a central straight line westward from Cochetopa Pass.

November 1—Fremont rejoins the others. He leads them from the Saline

River through a prairie fire at full speed. He orders the men to keep no diaries. Milligan refuses: "The sequel of this selfish demand of the Col. remains to be seen." The route along and from the Smoky Hill is much the same as that in the 1848 itinerary given above, except that they strike the Arkansas about 25 miles west of Dodge City. November 18 through 24—They camp at Bent's trading houses at Big Timbers on the north side of the Arkansas opposite future Prowers CO, 8 miles west of Lamar. Here Fremont leaves Milligan, who has bad feet and is still writing a diary. Milligan will record on February 2, 1854, "Commences hauling logs to build a new Fort, the rats having entirely ran away with this one [the trading houses]. Bent's New Fort of stone will arise here during 1854. Ft. Wise will be established in 1860, to be called Old Ft. Lyon from 1862 to 1867, when present Ft. Lyon will be founded 20 miles upriver.

November 25—Fremont leads 21 men and 54 shod animals up the Arkansas. Carvalho is now about the only chronicler; he writes his memoirs in 1856 to boost Fremont's presidential campaign (Spence 1984). His book is full of adulation for Fremont but is short on dates, because Fremont did not let him keep a journal. Fremont ascends the Arkansas to near Boone and goes up the Huerfano around the south end of the Wet Mountains. Then he crosses the Sangre de Cristos ("Sierra Blanca") through Sand Hill or Medano Pass into the middle of Great Sand Dunes National Monument on December 5. He peeked into this pass on his fourth expedition and should know that it is not fit for a railroad. Near the pass they find a destitute Mexican and add him to the roster. Fremont crosses San Luis Valley, goes up Saguache ("Sah-watch") Creek and through North Cochetopa Pass, December 14, and follows Gunnison's wagon tracks down to the Gunnison River.

A careful reading and mapping of Lt. Beckwith's 1854 words confirms the conclusion of Spence (1984) and Richmond that Gunnison (and Fremont) in 1853 use what is now called North (Cochetopa) Pass, elevation 10,149 feet. It is 4 miles northeast of the "Cochetopa Pass," elevation 10,032 feet, labeled on today's maps. This southern Cochetopa Pass probably is not Carnero Pass, however. Beckwith apparently can see the Carnero from the junction of West Pass and Cochetopa creeks. This would make it the 10,500-foot notch that is 8 miles southwest of Cochetopa Pass, or 12 miles from the North Cochetopa Pass. Just as Beckwith says, the eastern approach to the Carnero is much farther up toward the head of Saguache Creek than is the common approach to both of the Cochetopa passes. All this is admirably confirmed by Heap's 1854 map, which shows the Carnero about 10 miles from the Cochetopa. Heap may have gone through the southern Cochetopa, for he reported being west of Cochetopa Dome.

January 1, 1854—While skirting the south side of the Black Canyon of the

Gunnison River, Fremont is in what John Gunnison called the most cut-up country he ever saw. Braving temperatures of 30 below zero, the party pauses for a New Year's feast consisting, "besides our usual 'horse soup,' of a delicious dish of horse steaks, fried in the remnants of our '[buffalo]-tallow' candles." One day 50 baggage animals roped together all tumble down several hundred feet. Two are killed. Fremont still follows Gunnison, descending the Uncompahgre and crossing the Colorado at present Grand Junction. The dangerous crossing is made partly on ice and partly by swimming the animals in the swift, frigid waters. The route then leads along the base of the Book Cliffs.

Fremont crosses the Green River at the mouth of the San Rafael. He is forging a new path, Gunnison having gone too far north (for Fremont) and crossed at the modern town of Green River 15 miles upstream. Fremont ascends the San Rafael northwest until he is blocked where it cuts through the San Rafael Reef, which he calls the Anterria Range. He turns southwest along the base of the Reef for 50 miles, curving west along what is now the northern border of Wayne County UT (Spence 1984). He passes north of Thousand Lake Mountain on his way west into the Wasatch Plateau. The men are frozen, exhausted, and starving.

The Wasatch is almost the coup de grace. Carvalho writes, "We commenced the ascent of this tremendous mountain, covered as it were, with an icy pall of death." Somehow Fremont gets them over. From his astronomical observations he then guides them unerringly to the little Mormon settlement of Parowan. Probably they go from near today's town of Fremont west to Otter Creek and follow it south along the Fish Lake Branch of the Old Spanish Trail. This trail zigzags through present Kingston and Circleville on the Sevier River and then crosses west and southwest to Parowan and nearby Little Salt Lake. The men suffer from scurvy, dysentery, and frostbite-cracked fingers and toes. Oliver Fuller dies within a day of salvation, although his blackened feet probably would have been amputated had he survived.

February 8 through 20—The expedition regroups in Parowan. Fremont learns of Mormon John Steele's recent explorations on the Old Spanish Trail and Virgin River. Carvalho, Egloffstein, and probably two others must leave to recuperate in Salt Lake City. Fremont and the rest push on to the west on the 21st. Following his *Memoirs* map, with gaps filled in by the excellent notes of Spence (1984), by modern names they go to Cedar City and Enterprise UT, and on to Panaca and Castleton NV. They proceed west to White River, north around the end of the Seaman Range, and southwest past the north end of the Worthington Mountains. They cross Nellis Air Force Range north of the Quartzite and Helen mountains. Thence they go through Lida NV to south of Oasis CA. At places early in the route they follow the track of the Death Valley Forty-niners.

March 15—From the California-Nevada border about 8 miles southeast of Oasis, Fremont heads southwest across Eureka Valley and tries to cross the Inyo Mountains about 15 miles due east of modern Big Pine. Fremont says on page 6 of this reprint, "The first range we attempted to cross carried us to an elevation of 8,000 or 9,000 [about 7,500] feet and into impassable snow, which was further increased on the 16th by a considerable fall. [Fremont calls the Inyos the first range of the Sierra Nevada.] There was no object in forcing a passage, and I accordingly turned at once some sixty or eighty [about 80] miles to the southward [and 40 more southwestward], making a wide sweep to strike the *Point of the California mountain* [at Walker Pass]." Fremont's course, clearly shown on his map but with a gap in the middle, goes along the east side of the Inyo and Coso mountains, passing through the Eureka and Saline valleys and Darwin Wash before cutting southwest to Freeman Junction. (Spence proposes a route from Oasis to Big Pine and down Owens River past Owens Lake, but Fremont's map and words explicitly indicate otherwise.)

About April 1—Today's Freeman Junction is at the entrance to Walker Pass. Fremont's map shows that he goes 10 miles farther southwest and crosses back northwest by Humpayamap Pass, which parallels Walker Pass. From Lt. Williamson's 1854 map and elevations, this route has to follow up today's Little Dixie Wash and down Kelso Creek to Weldon. But Williamson, who has Godey and Preuss with him, states flatly, "I have conclusive evidence to show that this [Fremont's 1854 pass] was Walker's Pass…of which Colonel Fremont could have known nothing definitely, as he had never been there before." It doesn't make much difference either way. The Kern River Canyon farther west is no good for a railroad. From near modern Bakersfield Fremont takes the standard road north down the San Joaquin Valley to Stockton, where he disbands. He goes on to reach San Francisco on April 18.

Fremont spends 174 days going from Westport to San Francisco, not counting 26 days at Saline River and 12 at Parowan. He gives his mileage as 1,550, but that is only to Oasis and the Inyo Mountains. Adding 500 gives a minimum of 2,050 to San Francisco. The average rate is 12 grueling miles per day under severe conditions. Fremont long since has had to scrap his original nonsensical plan of zipping to the Pacific in 60 days and then zipping back on a "double expedition" (Stegmaier and Miller 1988).

Legacy   The only contribution that Fremont's last two foolhardy and unscientific expeditions made to railroad surveying was utterly to discredit his own touted central route. The Great Reporter could never bring himself to report fully these dismal failures. He could only lie about them. In 1849 he averred, "The result was entirely satisfactory. It convinced me that neither the snow of winter nor the mountain ranges were obstacles in the way of the [central] road, and furnished me with a far better line than any I had previously known" (Spence 1984). In 1850 he wrote a preposterous letter to a railroad convention: "this continent can be crossed, from the Mississippi to the Pacific, without climbing a mountain, and on the very [central] line which every national consideration would require." On page 7 of the 1854 letter reprinted here he claimed, "It is clearly established that the winter condition of the country constitutes no impediment, and from what has been said the entire practicability of the [central] line will be as clearly inferred."

Benton, of course, backed Fremont's lies to the hilt, even after the disasters that were obvious to all. In 1849 Benton told a convention that Fremont "wanted a road three or four degrees further south [than South Pass], and has found it, and gives the country the benefit of it" (Bancroft 24:509). During another speech Benton was repeatedly badgered about how his central railroad could possibly get through the Rocky Mountains. "Pointing to a liveryman in the audience, a man of large stature and well-known habits, Senator Benton said: 'When we get to the mountains, if we cannot get through any other way, we will get Bob O'Blenis to swear a hole through'" (Bernard 1906). The "central route" still needs Bob O'Blenis today.

Capt. James H. Simpson, with Fremont and Benton in mind, summed it up in 1859: "The truth is, facts are stubborn things, and he, be he engineer, statesman, or philosopher, who ignores them, will at length find that he has been following but a vain conceit, which will eventually land him…into a condition…of utter ruin."

REFERENCES

(See Preface for Heading and Author references, and for Bancroft, not listed here.)

Abel, Annie Heloise, 1915, The official correspondence of James C. Calhoun: Wash., Office of Indian Affairs, 554 p., Parke's folding map in pocket.

Beckwith, Edward G., 1854 (1855 pub.), Explorations for a route for the Pacific railroad near the 38th and 39th parallels, in Reports of Explorations and Surveys: Wash., 33/2 ("33/3") H91, serial 792, 2:48-49; see also Warren's General Map in v. 11.

Bernard, William R., 1906, Westport and the Santa Fe trade: Topeka, Kansas State Hist. Soc. Transactions 9:563.

Bigelow, John, 1856, Memoir of the life and public services of John Charles Fremont: N.Y., 4th Exped. p. 357-78; Fremont's 1854 letter reprint 473-80; 1849 letter to Jessie 365-76, quote on discouraged men 368.

Brandon, William, 1955, The men and the mountain, Fremont's fourth expedition: N.Y., 337 p.; route map 215; Leroux letter discussion 294-312.

Favour, Alpheus H., 1936, Old Bill Williams, mountain man: Chapel Hill NC, 229 p..

Fremont, Jessie Benton, 1887, Souvenirs of my time: Boston, p. 187-88.

Fremont, John C., 1850, The Pacific railroad, letter from Col. Fremont: [N.Y.], Stryker's American Register and Magazine, v. 4, p. 558-64, quote 560.

Fremont, John C., 1887, Memoirs of my life: Chicago, folding map at back.

Hafen, LeRoy R. and Ann W., 1960, Fremont's fourth expedition: Glendale, 319 p.; Itinerary diaries of B. Kern 79-108, R. Kern 109-34, E. Kern 289-95, with B. Kern quotes on icicles 97, belly 99, horrid 100, lost mules and the top 102, days of horror 103; R. Kern on Vincenthaler 130; quotes by Benton 59, Fremont to Benton 76, Martin 139, McGehee 159, Breckenridge 181, Simpson 247-48, Leroux letter 251-53, Godey 269, Lupton 284-85, Fitzpatrick 287.

Hamilton, William T., 1905, My sixty years on the plains: N.Y., p. 196.

Heap, Gwinn H., 1854 (1957 reprint), Central route to the Pacific; LeRoy and Ann Hafen, eds.: Glendale, folding map; see 139 for Cochetopa Dome.

Lecompte, Janet, 1978, Pueblo, Hardscrabble, Greenhorn, the Upper Arkansas 1832-56: Norman, 254 p., map viii.

Mollhausen, Baldwin, 1854 (1858 pub.), Diary of a journey from the Mississippi to the coasts of the Pacific: London, quote 2:82-84.

Preuss, Charles, 1848-49 diaries (1958 printing), Exploring with Fremont: Norman, quote on Williams p. 144; rescue party campfires 147.

Richmond, Patricia J., 1990, Trail to disaster: Denver, Colo. Hist. Soc., 117 p.

Simpson, James H., 1859 (1876 printing), Report of explorations across the Great Basin: Wash., Engineer Dept., quote p. 235.

Spence, Mary Lee, 1984, The expeditions of John Charles Fremont, 1848-54: Urbana, v. 3, Fremont's 4th Exped. 50-108; discussion of Mrs. Richmond xxix-xxx, 74, and map 108; make-up of 1849 CA party 51-53; Fremont to Jessie quotes on chocolate 75, error 76, baggage 77, courage 77, Godey goes back 80, survey 80, astonished 81; Fremont's 5th Exped. 379-608; Fremont's 1854 letter reprint 480-88; Carvalho reprint 383-405, 406-21, 423-68; notes on Great Basin route 475-77, 489; on satisfactory result 122.

Stegmaier, Mark J., and David H. Miller, 1988, James F. Milligan, his journal of Fremont's fifth expedition: Glendale, summary 75-99; double expedition 79; quotes on delay 107, patience 118, sequel 128, New Fort 161.

Torrey, John, 1850 (1854 pub.), Plantae Fremontianae: Wash., Smithsonian Contributions to Knowledge, v. 6, 24 p., plates; quote p. 4; see also Spence p. 573.

Upham, Charles W., 1856, Life, explorations, and public services of John Charles Fremont: Boston, p. 273-300, 327-34.

Weber, David J., 1985, Richard H. Kern: Albuquerque, Fremont's fourth expedition p. 17-50; Mrs. Richmond's map 41, arguments for it 298-300.

Williamson, Robert S., 1854 (1856 pub.), Routes in California, in Reports of Explorations and Surveys: Wash., 33/2 H191, serial 795, 5:1-43, quote 18.

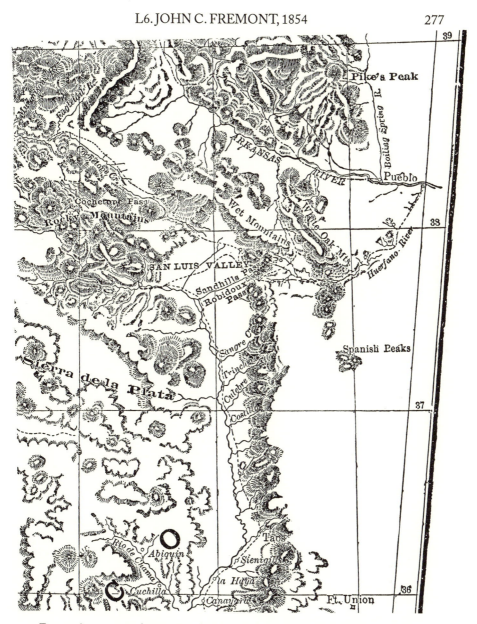

Fremont's own map of 1848–49 and 1853 routes. In the San Luis Valley, the southern dashed line is his 1848–49 route from the Great Sand Dunes southwest to the Rio
Grande, up its valley into the San Juans, and back out on the same path, thence to
descend the river to Taos. The northern dashed line is his 1853 route from the Great
Sand Dunes northwest to Saguache Creek and North Cochetopa Pass. From compiler's copy of "Map Showing Country Explored by John Charles Fremont from 1841
to 1854 Inclusive. Drawn and Engraved Expressly for Fremont's [1887] Memoirs."

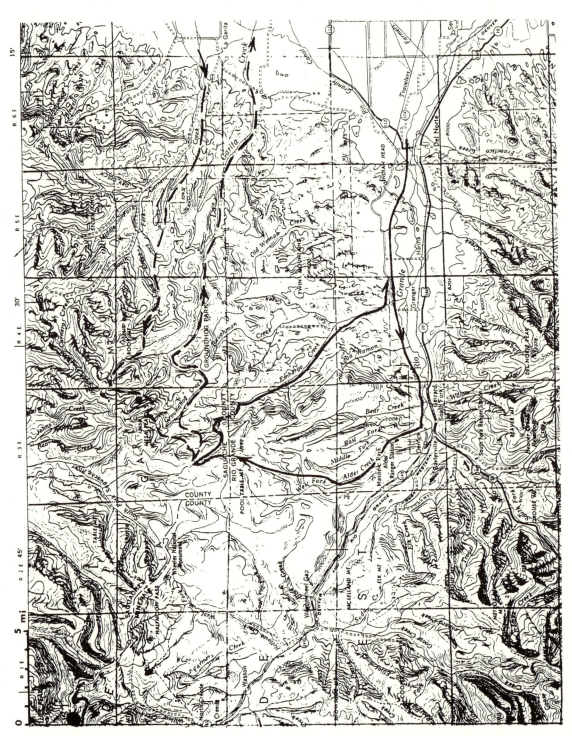

Map of Fremont's 1848-49 path in San Juan Mts. Solid line is the likely path (after Brandon 1955), except that Fremont's (1887) map shows his travel here on the south side of the Rio Grande. Dashed line is an unlikely path (after Richmond in Spence 1984). Carnero Pass is 15 miles due north of the northernmost point on the likely path, and North (Cochetopa) Pass is 12 miles northeast of the Carnero. Leroux Pass is just west of the large black dot at the northwest corner of this map. The inscription "1848" in a rock shelter is at the small black dot near Mesa Peak. It probably was written by a small party reconnoitering from the main path.

33d CONGRESS,   [SENATE.]   MIS. DOC.
  1st Session.   No. 67.

LETTER

OF

J. C. FREMONT

TO

THE EDITORS OF THE NATIONAL INTELLIGENCER,

COMMUNICATING

Some general results of a recent winter expedition across the Rocky moun-tains for the survey of a route for a roilroad [sic] to the Pacific.

JUNE 15, 1854.—Referred to the select committee on the Pacific Railroad and ordered to be printed.

COL. FREMONT'S EXPLORATION OF THE CENTRAL RAILROAD ROUTE TO THE PACIFIC.

To the Editors of the National Intelligencer:

GENTLEMEN: While the proceedings in Congress are occupying public atten-tion more particularly with the subject of a Pacific railway I desire to offer to your paper, for publication, some general results of a recent winter expedition across the Rocky mountains, confining myself to mere results, in anticipation of a fuller report, with maps and illustrations, which will necessarily require some months to prepare.

The country examined was for about three-fourths of the distance—from the Missouri frontier, at the mouth of the Kansas river, to the Valley of Parowan, at the foot of the Wahsatch mountains, within the rim of the Great Basin, at its southern bend—along and between the 38th and 39th parallels of latitude; and the whole line divides itself naturally into three sections, which may be conve-niently followed in description.

The *first* or eastern section consists of the great prairie slope spreading from the base of the *Sierra Blanca* to the Missouri frontier, about seven hundred miles; the *second* or middle section comprehends the various Rocky mountain ranges and inter-lying valleys, between the termination of the great plains at the foot of the *Sierra Blanca* and the Great Basin at the Parowan valley and Wahsatch mountains, where the first Mormon settlement is found, about four hundred and fifty miles; the *third* or western section comprehends the mountainous plateau lying between the Wahsatch mountains and the *Sierra Nevada,* a distance of about four hundred miles.

The country examined was upon a very direct line, the travelled [page2] route being about fifteen hundred and fifty miles over an air-line distance of about thirteen hundred miles.

The first section.—Four separate expeditions across this section, made before the present one, and which carried me over various lines at different seasons of the year, enable me to speak of it with the confidence of intimate knowledge. It is a plain of easy inclination, sweeping directly up to the foot of the mountains which dominate it as highlands do the ocean. Its character is open prairie, over which summer travelling is made in every direction.

For a railway or a winter travelling road the route would be, in consideration of wood, coal, building stone, water, and fertile land, about two hundred miles up the immediate valley of the Kansas, (which might be made one rich continuous corn-field,) and afterwards along the immediate valley of the Upper Arkansas, of which about two hundred miles, as you approach the mountains, is continuously well adapted to settlements as well as to roads. Numerous well-watered and fertile valleys, broad and level, open up among the mountains, which present themselves in detached blocks, (outliers,) gradually closing in around the heads of the streams, but leaving open approaches to the central ridges. The whole of the inter-mountain region is abundant in grasses, wood, coal, and fertile soil. The *pueblos* above Bent's fort prove it to be well adapted to the grains and vegetables common to the latitude, including Indian corn, which ripens well, and to the support of healthy stock, which increase well and take care of themselves summer and winter.

The climate is mild and the winters short, the autumn usually having its full length of bright open weather, without snow, which in winter falls rarely and passes off quickly. In this belt of country lying along the mountains the snow falls more early and much more thinly than in the open plains to the eastward; the storms congregate about the high mountains and leave the valleys free. In the beginning of December we found yet no snow on the *Huerfano* river, and were informed by an old resident, then engaged in establishing a farm at the mouth of this stream, that snow seldom or never fell there, and that cattle were left in the range all the winter through.

This character of country continued to the foot of the dividing crest, and to this point our journey resulted in showing a very easy grade for a road, over a country unobstructed either by snow or other impediments, and having all the elements necessary to the prosperity of an agricultural population, in fertility of soil, abundance of food for stock, wood and coal for fuel, and timber for necessary constructions.

Our examinations around the southern headwaters of the Arkansas have made us acquainted with many passes grouped together in a small space of country, conducting by short and practicable valleys from the waters of the Arkansas, just described, to the valleys of the *Del Norte* and East Colorado. The *Sierra Blanca*, through which these passes lie, is high and rugged, presenting a very broken appearance, but rises abruptly from the open country on either side, narrowed at the points through which the passes are cut, leaving them only six or eight miles in length from valley to valley, and entirely unobstructed by outlying ranges or broken country. To the best of these passes the [p. 3] ascent is along the open valley of water-courses, uniform and very gradual in ascent. Standing immediately at the mouth of the *Sand Hill Pass*—one of the most practicable in the *Sierra Blanca*, and above those usually travelled—at one of the remotest head-springs of the *Huerfano* river, the eye of the traveller follows down without obstruction or abrupt descent along the gradual slope of the valley to the great plains which reach the Missouri. The straight river and the open valley form, with the plains beyond, one great slope, without a hill to break the line of sight or obstruct the course of the road. On either side of this line hills slope easily to the river, with lines of timber and yellow autumnal grass, and the water which flows smoothly between is not interrupted by a fall in its course to the ocean. The surrounding country is wooded with pines and covered with luxuriant grasses up to the very crags of the central summits. On the 8th of December we found this whole country free from snow, and Daguerre views taken at this time show the grass entirely uncovered in the passes.

Along all this line the elevation was carefully determined by frequent barometrical observations, and its character exhibited by a series of Daguerreotype views, comprehending the face of the country almost continuously, or at least sufficiently so to give a thoroughly correct impression of the whole.

Two tunnel-like passes pierce the mountains here, almost in juxtaposition, connecting the plain country on either side by short passages five to eight miles long. The mountains which they perforate constitute the only obstruction, and are the only break in the plane or valley line of road from the frontier of Missouri to the summit hills of the Rocky mountains, a distance of about eight hundred and fifty miles, or more than half-way to the San Joaquin valley. Entering one of these passes from the eastern plain, a distance of about one mile upon a wagon road, already travelled by wagons, commands an open view of the broad valley of *San Luis* and the great range of *San Juan* beyond on its western side. I here connected the line of the present expedition with one explored in 1848-'49 from the mouth of the Kansas to this point, and the results of both will be embodied in a fuller report.

At this place the line entered the middle section, and continued its western course over an open valley country, admirably adapted for settlement, across the San Luis valley, and up the flat bottom lands of the Sah-watch to the heights of the central ridge of the Rocky Mountains. Across these wooded heights—wooded and grass-covered up to and over their rounded summits—to the Coocha-to-pe pass, the line followed an open easy wagon way, such as is usual to a rolling country. On the high summit lands were forests of coniferous trees, and the snow in the pass was four inches deep. This was on the 14th of December. A day earlier our horses' feet would not have touched snow in the crossing. Up to this point we had enjoyed clear and dry pleasant weather. Our journey had been all along on dry ground; and travelling slowly along waiting for the winter there had been abuudant leisure for becoming acquainted with the country. The open character of the country, joined to good information, indicated the existence of other passes about the head of the Sah-watch. This it was desirable [p. 4] to verify, and especially to examine a neighboring and lower pass connecting more directly with the Arkansas valley, known as the Poow-che.

But the winter had now set in over all the mountain regions, and the country was so constantly enveloped and hidden with clouds which rested upon it, and the air so darkened by falling snow, that exploring became difficult and dangerous, precisely where we felt most interested in making a thorough examination. We were moving in fogs and clouds, through a region wholly unknown to us, and without guides; and were therefore obliged to content ourselves with the examination of a single line, and the ascertainment of the winter condition of the country over which it passed; which was in fact the main object of our expedition.

Our progress in this mountainous region was necessarily slow; and during ten days which it occupied us to pass through about one hundred miles of the mountainous country bordering the eastern side of the Upper Colorado valley, the greatest depth of snow was among the pines and aspens on the ridges about two and a half feet, and in the valleys about six inches. The atmosphere is too cold and dry for much snow, and the valleys, protected by the mountains, are comparatively free from it, and warm. We here found villages of Utah Indians in their wintering ground, in little valleys along the foot of the higher mountains, and bordering the more open country of the Colorado valley. Snow was here (December 25) only a few inches deep—the grass generally appearing above it, and there being none under trees and on southern hill sides.

The horses of the *Utahs* were living on the range, and, notwithstanding that they were used in hunting, were in excellent condition. One which we had occasion to kill for food had on it about two inches of fat, being in as good order as any buffalo we had killed in November on the eastern plains. Over this valley country—about one hundred and fifty miles across—the Indians informed us that snow falls only a few inches in depth; such as we saw it at the time.

The immediate valley of the Upper Colorado for about one hundred miles in breadth, and from the 7th to the 22d of January, was entirely bare of snow, and the weather resembled that of autumn in this country. The line here entered the body of mountains known as the *Wah-satch* and *An-ter-ria* ranges, which are practicable at several places in this part of their course; but the falling snow and destitute condition of my party again interfered to impede examinations. They lie between the Colorado valley and the Great Basin, and at their western base are established the Mormon settlements of Parowan and Cedar city. They are what are called fertile mountains, abundant in water, wood, and grass, and fertile valleys, offering inducements to settlement and facilities for making a road. These mountains are a great storehouse of materials—timber, iron, coal—which would be of indispensable use in the construction and maintenance of the road, and are solid foundations to build up the future prosperity of the rapidly-increasing Utah State.

Salt is abundant on the eastern border, mountains—as the *Sierra de Sal*—being named from it. In the ranges lying behind the Mormon settlements, among the mountains through which the line passes, are accumulated a great wealth of iron and coal, and extensive forests of [p. 5] heavy timber. These forests are the largest I am acquainted with in the Rocky mountains, being, in some places, twenty miles in depth, of continuous forest; the general growth lofty and large, frequently over three feet in diameter, and sometimes reaching five feet, the red spruce and yellow pine predominating. At the actual southern extremity of the Mormon settlements, consisting of the two enclosed towns of Parowan and Cedar city, near to which our line passed, a coal mine has been opened for about eighty yards, and iron works already established. Iron here occurs in extraordinary masses, in some parts accumulated into mountains, which comb out in crests of solid iron thirty feet thick and a hundred yards long.

In passing through this bed of mountains about fourteen days had been occupied, from January 24 to February 7, the deepest snow we here encountered being about up to the saddle skirts, or four feet; this occurring only in occasional drifts in the passes on northern exposures, and in the small mountain flats hemmed in by woods and hills. In the valley it was sometimes a few inches deep, and as often none at all. On our arrival at the Mormon settlements, February 8th, we found it a few inches deep, and were there informed that the winter had been unusually long-continued, and severe, the thermometer having been as low as 17° below zero, and more snow having fallen than in all the previous winters together since the establishment of this colony.

At this season, their farmers had usually been occupied with their ploughs, preparing the land for grain.

At this point the line of exploration entered the *third* or western section, comprehending the mountainous *plateau* between the Wahsatch mountains and the Sierra Nevada of California. Two routes here suggested themselves to me for examination: one directly across the *plateau*, between the 37th and 38th parallels; the other keeping to the south of the mountains, and following for about two hundred miles down a valley of the *Rio Virgen*—Virgin river—thence direct to the Tejon Pass, at the head of the San Joaquin valley. This route down the Virgin river had been examined the year before, with a view to settlement this summer by a Mormon exploring party under the command of Major Steele, of Parowan, who (and others of the party) informed me that they found fertile valleys inhabited by Indians who cultivated corn and melons, and the rich ground in many places matted over with grape-vines. The Tejon Passes are two, one of them (from the abundance of vines at its lower end) called *Caxon* [*sic*] *de las Uvas.* They were of long use, and were examined by me and their practicability ascertained in my expedition of 1848-'49; and in 1851 I again passed through them both, bringing three thousand head of cattle through one of them.

Knowing the practicability of these passes, and confiding in the report of Major Steele as to the intermediate country, I determined to take the other, (between the 37th and 38th parallels,) it recommending itself to me as being more direct towards San Francisco, and preferable on that account for a road, if suitable ground could be found; and also as being unknown, the Mormons informing me that various attempts had been made to explore it, and all failed for want of water. Although biased in favor of the Virgin river route, I determined to examine this [p. 6] one in the interest of geography, and accordingly set out for this purpose from the settlement about the 20th of February, travelling directly westward from Cedar city, (eighteen miles west from Parowan.) We found the country a high table land, bristling with mountains, often in short isolated blocks, and sometimes accumulated into considerable ranges, with numerous open and low passes.

We were thus always in a valley, and always surrounded by mountains more or less closely, which apparently altered in shape and position as we advanced. The valleys are dry and naked, without water or wood; but the mountains are generally covered with grass and well wooded with pines. Springs are very rare, and occasional small streams are at remote distances. Not a human being was encountered between the Santa Clara road near the Mormon settlements and the *Sierra Nevada*, over a distance of more than three hundred miles. The solitary character of this uninhabited region, and naked valleys without water courses, among mountains with fertile soil and grass and woods abundant, give it the appearance of an unfinished country.

Commencing at the 38th, we struck the Sierra Nevada on about the 37th parallel about the 15th March.

On our route across we had for the greater part of the time pleasant and rather warm weather; the valley grounds and low ridges uncovered, but snow over the upper parts of the higher mountains. Between the 20th of February and 17th of March we had several snow storms, sometimes accompanied with hail and heavy thunder; but the snow remained on the valley grounds only a few hours after the storm was over. It forms not the least impediment at any time of the winter. I was prepared to find the Sierra here broad, rugged, and blocked up with snow, and was not disappointed in my expectation. The first range we attempted to cross carried us to an elevation of 8,000 or 9,000 feet and into impassable snow, which was further increased on the 16th by a considerable fall.

There was no object in forcing a passage, and I accordingly turned at once some sixty or eighty miles to the southward, making a wide sweep to strike the *Point of the California mountain* where the Sierra Nevada suddenly breaks off and declines into a lower country. Information obtained years before from the Indians led me to believe that the low mountains were broken into many passes, and at all events I had the certainty of an easy passage through either of Walker's passes.

When the Point was reached I found the Indian information fully verified: the mountain sudden terminated and broken down into lower grounds barely above the level of the country, and making numerous openings into the valley of the San Joaquin. I entered into the first which offered, (taking no time to search, as we were entirely out of provisions and living upon horses,) which led us by an open and almost level hollow thirteen miles long to an upland not steep enough to be called a hill, over into the valley of a small affluent to Kern river; the hollow and the valley making together a way where a wagon would not find any obstruction for forty miles.

The country around the passes in which the Sierra Nevada here terminates declines considerably below its more northern elevation. There was no snow to be seen at all on its eastern face and none in the pass; [p. 7] but we were in the midst of opening spring, flowers blooming in fields on both sides of the Sierra.

Between the point of the mountains and the head of the valley at the Tejon the passes generally are free from snow throughout the year, and the descent from them to the ocean is distributed over a long slope of more than two hundred miles. The low dry country and the long slope, in contradistinction to the high country and short sudden descent and heavy snows of the passes behind the bay of San Francisco, are among the considerations which suggest themselves in favor of the route by the head of the San Joaquin.

The above results embody general impressions made upon my mind during this journey. It is clearly established that the winter condition of the country constitutes no impediment, and from what has been said the entire practicability of the line will be as clearly inferred. A fuller account hereafter will comprehend detailed descriptions of country, with their absolute and relative elevations, and show the ground upon which the conclusions were based. They are contributed at this time as an element to aid the public in forming an opinion on the subject of the projected railway, and in gratification of my great desire to do something for its advancement. It seems a treason against mankind and the spirit of progress which marks the age to refuse to put this one completing link to our national prosperity and the civilization of the world. Europe still lies between Asia and America; build this railroad and things will have revolved about; America will lie between Asia and Europe—the golden vein which runs through the history of the world will follow the iron track to San Francisco, and the Asiatic trade will finally fall into its last and permanent road, when the ancient and the modern Chryse throw open their gates to the thoroughfare of the world.

I am, gentlemen, with much regard, respectfully, yours,

J.C. FREMONT

WASHINGTON, *June* 13, 1854.

Frederick W. Lander, 1854

Remarks On The Construction Of A
First Class Double Track Railway To The Pacific

Washington, Henry Polkinhorn, Printer, 1854, 14 p. [WC 277 note; WCB 240a;
UPRR p. 26; NUC NL 0065153.] Reset verbatim from a facsimile, by courtesy of
The Bancroft Library, University of California, Berkeley.

Significance To rectify its omission from the official surveys, Lander
explored the north-central railroad route via the Columbia River and South Pass
in 1854, at his own initiative and expense. Back in Washington, he wrote this
tract favoring a trunk line from South Pass through Salt Lake City to California;
he advocated a branch on one end to Puget Sound via the Columbia, and a branch
on the other end to St. Paul or Chicago. He deemed impracticable the northern
route through Montana, which he had covered in 1853 with Isaac I. Stevens's survey (2:D10). Lander's further explorations are reviewed in L8.

Lander also here poured out verbose and not very convincing arguments for
first building a quick, light, second-class railroad to use in building the main road
and in gaining a speedy return on investment. He did not spell out the costs of
upgrading. He thought that the idea of constructing three lines was fiscal mad-
ness (see L10). John G. Wells reprinted excerpts of Lander's report in 1857. The
first modern reprinting appears to be the one that follows.

Author FREDERICK WEST LANDER, 1821-1862, engineer, soldier, explorer,
would-be poet. Lander was born in Massachusetts and educated as a civil engineer, after accepting advice not to try to become a full-time poet. He made surveys for several eastern railroads. In 1853 he was on Isaac I. Stevens's exploration
for a northern Pacific railroad route. He returned east the next year via South
Pass, making his own daring railroad reconnaissance (see Itinerary). He became
chief engineer for the federal South Pass and Honey Lake wagon road in 1857,
and superintendent in 1858, after his predecessor wasted a season. (Lander later
was in two fist fights with this man.) Lander's trips for these years and for 1859-
60 are detailed in the L8 Itineraries and by Jackson 1952. In summary, he scouted

the area west of South Pass in 1857, built the Lander Cutoff in 1858, finished and promoted this trail in 1859, and worked the Honey Lake, California, end of his road in 1860. He skirmished with the Paiutes near Honey Lake but then made peace with them. He married Jean Davenport, a successful English-born actress, in late 1860 in San Francisco.

At the outbreak of Civil War, Lander went on an impossible mission to try to help Sam Houston prevent the secession of Texas. He wrote some patriotic poems. As brigadier general of volunteers he fought courageously in Virginia and was severely wounded in the leg in late 1861. Early in 1862 he successfully defended a Maryland town against a superior force under Gen. Thomas J. "Stonewall" Jackson. In a later conflict Lander gallantly led a brilliant charge. While preparing another attack he died suddenly, possibly from a stroke caused by a blood clot from his unhealed leg wound. He was a big man with great physical strength. He was a faithful public servant and an intrepid explorer. Jackson (1952) called Lander "one of the greatest road builders in the nation's history." (Branch 1929; DAB; NCAB; ACAB; Thrapp; Heitman.)

Itinerary, 1854   LANDER, SEATTLE TO COUNCIL BLUFFS VIA SOUTH PASS. March 18—Lander leaves the Seattle-Olympia area with only 6 men using pack horses. He has the moral support of a resolution from the legislature of Washington Territory, but the expenses are private. Lander and three of the men, including meteorologist J. F. Moffett, are veterans of Isaac I. Stevens's 1853 northern survey for the Pacific railroad (2:D10). None of the other men is identified. Geologist John Evans provides the only barometer on the northwest coast but does not go along.

From Ft. Vancouver the party ascends the Columbia to the Dalles and takes the Oregon Trail. At the Umatilla Agency near present Pendleton OR two of the Stevens veterans become disabled and are left behind. Lander scouts the options to the sides, including the connection between the Walla Walla and Grande Ronde rivers in the northern Blue Mountains. From Ft. Boise he follows the Snake nearly to Ft. Hall, where the barometer breaks. Thence he goes south up the Bannock and down the Malad to near the mouth of Bear River at Great Salt Lake. Here he envisions the possible connection of his branch line with the main California-bound trunk of the Pacific railroad coming from South Pass, or perhaps Bridger Pass. Lander estimates the distance so far to be 1,155 miles.

From Ft. Hall Lander records, "Leaving my own tired party and worn-out horses in camp, Captain [Hector] McArthur [former Hudson's Bay Company factor] accompanied me, with a single half-breed, in a long reconnaissance of the numerous passes of the upper rim of the Great Basin during many days' forced marches in hostile Indian country, and continued exposure to violent storms of snow and sleet." At this time he conceives and partially explores the future Lander Cutoff from South Pass to Ft. Hall: "By reference to the sketch [not published], it will be seen that a dotted line is carried from the South Pass, in a northwesterly direction, to the headwaters of the Snake [Greys River]. This line (so far as examined) extends over a broad gravel plateau…The engineering rule—in seeking location…at angles to the direction of great watercourses [here the Green]—is to skirt the country in which they head."

July 9—Lander reaches Council Bluffs with only one man, Moffett, who soon dies "of the privations incident to a passage of the continent without the comforts of a train, after his arrival at Missouri river." For part of the way they have survived on thistle roots and mule meat. These meager scraps of an itinerary come from Lander's 1854 official report reprinted in 1856, augmented by Branch in 1929. Adding the standard 1,140 Oregon-Trail miles, from Ft. Hall via Ft. Bridger to Council Bluffs, to the previous 1,155 miles gives a total of 2,295 miles. Traveled in 114 days, the average rate is an impressive 20 miles per day. These figures do not do justice to all the side excursions.

Legacy   Neither of Lander's 1854 reports, the one reprinted here or the one revised and published with the official Pacific Railroad Surveys, had much impact on the course of events. Jefferson Davis ignored the South Pass route in his final analysis. Nobody took the idea of initial temporary rails seriously, although Lander amplified it in 1858; his bold 1854 exploration did, however, influence the later construction of the South Pass and Honey Lake wagon road, with its Lander Cutoff (L8).

REFERENCES
(See Preface for Heading and Author references not listed here.)

Branch, E. Douglas, 1929, Frederick West Lander, road-builder: [Cedar Rapids IA], separate reprint from Mississippi Valley Hist. Review 16:172-87.

Jackson, W. Turrentine, 1952 (1979 reprint), Wagon roads West: Lincoln, p. 192-217; quote 232.

Lander, Frederick W., 1854 (revised and printed 1856), Reconnaissance of a railroad route from Puget Sound via South Pass to the Mississippi River, in Reports of Explorations and Surveys: Wash., 33/2 ("33/3") H91, serial 792, 2:1-45; quotes on sketch 36, Moffett 44, McArthur 45.

Wells, John G., 1857, Wells' pocket hand-book of Nebraska: N.Y., 90 p., 2 maps; Lander reprint 75-78, containing excerpts from Lander's p. 5 and 13.

REMARKS

ON THE CONSTRUCTION OF A

FIRST CLASS DOUBLE TRACK RAILWAY

TO THE

PACIFIC,

AND THE

DIFFICULTIES ATTENDING ITS SOLUTION

AS A

PRACTICAL AND SCIENTIFIC PROBLEM.

BY FRED. W. LANDER,

*Late locating and estimating engineer of the Northern Pacific Railroad
Exploration; chief in charge Puget Sound Central Pacific Railroad Exploration; accompanied by extracts from the reports
of F. W. LANDER, on the character of the Northern
and Southern routes to Puget Sound,
as instituted by reconnaissance.*

WASHINGTON:
HENRY POLKINHORN, PRINTER,
1854.

PACIFIC RAILWAY.

Within a period of ten years, the subject of the construction of a railroad to the Pacific, has passed through the various uncertain phases of a project, to the important position which it now occupies in the attention of the American nation.

A general study of the question has arisen throughout the country. Partisans have appeared in support of the various routes to which local interests refer. Plans of procedure have been offered by which this great work may be attempted.

While apprehensions have existed in many quarters that only by the extension of settlements can so stupendous an undertaking be accomplished, sanguine theorists have not been wanting, to propose the immediate construction of a first-class double track railway to the Pacific.

During the recent discussion of this question before Congress, it has even been proposed, to build three first-class grand trunk lines of elaborated character, to that distant terminus.

It may, therefore, certainly be regretted that an engineering study of this intricate subject has not yet been presented, by some individual of long practical experience, who has had opportunity of forming definite conclusions upon its peculiar merits, by a full study of the question in the far interior of the American continent. The deduction of the mere Theorist in railway construction does not afford data for definite knowledge of the stupendous nature of this national undertaking; while the practical individual who, from motives of patriotism or professional emulation, connects himself with the Pacific railway Explorations, endures the mortification of seeing the direct convictions—forced upon his mind by long experience in railroad building and honestly expressed—either assailed as unwarrantable, seriously modified, or wholly suppressed by official parties. Still it is evident that a very general and patriotic desire exists, that some well defined and tangible mode of operations may be devised, by which this important design may be successfully carried out, and that such a well-devised plan of operations can only occur by blending the information to be derived from various sources, and that this information should be presented at the present time, from the fact that a question so intricate can alone be solved by a full comprehension of every detail, while the project is embryo. [p. 4]

Now, assuming that this project is a practical and scientific problem of stupendous character, it may still be resolved to its salient points, and by simplifying and arranging those deductions which tend toward certain conclusions, may be placed fully within the comprehension of unprofessional parties, who may then appreciate its peculiar merits.

The whole engineering question resolves itself into obtaining some rapid and effective means of transportation along the route of the road, that it *may be constructed at all*. The pecuniary question to the application of the least amount of cash capital, without reasonable prospect of immediate return, and the proportioning of means to the end required. Both presentations of the subject, refer to the rapid extension of a railroad of a character adapted to the carrying trade of Western commerce through two thousand miles of uncivilized, hostile, and in many instances uninhabitable country, over mountain ranges, sterile deserts, mighty rivers, and regions devoid of wood or building materials, all obstacles to be overcome before connection can occur with a paying terminus.

It is the stupendous nature of these obstacles which renders the project an engineering problem, while the distance to be passed over ere connection can occur with a paying terminus, more particularly affects it as a pecuniary question.

The engineering problem should have been solved by the application of the best practical talent in the nation; the pecuniary question treated with caution from the experience gained of the late undue expansion of the credit system of construction under land grants, free charters, and multiplication of lines between non-paying termerni [*sic*].

By the bills as at present before Congress, it is proposed to construct a road of first class character from the outset; to use the road, to build the road, and by connection with wagon and stage coach transportation, to open the line of communication and develop national territory at once. This would lead to *over handling*, the costs and evils of which are well understood by every practiaal [*sic*] individual and resulting from even a break of guage [*sic*] on railways have been fully demonstrated both in Great Britain and America.

From the distance to be passed over, and the speed and amount of transportation required, neither wagon or plank roads are applicable to the necessity, which is the moving of weighty materials along the whole route of the road during the progress of its construction over the hundreds of miles from where existing in natural deposit, they may be supplied to the sections deficient.

Now it is a clear engineering proposition, and will not be disputed, that the use of the rail, as that method of transportation perfected by human ingenuity to the best practicable result for moving weighty material at high rates of speed and low cost, transcends all other modes of land locomotion. But the use of the rail for the mere purpose of moving supplies and materials of construction for the completion of a grand trunk railroad, need not involve the elaborate completion of such a road, to wear out and decay during the process of its construction, and of a character to which no remuneration can ensue until its connection with a paying terminus, or in other words the mere use of the road to build the road, and the extension of a line of first class character from the outset, [p. 5] is a chimera and would never be presented by an individual of reasonable comprehension of the stringent liabilities of the construction, decay and depreciation of railroads.

Over many portions of that broad division of the continent reaching from Missouri river to the Pacific, the mountainous, broken, and undulating country bears a very small proportion to the extent of elevated plateaux either level or of slight inclination to the horizon. These elevated plateauxs offer substrata of sand or gravel, easily excavated, slightly affected by the action of frost, and by nominal reduction of surface, affording a road bed or perfect drainage, and of superior quality, for the preservation of superstructure and machine, and also favoring those simple manual operations deemed sufficient to keep American railway lines in working order.

The ease with which a line of superstructure and turnouts can be extended over this plateau surface, warrants my proposing the extension of a rough American rail way, of first class superstructure, but of medium equipment, as the first step to be taken toward the completion of a grand trunk line to the Pacific, since a rough American railway can necessarily perform, at low cost, all that a grand trunk line can possibly perform until its connection with the terminus, and as a direct exponent of proportioning means to the end required, would absolutely exist as an effective solution of the Pacific railway problem, by procuring the earliest practicable connection with a paying business at low cost.

The insurmountable obstacles attending the elaborate construction of a line of first class character from the outset, is, as before stated, the difficulty of transporting supplies, materials, and appliances of construction along the route of the road. Long sections of the route are devoid of all available means of construction, and broad divisions appear not susceptible of development by settlements, while from the nature of the interests involved, this great project cannot await the extension of settlements for its development, neither can these stupendous operations of entire construction be attempted without some visible means of completing the work.

No estimate has ever been presented of the cost of renewal of superstructure and rolling stock during the period of construction of a Pacific Railroad. The whole question has been resolved into the *immediate* completion of an elaborated first-class road by the extension of settlements along the route of the line. Sanguine theorists have proposed the completion of the road within a period of years, during which the mere ballasting and laying of a double line of superstructure from the East to the Pacific, attempted by any amount of manual labor, but only aided by minor means of transportation, could not occur.

The cost of transportation for the mere building of a grand trunk road cannot be estimated as less than $50,000,000. The renewal of superstructure and rolling stock during the period of construction cannot rule less than $50,000,000. But the chief misfortune to be apprehended is the long period which must elapse before an overland communication would occur with the Pacific possessions. The insurmountable obstacle attending the ready completion of a first-class road elaborated from the outset is the difficulty of transporting supplies and materials along the route of the line; the long sections devoid of appliances of construction; [p. 6] the broad divisions not susceptible of development; the fact that neither wagon nor plank roads are suited to the imperative necessity of an abundant and rapid means of transportation. The character of the interests involved, and the knowledge that a stupendous system of construction cannot be attempted without some visible means of completing the work, should teach all individuals of reasonable comprehension that this great project is not of a character to be cursorily treated, and modify all attempts at its solution in a discursive and inconclusive manner.

It will require a period of twenty years to extend a grand line of first-class character to a Pacific terminus by ordinary methods of construction. During this period the superstructure and rolling stock would thrice need renewal, as worn out or decayed.

In the extension of a first-class line, elaborated from the outset, the first renewal of superstructure and rolling stock would occur at the period of its reaching the mountain sections, the rock cuttings, tunnels, main and minor summits of which would necessarily exist for many years as a terminus to the road.

The wear and tear of rolling stock and equipment upon American railways of single track is estimated at $1,300 per mile per year. Of the $500,000,000 invested in American roads, $125,000,000, or twenty-five percent has proved total loss to their projectors.

Within the period of (20) years required to extend a road of first-class character to the Pacific, such improvements will have occurred in railway locomotion as to have fully modified any plan of construction first adopted. Although the provisions of the present bill limits the completion of a grand trunk road to ten years, a road cannot thus be *legislated* to its terminus; contingencies will occur; the question of transportation is beyond control, and the needful supply of labor along the route of the road beyond the limits of practical application. The mistake of the nation has hitherto been in the construction of roads of too elaborated character, the multiplication of lines between terminii [*sic*], and the giving up of favorable projects to the interested operations of private parties seeking early remuneration to capital by monetary transactions of disastrous character to the business relations of the country.

The application of this experience to the present question should demonstrate that like evils may be apprehended in an attempt at the construction of three great lines by a system of land grants, as creating the danger of an immense paper issue by flooding the stock market with the hypothecated scrip of mammoth companies and the non-paying mortgages of unfinished roads.

It is therefore not warrantable to submit this question as a project to all the fluctuations of funds, labor, public appreciation, and the operations of interested speculators, merely to procure the purposes of a nominal way transportation, every need of which may be readily secured by the rapid extension of a rough preliminary road.

Therefore I present the following clear engineering proposition, that the whole question of the construction of a first-class railroad to the Pacific, resolves itself into the prior construction of a railroad to the Pacific of less elaborated character. That in attempting the construction of a first-class road from the outset, without a paying business, reaching its Pacific terminus [p. 7] at an indefinite period of time, and subject to the liabilities of speculations by private parties, to the depreciation of superstructure and rolling stock, and only aided by the gradual extension of settlements, this project is a chimera, and an attempt at its solution by the extension of three great roads of like elaborated character, will lead to the most disastrous consequences.

Inexperienced parties have slight knowledge of what may be performed with the rail and locomotive engine. The mere theorist in railway construction is often led astray, and forms conclusions neither suited to the country or the question, by the study of foreign sources of information. If there has been a leading mistake in American railway engineering, it has occurred from the laudable desire of erecting works of a character bearing favorable comparison with those of older and more densely populated countries. But the needs of a practical moving people in the thinly settled regions of the West have led to the extension of lines of less elaborated character. The ability of individuals of real genius has within a few years given the proper direction to the inquiries of the practical and scientific engineers of America, and the proportioning of means to the end required, and the restrictions applied by the prospect of real remunerative returns, is daily becoming better understood by parties employed by private companies in the building of roads.

A mere per centage of the amount of money already expended by Congress in attempts at the solution of this intricate question, if applied in a definite appeal to real sources of information or to the practical experience which has shown such admirable results in the extension of lines at low cost, through thinly populated regions, would have led to a direct presentation of the merits of the present problem. The principle of early communication, however, cannot be waived or ignored, because it has not yet been presented before Congress, or appeared in the provisions of a bill, providing for the gradual extension of a grand trunk road *towards* the Pacific. As before stated a road cannot be *legislated* to its Pacific terminus by the will of its well-wishers and under an uncomprehensive view of the difficulties attending its extension. The insurmountable obstacles to which I have referred will certainly occur, and must eventually be overcome by the means which attempted at the outset would prevent all evil consequences. To those of slight experience in the various classes of railways the extension of a rough preliminary Railroad to the Pacific may seem impracticable or absurd, but to the experienced railroad builder, who has seen the working locomotive and material train made the great vehicle of transportation over unfinished lines, and upon every variety of surface, this mode of transit will at once sustain its important character, in relation to the peculiar exigencies of the present case.

Passing over a level or slightly inclined surface of a gravel or sand substratum, superseding all necessity of ballasting, procuring practicable passage of favorable mountain passes by detour, and without breaking bulk, overhanding, or costly mechanical appliances, or stationary engines, and needing only a few unimportant changing stations in elevated regions, such a road would thence extend toward the Pacific, over the broad plains of the interior. The chief desideratum, (which is readily secured,) being an abundant supply of pure water for the use of locomo-[p. 8] tives and the principle necessity, the passage of long planes of surface of slight inclination to the horizon.

Such a line, would as far transcend all means of transportation by plank or wagon roads as possible to conceive. It would admit a speed of thirty miles per hour, with loaded trains, over the greater portion of its distance, and at least the passage of loaded trains over all portions of its distance.

It would appear as a direct exemplification of capital reserved. The whole amount of its cost would have been expended in the mere needs of transportation for the purpose of building a grand trunk road. Attempted without its aid, the construction of the grand trunk road may be regarded a chimera, and even if eventually completed, the mere depreciation and renewal of its superstructure and rolling stock, the loss of interest on dormant capital and the disastrous results attending its consummation, would thrice exceed the entire cost of a preliminary road.

The mere development of territory would remunerate the cost of constructing a road, only attempting in every stage of its completion a character or medium adapted to the simplest requirements of necessity; while no such minor sources of revenue would warrant the construction of a first class line or road assuming an elaborated character from the outset.

Reverting to the causes of the present crisis in the railway manias of the country, we may remark that it has been produced by an unhealthy spirit of speculation, not only unrestricted by wholesome legislation, but in a measure urged forward by an indiscriminate patronage by the bestowal of border land grants to aid the large monetary operations of private companies.

Under such contingencies, should it not seem a study to the strict constructionist of the Constitution, whether Congress possesses the power to aid the extension of several grand lines, or of even a single grand trunk line of elaborated character from the outset, by donating the public domain to private individuals, and thus eventually bearing the liabilities of their hazardous speculations, or at least whether this result should occur without due study of the peculiar merits of such an important national question.

The flooding of the stock market with the hypothecated land scrip of three great lines, all unfinished, and in different stages of construction, slowly verging toward that distant terminus from which remuneration can alone accrue, would undoubtedly produce a monetary crisis of disastrous character.

The national requisition is a Railroad to the Pacific: this, public necessity requires—but the desideratum involved, is not the aggrandisement of private speculations in border lands, or the augmentation of local interests; not how a land grant bill is to be pushed through both houses of Congress, but how this important line of communication is to be pushed across the American continent. If the completion of *one* line cannot await the gradual extension of settlements or the completion of the ponderous operations of entire construction, why should it be attempted upon three? Why attempted at all unless by systematic effort, and as liable to be achieved within the ordinary lifetime of a healthy man?

The belief that private parties will seek the earliest practicable connection with terminus, will prove a fertile source of error. Although abund-[p. 9] [ant] sources of revenue are therewith connected, other sources of revenue can be earlier made available. Millions of dollars can be more profitably expended by local parties in extending a line towards the mountains, claiming the distinctive term of Pacific Railroad, and by individuals holding the outlets of such roads to the furtherance of gigantic border speculation, than a single million can be applied to the reduction of those great obstacles, only reached at a distance of one thousand miles from civilization.

By the proposed method of extending a line of first class character, in sections of one hundred miles each, ten years will elapse ere the actual operations of construction can occur at the most difficult portions of the road.

The cost of a preliminary railroad rapidly extended and properly equipped and furnished, would not rule less than $50,000,000. The difference between the cost of a grand trunk road, built by the aid furnished by a preliminary road and its gradual construction by the extension of settlements, $100,000,000. The difference in result to the nation impossible to conceive; the one ranging over a period of twenty years, and attended by operations of disastrous character; the other, of ready consummation and carrying out the requirements of a direct national necessity. But such a line must necessarily adopt a peculiar location or take advantage of those broad plateaux extending from the western frontiers of Iowa and Missouri to the Rocky mountains. But if the development of this project is to rest on the basis of a system of land grants, then any circumstance which tends to restrict its consummation within reasonable limits, may be deemed a national benefit. The commencement of three great lines, Northern Central and Southern, would undoubtedly lead to a monetary crisis by flooding the stock market with the land scrip of the regions traversed by such costly and unfinished works. Neither can it be believed that the practical good sense of the community will confine the development of the project to an attempt at constructing but one great road. The nature of the first thousand miles contiguous to the States will have a greater effect (under a liberal system of land grants) in urging the attempt at construction, than any knowledge of insuperable difficulties existing upon the route in advance, will effect in restraining it.

But by the nature of the exigences involved, this subject is resolved into the completion of a single line, within a reasonable space of time, at the lowest practicable cost, and without invidious selection of a route by Congress from the mere circumstance that over the peculiar location of the central sections of the continent broad plateaux of slight inclination to the horizon warrant the immediate extension of a road of less elaborated character than could be attempted through broken, ledgy and undulating country.

A railroad of central position, readily constructed at low cost, say 50,000,000 dollars, extended through the Mormon settlements, and besides gaining an abundant and paying business by early connexion with San Francisco, occupying a location which admits of feasible connexion with the great North Western terminus of Puget Sound, is the exponent of a direct and plain construction of the limited powers of the Constitution. It is at such a distance from the frontier, as to be secure from [p. 10]molestation in event of war. It can be rapidly extended over a gravel plateau at the lowest practicable cost. It solves the Mormon question without legislation. It does not destroy the hunting grounds of the Indian, since it crosses territory where the yearly transit of the Pacific emigration has already driven the wild game of the prairies to more isolated localities. It is fully within the limits of construction by aid of legislation, and by land grants, under that power of the Constitution which admits of the completion of means of military defence, and to a rigid interpretation of the meaning of that instrument, it must seem a very open question whether, when a road of $50,000,000 cost, occupying a central position, a cheap location, touching at important local points, and developing the whole pacific coast by northern and southern branches, *will* solve this necessity, whether the power bestowed by the Constitution, would warrant the additional extension of Northern and Southern roads of more elaborated character, built on exposed frontiers, and needing thorough defence in time of war.

A railroad is not a Chinese wall or line of fortifications, but a structure peculiarly pregnable to the most insignificant means of attack, and must occupy a location at a distance from the frontier, or incur the hazard of needing protection by augmentation of the standing army.

A line extending westward from the mouth of Kansas or La Platte river through the great South Pass of the Rocky Mountains, can thenee [*sic*] reach the level plains of the Great Basin, and the broad plateaux of the great Columbia river, by the passage of a single summit of country.

The consummation of this project, by a line of reasonable cost, touching at the important way station of Salt Lake City, with a main trunk extending to California, and a northern branch reaching Puget Sound through the grand level pass of Columbia valley, is the resolution of a national question to its salient points as developing and defending insolated [*sic*] territory at minimum cost.

The following extract from reports of the difficulties attending the construction of the Northern route to Puget Sound, will explain the reason of the route, by Salt Lake City, and the South Pass to Mississippi river, having been examined under the unanimous action of the Legislature of Washington Territory.

"Gov. S.T. [I. I.] Stevens,

"Sir: The result of the reconnaisance [*sic*] for the location of a northern railroad to Puget Sound, has demonstrated its *practicability* as a railroad line, although the route of the road is not so well decided upon. A detour from the present line appears necessary, to avoid the severe valley of the Bitter Root river, which is nearly impracticable. This detour should be attempted through some southern pass of the mountain as tending more directly toward the great valley of Columbia river. The valley of the Columbia, as the only natural pass through the whole Pacific coast range of mountains, admitting a close approximation to level grade, being entitled to the serious attention of this survey.

"If the detour south cannot be made without losing the character of the whole northern route by deflection, then the examination of a line from the southern shore of lake Michigan and by the valley of the Platte [p. 11] through the South Pass to the valley of the Columbia becomes important, since the superior and distinctive feature of a northern route to Puget Sound, which is the short distance between Lake Superior and the Pacific, must be surrendered to procure location, and regarding an eastern connection and the uniting of important and conflicting interests, by becoming to the South Pass a portion of the main trunk to California, the latter line would present advantages the northern route does not possess.

"The examination of the line by the South Pass can be confined to that portion of country between the South Pass and the waters of the Columbia. Other examinations more discursive, are important, but appear in detour so far toward the south as to destroy their connection with the subject of the present report. This route by the South Pass as located farther south, will present a better character regarding the effects of severe frosts on superstructure and machine. It would become the direct continuation of the great eastern lines toward the Pacific, and upon that parallel of latitude teeming with population. It would secure a navigation on Lake Michigan not so liable to obstruction from ice. Regarding the growth of the new State in the valley of the Salt Lake, it would afford direct communication with that singular people, not subordinate to any other consideration, when their peculiar institutions, and isolated position in the heart of the American continent are considered. And the construction of a Pacific Railroad is so stupendous an undertaking, and will require such immense returns from transportation to afford remuneration to investments, that should divided interests be united in its construction and different sources of revenues combine in its support, the result would indeed be important. This whole subject must be studied by *future reconnaissance* made upon the Northern route by a system of southern detour, and continued to the Southern, from the due consideration of the question of detour upon the Northern route, *having caused the abandonment of the actual line of direction, and the examination of a distinct line presenting paramount and still more apparent claims for consideration.*"

In the above review of a question of detour, to avoid nearly impracticable country in seeking location for the Northern route to Puget Sound, it was first suggested to attempt a descent in better direction from some more southern pass of the Rocky mountains, than that first adopted for the passage of the northern line, thus securing an intermediate route to the grand pass of Columbia valley between the great Northern and southern passes of the Rocky mountains.

The second step in the premises, was to waive all claims of the extreme northern route to notice, until a route between Puget Sound and the southern waters of
Lake Michigan was examined—that a comparison between the two routes might
be instituted, and in the meantime to distinctly state to the nation that the primary object of the Northern Exploration, which was the seeking of a facile and
favorable railroad route of minimum distance between eastern navigable waters
and Puget Sound, had in a measure failed, having been surrendered to procure
location. This was the plainest and most definite view in the question.

The superior nnd [*sic*] distinctive feature of an extreme northern route to the
Pacific was the apparent short distance between eastern navigable [p. 12] waters
and Puget Sound. This distinctive feature was seriously modified by the fact that
the harbors of Lake Superior are frozen or obstructed by ice during a large portion
of the year; and that during that period a railway terminating so far to the north
would debouch directly into foreign or Canadian roads, and being therefore more
particularly the requirement of a foreign than a national interest, might more
properly exist as developed by the investment of foreign, rather than of American
capital. This presumption was guarded against by the sudden or abrupt deflection
of the Northern route toward the south, and its connection with the Mississippi
river at St. Paul, Minnesota, and by communication with railroads already constructed through Central American Territory, at the southernmost point of Lake
Michigan. The waters of the Upper Mississippi at Lake Pepin being also
obstructed by ice during a large portion of the year, the legitimate terminus of a
northern railroad from Puget Sound appeared to be at the southern point of Lake
Michigan. But the distinctive feature of the northern route to Puget Sound,
which was the shortest distance between terminii, having been surrendered to
procure location, the distance between the southern shore of Lake Michigan and
the western terminus is no greater upon the southern or South Pass line than
upon the northern route to Puget Sound.

It would not then appear a warrantable procedure to extend a railway over the
extreme northern route to Puget Sound, and so near an exposed frontier, unless it
offered superior facilities for developing national territory, or for ready railway
construction. But a line passing along the frontier is not in a position to develope
territory, and regarding railway construction, nearly impracticable obstacles had
already directed examinations farther south.

The last presentation of the problem was the engineering feature, and to this
requisition the examination of the new route from Puget Sound to Lake Michigan was distinctly referred. In the development of this engineering requirement,
the opportunity of a connection with the great Central railroad to California was
disclosed. When this consideration came into the study, it concluded argument

upon the subject, since it reduced the completion of a railroad to Puget Sound to the mere construction of a spur line from the vicinity of the South Pass to Puget Sound. Under these liabilities the citizens of the Northwestern Territories urge a national claim that the great Pacific route to California may occupy a central position, more especially is this claim instituted, since the recent exploration conducted under a unanimous vote of the Territorial legislature of Washington, has demonstrated the highly favorable character of the route.

It will therefore appear that this whole question of a railroad to Puget Sound has changed in its character and no longer presenting a single claim to notice, as arising from the short distance between Lake Superior and Puget Sound, is affected by interests in no degree subordinate, as engineering and national considerations are brought to bear upon it. It is no longer under the contingency of a terminus upon Lake Superior, but becomes distinctly referable to the location of a railroad to California.

In comparison of these two routes as railroad lines, the Southern extends over an open country traversed by the great Indian trails and [p. 13] buffalo paths leading north and south, offering every opportunity for constructing spur roads, and thus extending the benefits of railway development to distant localities.

The Northern is shut in by lofty mountains and passes for that portion of its distance beyond the first Rocky Mountain chain, through a very difficult and almost impracticable country. The difference in cost of construction between these lines, of 2,000 miles each, will not rule less $30,000,000 in favor of the South Pass route. From the facility with which a rough preliminary road can be extended over the latter route, and the absolute necessity of first resolving this Pacific question to the construction of such a simple and effective means of transportation, I can perceive no comparison between the routes as railway lines, under the remarkable exigences involved in the development of this peculiar question.

In reference to this Southern route to Puget Sound, or more particularly this Central route to California, with its branch of 800 miles to Puget Sound, I would especially refer to the imperative and striking feature that it would become, in its artificial relations, to Nebraska, Kansas and Utah, what the great rivers in our country have been in their natural advantages to the sections east of the Missouri.

This feature of local and domestic utility cannot be deemed subordinate to any other, and combined with its former important characteristics, gives the location of the Central line such importance, that to aid its construction would be national, and to achieve it patriotic.

Those great navigable rivers of the West, which have rendered the growth of the central sections of the union, unparallelled in the history of nations, cease at the Missouri, and the net work of steamboat navigation, transporting the appliances of civilization and the means of growing up populous communities in the wilderness, there finds its limit. For Minnesota, and that narrow strip of national territory far to the north, and between the British frontier and the upper Missouri, such facilities may exist by the waters of the Mississippi, St. Peters, and Missouri, but for the broad territory extending over the central portions of the continent of the far Pacific, they must be supplied by the triumphs of human ingenuity. And since the genius of Fulton first propelled his rude craft against the current of the Hudson, what changes have not occurred in the history of nations, in the different phases of human progress, in arts, mechanics, and the achievments of civilization? Even throughout the mighty West, the rapid growth of which must forever remain a monumemt of his genius, the shriek and rattle of the locomotive engine is heard, contending with the plash of the steamboat paddle, along the lake and by the mighty river, as the masterly energy of America wrestles for the great result—Prosperity.

Therefore it is within the power of man to supply the greatest deficiencies of nature, and even west of the Missouri, by the mere choice of location, in carrying out the more direct requirements of national necessity, to place a great railroad line in its passage to the Pacific, where full of important connexions, like the branches of a river, its arms extending upon either side, it may develope the important region which it traverses, and become to the Western portion of the American continent what the Ohio and the Mississippi have been to the Eastern. [p. 14]

By the proper location of a branch road, northern Minnesota may be drained of its rich lumber upon the line of this central road, aid in its construction and find a market for a valuable home product, absolutely needed in Nebraska, Kansas, and Utah. British interest will eventually attempt the construction of an extreme northern route, and a like market will be afforded for such products.

It is more expedient to build a Minesotian [sic] American railway, to tap the carrying trade of a British Pacific road, than to build an American road over nearly impracticable mountain ranges to be drained of its business on reaching level country, by a British line.

Finishing then, the comparison of these two great routes to Puget sound, I will conclude by remarking that, while the impracticable nature of the western mountains shut the Northern route from the Pacific terminus—it was the very facility of connection with the Pacific that first gave character to the Southern. While the one passes along exposed frontier for a distance of fifteen hundred miles, and in direct vicinity of a great navigable river—the other becomes, for over half its length, the main trunk of a more important road, through central American territory.

The one has been reduced to a local, the other is still a national requirement. Upon the one, facilities for communication can only exist by artificial means— upon the other, they are already abundant by the act of nature, The lumber of the North is needed in the South. Connection with the West is claimed by the East. The Northern route affords neither, and the Southern route offers both. I claim, then, the question for the southern.

NOTE.— The question of guage [*sic*] of a Pacific railroad should not be agitated at the present time, neither should legislation now fix the width of guage from the following reasons.

The guage of the three tracks, Northern, Central, and Southern, should correspond with the grand trunk lines of the east, into which they severally debouch during early construction, and in the extension of a prelimi- nary railroad, to prevent the evil consequences of a *"break of guage"* In some portions of the union, a majority of these eastern lines are of the narrow guage. The narrow guage is preferable to the intermediate, or that of 5½ feet, in the passage of a rough superstructure in frost country. Although the lowering of the centre of gravity in the machine, arising from the extension of the base by adopting a wider guage, is a desideratum in the passage of a rough undulating surface, it is unwarrantable to attempt it by lengthening the axle. The guage eventually adopted on the elaborated grand trunk line, hereafter to exist, should be governed in application by experience gained from those improvements in transportation which inevitably occur, and which, during the period of years over which the process of constructing a grand trunk line must necessarily extend, will seriously modify all pre- sent conclusions on the subject.

Frederick W. Lander, 1858

Practicability Of Railroads Through The South Pass

Washington, 35/1 H70, serial 955, February 26, 1858, 20 p. [WC 277 note; WCB
301b; Hasse p. 43; Holliday 626; NUC NL 0065152.]
Reset verbatim from compiler's original.

Significance Lander here proposed that a preliminary Pacific railroad be
built over his new Lander Cutoff northwest from South Pass to Ft. Hall. As
superintendent of the federal South Pass and Honey Lake wagon road project,
one of the largest in the history of the West, he constructed this cutoff in 1858
after scouting it in 1857. He went on in 1859 and 1860 to make road improvements to City of Rocks and to Honey Lake via the California and Nobles trails
(see Itineraries). California's Senator John B. Weller, armed with a petition signed
by 75,000 constituents, gained Congress's approval in 1856 and early 1857 for
building several wagon roads west, the most important being to Honey Lake.
Lander energetically finished work on his road, while work by others on other
roads west from Texas and Minnesota (5:J8) bogged down in fraud and failure.

Lander wanted to build his temporary railroad cheaply and quickly—within
three years. He even proposed using wooden rails part of the way. He sincerely
praised the helpfulness, hard work, and perspicacity of the Mormons. He wrote
this admittedly "imperfect" and "discursive" report in his spare time in ten days, at
the request of Representative Francis P. Blair of Missouri. Lander was a doer, not
a writer. This probably is the first reprint.

Lander here avoided criticizing the official choice of the southern route. But
when he did, survey chief Andrew A. Humphreys shot back in 1860: "As Mr.
Lander has not passed over any portion of the southern line, his opinion as to the
character and cost of that route is not based upon personal observation."
Humphreys also thought that the railroad should not pass through the Mormon
settlements, because "they could and very probably would interrupt this line of
communication."

Author FREDERICK WEST LANDER, 1821-1862. See L7.

Itinerary, 1857 LANDER, INDEPENDENCE TO SOUTH PASS. June 15—Chief engineer Lander and his 14-man advance reconnaissance party leave Independence. They have 2 light wagons, 27 mules, and 2 horses. They carry bacon and flour for only two weeks, and coffee and sugar for 60 days, expecting to pick up full rations at Ft. Leavenworth. An administrative foul-up delays rationing until they reach Ft. Kearny, however. Lander hurries on, with supply wagons trailing behind, and reaches South Pass on July 15. He has traveled 950 miles in 31 days at 31 miles per day. In the next 69 days until September 22 he covers about 2,000 miles at 29 miles per day on zigzag scouts between South Pass and City of Rocks in south-central Idaho. One of the routes explored is the Lander Cutoff to be opened next year. The Mormon War hastens the end of operations. The main party under the superintendent of the project arrives too late to do anything and goes into winter quarters at temporary Ft. Thompson on the Popo Agie near present Lander WY.

Itinerary, 1858 LANDER, INDEPENDENCE TO SOUTH PASS THENCE BY LANDER CUTOFF TO CITY OF ROCKS. April 29—Lander, now the superintendent, leaves Independence with a crew of Maine lumberjacks. April 30 through May 3—He stops at Ft. Leavenworth to arrange for a provision train to follow. With what he carries along he has to feed destitute teamsters returning from the Mormon War. At Ft. Laramie he buys a train loaded with Mexican flour and beans. June 14—Lander reaches South Pass, from Independence 950 miles in 44 days, not counting 3 at Leavenworth. Average rate is 22 miles per day.

June 18 through September 15—Lander's crews construct his cutoff from South Pass to City of Rocks, 345.54 miles in 90 days at 4 miles per day. The road goes from South Pass to the modern town of Big Sandy, over the Green River to Marbleton, across the head of Greys River and through Salt River Pass, to Afton and Auburn WY, and on to Wayan and Ft. Hall ID, north of Pocatello, 252.49 miles. The remaining 93.05 miles is along the old emigrant road through today's American Falls, Raft River, Malta, Elba, and Almo ID to City of Rocks National Reserve. Lander estimates that they have excavated 62,310 cubic yards and cleared 23 miles of heavy pine and 11 miles of willows. Itinerary is from Campbell 1859, Jackson 1952, and Forest Service 1968.

COMMENT. Lander's emigrant guide appeared in Campbell's 1859 report. Lander bragged of the abundant grass, wood, and non-alkali water on the new cutoff, and the absence of ferry tolls. He designed the route for ox-team emigrants, but it "will prove to be the very best northern railroad line across the continent." He admitted that it was not as good for mail as the line through Salt Lake

City, however. Lander's hired Mormon workers "are very excellent laborers, many of them Cornish miners, who understand all sorts of ledge work, masonry, &c." The crews were threatened by Indians toward the close of the season. Lander spoke with Shoshone chiefs Washakie and Pocatello, and with some of the Bannocks who were out to kill Mormons. Lander worried about next year's reception, and he urged the government to compensate the Indians for building a road through their territory.

Itinerary, 1859 WAGNER, TROY KS TO CITY OF ROCKS VIA SODA SPRINGS. April 30—William H. Wagner, Lander's chief engineer, leads the advance party from Troy KS, 15 miles west of St. Joseph MO. He is at Ft. Kearny May 8, Ft. Laramie May 17 through 20, and South Pass May 27. On this leg he races 880 miles in 28 days at 31 miles per day. He takes the Sublette Cutoff to be at Soda Springs, June 10 through 17, waiting for reinforcements from Salt Lake City. From here he sends a group back east to improve the Lander road, while he and 12 men take the Hudspeth Cutoff to reach City of Rocks on June 26. On this leg he is mending bridges and surveying. He covers 320 miles in 23 days, not including 7 waiting at Soda Springs. The average rate is 14 miles per day. Wagner goes on 470.5 miles to California's Honey Lake, as reported in his emigrant guide in Lander's (1861b) report. The road is the usual California Trail to and down the Humboldt to Lassen Meadows. Thence west to Honey Lake it is Nobles Trail (5:J8 and map 5:J9). On the way Wagner explores as far as 70 miles north of the Humboldt but does not find a better route.

COMMENT. Lander's main party reached South Pass on June 24, 1859. Albert Bierstadt "accompanied the expedition with a full corps of artists, bearing their own expenses. They have taken sketches of the most remarkable of the views along the route, and a set of stereoscopic views of emigrant trains, Indians, camp scenes, &c." (Lander 1861b). This was Bierstadt's first trip West. The famous artist pioneered the expeditionary use of wet-plate photography. The few surviving photographs, "while unimpressive visually, represent a key moment in American landscape consciousness" (Naef and Wood 1975). Within two or three years, remarkable technical advances produced outstanding results.

Because Lander's emigrant guide was not printed in time, he had 1,000 of them written out by hand and given to emigrants at South Pass. Traders and ferry operators on the older roads had been trying to keep travelers off of the new Lander Cutoff. At the end of the season Lander claimed, "Thirteen thousand emigrants travelled the road the present year; over nine thousand—all the males of the trains—signed papers" certifying how good the road was, except for the

Green River crossing, which needed a bridge. Lander himself obviously drafted these testimonials for the emigrant signatures. One of his reports (1861a) contained tables listing some of the signers and their destinations and numbers of wagons and people. The 471 signers with wheels had 1,552 wagons with 4,646 people, or almost exactly 3.0 persons per wagon on average. Of these, about 70 percent were headed for California and 30 percent for Oregon. About 12 head of stock accompanied each wagon. In early 1860 Lander wrote a perceptive report on the Indians and mountain men that he had met in 1859.

Itinerary, 1860   LANDER, HONEY LAKE TO LASSEN MEADOWS AND BACK. July 4—Lander and about 50 men leave Susanville CA near Honey Lake. They go east on Nobles Trail (5:J8) through present Gerlach NV to reach Lassen Meadows on the Humboldt River at today's Rye Patch Reservoir, August 5. On the way they grade rough places in the road, dig wells, clean out springs, and make masonry tanks at these water sources. August 21—On their return, by arrangement, Lander counsels with Paiute Chief Namaga near Gerlach. Namaga tells Lander, "The white men were coming into the country and taking up the finest valleys, driving the red men from their fishing grounds and giving them nothing in return…The white man had plenty, but the Indians were poor…The Indians were very mad and they made fight, but now they were willing for peace." Lander agrees to do all he can to get the government to pay for the lands. Namaga makes a year's truce.

August 26—Lander's party is back at Honey Lake, after working hard both out and back. The round trip of 270 miles takes 54 days with an average progress of 5 miles per day. Itinerary is mainly from Fairfield 1916; Lander's official report (1861b) is sketchy.

COMMENT. Lander went to California by sea in 1860 and arrived at Susanville about June 1 with his 50 men, including 30 armed with Sharps rifles and dragoon pistols. In early May some Paiutes had killed, apparently with good cause, five whites at a station on Carson River (4:G Perspective). On May 12 the Paiutes at Pyramid Lake killed some 48 of 105 in the advancing ragtag militia under Maj. William M. Ormsby. On June 2 on the lower Truckee River, Col. John C. Hays with 750 men killed 20 to 50 Indians (the Paiutes said only 4). The whites lost 3 men and one more soon afterwards. The settlers were in a panic when Lander arrived at Susanville. (Fairfield 1916.)

Indians killed a rancher near Honey Lake on June 17. Lander picked up their trail on a 50-mile scout on the 18th. On the 19th, with 35 of his men and 30 local rangers, he set out northeast from Susanville in pursuit. About 40 miles away, near Observation Peak the Indians attacked, mortally wounding one ranger. Lander bravely led the counterattack that killed "several" Indians. Then he went toward them unarmed to parley, without success. His later truce council with Namaga, who was called "Young Winnemucca" but who was no kin to Old Winnemucca, was on August 21, as noted above. The citizens of Honey Lake Valley met on September 10 and declared that "the energy of Col. Lander in protecting the settlers during the war, carrying on the work he was sent to do, and obtaining an interview with [Young] Winnemucca and making an armistice with him merited their admiration and respect." (Fairfield 1916; this account agrees with Eagan 1972 but is at odds with others, such as Madsen 1985 and some of the Lander biographers, who claim that Lander was part of Hays's force.)

Itinerary, 1860   MOORE, SOUTH PASS TO FT. HALL ON LANDER CUTOFF. July 29 through August 16—Emigrants Martha Bishop Moore and her husband go over the 252 miles of the Lander Cutoff in 19 days, averaging 13 miles per day. The cutoff starts at Gilbert Station, or Burnt Ranch, about 10 miles east of South Pass. They drive along 5,100 sheep, with three dogs and one good man per thousand sheep. The sheep are shorn, so that excess wool will not absorb water and weigh them down in crossing streams. Mrs. Moore writes in her diary, "Nothing about the stream [Green River] to excite terror though so many sad accidents have happened here." Next it is "Over mountains, down canons on heights that make one dizzy to look down[;] such has been our road all day & tonight watchworn & weary we are camped in a valley where there are plenty of strawberries but not much else…The Indians attacked us…We hastened away thankful that our lives have been spared, but the roads were miserable and…upset my wagon."

Medorem Crawford, 2:D11, goes over the Lander Cutoff from August 7 through August 27, 1862, in 21 days. He remarks that "unless some repairs are made the road will have to be abandoned." Ferrymen have tried to increase their business by destroying Lander's bridge over the Portneuf River. Mrs. Harriet Buxton Loughary makes the same trip, June 28 through July 15, 1864, in 18 days without any sheep and with no serious complaints. Mrs. Loughary always seems to see the beauty along the way.

Highlights   Lander was an exemplary public servant. Secretary of Interior Jacob Thompson said of him in 1860, "The zeal and indomitable energy with which this work has been prosecuted, through several years, by the superintendent, reflects the highest credit upon him. No officer could have performed this arduous duty with more ability and fidelity to the government. His successful efforts to improve this great highway…will be duly appreciated by the hardy emigrants who will enjoy its advantages."

Some emigrants had mixed feelings about Lander's work. Randall H. Hewitt reminisced in 1906 about his 1862 journey: "the road was simply superlatively execrable. When first viewed and constructed by…F. W. Lander, it was undoubtedly a fairly good wagon road…But at the time I write of, it was badly washed by mountain floods and was in a horrible condition, as no repairs were at any time made except such as passing emigrants found necessary in order to get through at all." Later, "The tent was pitched in the dust, but I made it my business to cut willow brush to carpet the floor so the ladies might have a comfortable place to rest."

Legacy   Lander's suggestions as to location and mode of construction of the Pacific railroad were ignored. Lander built his cutoff for ox-team emigrants, and they did use his road, although with decreasing frequency as it fell into disrepair, until the Union Pacific replaced most covered-wagon travel after 1869. The road never was quite finished, anyway. The legislated end of it at Honey Lake was not a real end; emigrants still had to get to the Sacramento River on trails not recently improved. Lander felt that Capt. James H. Simpson's Central Overland Trail (5:J9), direct from Salt Lake City to Sacramento, was not suitable for emigrants. But Simpson's route carried the mails after 1859, including the Pony Express.

Chief Namaga died of tuberculosis in 1871. The Paiutes in the region of Pyramid Lake suffered from disease, white squatters, dishonest agents, army attacks, exile, and loss of water rights (Egan 1972).

REFERENCES
(See Preface for Heading references not listed here.)

Branch, E. Douglas, 1929, Frederick West Lander, road-builder: [Cedar Rapids IA], separate reprint from Mississippi Valley Historical Review 16:172-87.

Campbell, Albert H., 1859, Report upon the Pacific wagon roads: Wash., 35/2 S36, serial 984, 125 p., maps; Campbell's report 3-12, summarizing Lander's 1857-58 routes 5-8; Lander's reports 30-35 for 1857, 47-57 for 1858, emigrant guide 58-62 with comment 63-73; quote on railroad 63, Mormons 67.

Egan, Ferol, 1972, Sand in a whirlwind, the Paiute Indian War of 1860: Garden City NY, Paiutes p. 252-83.

Fairfield, Asa M., 1916, Fairfield's pioneer history of Lassen County California: San Francisco, 1860 campaign p. 207-26; itinerary 226-33; quote by Namaga 229, settlers 232.

Forest Service, 1968, Guide to the Lander Cut-off: Ogden UT, brochure with map.

Hewitt, Randall H., 1906 (1964 reprint), Across the plains in 1862: N.Y., quote on execrable road p. 236-37, tent 241.

Humphreys, Andrew A., 1860, Routes for a railroad to the Pacific, in Samuel R. Curtis, Reports of the majority and minority of the Select Committee on the Pacific Railroad: Wash., 36/1 H428 Report, serial 1069, p. 43-46.

Jackson, W. Turrentine, 1952 (1979 reprint), Wagon roads West: Lincoln, Lander's routes p. 192-96 for 1857, 207-09 for 1858, 212-15 for 1859, 216-17 for 1860.

Lander, Frederick W., 1860, Report on Indian affairs, in Massacre at Mountain Meadows: Wash., 36/1 S42, serial 1033, p. 121-39.

Lander, Frederick W., 1861a, Additional estimate for Fort Kearney [sic], South Pass, and Honey Lake wagon road: Wash., 36/2 H63, serial 1100, 27 p.; tables 5-27.

Lander, Frederick W., 1861b, Maps and reports of the Fort Kearney [sic], South Pass, and Honey Lake wagon road: Wash., 36/2 H64, serial 1100, 39 p.; Lander's 1859 report 2-20, quotes on Bierstadt 5, emigrants 9; Wagner's 1859 report 20-26; emigrant guide 27-30; Lander's 1860 report 31-35; Wagner's 1860 report 35-39; no maps issued.

Loughary, Harriet Buxton, 1864 (1989 printing), Diary, in Covered Wagon Women, Kenneth L. Holmes, ed.: Spokane, 8:142-48.

Madsen, Brigham D., 1985 (1995 reprint), The Shoshoni frontier and the Bear River Massacre: Salt Lake City, p. 120-21.

Moore, Martha Bishop, 1860 (1988 printing), Journal, in Covered Wagon Women, Kenneth L. Holmes, ed.: Glendale, 7:259-95, quotes on Green R. 283, dizzy 284.

Naef, Weston J., and James N. Wood, 1975, Era of exploration, the rise of landscape photography in the American West: N.Y., quote p. 31.

Thompson, Jacob, 1860, Report of the Secretary of Interior, in Message from the President: Wash., 36/2 S1, serial 1078, quote p. 47.

PRACTICABILITY OF RAILROADS THROUGH THE SOUTH PASS.

LETTER

FROM

THE SECRETARY OF THE INTERIOR,

Transmitting a report from F.W. Lander, esq., relative to the practicability of a railroad through the South Pass.

FEBRUARY 26, 1858.—Referred to the Select Committee on the Pacific Railroad.

DEPARTMENT OF THE INTERIOR.

February 24, 1858.

SIR: I have the honor to transmit herewith a report from F.W. Lander, esq., civil engineer, upon "the practicability of a railroad through the South Pass," and the best method of constructing the same, in response to a resolution passed by the House of Representatives January 26, 1858.

I am, sir, respectfully, your obedient servant,

J. THOMPSON, *Secretary*

Hon. JAMES L. ORR,

    Speaker of the House of Representatives.

IN THE HOUSE OF REPRESENTATIVES, *January* 26, 1858.

On motion of Mr. BLAIR,

Resolved, That the Secretary of the Interior be requested to furnish this House with any information that may be communicated to him by F.W. Lander, esq., engineer of the wagon road, as to the practicability of railroads through the South Pass, and the best method of constructing a road, and any other information in regard to the same obtained during his late expedition.

    Attest: J.C. ALLEN, *Clerk.*

[p. 2]

DEPARTMENT OF THE INTERIOR,
February 1, 1858.

SIR: Enclosed please find a copy of a resolution of the House of Representatives, passed January 26, 1858.

As you were not instructed to furnish the department with a report upon the practicability of a railroad through the South Pass, &c. I am unable to comply with the resolution unless you have some information upon this subject which you are willing voluntarily to furnish at the earliest practicable period.

I am, sir, respectfully, your obedient servant,

J. THOMPSON, *Secretary.*

F.W. Lander, Esq.,
    Superintendent Fort Kearney, S.P., &c., Road.

WASHINGTON, *February* 13, 1858.

SIR: I have the honor to reply to your letter of the 1st instant, and to transmit a report "on the practicability of a railroad through the South Pass, the best method of constructing a road, and such other information in regard to the same, obtained during my late exploration, as I am able to furnish at the earliest practicable period."

Very respectfully, your obedient servant,

F.W. LANDER.

Hon. J. THOMPSON,
    Secretary of the Interior.

REPORT.

The term "a railroad" is susceptible of many definitions. A commercial railroad, an agricultural railroad, or a means of transportation by rail, cheap, effective and to be immediately made applicable to the claims of mail and military service across the continent, might each be considered in a more desultory treatment of the subject than is now required. A commercial railroad, or one adapted to moving the immense freights of Pacific commerce at rates of speed or cost, which would enable the line to successfully compete with the carrying trade of the ocean, is a road of a class not now in use; a permanent work, which cannot be built without the aid of a preliminary or light railway to transport materials and supplies of construction. It is beyond the reach of the present report.

An agricultural railroad may be defined as a road of the classes now in operation throughout the western States; a road of masonry and bridging, graded, ballasted, furnished and equipped to the claims of a large way and through transportation. Such a road is well adapted to the development of those routes across the continent which extend over undulating and broken surfaces, and require the labor of reduction [p. 3] to practicable gradients by the excavation of cuts and the erection of embankments, before the locomotive can be made of use; routes over which the superstructure must necessarily progress so slowly as only to keep pace with the progress of settlements. Structures of reasonably permanent character, under these contingencies, being the surer economy from the outset. In my own view of the question, a road up to the Republican fork of Kansas river, through a very fertile and well timbered region, but passing over an undulating surface, would be described as an agricultural railroad, and would eventually reach the South Pass. Numerous other roads of similar character could find direction toward the Upper Platte valley, and the same important point from the whole eastern border further north. But an experience of over fifteen years of the building, workage, wear, depreciation and renewal of railways, has rendered it evident to me that no estimate of the cost of a permanent road over a route of nearly two thousand miles of broken surfaces can be deemed reliable, and that the desideratum of overland communication by rail and steam power must take place by those irregular but progressive steps by which the practical talent of this nation has so repeatedly solved the various experiments and necessities of progress.

The route to the South Pass by the main Platte valley permits the adoption of modes of construction which will cover the liability last referred to, for it can be developed by railways without material reduction of the natural surface of the earth.

In my report of 1854, I proposed the extension of a surface railroad from Missouri river through the South Pass, by a superstructure capable of sustaining the tread of a class of locomotives suited to surmounting steep gradients. Near the Missouri river this road to consist of a T. rail of sixty pounds per yard, applied to a ditched and drained road-bed, but as it progressed towards the mountains to assume a different style of construction, regarding the contingencies of transportation and building. My examinations of that year were confined to the north side of the river Platte, where long distances of the route are untimbered. The discoveries of the present season led me to suggest that the mode of construction then proposed shall be modified. There is timber enough on the south side of the Platte to build a road to the mountains, and when the foot hills are reached all difficulties of this nature are overcome. It is about five hundred and thirty miles from Missouri river to the Black hills, and over this distance the route is a perfect flat plain of gravel sub-strata

The published report of the War Department leads the reader to infer that from the entrance of the Black hills to the South Pass a railroad must make passage of one of the routes of the natural wagon roads used by emigrants. The barometric profile of Colonel Frémont, taken over the old emigrant road, was made the basis of a detailed estimate, and by the system of equated distances of maximum loads applied to this profile the line was much lengthened, and the favorable nature of the route entirely lost. The same report offered the deduction that the only practicable method then known of reaching the plains of the Great Basin from the South Pass was to descend Green river, and thence rise again from a much lower plain than that [p. 4] of the South Pass, over the great Wahsatch mountain range, placing the line under the further liability of subsequent descent to the level of the Salt Lake valley.*

My own report removed the objection to that portion of the route through the Black hills, because I adopted a different line of exploration, availing myself of all side hill approaches of a section of country over sixty miles in breadth; but I was unable to do more than suggest an entire change in the system of location regarding the lines west of the South Pass. Instead of descending the rapidly falling valley of Green river, which would be decidedly against that important and well known rule of railroad engineering, never to surrender height accomplished in mountain approach, and while the summit was still unsurmounted, I proposed heading Green river valley, and by the line of the foot hill springs, passing over the Wahsatch mountains to the waters of Snake river. The grand summit section of the continent having thus been overcome without difficulty, and by low grades, the passage from Snake river to Oregon and Puget's Sound, and from Snake river to the plains of the Great Basin, was very highly practicable. But by reference to my report of 1854 it will be seen that I apprehended the route from the South Pass to the head waters of the Snake to be an untimbered, ungrassed plain; a portion of that terrible region yearly traversed by our overland emigration, and so graphically described by Colonel Cooke of the Utah army. It was explored the present season, and found not only to be adapted for the route of a wagon road, avoiding the deleterious and ungrassed regions of the south, but also to be a most richly timbered, arable region for the passage of railroads. The immense forests of yellow pine and fir which line this route, and the easy grades by which a railroad may make passage from the South Pass to the valley of the Snake, and thence over a flat gravel plain to the edge of the Great Salt Lake, have caused me to change the whole programme of the construction of a railroad through the South Pass. Not only are those claims of the question suddenly made prominent by the present

---

*The officer in charge of the resolution of the rough data of the old reconnoissances, made the best use of the materials of his command, and no remarks of this paper must be interpreted as a reflection upon the able and scientific labors which have given to the country so much valuable information on the subject of railroads to the Pacific, on climates, soils, and resources of routes.

aspect of the Mormon population thus best answered, but the whole solution of
the great problem of overland transportation by rail equally aided by the discoveries of the present season.

My reply to that clause of the resolution requesting information as to the practicability of railroads through the South Pass, might be to state that any class of
railroad is practicable through the South Pass; but in reply to those clauses desiring "the best method of constructing a road through the South Pass, and any
information in respect to the same, obtained in my recent explorations," I transmit my professional opinion of what I believe to be the most rapid and expedient
method of building a road. A railroad which, suited to military and mail transportation, can reach the waters of Salt Lake and the Salt Lake city in *three* years
from the time of its commencement, if forwarded [p. 5] with the usual energy of
American movements, and under a proper programme for overcoming the difficulties of construction.

From the mouth of the Platte river to the base of the Black hills, a distance of
over five hundred miles, as before described, the route of the South Pass is a flat
plain of gravel sub-strata, rising at an inclination of about eight feet per mile, and
without a break in surface, towards the mountains. The lower end of the river valley is fairly wooded with the cotton. Nearer the mountains the foot hills are well
timbered with cedar, yellow pine, and fir. Excellent building stone is abundant
along the line, and large coal fields occur at various points, and at the eastern
extremity. Upon this flat plain rails can be laid without grading. The superstructure can progress at the rate of one mile per day, or faster, if circumstances justify
the additional expense. A light railroad, over which trains can pass with facility,
and even at high rates of speed, would thus reach Fort Laramie in less than three
years, and become the initiative or preliminary step toward the building of a railroad of a more ponderous class, either for the transportation of Pacific commerce,
or as adapted to the increased business of the line, when developed by settlements.

The Road.

The class or medium of the preliminary or light railroad would be governed by
circumstances; but, under the present contingency of the Mormon war, and the
absolute necessity of some rapid and effective means of military transportation to
be immediately applied, I would advise the preliminary use of as light a rail as
forty pounds per yard. The natural gradient of the Platte valley of eight feet per
mile, does not require weighty tread of locomotives "to procure adhesion," and, as
very light engines can thus be made of use, a heavy rail is not required.

The rail of forty pounds per yard is easier laid than that of sixty pounds, the class now in general use for light roads. Two men can readily handle and place the lighter rail, and adjust chairs at joints, while, in cold weather, the laying of heavier rails is a more ponderous and tedious operation. One third of the transportation is saved by the use of the lighter rail. If laid in the winter upon ice, snow, or over frozen earth, when the superstructure settles out of line and level during spring thaws, it can be brought to surface again by shimming and chucking for the passage of locomotives, and by the use of the weighty lever bars used in repairs, while to place a weightier rail in running order after it is bent over uneven surface, it is often necessary to take up the road that the bars may be straightened by a machine.

The light rail therefore is preferable to the weighty one because it is cheaper, because with the same cost of transportation a third more length of rail can be furnished and laid in a shorter space of time, because when out of surface it is easier brought back to line and level, and because when in operation it will, from the nature of the work, permit the performance of all that a heavier rail would admit of doing. Such rails can be procured in quantity at various points along the western [p. 6] navigable rivers and can be deposited by water transportation, without breaking bulk at the mouth of the Platte. Working parties being kept in advance of the line of superstructure, dressing the surface, making the necessary small water drains and preparing the cottonwood cross ties for service, during the summer season the road could progress very rapidly. Even in winter, by the use of houses upon car wheels and turn outs, the road could progress.

The road from Fort Laramie to the South Pass.

Thirty miles beyond Fort Laramie the broken and undulating surfaces of the Black hills are encountered, precluding the use of the preliminary iron road with economy, unless by the laying of a weighty rail and the application of the high grade locomotive. It is not advisable to attempt the expense of transporting heavy rails to this part of the road, to be worked at high cost and eventually renewed, even if the nation could wait for it, when there are other more applicable means of solving the question. Neither is it expedient to postpone the development of the route by rail, until a graded road could pass through this broken section by reduction of surface.

I propose therefore that on the commencement of the light iron road at Missouri river, steam saw-mills and pile drivers shall be transported by wagon trains to the entrance of the Black hills, and a simple piling road, elevated above the surface of the earth as circumstances require, shall supersede wagon and precede steam transportation. This road to consist of sawed wooden rails, and be worked by draught animals for the transportation of mails, passengers, military supplies, and troops. Through the great timbered regions of the upper Wahsatch mountains this road could progress very rapidly. Along the whole line all subsequent works of construction could be carried on with economy and despatch from the cheap and effective transportation afforded. There is hardly a large public work in the United States attempted or built without the use of the wooden rail. In northern Maine and Wisconsin rafting waters and "log driving" streams are united, and sections of country offering great natural obstacles to their extension are thrown open by wooden railroads. Coal mines, ice lakes, quarries, all natural depots of supplies, are developed by our energetic population by wooden railroads, when the iron road is inapplicable or too extensive [expensive?]. When constructed, iron rails and locomotives could be carried upon the one named, at very low cost, to the flat plains of Humboldt river, 350 miles in length, and extending to the eastern settlements of the Pacific. Much of the intermediate section is suited to the use of the iron rail without grading. Not less than 1,200 miles of the route described could thus be worked by locomotives at a speed of 18 miles per hour. The wooden road over steeper grades, worked by mules and horses, would admit of passenger, mail and military transportation at a speed of ten miles per hour. There is no danger to be apprehended from snow upon the iron rail from Missouri river to Fort Laramine; from Fort Laramine [sic] to the plains of Snake river the elevation of the road guards against it, and the entire route could be worked throughout the year. The passage of the South Pass [p. 7] would be made at a point about 7,400 feet above the sea. The descent to the heads of the Big and Little Sandys, to the new forks of Green river to the main stream, to the long plain where the line would again ascend towards the summit of the McDougal Pass, involves but slight loss of grade. The average height above the sea of the section, which is over one hundred miles in length, is from 6,900 to 7,000 feet. The passage to the first water of the Snake by McDougal's Gap can be made without ledge-cutting, upon grades of 40 feet per mile. But by detour the line can pass to the flat plains of Snake river without serious loss or gain of grade. Through this pass by detour the meat packers of old Fort Bonneville "went to Buffalo" (a technical term) throughout the year. A cut-off can be made on the Salt Lake route, if deemed expedient in permanent construction, by the line of Thompson's Pass, through which it is now proposed to build the new wagon road. This cut-off reaches the Bear river valley and the Salt Lake on grades of 50 feet, but regarding a connexion with Columbia valley and Puget's Sound is not, in my own estimation, the best line. It requires a tunnel of half a mile, and is therefore not available for a preliminary railroad. The reason for placing the wagon road through this pass is because the appropriation is so reduced, by the operations of the present year, that the more northern line cannot probably be built with the sum remaining. The northern is the shortest route to California.

Resources of the country.

This line of communication, which passes near the head of Green river, is the best approach to some of the most important sections of the interior.

Little reliable information exists of these very valuable regions, which, in view of a pending national calamity, are especially worthy the attention of government. From the arable grounds of the Salt Lake valley, through the numerous valleys and timbered regions of the Wahsatch mountains, towards the head of Wind river, to the Beaver Head, and to the St. Mary's valley of the north, occur available and peculiarly favorable locations for settlements. There are the numerous herding grounds of the Indians and mountaineers, and here are recruited and fattened in the open air and during winter the worn down cattle, mules, and horses bought up by traders from the later overland emigration. It is from these valleys that Colonel Johnson has recently been furnished with a drove of fat cattle, needed during his present necessities from wintering among the sand plains of the south. The half-breed horses raised by the mountaineers from a cross between the larger animals of the settlements and the Indian pony, reared in the open air and without forage, are some of the finest animals I have ever seen. Durham short-horned cattle, a delicate breed, and not usually thought adapted to exposure, are raised here, and wintered without shelter, upon the natural grass of the mountains. Hay is never cut by the mountaineers, yet this celebrated stock, fattened upon the bunch grass, grows larger than any I have seen in the States. John Grant, a well known trader, who has raised a large [p. 8] stock of Durham milch cows and steers and American horses, winters yearly in the great valleys of the mountains, with no shelter but the common Indian lodge of dressed elk or buffalo skin.

It is very evident that if government would take steps to throw open the Black hills region and this cordon of beautiful valleys by grants of lands to actual settlers, and by providing some effectual means of transportation through the South Pass, or the pass about 30 miles north of it, the Mormon question would not long require solution by an increase of the standing army.

In this view the information gained by the late expedition is very important. If the Mormons are attacked by such forces of military troops as to be driven from their present localities, they will undoubtedly occupy the very valleys to which I refer. Reaching the wildest fastnesses of the mountains, and becoming more assimilated with the Indians, they would at length extend their predatory bands to the Saskatchawan of the north and the great eastern bison ranges. From these points they could for many years harass and obstruct all northern and central overland emigration.

Again, if they are compelled to forsake their present farms, destroy their costly irrigation ditches, and the improvements by which alone the valley of the Great Salt Lake has been made suitable for the permanent abiding place of a white population, and go to the south, or even leave the continent, our overland emigration will be deprived of those great way stations of supplies, which have been of such service to it in the interchange of cattle, horses, and the furnishing of provisions at low cost. Either of these is a conclusive argument in favor of the development of the more northern valleys by settlements.

The nation, especially the northern and central sections of the Union, cannot afford to lose the advantages of the Mormon supply stations, unless others are provided. It costs twenty (20) cents a pound to transport provisions from Missouri river to the mountains; but flour could be bought at the Mormon settlements (1854 and 1857) at four (4) cents the pound; at the emigrant road Mormon stations of the South Pass for ten (10) cents. Even should this question of Mormon hostilities eventually bear a different aspect, the development of the northern valleys by settlement is imperative.

Having been much exposed in the passes of the central mountains during two protracted explorations, with very small parties of men, and especially the last season, when the Mormons were expecting attacks from the government military forces, I wish, in this connexion, to place on record my own opinion and that of my party in favor of the masses of the Utah population. This opinion is not unimportant at a time when the public mind is so inflamed against the Mormons as to believe that no good can come of any further connexion with them. Often reduced to great straits for provisions and supplies, I was uniformly relieved, and in several instances most kindly and hospitably entertained, by that distant class of our fellow citizens. It cannot be denied that among this peculiar people exists as much thorough push, practical energy, and determined movement as are found in the republic. Both in founding the colonies of Salt Lake and throwing open that arid desolate section to settlements, they have [p. 9] overcome some of the most remarkable obstacles of nature. In fact, the initiative steps taken by this singular people first gave great impetus to our own overland emigration, by imparting knowledge of the resources of travel, and by furnishing the supplies.

Such is their aptitude to hard work under great privations, their practical knowledge of tilling the soil by irrigation, their experience of the irregular modes of subsistence in mountain life, that if their information and example could be retained to the nation by intermingling with them, or placing adjacent to them a Christian population, and by the influence of a more enlightened public opinion, the result would indeed be important.*

---

*The Mormons have already established settlements upon the headwaters of Salmon river, adjacent to the valleys described, and about two hundred and fifty miles north of the city of the Great Salt Lake.

But there are other reasons for the development of these mountain valleys. Our hardy frontier population is now pushing up against the sand plains, and necessity will soon compel them to occupy the arable regions of the great interior.

Therefore, if we absolutely need the light military railroad as soon as it can be built to transport military supplies and troops, if the Mormons are to be fought, if we need it as soon if they are to be overcome by more peaceful means, so, too, we need it at once to solve a necessity of American progress.

The settlements of the Pacific coast have the transportation of the ocean to bring the weighty supplies and resources of civilization to their doors. Those of the eastern frontier the navigable waters of the lakes and rivers. But all water transportation must cease at the Missouri, for the whole great central interior region is without a navigable river.

The route of approach to the South Pass.

The route of the main Platte valley, which I have repeatedly described as the best approach to the South Pass, regarding the earliest practicable consummation of facile and speedy transportation by railroad, is a narrow strip of fertile, arable soil, from 10 to 20 miles in breadth, extending from the eastern settlements, across the sand plains, to the Black hills. It furnishes abundance of grass to animals of transportation, and has long been travelled by the California, Oregon and Utah wagon emigration. It is the main stem of the great forked route of the nation, going west from the northern and central States of the Union to the Pacific coast. The first 530 miles of this route reaching to Fort Laramie differs from all others across the continent, in affording a long, flat plain of gravel substrata, with no natural obstructions to prevent the immediate use of the light iron rail and grasshopper engine along the surface of the earth, without grading. Superior localities for settlement can be found both north and south of Platte valley. The valley of the south fork of the Platte is preferred by some mountaineers, for farming grounds, to locations north of it, but would be occupied to the mountains if a road [p. 10] passed up the main river. Mons. Dessou, a half-breed trader, who has raised large crops of Indian corn at Fort Laramie, prefers the valley of the South Platte to that of the main river. His farm at Fort Laramie was at the edge of the Black hills region, the whole of which great fertile section is adapted either to herding or agricultural purposes.

The development by railroad of the first 530 miles of this main stem of the forked emigrant road is very important, as occupying a position between the forests of timber, depots of coal, broad regions adapted to settlement, and the arable lands of the frontier. But the development of the route in a proper manner, that it may aid the further overland emigration by offering low rates of transportation when the road is worked, is as important. I will therefore refer to this subject in detail.

Loss of stock by overland emigration.

It is over two thousand miles from the starting point of the overland emigrants to the Pacific. The points of departure are the western borders of Iowa and Missouri. The emigration traverses the flat plain of Platte valley, and near the South Pass breaks up for the destinations of Utah, California, Oregon and Washington. The great stock drovers, who are in the yearly custom of crossing the plains with horses, cattle and mules, make their preparations the preceding autumn. They are thus enabled to reach the Pacific coast in a single season, with their droves low in flesh, but without over 25 per cent. loss from the number of animals. But the wagon emigration, that of mechanics, farmers, and laborers, who are seeking the Pacific shores for a home, cannot make these extensive arrangements. They reach the starting point of Missouri river later in the spring, and the grass of the plains is often eaten up by the stock driven in advance of them. Thus, with the animals broken down in the journey of the first thousand miles, they are frequently compelled to winter at Salt Lake. If, on the contrary, they push on and endeavor to keep up the character of their means of transportation by barter with the traders along the road, often by submitting to the losses of the exchange of their worn horses, oxen and mules, for the vamped up animals of the earlier emigration, or for the Indian ponies of little comparative value in the regions of their destination, they reach the western coast, broken in health, energy and means, to be exposed during the awful first winter to the tender mercies of those influences which all overland emigrants have tested, and to which it is not necessary here to allude. The bridging of streams, the removal of the artemisia shrub by fire from regions along the road, thus favoring a bunch grass growth, the giving of information to the emigrant regarding the poisonous waters, the opening of abundant sources of supply of the pure element, the building of the grand northern or southern cut-off route discovered by the wagon road expedition of the present year, will prove of aid to overland emigration, but in a national treatment of the question should only appear as adjuncts and auxiliary steps towards more important measures. To efficiently aid and promote overland emigration the [p. 11] time of transit must be shortened. The point of departure should be moved thirty or forty days nearer the Pacific, and means afforded by which the emigrant can reach the new starting point and leave it at the same time of year that he now leaves Missouri or Iowa.

The passage of the overland emigration may be shortened by extending the railroad I have described over the first five hundred miles of this main stem of this great forked route of the nation to Utah, California, and Oregon. If the railroad of 530 miles, from the borders of Iowa to the Black hills, is built, and operated at such rates of fare as to place it within the command of the overland emigrant, the desideration would be accomplished. The frontier would have been moved 500 miles nearer the Pacific. The stock of the overland emigrant, fresh from the rich prairies of the west, would first put neck in yoke in the rich bunch-grass pasturage of the numerous routes which would be opened through the Black hills. Not only would the time of transit be shortened, and the loss of stock guarded against, but communities of stock raisers and herdsmen would grow up at the Black hills terminus of the road, great way stations of population soon reach the outlying farms of the Mormons, and even to those rich arable regions of the upper mountains to which I have heretofore referred. The flat inclined plane, reaching from the mouth of the Platte to the Black hills, would also be developed by settlements, and the citizens of a narrow State soon support and protect their railroad. In fact, the protection of this road is one of the least of the many arguments offered against overland rail-ways. The leading chiefs of the Indian tribes would provide for its protection. When treated like human beings, the Indians are perfectly reliable for almost any service required. This remark is justified by my own experience among them, and constant success while exploring with small parties without escort.

The development of the country would soon lead to the extension of a more permanent line, perhaps placed in some adjacent location over a broken but more advantageous region, for the support of a large population.* None of these lines of country can be opened by wagon roads. Like the rich prairies of Illinois, lying for years undeveloped in the heart of civilized communities, effective means of transit must [p. 12] be provided before settlements can occur. Timber for cabins, and the appliances of civilization being borne upon the rail, as by trains of the Illinois Central railroad, the routes will be populated, but not before. This is an evident

---

*"I bring this whole view of the engineering merits of the question as giving great character to a forked road, which, reaching by a main stem from the central border of eastern civilization to the Mormon settlements, would there permit of the connexion of a short branch line to Puget's Sound, and of the extension of a main trunk to California."

"This road, as first extended, would represent the word *line* as *delineated,* or placed by the requirements of location, by the trace of actual survey for preliminary service. But, as eventually elaborated, it can only be described at the present time, by the report of reconnoissance, as within the limits of all future claims of location by the word *route.* The rough road, built for the purpose of military transportation, must be placed by engineering study over a surface adapted to rapid extension, and be adjusted with great care at water crossings, summits of country, and all positions of character to postpone early communication. But it may, nevertheless, become the means of constructing a grand line, not necessarily contiguous to it, as the term would be applied in civilized regions; for, reaching by any line of approach the vicinity of the plains, and rim of the great basin, where occur sources of supply of iron, coal, building materials, and way stations of population, a preliminary road would become the carrying line for developing and transporting these resources."

"This view of the question should, also, practically refer to all routes of such undulating and broken surface as to postpone *early* communication if adopted."—(Extract from report of F.W. Lander, printed under resolution of House of Representatives of February 14, 1855.)

conclusion; it now costs two hundred dollars ($200) per ton to move military sup-
plies from Missouri river to Fort Laramie, over this very line of five hundred
miles, the most favorable of all routes, and the best natural wagon road in the
world, by wagon trains.

Cash and credit systems, land grants, &c.

All advocates of a Pacific railroad seem to believe that the question of overland
travel is settled when the road is built. This is a mistake. If the road is in the hands of
a company who desire a per centage on the cost of building, and especially on workage and renewal, fares must be so high as to place the road beyond the reach of the
travelling population. The basis of bills has hitherto been to have military supplies
and mails go free, but the population pay. As a builder and superintendent of the
workage of roads of many years' experience, I think the system should be reversed.
Government desires speedy and effective military and mail transportation over our
own soil, and is able and willing to pay for it. Why, then, may not contracts be made
to have this transportation furnished with such arrangements, included in the contract, as will enable the carrying party to offer low fares to emigrants, until the routes
are populated, and other sources of revenue have grown up. Even in reference to the
land system, it requires no prophet to show that the domain west of the Missouri
must be developed by railways. In many respects a desolate region, and without navigable rivers, it is interspersed with valleys, hills, and plains, of remarkable fertility,
but at long distances apart. Much of the country will require irrigation. The lands
must come to the settler at low rates, or he cannot afford to improve them. If given
away to companies who will extend railroads to develope them, they are augmented
in price to the actual settler. If no provision is made to cause these companies to run
their trains at low rates to the emigrant, the whole system of development is a
patronage of capital to the detriment of the poorer citizen, who, gaining no advantage from the railroad, pays two prices for his land. The unfortunate experience of
the Illinois Central Railroad, in the attempt of its managers to run trains at non-
paying rates, for the purpose of developing their lands, conclusively shows that
some means must be provided for cheap workage, or the result will be ruinous to the
company that attempts it under the mere apprehension of immediate results from
the most excellent speculations in land. As to the road up the Platte, emigrants had
better keep to their ox-teams and wagons than to think of paying such rates of fare
as would remunerate transportation without government aid. It has been proposed
to overcome these prospective liabilities by increasing the amount of land donated,
so great a breadth of surface of alternate sections along the route being secured to
first holders, as to warrant the company a grand bassis [*sic*] of stock issue, [p. 13]
over which they can bond and borrow. Now, beyond conflicting with the claims of

the actual settler, and the truly national plea of developing the route at short notice with a population, this course of procedure inaugurated a system of credit issue over the intangible and fluctuating value of wild lands. It would place this road not only under the contingency of workage without revenue, loss of interest on dormant capital, deterioration, and renewal, but ever exposed to the mere chance of progression by the fruits of a speculation in sand plains. This would not be expedient. The public would be deceived at first, but, as the road could not pay its own expenses and per centage, and the lands of many of the alternate sections would be soon known to be valueless, public appreciation would be lost, all credit would be withheld, and the whole affair appear as a visionary folly. Congress would again and again be appealed to, and again and again compelled to make advances in money or substantial credits. But the worst feature of the case would be, that the only route to the mountains, graded and ballasted by nature for the laying of rails without delay would be taken up and occupied by a mammoth monopoly, and prevent the extension of a road by some simple and effective mode of building. We cannot but assert, then, that the land grant system of building, not an objectionable system along the fertile border, should be applied to this project with great caution. The arable portion of Platte valley is very narrow; the adjacent scattered fertile sections limited in extent. The danger of pushing the squatter to extremity is well known, and in the fastnesses of the mountains, at a distance from civilization, he is the lord supreme of his own little domain. Moving with axe and plough in advance of this road, taking the chances of securing the best locations by his own scanty means of transportation, of fighting Indians, and irrigating sterile land plains, he possesses the indomitable spirit of the American frontier yeoman. Not always understanding the subtler distinctions of laws, which place him at the mercy of landed monopolies, he is ever ready to argue whether the patronage of capital, without corresponding advantages secured to labor, is not at conflict with a true interpretation of the strictly defined powers of a government emanating from the people, and based on the idea of elevating the working man to his true position in nature. On the other hand, the company should certainly retain all those privileges which, by legitimate speculations near depot grounds and town sites developed by their own energy and foresight, will help to reimburse them for outlay incurred, and lead to the cheap running of trains.

These remarks cannot appear out of place in reply to a resolution asking information as to the best method of building a road through the South Pass, and while the country is still suffering under the third great crisis, which, in the course of my own experience, has resulted by the literal overworking of the credit system of railroad construction, and credit issues over the basis of wearing and deteriorating railroads. [p. 14]

How cheap workage might be secured.

Looking at the sums expended for the last five years for military transportation along this important route, it will be seen that government can afford to pay a sum for facile means of moving troops and supplies, amounting to six per cent. per annum, on a cost of fifteen thousand dollars ($15,000) per mile. Under the present contingency of the Mormon war, government could certainly afford to pay this sum per year, and continue it for a reasonable length of time.

But beyond this, government could afford to pay a certain price per mile, say five thousand dollars, ($5,000), for the establishment of a means of military defence and for the development of a portion of the public domain which no navigable river traverses, and the peculiar character of which precludes settlement, until the river of iron, the means of transit projected by human ingenuity, is applied.

But, in addition to this, government can afford to bestow on the projectors of the line sections of land at each watering station as town sites. In the working of a road of nearly level grades during the service of military transportation, trains could afford very low rates of fare to emigrants. In return for privileges accorded, its owners could even contract with government to draw cars during the two months of spring emigration at mere nominal cost, thus placing its facilities as fully at the command of the poorer class of emigrants as are the low fare steamboats of the great rivers and lakes.

The sources of emolument herein embraced are ample for building and working a road over the Platte valley route, and will cover the cost of its expansion by renewal of cross ties from the firmer timber of the mountains, and the raising of the track two feet above the flat surface of the valley to a drained, ditched, and dressed road-bed, with culvert masonry and more permanent bridges than would be used at the outset. By such a simple mode of extension government takes no part in the testing of the experiment. The very iron laid upon the earth secures, better than the most costly cordon of forts, the absolute safety of the Pacific possessions by military service, without increasing the standing army. It likewise affords the means of solving the Mormon question without difficulty, and is certainly worth to the nation thrice the amount advanced. Government, taking no part in the experiment of laying the road, or of the testing of the difficulties of doing so, applies at low cost a means of augmenting the value and of throwing open the public domain, while retaining to its own benefit *all*, and not merely one half or only alternate sections of the route developed. It retains, too, at its own option, the right of fixing the price of lands to the actual settler, or of giving portions of them away, if deemed more expedient; it provides for the cheap running of trains that the routes may be populated; it ceases to pay when the routes are populated, and it pays nothing until trains are actually running. In fact, prior to any disbursement by government, lands sold along the route will have provided for all expenditures required, and adjacent to the present border there is no existing reason why they should not thus be sold. [p. 15]

Reviewing, then, this whole question, we may remark that it is the desire of the nation that some step be taken towards the construction of a Pacific railroad. Congress hesitates to set apart two hundred millions of dollars for this purpose of building one road on any plea of military defence. Neither will it give up the control of the public domain to private parties to aid the attempt at building three. All routes are of extreme length, and extend over mountains and sand plains. The workage of the road, when built, its wearage and renewal are great experiments. Most especially and decidedly a national mistake is the belief that six per cent. can be paid on the dead stock or dormant capital of such a road by any future earnings. With the present means of transportation by wagons, it will require twenty years to build it, for all the bills before Congress are based on the reports of the War Department and imply permanent construction from the outset. This makes even building as well as workage an experiment.

In view of the progression of practical experience of construction in our own country, of late improvements in France, and the peculiar claims of this new problem of transportation of long traffic, any road started of the class of the present day, and without comprehension of the system of expansion, must become obsolete as a means of transportation during the twenty years of its progression to the Pacific. This is evident; for after observation of the achievements of the mechanic arts even of the last ten years no individual can now define the character of a Pacific railroad twenty years from 1858.* Although bills provide for the construction of the road in ten years, the magic of a bill cannot create a road, neither can it

---

*A doubt exists in the minds of practical individuals whether the traffic of a grand trunk overland railroad will ever support its running expenses. Hence there is an experiment to be tried. **** Again, should this experiment prove successful, then the grand trunk railroad of the present day would be wholly inadequate to the amount of transportation required. The broad uncultivable wastes of the American continent (over any route whatever) are unlike the present railroad routes of civilized regions. They compare with them as the drear expanse of the ocean contrasts with the inland navigable waters of our lakes and rivers. When this sea of space is to be traversed with the certainty of a paying business, and an enormous through traffic to warrant the running of trains, the locomotive engine will make passage of the level sand wastes of the wild interior at rates of speed which will startle human credulity. And when the same inventive genius which once so readily modified the costly modes of building of older nations to the means and demands of our own new and undeveloped country is called upon to grasp the broader conclusion and solve this future necessity of civilization and of progress, then the Pacific railroad will resemble the present grand trunk road of populated countries as the new British steamship Great Eastern compares with the first class steamer of the coast. Thus, while the first study of this question should be grounded on a comprehensive desire to answer at once, and in the best manner, that which is at present required, yet, in view of the grand prospective contingencies presented, it should also be definitely guided by a full apprehension of that which is liable to occur. The conclusion is, that if government should see fit to construct a railroad, necessarily in connexion with, but in preference to, a wagon road, then a railroad suited to military transportation, and to the mere testing of this experiment, is the class of road to be attempted.—*Extract from Report of F. W. Lander, printed under resolution of the House of Reps. of February* 14, 1855.

grow up like the fabled palace of Aladdin in a single night. There is too much good sense in the nation to propose that it should not embrace all the perfections of the future, yet it must progress at once, and, if step by step, with the celerity commensurate with the importance of the undertaking [p. 16] and the present needs of the country. The difficulty of choice of route is obviated by the adoption of the line of a flat plain. It is the belief of professional parties that a route of equal character exists in the south. Thus, then, we may close this statement. By extending the cheapest practical means of moving military supplies and troops to Fort Laranie [sic], laying an iron road which can be worked by locomotives and supersede wagons, without embracing the more elaborate triumphs of steam power, and gaining many attendant advantages, we also take the simplest and most effective step towards solving the experiment of an overland railroad to the Pacific. There is no invidious selection of a route by legislation, because the only route graded and ballasted by act of nature is adopted. This route is of national position for military defence in time of war, because, while providing means of transpoaration to Utah, California, and Oregon, it is located at a distance from the frontier and cannot easily be assailed by an enemy.

Equipment and Furnishing.

No practical engineer or railroad superintendent would advise the immediate furnishing of this road throughout its length to Fort Laramie. It should be provided with turnouts and watering stations, but with no costly or ponderous works to entail cost. The first one hundred (100) miles nearest Missouri river might reasonably be provided with a small equipment for daily service. The trains could on occasion work the whole length of the line. The line could be kept in surface [sic] throughout its length without daily workage of locomotives; for it would afford like conveniences to those of a canal or of navigable waters to local emigration by being provided with light freight cars, these cars to be drawn by the animals of the population seeking location for settlement along the line. For the low tolls charged for the use of such cars the company could afford to keep the line in surface [sic]. Thus, for mail or military use, the route would always be ready for the passage of trains up the road. It would be for the interest of the population to protect it, without reference to the other modes of protection hitherto stated. The danger of destruction of a military railroad is the very least of the many arguments made against it. Although a permanent railroad is a class of line peculiarly pregnable to the most insignificant means of attack, a common line of superstructure, light rail, flat chair, hook spike, and plain cross tie, extended over a flat gravel plain, is readily renewed, and, if the line of communication is broken, can be relaid at a few hours' notice.

Conclusion.

The whole conclusion of this paper is that Congress by authorized agents can, without danger or loss to the country, and with great prospect of gain, contract for the transportation of military supplies from some point on Missouri river to Fort Laramie, the transportation to be furnished by railroad within three (3) years from the com-[p. 17] mencement of the work. On the passage of a train over the first one hundred (100) miles of road, a payment to commence upon the terms of whatever contract has been the result of proposals issued. These payments to extend ten years, by which time the route will have become populated, the expansion of the road taken care of itself, or the line worn out and superseded by a more direct and permanent one. In reference to the wooden road from Fort Laramie to the plains of the Great Basin, with its intermediate sections of iron, eventually reaching the eastern boundary of California, Congress can further safely contract for the carriage of mails throughout the year by railroad, from the point on Missouri river, in twenty days to California, requiring sufficient surety for the performance of the work; and, in view of the importance of the great advantage gained, paying such a price as will justify the wooden rail being extended at once.

The importance of this road in reference to the proposed new territory of Carson and the solution of the Mormon question is obvious. The expansion of the wooden road to a steam carrying line need not be immediately provided for by government. In reference to this expansion, but out of the limits of treatment of a report relating to railroads through the South Pass, I may remark that north of the Wind river mountain lies a route of the Snake river, through a less elevated region of country. This route may, on exploration, offer greater facilities for railroad workage, during winter, and regarding difficulty from snow than that of the South Pass. It extends through a pass used by the Shoshonee tribe of Indians, in returning from "buffalo" during the winter season. I have reason to suppose that the explorations of Lieut. Warren, an able and scientific topographical engineer, will be extended so near the pass as to permit of the connexion of it with the base line of his system of examinations. The resources of the country will undoubtedly engage his attention; but the more practical building question, although beyond their field of labor, might properly be observed by the civil engineers of the wagon road, if directed by the department, under the following statement of a portion of my report to you of the 4th instant:

"If you think it proper to have a route explored from Fort Hall to the north fork of the Humboldt river, and desire the connexion of the important general reconnoissances of last summer, with other surveys pursued north of latitude 43°, which, I am unofficially informed, are to be continued next season, it is a question whether it should be done out of the present appropriation. But it would be an omission of engineering duty not to call your attention to this subject. The new northern line from the South Pass to Fort Hall loses much of its character if it is not connected with the valley of the Humboldt by a more direct route than is now travelled by emigrants."

"Again, reaching the great plains of the Snake, either from the east, say Fort Thompson, on Wind river, or from the south, say Green river valley, approaches are fully practicable to the unopened agricultural regions of the Deer Lodge and Beaver Head vallies, and to the Flat Head or St. Mary's valley of the north. Both of these reconnoissances might properly be embraced in the programme of future engineering work, at the discretion of the department. The more [p. 18] westerly one from Fort Hall, towards the north fork of the Humboldt river, should, however, be pursued, as the legitimate deduction from, and conclusion of the engineering service of the last season. The one towards the north, although as important to the country, can only be embraced within the programme of survey of the engineers of the wagon road expedition, for the purpose of connecting their work with the base line of accurate surveys of other parties." * * * * * "An additional appropriation of eight thousand dollars ($8,000) would cover the whole field."

"Pacific Railroad."

"The House of Representatives has just passed a resolution, enclosed in your letter of this date, calling for information of railroad routes through the South Pass. I gained much information of railroad routes through the South Pass during the exploration of last season, and will immediately transmit to you such a report in reply to the resolution as can be made up without interfering with the work entrusted to my charge by your instructions. But such contradictory opinions exist among unprofessional parties, as to the value of engineering reconnoissance, that it might seem proper to have this information tested by survey. My own view of Pacific railroad exploration has been to defer all costly mapping, engraving and elaboration of rough field data, until more accurate surveys were obtained than I believe have yet been carried on, or until the lines of routes are actually placed."* [p. 19]

---

* *Railroad reconnoissance.*—To look; to view; the study of country with limited use of instruments; to procure information of its characteristics regarding railroad construction.

Report of reconnoissance.—To describe and submit conclusions from inferences drawn.

Railroad survey.—Instrumental examinations, by which surfaces are measured.

Report of survey.—To state, by accurate deductions, from data gained.

Explorations of the wild interior, for the purpose of ascertaining the most economical and practicable route for a railroad to the Pacific, are reconnoissances rather than surveys. They are engineering studies of *routes* or belts of country, often of two hundred miles in breadth, of two thousand miles in length, extending from the verge of the eastern border to the Pacific, of which the characteristics are to be known regarding railroad construction.

Routes are not lines; several lines might occupy relative positions on a single route.

[continued on next page]

"For the sum of ten thousand dollars ($10,000) such a survey as is pursued in civilized regions can be carried from the South Pass, across the dividing range of the Wahsatch mountains, to the plains of Snake river and to those of the Great Basin, and the actual amount of work be shown in profile section, as taken by the spirit level along the whole surface of a located line. The barometric approximations of an unplaced line, put upon such scales as have been presented to the country, perplex, confuse, and mislead the unprofessional observer. Such a survey as I describe, and which, if connected with the wagon road expedition, can be made for $10,000, would fix the character of the forked route of the South Pass. The northern branch of this route to Puget's Sound was explored by me in 1854. The southern fork of it, through Humboldt river valley, has been examined by numerous individuals. All operations of the study of this national subject can be carried on at less expense when connected with large expeditions organized for other purposes. I have not hitherto thought it proper to allude to the subject of a Pacific railroad in my correspondence with the department beyond the statement of my report of December 1, 1857, that numerous routes," &c.

"But if it is assumed by Congress that the wagon road is an adjunct to a Pacific railroad, or that the duty of the engineer of the wagon road is to cover the subject of Pacific railroad building, I suggest the propriety of a fund being provided for carrying on the work and the manner in which it might be used."

Schedule of lines from the valley of the Platte to the waters of Snake and Bear rivers.

The Wind River mountains breaking down to a flat plain at the South Pass, divide the waters of the Atlantic from those of the Gulf of California or its affluent, Green river.

The lineal section, rapidly placed by the labors of a single season, and presented as the result of a Pacific railroad exploration, must not always be presumed to be a profile of the preferable, or the very best trace for location existing upon the divison examined. From the limited time prescribed for making these examinations, and from the vast extent of country explored, the first line of barometric levels does not always occupy the best position of the route to which applied.

The engineering features of the whole broad division passed over are connected with this base line, and stated in the form of opinions or convictions forced upon the mind of the engineer by former experience of the necessities of location in all varieties of country.

No elaboration in office of the rough data of field reconnoissance can entitle them to be regarded as the results of survey. When the preferable route is selected, by the comparisons of reconnoissance, the location line of that route will be placed by careful instrumental survey, and it may then be accurately delineated; but the lineal section of barometric levels, with which the side examinations of reconnoissance have been connected, must not be supposed to occupy that position. Presented as the profile of a route, when *not* accurately placed, it will lead to erroneous conclusions on its merits; and even *when* accurately placed, the mere approximations of the instrument used do not furnish a result regarding minor undulations of surface. Again, from the small scale on which a profile of two thousand miles of line must be presented, the remarkable differences between the flat plain over which rail must be used without grading and the broken country, which needs costly and tedious operations for reduction to grade, are not perceptible.—(Extracts from report of F.W. Lander, printed under resolution of House of Representatives of February 14, 1855.)

The Wahsatch mountains divide the waters of Green river from those of the Great Salt Lake and its affluent, Bear river.

This range also divides the waters of Green river from the great Snake. Just north of the Wind River mountains, latitude 43° 30', occurs the Buffalo gap, affording passage to a break down of the Wahsatch mountains at the head of Green river, and to the tributaries of the Snake.

Railroad lines to Snake or Columbia river.

A line from the South Pass skirting the southern base of the Wind River mountains to the head of Green river and Onion creek to the Snake.

A line from the South Pass skirting the southern base of the Wind River mountains, and by Little Jackson's river to the Snake.

A line from the South Pass to Marsh creek and through McDougal's gap to the Snake. This is the direct route of parallel 43°. It reaches Great John Gray's river, a main tributary of the Snake, by a tunnel of half a mile, and is a route for permanent construction.

All the above lines find excellent passage to the Salt Lake Basin, west of the valley of Bear river, and, with the exception of the McDougal route, require no tunnels. [p. 20]

Lines to the plains of the Great Basin by Bear river.

A line in a due westerly direction from the South Pass to the mouth of Piney creek; thence south along the base of the hilly country to the Labarge; thence in a direction north of west up Labarge creek to the foot hill springs of the Wahsatch mountains has a tunnel section of two miles. It was examined by John F. Mullowny. The tunnel gives a passage to the valley of Smith's Fork, the great tributary of Bear river. Thence the passage to Salt Lake is a flat plain, with the necessity of some few bridge crossings of Bear river of 150 feet in length, in an excellently timbered country.

The passage to the Salt Lake valley by this line involves great loss of directness, but the route after tunneling is nearly level.

A line from the foot hill springs of Labarge creek through the Wahsatch mountains by a tunnel of one and a half miles to the head of the upper branch of Smith's Fork; thence by a tunnel of half a mile to the head of Salt river, a great tributary of the Snake, is probably a preferable line, and offers opportunities of connexion with Oregon and Puget's Sound by eight hundred miles of branch road.

All of the above lines, which reach the waters of Snake river, afford favorable routes of connexion with Puget's Sound and Oregon.

A map.

The work of the large map of the wagon road explorations of the present year, delineating these routes and the wagon roads, can be reduced and placed upon the lithographed map of the Pacific Railroad Explorations in about three days, free of expense to the department. This lithographed map is now in the hands of the Superintendent of Public Printing. The engraving to fill up the blank spaces will cost about fifteen dollars, ($15.) The maps can then be furnished by the printers in New York at seven dollars ($7) per hundred. They can be delivered eight days after the order is received. It may not seem expedient to you to have the large wagon road map printed at the present time. Many additions will be made to it during next summer, and the engraving of so much work would postpone so long the transmission of the map to Congress as to prevent its being of immediate service in illustrating the present hurried report.

The general description of the lines of the route of the South Pass, and which permits any map of the central interior illustrating them, is that the route passes west from the South Pass, along the 43d parallel, to a point south of Fort Hall, and thence in a direction south of west to the valley of Humboldt river. The connexion line to Oregon and Puget's Sound passes northwest in the vicinity of the valleys of the Snake and Columbia, from a point of departure near the South Pass.

The very imperfect manner in which I have replied to the terms of the resolution, and the discursive style of my remarks, may be excused, when it is known that the report has been written during the last ten days, at intervals of time not occupied by the regular business of the office.

Thomas J. Cram, 1858

Memoir…Project Of A Rail Road Through Sonora, To Connect With The Pacific Rail Road In Arizona

Troy, N.Y., R. V. Wilson, Book and Job Printer, 1858, 9 p., map. [WC 299a note; WCB 299a:2; Holliday 242; Streeter 491; NUC NC 0771573.]
Reset verbatim from a facsimile, and reproduced by permission of
The Huntington Library, San Marino, California.

Significance   In this perplexing unofficial tract, a Northern army officer unaccountably went public to espouse two explosive Southern crusades, one for a southern Pacific railroad and the other for U.S. acquisition of Sonora. Both of these measures could have promoted the extension of slavery into the territories. The Gadsden Purchase from Mexico in 1853 gave the United States a corner of land south of the Gila. Jefferson Davis and others favored the purchase to secure the right of way for a southern Pacific railroad; the Senate ratified it in 1854 only after bitter sectional strife. As late as 1855, Davis wanted to acquire the northern provinces of Mexico (Goetzmann 1959). Cram must also have known of filibustering Henry A. Crabb, whose fate was in all the newspapers. Crabb and his gang of 68 Californians were besieged and executed by Mexicans in Caborca, Sonora, April 1-7, 1857. The *New York Tribune* carried a report datelined "Sacramento, May 19, 1857," that "Mr. Crabb left here about January last, ostensibly for the purpose of mining in the Gadsden purchase, and settling there; but really intending to conquer Sonora, and in process of time add it to the slave States. He was…ever an active politician and ultra pro-slaveryist" (Buchanan 1858). The Mexicans preserved Crabb's head in a jar of mescal.

Capt. Cram was not one to duck controversy, but his jumping into these sides of these issues is extraordinary. See the Highlights for his vehemently opposite views of 1864.

Cram argued in 1858 that it would be more than twice as far by railroad from the "heart of Arizona" (about 30 miles east of Tucson) to San Diego than it would be to Guaymas, Sonora. Although Cram fudged the numbers somewhat to suit his purpose, Lt. Robert S. Williamson's 1854 preferred railroad route from Ft. Yuma to San Diego did indeed go the long way around through San Gorgonio Pass

(Palm Springs) and Los Angeles. Cram also showed that Guaymas was 453 miles closer than San Diego to any Atlantic port by any then considered isthmus crossing. His main object was to transport the weighty products of Arizona's mines economically. But he acknowledged in his title that the tracks to Guaymas would be just a branch from a southern Pacific railroad necessarily destined for California. In his 1857 Annual Message, President Buchanan, a Pennsylvanian trying to appease the South, had noted that "a military railroad to connect our Atlantic and Pacific States...on the Arizona route" was both feasible and constitutional.

Another 1858 issue of this pamphlet has a Washington, D.C., imprint (WCB 299a:1); it has 12 pages, no map, and only one recorded copy. The present reprint appears to be the first for any issue.

Author   THOMAS JEFFERSON CRAM, ca. 1803-1883, topographical engineer, Civil War general. A New Hampshire native, Cram graduated fourth in his West Point class of 1826. Until 1836 he remained at the Military Academy as assistant professor of mathematics and of natural philosophy. He resigned and for two years did engineering work for eastern railroads. He re-entered the service as a captain in the topographical engineers in 1838 and performed various surveys in the midwest for the next seven years. For example, he reported in 1841 on marking the boundary between Wisconsin Territory and Upper Michigan. He found that the legislated boundary was based on "imaginary" geography. He made military reconnaissances in Texas in 1845-46 and geodetic surveys of the New England coast in 1847-54. He was chief topographical engineer of the Department of the Pacific under Gen. John E. Wool, 1854-58. In 1855 he surveyed the Columbia River from Ft. Vancouver to Walla Walla (Pierce 1856).

Cram wrote yet another astonishing report in 1858. It was called *Topographical Memoir of the Department of the Pacific.* It was warmly endorsed by Wool but totally repudiated by Secretary of War John B. Floyd, who suppressed it for a year, until Congress called for it. In it Cram provided a wealth of data on inland routes and distances, passes, and Indian battles. In it he also condemned or ridiculed a long list of public officials. He chided "an ex-Secretary of War" for wanting to fortify the entrance to the Columbia. He accused a future Indian sub-agent of one of the "infernal acts of cruelty" in 1852 that set off the Rogue River War: "Captain Ben. Wright massacred over thirty [38] Indians out of forty-eight, who had come into his camp by invitation to make a 'peace.'" Cram said that Oregon's Gov. George L. Curry, in waging in 1855 "a war of extermination" with volunteers, showed a "marked contempt of the authority of the President's commander of the department [Wool]." Cram derided Gov. Isaac I. Stevens's 1856 Washington volunteers, whose "whole object was to plunder the Indians of their horses and cattle." Stevens's 1855 treaty retinue, in contrast to the "magnificence in the extreme" of the assembled Indians, was "shabby, diminutive, and mean in appointments...The pitiful escort [was]...mounted on lame, gaunt horses...[which] jeopardized the very object of the negotiation."

In his *Topographical Memoir* Cram also deplored "that unfortunate jealousy, or something worse, existing between the Indian Bureau and War Department, the fruits of which are most pernicious." He criticized "The hot haste and grasping disposition evinced by the senior commissioner [Stevens] in his speeches in council" (see also 2:D10 Highlights). He characterized the gold rushers to Ft. Colville as "Anglo-Saxon devils, in human shape." He even tweaked Secretary Floyd's claim that "most" tribes conspired to wipe out the whites: "I think the Hon. Secretary may have forgotten the number of tribes in those Territories." He castigated the Oregon legislature, which, "as an everlasting monument to its members, passed a memorial requesting the President to recall General Wool...a more unjust document never emanated from a legislative body. I will not pollute this paper with its contents." He concluded, "The Indian Bureau should never have been severed from the War Department." Wool agreed with all these criticisms. Bancroft (31:117), on the other hand, was highly critical of Wool's opinions and actions.

Cram surveyed the North Carolina coast 1858-61. In the Civil War he was aide-de-camp to General Wool and was involved in the capture of Norfolk, Virginia. He was transferred to the engineer corps in 1863 and was brevetted a major general at war's end. He supervised harbor improvements in the Great Lakes until his retirement in 1869. (ACAB; Heitman; Cullum 432.)

Highlights   In an 1864 letter to Northern Pacific Railroad promoter Edgar Conkling, Cram completely reversed his 1858 endorsement of the southern route: "Now that the 'slave interest' no longer sets its ogre shape in direct opposition—as it has done for the last quarter of a century—to all attempts to develop our great Northwest, it seems to me that the very present—while the incubus is being removed—is the time when the advocates of the Northern route may step forward, as you have done in this pamphlet, with a prospect at least of a fair hearing being vouchsafed, which was not the case while the Pacific Railroad explorations were under the entire management and artful dodging of one [Jefferson Davis] who was exerting all his influence—powerful from the official position he held and the authority with which he was clothed in connection with these explorations—to bend every argument, by special pleading, to induce the Government, which subsequent proof shows he was then betraying, to construct the railroad on the extreme Southern route.

"The controlling influence of the slave oligarchy was, to my mind, never more successfully, or covertly and adroitly wielded that it was by the conspirator in whose hands these explorations were placed and firmly held during two Presidential administrations.

"I repeat, now is the time to press the importance of the northern route, without condemning the central route, upon the notice of the World."

Cram did not here criticize the distinguished Union General Andrew A. Humphreys, who had administered the Pacific railroad surveys under Davis, and who had favored the southern route. (See 5:J Perspective.)

Legacy In another turn of events, Union General James H. Carleton in 1863 advocated purchasing northern Sonora for railroad access to the Gulf of California (L11). He wanted to supply his Arizona troops cheaply from Lobos Bay (now Puerto Lobos), midway between Guaymas and Ft. Yuma. He pointed out, "When the vast mineral resources...become better known...the government will see that a port on the gulf of California should be ours, at any cost." It never happened. But the Atchison, Topeka and Santa Fe completed a transcontinental link to Guaymas via the Sonora Railway in 1882.

REFERENCES
(See Preface for Heading and Author references, and for Bancroft, not listed here.)

Buchanan, James, 1857, Annual Message: Wash., 35/1 H2, serial 952, p. 27.

Buchanan, James, 1858, Execution of Colonel Crabb and associates, in Message from the President: Wash., 35/1 H64, serial 955, 84 p.; quote 71.

Conkling, Edgar, 1864, Benton's policy of selling and developing the mineral lands, and the necessity of furnishing access to the Rocky Mountains by the construction of the Northern and Central Pacific railroads, with a letter endorsing the policy, from Lt. Col. T. J. Cram: Cincinnati, 16 p.; Cram letter 15-16, quotes 15.

Cram, Thomas J., 1841, Boundary-line between the State of Michigan and the Territory of Wiskonsin: Wash., 26/2 S151, serial 378, 16 p., 5 maps; quote on imaginary 4.

Cram, Thomas J., 1859, Topographical memoir of the Department of the Pacific: Wash., 35/2 H114, serial 1014, 126 p.; quotes on ex-Secretary 9, Ben Wright 40, Curry 44, WA volunteers 60, Stevens's retinue 81, jealousy 82, hot haste 85, devils 86, Floyd 88, OR legislature 103-04, Indian bureau 122.

Goetzmann, William H., 1959, Army exploration in the American West 1803-63: New Haven, p. 274.

Pierce, Franklin, 1856, Indian disturbances, in Message of the President: Wash., 34/1 S26, serial 819, 68 p.; Cram report 38-44.

Williamson, Robert S., 1854 (1856 pub.), Routes in California, in Reports of Explorations and Surveys: Wash., 33/2 H91, serial 795, 5:41.

MEMOIR

SHOWING HOW TO BRING THE

LEAD, COPPER, SILVER AND GOLD

–OF–

ARIZONA

INTO THE MARTS OF THE WORLD,

AND

PROJECT OF A RAIL ROAD THROUGH

SONORA,

TO CONNECT WITH THE

PACIFIC RAIL ROAD IN

ARIZONA.

BY
CAPT. T. J. CRAM,
U. S. Corps Top'l Eng'r.

———————

TROY, N. Y.:
R. V. WILSON, BOOK AND JOB PRINTER, 225 RIVER STREET.
1858.

I.   NEW MEXICO....The more our explorations are prosecuted in this territory, it seems, the more it is discovered to possess advantages beyond what were dreamed of before it came into our possession, in regard to fertility of the soil of its valleys, the salubrity of its climate, and the richness of its minerals.

But, how fertile soever may be the valleys of New Mexico, and how rich soever may be the foot hills of its mountain slopes in copper, silver and gold, as no doubt they are, still, this country containing 250 to 300 thousand square miles of the earth's surface, cannot become a profitable one for the Anglo-Saxon race to occupy so long as it has no sea-coast front—being so destitute as it is generally of interior navigable rivers leading to sea-ports.

It is in this view, that the Department (or State) of Sonora (see map) belonging to Mexico, lies directly in the way of all our New Mexico possessions; and until we have the ownership of Sonora, our whole possessions north of it will be comparatively of little avail for flourishing territories or States.

Railroads may in some measure supply the deficiency of navigable rivers; but they can never be constructed without means to an enormous amount; and although there are doubtless riches enough now undeveloped in this country to justify the construction of certain parts of a railroad through it, yet there are other more extensive portions which have no such inducements to further the construction of a railroad through them—to the end of forming a connected line all the way from the Atlantic to the Pacific.

I would by no means have it inferred that these remarks are penned for the purpose of dampening the project of a railroad on the southern route: on the contrary, this project I would advocate with what little I may be capable of [p. 4] contributing; but while so doing, I would, at the same time, call attention to some collateral circumstances which must ever have an influence, more or less controling [sic], over the effects expected to be realized by the construction of a railroad to the Pacific on this route; and these circumstances will be found in the position, wealth and ownership of Sonora—as may be seen by any one having the patience to follow me through this memoir.

II.   ARIZONA, or that portion of New Mexico south of the Gila River (known as the Gadsen purchase,) contains 45,700 square miles: and there is surface enough in it for a State about equal in size to Tennessee; but at present little is known of the proportion of waste land in it, and therefore it cannot be said how well it would compare in respect to the amount of its cultivable surface. In many places it would grow cotton, wheat, fruit, sugar and hemp in the greatest abundance; but the natural directions of the lines of trade or export of any surplus staples are not east and west: they are towards the south, and therefore intercepted by Sonora.

The organization of Arizona into a separate territory, would no doubt have the desirable tendency in some degree to Americanize that district: and the construction of a railroad through it from the Rio Grande to the Colorado, thence to our Pacific coast, would greatly facilitate the development of its emboweled wealth into a condition of practical utility; but it would not answer all the requirements essential to render Arizona a promising State. It should be put in possession, or within convenient reach of a sea-front having one good natural harbor at least.

The distance from the Rio Grande through Arizona to the Colorado—which is the eastern boundary of the State of California—is 576 miles to Fort Yuma; thence to San Diego, 375 miles on the railroad survey. From the centre or heart of Arizona, therefore, to San Diego Harbor it would be 663 miles. It is here to be observed that San Diego is the nearest Pacific coast harbor we have to our [p. 5] Atlantic ports—as it is also the nearest good harbor, we own, to Arizona. The port of San Pedro is 20 miles nearer to Arizona than San Diego; but for harbor purposes the latter is far superior.

Now, suppose the Pacific Railroad constructed on the southern route to San Diego; this 663 miles would be the mean or average extent of land transportation for imports and exports of Arizona: whereas, the distance from the heart of Arizona to Guaymas—a most excellent harbor of great capacity—in Sonora, on the Gulf of California, would be only about 300 miles; and from the eastern portion of Arizona down through the valley of the Yagui River to Guaymas, it would not exceed 350 miles; and it is also to be observed, that the valleys of Sonora trend, in their general direction, southerly—affording natural routes from Arizona to the sea-ports on the gulf. From the head of the gulf coastwise to Guaymas, it is only about 400 miles, and in this sea-front there are several small ports.

The distance from the heart of Arizona by railroad to Fort Yuma would be very nearly 300 miles. If then its exports should go west to the Colorado, and then be transhipped upon light draught steamers to descend the river to the Gulf, where they would again have to undergo transhipment, the expense would be far greater than if they could be sent 300 miles by a railroad down through Sonora directly to the Harbor of Guaymas.

Again: another difficulty presents itself in carrying on the commerce through the Colorado. The same class of steamers that navigate the river would find it impossible to navigate the Gulf, in safety, to any place of transhipment into vessels drawing over 12 feet water.

Let us now consider briefly the commercial connection—via the Isthmus routes—between our Atlantic ports and Arizona.

In going from which ports—whether by the Panama, the Nicaragua, the Honduras or the Tehuantepec transit—to San Diego or to Guaymas, the Pacific por-

tions of [p. 6] the routes from the termini of the transits, all come together at Acapulco, Mexico. (See map.)

The following Table exhibits all information desirable, in relation to the distances in statute miles, by the sea-steamers' runs, from New York and New
Orleans to San Diego and Guaymas:

FROM	VIA ISTHMUS,	TO	MILES.
New York.....	Panama	San Diego,.	5640
	Nicaragua		5147
	Honduras		.4737
	Tehuantepec		4523
New Orleans...	Panama	San Diego,...	5141
	Nicaragua		4174
	Honduras		3726
	Tehuantepec		3166
New York.....	Panama	Guaymas,....	5187
	Nicaragua		4694
	Honduras		4284
	Tehuantepec		4070
New Orleans...	Panama	Guaymas,....	4688
	Nicaragua		3721
	Honduras		3273
	Tehuantepec		2713

From the foregoing Table we perceive that Guaymas, Sonora, is nearer to any
of our Atlantic Ports, by 453 miles, than San Diego.

Once into the Pacific, there are three ways for commerce to reach to the heart
of Arizona, which will be seen by the following

DISTANCES.

MILES.

Acapulco, by sea, to San Diego,.. 1533
San Diego, by the proposed Pacific Railroad, to the
    heart of Arizona,... 663
Acapulco via San Diego, to the heart of Arizona,........................... 2196

[p. 7] Acapulco, by Gulf California, to mouth of Colorado, ... 1480
Mouth of Colorado to Fort Yuma,.. 125
Fort Yuma, by proposed Pacific Railroad, to heart of Arizona,.......... 288
Acapulco via. Colorado and Pacific Railroad, to heart of Arizona,... 1893

Acapulco, by sea, to Guaymas,... 1080
Guaymas, by proposed Railroad through Sonora, to the
    heart of Arizona,...300
Acapulco via. Sonora, to the heart of Arizona,................................ 1380

Hence we perceive the possession of Sonora would place us 513 miles nearer the heart of Arizona than we are by going up the Colorado, and 816 miles nearer than by going around by San Diego.

The sea-steamer track from San Francisco is 1680 statute miles to the harbor of Guaymas, requiring six days to make the run, according to the present best steamer speed on the Pacific.

Arizona is by no means a newly known district. It was settled in many places more than 100 years ago by Spaniards who were attracted thither by the representations of the Jesuit Missionaries, of the precious metals it was known to contain. Many of the small valleys were cultivated and produced all that was required for home consumption of those engaged in the mines. No sooner, however, had the district well began to thrive, than troubles commenced with the powerful tribes of Indians to the immediate north, and what little leaven of civilization had been introduced by the Jesuits, was swept away by these savages, who, ever since, have devastated the country and driven out all or nearly all persons attempting to work the mines. It is in this way that this valuable district has been kept down.

Under a Territorial organization for itself, and supported by two regiments of U.S. troops, however, it would immediately spring up from the pressure it has endured for [p. 8] a century at the hands of the barbarous Apaches, who are still formidable in all the southern portion of New Mexico.

With such an organization and so protected, *the copper mines alone*—that are as well known to exist in Arizona as that coal mines exist in Pennsylvania—would justify the construction, *at the present time,* of a railroad from the heart of the district, 300 miles to the mouth of the Gila, or 300 miles down through Sonora to Guaymas. The latter route would be the most profitable not only to Arizona, but likewise to the capitalists embarking in the enterprise. The former route, however, would subserve the interest of the greater project of the Pacific Railroad, whilst the latter would meet with an obstacle in our non-possession of Sonora.

III.   GULF OF CALIFORNIA....It is in relation to our New Mexico possessions that this Gulf is becoming every day of more and more commercial importance to the United States. It is to be regarded as one of the seven seas of the North Pacific; and though one of the least in size, it is by no means the least important. It is embraced by the Mexican shore line of 1600 miles in extent. It is 800 miles in length, and its mean breadth is 100 miles. It is admirably adapted to sail navigation, and but for the absence of fuel on its shores, the same might be said of it for steam navigation. As yet no coal has been discovered on its coast. It has several excellent harbors, among the principal of which is Guaymas, already referred to. The tide rises about seven feet: the waters of the Gulf abound in whales, seals, turtles, pearls, &c.: its coast is rich in valuable minerals; but the genius of the inhabitants has not yet been active enough to fully develop the wealth of the mines of copper, lead, salt, gold, silver, sulphur, &c., which are acknowledged to exist in great abundance interior to its coast, and on its shores and islands.

IV.   LOWER CALIFORNIA contains, in area, 80,812 square miles. It is not an inviting country: it is dry, [p. 9] mountainous, and destitute of wood; it however has numerous little valleys well adapted to stock-raising. Its mineral resources, if it have any, have not yet been discovered. It is probable, however, that proper geological surveys extended systematically over this peninsula, would bring to light hidden treasures.

V. SONORA....This department of Mexico contains 78,530 square miles. It has a sea-coast front on the Gulf of 500 miles. It lies between the parallels of 27 and 32 degrees north latitude and extends in longitude from the Sierra Membres (Willow Mountains) to the Gulf. It has many beautiful and luxuriant valleys, watered by as many beautiful rivers. Of these, the Yagui, which enters the Guaymas Harbor, is the most extensive. The length of this valley is about 300 miles. The agricultural products of this Department are very considerable, including sugar and wheat. But the sources of the greatest wealth are the mines, from which millions of dollars in silver are obtained and exported from Guaymas annually. Sonora has been greatly ravaged, as well as Arizona, by the Apache Indians; and from this cause the development of its vast wealth has been sadly retarded. Under an enterprising population, with a good government, it is not extravagant to say that the mines of Sonora would yield from 50 to 80 millions per annum immediately; and that through the port of Guaymas and the valley of the Yagui commerce would receive an impetus not inferior to that realized through the Golden Gate and the Sacramento valley, from the gold mines of the western slope of the Sierra Nevada in California.

It is not to be doubted that a Railroad from the Harbor of Guaymas, up the valley of the Yagui, or up one of the other valleys through Sonora to Arizona, would be amply productive: it would open our New Mexico possessions to their nearest Harbor, by the most natural route, all the way through a country full of the richest known deposits of lead, copper, silver and gold.

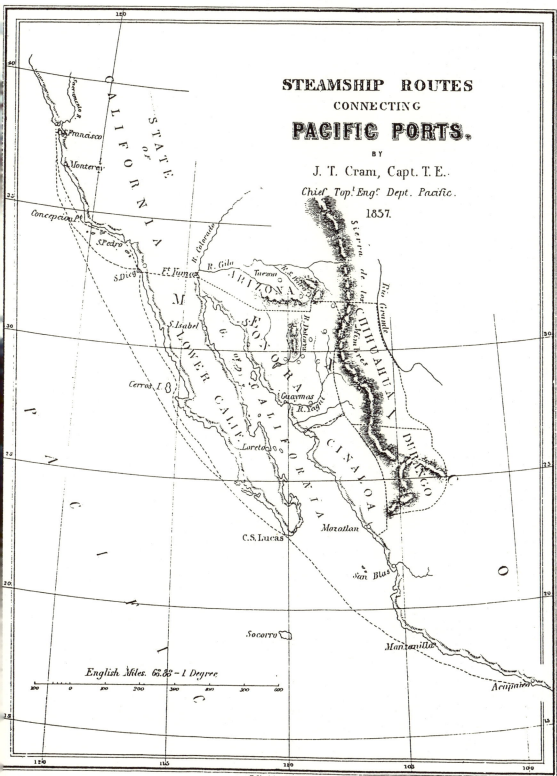

STEAMSHIP ROUTES
CONNECTING
PACIFIC PORTS.
BY
J. T. Cram, Capt. T. E.
Chief Top! Eng! Dept. Pacific.
1857.

English Miles. 65.83 = 1 Degree.

A

PLAN

FOR

THE SPEEDY CONSTRUCTION

OF

A PACIFIC RAILROAD

WITH

THE DRAFT OF A BILL

BY

HON. B. B. MEEKER

OF MINNESOTA

—⟶✦⟵—

ST. LOUIS:

GEORGE KNAPP & CO., PRINTERS AND BINDERS

1860.

Bradley B. Meeker, 1860

A Plan For The Speedy Construction Of A Pacific Railroad

St. Louis, George Knapp & Co., Printers and Binders, 1860, 15 p. [WCB 361b; Graff 2739; UPRR p. 42; NUC NM 0400869.] Reset verbatim from a facsimile, by courtesy of The Newberry Library, Chicago, Illinois.

Significance   Meeker's proposal to build three Pacific railroads simultaneously, in dozens of segments by dozens of different State-chartered companies, was naive and impractical. He was trying to secure a northern route for Minnesota by giving the other sections their desired central and southern routes. This likely is the first reprint.

Author   BRADLEY B. MEEKER, 1813-1873, lawyer, judge, Western promoter. A Connecticut native and graduate of Yale, Meeker studied law in Kentucky and practiced there 1838-48. He was an Associate Justice of the Supreme Court of the new Minnesota Territory 1849-53. During this time he was a founder of the Minnesota Historical Society and a member of the first Board of Regents of the University of Minnesota. He ran the first court in Minneapolis in an old government grist mill at St. Anthony Falls.

In 1854 at Minnesota's first agricultural fair, Meeker gave a "high-sounding" address "typical of the day." He was a member of the constitutional convention of 1857, and Meeker County was named for him. He engaged in real estate and owned a large tract of land in the Twin Cities along the Mississippi River. He wrote promotional pamphlets like this one on the Pacific railroad, and the one reprinted in 7:M3 on the overland mail route. "He was a queer genius in his way." He died suddenly in Milwaukee on a trip east. (Minnesota Historical Society 1898, 1920, 1941; Holcombe 1908.)

Highlights   Navy Commander Matthew F. Maury, Superintendent of the National Observatory, was another who favored more than one Pacific railroad at this time. He had promoted the railroad since 1849 (Perspective L). He brought forth the first textbook on oceanography in 1855. In 1860 he presented a unique oceanographic argument for having both northern and southern railroad routes (Curtis 1860, Taylor 1860). He pointed out that the fastest outward commercial shipping to China must take advantage of the trade winds blowing westward from San Diego. The fastest return, however, must be by the "brave west winds" blowing eastward to Puget Sound. Maury thought that the most efficient use of these wind patterns would require railroad termini at both coastal points.

Legacy   Meeker's effort probably had no national impact whatsoever. But it stands as a type example of sectional boosterism. Every city up and down the Mississippi aspired to be the starting point for a Pacific railroad.

REFERENCES
(See Preface for Heading references not listed here.)

Curtis, Samuel R., 1860 (June 19 reprint with map), Reports of the majority and minority of the Select Committee on the Pacific railroad: Wash., 36/1 H428 Report, serial 1069, 72 p.; Maury's letter 48-55.

Holcombe, Return I., 1908, Minnesota in three centuries: Mankato MN, 2:428 biography.

Maury, Matthew F., 1855 (1856 new edition), The physical geography of the sea: N.Y., 348 p., 13 plates.

Minnesota Historical Society, 1898, Collections: St. Paul, 8:69, quote on queer genius 8:99.

Minnesota Historical Society, 1920, Collections: St. Paul, 17:338.

Minnesota Historical Society, 1941, Minnesota History: St. Paul, quote on high-sounding 22:252.

Taylor, James W., 1860, Northwest British America and its relations to the State of Minnesota: St. Paul, 54 p.; Maury's letter 42-47.

PACIFIC RAILROAD.

GENERAL VIEW OF THE SUBJECT.

Since a distinguished capitalist of New York, some 18 years ago, first broached the question of a Railway communication with the Pacific Ocean, it has never ceased to be a matter of vital interest to the American people. Press, Politicians, Legislatures, State and National, have canvassed and discussed the measure till all sections and parties, however different and differing in other respects, acknowledge its importance and concede its necessity. To protect our cities and settlements on a distance coast of more than 1600 miles in length—to defend our borders along our Northern and Southern co-terminous boundaries with foreign nations, as well as our vast Western interior—to develope the dormant wealth of our mineral regions of almost limitless extent and but little known—to facilitate foreign and internal commerce and the Postal service of the nation—are among the leading objects of this Great Continental Work. But there is a moral necessity for it of no less urgency and demand. We need some mighty enterprise worthy our unparalleled career as a nation, to engage our energies and attention. Our country is vast and our people restless. We are at peace with the world and conquest is not our mission. If war does not employ us, the arts of peace must, or we shall degenerate into a nation of political scramblers and skirmishers. Factions will assume the place of parties, and demagogues that of statesmen, till the Government and its revenues are used for no [p. 4] other purpose than to mete out rewards and punishments as they alternate in the hands of contending leaders. It is already a subject of serious doubt whether our system is capable of carrying out the will of the nation in aiding to construct a work of such vast and varied utility—such a bond of union—such a monument of wisdom and patriotism, as a Pacific Railroad.

Several causes have conspired to delay this great work in spite of its popularity with the people. One is the constitutional scruples entertained in reference to it by what is called the States-rights party. They have feared that such a thoroughfare built by the General Government, and traversing a number of States and Territories soon to become States, might be invasive of their sovereignty, and for that reason, if no other, might be unconstitutional and unauthorized. Others again, and they not a few in number, could find no provision in the Constitution to justify Congress in incorporating a Pacific Railroad Company; and though they deemed the measure important to the Union and our defence as a nation, they considered an amendment to the Constitution necessary before they could sanction the measure. Until 1856, the leading spirits and politicians of the whole

South were opposed to it for one or the other of these reasons. Northern men, too, were afraid of committing themselves upon the subject for fear of offending the jealous advocates of States-rights in the South. President Taylor was the first Chief Magistrate that ever officially broke ground in its favor, from which time to the present, though more or less before each successive Congress, it has not as yet reached a legal or practical form.

Sectional interest, too, has had its full share of influence to defer efficient action. The friends of the Northern, Southern and Central Routes could never be prevailed upon to surrender the claims of their respective sections. It is believed that the following plan, respectfully submitted to the public, avoids all these difficulties and objections.

ROUTES.

When the subject first seriously engaged the attention of Congress, three Routes were proposed, and an appropriation [p. 5] was made for three surveys—the Northern, Central and Southern. If it is for Military purposes, and purposes of National defence merely, that justifies the aid of the Government, the extreme Northern and the extreme Southern certainly have the best claim to assistance; for though along the Central are a few weak and detached bands of Indians that need looking after, along the *Northern* and along the *Southern* are the most powerful and warlike nations on the Continent, many of whom have never known nor felt the yoke of subjugation, and who will always be the more dangerous because of their proximity to foreign nations, that might at any time incite them to hostility or war. In the event of a conflict with Mexico, who does not know that she could easily confederate with all the bands in her neighborhood in an effort to burn or plunder our settlements, or increase the annoyance to our people, who have never enjoyed a day's repose from their incursions since we acquired the territory? Nor should it be forgotten, that during the last war with Great Britain, the border Indians of the North-west were a more determined and terrible foe than the royal troops themselves. Along the proposed Northern Route, we now have the Chippewas, the Sioux, the Blackfeet, the Flat-heads, not to mention other numerous and hostile tribes in Oregon and Washington. In the event of another war with England, these natives, not over friendly even at *this* time, could be easily spirited to hostilities against our pioneer settlements, long before relief could be afforded in that distant region without a Railroad.

Besides, the Northern is by far the shortest route, and communicates directly with two rising States on the Pacific, each of which might claim as much consideration at the hands of Government as California, that has hitherto enjoyed a monopoly of postal service, and a precedence in every thing in that distant region of the Republic. In the event of future wars with Maritime Powers, would San Francisco be the only point exposed to foreign Navies? What would be the fate of the rising towns and cities clustering around the mouth of the Columbia, and the splendid harbors of Puget's Sound, more than 800 miles distant and perfectly inaccessible by land, if we could concentrate our military force *only* at the former place? These [p. 6] last named cities are within *hearing* of British cannon *already* mounted, and within four hour's sail of the British Navy, that, like the mystic sword, guards, day and night, the growing power of England on the North-west coast of this Continent. If the aid of our Government is to be invoked to construct military defences by building a Pacific Railroad, surely, all other things equal, it should be built in that direction whence we have reason to expect the first alarm and the greatest danger.

But Congress has the power by express grant, and it is a duty which it owes to the whole country to establish Post Offices and *Post Roads* wherever they are needed. This grant has been construed by commentators on the Constitution, and especially by the late Justice Story, the ablest of them all, to carry with it the power not only to repair, but also to construct or build Roads in any of the States or Territories over which to transport the public mails. It would seem that in our efforts to accommodate the Mail service to the reasonable wants of the people, the great North-west, including Oregon and Washington, have been too much overlooked in the extraordinary efforts of our Government, by land and by ocean, to reach the Golden Gate. The correspondence and intercourse of the people of Oregon and Washington are primarily with the States in the same latitude from which they emigrated, and the means for carrying it on should be, if practicable, direct; yet not a dollar has ever been expended to connect, in this respect, the Great Lake Valley and North-west with their neighbors across the mountains, whilst millions have been expended without the limits of our own country and millions more within, to get the mail to California. If it is to facilitate the Mail service of the Nation, as well as to aid in its defence, that Congress is authorized to aid in this great work, why overlook two-thirds of our possessions on the Pacific coast and the entire North-west?

The great argument, however, in favor of the constitutionality of this measure is the control surrendered by the people to the General Government over the commerce of the Nation, both foreign and international. To regulate and facilitate this leading interest, is one of its principal duties. The greatest commercial facilities, thoroughfares, and centres, the world round, are in a line with the proposed Northern Route. The [p. 7] maritime experience that mans and supplies the navies, the capital and shipping that controls and carries on the commerce of the Nations, are found in the same latitude; and, as if God and nature designed to favor this above other routes, the best harbors of the world are placed on its two extremes—New York, Boston, Portland and Halifax on the east, and the deep and well protected bays with which Puget's Sound is indented. The commerce of our Great Lakes, too, which with their navigable outlets by rivers, canals and gulf to the Atlantic, stretch along our Northern boundary more than half across the continent in the direction of Puget's Sound, is more than our entire foreign trade. Just south of this line and parallel with it, four Grand Trunk Railroads, in the *same direction*, have already been constructed to the Mississippi, and some of them beyond, from Portland, Boston, New York and Philadelphia, respectively, at an expense, too, that would have more than built one through to the Pacific. It should also be borne in mind that this chain of inland seas along our northern borders and the capacious ports around Puget's Sound lie on the same parallel of latitude with the great Ocean road of America to Europe and Europe to America—on the track that the commerce of the world has beaten for ages, and that the further south or the further north you diverge from this line, the greater will be the detour you make from this highway of nations. Can this Route therefore be overlooked altogether in providing for others? Can a work intended to be as lasting as our government, and as comprehensive as the wants of this great nation, be contracted to a Central or to a Northern or a Southern Route? Shall local or sectional interests be *permitted* to influence the Representatives of the American people in the construction of a system of military defences, postal facilities, and commercial intercourse, intended to be co-extensive with our existence as a nation? Least of all, would it be wise in Congress to delegate to interested parties, corporators, or grantees, the important duty of locating these roads, or their termini, or to embarrass a work that should be open to the free competition of the labor and capital of the nation, by conferring exclusive privileges on a few?

No one company in America or Europe is or *can* be equal to [p. 8] such a task, whether one, two or three roads are authorized. In any event, it will be a work of years, and the plan adopted should be such as to invite and interest hundreds or even thousands of companies, and armies of laborers to shorten the period of construction, by competition, and rivalry. To inaugurate the work as soon as possible, and to satisfy contending sections, three routes, a Northern, Central, and Southern, will have to be equally favored, as they seem to be equally necessary. Can three greater monuments of American power, progress, or prosperity, be devised?

It would facilitate emigration, Northern, Southern and Central—thus strengthening the three sections equally. All know that emigration has certain laws which, in the history of this continent, it has rarely ever departed from. One of these is, it uniformly follows its native latitudes. Three roads would just accommodate this natural propensity of our people in their migrations from the old States westward. Northern people would pour along the Northern route, Southern along the Southern, whilst those from the Middle States would incline to keep the Central. The effect of this would be to form and to preserve a proper balance in the population and settlement of a common Territory. It would do more. It would be a grand and glorious compromise, doing more to banish sectional animosity and restore harmony than all other measures that were ever devised by the patriots and peace makers of the Union; *whilst any plan less than this, should it ever be successful, would only widen the breach, and aggravate the evils of discord and dissension.*

CAN THE GOVERNMENT, AS SUCH, BUILD AND OPERATE THESE ROADS?

Conceding for the sake of argument that there is no difference in the routes, and that one would be as cheap and as practicable as the other, a preliminary question of the highest importance should be well considered. Shall the Federal Government, or shall corporations independent of the Government, build *the* road or roads? A mistake in this respect might be worse than fatal—it might not only be destructive of the measure as now contemplated, but by disastrous delays and wrang-[p. 9] lings discourage and dishearten our people from ever hoping so grand a consummation.

Were our Government more or less despotic than it is, we might expect better results from its participation in this great work. An ALEXANDER, a CAESAR, a NAPOLEON, at the head of such a Republic as ours, and as far removed from foreign wars as we are, would not hesitate to address himself to this National work with all the energy, power, and resources of the country whose destinies he ruled. The defence along our Northern and Southern borders, which it would constitute, and which would be more effectual than a Chinese wall, as it would certainly be cheaper, the cement and consolidation of the Empire, and the fame of achieving such a monument in one's lifetime, would be sufficient motive for a great and patriotic ruler, whose soul was animated and ennobled with the love of true glory. The first of Romans—the world's greatest man—the noble CAESAR, when he had become Master of an Empire which was only fit to be his slave, literally planned a similar scheme to tie and hold together the distant members of that mighty Republic. There is some advantage in having one mind to direct, one soul to animate, and one heart to encourage such a noble enterprise. The grand results would be order, energy, economy, and success. On the other hand, when the people are yet free—free from the despotism of faction and demagoguery—the meanest and most corrupt of all tyrannnies, lasting monuments of National glory and utility like this have, in better times, been achieved under the care and direction of Government itself. But in the present degenerate and demoralized condition of parties that alternately administer our Government, State and Federal, with hardly any aims in view above the spoils of place, no one at all acquainted with affairs should wish to see committed to unscrupulous partisans this great National charge. Like Postmasters, Custom House Officers, Land Officers, Indian Agents, and all that innumerable fry of place-holders, from the head of a Department to the tipstaff of a Court, the hosts of governmental employees on such a National work would hold their trusts as they would hold their souls— pledged to the faction in power. Each change of National Ad-[p. 10] ministration would be followed by a change of employees. There would be no such thing as pecuniary responsibility to guard the nation's treasure or to guaranty fidelity and efficiency. *Political* would be all the accountability expected on the one hand or demanded on the other. But the worst of all, the work would never be finished, and if it *were,* it could not be operated successfully, nor kept in repair by the Government. One has only to turn to the manner in which public works are carried on around him, in any town, city, or State, for demonstration and proof of all that is here said. The abuse of public confidence in every shape, involving pecuniary trust, is the flagrant sin of the times, and from the just apprehensions of which, neither Church nor State, in any of their departments, is exempt. Should the Government, as such, undertake to build a pacific Railroad, all the Nation could surely promise itself would be the certain loss of its treasure, and the ultimate failure and abandonment of the measure.

Nor should Congress charter or incorporate any Pacific Railroad *Company.* If it create it, it must control it; and if it control it, it will assume powers dangerous to the States that in future years will grow up along the line. A law of that kind might be as unconstitutional as it was claimed the old United States Bank was, and far more likely to be used for political and partisan purposes. One was limited in its duration, the other is to be perpetual. Will the jealous advocates of State rights sanction such a law?

PLAN FOR BUILDING THESE ROADS.

What then should Congress do, and how aid in this great national work? I answer by repeating that for military, commercial, and postal purposes, it should favor a Northern, Southern, and Central route, and should indicate the line and fix the principal points to be touched or reached by each. It should then make provisional grants of land and money to individuals or companies, to be vested or paid on the completion of sections or portions of one hundred miles each of the roads. Suppose Congress afford pecuniary aid to the amount of $30,000 and land at the rate of forty alternate sections for each mile finished [p. 11] and in runing [*sic*] order. From the western boundary of Minnesota to Olympia on Puget's Sound is 1500 miles. The pecuniary cost of the Government for the construction of the entire road would be $45,000,000, and 38,000,000 acres, now and forever worthless to the Nation till the road is built. From the western limits of Missouri to the eastern boundary of California may be about 2,000 miles. With the same aid to the Central route, this road would cost in money $60,000,000, and in land 51,200,000 acres, likewise of no available worth to the Government before the road is completed. What is said here of the Central may be fairly applied to the extreme Southern route from the western borders of Texas to the eastern confines of the gold-digging State, making an aggregate of only $165,000,000, less than the probable cost for the next twenty years arising from Indian wars and wars to protect or defend our borders which these very roads would prevent or render unnecessary.

How should the work, then, be undertaken and made to progress?

Let the States and Territories traversed by these several routes charter companies, or pass a general Railroad Law, under which sections, or so much of the Pacific Road located by Congress as falls within the State or Territorial jurisdiction, can be built. Let these companies or corporations undertake for the compensation offered to build a portion of any of the three roads, and at any point or points they may elect to begin at, provided they have no aid from Congress till at least one hundred miles are completed, and so on as often as one hundred are finished and equipped.

This would preserve the rights and independence of the States by making them sovereigns over the soil or territory within their limits, and prevent the assumption of a colossal power on the part of the Central Government. It would create a competition among all the States and Territories along the line to hasten on the work through their respective limits, even by resorting to additional aid by taxing themselves that they might be the first to enjoy the benefit of this great thoroughfare. More than all this, cities and States beyond the im-[p. 12]mediate reach of these roads might, under this plan, be moved to a patriotic rivalry in one of the greatest works of this or any other age of the world. The city of St. Louis and State of Missouri might deem it their interest to push forward the Central Road to Pike's Peak a little faster than the bonus offered by Congress would take it, and therefore might donate, or take stock in aid of a company to the amount of $1,000,000. Other States and cities more interested in the other routes, might do the same. In the same way the South might enter into a competition with the North, and the North with the South, and both find a glorious field for their enterprise and a glorious reward for their labor.

It may be said by some that the Government ought not to aid in the construction of several chapters of these roads, situated, it may be, for years remotely from each other. Companies would, of course, build those sections first that would pay best when built. If there should be a departure from this rule, it would be in favor of those that could be constructed the cheapest. But there could not be one hundred miles of continuous railroad on any of these routes that would not be of great service to the Government in a military, commercial, or postal point of view. One hundred miles of continuous railroad pointing east and west on the Rocky Mountains, even a thousand miles from any road of the kind would be a *National* road, and *needed* by the Nation. But this is the way all of our great lines of railway have been built. We can travel from Bangor to New Orleans now by railroad, a greater length of railway than any of the three routes to the Pacific. Some of the roads that help to make this great thoroughfare were built years before it was dreamed a man would ever travel by railroads from Maine to Louisiana. But by many companies working on different and distant sections, some building fifty, some an hundred miles, rarely more than that by any one, each gap has been closed, completely revolutionizing the travel and trade of the country.

The advantages of this plan can be seen at a glance.

1. By favoring three routes, all opposition in Congress of a sectional character will be at once removed.

2. By Government's affording, on certain conditions, aid to [p. 13] companies chartered or to be chartered by States and Territories traversed by the Roads, it but follows precedents heretofore established in granting lands to States and incorporations in aid of State improvements, thereby relieving itself from constitutional embarrassments that would grow out of a direct participation in the works themselves.

3. It saves the rights of the States against Federal encroachments, by leaving the companies responsible to the States and Territories within whose limits they operate, subject only to such conditions and impositions as Congress may justly create to guaranty the transportation of the public mail, military stores, &c.

4. This plan makes the bonus in land or money to be advanced by the United States constitutionally as available in States as in the Territories.

5. As soon as the routes are surveyed, fixed, and marked along the lines, the

State and Territorial Legislatures will charter companies numerous enough to take every section of a hundred miles, from one extreme of the route to the other; and the interest, energy, and competition which a law embodying these views would stimulate, would fill up every gap not at first taken, from Missouri to California, and it would hardly be visionary to suppose that in less than eighteen months one could travel from St. Louis to San Francisco, and not be out of sight of operatives on the Central route one day during his journey. The other routes, if equally feasible, would be pushed with the same zeal and interest. Who that is acquainted with the northwest does not know that with the aid herein assured, the first segment of the Northern Pacific from the head of Lake Superior to the Mississippi, a distance of less than 100 miles would be finished and in running order in two years from the date of such an act of Congress, thereby uniting the two mighty valleys of this continent? And if this should be all that would ever be done on the Northern route, it would be all the Government would have to advance aid for; whilst for military, postal, and commercial purposes, it would be of more service to the United States than any other hundred miles of all three routes.

6. This plan gives *all*—individuals, companies, towns, cities, [p. 14] States, and Sections—a chance to lend a helping hand to construct these iron bonds of Union, and to erect the most enduring monument to American glory. It looks to a speedy commencement in good *faith* and successful prosecution of the greatest work of this or any other age or country, instead of frittering away ten or fifteen years more in transferring, assigning, and trading in privileges, and dickering in stocks, which would naturally follow the incorporation by Congress of a company of distant and scattered speculators who would never live to *finish* if they even *began* the work.

7. It guards the National Treasury by withholding any aid till the Government has received a substantial benefit, to wit: the construction of one hundred miles on the line and at the guage [*sic*] which it may prescribe, and the execution of ample assurances by each company to convey the mail, transport the public stores, army, &c., at prices not to exceed the charges of other railroads for similar services, till the advancements are extinguished.

8. Should either Route, as the work progresses by this plan, be found, on experience, impracticable, the further prosecution of it can be at once abandoned, without any loss to the Government, or injury to any company. It will be an acquisition to the Government as far as it goes, useful to its postal and military service, and needed by the public. No company would be apt to build 100 miles of Railroad anywhere, even for the bonus offered, did it not promise remuneration to

own and operate it afterwards. A Railroad from Missouri to Pike's Peak, or from the head of Lake Superior to the Mississippi river, would in every sense be a national thoroughfare. In the meantime, if the extreme Northern or the extreme Southern Route should finally be abandoned by reason of its impracticability, capital and labor of both sections would speedily fall to the Central without a murmur or a complaint that they had been neglected.

BILL.

Be it enacted by the Senate and House of Representatives of the United States of America in Congress assembled: That it shall be the duty of the President of the United States, on the [p. 15] passage of this act, to cause three Railroad Routes to be surveyed and marked; one from or near the head of Lake Superior to some point on Puget's Sound, or near the mouth of the Columbia river, on the Pacific Ocean; one from ———, on the western boundary of the State of Missouri, to — ———, in California, and a third from ———, in Texas, to San Diego.

SEC. 2. *And be it further enacted,* That there be, and are hereby granted and guaranteed to any Company or Companies, chartered, or to be chartered, by any State or Territory, traversed by said Routes, when surveyed and fixed, the right of way through the public lands, the sum of ——— thousand dollars, and every alternate section of land, designated by even numbers, for ——— sections in width, on each side of any of said roads for each mile of Railroad finished; provided, that said right of way, title to said lands, and said money shall not vest, nor be paid, nor secured, till the Company shall have finished and equipped, one hundred miles of continuous Railroad on any of said routes or lines as surveyed, and marked by the United States, and with a guage of——— feet, which shall be the guage, on each of said routes, and of each segment or section thereof: and so on, and at that rate, and on the same terms, as often as any Company so chartered, shall finish and equip a hundred miles of continuous Railroad, at any point on any of said lines; Provided further, that said right of way, land and money shall not vest, nor be paid before each segment of one hundred miles shall be approved by either the War or Post Office Department, and the Company building the same shall have executed bond to the U. States, with adequate security, faithfully to operate and keep in repair said hundred miles of Railroad, and to transport the Indian annuities, the army and forces of the United States, public stores and mail, at rates not to exceed the charges of other roads of the same class, which charges shall be accredited to the Company or Companies, and be applied in payment of the advancement in money or scrip made by the United States to aid said roads through to the Pacific.

David Fergusson, 1863

Route Between Tucson And Lobos Bay

Washington, 38 ["37"] Special Session S1, serial 1174, March 14, 1863, 22 p., 3
maps. [WC and WCB 387; Eberstadt 120:86; Graff 1306; Howes F87;
Wheat Transmiss. 5:map 1042; NUC NU 0262614.]
Reset verbatim from compiler's original.

Significance   This richly informative report revealed much about the lands
and resources of northern Sonora in the 1860s. Maj. Fergusson provided worthy
data on the possibilities for obtaining supplies in Sonora and transporting them
by wagon or future railroad to U.S. troops in Arizona. He carefully noted topography, roadbeds and distances, climate, water, grass, wood, crops, cattle and sheep,
prices, mines, town populations, mills and stores, harbor water depths, and key
inhabitants and their occupations. He made all of these observations in a month.
He benefited from some excellent maps made by a Mexican scientific commission. Yet he modestly apologized for his report: "All is crude and undigested, principally for want of talent in this line, and for want of time, instruments, &c."
Nevertheless, the quality of his work exceeded that of many professional military
explorers.

The Mexican Congress had granted permission in June, 1861, for the U.S.
army to investigate this supply route (Hunt 1958). The subsequent presence of
French troops in Mexico complicated the issue, but the town officials in Sonora
aided Fergusson graciously in every way. They appeared to feel that cooperation
would be to their ultimate economic benefit.

This apparently is the first reprint.

Author   DAVID FERGUSSON, soldier. At the outbreak of Civil War, Fergusson
became a major in the First California Volunteer Cavalry. He was part of the
2,500-man California Column that moved in stages under Gen. James H. Carleton from Los Angeles to New Mexico. In late 1861 Fergusson was posted near
Warner's Ranch, now Warner Springs, where he tried to prevent secessionists
from causing trouble or going east. In early 1862 he moved to San Bernardino,

where he found the majority of citizens to be treasonous and a danger to the few unionists. Then he went to Los Angeles to prepare for marching east. Carleton, who managed every detail, admonished that "The horses must be kept fresh and in good condition, even though the men must walk most of the way." Fergusson tried to get two trumpets before he left for Tucson: "They are indispensable."

In June, 1862, Carleton sent Fergusson as chief commissary to Magdalena, Sonora, "to ascertain the resources in the way of forage and subsistence…Cultivate with them [the people] such feelings of kindness and good neighborhood as shall show to them that we are friends who wish to deal honorably and frankly and pay fairly for what we get." Fergusson's report listed all the towns and crops; he bought all the flour in sight, even though prices kept going up. In July he was placed in command of western Arizona, with headquarters in Tucson. In September Carleton commended Fergusson for his "most arduous" services and ordered him on the survey from Tucson to Lobos Bay that is outlined in the Itinerary. (War of the Rebellion 1897.)

Fergusson was on his survey to Lobos Bay from October 10 to November 22, 1862. He finished his report back in Tucson and moved on to Mesilla, New Mexico, "crippled with lumbago and rheumatism" (p. 13 of report). He made a map and census of Tucson before he left, and measured 261.87 miles from there to Mesilla (Hunt 1958). In 1863 he was promoted to colonel of a battalion but was soon "dismissed for leaving his post" (Bancroft 24:469).

Itinerary, 1862   FERGUSSON, TUCSON TO PUERTO LIBERTAD, VIA ARIVACA, SASABE, AND ALTAR. October 10—With an escort of 17 men of the First Volunteer Cavalry under Lt. C. P. Nichols (Nicolas?), plus interpreter and surveyor J. B. Mills, Maj. Fergusson leaves Tucson. They have at least two wagons and carry along a boat frame. The route goes south-southwest past abandoned ranches and the mining town of Arivaca AZ, deserted because of Apaches. Fergusson keeps careful track of water, grass, wood, and topography. Except for a few vaqueros and their families, this route has no settlements until Altar, Sonora, reached October 15. Altar and vicinity hold about 2,000 people on the Altar River, which is "only an insignificant rivulet." The inhabitants here and at all other towns receive Fergusson cordially. Judge Miguel Zepeda goes with the party through the town of Pitiquito, population 1,200, to Puerto Libertad on the Gulf of California, October 20. Zepeda owns the only building, a dilapidated warehouse, in the platted but otherwise empty townsite.

Fergusson travels 225 miles in 11 days at 20 miles per day. He sets up his boat and takes soundings in the harbor. Mills triangulates the landmarks. They later trace fine maps of Libertad and Lobos made by a Mexican scientific commission headed by Thomas Robinson of Guaymas. The absence of grass at Libertad forces a return to Pitiquito, October 25-27. Thence via Caborca they return to the Gulf at Puerto Lobos, which is 30 miles north of Libertad. Antonio Ramirez of Caborca is an excellent guide. Lobos has no water, so they stay only a few hours.

Itinerary, 1862   FERGUSSON, PUERTO LOBOS TO TUCSON VIA CABORCA, ALTAR, SERIC, AND ARIVACA. November 1—Fergusson leaves Puerto Lobos and reaches Caborca on the 3d. Its 800 people engage in agriculture and mining. Fergusson follows the Altar River east through the towns of Pitiquito and Altar, and on north-northeast to Oquitoa, El Atil, and Saric (populations 500, 100, and 500, respectively). Thence he goes to Arivaca and retraces his outward path to reach Tucson on November 11. On his return he goes 215 miles in 11 days at 20 miles per day.

Fergusson's itinerary tables contain two confusing mileage entries. The "43.62" for October 31 on his page 18 should read 0.99, including which the cumulated subtotal is 43.62 miles. Similarly, the "39.49" for November 8 on his page 21 is a cumulated subtotal down to and including the 1.27 listed above. In all itineraries, the final cumulated grand totals are correct.

Highlights   Francisco de Ulloa sailed to the head of the Gulf of California in 1539. The next year Hernando de Alarcon did the same and entered the lower Colorado River. Juan de Oñate arrived at the mouth of the Colorado by land in 1605. Maps showed the Gulf correctly until the 1650s, when California appeared as an island on some influential charts. By 1700 the island fantasy was the ruling hypothesis. (Wagner 1937.)

The first European to visit the coast of the Gulf of California near Caborca was Father Eusebio Francisco Kino in 1692. He established the mission in Caborca in 1694. In 1701 and 1702 he explored the mouth of the Colorado and the head of the Gulf. In his map of 1705 and his Relation of 1710 he laid to rest the idea that California was an island. (Bolton 1908.)

Alexander Humboldt's great 1804 map of New Spain showed the towns of Caborca, Pitiquito, Altar, Oquitoa, El Atil ("Ati"), Tubutama, and Saric.

Lt. Robert W. H. Hardy, formerly of the Royal Navy, explored both coasts of the Gulf of California in 1826, looking for pearls. He made the first modern map of the Colorado River up to the mouth of the Gila. He found available charts north of Tiburon Island in the Gulf to be inadequate. He went ashore near Libertad, but the land was parched.

The 1849 book of Escudero on Sonora and Sinaloa contains nothing on the Libertad-Lobos area.

Andrew B. Gray with the Texas Western Railroad Company surveyed a route for a southern Pacific line from San Antonio to San Diego, January to June, 1854. He was another Southerner who envisioned branch tracks to Sonora, "toward Guaymas or to the harbor of Tiberon." He noted, "From Altar to the Gulf of California, where there is represented to be a good harbor, it is 55 miles." Gray went from Altar 100 miles northwest to Sonoita and thence 60 miles west-southwest to Adair Bay on the Gulf. Named by Hardy, Adair Bay had mud flats unpromising for a harbor. The local Papagos rotted their teeth on the roots they ate.

In 1861 mining engineer Raphael Pumpelly and Charles D. Poston (3:F10) made a desperate escape from Arivaca. The army had pulled out its regulars to serve elsewhere in the Civil War. The Apaches and bandits raged unabated. Pumpelly's account of their incredibly dangerous journey to Los Angeles through Caborca and Yuma is one of the classics of Western adventure. They were headed for Lobos Bay, but the expected vessel did not come. Pumpelly observed that Fergusson considered Libertad to be a good port.

In 1864 Sylvester Mowry announced that "A new port, La Libertad...has been opened, giving an immediate outlet to the valuable district of Altar and northeastern Sonora, and to Arizona." Mowry was a Northerner and a West Point graduate, but as a mine operator in Arizona surrounded by Southerners, he opportunistically leaned toward the South during the Civil War. He favored the southern Pacific railroad and stated flatly, "The first terminus of the Pacific railroad will be Guaymas, on the Gulf of California." He added, "A liberal grant has been made by the Legislature of Sonora to an Eastern company...for the right of way of a railroad from Guaymas to El Paso, to connect with the Southern Pacific Railroad."

Mowry hated Apaches: "There is only one way to wage war against the Apaches. A steady, persistent campaign must be made, following them to their haunts...They must be surrounded, starved into coming in, surprised or inveigled—by white flags, or any other method, human or divine—and then put to death. If these ideas shock any weak-minded individual who thinks himself a philanthropist, I can only say that I pity without respecting his mistaken sympathy. A man might as well have sympathy for a rattlesnake or a tiger." Pumpelly quoted this passage and fired back: "If it is said that the Indians are treacherous and cruel, scalping and torturing their prisoners, it may be answered that there is no treachery and no cruelty left unemployed by the whites. Poisoning with strychnine, the wilful dissemination of small-pox, and the possession of bridles, braided from the hair of scalped victims and decorated with teeth knocked from the jaws of living women—these are heroic facts among many of our frontiers-men."

Legacy Gen. James H. Carleton ordered this reconnaissance with the long-range view of forestalling the seizure of Sonora by the Confederacy. Crabb had wanted to add it by force to the slave states in 1857, and Cram urged its purchase in 1858 (L9). In 1863 William M. Gwin was actively scheming to exploit the mines of Sonora by settling Southerners there (L3). Carleton favored its purchase by the Union. None of these efforts came to fruition. After the Civil War a few ex-Confederates tried to scratch out a living on Sonora's fields, but they gave up after a year (Monaghan 1955). As noted in L9, the Atchison, Topeka and Santa Fe completed a link from Arizona to Guaymas via the Sonora Railway in 1882.

REFERENCES
(See Preface for Heading references and for Bancroft, not listed here.)

Bolton, Herbert E., 1908 (1976 reprint), Spanish exploration in the Southwest 1542-1706: N.Y., p. 429, 441-45.

Escudero, Jose A. de, 1849, Sonora y Sinaloa: Mexico City, 148 p.

Gray, Andrew B., 1856 (1963 reprint), The A. B. Gray report: Los Angeles, 240 p.; quotes on Altar 85, Guaymas 119, Adair Bay 88-89, 219-20.

Hardy, Robert W. H., 1829, Travels in the interior of Mexico 1825-28: London, p. 293, 304; maps at front and 320.

Humboldt, Alexander von, 1804 map (1814 reprint), in Political essay on the Kingdom of New Spain: London, map in vol. 1 of 4.

Hunt, Aurora, 1958, Major General James Henry Carleton: Glendale, p. 237.

Monaghan, Jay, 1955 (1984 reprint), Civil War on the Western border 1854-65: Lincoln, p. 348.

Mowry, Sylvester, 1864 3d ed., Arizona and Sonora: N.Y., 251 p.; quotes on first terminus 52, Apaches 68, Libertad and Guaymas-El Paso railroad 92.

Pumpelly, Raphael, 1870, Across America and Asia: N.Y., p. 1-67, Libertad 31; quote on cruelties 34.

Wagner, Henry R., 1937 (1968 reprint), Cartography of the Northwest Coast of America to 1800: Amsterdam, 543 p.; Ulloa 20-21, Alarcon 30-35, CA island 127-29 and 144-47.

War of the Rebellion, 1897, Operations on the Pacific: Wash., Part 1, p. 92, 115, 748, 762, 840, 877, 945; Magdalena report 1159-62; quotes on arduous 104, horses 1019, trumpets 1024, Magdalena orders 1133.

LETTER

OF

THE SECRETARY OF WAR,

COMMUNICATING,

In answer to a resolution of the Senate, a copy of the report of Major D. Fergusson on the country, its resources, and the routes between Tucson and Lobos Bay.

MARCH 14, 1863.—Read and ordered that 2,200 extra copies be printed—2,000 for the use of the Senate and 200 for the use of the governor of Arizona.

WAR DEPARTMENT,
Washington City, March 14, 1863.

SIR: In compliance with the resolution of the Senate of the 11th instant, I have the honor to transit herewith a copy of the report of Major D. Fergusson on the country, its resources, and the route between Tucson and Lobos bay.

I am, sir, very respectfully, your obedient servant,

EDWIN M. STANTON,
Secretary of War.

The PRESIDENT OF THE SENATE

Headquarters Department of New Mexico,
Santa Fé, New Mexico, February 1, 1863.

GENERAL: I have the honor to herewith enclose the report of Major David Fergusson, 1st cavalry California volunteers, whom I ordered to make a survey of port Lobos and Libertad, on the gulf of California. This is a report of great importance, as showing how much cheaper supplies can be gotten for Arizona and the Mesilla valley, *via* Libertad, than from Indianola, Texas, or from Kansas City. The report is of still greater importance when considered with reference to the political and commercial geography of our country. It shows how practicable it is to make a railroad from the Rio Grande to the gulf of California and thus to the Pacific. It shows why the southern confederacy wish to hold the Territory of Arizona and wish to have a part of the State of Sonora. It shows how very important it is for us to purchase from Mexico, before it becomes a possession of, say,

France, a strip of territory which will give us so fine and accessible a port on the gulf of California.

When the vast mineral resources of Arizona and of the Pinos Altos region have become better known, (and not one year will pass away before their import-[p. 2] ance will be appreciated,) then the government will see that a port on the gulf of California should be ours, at any cost.

I am, general, very respectfully,

JAMES H. CARLETON,
Brigadier General Commanding.

Brigadier General LORENZO THOMAS,
Adjutant General United States Army, Washington, D.C.

MESILLA, ARIZONA, *December* 2, 1862.
SIR: On the 26th of September last I received instructions as follows:
"HEADQUARTERS DEPARTMENT OF THE PACIFIC,
July 26, 1862.

"General Carleton will send Major Fergusson, with a sufficient escort, to examine the country, its resources, and the *route* between Tucson and Lobos bay, (places known as Libertad,) *via* Arivaca and Altar or Caborca.

"By order of Brigadier General Wright.

"RICHARD C. DRUM,
"Assistant Adjutant General,"

Lieutenant J.F. BENNETT,
1st Infantry California Volunteers, Acting Assistant Adjutant General, Headquarters Column from California, Santa Fé, New Mexico.

(General Orders, No. 20.)
HEADQUARTERS DISTRICT OF ARIZONA,
Las Cruces, New Mexico, September 5, 1862.

*   *   *   *   *   *   *

Major Fergusson will proceed, *via* Arivaca and Altar or Cubave, without delay, to a point at or near Lobos bay, on the gulf of California, known as Libertad, and examine the intermediate country, with a view to the transportation of supplies He will ascertain the resources of the country on the route, also the availability of Lobos bay as a port where military supplies destined for Arizona may be landed. Major Fergusson will then repair in person to the headquarters of the district of Arizona, and make a report of his examination of the port of Lobos route to the general commanding the column from California.

*   *   *   *   *   *   *

By command of Brigadier General Carleton.

BENJAMIN C. CUTLER,
First Lieutenant 1st Infantry California Volunteers,
Acting Assistant Adjutant General.

There being no cavalry at the disposal of the commanding officer at Tucson for an escort, I was delayed until the 10th of October from proceeding to carry the above instructions into execution. On the afternoon of that day I started, with an escort of seventeen men of company "E," 1st cavalry California volunteers, commanded by First Lieutenant C.P. Nicolas, of the same regiment, *en route* to the port of La Libertad, *via* Arivaca, Altar, and Pitiquito, and arrived at La Libertad on the 20th of October. I append hereto an itinerary of the route. The distances were measured by an odometer, which I was fortunate enough to get the loan of from Mr. J.B. Mills, jr., interpreter to Lieutenant Nichols, commanding my escort, and acting assistant quartermaster thereof. [p. 3]

The port of La Libertad is not on that part of the gulf of California known as Lobos bay, but at a distance which I estimate to be about twenty (20) miles south of it. I enclose herewith traced copy of map of the "Ensenada de Los Lobos" so called, and the port of La Libertad, made by the scientific commission of which Don Thomas Robinson, of Guaymas, was chief.

Previous to obtaining or seeing the original map of the commission, by aid of a boat, the frame of which was got out in Tucson by mechanics of the quartermaster's department, and put together at La Libertad, I took soundings in the port, which are marked on the maps in red ink in feet. The figures indicate the depth at low water.

To Mr. J.B. Mills, jr, I am indebted for the triangulation of the bay, and for tracing the result, in red ink, on the map, time not permitting the making of an original, and, as the result of both surveys are so nearly alike, I did not consider an original map necessary. Where there is any difference in the soundings I have no hesitation in saying that the result of my own labors, marked in red ink, are as correct as circumstances and time would permit. Having arrived on the 20th, and the 21st, 22d, and part of the 23d of October being taken up in putting the boat together, I could not, considering the quantity of provisions and forage on hand, and the absence of grass, remain more than a day and a half longer to make soundings, reconnoitre the vicinity, &c.

Of the value of this ensenada of Libertad as a port no one who sees it can doubt. The soundings show a depth of water sufficient for vessels of any tonnage; the holding-ground is excellent, being generally of fine white sand and shell, at that part marked out on the map as "El Puerto de la Libertad," except where the ledges of rock are carefully laid down. These rocks are low, flat croppings of the bed-rock, and visible in the water in fair weather.

The bottom in the upper, or Cobode Lobos part of the bay, is sandy in parts, gravelley and pebbly in others, and near the shore composed of cobble-stones, gravel, pebbles and sand. The shore or beach is generally sandy, gravelly, and pebbly. The banks are low sandy loam, except the southern part, which consists of high bluffs of sand and shell of about a mile and a quarter in length, broken by ravines and gullies. From Point Kino to Cabo de Lobos the bay extends about 5 3/4 miles, and has a depth of about two miles near the centre; at Point Robinson a ledge of broken jagged rocks extends into the sea about 400 yards. The constant ripple at this place indicates the presence of rocks. By extending a mole or breakwater in the direction of these rocks four or five hundred yards, vessels could ride at anchor in the bay to the south with the greatest security in almost any storm.

The soundings on the map will show that the part of the bay between Point Robinson and Cabo de Lobos has deep water and a bold shore, where vessels may discharge within a few yards of the bank.

The beach is, in nearly all its extent, admirably adapted to beach vessels upon for repairs.

The rise and fall of the tides I cannot give an exact account of for want of time and instruments, but I think from nine to ten feet is a fair average. There is nothing on the beach to indicate heavy storms, surf or breakers. During my stay there the climate was delightful; the winds commencing very lightly in the mornings about four o'clock, from the east, changing gradually to the northwest, blowing a pleasant breeze from ten to one and then ceasing at sunset. The nights were cool but not chilly. I should judge, though I do not pretend to any nautical experience, that vessels may safely anchor in this bay and ride out any storm, except from the southwest, and even then unless it be unusually severe, when there is enough sea room to make sail and leave the bay, should it be necessary. What are termed the "Cordonazos," which take place in September, are the severest storms in the gulf, and then it is said the bay is comparatively smooth. [p. 4]

With the exception of San Diego and San Francisco, California has no harbor comparable to La Libertad.

The intended town of La Libertad is laid out on the shore, having the centre of the principal plaza about 400 yards back from the "pozo" or well, which latter is about fifty yards from the shore, at the rock called "La Piedra Parada."

This part of the bay is the best for landing goods at present. According to the observations of the scientific commission, above referred to, the centre of the plaza is in latitude 29°, 53', 47", 48''' north, and the longitude 112° 32', 45", 43''' west of Greenwich.

The port and town are surrounded by sierras of some height, between which and the sea there is an inclined plane, devoid of water or grass, and of a sterile, rather loose soil, bearing a growth of mesquite, torote, hediondilla, sahuaeo, pita-haya, ocuatilla, pallo-verde, pallo-fierro, &c. It is true that one of the ridges of sand, about four and a half miles to the south, (from the well,) near the beach, yields some "galleta" grass, but to no great extent from the absence of rain; but the dried-up remains of last year's growth were all that could be seen this season.

Fresh water is obtained in abundance in the well ("pozo") near the beach at "Piedra Parada," at a depth of twelve to fifteen feet; it is clear, pure, but warm. From the Piedra Parada, along the beach for about 250 yards, fresh water, of about a temperature of 98° Fahrenheit, issues from the sandy beach, to which wild animals come to drink at low water.

At La Piedra Parada, which is south 3° east from the "pozo," and about fifty feet long by forty feet wide and covered at high tide, there is a warm spring in which one can enjoy a luxurious warm bath. The water is fresh enough for drinking and cooking purposes, although it has a slightly mineral taste.

There is a house partially fallen down (the only one there) on Point Robinson, which was built by Don Miguel Zepeda, of Altar, for a warehouse. Last year ex-Governor Cubillos, of Sonora, shipped a quantity of copper ore from this port to England, in a vessel of over 1,000 tons burden.

The harbor is full of a great variety of fish, such as bass, mullet, sardines, flounders, rock-cod, shark, turtles, crabs, black-fish, gold-fish of a large size, &c. Clams and a species of oyster were also found. Very few shells were found on the beach; an evidence of the absence of storms, breakers, and surf.

The nearest settlements to the port are Caborca and Pitiquito. There is a deserted ranch belonging to one Don Fernando Cerna, about fifty miles from the port, situated about six miles to the south of the road, where there are two inexhaustible wells of water and an excellent grazing range.

Until wells are dug or water discovered on the road between Pitiquito and Libertad, each wagon should carry a barrel to contain about forty gallons of water; or trains of fifteen wagons have each a water-tank of 600 gallons capacity. This would avoid the necessity of going to the picu—four or five miles off the road—for water. Several parties are now, however, ready to sink wells, make dams, ("represas,") and settle on the road, provided the surplus for our troops are transported over this route. There will be no doubt or danger of scarcity of water in that event. The whole route from Tucson, with but short intervals excepted, can be settled by rancheros, and grain, hay, and other resources will be forthcoming in abundance when the occasion calls for them. The people and authorities along the route are alive to the advantages they can reap should this route be established.

Don Miguel Zepeda, judge of the first instance of the district of Altar, who accompanied me to Libertad, and who has an interest in its advancement, is compromised to obtain a supply of water by either a well or "represa" at La Angostura, thirty-five miles from La Libertad. Angostura is admirably adapted for a stock ranch, and with water enough much land could be cultivated and good hay cut every season. [p. 5]

In the way of timber there is nothing near Libertad, and none on the route nearer than Busani rancho, where there is considerable oak, ash, walnut, and cottonwood. The whole of the district of Altar is barren of good timber, with the exception of Busani, I am informed. However, I must except mesquite, which, in some parts, grows to quite a respectable size, and nearly all the lumber used in the district is of mesquite. Limestone of a very superior quality is found near La Libertad, and at all the settlements and pueblos on the Altar river. The sierras are said to be rich in minerals near the port; of this I can say nothing of my own knowledge.

There can be no agriculture nearer La Libertad than the Picu valley and the pass of the Angostura, twenty-four and thirty-five miles distant, respectively; and there only to a limited extent, except in very rainy seasons, or after abundance of water for irrigation is obtained from wells or artificial lakes. The whole country from Pitiquito to Picu in the valleys is good for grazing, and in the Bajio de Aquituni large crops can be raised without irrigation, the rains sufficing.

I transmit herewith a small map with the routes to La Libertad and Lobos and back, *via* the Altar river, traced thereon in red ink. A glance at the map will demonstrate that, in a geographic point of view, La Libertad or Lobos bay are the nearest ports to the northern districts of Sonora, all of Arizona, New Mexico, and parts of Texas and Chihuahua, and time will show that the routes are not only favorable in regard to distances, but in respect to superiority of roads and economy of time and means. From La Libertad to El Paso, *via* Tucson, the longest route, the distance is but, say 500 miles; from Indianola, Texas, to El Paso, the distance is 798½ miles; from Tucson to La Libertad, I can say with confidence that I never saw a better natural road for such a distance, or one more favorable for a railroad, so far as the topographical features of the country are concerned. Government surveys have shown the practicability of railroads from Tucson to La Mesilla, &c. From Los Paredones, *via* Pozo Verde and Fresnal, it is said, a more *level* route exists than from Tucson, *via* Arivaca, to Libertad. It is worth examination, for lately many discoveries of silver have been made at Fresnal, and the whole of the Baboquivari range is said to be rich in argentiferous galena ore; the country is covered with excellent grass, and at Fresnal and Pozo Verde water exists in great plenty. There is now a population of 500 Mexicans at Fresnal, mining for silver. There is great danger of these people ruining valuable leads, by their grasping and unprofessional mode of opening and working veins of metal. They yield no revenue to the government and are under no legal restraints; as foreign miners, it is but just they should at least pay the taxes usual in California. From the Pimo villages to Altar, *via* Los Paredones, there is a good hard level road.

On the 25th of October I left La Libertad on my return, having left the boat in a gulley near the beach and the "Pozo," partially filled with sand, and arrived at Pitiquito on the 27th of October. On the 28th I went to Caborca to make inquiries in regard to the port of Lobos and to get a guide. On the 29th, having left all my escort except five men, I took one wagon and started *en route* for Lobos. The presidente de la municipalidad of Caborca, and Don Jesus Rivera, of that place, accompanied me. Don Antonio Ramirez voluntarily offered his services as guide *gratis*.

To these three gentlemen I am under many obligations for courtesy, kindness, and many favors. Ramirez is one of the best of guides, and to him belongs the honor of first guiding wagons over a practicable route to both La Libertad and Lobos. He it was who guided Don Miguel Zepeda, who opened the Libertad route. I enclose an itinerary of the route from Caborca to Lobos, and transmit also a traced copy of a sketch of the port of Lobos. It not being practicable to carry the boat here, no soundings were taken; and as no fresh water is found at Lobos our stay was limited to a few hours, having arrived there on the morning of the 1st November, at 9 o'clock, and left at 3 p.m. same day. The [p. 6] sketch herewith gives as nearly correct an outline of Lobos as could be well done without an actual survey. The harbor appears to have deeper water than Libertad, except at the cove at the north end, near the low spit of land. The southern point is formed by a high mountain ridge called the Sierra del Tolouche; the northern by a low spit or tongue of land, which, though not so good as the southern still shelters the bay from heavy seas, if not from high winds. The topography of Lobos is not so favorable for a town or settlement as La Libertad, the ground being more desert, more rough and broken up by ridges and gullies. The shore in the central and southern parts is a high bluff, composed of limestone, shell, and sand; elevation from 75 to 150 feet, broken by deep ravines. Where the "jacales" are marked on the map, however, the position is favorable for building houses, and for landing goods. From the elevated shore I could discover that the water is deep, and near the beach the bottom the same as at La Libertad; the water is deeper near the shore, except at the "spit," where, at low tide, several hundred yards are laid bare, and some rocks exposed. Except at this part of the bay, there appears to be [no] rocks or shallows. I consider the harbor, or rather roadstead, safe and commodious, and would recommend that the first time a public vessel comes to La Libertad that soundings be taken at Lobos. Water in abundance for shipping can be had at the "Desemboque" mouth of the Altar river, at a distance, by sea, not exceeding 12 to 15 miles, which is at the foot of La Sierra de las Espinas, N. 6° W. No agricultural lands are nearer Lobos than the Bajio de Leon, 12⅓ miles distant. The northern point of La Libertad bay is seen from Lobos, viz: Cabo de Lobos, about 20 miles S. 18° E. The port is like La Libertad, surrounded by a semi-circular range of hills, or succession of sierras, situated as follows:

Sierra de la Cascarita, on the gulf, N. 4° W.; Sierra de las Espinas, at the foot of which is the "Desemboque" and fresh water, say 15 miles N. 5°W.; La Sierra del Tanque, N. 11° W.; Cerro Pinto, a whitish detached hill, N. 15° W.; Cerro del Copal, N. 5° W.; the Sierra del Puerto de Lobos extends from N. to E., the greatest distance from the beach being 4 to 5 miles; Las Sierras del Mescal, (two detached hills,) N. 80° E.; Sierra del Datil, east; Sierra del Tolouche, southern point of Lobos bay, S. 26° E.; point of low spit of land, forming northern extremity of the bay, S. 52° W.; knoll near the spit, S. 76° W.; large island, probably Tiburon, S. 40° W.; knoll near the spit, S. 76° W.; large island, probably Tiburon, S. 40° W.; Isla del Angel de la Guardia, S. to S. 20° W., about forty miles distant.

The observations were taken one mile north 71° east from the point marked "jacales" on the map.

The growth of wood at Lobos is the same as at Libertad, with the addition of the copal tree, which grows on the Cerro del Copal and neighboring ridges and ravines.

In regard to water, I refer to my itinerary of this route. I have no doubt abundance can be obtained by artesian boring.

Fish in more abundance even than at La Libertad were seen here; and in a small cove to the north were seen about three hundred seals on the shore, one of which was killed by one of our party. As at La Libertad, we found abundance of pumice-stone near the beach. Good building stone is abundant in the hills, but no timber; fuel is plentiful.

The first known of this bay by the people of Caborca was in 1840 or 1841, when the Papago Indians discovered a wreck of a vessel, upon advice of which several parties went to the port from Caborca by way of the Alamo Muerto ranch, and the "Desemboque" by the beach.

I have seen no map having anything like a correct representation of the bay of Lobos, and none previous to Robinson's having La Libertad on at all.

In the whole district of Altar the most confused and undefined ideas existed in regard to Lobos bay, and my guide, Antonio Ramirez, was the only person [p. 7] who gave me assurance of finding a practicable wagon route, and he redeemed his promise. I was told by a person who had been at Lobos several times that it was "impracticable to take an empty wagon." I took a half loaded wagon, drawn by a very poor team, without the slightest difficulty; without using an axe, a spade, or crowbar, or moving a single obstruction on the road, or going over any sand hills. I was assured by parties pretending to respectability that for sixteen miles the route lay over mountains of shifting sand hills. Sand hills are seen, but none but a simpleton would cross them, as they are no more in a direct route than a good hard road is.

I hope I have dispersed an illusion and a delusion wide spread in regard to the impracticability of the Lobos and Libertad routes. This delusion was fostered with great care by parties in and out of Sonora, whose love of gain exceeds their love of truth and manly honor. It is proper to say that Lobos is not yet a port of entry, not being, as it is termed in Sonora, "habilitado."

On the coast above the Lobos bay are two estuaries ("esteros") affording safe anchorage for small vessels. The first is between Lobos bay and "El Desemboque." It is a kind of canal, about 500 yards long by 150 yards wide, having five to six feet water at low tide; it is two leagues south of the "Desemboque," and is well sheltered from winds. In case of the neighboring hills being rich in minerals, as it is averred they are, this will be a valuable anchorage. The second estero is at "La Salina," where large quantities of salt are found. It is fit for small schooners only. Fresh water is at the distance of 1,500 yards, within five feet of the surface. Guano is got from "La Isla Blanca," in the vicinity. Fine white salt is found at La Sierra de la Cascarita and the Sierra del Tanque.

On the morning of the 2d of November I arrived on my return at the Pozo Morenéno, described in the itinerary of this route. There are several gold and silver mines in this neighborhood, in the Sierra del Alamo, namely, of silver: La Morenéna a "Real," one league due north from the "pozo;" El Agua Nuevo, one league northwest from the "pozo;" besides La Purisima, San Francisco, Zepedas, &c. Of gold, the "Placer de las Palomas" is the principal, being two leagues north, sixty degrees west from the pozo; it yields from 50 cents to $16 per day to the hand. There are seven arrastras at work at the pozo reducing silver. The Alamo Muerto rancho is seven leagues distant to the northwest, where there is wood, water, and grass in abundance, and by which the wagon road to the Desemboque passes.

In the Sierra del Alamo are five "aguages," (watering places,) viz: La

Morenéna, El Agua Nueva, Agua de las Palomas, Chucubabi, and Pozo Morenéno.

On the morning of the 3d the wagon returned to Caborca, which is 53⅔ miles from the port, and 6.54 from Pitiquito.

CABORCA

is situated on the right bank of the Altar river; has a population of 800 souls, chiefly engaged in agriculture and mining. The land on the river bottom is very fertile, and yields annually about 6,000 fanegas of wheat, 2,000 fanegas of corn, some barley, beans, &c. The land in cultivation is about four miles square in extent, and is but a fraction of what is susceptible of cultivation. The sugar-cane, tobacco, and cotton flourish here. All the fruits usual in this latitude grow in abundance. About thirty years ago the river changed its course, having formerly gone to the west, or nearly so, when it afforded much more water for irrigation than now. In those days there was sufficient water at Bisani (fifteen miles from Caborca, and one and a half miles to the right of the road to Lobos) to raise large quantities of grain. Now there is no water at that point. It is a very fertile rancho belonging to Don Dionisio Gonsalez. There is a rancheria of about 300 Papago Indians here, who cultivate enough to subsist on, [p. 8] and who have to draw their water from La Culera, a distance of *nine miles*, and drive their cattle to water at the same place.

It is very difficult to collect statistics from the Mexicans of the amount of wheat raised on the Altar river, at the various towns. I got official information from the prefect, and had his statements fully corroborated by the principal merchants. Barley is raised in limited quantities, from the fact that there is no demand for it. In the hope, however, that the route from Libertad to Tucson shall be opened, the farmers have sowed much more barley this season than usual. The time of sowing wheat and barley is in the beginning of November. I recommended that barley should be raised in considerable quantities.

The prices of wheat and barley are about the same at all the pueblos, viz: wheat, at harvest time, $1 50 per fanega, (150 pounds;) wheat, at seed time, $3 per fanega, (150 pounds;) barley, at harvest time, $1 per fanega, (120 pounds;) barley, at seed time, $2 50 and $3 per fanega, (120 pounds;) beans cost from $3 to $8 per fanega, average $5; corn the same as wheat, but the fanega weighs about 200 pounds.

Beef cattle and all kinds of stock are scarce. I estimate that about 4,000 head of cattle pertain to Caborca, and perhaps 5,000 to 6,000 are on the Calera rancho; six miles from there, amongst themselves, they sell steers for $5 to $12. There are no butchers; animals are generally fattened for slaughter in the towns, and then they sell for about $20. Heavy fat oxen, from $40 to $60; tallow bringing a high price.

An abundance of corn fodder is always to be had at the pueblos, as two harvests are raised annually. They have no way of selling it by weight. It is made in bundles (tercios) of from 6 to 12 pounds, according to the age of the corn, and sold for 6¼ cents per *tercio* at *retail*. It is an excellent food for animals, as the ears as well as the straw are sold.

At this place there are 1 flour mill, (belonging to Don Manuel Carmelo,) 4 stores, 2 carpenters and wheelwrights, 1 blacksmith, 6 to 8 shoemakers, 3 or 4 tailors, and 2 silversmiths.

From the top of the church, the finest in Sonora, are seen the following mountains:

Sierra del Saucito, say, 5 leagues distant, N. 15° W.; Sierra de la Vasura, 6½ to 7 leagues distant, N. 40° W.; Sierra de Santa Teresa, 40 miles distant, N. 60° E.; Puerto Blanco, 2½ leagues distant, N. 85° W.; Cerro del Potrero, about 1 mile distant, S. 65° W.; Cerro de la Colera, 2½ leagues distant, S. 70° W.; Cerro del Alamo Muerto, 10 leagues distant, S. 87° W.; Sierra de la Mosca, (Cordillera,) S. 45° W.; Sierra del Viego, 7 to 8 leagues distant, S. 30° W.; Sierra de Aqintani, 8 to 9 leagues distant, S. 5° W.; Cerro de Canedo, (range) E. to S., 30° E.; Puerto del Alamo, 5 leagues N., 10 ° E.; Puerto del Chanate, 5 leagues N., 20° E.

The two last are passes in the mountains, through which it is said good direct roads can be found from Caborca to Los Paredones, which would shorten the road from Libertad to bring it, *via* Caborca, and these passes to Los Paredones. Don Jesus Rivera and Don Miguel Carmelo agreed to examine these passes and the routes; to take a cart and test them thoroughly, and inform me of the result. They say that water and grass can be found at convenient distances. The Chanate ranch is *en route via* the Chanate pass. There is good water and grass.

I can recommend the following residents of Caborca as excellent guides, viz: Antonia Ramirez, in regard to the coast; José de los Santos and Marino Molino to Arizona, and various routes to different sections of Sonora.

The district of Altar is supplied with salt to a great extent from Caborca. It is brought from La Salina and Cerro del Panque.

On the 4th I left Carborca, and the same day arrived at [p. 9] a town of

PITIQUITO,

1,200 inhabitants, including the small farmers in the immediate neighborhood.

Pitiquito is on the right bank of the Altar river, 6.54 miles east of Caborca, and 14 miles S. 82° W. of Altar, and about five miles below the confluence of the Altar and Magdalena, or San Ygnacio rivers. This is the first pueblo, in point of agriculture, in the district. The soil is very fertile, and the quantity under cultivation is limited, compared with what can be cultivated. The extent at present under cultivation is about four miles in length by two along the river banks, all irrigated.

Of wheat they raise annually 8,000 fanegas; of corn, say, 2,000 fanegas. Some barley, beans, sugar-cane, tobacco; the usual fruits and vegetables are raised in sufficient quantities for home consumption. Prices the same as at Caborca; some little crystalized sugar and considerable panocha are manufactured here. Tobacco and cotton thrive well also. There are about 2,000 head of cattle owned in this pueblo; a few sheep, horses and mules, but very few burras ninchas.

There are two flour mills; one owned by Don Pedro Selaya, and the other by Don Dionisio Gonsalez; both horse or mule power, there being no waterpower on the river below Oquiton. There are three arrastras, crushing quartz, belonging to Don Francisco Gastela. The quartz is brought from El Saucito, 4½ leagues west; yield of gold, about $56 per ton. The sierras in this vicinity, as well as those near all the pueblos, are mineral.

In Pitiquito there are four stores, one blacksmith shop, one millwright, (American,) one carpenter, and shoemakers, silversmiths, saddlemakers, &c.

Don Faustine Feliz is the mayor, or "presidente de la municipalidad." To him, to Don Salvador Mendez, Don Francisco Gastelo, and Don Rafael Rivera, we are indebted for much kindness. Those gentlemen are public spirited and intelligent; they took immediate steps to improve the roads to and from their town, and, on our return, we found two miles of a new road made, and the road over the hill towards Altar smooth and level, they having removed the loose stones and rocks therefrom. They and the people of this place are to make a new road for six to ten miles towards Libertad, which will shorten and improve the route considerably.

The following sierras are seen from the church top, viz: Sierra Alta de Pitiquito, just at town, N. 60° W.; Sierra de San Hilario, N. 30° W.; Sierra de Chucurate, three to four leagues, N. 20° E.; Sierra de la Gamuza, S. 45° E.; Sierra de Aquituni, eight to nine leagues, S. 17° E.; Cerro de la Campana, S.; and the Sierras del Quizuan and del Agua Salada, (direction lost.)

On the morning of the 5th of November left Pitiquito, and arrived the same day at

ALTAR,

the capital of the district of the same name, situated on the right bank of the river. It has a population of 1,050 within the town, and including the farms and small ranchos in the vicinity, 2,000 in all.

The extent of land under cultivation here is limited; scarcely enough is raised for home consumption. The town is, like the others on the river, built of adobes; the houses being, with one exception, only one story high. The productions are the same in kind as in Pitiquito and Caborca, with few exceptions. The water of the river (called so by courtesy, I suppose, for it is only an insignificant rivulet) diminishes in volume every year. The rains for many seasons have been very light, and many of the springs and little affluents to the river lose themselves in the sand. [p. 10]

Agricultural and other products can be obtained here at the same prices as at the other towns.

There is no flour mill. There are ten stores, two blacksmiths, two tailors, one wheelwright, six silversmiths, &c. There is an old church, and the only priest in the district resides here.

Here, I may say, *en passant,* that everything in the way of buildings, mills, workshops, mechanical labor implements, &c., are of the most primitive description; though the Mexicans have been in great numbers from this district in California, they appear to have profited but little by the example of American mechanics and American industry.

The district is sparsely settled, more from fear of the dread Apache than anything else. The country has been laid waste and desolate by these Indians. Cattle have been entirely run off ranches having tens of thousands, and lives sacrificed in such numbers as to make the recital cause one to shudder.

There is so little stock left now in Sonora that the Indians are obliged to come to the very corrals in the towns and steal animals. Without the extermination of the Apaches, or the settlement of Sonora by a different race, the entire depopulation and ruin of the State is only a question of time. In former years horses, cattle, and sheep were in such numbers over the whole country that the owners had but a vague idea of the numbers they possessed. Horses were sold at from five to ten dollars; cattle, two to three dollars; now a good horse of the Sonora stock, small, ugly, but of the most surprising endurance, costs $100.

The mountains surrounding Altar are the "Carnero" range to the east, two to three miles distant; through this sierra there is a pass to La Magdalena. Highest point of the Sierra del Chino, 13 miles, S. 20° E.; Sierra del Chante, 15 to 18 miles, westerly.

The prefect, Don José Maria Redondo, lives in Altar; he politely gave me letters to the presidentes of Pitiquito and Caborca, instructing them to afford me every facility possible in the performance of my duties, and to furnish guides free of charge.

From the principal people of Altar, as well as of the other towns, we received proofs of friendship and hospitality, though their country has been cursed with the presence of straggling bands of vagabond Americans, and others, speaking the English language, mistaken for Americans, who are not only a disgrace to themselves, but to the Anglo-Saxon race. The prefect issued instructions to the authorities on the river at Oquitoa, El Atil Tubatama, and Saric, to repair roads and make new ones when necessary on the route to Tucson by the river.

On the morning of the 6th started for

OQUITOA,

a small town of 500 inhabitants, 6.20 miles from Altar, N. 25° E., on the right bank of the river.

This is entirely an agricultural population. The harvest of wheat is 5,000 fanegas, about 2,000 corn, some barley, beans, &c. Barley is sown in larger quantities this year. The usual fruits, sugar cane, tobacco, &c., flourish here. The river bottom is very fertile, and yields prolific harvests where the soil is irrigated. There are four flour mills, having each one run of stones. There is a good deal of water-power; it is very favorably situated for manufactories.

The town is surrounded by hills—barren, bleak, and said to be mineral. Fuel is abundant, and in the immediate vicinity. Beef cattle and grazing scarce. There is a church; no stores or mechanics. The presidente de la municipalidad is Basilo Cabellero. At two p.m. same day arrived at [p. 11]

EL ATIL,

a village 11⅔ miles from Oquitoa, on the river. It contains about 100 inhabitants—Indians, with the exception of five or six Mexican families. There is considerable good arable land under cultivation here, yielding annually 7,000 fanegas of wheat, and 1,000 to 2,000 fanegas of corn, and some barley; of the latter, as in other puebloes, more than usual has been sown this season, and for the same reason. There is some water-power here also; the only flour mill (belonging to Don Miguel Zepeda) being propelled by water.

There is an old church; no stores or mechanics of any kind; but very few cattle or stock. Abundance of corn fodder and grain can be had here for trains at the usual prices.

Don Manuel Hugues is the "juez local," and only authority in El Atil.

The sierras in vicinity and view are: Santa Teresa, five miles northeast, said to be rich in copper; El Carrisal, a range running east and west, nearest point six to nine miles distant, northerly; El Atil, a small hill, half a mile south.

On the morning of the 7th started for

TUBATAMA,

a town of 800 inhabitants. It is entirely surrounded by hills, and stands upon a knoll seventy-five to eighty-five feet high, on the left bank of the Altar river, the bottom lands of which are here extremely fertile, and well cultivated under corn, wheat, sugar-cane, tobacco, beans, some barley, and the various fruits and vegetables of this latitude.

The annual crop of wheat is 4,000 fanegas; of corn, about 1,500 fanegas.

The castor-oil bean grows here in the rankest luxuriance. Corn-broom and wild cane obtain a growth of fifteen to twenty-five feet high. There is but little commerce; only one store, and no mechanical industry, except, perhaps, one carpenter and blacksmith. Here is a very old church, of which one bell has the date of 1738. The church walls are hung with life-size portraits of saints and various tableaux of a religious character, of no mean style of art. Here the erratic Count Raousset de Boulbon and his misguided followers made their headquarters. Tubatama is eight miles N. 70° E. from El Atil. There are four flour mills here, all driven by water-power, of which there is an abundance, considering the volume of water in the river. Many factories could be established here. There is but one store, owned by the presidente, Don Francisco Ochoa.

The sierras in view from the top of the church are: El Carrisal, 2 leagues NW.; El Sombreretillo, a conical hill, 5 leagues N.; Santa Teresa, 2 miles S. 40° W.; Joanaqui, 1 mile NE.; San Juan, 4 miles N. 15° E.; Cerro del Chile, 9 to 10 leagues N. 26° E.; Babocomari, a low hill, 4 to 5 leagues N. 29° E.

Encamped this day at Babocomari rancho. Next day, the 8th, passed through the town of

SARIC,

the last on the river. A colony of Chilenos settled here in 1858, then an old mission. It is situated on the right bank of the Altar river, nestled in a valley entirely surrounded by hills. The population is 500, principally engaged in mining and agriculture. The river bottom in the vicinity is very fertile, with abundance of water for irrigation.

Here the harvest of wheat is 2,000 fanegas; of corn, say 1,000 fanegas; barley uncertain. For the supply of future demands the barley crop will be much increased here, as on all the river bottom. The usual vegetables are raised, but fruit is scarce on account of the recent settlement of the place. [p. 12]

The valley is cultivated for a mile below, and three and a half miles, above, the town. In the vicinity there is a considerable growth of mesquite, ash, cottonwood, and some oak and walnut fit for lumber. There are here two flour mills, one carpenter and wagonmaker's shop, one blacksmith shop, three shoemakers, four smelting furnaces for silver ore, one silversmith, one saddler, one quartz mill, and four stores.

The "presidente" of the municipality is Don Bartolo Barcelo, who, under instructions from prefect, has set about repairing and changing the road in the vicinity. Part of this labor was performed when I passed, and the work was to proceed to completion at once. I enclose, also, an itinerary of this route from Altar to Tucson, in which, and in the two others appended, I have endeavored to give every object of interest a place, and to represent with fidelity the features and resources of the country with respect to the object of my mission. Having spent only four days at La Libertad, a few hours at Lobos bay, one day going and one returning at Altar, and one day at Pitiquito, and riding, on an average, twenty-five miles per day during the trip, I hope my efforts may prove more satisfactory to the commanding general than they do to myself.

The rest of the routes are described in the itineraries. All is crude and undigested, principally for want of talent in this line, and for want of time, instruments, &c.

I am in hopes that, with some trouble in making the proper reconnoissances, better and shorter roads may be discovered from Tucson to the gulf, and also from, say, Tubac to the Rio Grande. I am informed that sixty miles can be saved by taking a route from Tubac to Mesilla, instead of going *via* Tucson and the present road, and over a superior road, having wood, water, and grass at convenient distances.

To sum up: both routes travelled by me to La Libertad are practicable for heavy freighting. Each possesses some advantages over the other; the one *via* Altar river possesses the advantage of passing through towns and settlements where all the requisites of water, fuel, forage, &c., are obtained in great abundance at short intervals; but the roads are not so level nor so well adapted for very *heavy* loads as the route *via* Zazabe and Los Paredones, which route, however, has no settlement whatever between Zepedas ranch (fourteen miles from Altar) and the Mina Colorado, (near Arivaca,) though, as before stated, the whole country almost is adapted for stock-raising and for ranchos, where produce can be raised, should wells be dug and artificial dams made when required. The difference in distance is in favor of the latter route, as by avoiding Altar, and going direct from Zepedas rancho to Pittiquito, fourteen miles can be saved, thus reducing the distance on that route to 211.24 miles, while the route *via* the Altar river is 226.11 miles.

About the middle of November the country in Sonora, towards the Gulf, is visited with rains called "Las Equipatas." The winter rains fall in December, January, and February. The rainy season commences about June 20, and continues until September.

Trains en route from La Libertad to Tucson will require to be guarded against Apaches; that a military escort will be necessary I do not believe, *provided* teamsters and herders are well armed, under a careful wagonmaster, who will exact vigilance and obedience.

Mexicans travel safely, and herd their animals at night.

At La Libertad the danger from Indians is but very little. Apaches have been known to visit there only once. The Tepoca and Ceres (or Seris) inhabit the coast to the south of the port. They depredate upon the settlements on the Sonora river generally, and when pursued cross to Tiburon island, in the gulf.

It is very unusual for them to come further north than La Cienaga, *(vide* Ehreberg's [*sic*] map.) One man was left in charge of produce stored at Libertad [p. 13] for several months lately; so that, if any settlement be formed at the port, a military force will not, in my opinion, be required.

I returned to Tucson November 11, having been absent since October 10. Left Tucson for Mesilla with the first escort (Major Watts) November 22, and arrived at Mesilla December 1. At Tucson I arranged my notes, and sent a report almost literally the same as this, with maps, &c., to headquarters department of the Pacific.

I have the honor to be, sir, very respectfully, your obedient servant,

D. FERGUSSON,
Major, 1st Cavalry, California Volunteers.

P.S.—Since the 26th November I have been crippled with lumbago and rheumatism, and am unable to put my report in such a shape as I wish in consequence. D.F.

MESILLA, *December* 6, 1862.

FEBRUARY 1, 1863.

Approved and forwarded to the War Department.

JAMES H. CARLETON,
Brigadier General Commanding.

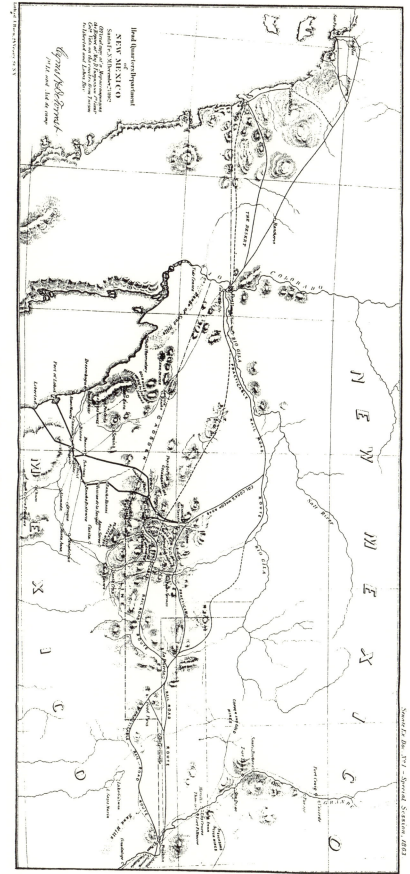

Routes from Tucson to Libertad and Lobos Bay

Senate Ex. Doc. No. 1 – Special Session, 1863

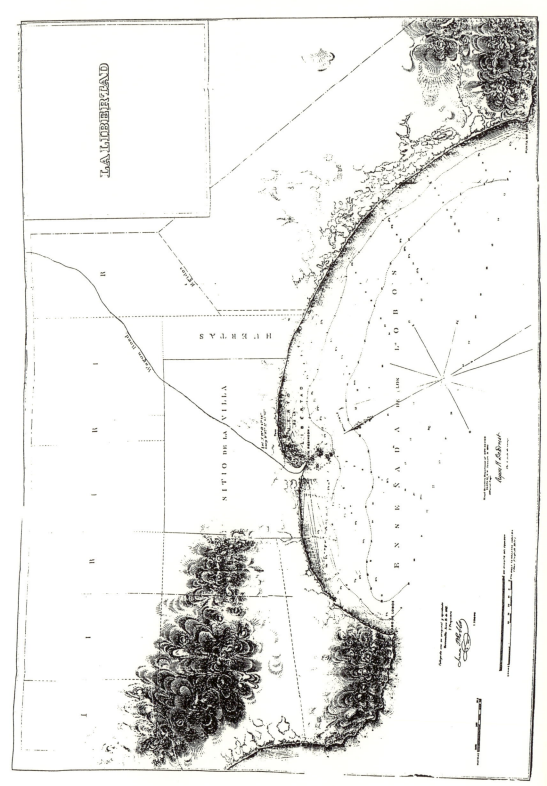

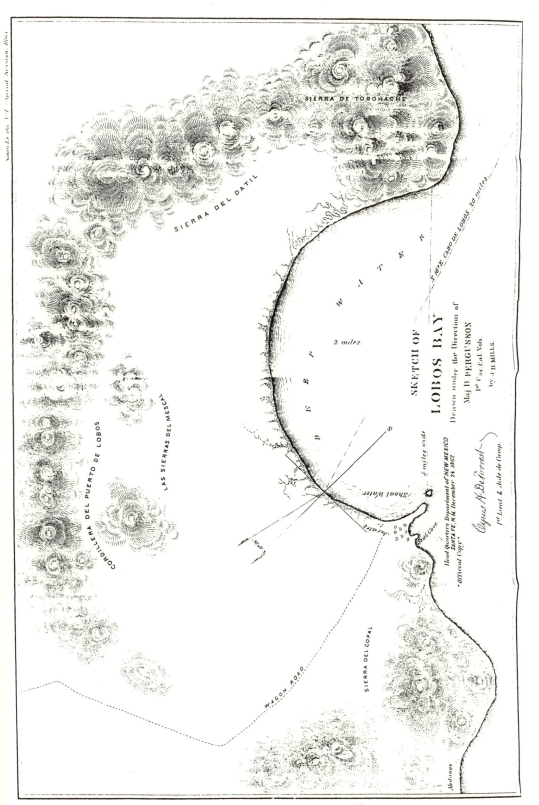

Itinerary of the route from Tucson, Arizona, to the port of La Libertad, on the Gulf of California, State of Sonora, Mexico, via Arivaca, Zazabe, Paredones, and Altar, by Major D. Fergusson, first cavalry, California volunteers.

Date.	Distance in miles.	Route and remarks.
1862. October 10, 3 p. m.	8.89	From Tuscon to— MISSION OF SAN XAVIER DEL BAC.—Good level road; wood, water, grass, grain, corn, fodder, &c. Course of route S. by W. ¼ W.
	1.71	EL RANCHO VIEGO.—Good road through meadow; running water 200 yards to left of road; wood and grass; an abandoned ranch belonging to San Xavier mission.
7 p. m. October 11, a. m....	.79	PUNTO DE AGUA, also known as Struby's rancho. Good road through dense mesquite; running water 150 yards to left of road; wood and grass; shade; ranch abandoned. Course SW. by W. ¼ W.
	8.38	SAHUARITO, also known as "Columbus," a deserted rancho; good road, somewhat dusty; grass; an old well caved in, water near the surface; wood.
	8.56	ROADE'S RANCH.—Good road; at the forks of the road take the left; permanent water in well, about 12 feet deep; a good curb well should be made here to *secure* water for large trains; grass, cottonwood trees; shade. Ranch abandoned.
	2.82	LOS TARAISES.—An abandoned ranch; an old filled-in well, water found 10 to 12 feet down; field of 10 to 12 acres enclosed; good grass; wood; at forks of road go to the right, the left is the Tubac road; good hard road. Course from Punta de Agua, S. ¼ W.
	2.98	REVENTON, or KITCHEN'S RANCH.—Good road, grass, and wood; permanent water in gully 200 yards to left of road, amongst the cottonwoods. There is a well partially filled in at the house, where water was formerly obtained, 10 to 12 feet from the surface; ranch abandoned. The ranch formerly belonging to Brevoort is called "El Reventon de los Patos." The cañon ranch is nearly opposite, to the left, where water is always found in the arroyo bed. Course from forks of road, S. ¼ W.
3 p. m. October 12, 4 a. m.	5.70	SOPORI RANCHO.—Good road; gentle ascent on mesa yielding fine grass; ranch abandoned; traces of former cultivation; acequias with running water. Good grass, groves of cottonwood, walnut, and mesquite, beyond the ranch, in the valley; several abandoned silver mines in this neighborhood; old arrastras seen at the ranch. This is an excellent grazing ranch of great extent. Course from Reventon to turn of road, SW. by S. ¼ W. Course of Sopori valley, W. ¼ N.
	11.36	MINA COLORADO, also known as the "Heintzelman mine."—Road through a fertile valley yielding abundance of grass; indications of water near the surface; cottonwood and walnuts for some distance from Sapori. Fine sheep ranges on the hills on each side of the valley; road good when dry. It is doubtless muddy, in parts, after heavy rains. Water from well in abundance at the mine; grass and some wood. Course from Sopori, W. ¼ S.
	7.76	ARIVACA.—Excellent hard road over mesa, yielding fine nutricious grass: open country. Fine running stream of water, (permanent,) good grass, wood. This was the reduction works of the Mina Colorado; they were extensive and costly; now abandoned. This is one of the finest ranches in Arizona, contains about 20,000 acres of fine grazing land, and is rich in silver mines. There is a cienaga of considerable extent that can easily be drained, and several hundred acres of valuable arable land reclaimed. From the Mina Colorado is seen the Picacho de Baboquivari, a very high conical mountain and noted landmark in Arizona and Sonora. From Arivaca it bears N¾ 70° W. Course from Mina Colorado, SW. by S.
	.50	LOS ALAMOS, or OLD ARIVACA.—Road level and hard in dry weather. In the bottom the road will be soft and muddy in rainy season, but a detour can be made to the right along the foot of the mesa. Here are the old reduction works; several mines in vicinity, fine grazing, cottonwood groves, laguna of permanent water 50 yards to left of road, in clump of cottonwoods.
	6.13	CORODEPE CUESTA.—Road down valley and along foot of Mesa; good and hard valley, well wooded, and good grass all along. About three miles before arriving at the foot of the hill the valley expands, yields fine grass; and from the vegetation water is supposed to be very near the surface. At Corodepe arroyo, at the foot of the hill, it is said water is found by digging a few feet in the sand in dry seasons. Course, W. by N. ¼ to valley, and then W. to Corodepe.
October 12, 1 p. m.	5.39	SPRING IN BED OF ARROYA.—Road ascends over a low hill to mesa, at Corodepe, then over hard mesa, rolling, with fine grass; easy grades. The spring is probably permanent, but not now yielding much water. A mezquite tree on the right of the road is blazed, and marked "water and agua." This is likely the Agua Zarca.

Itinerary of the route from Tucson, Arizona, &c.—Continued.

Date.	Distance in miles.	Route and remarks.
1862. October 14, 4 a. m.		From Tucson to—
	8.62	Z'azabe.—Road until within five miles of Z'azabe over gently undulating, open, grassy mesa; hills to the left dotted with oaks; Baboquisari range and valley to the right; grass as far as the eye can reach; excellent ranges for sheep and cattle. For five miles before arriving at Z'azabe the road is through a level valley; soil rather sandy loam; grassy. For this distance, with much travel, the road will be dusty; but there is abundance of room to make new roads as fast as the old get cut and dusty. Camp at mouth of ravine to the right of the road, 23-100ths of a mile. Course of ravine, N. by W. Permanent water abundant up the ravine about one mile from the road; wagons left at mouth of ravine and animals driven to water; a large cumaro tree at mouth of ravine, on right of arroyo, marked "water;" and on the right of the road, opposite the ravine, I put up a guide-post, giving directions to find the water; fine grazing and plenty wood and shade. Course from Corodepe, SW. by S.
	6.42	Charco de los Mesquites.—A water-hole, now dry, on left of road, at a clump of eight mesquites.
	.08	Tecolote trail crosses the road; direction to Tecolote rancheria, NW.
	4.58	Charco.—Water-hole, (evidently rain water.) Here animals were watered; good grass; wood; a mezquite tree, on right of road, blazed, and marked "water."
	2.27	Rancheria.—A few abandoned Indian huts. The luxuriant vegetation and "sacaton" grass here indicate water near the surface.
	.50	Forks of road.—The road from Tubatama to Fresnal leaves the road here; its direction is N.
	.35	Forks of road.—Where the Tubatama and Fresnal road join the Paredones road, take the right hand road.
	.95	Ascent to mesa.—Here is a short but not steep or bad ascent of about 100 yards; no doubling necessary.
	6.39	Tinaga or Charco, on left of road, containing some rain water; good grazing; wood.
4¼ p. m. October 15, 4 a. m.	15.01	Los Paredones.—Good, hard road all the way. From Z'azabe it follows over a succession of hard mesas and valleys; it winds considerably to rise into the first mesa. From the Charco de los Mesquites to the point of the range of hills on the right, the course is SW.; thence to the Paredones south. The Sierra del Carrizal (where there is a deserted ranch and plenty of water) is about six miles to the left of the road. About four miles before arriving at Los Paredones the road passes two symmetrical, detached, conical hills near the point of the range to the right. La Sierra del Humo is just to the right (NW.) of Los Paredones; water is obtained in a well in the bed of arroya at foot of high bluffs (called "Paredones") to the right of the road. The quantity at present obtained in the well is not sufficient for large trains; depth of well about eight feet. It is almost certain a large quantity of water may be obtained by digging proper wells, an easy work, and securing them from injury from travellers and wild animals; good grazing here; abundance of wood; mesquite beans in season. The country passed over this march is pleasant and open, yielding excellent grass as far as the eye can reach.
	14.73	Jesus Maria.—Ranch of Don *Miguel Zepeda;* road over level plain; mesquite and chapparal; grass on route; water at ranch from a well, *noria,* abundant; grass in vicinity of rancho, being kept down by stock, is scarce; grain and wood; about three miles to NW. is Bamori, where there is an inexhaustible supply of water in an artificial lake, made by constructing a dam in bed of arroyo. Here are fifteen to twenty vaqueros, with their families, in charge of cattle belonging to Altar and vicinity; some cultivation around the lake. Course of road, south.
	8.58	Altar.—Good, hard, level road, (a few hundred yards of sand in arroyo near Altar;) no grazing of any consequence in vicinity of Altar; abundance of grain, principally wheat and corn, and corn fodder abundant, at about one half cent per pound; wheat, $1 50 to $3 per fanega; barley same price; fuel has to be purchased; water abundant in acequias from the river. The amount of produce raised at Altar is inconsiderable, but at the other towns on the river large quantities are raised. Course, south.
	4.05	Dry arroyo.—Good, hard, level road.
	6.20	Road to Zepeda's ranch, (Jesus Maria.)—Leaves Pitiquito and Altar road, running in a northeast direction in a nearly straight line over level plain to Zepeda's ranch; distance from Pitiquito about fourteen miles. This road is the shortest, avoiding Altar en route to Pitiquito and saving about fourteen miles.
	2.23	Foot of hill.—Good, hard road.
	.36	Summit of hill.—Hard rocks; road not steep; loose stones and rocks on this hill removed by the people of Pitiquito, making the hill easy to cross on our return. Course, from Altar, S. 82° W.
October 17, 11¼ a. m.		Foot of hill.—Good, hard road; descent easy.

Itinerary of the route from Tucson, Arizona, &c.—Continued.

Date.	Distance in miles.	Route and remarks.
1862. October 18, 11 a. m..	1.16	From TUCSON to— PITIQUITO.—Good, hard road. Here grain, corn, fodder, and other produce are raised in abundance, at same prices as at Altar; water from river in acequias in town; but little grass within two miles; fuel has to be purchased in town, mesquite abundant in immediate vicinity, however; water-casks should be filled here; no more water on road, in very dry seasons, for 52 miles, to the Picú. Course, S. 82° W.
	7.59	CIENAGA AND CABORCA ROAD.—This road crosses it at nearly right-angles, running to Caborca, N. 80° W.; road, for 31 miles, level and hard, then gentle rise for about two miles, then gradual descent over rather loose, sandy loam. The authorities of Pitiquito have already shortened and improved the road, and the "presidente" of the municipality has given orders to construct a new road to the left of the present, over a different pass, that will shorten the distance to the port six miles, and avoid the loose, sandy soil referred to on the present road.
	5.00	LAGUNA MOSCA.—No water in dry season; good, hard road; good grass; some bare plains, called "playas," crossed rest of road over grassy plain. Course, S.W.
October 18, 8 p. m... October 19, 1 a. m...	6.58	BAJIO DE AQUITUNI.—Good, level road; good grass all the way; no water; plenty wood. In this valley, when the placers at the Cienaga were worked, large crops of grain were raised; no irrigation required, rains sufficing In the event of the route to Libertad being opened, several parties will settle in this valley and sink wells.
	2.97	EL ZANJON, (DRY ARROYO.)—Good road, level; some levelling of banks about four feet high required here; arroyo only twelve to fourteen feet wide; wagons passed easily; wood and grass.
	7.39	TINAJA DEL VIEJO.—A natural tank in the point of Sierra del Viego to the right of the road; water in rainy seasons, and generally all the year. At this point in the valley the people of Caborca and Pitiquito expect water can be obtained at no great depth from the surface.
	7.17	ANGOSTURA PASS.—Good, hard road; ascent gradual for eight or nine miles; good grass on route. This pass is about half a mile long by about 100 yards wide; road hard and level; Sierra del Viejo on the right, Sierra de Aquituni on the left. About half a league to the right of the road, just beyond the pass, where there is a wooden trough, Don Miguel Zepeda dug a well for about 40 feet, where moist earth was reached, indicating water very near; but as the provisions of the workmen gave out, the work had to be abandoned, or rather suspended. In this pass, at an expense of from $600 to $800, a "represa" or dam can be made (there being abundance of limestone) to collect water for any number of animals; and several persons are about applying for a grant of the land with a view of doing so, and making a stock ranch here, for which it is admirably adapted. Wood in great abundance at the point of a "loma" beyond the pass; to the left of the road there are several lagunas and water holes, ("charcos,") where rain-water is collected, and found generally the greater part of the year; none there when we passed; there was no appearance of its having rained this season. Course, from Bajio de Aquituni, S. 16° W.
October 19, 12 m ... October 20, 9 a.m...	11.14	PICU.—Good, hard road; passes over several grassy bottoms, giving signs of water near the surface. The trail to the water at the Picu leaves the road at the mouth of the ravine. There is a mesquite tree on the right of the road, to which I nailed a board with "Picu" cut in it. Course of ravines to water about southeast; trail well defined, is rocky and hard on animals' feet; wagons are left on road and animals driven to water four and a half to five miles; the first water issues from a low, white limestone rock near a stone corral; water good and plentiful. Following in the same direction 1,331 paces there are seen several corrals and a ravine leading at right angles to the right, 1,110 paces up which there are several pools of living permanent water; the grass is not plentiful within one mile of the first water; large herds of wild and other cattle come nightly to these "aguajes," or watering places; wood; fine grazing and plenty wood at camp below on the road. Course, from Angostura, S.W.¼W.
	.57	POZO DE LOS CRISTOLAS.—To the left of the road about 75 feet, well 12 feet deep, but no water now—signs of water, however. Course, S. W. ¼ W. Cerro del Carbon to the right, El Picu to the left.
	1.00	CHARCO DE LOS PAPAGOS.—Trail leads to the Charco to left of road 60 to 70 feet; old camp fires; "Sacaton" indicates water near surface. Course, west.
	4.12	TINAGA DEL TULE —There is a serguard on the left of the road, having a cross (†) cut into it. From this point go to the foot of the red bluffs to the left where the Tinaga is to be found. The rain-water remains in it for many months; none now; but little grass from this point to the port. Course, S. W. ¼ W.
	4.50	DEVISADERO PRICTO.—Good hard road; no grass; wood.
	.83	POINT WHERE THE GULF IS FIRST SEEN.—Good hard road; no grass. Course, S. W. ¼ W.

Itinerary of the route from Tucson, Arizona, &c.—Continued.

Date.	Distance in miles.	Route and remarks.
1862. October 20, 5 p. m.	12.93	From Tucson to— Port of La Libertad.—At the well or ("pozo;") road over an inclined plain; desert, sterile soil, rather stony and loose; crosses many small arroyos, (dry.) The road improves by travel as the soil *packs*, yet this is the worst part of the whole route. Abundance of water for large trains in a well (12 to 15 feet deep) a few yards from the beach at La Piedra Parada, (the name the port was originally known by.) Fresh water issues from the beach, at low tide, at this point, and for 200 or 300 yards towards Point Robinson; it, as well as the water in the well, is warmer, but clean and pure. No grass *en route* for the last 18 miles, or thereabouts; about 4¼ miles towards Point Kino, on a sandy ridge, near the shore, there grows some "galleta" grass, but to no great extent; now there are only the remains of last season's growth; no appearance of rain having fallen this season at La Libertad; wood plentiful and near the beach. Course from Devisadero Prieto, *west*. Game; deer and mountain sheep frequent the beach for water.
	225.24	Total distance from Tucson to La Libertad.
	14.00	From the above may be deducted 14 miles in going direct from Zepeda's ranch to Pitiquito instead of *via* Altar, reducing the distance to 211.24
	211.24	miles.

D. FERGUSSON,
Major 1st Cavalry, California Volunteers.

Approved, and respectfully forwarded to the War Department.

JAMES H. CARLETON,
Brig Gen. Commanding.

February 1, 1863.

Itinerary of the route from Pitiquito to Lobos bay, on the Gulf of California, via Caborca, La Calera, and El Pozo, Moreneño, Sonora, Mexico, by Major D. Fergusson, 1st cavalry, California volunteers.

Date.	Distance in miles.	Route and remarks.
1862. October 29, 11 a. m.. 1 p. m.. October 30, 1 p. m..	6.54	From PITIQUITO to— CABORCA.—Level road, good and hard most of the way; a bridge requires repairs of a trifling nature; the right hand road, through the dense mesquites, is the better one, as it avoids the sand in river bottoms; grain and corn fodder in abundance at Altar and Pitiquito prices; population 800; water from Altar river in acequias, &c.; no grass within a mile; but corn fodder can always be had here, being two crops, in June and November. Course, *west*.
	5.91	LA CALERA.—A stock ranch, the property of Don Dionisio Gonsalez; good road, level, but somewhat dusty and sandy within a mile of the ranch; water abundant, and just at the ranch; no more water until arrival at Poza Moreneño this season; grass and wood. Course, S. 60° W.
	4.58	CROSSING OF RIVER BED, (now dry;) level road, but dusty; grass all the way; wood.
	.50	LOS PUERTECITOS.—Point of hill to left of road; good level road; grass and wood on route. Course, S. 60° W. from La Calera.
October 30, 8 p. m..	6.82	ZANJON DE AQUITUNI.—Narrow, dry arroya, with banks about three feet high; no difficulty in crossing; good road, level; wood and grass.
October 31, 4 a. m..	2.65	MESA DEL PINTO.—Wood and grass; good level road; camped here.
	2.22	PUERTO DE LAS CASCARITAS.—Point of mountain coming to the road from the left; wood and grass; road level and good; very gentle ascent. Course, S. 60° W.
	5.31	EL POZO MORENENO.—Road from last point ascends over a desert, rocky, hard mesa, (easy grades,) with many dry arroyos and some shallow gullies; by removing loose stones the road would be much improved; no heavy pulls, but hard on animals' feet. The Pozo Moreneño is a well and excavation in the rock, where water is found in abundance, and easy of access to animals; it is good and permanent. Here are the reduction works of several silver mines in the Sierra del Alamo, which is rich in silver, gold, and copper, and other unknown minerals; but little labor is necessary to make the crossing of the ravine at this point easy for heavily loaded wagons; our wagon, half loaded, crossed with facility; wood in vicinity; grass scarce within three miles; no more water on route to Lobos, or even there; a supply to go and return is necessary in dry seasons. Course from Los Cascaritas, S. 85° W.
	5.30	ARROYA DEL BAJIO DE LAS CASCARITAS.—Road for about three miles down easy grade, on rocky hard mesa; but little grass; then commences the Abra de las Cascaritas, a large plain, about 30 by 12 miles, extending to the gulf. To the right, towards the gulf, are sandy stretches, unfavorable for roads. The plain is bounded by sierras, except on the gulf. After the first three miles the road is hard, level, and good; good grazing; plenty of wood. Course, first three miles, S. W., then nearly S.
	2.80	BARRANCOS.—Just on right of road; level road; soil, sandy loam, with many squirrel holes, (tuserales;) good grass all the way. Course, S. 33° W.
	43.62	LOS HUERFANOS.—From detached hills in the plain, two large and two small; the nearest 125 yards to the left of the road; good road; grass. Course, S. 33° W. from last point. Course, since heading for Los Huérfanos, S. 55° W. Half a mile to the left of the road, before arriving at the Barrancos, is a stock ranch, at present uninhabited, belonging to Don Mariano P. Serrano and Antonio Ramirez, of Caborca, who have raised grain and vegetables there without irrigation. They sank two or three wells, about 70 feet, without obtaining water; there is every prospect of doing so, however, by going to a greater depth, or trying in other places, for there are various shrubs and plants that Mexicans universally believe are sure indications of water. There is an excellent grazing range and much fertile arable land here. Animals range for weeks without water.
	4.22	BAJIO LEON.—Level road; ground not very hard in dry weather; some squirrel holes, but a very fair road, and plenty room in the plain for roads. Fine grazing; abundance of wood; land fertile. Course S. 33° W.
	4.38	LA LOMITA BLANCA.—A detached whitish hill, about 500 yards to the left of the road. The road ascends gently; grass becomes scarce, until at this point there is none. Course S. 42° W.
October 31, 11 p. m.. November 1, 5¼ a. m.	2.48	PUERTO OR PASS IN THE SIERRA.—Road up an easy grade over desert and rather loose, black, stony soil; many little dry arroyos are crossed. From this point, it is said, there is another route, diverging to the right, from La Lomita Blanca, and going back, *via* the Pozo Grande and Pozo Prieto at the foot of Sierra del Viejo, to the Calera, but it appears the ground is loose and unfavorable for teaming, though it appears some distance would be saved, and it is doubtful if water sufficient is always at the wells. Course from La Lomita Blanca to Puerto S. 20° W.

Itinerary of the route from Pitiquito to Lobos bay, &c.—Continued.

Date.	Distance in miles.	Route and remarks.
1862. November 1, 5¼ a. m.	1.22 4.28 60.20	From PITIQUITO to— MOUTH OF CANON.—Road descends between two hills; descent gradual; soil as on last stretch; no grass; woods. Course S. 76 W. PORT OF LOBOS.—At old Jacales. The road descends at an easy grade; soil dark, loose, broken rock and sand; nothing to prevent a very fair road being made at a trifling expense; some ravines and gullies to cross one to two miles before arriving at a dense choyal, which extends back from the beach about one thousand yards. To the right of the bay, along the shore, there is a strip of sand hill on which galleta grass grows, the only grass within ten miles of the beach; fuel, mesquite, torate, copal, &c., growing near the beach. No fresh water has yet been obtained here. In 1852 Don Thomas Spence, of Guaymas, sunk a well a few varas deep, where salt water was struck. Don Miguel Zepeda and others sank wells from twenty to thirty feet, and upwards, without reaching fresh water. As the port is nearly surrounded by high sierras having water, and the fact that water is generally found on the beach, at no great depth, along the gulf, it is fair to presume that at this point also it can be struck, at least, by boring artesian wells; at the Desemboque, mouth of the Altar river, about twenty miles up the gulf, fresh water is obtained in abundance at all times. Course from cañon to Lobos S. 13° W. Total distance from Pitiquito to Lobos.

D. FERGUSSON,
Major 1st Cavalry, California Volunteers.

JAMES H. CARLETON,
Brig. Gen. Commanding.

Approved.

FEBRUARY 1, 1863.

Itinerary of the route from Altar, via Oquitoa, El Atil, Tubatama, and Saric Sonora, Mexico, to Tucson, Arizona, by Major D. Fergusson, 1st cavalry, California volunteers.

Date.	Distance in miles.	Route and remarks.
1862. November 6, 7 a. m..	6.20	From ALTAR to— OQUITOA.—Good, hard, smooth road; abundance of water in acequias; but little grass *en route*; grain and corn-fodder at Altar and Pitiquiti prices in great abundance; population about 500; four flour mills; harvest of wheat 5,000 fanegas, and 2,000 of corn; fifty per cent. more can be raised, and also barley, if the demand should require it; have no doubt grain of all kinds can be obtained at all the towns, in future, on the river, at an average of one cent per pound, by *contract*, and corn-fodder, in the ear, at $7 to $10 per ton; wood. Course N. 55° E.
	1.23	GONZALEZ'S MILL.—At foot of low range of hills, on the left, running E. and W. To the right are cultivated fields and gardens on the river bottom; abundance of water and water power; 120 inches in mill-race, having a fall of 15 to 20 feet; wood abundant; some grass; road smooth and hard along foot-hills.
November 6, 2 p. m..	1.94	EL RANCHO REALITO.—Good hard road.
November 7, 5 a. m..	8.48	EL ATIL.—Hard road all the way from Oquitoa; a few small rises within two miles or so; then almost level; growth of mesquite, palo verde, palo fierro, lahuaro, pitahaya, &c., *en route* from Altar; some grass here; 7,000 fanegas of wheat are raised every season, some barley, and considerable corn, and the place is capable of yielding 50 to 100 per cent. more. There is good soil, and abundance of water in Altar river. This is principally an Iudian pueblo. There is one flour-mill. Population about 100 Indians and five or six Mexican families. Country open, rolling, and desert, except in river bottom.
	4.13	SANTA TERESA.—An old mission a few yards to the west of road; only two families living here; it is the property of Don Luis Redondo, formerly governor of Sonora, and in the time of the Jesuits was cultivated to a considerable extent and irrigated from the Altar river; about 200 yards from the church, at the foot of the hill, is a spring of good water, by which the old road passes over the hills; the new road forks to the right and joins the old about a mile in advance. The old road is preferable, as it avoids sand in the river bed, which makes heavy pulling for a short stretch; good grass at mission; wood also. Course from El Atil NE. Good hard road. Sierra de Santa 500 yards east of road at mission.
	.61	FIRST CROSSING OF RIVER.—Good hard road.
	.85	LEAVE RIVER BOTTOM —The river is crossed three times; road through river bed is in heavy sand; a new road is to be made from the river to avoid the sand; it goes to the left from the first crossing up a small bank, past a house on the right, through some fields, the owners of which have promised to construct this road, which will be very good.
	.91	LA PUENTA.—Hard road, mostly over slaty rock at the edge of the valley; hill on the left, about 100 yards over a bare rock, to be avoided by the new road.
	1.56	TUBATAMA.—Fair road, but it is to be improved by the town authorities, by order of the prefect. Town situated on a knoll; population 800; four flour mills; good water-power; 4,000 fanegas of wheat and 1,000 to 1,500 of corn raised annually; crops can be increased 50 to 100 per cent.; corn-fodder abundant and cheap; river bottom extremely fertile and productive here, town surrounded by hills. Course from El Atil N. 70° E.
	.30	FORD OF RIVER.
	.46	MORENO'S MILL.
	.52	ZIG-ZAGS.
	1.46	DESCENT INTO VALLEY.
	.85	EL RANCHITO.—A few hundred yards from town the road takes a turn to the left to ascend a low hill; then follows smooth, hard, rolling mesa, making a semi-circle, and comes again into the river bottom; this is not necessary, and the new road is to follow the bottom at the edge of the *lomas*, where it will be good, and inside of some of the fences, about to be removed.
	1.11	TOP OF HILL.
	1.07	TOP OF HILL NEAR ESTANCIO.
	.48	EL ESTANCIO (rancho) road crosses two hills, hard and rock, but not very steep; no doubling of teams required. The last hill can be avoided by going the old road, which forks to the right about a quarter of a mile from the ranch, and follows a cañon and arroyo, where some rocks and stones can be removed with but little labor, and road made very passable. The whole river bottom to the right of the road is cultivated from Tubatama hither. There are quite a number of orchards, (small,) yielding the usual variety of fruits of this latitude; also excellent sugar-cane, castor-oil bean, &c. Formerly the road passed through and along the river bottom, and saved some distance, besides being very good. The local and district authorities and people have agreed to open and improve the old road, which passed through fields now under cultivation and fenced. There is abundance of grass and running river water at Estancio, also abundance of wood and shade. Around the point to the right there is considerable land cultivated. Don José Moreno's fine ranch "*La Aurora*" is within half a mile of this place; it produces grain, fruits, &c., in great abundance.

Itinerary of the route from Altar, via Oquitao, &c.—Continued.

Date.	Distance in miles.	Route and remarks.
1862. November 7, 5 a. m..	1.14	From ALTAR to— VAN ALSTINE'S RANCHO (El Inerto) road passes through a dense grove of large mesquite, interspersed with some ash, oak, walnut, &c.; soil fertile, grass and water abundant; some grain and porduce raised on this ranch.
	3.05	FORKS OF ROAD, (Fresnal and Saric roads.) Road still through some growth of timber, level plain, fine grass; keep to the right. The road to the left goes to Fresnal. About three miles from Van Alstine's there is an old road, leading to the right of the present road, which requires some repairs to level the bank of an arroyo a few yards from the forks. The old road is one to one and a half mile shorter than the new, and equally good.
November 7, 2 p. m.	1.87	BABOCOMARI HILL.—(Point on road opposite the hill.)
November 8, 5 a. m.	1.27	BABOCOMARI RANCHO.—Good hard road over level grassy plain ; running water, grass, wood, and shade near the house. Good arable land under cultivation here, by Don José Moreno, the proprietor. About one mile beyond the house is the best place to encamp. Babocomari hill is S. 5° E. of road. Course from Tubatama W. 26° E. This is a fine ranch.
	39 49 3.58	CANON DE QUIMORI.—To the left of the road; much land under cultivation here.
	.54	SARIC or ZARIC.—Good hard road through valley, somewhat narrow, with low hills on each side ; good grass *en route.* On approaching the hill near the town take the right hand road ; the left has a steep grade to cross the hill or ridge. Here, also, the local and district authorities and people have agreed to change the road where a necessity exists. Instead of crossing the hill the new road turns the left end of the *lourd,* and comes into the pueblo through the " *milpas*" or fields. There is considerable cultivation at this place ; about 2,000 fanegas of wheat, 1,000 of corn, and some barley are raised annually. The crops can be doubled ; and, in expectation of the Libertad route passing this way, much more land has been put under grain this season than usual. Abundance of water for irrigation supplied here by the Altar river. Grain and corn fodder at same prices as the other pueblos. The town is surrounded by low hills, said to be rich in silver ore, &c. There are a quartz mill, four flour mills, and four smelting furnaces here. Course from Babocomari N. 6° E.
	3.46	LAS GALERITAS.—The road winds along foot of hill on the right of the river ; it is rough sidling, and narrow in some places ; in others injured by the breaking of the acequia which runs alongside. The new road which was commenced will avoid all the bad stretches in the old, and be quite a good road no doubt. Even this one offers no obstacle to travel through ; it is rough for about half the distance, (13,) four miles, the rest is good and hard. The course of the river is tortuous, valley narrow. The valley is under, and being put under, cultivation. There is quite a heavy growth of mesquite, oak, ash, walnut, and cottonwood. At Los Galeritas are only a few houses, where five or six fugitive secessionists and outlaws were seen.
	1.79	RANCHO DE BUSANI.—Good hard road. The houses are on a knoll overlooking a very fine, extensive, fertile valley. Here is a cienaga to the right of and near the house where the Altar river takes its rise. Busani is one of the finest ranchos in Sonora, is the property of *Don Luis Redondo,* of Altar; it is not now stocked, however, on account of the Apaches, who have robbed, plundered, and murdered to an extent incredible in the State of Sonora. The low hills bounding the rancho are covered with fine grass as far as vision extends; wood and shade here. Course from Saric N. ¼ E.
	3.16	FORKS OF ROAD.—Take the right hand road.
	8.00	CHARCO DE LOS FUSONES.—Good, hard, level road; at the forks of the road keep to the right; it is about one and a half mile longer, but it avoids a hill, nearly seven miles from Busani, over which we passed by mistake. Excellent grass in every direction; water, in the rainy season, in the '' Charco," 75 yards west from the road, where there is a clump of trees.
	1.32	AGUA ESCONDIDO.—Good level road still in the valley, which is from one half to one and a half mile wide, and dotted with oaks, ash, walnut, cottonwood, mosquite, and mulberry. The water is up a ravine to the left, running N. 30° W., and about 1,000 yards from the road. It is at the foot of a high round hill. There is a cross cut into a mosquite tree on the left of the road, where wagons can turn off and encamp at mouth of ravine, 300 yards from the water, which is abundant, permanent, and good; trail to water easily followed. Ravine bears a growth of mosquite, cumero, oak, walnut, and mulberry, &c.; excellent grazing. Course from Busani north.
November 8, 3 p. m. November 9, 5 a. m.	2.91	LA TINAJA.— Fine, level road. The road forks about three-quarters of a mile before coming to the Tinaja, and they join again 36-100 of a mile beyond the Tinaja ; keep the left road to the Tinaja. The water is up a ravine, opposite high, blue, precipitous, honey-combed bluffs to the right, and 200 yards from the road, at the foot of a perpendicular rock ; it is not sufficient for more than 30 to 40 animals at this season ; is mostly rain water, though there is, apparently, a spring ; fine grass and abundance of wood.

Itinerary of the route from Altar, via Oquitao, &c.—Continued.

Date.	Distance in miles.	Route and remarks.
1862. November 9, 5 a. m..	4.90	From ALTAR to— LAS TRES BELLOTAS.—(The three black oaks.) Here the boundary line between Arizona and Sonora crosses the road ; the three oaks are about 30 feet to the right of the road ; one has fallen; they are the largest trees in the valley. There is considerable black oak in this part of *Basani* valley; the white oak dots the hill sides. From this place, it is said, a good road can be found *via* Urias ranch, to the right, (east,) coming into the Arivaca cienaga, and avoiding the worst part of the entire route. It is well worth examining. It is probable a good, direct road could be found to Tubac.
	1.09	ARIVACA AND TUBATAMA TRAIL.—The trail here leaves the road and crosses the hills to the left, and joins the road again near Las Fraguitas.
	1.33	FOOT OF HILL.—Road continues good and hard along the valley, which is from 200 yards to one and a half mile wide ; abundance of grass; black and post oaks, mulberry, &c.
	.30	FIRST BENCH OF HILL.
	1.61	SUMMIT JUST BEFORE DESCENDING.
	.57	FOOT OF HILL IN DRY ARROYO ROAD.—The first pitch is not steep enough to require doubling with heavily loaded wagons; the road can be improved by keeping to the right in ascending the first rise ; after 75 to 100 paces the second pitch commences; this is longer and steeper, but a little judgment shown in ascending this road, by keeping to the left and winding up it, will be much easier; the ground is hard, somewhat stoney, but not rough. The steepest parts, being short, are not impracticable for heavy loads. Mexican 8 and 10 mule teams haul 3,500 to 4,000 pounds over this hill. The descent is rather steep and stoney ; to ascend here doubling will be necessary until the road is differently laid out and improved. It appears as if a much easier grade could be got through ravines to the left, (west,) and over lower ridges or cuestras. It appears no effort has been made to find a better road in this section. Old Indian trails have been followed without an effort to discover a better route over the hill ; fine grazing along the route, and in this section of country. Course from Las Tres Bellotas to summit N. 17° E.
	1.06	ARIVACA TRAIL.—Joins road from the left, (S.)
	1.21	LAS JARRETILLAS.—Water in spring 150 yards to the right of the road, direction S. 60° E., in open ravine, towards high, round hill ; willows, sacaton, &c , indicate water here unmistakeably ; it is quite abundant for large trains; fine grass and wood.
	.80	ANGLE IN ROAD TO GO NORTH.
	.70	MOUTH OF CANON.—From the foot of the hill the road follows a ravine, which is quite tortuous and stoney until reaching this cañon ; grass en route, and oaks, walnut, &c.
	.48	MINA DE LOGAVINA.—Knoll at the end of the cañon; cañon most of the way only wide enough for wagon road ; it has a high hill on each side, rocky and precipitous ; fair road. Course of cañon E. and W.
	.30	LAS FRAGUITAS.—Road rocky and winding to W. 10° E. Here are deserted reduction works of some silver mines in vicinity ; no water at present ; usually running water all the year here ; scarcely any rain fell this season in this section.
	.74	HILL ABOVE ARIVACA VALLEY, where the houses are first seen.—From Las Fraguitas the road curves to the N., then to NW., then changes to N. 10° E. direct ; a few yards past the reduction works some rocks and stones require removal, and levelling and some grading is required for 200 and 300 yards. A road could be made with very little labor along the arroyo much preferable to the present.
	2.03	ARIVACA.—Good road over gently descending, grassy plain ; abundance of fine grass, and living, running water; wood. Course N. 10° E.
November 11, 1 p. m.	58.95	TUCSON.—Good road already described in itinerary from Tucson to La Libertad.
	140.32	Total distance from Altar to Tucson.
	85.79	From Altar to La Libertad.
	226.11	Distance from Tucson to La Libertad.

D. FERGUSSON, *Major 1st Cavalry, C. V.*

HEADQUARTERS DEPARTMENT OF NEW MEXICO,
Santa Fé, N. M., January 31, 1863.

Official:

Approved.

FEBRUARY 1, 1863.

BEN. C. CUTLER, *Captain and A. A. General.*

JAMES H. CARLETON, *Brig. Gen., Commanding.*

James A. Evans, 1865

Union Pacific Railroad. Report Of Jas. A. Evans Of Exploration From Camp Walbach To Green River [in 1864]

Letter of January 3, 1865, Montrose, Pennsylvania, to T. C. Durant; New York, 24 p.
[WC and WCB 414; Graff 4246; Holliday 351; Howes E223; UPRR p. 48; NUC
NU 0027552. Reset verbatim from compiler's copy of 1866 reprint in *Union Pacific
Railroad, Report of Thomas C. Durant, Appendix A*.

Significance   Evans made the first serious railroad survey along much of the
future Union Pacific line across Wyoming, from the head of Lodgepole Creek to
Green River via Bridger Pass, in 1864. He pretty much followed the route of Capt.
Howard Stansbury in 1850 (5:J3), a portion of whose map is reproduced here. Lt.
Francis T. Bryan traversed this same route in 1856 and 1858 (5:J11 and 4:G8).
However, it was not until 1865 that Evans surveyed the finally chosen "Evans
Pass" across the Laramie Mountains, ten miles south of the head of Lodgepole
Creek. Jim Bridger had led Stansbury across this very area, but the Union Pacific
people (excepting Francis M. Case, L3) assumed the pass to be their own discovery. Concerning another part of the line, Evans astutely observed that the route
might best go 20 miles north of Bridger Pass; the final selection indeed took it
there, through Rawlins. (See Randolph Marcy's 1858 route, 4:G8.) Evans saw that
the Laramie Canyon would be a direct possible link between this Rawlins location
and Ft. Laramie on the North Platte. He may have been the first white man
(Howes E223) to crawl through this gorge; he found it to be utterly hopeless for a
railroad. John Bartletson, 5:J11, had been nearby in 1857. Evans did not go to
South Pass, because of Indian troubles, but he rejected it from prior data.

The first edition of Evans's report was a separate pamphlet, similar to those
reprinted in L13 and L14, with the complete title as given in the heading above.
The present L12 reprint, however, is taken from the 1866 second edition embodied as Appendix A in the *Report of Thomas C. Durant*, which also has the Case and
Reed reports, and plates and maps not present in the first editions. The plates
gave the stockholders visions of the wilderness and of the construction challenges. The first plate, depicting Camp Walbach, is included in this first modern
reprint of the Evans report.

Author JAMES A. EVANS, explorer, surveyor, railroad builder. Following up his 1864 surveys recounted here, Evans in 1865 ran a new line from Lodgepole Creek by way of Crow Creek to what Durant named Evans Pass over the Laramie Mountains. In 1866 Evans made more detailed surveys there and also checked more closely the nearby approach by the Cache la Poudre. From 1867 he and Samuel B. Reed supervised the actual building of the Union Pacific—grading, bridging, tunneling, supplying, laying track, etc. (Galloway 1950.)

Consulting engineer Silas Seymour with Chief Engineer Grenville Dodge and Evans in September, 1866, "ascended the westerly slope of the Black Hills [Laramie Mountains] to a depression in the summit...named Evans' Pass, in honor of the Engineer of that name, who formed one of our party; and to whose energy, and skill in his profession, the Railroad Company are indebted for most of the information in their possession respecting the region." Despite this high praise, the next year Seymour tried to relocate the line to the pass. Dodge denounced Seymour's proposal as being a detriment rather than an improvement.

Itinerary, 1864 EVANS, OMAHA TO LARAMIE MTS. VIA LODGEPOLE CREEK. April 16—Division Engineer James A. Evans, his first assistant F. N. Finney, 5 named men, "and the remaining members of the corps," leave Omaha with wagons. They follow the north side of the Platte, cross to Ft. Kearny, and continue along the south side of both the Platte and the South Platte to Julesburg CO. Thence they ascend Lodgepole Creek westward into the Laramie Mountains ("Black Hills") to abandoned Camp Walbach on the South Lodgepole, May 16. They are joined enroute by a lieutenant and escort of 20 soldiers supplied by Col. W. O. Collins at Ft. Laramie, at the order of Gen. Robert B. Mitchell. Evans has traveled 575 miles in 31 days at 19 miles per day.

The army occupied Camp Walbach, located 20 miles east of present Laramie WY, from September 20, 1858, to April 19, 1859 (Ryan 1963). Two companies under Maj. Thomas Williams spent a wretched winter guarding the little used Ft. Riley-Bridger Pass wagon road explored by Lt. Francis T. Bryan in 1856 (5:J11). Bryan opened this road in 1858 as a supply route to the Utah Expedition, but it was not popular with the army (4:G8), and few emigrants used it. The men of Camp Walbach spent most of their time on survival. They piled sandstone blocks in walls around their tents. They built a hospital and some storehouses of logs. These were the "deserted ruins" found by Evans and portrayed in his drawing.

Itinerary, 1864 EVANS, LARAMIE MTS. TO GREEN RIVER VIA BRIDGER PASS. About May 18—Evans starts his survey from Camp Walbach up South Lodgepole Creek 14 miles to the summit of the Laramie Mountains at "Cheyenne

Pass." A descent of 8 miles takes him to the Laramie River near present Laramie WY. He thinks that a 1,500-foot tunnel would be needed at the summit. From the Laramie River Evans generally follows Stansbury's 1850 route as improved into a road by Bryan in 1858. The road goes northwest across the Laramie Plains to today's town of Elk Mountain. Then it proceeds west past Ft. Halleck, established 1862, and Rattlesnake Pass, both at the north base of Elk Mountain itself. From here the road crosses the North Platte and ascends a branch of Sage Creek to Bridger Pass on the Continental Divide, 20 miles south-southwest of modern Rawlins. Evans surveys on west down Muddy Creek and across to Bitter Creek, which passes Rock Springs and reaches the Green River at today's town of Green River WY, July 26.

Evans has been painstakingly measuring latitudes, longitudes, distances, elevations, grades, curvatures, and needs for bridges, culverts, tunnels, masonry, sluices, and excavations. He goes 270 miles in 70 days at a busy 4 miles per day.

Highlights   In the first report issued by the Union Pacific Company in 1864, President John A. Dix included accounts of its earliest surveys. Vice President Thomas C. Durant noted that the initial survey parties were "employed by individuals, and not by the Union Pacific Company," since they were sent out before the company was fully organized. Chief Engineer Peter A. Dey in late 1862 and early 1863 made a quick trip to Salt Lake City. He liked the directness and grades of Lodgepole Creek but worried that "it fails to meet the wants of the Denver gold region." He reported coal and iron ore in the Laramie Plains and saw no special problems westward until the Wasatch crossing. He also checked out the Cache la Poudre access to the Laramie Plains from present Greeley on the South Platte. This route "would require heavier grades and more curvature than the line through the Cheyenne Pass…[and] increasing the distance sixty or seventy miles." And as for the Berthoud Pass road that would meet the wants of the gold region, "Mr. [Francis M.] Case's survey of this route from Denver, shows a heavy and expensive line up this [Clear Creek] valley" and a 3.5-mile tunnel at the top. (See L13.)

In 1863 Dey had six lines run from the Missouri River north and south of Omaha to Fremont on the Platte. He preferred the line from Bellevue and the one from the south end of Omaha. Late that year engineer B. B. Brayton and geologist James T. Hodge visited Cheyenne Pass at the head of South Lodgepole Creek. They had just finished their examination, Brayton wrote, when "a storm set in which, for fierceness, intensity, and duration, I never saw equaled. It lasted ten days…Prof. Hodge urged me strongly to abandon the survey at Bridger [Pass]. I said to him, that I was sent to make it, and I intended doing so before I returned." Hodge, looking for iron and coal, found "the country covered with snow, rendering geological explorations altogether impracticable." Brigham Young sent his son Joseph A. Young to survey Provo Canyon "until rough weather drove the party from the field."

With this background, Evans, Case (L13), and Reed (L14) set out in 1864 to make more detailed surveys of the possible routes from the South Platte to Great Salt Lake.

Legacy   Today's Union Pacific crosses the Laramie Mountains by "Evans Pass" (or "Sherman Summit" or "Lone Tree Pass") on the ridge between South Crow and Lone Tree creeks near present Buford, 25 miles west of modern Cheyenne and 10 miles south of South Lodgepole Creek. Union Pacific lore credits B. B. Brayton with first spying this better route from a viewpoint at South Lodgepole Creek's Cheyenne Pass in 1863: "I, with a field glass, observed a route to the south…which would enable us to reach the summit by a grade apparently easier" (Dix 1864). Brayton could not follow up, owing to short rations, a big snow storm, and orders to go on to Bridger Pass.

In 1864 Evans made an effort to check Brayton's suspected pass but did not get far enough south. Then in his 1910 book, Gen. Grenville M. Dodge claimed that in 1865, while scouting in the Laramie Mountains with a few cavalrymen, he was cut off from his main command by Indians: "we took the ridge between Crow Creek and Lone Tree Creek, keeping upon it and holding the Indians away from us, as our arms were so far-reaching…We were on an apparently very fine approach to the Black Hills…I said, 'If we saved our scalps I believed we had found a railroad line over the mountains'…As soon as I took charge of the Union Pacific I immediately wired to Mr. James A. Evans…describing this ridge to him…He immediately made an examination and discovered a remarkably direct line of only a 90-foot grade." Goetzmann (1966) notes, however, that Dodge's 1865 diaries and letters did not record any such hostile Indians or pass discoveries.

The much duller actuality is that Jim Bridger led Capt. Howard Stansbury right over "Evans Pass" on September 28, 1850 (see map). Stansbury was returning east from Salt Lake City, and Bridger was going to show him the Lodgepole Creek route to the South Platte (5:J3). Stansbury wrote, "Ascending the western slope of the Black Hills…we reached the summit of the ridge, which gives rise to the head of Lodge-pole Creek…falling with a rapid and sudden descent…The ridge appeared to be much lower to the southward…We accordingly followed down the ridge in a S.S.E. direction for six miles, when we struck upon a little stream…a branch of Crow Creek." Even if this were Middle rather than South Crow Creek, Stansbury was no more than 3 miles from present Buford.

Stansbury turned north from his pass and found a north-south depression along the east flank of the Laramie Mountains, extending 30 miles to Chugwater Creek: "The depression thus formed is called the 'Cheyenne Pass,' from the constant use made of it by that tribe in their migrations." All this Stansbury showed on his accurate and later readily available 1852 map. On his 1859 General Map, Lt. Gouverneur K. Warren plotted Stansbury's track but moved the label "Cheyenne Pass" to where Buford now is. Then the Union Pacific people called the head of Lodgepole Creek "Cheyenne Pass." It's too bad that this name has three different meanings. It's also too bad that neither Stansbury nor Bridger was given much credit for discovering the pass near Buford. Goetzmann called it "fully as important as the South Pass." (Fremont in 1842, 5:J1, and Kearny in 1845, 4:G5, had both followed the north-south Trappers Trail between the South Platte and Ft. Laramie.)

The also unheralded Francis M. Case, in his report written December 15, 1864 (L13), was the first Union Pacific man explicitly to locate "Evans Pass" by the creeks involved. He even specifically cited Stansbury's discovery account. Seymour and Dodge toured the pass in September, 1866. It is ironic that certain parties later claimed, for personal gain, that the company did not know of this easy pass until after a construction contract was signed on August 16, 1867 (Fogel 1960).

REFERENCES
(See Preface for Heading references, and for Howes, not listed here.)

Dix, John A., 1864, Report of the organization and proceedings of the Union Pacific Railroad Co.: N.Y., quotes by Durant 41; Dey on Cache la Poudre and Berthoud 5, and on Denver 7, of Appendix 1; Brayton on glass ii, and on storm iii, of Appendix 1B; Young on weather ix of Appendix 1C; Hodge on snow iii of Appendix 2.

Dodge, Grenville M., 1910, How we built the Union Pacific Railway: Wash., 61/2 S447, quotes on ridge 86, grade 87.

Durant, Thomas C., 1866, Union Pacific Railroad, report of Thomas C. Durant, Vice President and General Manager, to the Board of Directors, in relation to the surveys made up to the close of the year 1864: N.Y., title leaf and 8 p.; Appendix A, Evans's report, 24 p., 2 maps, 2 plates; Appendix B, Case's report, 11 p., 7 plates; Appendix C, Reed's report, 15 p., 2 maps, 5 plates.

Fogel, Robert W., 1960, The Union Pacific Railroad, a case of premature enterprise: Baltimore, p. 117-19.

Galloway, John D., 1950 (1989 reprint), The first transcontinental railroad: N.Y., p. 251, 254-56, 263, 301.

Goetzmann, William H., 1966 (1971 reprint), Exploration and empire: N.Y., on Dodge 300; quote on pass 301.

Ryan, Garry D., 1963, Camp Walbach: Cheyenne, Annals of Wyoming 35:5-20.

Seymour, Silas, 1866 (1867 pub.), Incidents of a trip...to the Rocky Mountains and Laramie Plains: N.Y., quote p. 40.

Stansbury, Howard, 1852, Exploration and survey of the Valley of the Great Salt Lake of Utah: Phila., 32/Special S3, serial 608, quotes on Black Hills 257-58, Cheyenne Pass 260; map in separate folder.

Map of "Evans Pass" by Stansbury 1850 (published 1852), showing Lodgepole Creek (A), Crow Creek (B), and Cache la Poudre River (C). The pass is at the crest of the Laramie Mountains ("Black Hills") near the camp of September 28, 1850.

UNION PACIFIC RAIL ROAD
SURVEY OF 1864.
CAMP WALBACH FROM THE EAST.

J.A. EVANS. DIV. ENG'R. DEL.

The Major & Knapp Eng'g Mfg & Lith Co. 449 Broadway N.Y.

APPENDIX A.

Report of JAMES A. EVANS, *Division Engineer, of Exploration from Camp Walbach to Green River, made in*

1864.

Montrose, Penna., *January* 3, 1865.

Sir,—I have the pleasure of submitting the following report of explorations and surveys, extending from the eastern slope of the Black Hills, to Green River:

On reporting for instructions, at Omaha, Nebraska, early in April last, it was found, in consequence of the non-acceptance of one of the appointments made by the company, that the work originally designed for two distinct parties would have to be done by one. By giving that single corps additional strength, the supposition was entertained that it could cover the ground. Subsequent events fully justified the arrangement; hence the portion of the line first assigned to the undersigned for examinatiog [*sic*], formed but part of the country covered by this communication.

Preparations for our journey up the Platte River having been completed, I left Omaha on the 16th day of April, looking to Old Camp Walbach, at the eastern slope of the Black Hills, and on Lodge Pole Creek, as our point of commencement.

In consequence of Indian difficulties on the border, I made application to Brigadier-General Mitchell for authority to procure escort, which was very cheerfully granted by him, and very promptly complied with by Colonel Collins, then in command at Fort Laramie. [p. 2]

Our line of travel was on the north side of the Platte River as far as Fort Kearney, where we crossed, thence on the south side to Julesburg, on the south fork, distant from Omaha 400 miles. At this point, in consequence of the hostility shown by the Cheyenne tribe of Indians, I telegraphed to the commander at Fort Laramie (Col. W.O. Collins) for escort. With promptitude highly commendable, he immediately sent a detachment, composed of a lieutenant and twenty men of the Eleventh Ohio Volunteer Cavalry.

At Julesburg we crossed the south Fork of the Platte River, a short distance below the mouth of Lodge Pole Creek, up the valley of which we continued our journey. Some forty miles up this tributary we met our escort, they having crossed the country from Fort Laramie for the purpose of intercepting, or rather meeting the party; they remained with us until the completion of our field work in September.

We reached the deserted ruins of Camp Walbach, situated in latitude 41° 21' N., longitude 105° 15' W., distant by travelled road from Omaha, 575 miles, on the 16th May. The instructions given me contemplated my noting the country along the line of travel.

As far as Fort Kearney the country is favorable for the construction of a railroad; and the same is true of the entire route until we approach to within fifty miles of the Black Hills. For that entire distance, the uniformity of surface, the superior character of the material and the small amount of mechanical work required, as bridge superstructure, masonry, &c., combine to make this portion of the line everything that can be desired. When we consider that such is the topography of the country extending over nearly ten degrees of longitude, we can safely come to the conclusion that a region more favorable for railroad purposes does not exist in this or any other country.

As we approach to within fifty miles of the mountains, the valley of Lodge Pole Creek gradually changes; the distinctive smoothness of surface ceases, giving place to a more broken topography—by no means making necessary heavy or expensive grading, yet in marked contrast to the extreme uniformity of the lower part of its course, and of the Valley of the Platte.

The only difficulty in the way of the engineer on the portion [p. 3] of line above referred to is the scarcity of timber. Confining my observations to the Platte Valley, it may be stated that as far west as a point 80 miles above Fort Kearney, all the timber that seems to be available occurs at Loup Fork of the Platte, and on the Platte itself; principally cottonwood, with some cedar interspersed.

At and near Cottonwood Springs, distant from Omaha 285 miles, from Fort Kearney 90, the bluffs on the south side of the valley tend towards the river, approaching to within half a mile of the stream, and continuing parallel with it for some distance above and below. Here, in a district very broken, and somewhat difficult of access, a considerable growth of cedar is found, of excellent quality for cross-ties and kindred purposes. From this point to the mountains no timber is found, neither on the streams nor contiguous to them. The manner of supplying this portion of the line will be hereafter indicated.

BLACK HILLS.

On reaching the base of this chain of mountains, after a reconnoissance of the country in the vicinity of old Camp Walbach, I fixed the starting point of my survey directly south of the ruins, at a point distant 1,200 feet, and on the opposite bank of Lodge Pole Creek. The line follows that tributary of the South Platte to its source at the summit of the range, overcoming, in a distance of 14 11/100 miles, an elevation of 1,612 feet, giving an average grade of 114 25/100 per mile. It was found necessary to undulate this grade, not, however, to an extent seriously to interfere with any traffic this part of the road may be called upon to do.

The accompanying map and profile will show the direction and arrangement of grades.

A sufficient supply of timber (yellow pine and spruce pine) can be obtained in this mountain chain, and contiguous to the line, to supply all the wants of construction, besides furnishing a large surplus for the line to the eastward, and for fuel.

The character of the material in excavation is indicated on the profile; specimens have been furnished. On the eastern slope it will prove to be granite, of different degrees of hardness and coarseness; on the western slope, sandstone exclusively. A tunnel 1,500 feet long is found necessary at the summit. [p. 4]

The gradient used from the summit of this range to the Laramie Plains is 2.5 per 100 feet, 132 feet per mile. A lighter grade cannot be used over this ground without a large sacrifice of profile and direction. A reference to the accompanying profile will show this grade to be continuous for 8 17/100 miles. Should this, or any other line crossing the Black Hills be the one finally adopted, additional or extra power will be required to make the ascent; knowing this to be he [*sic*] case, and knowing too, that any attempt to use a lighter gradient over the ground would result in giving a very expensive line, I came to the conclusion that a sufficient saving in grades could not be made to compensate for the additional material it would be necessary to move.

Efforts were subsequently made by me and the party under my charge, to obtain a more favorable crossing of this range of mountains, but without success, the details of which will be submitted in their proper place.

By reference to the profile, it will be seen that on the western slope of the Black Hills depression amounting to 1,080 feet is overcome by means of a gradient of 2.5 per 100 feet. To reduce this to our maximum grade would require additional distance as follows:

43,200 feet at 2.5 per station	=	1,080 feet.
49,091 " at 2.2 per "	=	1,080 "
5,891 " additional distance required.		

By using a 2.2 grade, 116 feet per mile from the mouth of the tunnel, say station 780 to station 881, there inserting a switch, and running back half the distance, or 2,945½ feet, then switching again, we would be placed 99 feet lower at station 881 than we are now, and could reach the foot of the slope from that point with a grade of 116 feet per mile, striking the table at the foot, as we do now, which I consider important.

My reason for fixing upon station 881 as a point from which to switch back, is, that the requisite distance can be obtained there on a smoother slope, less cut up by ravines than elsewhere. [p. 5]

LARAMIE PLAINS.

Soon after leaving the base of the Black Hills, our line crosses the main fork of the Laramie River.

From thence to the Rattlesnake Pass, at a point where the Medicine Bow range of mountains drop off into low ranges of hills of comparatively slight elevation, our line crosses the drainage of that mountain chain, and of the plains at nearly right angles. Some bridging will be necessary on this part of the route. For amount see item of "Bridging." The principal streams crossed are—

> Main Fork of Laramie River.
> Right hand Fork "   "
> Cooper's Creek.
> Rock or Frappe's Creek.
> Medicine Bow River.

The amount of grading necessary for the distance is light, the alignment excellent, the material good.

The Medicine Bow Mountains, distant from our crossing of the Laramie River 16 miles, are in good part covered with timber suitable for all kinds of construction. As our line proceeds westerly we gradually approach them, at Cooper's Creek we are distant but 2½ miles; from thence we run nearly parallel with the range until we flank or turn it by the Rattlesnake Pass.

The large amount of timber found here renders easy the solution of a problem that would otherwise be extremely difficult to solve, viz., the supply of timber for that part of the line west of the North Platte River, a country desert in character, destitute of vegetation, and impossible to avoid by any line following the valley of the Platte. This consideration alone should, and doubtless will, have great weight in the comparison of routes—when we consider, further, that the timber of this region is indispensable for the purpose of developing and making available the coal of Bitter Creek, too much importance cannot be attached to its fortunate proximity to the line.

Distance from the main fork of Laramie to the head of Rattlesnake Pass, 69½ miles. The only difficult point for that distance [p. 6] is the dividing ridge between Rock Creek and the Medicine Bow River.

Should it be considered desirable to lessen the gradients and obtain a smoother profile, by a sacrifice of distance at that point, a detour of four or five miles to the northward will accomplish it, as indicated by the dotted line on the map.

The fixed points on this section of line are, in my opinion, Station 1,520, near the crossing of the main Laramie—the crossing of the Medicine Bow River—the head of Rattlesnake Pass.

Should explorations already or hereafter to be made, demonstrate the practicability of a line *via* the South Fork of he Platte and the Cache-la-poudre Creek, the first point mentioned above would have to be made for the purpose of avoiding the broken ground at the base of the Medicine Bow range of mountains.

Our descent from the head of Rattlesnake Pass is made by a gradient of 116 feet per mile for five miles nearly.

This Rattlesnake Pass is a marked depression in the spurs forming the termination of the Medicine Bow range, which here loses the distinctive character of a mountain chain, dropping off into ridges of slight elevation, stretching far to the northward, and forming the eastern boundary of the

VALLEY OF THE NORTH PLATTE.

The line here offers nothing remarkable, aside from the crossing of the North Platte River, which proves to be extremely favorable, being rectangular, and affording reliable foundations for piers and abutments. The amount of bridging required is 600 feet. It will be seen that our line makes considerable southing to reach this point. A short distance below our crossing the river enters a cañon extremely crooked, bounded by perpendicular escarpments of sandstone rock, which feature it continues to have so far as the mouth of Pass Creek, some fifteen miles below.

Any line *via* Bridger's Pass will, from necessity, make this crossing of the river a fixed point, there is no means of avoiding it; hence I look upon the favorable character of the crossing as fortunate.

After passing the Rattlesnake Pass, the country changes sensi-[p. 7] bly— everything indicating the approach to a barren region. The abundant pasturage of the Laramie Plains being here replaced by a stunted growth of sage brush. Grass is only found on the water courses, the more elevated points being almost entirely destitute of vegetation. This feature of extreme barrenness increases in intensity until the western terminus of the division is reached at Green River.

The topography of the valley of the North Platte River immediately bordering on the stream, and in the vicinity of our line, has been already referred to. The perpendicular walls of sandstone commence a very short distance below our crossing on the *eastern* or right bank. On the *western* side, the slopes are gentle for nearly four miles, from thence the vertical rock borders closely both sides of the river, continuing, as stated before, to the mouth of Pass Creek.

After crossing this river, our line continues down it to nearly the commence-ment of the cañon. We then leave the valley, and by easy grades reach Sage Creek, striking the latter stream about two miles above its mouth.

No information can be given in a report of this part of the line other than what may be conveyed by the accompanying map and profile. The grades are light, the amount of excavation necessary small; building stone for what light structures may be needed, abundant.

Thirty-one and one half miles from the crossing of the North Platte River, brings our line to the summit of

BRIDGER'S PASS.

Although this is a point of some geographical importance, as forming the water-shed of two oceans, nothing formidable is encountered either in approach-ing or leaving it. The maximum grade on the eastern side is 2.05 per 100 feet. On the western, 2.18 per 100, and only for short distances.

The approaches to this and the Rattlesnake Pass are the points where the greatest obstructions from snow may be looked for. The location of the line in the vicinity of both has been made with reference to such contingency. In every instance where the nature of the ground admitted without sacrificing [p. 8] pro-file, the line has been thrown to the right, by that means placing valleys and depressions between it and the prevailing northwesterly winds.

Soon after crossing the divide or head of Bridger's Pass, we reach a branch of Muddy Creek, down which our line runs to its junction with the main stream, which we follow a distance of fifteen miles to a point where it bends strongly to the southward to form its junction with Little Snake River, of which it is a tributary.

The valley of Muddy Creek, as far as followed by our line, is extremely nar-row, having but little flat or bottom land on its margin—much of the distance being what is termed in the phraseology of the mountains, a cañon. Our line, in consequence, comes in frequent contact with the stream, and several changes of channel will be necessary.

By a judicious arrangement of grades, the work is rendered light in character. Where changes of channel are necessary, the embankment will require protection on the exposed side, by a lining of loose rock (rip-rap), the material for which pur-pose is convenient, abundant, and easily quarried. This stream (Muddy Creek), it may be stated, is comparatively small and insignificant,—in June last it was nearly dry. During the melting of the snow its section is much increased.

From what observation I was able to make, I estimate its flood section to be 180 square feet.

After leaving the elbow of Muddy Creek, the line passes over a country of long, flat slopes, crossing Bridger's Fork of Muddy. By means of a tributary and easy grades, we reach the broad table-land at the head of

BITTER CREEK.

The distance from the broad dividing ridge at the head of this stream to its junction with Green River, is 79 miles by our line, which keeps the valley for the entire distance with one exception, where we cut off a bend the stream makes to the northward, saving a distance of four miles at a very slight sacrifice of grade and profile.

The extreme scarcity of herbage for our stock made it neces-[p. 9] sary to push over this part of the line with great rapidity. Extraordinary exertions were made by the party to reach Green River at the earliest possible time compatible with the interests of the survey. When I state that runs of 12 miles per day were made over this portion of the line, engineers will understand the anxiety manifested by those engaged in the work. The favorable nature of the surface (affording no choice of ground but that could be readily detected by the eye) enabled us to reach our terminus at Green River, in nine working days from the time we first touched the drainage of Bitter Creek. The profile shows very light work until we approach to within six miles of Green River. It seems to be a characteristic feature of this region that streams form their intersection by means of narrow gorges, Bitter Creek is no exception; the last six miles of its course is through a crooked cañon, the sides of which are composed of friable sandstone and shale.

Having understood that Mr. Reed, in charge of the party west of Green River, made his connection near Rock Springs, some 18 miles above the mouth of Bitter Creek, it does not seem necessary to be minute in description of that part of the line.

TIMBER—FUEL—COAL.

From what has been already said in the first part of this report in reference to the supply of timber for the line east of the Black Hills, viz.: the valley of Lodge-Pole Creek and the South Platte, it is evident that the surplus in the Black Hills and along the Medicine Bow Mountains, will have to be made available to supply the almost entire want of so important an item of construction on that part of the route. From Julesburg, on the South Platte, to Camp Walbach, at the foot of the mountains, is 175 miles. This distance will require 394,000 cross-ties alone. As the building of the road will probably be from east to west, this material will have to be furnished in advance of construction, by teams.

The superior direction, and consequent saving of distance from the Missouri River to Salt Lake City, via Lodge-Pole Creek Cheyenne Pass, Fort Halleck, and Bitter Creek, over the much [p. 10] longer road, via the North Fork of the Platte, and the South Pass, is fast diverting the travel to the former.

During the past season a large proportion of the emigration has travelled it in preference to the latter and older route. It is believed the Lodge Pole road will continue to grow in favor. By establishing proper and convenient places of deposit for ties along the Lodge Pole Creek, much, and perhaps all this hauling could be done by empty return trains from Salt Lake. The mode of supplying the desert country on this division west of Rattlesnake Pass with fuel, wood, ties, timber for bridges, &c., is obvious.

COAL.

The first indication of this mineral in place on the line occurs on Rock or Frappe's Creek, in Latitude 41° 43'.

On the other side of the divide, near the Medicine Bow River, at station 3640 of our line, a seam of coal can be seen two feet thick, dipping south southeast, at an angle of 20 degrees. The coal is inferior in quality, being extremely dry and brittle.

East of Fort Halleck, coal is again found, probably of the same formation. At both of the places mentioned, some mining has been done, the coal from each having been used for blacksmith purposes with success. As to the extent of the deposit east of the North Platte River, the undersigned has no means of basing an intelligent opinion. It may be stated, however, that the places mentioned are not the only ones where coal is found east and north of the Medicine Bow Mountains. The next coal found is near Sulphur Springs stage station of the Overland Stage Co., on Muddy Creek, 14 miles west of the summit of Bridger's Pass. It is seen at the mouth of the cañon, at a considerable elevation above the stream, and gives the following section. [p. 11]

Coal.

Shale 3.

Coal.

Shale 3.

Coal.

This opening has been worked systematically, and is carried in a distance of 40 feet, with but little appreciation in the quality of the coal, it being like that found to the eastward, brittle and imperfectly mineralized. The station of the Overland Stage Company, at Sulphur Springs, is the headquarters of one of the divisions of their line; their blacksmith and repair shops are here. The object in making the coal opening, of which a section is given on the other side, was to save the hauling of coal from Bitter Creek, whence they procure their supply.

At the shop I found some good specimens from that locality. I afterwards visited the opening from which they were obtained, and a specimen is now in your possession; an analysis of it will probably be made. At Black Buttes, 30 miles from the summit of Bitter Creek, and on our line, where this coal occurs, several seams have been opened, one 5 feet, and one 3½ feet of clean coal. Frequent propping is required, in consequence of the broken, fragmentary nature of the roof. This is the hardest and best quality of coal found on the line. It may be stated that these are merely surface openings—other seams may occur at a greater depth; if so, they will be found of a superior quality, having a better roof. Some expenditure in sinking shafts will probably be necessary to determine fully the extent and value of this coal basin. As far as my examination and observation went, from this point (Black Buttes) to near Green River, the coal crops out of the bluffs frequently, and seems abundant. [p. 12]

Approximate Estimate of Quantities.

Reference to Profiles.	From Station.	To Station.	Miles.	Cubic yards earth excavation.	Cubic yards solid rock.	Cubic yards tunneling.	MASONRY. Cubic yards rec culvert.	Cubic yards arch culvert.	Cubic yards bridge abut's and piers.	Timber in sluices and foundations.	Lineal feet truss bridging.
Black Hills	0	1230	23.29	12,100	804,700	14,000	1,171	3,012	1,107	2,800 ft. B.M.	600 feet.
Laramie Plains, No. 1	1230	2770	29.11	355,466	24,000		163	528	225	1,700 " "	300 "
" " " 2	2770	3660	16.86	375,312	120,274		365	536	178	5,000 " "	280 "
Laramie P. & Rattlesnake Pass	3660	5520	35.21	478,150	205,462		478	134	992	5,000 " "	600 "
Platte Valley & Saige Creek	5520	7370	35.04	433,390			423	254	1,088	8,000 " "	
Bridger's Pass & Muddy Creek	7370	9350	37.50	510,230	20,000		94			4,000 " "	
Bitter Creek, No. 1	9350	10970	30.70	209,650					930	12,800 " "	
" " " 2	10970	12950	37.50	366,730					1,280	13,400 " "	400 "
" " " 3	12950	Green River.	24.48	267,820	96,280				1,840	14,400 " "	800 "
Total			269.69	3,008,778	1,270,716	14,000	2,694	4,464	7,640	67,100 " "	2,980 ft.
Average for 1 mile				11.156	4,712	51 9/16	9 9/16	16 5/16	28 3/16	248 ft.	11 5/100 ft.

[p. 13] It may be proper to state here, that no temporary structures are contemplated in the foregoing estimate. In all cases, even when there is a want of material, and where no located line would balance the excavation and embankment, the estimate has been made under the supposition that material would be borrowed for the purpose of making the fills. This has been done for the purpose of simplifying the estimate, and affording a basis to work from, in arriving at the cost of construction. The Black Hills are peculiar, in that the principal ravines on either slope are deep and narrow, with no ridges between, making it difficult obtaining the material necessary to fill them from the adjacent cuttings. On this part of the line the material is all rock. It is a question to what extent truss bridges or short viaducts may be used with advantage and economy. The crossing of Lodge Pole Creek, on the eastern slope, a type of all of them, would compare in quantities, as follows:

1st.	Estimate for full embankment, cubic yds..............		60,920
	Arch culvert masonry	"	810
2d.	Estimate for truss bridge:		
	Embankment,	"	12,360
	Masonry in piers and abutments,	"	1,856
	Truss bridging, lin. feet............................		300

BRIDGING.

	LIN. FEET.
Main Fork, Laramie River.....................................	350
Left hand Fork, Laramie River...............................	250
Cooper Creek..	50
Rock, or Frappe's Creek.....................................	250
Bear Creek..	50
Medicine Bow River..	150
Pass Creek..	80
North Platte River..	600
Bitter Creek, 17 crossings..................................	850
Green River...	50
Total..	2,980

TABLE OF GRADES.—ASCENDING.

Distance.		Grade per 100 feet.	Grade per mile.
Feet.	Miles.		
7,000	1.?25	2.8	147.84
43,700	8.276	2.2	116.16
44,400	8.409	2.0	105.6
7,600	1.439	1.9	100.32
16,600	3.143	1.8	95.04
22,500	4.240	1.6	84.48
42,500	8.049	1.5	79.20
37,700	7.140	1.2	63.36
30,700	5.814	1.0	52.80
83 000	15.719	0.8	42.24
94,400	17.878	0.5	26.40
34,400	6.515	0.3	15.84
32,400	6.136	0.2	10.56
46,900	8.880	0.1	5.28
Total....	102,963.....Miles.		

TABLE OF GRADES.—DESCENDING.

Distance.		Grade per 100 feet.	Grade per mile.
Feet.	Miles.		
56,000	10.606	2.5	132.09
48,100	9.110	2.2	116.16
34,600	6.553	2.0	105.6
8,600	1.628	1.9	100.32
4,800	0.909	1.8	95.04
14,200	2.689	1.6	84.48
39,600	7.5	1.5	79.20
46,300	8.768	1.2	63.36
22,900	4.335	1.0	52.8
62,500	11.837	0.8	42.24
94,200	17.84	0.5	26.4
58,900	11.155	0.3	15.84
59,900	11.344	0.2	10.56
161,800	30.643	0.1	5.28
Total...	134.917.....Miles.		

Distance ascending......................... 102.963
    " descending......................... 134.917
    " level............... .... 31.81

Total distance................. 269.69

TABLE OF ALIGNMENT.

½°	1°	1½°	2°	2½°	3°	3½°	4°	5°	5½°	6°	8°	Tangent
Rad.	Rad.	Rad.	Rad.	Rad.	Rad.	Rad.	Rad.	Rad.	Rad.	Rad.	Rad.	
11,459 feet.	5,730 ft.	3,820 ft.	2,865 ft.	2,292 ft.	1,910 ft.	1,637 ft.	1,433 ft.	1,146 ft.	1,042 ft.	955 ft.	716 ft.	Tangent
1.05 miles.	24.89 m.	1.06 m.	6.12 m.	1.17 m.	22.23 m.	1.42 m.	6.13 m.	5.45 m.	0.28 m.	3.38 m.	1.49 m.	195.02 miles.

Tangent.. 72.31 per cent,
Curve... 27.69 "

Length of Tangent line.......................... 195.02 miles,
    "   Curve   " .... 74.67 "

Total length of Division.......................... 269.69 "

TABLE.

	LATITUDE.	LONGITUDE.	ALTITUDE, FEET.
Camp Walbach	41° 18'	105° 15'	7,000
Summit of Black Hills	41° 16'	105° 29' 48"	8,656
Crossing of Main Fork of Laramie	41° 18' 17"	105° 34' 18"	7,175
Rattlesnake Pass	41° 45'	106° 39' 12"	7,560
Crossing of North Platte River	41° 42' 20"	106° 59'45"	6,695
Bridger's Pass	41° 41' 09"	107° 30' 48"	7,534
Head of Bitter Creek	41° 31' 56"	108° 16' 48"	7,090
Green River	41° 32' 51"	109° 30' 20"	6,092

REMARKS.

Soon after crossing the Black Hills with my line, I was impressed with the necessity of making a further examination of that range of mountains, both to the northward and likewise to the southward of the ground covered by my instructions; I should have done so then but for the following consideration: As stated before, my work was largely increased and extended in consequence of the non-acceptance of one of the appointments. I looked upon the necessity of having a line through as of the first importance. In accordance with that supposition, I resolved to push my line to Green River, for the purpose of making my connection there, then, if time permitted, to return to the Black Hills for further examination.

The country west of the North Platte River proving much more favorable than was anticipated, enabled the party to reach the terminus on the 26th July. On the following day (27th) we started on our return journey.

I expected, if time permitted, on my return, to examine the country south of our main line over the Black Hills (the range being considerably less in elevation there), if possible avoiding the drainage of Crow Creek, and finally reaching Lodge Pole Creek by means of a tributary of that stream (south of the main branch which we followed on the eastern slope), and designated on the maps as Muddy Creek. After that was done, it was my purpose to examine the Cañon of the Laramie River, supposing that if [p. 17] the latter afforded but ordinary obstacles to construction, the question of grades there would be an easy one, running, as this river does, completely through the range.

On reaching Fort Halleck, on my way back to this work, I found instructions requiring me, if possible, and if the state of my supplies warranted me in so doing, to return by way of the South Pass.

To make this part of my report intelligible, it becomes necessary to state here, that Fort Halleck was fixed upon as our base of supplies, and for obvious reasons, among which may be stated its central position with reference to the division, and the superior facilities it afforded for storage.

In pushing our line west, we left Fort Halleck with rations sufficient to take us to Green River and back to the fort. When we reached there on our return our stock of provisions required replenishing.

Had my instructions, therefore, found me at Green River instead of Fort Halleck, it would not have been possible to have complied with them.

I regard it as unfortunate that the possibility of our being able to return by way of the South Pass was not foreseen and provided for, and a different arrangement of supplies made to meet the emergency, as it would have enabled me to have based upon actual observation, what is now but conjecture and the observation of others.

When we left Omaha, the impression prevailed that the extent of the division would prove to be all one corps could accomplish during the season.

As stated before, the favorable nature of the ground, the fortunate proximity of the travelled road to our line, enabling us to move our transportation readily and with despatch, combined with the strength and efficiency of the party, brought us to our terminus at least six weeks earlier than I anticipated.

The geographical position of Fort Halleck with reference to the South Pass will show the difficulty in reaching the latter.

Had our supplies been in shape it is very questionable if the integrity of the party could have been preserved. The ordeal our stock had passed through west of the North Platte River, made our teamsters extremely reluctant to traverse a similar [p. 18] region still more extensive. That reluctance (had the order been given to retrace our journey) would have resulted in insubordination, and other and different arrangements for transportation would have become necessary. This I should not have hesitated about, however, had it been the only difficulty in the way.

Here Mr. Finney, first assistant, left the party and returned to the States.

I concluded, however, that I would carry out the programme I had already marked out, with reference to the head of Crow Creek and the Laramie Cañon; then, if rapid transportation and escort were provided me through the military authorities at Fort Laramie, I would go to the South Pass, taking with me a few men, for the purpose of examining the salient points on that line, the party returning to the Missouri meanwhile.

The result of our labors in the Black Hills, south of our main line, may be summed up thus: The starting point (running back) of the branch line is a little west of our crossing of the main fork of Laramie River. Distance from the point of divergence to the foot of the range by main line 5½ miles, by branch line 9 miles, caused by the latter striking the range more diagonally. The broken nature of the surface after touching the Black Hills, had the effect of keeping us constantly at the foot of the slope. When it became necessary to turn to the left for the purpose of preserving our direction and to prevent our being thrown into the tributaries of Crow Creek, the elevation was found to be greater than we could surmount.

Explorations have been made since on the Cache-la-Poudre Creek, in the country to which this line would have carried us, had we continued it, and is probably the line with which Mr. Case connected his survey.

It must be understood here, that our labors were done with a view of still making the valley of Lodge Pole Creek our eastern continuation.

Our journey to the Laramie Cañon was by way of Camp Walbach and the Valley of the Chugwater to near its mouth, where we crossed a low divide between it and the Laramie River; thence up the latter to near the mouth of Sibylle's Fork, [p. 19] where we established a camp, intending to devote some time to an exploration of the hills in that vicinity, the Cañon of the Laramie and the Valley of Sibylle's Fork. On producing a line 25 miles up the latter, we found it did not penetrate the range with anything like a distinct valley, besides carrying us far to the southward. My explorations and observation now enable me to form an idea of the several crossings of the Black Hills. The sections will compare as follows:

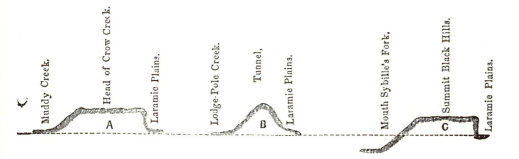

Section A. — From Muddy Creek to Laramie Plains.
      B. — Section on main line.
      C. — Sybille's Fork to Laramie Plains.

It will be seen that both the sections A and C are lower than the crossing of our main line. What constitutes their inferiority is the great rapidity of the descent where it does occur. The Laramie Cañon remains to be noticed.

I approached this part of my labor in the mountains with no little interest and solicitude. As our main line progressed across the North Platte River, over Bridger's Pass, and over the country between Muddy Creek and Bitter Creek, a sufficient knowledge of the country north was obtained to show the feasibility of a line, striking the Medicine Bow River at its elbow, the North Platte below the mouth of Pass Creek, then north of Bridger's Pass, and by means of some one of the valleys leading into Bitter Creek from the northeast, forming a junction with our line in the valley of that stream.

The Laramie Cañon seemed to be the key to this route.

It will be understood, then, that the importance of this gorge was not under-estimated by me—no information could be obtained as to its character, even from mountain men, supposed to [p. 20] be familiar with all the nooks and gorges of a country in which they had spent the whole of their manhood, and no small portion of their declining years. While camped within a mile of its terrible chasm, projecting points obscured it so entirely from view, that had it not been for the river rushing by our tents and the previous knowledge of its existence, it might have been passed unnoticed.

Taking with me Messrs. Dutton, Sladden, O'Neil, and Booze, of the party, I started from camp 74 on the morning of August 30, with the intention of tracing the river through the gorge. It is unnecessary to detail the difficulties we encountered in proceeding up it on merely a prospecting tour.

The river has evidently cut its way through the range, composed principally of granite and gneiss; its channel is extremely crooked, hemmed in closely by (for the greater part of the distance) vertical walls of rock, ranging in height from 500 to 1,500 feet—what room there is is occupied solely and exclusively by the bed of the torrent. Where it cuts through the cone of the range it forms a succession of rapids for miles, descending, it is estimated, from 3 to 5 feet in 100; these rapids would form a great obstacle, were the sides of the gorge otherwise favorable and the curvature such as could be overcome. From the necessity of keeping close to the water, (as where the walls are not vertical, the talus, at the foot is insignificant, and by no means continuous,) it will be seen that the grade would have to undulate with the descent of the stream, and no advantage could be taken of distance to overcome *extraordinary* elevation at any one point. In overcoming a distance of 12 miles in a direct line, this river must run through 22 miles at least of cañon. For a portion of the distance it more than doubles itself. Two cases were noticed, particularly where the stream is only prevented from forming a perfect ellipse, by a vertical wall of gneiss 1,000 feet high and 700 feet through from water to water. The cases above were noticed as extraordinary, but the whole distance is a succession of short bends, many of them forming greater obstacles still to the construction of a line. A succession of tunnels and bridges would be required for almost the entire distance. Taking this view of it, I did not think it necessary to run any line up it. It seemed now that we had, either by actual trial or observation [p. 21] examined everything within accessible distance that promised an opening.

On the 1st September, I started for the eastward with the party, expecting, when I reached Fort Laramie to learn by telegraph, something to govern my future operations.

At Fort Laramie I telegraphed for instructions. The reply was, in effect a permission to send the party back, and a request to go the South Pass myself for the purpose of observation.

In accordance with, and from a strong desire to comply with the request, as well as a wish on my own part to be in possession of facts necessary to institute a comparison between routes that seemed likely to come into competition, I started the party from Fort Laramie for the Missouri River, on the 5th September, remaining myself, with the intention of going up the North Platte for the purpose mentioned.

My only reliance for transportation, rations, &c., being on the ability and courtesy of the commanders of the different military posts, no arrangements having been made through the commander of the district.

The Indian difficulties having their origin in the spring, had increased intensely, until during the summer, the whole frontier (including the valley of the North and South Platte) was rendered insecure. At the time of my arrival at Fort Laramie, the several posts along the North Platte River, from Fort Laramie to the South Pass, were considered in danger. It is certain they were but feebly garrisoned, and incapable of offering anything like a protracted defence. This feeling of insecurity. [,] coupled with the difficulty of procuring transportation and the consciousness of being so entirely subject to the movements of others, forced me reluctantly to the conclusion that I could not do what I desired with the requisite despatch, if at all. I, therefore, left the post with the purpose of overtaking my party, which was done on the following day.

Our return was along the telegraph road, striking our outward line of travel, on the Lodge Pole Creek, 40 miles above its mouth.

By the exercise of constant vigilance, through a country from which the inhabitants had been forced to flee, and where the savages were decidedly hostile, we safely reached Omaha, with but slight interruption, on the 25th day of September. [p. 22]

It may be deemed a subject of congratulation that we returned without the loss of a single member of the party, with our stock entire, and everything in good order.

CONCLUSION.

By using the accompanying table of latitude and longitude in conection with a map of the country, it will be seen that in point of direction, the line of which this report is descriptive, stands pre-eminent. Taking the junction of the North and South forks of the Platte River, as a common starting point, the distance by way of Fort Laramie, through Valley of the Sweetwater, and through South Pass, would, under the most favorable circumstances, be increased 70 miles over this line.

In addition to the above, the Bridger's Pass route affords a much larger amount of valuable timber contiguous to it, than the line by the South Pass. A very important consideration, and one by no means to be overlooked.

Coal is said to occur on the North Platte, above Fort Laramie, as well as on Bitter Creek; both of these coal deposits should receive the closest scrutiny before any route is finally decided upon. My opinion is, and I give it with diffidence, that the result of such investigation will be to entitle the route *via* Bridger's Pass to still greater consideration. From some little observation of the valley of the North Platte, near Fort Laramie, from hearsay, and from the profiles of military engineers, I am led to believe that the upper route is by no means one of continuously ascending and easy grades, as far as South Pass, even,[.] In some instances it will be found necessary to leave the valley of the stream on account of cañons and narrows.

Some distance below Fort Laramie the North Platte ceases to be a river of the plains.

Twenty-five miles above that military post, it runs through what is called Horseshoe Cañon. Here spurs of the Black Hills extend some distance to the eastward and across the river. Major Bridger, in a conversation I had with him at Laramie, was very emphatic in stating that no line could pass up it. The alternative, in his opinion, was to have [leave] the valley of the river below the Fort, follow up the Rawhide Creek, striking [p. 23] the Platte again at or nearly opposite the mouth of La Bonté Creek. This would be leaving the valley of the Platte for a distance of 45 miles.

I do not mean to be understood that there is anything insurmountable here; only to show some of the obstacles that may be expected on this route, not only at the Horseshoe Cañon, but at Red Buttes, still further up, at the mouth of the Sweetwater, and at Devil's Gate, on the latter stream.

As the South Pass route will probably be examined, it does not seem necessary for me to follow the comparison further. I have merely given what information I was able to obtain.

I cannot close this communication without making one or two suggestions for the benefit of the Company in future explorations, as conducing to the efficiency of parties in the field, as well as the comfort mentally of those who may have charge in conducting the surveys.

There is no probability that the Indians will be more peaceable during the coming season that they have been during the one just past. Parties of engineers going there, unless protected by escort, will be subject to interruption and delay, if nothing more. The efficiency of the escort depends in a great degree upon the ability and attention to duty of the officers temporarily in command. My suggestion is, that the engineer in charge of the party should, by means of some arrangement with the War Department, be able for the time being, to outrank the commander of the escort. By no other means can unity be preserved and a conflict of authority prevented.

The other suggestion is, that either the Company, or head of the party should *absolutely own* the means of transportation. We suffered no inconvenience in consequence of this defect in our organization, but I can now see, how easily contingencies might have arisen, making it necessary to remodel this part of the organization of the party—a thing difficult of accomplishment in the Rocky Mountains.

In conclusion, I wish to acknowledge my obligations to the members of my party.

To F. N. Finney, 1st Assistant, I am particularly obliged for his valuable assistance so cheerfully rendered while he remained with the party. [p. 24]

From Messrs. Dutton, O'Neil, Furguson, and the remaining members of the corps, I received valuable assistance, for which they are not only entitled to my thanks, but to the consideration of the Company.

Praise is due Colonel W. O. Collins for his promptitude in furnishing escort.

To ———Jones, Esq., now of Salt Lake City, then in charge of the sutler's establishment, at Fort Halleck, I am obliged for several acts of kindness, among which may be mentioned his liberality in furnishing us with room for storage without charge.

Respectfully submitted,

JAS. A. EVANS,

Div. Eng.

To T. C. DURANT, Esq.,
    Vice-Pres't, U.P.R.R. Co.,
       13 William St., New York.

Francis M. Case, 1865 [+ Berthoud]

Union Pacific Railroad...Surveys Of Cache La Poudre & South Platte Routes [in 1864] [+ Denver City To Utah Lake, 1861]

Letter of December 15, 1864, Omaha, Nebraska, to T. C. Durant; New York, 11 p.,
presumably printed in 1865. [WC 414 note; WCB 412a; Graff 4243; UPRR p. 46;
NUC NU 0027555.] Reset verbatim from a facsimile, by courtesy of
The Newberry Library, Chicago, Illinois.

Significance   Case fruitlessly checked out the passes west of Denver in the vain hope that the Union Pacific main line could directly serve that city's business and mining interests. The best possibility was Berthoud Pass, but it required a 3.5-mile tunnel at the top and had complex terrain beyond. Engineer Edward L. Berthoud went through this pass in 1861 with guide Jim Bridger on a survey for a mail route from Denver to Provo, Utah (see Itinerary). In 1862 Case, then the Surveyor General of Colorado Territory, ran a line of levels over the crest and a short way down Fraser River ("Moses Creek"). His report, which first appeared in the Union Pacific's organizational document (Dix 1864), cast a chill on the Berthoud Pass idea. Case repeated this 1862 report with minor modifications here in his 1865 publication. His surveys were aided by the barometer elevations provided by botanist Charles C. Parry, who happened to be collecting alpine plants in the area (see Highlights).

Regarding the other passes, Case thought that the Continental Divide west of Boulder was too high and too steep even to warrant a visit. Three other possible passes were up westering branches of the South Platte after it entered its canyon into the mountains south of Denver. The first pass, at the head of the North Fork, connected to the Snake and then the Blue River and the mining towns of Keystone and Dillon. The second pass, the Boreas at the head of Tarryall Creek, connected to Breckenridge. The third pass, the Hoosier at the head of the main South Platte after it loops back north through South Park, connected to the Blue and Breckenridge. All of these passes were high, steep, tortuous, snowy, and out of line with the west direction of the Union Pacific from Omaha. Bayard Taylor wrote in 1866 that "The main branch of the South Platte finds an outlet to the plains through a cañon which is yet impassable."

Case's final possibility, the Cache la Poudre River route well north of Denver, would connect Laporte and Ft. Collins over Antelope Pass to the Laramie Plains. It was the route of the Overland Stage, roughly paralleling modern Highway 287; Case mentions stations or locations at Cherokee, Bonner ("Boner"), Stonewall, and Virginia Dale. Case's Antelope Pass lay between a branch of Dale Creek and Willow Creek near today's Tie Siding, Wyoming. The Cache la Poudre route, however, was not as straight or direct as the Lodgepole Creek route; Peter A. Dey thought that it would add 60 or 70 miles (L12 Highlights).

Case here was the first Union Pacific man in print to pinpoint "Evans Pass," the one actually adopted by the railroad (cf. L12 Legacy). On page 10 he stated, "allow me to suggest that a thorough examination should be made of the divide, east of Dale creek, and a few miles north of Virginia Dale, at the heads of Crow creek and Box Elder...Now, if by some branch of Crow Creek or Howard's Fork [Lone Tree Creek; see Warren's General Map], we can find a uniform grade to the summit, I think such grade will be within the limit fixed by the charter of the road...[Such a route] would connect with the Lodge Pole Route, by way of Muddy Fork [east of modern Cheyenne], without a serious sacrifice of alignment." This is precisely the line upon which the Union Pacific was built. And Case cited Stansbury's 1852 account of the discovery of "Evans Pass," to the page.

Vice President Durant in 1865 commented that Case's suggested line up Crow Creek "to my mind promises many advantages over the routes heretofore examined." Lt. Francis T. Bryan's topographer John Lambert had been in this area in 1857 and named Howard's Fork after one of his men; but Lambert was impressed mainly by "The inferior character of the whole region."

Case's report was reprinted by Durant in 1866. This probably is the first reprint since then. Although not issued with the first edition, one of Case's lithographs from the Durant edition, showing the mouth of South Platte Canyon, is reproduced here.

Author   FRANCIS M. CASE, explorer, surveyor, engineer. Case, from Ohio, became the first Surveyor General of the new Colorado Territory on June 17, 1861. That summer he completed surveys of township boundary lines and reported, "In the South Park are extensive settlements, and during the present season there has been a very considerable emigration of settlers to the Middle Park." In 1862 he reported preparation of a new map of Colorado and summarized the geology, mineral resources, climate, agriculture, and the stock-raising industry. He submitted several coal samples to Washington from along the Rocky Mountain Front, plus one collected by E. L. Berthoud in 1861 "from an outcrop in the valley of White river, near the western boundary of the Territory." In June, 1862, Case and Gov. John Evans examined Berthoud Pass, as reported in this present reprint. Case ceased being Surveyor General in April, 1863. In 1864 he performed the surveys outlined here. In 1865 he rechecked the Laramie River route from the North Platte to the Laramie Plains (Galloway 1950). In 1867 the Union Pacific loaned him to run a survey from Denver to near Cheyenne (Hafen 1948).

Participant   EDWARD LOUIS BERTHOUD 1828-1908, explorer, engineer, soldier, scientist. Berthoud was born in Switzerland, came to America in 1830, was educated in New York, and did engineering work on midwestern railroads in the 1850s. He and his wife settled in Golden in 1859 or 1860. On a first short exploration sponsored by local citizens to find a mail route from Denver to Salt Lake City, Berthoud found Berthoud Pass, 55 miles west of Denver, on May 12, 1861. He went on to Hot Sulphur Springs before turning back. Soon afterward the Central Overland Express Company sent Berthoud and mountaineer James Bridger through that pass and on to Provo, Utah, to mark out a wagon road (see Itinerary). A pamphlet, *The Rocky Mountain Gold Regions,* by Silas W. Burt and E. L. Berthoud, civil and mining engineers, appeared in 1861. The authors' aim initially was "to obtain reliable statistics in regard to the Quartz Mining in the Rocky Mountains for their own personal purposes." They hoped that future editions, which never materialized, would include information on natural history and "data affecting the location of the Pacific Railroad through the Mountain Range." The first edition contained Berthoud's observations on botany, mammals, reptiles, geology, and mineralogy.

Berthoud was commissioned in the Second Colorado Volunteers in 1862. He served in Colorado, Kansas, and Missouri. As a captain he erected the fortifications that helped save Jefferson City during a Confederate assault. From 1866 to 1880, as chief engineer and secretary of the Colorado Central Railroad, he built lines to the mining towns. He made route surveys as close as the link with the Union Pacific and as far afield as Idaho. In the 1870s he was the first registrar and secretary of the Colorado School of Mines. He also served on its first board of trustees and was the first professor of civil engineering and geology. In addition he taught botany, wrote papers on archeology and birds, and kept weather records. He was elected to the New York Academy of Sciences. He helped the State Library obtain scientific publications. He died of a fall. (Ryland 1965; Ewan; Hafen 1948).

Itinerary, 1861 BERTHOUD, DENVER TO PROVO. July 6—Edward L. Berthoud and a small pack party, guided by Jim Bridger, leave Denver and camp at Golden City. They ascend Clear Creek on the wagon road through Idaho Springs to Empire City. Berthoud writes, "We resumed our journey on the 9th up Clear Creek, and encamped at night on the summit of the Rocky Mountains, in Berthoud's Pass [11,307 feet], fifty-five miles from Denver…in a beautiful prairie covered with a luxuriant growth of grass, interspersed with a great variety of flowers." They descend Fraser River to the Colorado in Middle Park. July 11— By pre-arrangement they are joined by Indian agent Harvie M. Vaile and 4 men. The next day they reach Hot Sulphur Springs and lay over "to arrange our packs and enjoy bathing and fishing. The trout in the river were splendid." They cross the Colorado and proceed west past modern Kremmling and on over the Gore Range. Vaile notes, "Major Bridger, our guide, conducted Lord [George] Gore through this pass over eight years ago, with a train of some twenty wagons, hence we gave it the name of 'Gore's Pass'…our passage over was a gentle inclined plane on both sides, an easy and practicable grade for a railroad."

July 15—They reach the head of the Yampa near present Toponas CO. Berthoud records, "laid over a day, on account of the sickness of Major Bridger, and then bore him on a litter between two mules for two days." They follow down the Yampa, cutting off its northern bend by going through today's Pagoda. Before entering the canyon at what is now Dinosaur National Monument, from about the mouth of Little Snake River, they drop south through modern Elk Springs to the White River. This they descend to the Green River, cutting off the last bend at today's Bonanza UT. Berthoud describes the Green as "about one hundred and fifty yards wide, and quite deep. We made a raft, with which we crossed our provisions &c., in two trips, and swam our animals across, drowning two mules."

August 2—They arrive at Provo City. From the Green they have followed Fremont's 1845 track (5:J1). It ascends the Uinta, the Duchesne, and the West Fork of the Duchesne, thence crossing to and descending Provo River. So they pass the modern towns of Ouray, Randlett, Duchesne, Stockmore, and Heber City. Itinerary is from Berthoud's 1861 journal extracted by James D. Doty in 1862, from Vaile's 1861 report printed in 1862, and from Hafen 1926. Vaile dates only his Denver departure, July 8, and return by the Cherokee Trail, September 1. Berthoud states, "we arrived [at Provo] on the 18th [2d] of August, making the trip in twenty-seven and a half [28] days, including the loss of five and a half [6] days in exploring the route and resting in camp." He writes a report from Salt Lake City on August 4; on his way back he locates, surveys, marks, improves, and shortens the road to 426 5/8 miles (Hafen 1926). He returns to Denver on September

19, according to Ryland (1965). Assuming that the outward journey of about 500 miles takes 28 days including 6 layovers, the average rate is 18 miles per day.

Berthoud's shortened return route is given by Wheat (5:32-35, map 1019). Berthoud stays on the White River eastward all the way to present Meeker CO, thence curving northward around the Flat Tops to rejoin his outward path southeast of Pagoda.

Highlights   William Gilpin, Colorado's Governor and Superintendent of Indian Affairs, on June 19, 1861, outlined agent Vaile's assignment: "The necessities of our country render necessary the establishment of a great road from Denver to Salt Lake City. This road crosses the Cordillera about 60 miles due west from Denver, and then traverses the northwest quarter of Colorado diagonally. Harvie M. Vaile has been assigned to this region. Availing myself of the departure of a well selected surveying party, conducted by E. L. Berthand [sic], a most skilful engineer, and accompanied by the experienced guide, James Bridger, I have instructed Agent Vaile to accompany them."

Case mentioned that botanist Charles Christopher Parry made a number of key barometric observations of elevation near the Continental Divide. Parry, 1823-1890, was a genial little botanist, physician, and veteran of the Mexican Boundary Survey (DAB; Ewan; see 5:J7). In the summers of 1861 and 1862 Parry collected alpine plants from his base at a lonely cabin high on South Clear Creek. He reported in 1862, "In my solitary wanderings over these rugged rocks and through these alpine meadows, resting at noon-day in some sunny nook, overlooking wastes of snow and crystal lakes girdled with mid-summer ice, I naturally associated some of the more prominent mountain peaks with distant and valued friends." He named peaks after botanists John Torrey, Asa Gray, and George Engelmann. Parry spent many more years in the Rockies, and a peak was named for him, too.

Two men wrote about their visits to Berthoud Pass in 1866. Silas Seymour, consulting engineer to the Union Pacific and a thorn in the sides of the operating engineers, dashed up and back from Empire City in the afternoon of September 18. He remarked, "we made our way slowly up the trail without much difficulty, although in many places the path was quite steep and sideling." He and his companions sang patriotic songs on top. Out-of-shape adventurer Bayard Taylor, on the other hand, agonized his way up in late June: "It was, indeed, a terrible pull...our horses stopped, almost gasping for breath." Dismounted, "our knees tottered, our bodies were drenched with sweat, our eyes dim, heads giddy, and lungs utterly collapsed." Then he ran into deep snow at the top and really had something to complain about.

Legacy   All Union Pacific thoughts of tackling the big mountains back of Denver were abandoned when Congress's Act of July 3, 1866, allowed the Central Pacific to build east until it met the track coming west. In that race, the shortest and easiest route was the only way to go. Gen. Dodge told the Directors, "The Lodge Pole Creek main line...has the best alignment, costs less per mile, has the best grades and less bridging...and has less road to run and build than any of the other lines...[It] is superior to all others and should be adopted" (Galloway 1950). It was adopted on November 23, 1866.

Denver did not get its railroad straight west to the Pacific until 1934. At first the routes were all roundabout. Berthoud and Case made separate surveys to link Denver to the north with the Union Pacific main line near Cheyenne in 1867. Ex-Governor John Evans finished that line in 1870. A narrow gauge track went up Clear Creek to Central City and Georgetown in 1877. Another was built up the South Platte Canyon and its North Fork 66 miles to Grant (Campbell 1922). The Denver & Rio Grande laid narrow gauge tracks south to Pueblo in 1872 and slowly worked west from there to Ogden, Utah. The tracks were converted to standard gauge in 1890.

The big push straight west started in 1903. The tracks crept up South Boulder Creek—the first route summarily rejected by Case—to Rollins Pass at 11,680 feet. They descended to the Fraser at Winter Park, below Berthoud Pass. Promoters were David Moffat, Walter Cheesman, and William G. Evans, son of Gov. John Evans. The line ultimately went partly along Berthoud's 1861 trail down the Fraser and Colorado rivers through Gore Canyon to Bond. Thence it crossed to the Yampa and followed it north to Steamboat Springs and west to stop in 1913 at the coal fields at Craig.

After a string of 20 annual deficits the line was rejuvenated by a government subsidy and increased freight in coal and oil and lettuce. The company drove the 6.09-mile Moffat Tunnel right under Rollins Pass and the Continental Divide during 1923 to 1926. The tunnel buckled under the intense pressure but was successfully shored up. Still the road went only to Craig. In 1934 the critical 38-mile segment was completed down the Colorado from Bond to Dotsero that linked the Moffat line with the main line of the Denver & Rio Grande Western. Now trains could go from Denver to Dotsero to Grand Junction to Green River to Price to Provo (down the Spanish Fork, not the Provo River) to Salt Lake City to Ogden. "Denver's dream of a direct transcontinental railroad was realized at long last. The 606.9 mile direct line from Denver to Ogden completed a central route." (Hafen 1948.)

REFERENCES

(See Preface for Heading and Author references, and for Warren,
Wheat, DAB, and Ewan, not listed here.)

Berthoud, Edward L., 1861 (1862 printing), Extract from E. D. [sic] Berthoud's journal of his trip from Denver City to Utah lake, by J. D. Doty: Wash., 37/3 S unnumbered, p. 346-48; quote on pass 346, all others 347.

Burt, Silas W., and Edward L. Berthoud, 1861 (1962 facsimile reprint), The Rocky Mountain gold regions: Denver, 132 p., quotes 2-3.

Campbell, Marius R., 1922, Guidebook of the Western U.S., Part E, The Denver & Rio Grande Western Route: Wash., U.S. Geological Survey Bull. 707, p. 13-21.

Case, Francis M., 1861, Surveyor General's Office, Denver City: Wash., 37/2 S1, serial 1117, p. 616-17.

Case, Francis M., 1862, Surveyor General's Office, Denver: Wash., 37/3 S unnumbered, p. 112-17, quote on coal 117.

Dix, John A., 1864, Report of the organization and proceedings of the Union Pacific Railroad Co.: N.Y., Report of F. M. Case, Appendix 3, iv p.

Durant, Thomas C., 1865 (1866 printing), Union Pacific Railroad, report of…surveys made up to the close of the year 1864: N.Y., quote p. 4; Case report reprint, Appendix B, 11 p., 7 plates.

Galloway, John D., 1950 (1989 reprint), The first transcontinental railroad: N.Y., Case p. 251; Dodge quotes 213.

Gilpin, William, 1861, Report of June 19 from Denver, Colorado Territory: Wash., 37/2 S1, serial 1117, p. 709.

Hafen, LeRoy R., 1926, The overland mail: Cleveland, p. 222-223.

Hafen, LeRoy R., 1948, Colorado and its people: N.Y., Berthoud 1:295, 2:543, 639; History of Colorado Railroads by Herbert O. Brayer, 2:635-90, quote 688; Case in 1867 2:641.

Lambert, John, 1857, Report on the topography of the country between Lodge Pole creek, Cache la Poudre, and the South Platte: Wash., 35/1 H2, serial 943, p. 481-85, quote 484.

Parry, Charles C., 1862, Physiographic sketch of that portion of the Rocky Mountain range, at the head waters of South Clear Creek…with an enumeration of the plants: New Haven, American Journal of Science and Arts, 33:231-43, quote 234-35.

Ryland, Charles S., 1965, The energetic Captain Berthoud: Boulder, The Denver Westerners Monthly Roundup, v. 21, n. 9 & 10, p. 3-11.

Seymour, Silas, 1866 (1867 pub.), Incidents of a trip…to the Rocky Mountains and Laramie Plains: N.Y., p. 15-18, quote 15.

Stansbury, Howard, 1852, Exploration and survey of the Valley of the Great Salt Lake of Utah: Phila., 32/Special S3, serial 608, p. 258.

Taylor, Bayard, 1866 (1867 pub.) Colorado, a summer trip: N.Y., quote on Berthoud Pass p. 81-82, on South Platte Canyon 144.

Vaile, Harvie M., 1861 (1862 printing), Report of H. M. Vaile, on his expedition from Denver, Colorado, to Great Salt Lake City, and back: Wash., 37/3 S unnumbered, p. 376-82, quote on Gore 377; date of departure 376, and of return 381.

UNION PACIFIC RAILROAD

REPORT OF F.M. CASE.

OF

Surveys of Cache La Poudre & South Platte Routes,

AND

OTHER MOUNTAIN PASSES IN COLORADO.

OMAHA, Neb. T'y, Dec. 15, 1864.

SIR,—Under my instructions to gather, by actual survey and otherwise, whatever information I could relating to the mountain passes of Colorado, I have the honor to submit the following:

REPORT.

These passes, or such of them as have been spoken of as possible or practicable for railroad purposes, are, the Caché La Poudre, the Boulder, the Berthoud, a pass at the head of the North Fork of the South Platte, one at the head of Tarryall creek, and the Hoosier Pass near Montgomery.

THE BOULDER PASS.

From information obtained from Mr. D.C. Collier, a very intelligent explorer of Colorado, and now editor of the *Miner's Register*, of Central City, and from other sources, I judge the Pass to be at least $11,900 [*sic*] feet above the level of the sea. The [p. 2] valley (of S. Boulder) at the foot of the mountains cannot be more than 5,600 feet. The elevation of Boulder City, six miles' north, on North Boulder, being 5,536 feet. This leaves a difference of elevation of 6,300 feet, and this elevation must be overcome in a distance at most of 35 miles. Knowing these facts, I have not even visited the Boulder Pass.

THE ROUTE OF THE NORTH FORK OF THE SOUTH PLATTE

Would enter the mountains at the cañon of the South Platte, follow up that stream about ten miles to the mouth of the North Fork, thence up that stream 35 miles to the range, and thence connect with one of the heads of Snake River, an

F. M. CASE DIV. ENG.ʳ DEL.

UNION PACIFIC RAIL ROAD
SURVEY OF 1864.
MOUTH OF CAÑON OF SOUTH PLATTE.

The Mayer & Knapp Eng. M'f'g & Lith Co. 449 Broadway N.Y.

affluent of the Blue. The pass is represented by Hon. Daniel Witter, another very intelligent explorer of Colorado, as being a little below the "timber line," probably about 11,500 feet above tide-water. From elevations kindly furnished me by Dr. C.C. Parry, I am enabled to give some information that may be of use in judging of this route. At a point 12 or 15 miles below the pass ("The Forks,") the elevation is 9,153 feet, at 7 miles below it is 8,405, and at a point 4 miles further down 8,018, indicating that a practical grade would follow the valley to "The Forks." The trouble I apprehended would be to overcome 2,300 feet elevation in the 12 or 15 miles from that point to the pass, without a very long tunnel.

The descent upon the western slope to the mouth of Snake River, a distance of not more than 20 miles, is 2,700 feet, upon the hypothesis that the pass is 11,500 feet above tide-water. The route for the entire distance from the plains to the Blue is through a narrow valley, and in many places doubtless very tortuous.

THE TARRYALL CREEK ROUTE

Enters the mountains *via* South Platte, and follows up the main stream 10 or 12 miles further than the last mentioned route, where it diverges, following up the valley of Tarryall Creek some 25 miles to the South Park, thence near the creek across the Park to Hamilton and Tarryall, thence up the main stream to [p. 3] a pass about the height of Hoosier Pass, from which it descends Indiana Gulch to the Blue above Breckenridge.

Of this route I can say but little advisedly. Dr. Parry gives the elevation of Tarryall (old town) at 9,932 feet. The pass, at a distance, in my opinion, not exceeding six miles, is 1,500 feet higher. I do not think that the maximum grade allowed by the charter would go within two miles of the pass, following the stream. Whether there is any way of making distance on this approach or not I cannot tell, as I have not had an opportunity of examining the route from Tarryall to the pass. I have been down Indiana Gulch to the Blue, and should say the descent was 150 or 200 feet to the mile.

THE SOUTH PLATTE ROUTE.

I have made a partial survey of this route, and report herewith a profile of Hoosier Pass, a profile of a line 18 miles down the Blue, and one of a line 48 miles down the South Platte, through the South Park to the head of the cañon.

A tunnel of 2½ miles in length would be required at the crossing of the range. This tunnel would be through granite the entire distance, and would doubtless cross several gold lodes, which crop out upon the western, or rather northern slope.

The line upon the western slope would have to follow the side of the mountain to get a practical grade. I should think distance sufficient could be gained upon the east side of the Blue to allow the grade to reach the valley a few miles below Breckenridge, from which point to the mouth of the Blue the line would follow a fine wide valley, with easy grades, as indicated by the profile, and good alignment; except that the valley makes but very little westing in its entire length.

A line down the South Platte may be located so as to secure, very nearly, a uniform grade from the mouth of the tunnel to the head of the cañon, where my line terminates, with light curves and light work, as the profile indicates.

When I reached the head of the cañon, I found, by examination, that it extended 9 or 10 miles, and there being no way of moving camp down the valley, except by "packing," I concluded [p. 4] to abandon the survey. From the head of the cañon to the plains, a distance of some 40 miles, the river runs all of the way through the mountains. The greater portion of the distance the valley is of sufficient width to admit of a good location for the road, but there would probably be 20 miles, at least, of "close" cañon, or one both walls of which are washed by the stream. There would necessarily be a good deal of tunnelling in the cañon—how much I cannot say. I estimated the height of Hoosier Pass to be 11,500 feet above the sea. This estimate I formed from its being about 200 feet below the limit of arborescence or "tree line," which in that locality is about 11,700 feet above tidewater.* Allowing the pass to be as estimated, the elevation at the head of the cañon will be 8,432 feet. Calling the mouth of the cañon 5,700, it would leave a difference of elevation of 2,732 feet between the mouth of the cañon and its head, making an average grade of less than 70 feet per mile.

In the matter of grades, I do not hesitate in the opinion that there is no route in Colorado with so easy an approach, on both sides of the main range of mountains, as this route. Yet the easy grades are made at the sacrifice of general alignment. There will be a line of about 145 miles in length to make 76 miles of westing between Denver and the mouth of the Blue.

There is an abundance of timber, the mountain varieties of fir, spruce, and pine, along the whole route, except that in the Park it is some distance from the line. Good building stone and limestone may be easily procured from the ridges of stratified rock that intersect the Park, and in the same formation in the valley of the Blue.

From what information I have gleaned, in three and a half years residence in Colorado, the snow falls in the basin of the Blue and in the vicinity of Hoosier Pass

---

*I have since learned from Dr. Parry that the "tree line" at Georgia Pass, the nearest point to the Hoosier Pass, at which it has been taken, is 11,487 feet. F. M.C.

deeper than in any part of Colorado. From some person (I cannot now remember who gave me this information,) who kept a meteorological record [p. 5] at Georgia Gulch, during the winter of 1861-2, I learned that the total fall of snow at that place was 37 feet; and in one storm in February, 1862, 11 feet. Georgia Gulch is on the western slope—one of the gulches of Swan river, an affluent of the Blue.

THE BERTHOUD PASS ROUTE

I did not have time to make any further examination of this route the past season, and have but little information to report that is not contained in my report to Gov. Evans in 1862. Which report, with a few corrections, such as further experience in the geology and climatology of Colorado dictates, I here insert, that I may embody in one paper all the information I have been able to obtain upon the subject, up to the present date.

"COLORADO TERRITORY,
Denver, August 15th, 1862.

"HON. JOHN EVANS, GOV.
     Col. Territory:

"Sir,—In submitting to you this report of my late instrumental reconnoissance of the Berthand [sic] Pass and its eastern approach, with the view of its being by you laid before the Board of Corporators of the Pacific Railroad, I am aware that the facts which will be of real interest to practical railroad men are very meagre; yet, as many misrepresentations have been made upon mere opinion, the few facts I have gleaned may be of interest to the Board of Corporators, of which you are a member.

"I have had a connected line of levels run from the Platte River (at the upper bridge in Denver) to the summit of the Pass and two and three fourths miles down Moses Creek, on the Pacific slope. From one mile below Empire City a transit line has been run over the Pass—levels have been run up Clear Creek, a mile and a half above the mouth of Hoope's Creek, opposite the pass, and also from Empire City to the low pass between Bard Creek and the south fork of Clear Creek. Between this low pass and Georgetown, one and three-fourths mile south, the relative elevations have been ascertained by barometric [p. 6] observations, by Dr. Parry, a gentleman who is spending the summer near the Range, making scientific explorations.

"I submit herewith a map of the route from Denver, westward, embracing the Pass, giving a very fair representation of the topography of the country in the vicinity of the Pass, with the relative elevations at certain points, as ascertained by the levels. Upon this map I have drawn a proposed location of a railroad line, which, in my opinion, will be near the most practicable route for the real location. The length of the tunnel I make three and a half miles. I have made this length by supposing an up-grade of fifty feet to the mile, running westward in the tunnel from the entrance, for two miles, and thence running a down grade of ten feet to the mile, to the exit.

"An up grade in the tunnel of one hundred feet to the mile for the first two miles, instead of fifty, would shorten the tunnel about one-fourth of a mile. The grade, as you will notice, is less than 116 feet to the mile from the forks below Empire City to the tunnel, but the equation for curvature, on the line I have drawn, would probably bring the grade up to this maximum.

"This range of mountains, on its eastern slope being subject to a very considerably less fall of rain during the year than the Alleghanies or New England mountains, are much less disintegrated, and are fitly called "Rocky Mountains." The mountains on either side of the valley of Clear Creek are "rugged," with frequent points of rocks projecting into the valley; for this reason I have drawn the line so as to get down into the valley with the grade as soon as possible.

"I might say in this connection, that there would be a *possibility* of striking rich gold lodes in the construction of the tunnel, for it is in the "Gold Belt" there being lodes on each side of the pass, yet, I would not like to undertake the construction of the tunnel with the understanding that I should take this "possibility" in "part pay."

"Of the Western approach to the Pass I will hazard no opinion as to gradients or courses. The Western slope of the Range seems to be covered with a much deeper soil, as it is covered with a much denser foliage, which is doubtless owing to the arrest and precipitation of the spring and summer rains by the snow of the Range; the prevailing winds being northwesterly. [p. 7] This fact, in case of having to keep the mountain sides to get down to the valley of the Grand River, would render the cost of construction much less than upon the Eastern Slope.

"I have made considerable inquiry as to the winter snows in the neighborhood of the Pass, and find that at Empire City, they have wintered cattle every winter without hay. From all the statements of settlers on the experience of three winters, I am of opinion that the winter snows would form no serious obstacle to the running of railroad trains from the tunnel eastward. About three-fourths of a mile from the Pass, on the western slope, we passed a camp where a family were snowbound last winter, for some weeks, and judging from the height of the stumps of trees cut by them while there, should think the snow must have been five or six feet deep. This depth, from all the information I can glean, would be about a fair average for about fifteen or twenty miles west of the Range, in the vicinity of the Pass. The prevailing winds being from the northwest, the snow piles in immense drifts on the southeastern slopes of the range. These slopes, in the vicinity of the Pass, being very precipitous near the summit, arrest the snows before they reach the valley of Clear Creek. This fact may account for the light fall of snow near Empire City.

"The following table will show very nearly the distances between the points at which I have ascertained the elevations above the Platte at Denver, along the proposed route from Denver, westward to the Pass:

Places.	Distances.	Elevation.
Platte River, at Denver.	0 miles.	0.
Divide between Denver and Golden City	7.5 "	544.
Golden City	5.0 "	500.
Ten miles up the Cañon	10.0 "	1580.
Where Idaho road enters valley of Clear Creek	6.8 "	2019.
Idaho	5.2 "	2395.
Forks of Clear Creek below Empire City	7.3 "	3117.
Georgetown	4.0 "	3519.
Entrance of Tunnel	13.0 "	4820.
Total distance from Denver.	57.8 " [58.8]	

[p. 8] "In entering the Cañon of Clear Creek, either from Denver or the mouth of Clear Creek, the road can go into the Cañon from one to five hundred feet above the water of the creek, if a better line can be found at such elevation.

"Of the cost of construction of a railroad from Golden City to the entrance of the tunnel, I cannot, of course, make an estimate upon this reconnoissance, but should say the expense would not be greater than the average of eastern mountain roads for the same distance.

"Hoping these few facts may be of service to you and the Board of Corporators of the Pacific Railroad, I am,

"Very truly your obedient servant,

"FRANCIS M. CASE,
Civil Engineer."

Since writing the foregoing report I have obtained from Dr. Parry the elevation of the head of Middle Park, about ten miles from the pass on the western slope, which is 8,949 feet, or 1,340 feet lower than the mouth of the proposed tunnel 7½ miles above. The Hot Springs on the Grand river, 20 miles farther down, he makes 7,546 feet, showing an average grade from the head of the park to the Hot Springs of about 70 feet to the mile.

There is one difficulty that would be encountered upon this route not mentioned in the above report, and that is in the form of avalanches or glaciers, which occur occasionally at two different points near the foot of the pass, upon the mountain side south of Clear creek. The mass of snow and ice which accumulates at the head of gulches at these points, loosening next to the mountain by the action of the water from the melting snows, sweeps down the mountain side with a velocity that carries everything before it. At the one above the mouth of Hoope's creek, I saw trees and rubbish which had been driven before the avalanche across the creek, and four or five hundred feet up the northern slope of the valley. A located line would cross the track of both these avalanches.

THE CACHE LA POUDRE ROUTE.

Over this route I have run a preliminary line, commencing at [p. 9] La Porte, and running as indicated by the red line upon the accompanying map, I connected with Mr. Evans' line at his station 1,360, near the crossing of Laramie river.

Being entirely unacquainted with the topography of the country along this route, I kept my line in the valley of streams until I passed Cherokee station, and thence along what appeared at first sight to be the most feasible route. My party being short I was obliged to be with them so much that I could not devote as much time to reconnoissance as I otherwise would. I very much regret that I had not time to run a new line nearly or quite the whole distance from La Porte to the summit; and also to try a line over the divide to the head waters of Crow creek. I think I can get a fair line with lighter grades from La Porte to the Laramie Plains than are shown by any line yet surveyed over the Black Hills. Yet this is only my opinion. An actual survey only will determine this point. Some points are already settled by the present survey. One is, that Antelope Pass is 593 feet lower than the summit made upon the Cheyenne Pass route. Another is, that the descent to the Laramie Plains from Antelope Pass may be made with a grade not much, if any, exceeding 80 feet per mile.

I have indicated, by a red dotted line upon the map, my proposed location. I think a line may be obtained with a practical grade by keeping in a valley to the right of the stage road, and coming into the road, or near it, above Boner station. If so, it would be very much preferable to any line following the Cache La Poudre and Dale creeks. For those valleys being so narrow the grade must, of necessity, be laid at least 25 feet above the bed of the stream. Evidences of the flood of last spring show that the water was 20 feet above its present stage.

If this route should be found to be impracticable, I would try a route as indicated by the westerly dotted line passing over (or rather going through with a thousand feet tunnel) a low pass, about opposite the junction of Dale and Cache La Poudre creeks, and keeping along the eastern slope of the valley of Dale creek join the other line near the crossing of Stonewall creek. From this point, I think, by keeping up the divide west of this creek, the line would enter Stonewall cañon at a height sufficient to get a fair line through the cañon, and reach an elevation at its head [p. 10] which would admit of getting up the divide beyond and near the stage road with a grade not exceeding 2.2 feet per station.

Much time and care should be bestowed upon a located line, as the country, especially from Poison creek to the pass, is very rough, broken by points, and ledges of granite thrown up promiscuously. In some places you see only bare and isolated peaks, in others, ledges, trending in every conceivable direction.

In this connection allow me to suggest that a thorough examination should be made of the divide, east of Dale creek, and a few miles north of Virginia Dale, at the heads of Crow creek and Box Elder. From what information I can get, the foot of the mountains east of this point is as high, or even higher than the starting point of Mr. Evans' line. That point is 1,953 feet higher than my starting point at La Porte. Now, if by some branch of Crow Creek or Howard's Fork, we can find a uniform grade to the summit, I think such grade will be within the limit fixed by the charter of the road. By reference to the map you will see that such a route would connect with a line up the South Platte, with a much better general alignment than by La Porte; or would connect with the Lodge Pole Route, by way of Muddy Fork, without a serious sacrifice of alignment. (See also Stansbury's Report, p. 258, *et seq.*)

If a route can be obtained up the valley, east of Boner station near the line I have drawn, it would pass over, from La Porte to Stonewall Cañon, soil that is underlaid by stratified rocks, with occasional outcrops of the latter. From Stonewall Cañon to Laramie Plains, the formation is all primitive; most of the way however, the surface is covered with a soil—the result of the disintegration and decomposition of the granitic rocks. In the Stonewall cañon the granite is close grained, hard, and intersected by veins, or dykes of some basaltic rock. Toward the Laramie Plains, the feldspar predominates, rendering the rock more friable, and susceptible to disintegrating agencies.

As far as my observation extended, the primitive formation along the route shows no traces of any mineral veins whatever. My 2d assistant, Mr. Pim, says there is no doubt that Rock creek, furtherwest, comes down from a gold region. That he has seen the evidences himself; and also assured me that there [p. 11] was a large body of iron ore in the vicinity of our line, (he would not say where,) that he had also seen himself.

I did not see any indications of coal, in the later formations along the route. I did not look for them in the vicinity of the primitive rocks, believing that coal will not be found in such localities. The intense heat, at some period of their geological history, having driven off, or consumed the carbon, if it were ever there.

There is a sparse growth of timber, in places along the route, mostly a dwarfed variety of pine. South of the line, and at no great distance, appears to be a heavy growth of good timber.

I think that there would be little difficulty in rafting timber down the Cache La Poudre, and less still in getting it down the Big Laramie.

Accompanying this report I have the honor to submit condensed profiles of the Cache La Poudre, the Berthoud, and the South Platte routes. These profiles are made from my own surveys, and from such other data as I have been able to obtain. The grades in these profiles are broken to show the general undulations of the surface only. I also submit maps of the lines run during the past season, together with a map of Colorado, showing, approximately, all the different routes.

I have made no estimate of quantities upon any of these routes, for the reason that as yet I have not had time to run a line approximating the best location sufficiently near to make an estimate upon.

Respectfully submitted,
FRANCIS M. CASE,

Div. Engr.

To T.C. DURANT, Esq.,
    Vice-Pres't U.P.R.R. Co.,
        No. 13 William st., New York.

Samuel B. Reed, 1865

Union Pacific Railroad...Surveys And Explorations From Green River To Great Salt Lake City [in 1864]

Letter of December 24, 1864, Joliet, Illinois, to T. C. Durant; New York, 15 p. [WC 414 note; WCB 422a; Flake 9086; Graff 4247; UPRR p. 46; NUC NU 0027554.]
Reset verbatim from a facsimile, by courtesy of The Bancroft Library,
University of California, Berkeley.

Significance   Reed carefully pointed out the superiority of the line ultimately adopted by the Union Pacific through the Wasatch Range via Echo and Weber canyons into the Great Salt Lake Valley at Ogden. Reed had to be careful, because Brigham Young, who donated Reed's crew and supplies, dearly hoped that one way or the other the line would go through Salt Lake City and west along the south shore of Great Salt Lake. The alternate to Weber Canyon was the previously favored Provo ("Timpanogos") Canyon into Provo. In addition to the Weber-Echo leg, the Company accepted most of Reed's surveyed route east from the head of Echo Canyon. This route reached the Bear River at present Evanston, Wyoming, and descended Muddy Creek and Blacks Fork. Reed crossed to the Green and descended about 20 miles to the mouth of Bitter Creek, up which the line continued east from the modern town of Green River. The final railroad goes farther south on Blacks Fork and then due east to the mouth of Bitter Creek, avoiding Reed's line down the Green. Hostile Indians prevented him from better solving this problem.

Reed checked and rejected other adjacent Wasatch crossings, all of which were higher than the head of Echo Creek. He examined two Weber affluents on either side of Echo Canyon—Lost Creek, which comes in at Devils Slide, and Chalk Creek, which joins the Weber at modern Coalville. He surveyed the Weber up to the Kamas Prairie, where the town of Kamas now is. He went on to the head of the Weber. He came back to Kamas and crossed over to the Provo, descending it from Heber City to Utah Lake. He found the Provo Canyon to be steeper and more crooked than the lower Weber.

Previous explorations had covered this ground, but not as effectively. Capt. Howard Stansbury (5:J3) in 1849-50 entered the Great Salt Lake Valley by

Ogden River and left by Parleys and Echo canyons. He was told that the grades up Provo Canyon, and the tie to the upper Weber, were easy. From what one of his Mormon guides said, he put on his map a line from the head of the Weber to the mouth of Henrys Fork at Green River; this he labeled, "Reported to be a level and practicable route for a road." Reed found the Weber end of such a line to be unsuitable for a railroad. Stansbury did, however, spot the good connection between the head of Echo Canyon and Muddy Creek. He speculated that the best route west from Salt Lake City lay to the south of Great Salt Lake.

Lt. Edward G. Beckwith (L3) in April, 1854, explored for railroad routes from Salt Lake City via Weber River to Ft. Bridger and via Provo River on the way back. He considered both routes practicable. Beckwith went up Chalk Creek instead of following the emigrant road up Echo Creek. Reed found out that, as usual, the emigrants had made the better choice. Beckwith also favored a route south of Great Salt Lake for the way west from Salt Lake City. Capt. James H. Simpson's 1859 explorations mainly concerned the south-of-the-lake route west from Salt Lake City, but his report included an odometer table for a wagon road from Ft. Bridger down Chalk Creek and Provo River to Camp Floyd. Simpson concluded, regarding the Stansbury-Beckwith Utah railroad proposal, that "its cost will never justify its construction."

In 1863 the Union Pacific arranged for Chief Engineer Peter A. Dey to make a reconnaissance to Salt Lake City, and for civil engineer Joseph A. Young, Brigham's son, to survey Provo River and Chalk Creek (Dix 1864). In this same report Brigham Young wrote, "permit me to suggest whether it will not be well, previous to surveying and estimating for either the Timpanogos or Weber Lower Canyon line in detail, to first make a comparatively speedy and inexpensive survey of both those lines." That is just what Reed did.

Union Pacific Vice President Thomas C. Durant reprinted Reed's report in 1866, adding 5 plates and 2 detailed maps of Weber Canyon not present in the first edition. To this present reprint of the first edition we add the lithograph depicting the "Mouth of Timpanogos Canyon" at Provo.

Author SAMUEL BENEDICT REED, 1818-1891, explorer, engineer, railroad builder. Born in Vermont and trained in engineering, Reed worked on the Erie Canal in 1841. He soon went to Michigan and Illinois to be a locating engineer for a succession of midwestern railroads. He married Jane Eliza Earl in 1855. He began work for the Burlington Railroad in Iowa in 1859 and for the Union Pacific in Utah in 1864 to make the surveys reported here. In 1865 he ran more lines across the Wasatch Mountains and checked the route south of Great Salt Lake to the Humboldt River. He then headed the construction forces that for the next three and a half years successfully carried the Union Pacific to Promontory. He overcame many difficulties, including the unhelpful interference of Vice President Thomas C. Durant. In 1922 an 18-ton granite boulder from Echo Canyon was placed in his honor in the courthouse yard at Joliet, Illinois. (Galloway 1950.)

In the 1880s Reed was a consultant during construction of the Canadian Pacific Railway. He temporarily replaced an ousted chief engineer and disciplined the staff, which did not make him popular. On one junket in the Rockies he and the general manager were waist-deep in icy mud and two days without food. Both were Americans. "It is an irony that from the very beginning the CPR, that most nationalistic of all Canadian enterprises, was to a very large extent managed and built by Americans...But in the eighties, most of the experienced railway talent was American." (Berton 1970.)

Itinerary, 1864 REED, SALT LAKE CITY TO ROCK SPRINGS. June 1—Reed starts his survey from Salt Lake City. Although his actual course is much more complex, he gives the final distance of 233.46 miles from Salt Lake City to Ogden and up the Weber and Echo canyons and on to Green River and up Bitter Creek to Rock Springs. He does not give any more dates.

Highlights The Legislative Assembly and Governor of the Territory of Utah sent a memorial to Congress in relation to the Pacific railway on January 14, 1854. They wrote, "the route in question should commence at Council Bluff city, keep up the main Platte to its south fork, and up the south fork to the proper point for diverging to the summit of the Black Hills [Laramie Mountains], in the neighborhood of what is known as the Box Elder pass [Boxelder Creek heads about 8 miles south of Sherman Summit or "Evans Pass" on the modern Union Pacific]...across the southern portion of the level, well watered, and grassy Laramie's plains, to...Bridger's pass...by the waters of Muddy and Bitter creeks...across Green river...up Henry's fork...across Bear river and Weber river...down the Timpanogos or Provo river into Utah valley...[and] by the north end of Utah lake to Walker's river pass in the Sierra Nevada." Up to the Green River, this was about the way the Union Pacific was built. These recommendations mainly followed Stansbury's conclusions.

Legacy Union Pacific's Chief Engineer Grenville M. Dodge recalled in 1910, "We had only one controversy with the Mormons, who had been our friends and had given the full support of the church from the time of our first reconnoissances until the final completion. It was our desire and the demand of the Mormons that we should build through Salt Lake City, and we bent all our energies to find a feasible line through that city and around the south end of Great Salt Lake and across the desert to Humboldt Wells, a controlling point in the line. We found the line so superior on the north of the lake that we had to adopt that route with a view of building a branch to Salt Lake City, but Brigham Young would not have this...[He] gave his allegiance and aid to the Central Pacific, hoping to bring them around the south end of the lake and force us to connect with them there...[But] they, too, were forced to adopt a line north of the lake. Then President Young returned to his first love, the Union Pacific."

REFERENCES

(See Preface for Heading and other references not listed here.)

Beckwith, Edward G., 1854 (1855 pub.), Explorations for a route for the Pacific railroad near the 41st parallel, in Reports of Explorations and Surveys: Wash., 33/2 ("33/3") H91, serial 792, 2:9-19, 60-61.

Berton, Pierre, 1970 (1972 reprint), The impossible railway, the building of the Canadian Pacific: N.Y., p. 298, 450; quote 301.

Dix, John A., 1864, Report of the organization and proceedings of the Union Pacific Railroad Co.: N.Y., letters of Brigham Young and report of Joseph A. Young, Appendix 1C, viii-xiv, quote viii.

Dodge, Grenville M., 1910, How we built the Union Pacific Railway: Wash., 61/2 S447, quote p. 27-28.

Durant, Thomas C., 1865 (1866 printing), Union Pacific Railroad, report of...surveys made up to the close of the year 1864: N.Y., Reed report reprint, Appendix C, 15 p., 5 plates, 2 maps.

Galloway, John D., 1950 (1989 reprint), The first transcontinental railroad: N.Y., Reed biog. p. 190-91, 244-45.

Legislative Assembly, Territory of Utah, 1854 (1855 pub.), Acts, resolutions and memorials: Salt Lake City, memorial on Pacific railway p. 412-14, quote 413.

Simpson, James H., 1859 (1876 printing), Report of explorations across the Great Basin: Wash., Engineer Dept., odometer table p. 155, quote 238.

Stansbury, Howard, 1852, Exploration and survey of the Valley of the Great Salt Lake of Utah: Phila., 32/Special S3, serial 608, p. 82, 217, 220, 224-27, 263-66; map in folder.

UNION PACIFIC RAILROAD.

REPORT OF SAMUEL B. REED,

OF SURVEYS AND EXPLORATIONS FROM

Green River to Great Salt Lake City

JOLIET, Illinois, Dec. 24, 1864

SIR,—According to instructions, dated March 7th, 1864, I have the pleasure of submitting the following report of my explorations and surveys in the mountains east of and in the vicinity of Great Salt Lake City:

On reporting in Omaha, Nebraska, the 2d day of April last, I found that arrangements were not made for me to leave immediately for Great Salt Lake City.

While in Omaha, information was received that the 1st Assistant assigned to my party declined the appointment—Mr. A.J. Mathewson was transferred to fill the vacancy.

Arrangements for our journey being completed, we left Omaha April 30th, on Western Stage Company's line, for Atchison, Kansas, where we were delayed until the 7th of May before we could secure our seats in the Overland stage for Great Salt Lake City.

I was informed that Governor Brigham Young would furnish all my men teams and supplies for the survey.

When I arrived in Great Salt Lake City, he was absent on a tour to Bear Lake Valley, in the northern part of the territory.

His absence caused a few days delay; however arrangements were soon made, and we commenced field work the first day of June last. [p. 2]

GREAT SALT LAKE CITY TO THE MOUTH OF WEBER CANON.

The point of commencement is in the northwest part of the city, near Jordan River, which is connected by courses and distances with the monument at the southeast corner of Temple Block, in north latitude 40° 45' 44", west longitude 112° 06' 08". The altitude of the beginning of the line, as shown on the profile is 4,285 3/16 feet above the sea.

From the point of commencement the line runs near the base of the mountains, in a northerly direction, past Warm and Hot Springs, and in the vicinity of the Great Salt Lake, to the mouth of Weber Cañon, a distance of 36½ miles.

By referring to the map and profile, you will observe, that five or six miles of this distance can be saved by making a short tunnel through the low hills near the base of the mountains.

Careful surveys and estimates will determine between the line run, and the one suggested. The amount of excavation and bridging on this portion of the line is light, grades easy, and alignment good.

The altitude at the mouth of the Weber Cañon is 4,655.5 above the sea.

WEBER CANYON

On arriving at the mouth of this cañon we found it to be very narrow. The general course is direct. The sides of the cañon slope back at an angle which will admit of the road bed being made on the slope when necessary.

The river at the mouth of the cañon is 120 feet wide, and from four to six feet deep, being swollen at the time of the survey by melting of snow on the mountains. It has a strong, powerful current over a bed of water worn stones, and fallen rocks of immense size.

There is one obstacle to be overcome in this narrow gorge, known as the Devil's Gate.

A heavy point projects from the south into the valley. This deflects the river 600 feet north of its general direction. The water rushes around this bend with tremendous force, where it [p. 3] is impossible to build the road on account of the short crooks, and the rapid fall in the river.

To overcome this obstruction 1½ miles of maximum grade (116 feet per mile) will be required.

The line below the *Gate* winds along the side of the cañon, crossing ravines and projecting points of rock. From the *Gate* to the head of the gorge no heavy work is encountered.

The excavation through the cañon will be loose or solid rock. Granite and gniess [gneiss] predominate.

At the upper end of the gorge 40½ miles from Great Salt Lake City, the mountains recede to the right and left, leaving a valley from one-half to three miles wide, and 15⅛ miles in length.

Here the grading and bridging will not be expensive. Easy grades and curves of long radius are obtained.

There is rock for masonry at convenient distances on either side of the valley.

A limited supply of timber can be obtained in the cañons for cross ties and bridge purposes.

The place from which a supply of timber for railroad purposes through the mountains can be procured, will hereafter be described.

From the upper end of this valley the mountains close in upon the river, forming a narrow crooked cañon six miles long. The river winds from side to side of the narrow gorge, making frequent crossings necessary. The excavation and bridging will be expensive. About one-half the excavation will be rock. Black limestone, carboniferous sandrock, and clay slate are the prevailing rocks.

Two short tunnels will be required, one at station 1,043, three hundred feet long, and one at station 1,085, four hundred feet long.

The high point crossed by the line at station 1,053 to 1,072, can be avoided on the located line. (See map and profile.)

In this cañon there is one mile that is very narrow.

The *"debris,"* on both sides of the river, slopes to the water's edge. During storms of rain, or sudden melting of snow, great quantities of loose rock slide down the side of the mountain into the river.

Expensive retaining walls will be necessary to protect the road-bed. [p. 4]

From this place to the mouth of Echo Cañon (5½ miles) the valley is wide and of a very uniform surface. Excavation and bridging not expensive. Stone, for what few bridges are required, can be obtained at convenient distances on both sides of the river.

Mineral coal was seen in place, in the Weber Valley, two miles below the mouth of Echo Creek.

The dip of the rock indicates that if coal is found north of this place it will be below the bed of Weber River.

Numerous indications of iron ore were seen. The farmers living in the Weber Valley informed me that there are large deposits of this mineral on one of the small tributaries of the Weber, on the north side of the river.

The altitude of Weber Valley, at the mouth of Echo Cañon, is 5,535 above the sea.

The average grade from the Devil's Gate, 29½ miles, is 22 95/100 feet per mile. The grade is somewhat undulating, but generally very uniform, as a reference to the profile will show.

From the mouth of Weber Cañon to this place there will be sixteen bridges over Weber River. Some tributary streams and numerous irrigating ditches will have to be crossed.

I will here remark, that the profile of the line from Great Salt Lake City through the Wahsatch Mountains *via* Weber Valley to this place, 78 3/10 miles, is much more favorable then I expected to find.

From the mouth of Echo Cañon to the east branch of Sulphur Creek two lines were run—one *via* Echo Creek, crossing the divide between Weber and Bear Rivers, at the head of Echo; thence down a tributary of Bear River to the same, up Bear River to the mouth of Sulphur Creek, and up Sulphur to the east branch of the same stream. This line will hereafter be more fully described.

The other line continues up the valley of Weber River, 6. 44 miles, without encountering any heavy work to the mouth of

CHALK, OR WHITE CLAY CREEK.

From information received from various sources before leaving Omaha, and after arriving in Utah, I was led to believe that this [p. 5] valley would prove to be the most favorable, if not the only practical route over the high divide between Weber and Bear Rivers. It was, therefore, with great anxiety that we worked our way up the valley of this stream to the summit.

The first two miles up Chalk Creek Valley is through well cultivated farms. Then the valley narrows to a cañon one mile in length, only wide enough for the bed of the stream and quite crooked. The rocky points from opposite sides of the creek projecting past each other will cause heavy rock excavation. From here the valley opens, and for a distance of 18⅓ miles the excavation and embankment will be comparatively light.

The average ascending grade from the mouth of the creek to this place is 64. 33 feet per mile, almost three times as much as the average in the Weber Valley above the Devil's Gate.

The approach to the summit is made with 5¾ miles of maximum grade. The excavation and embankment will be expensive. At the summit a tunnel, 2,700 feet in length, will be required, through carboniferous sand rock, with expensive approaches at each end.

The altitude is 7,834 feet above the sea. This is the highest point reached on the survey.

In the mountains, to the south, there is a large tract of pine timber, suitable for railroad purposes, accessible from this point.

From the summit to Bear River the country is very much cut up by the various small tributaries of Yellow Creek. It is necessary to cross the drainage with the line. This makes heavy work, as will be seen on the profile.

While exploring the country at the head of Chalk Creek, I became satisfied that it was impossible to cross the divide between Weber and Bear Rivers, south of Chalk Creek, on account of the near approach to the Uinta Mountains. Subsequent explorations fully confirmed this opinion.

From Bear River, which is 150 feet wide and one foot deep at low water, to the east branch of Sulphur Creek, 11. 74 miles, the grading and bridging is light, alignment good, and timber convenient.

As two lines were run to this place, I will return and describe some of the distinguishing features of the [p. 6]

ECHO CANON LINE.

Echo Cañon is a deep gorge worn in the soft sand rock, 100 to 1,000 feet wide, and 23 ½ miles long. Bold escarpments rise almost vertical from five to eight hundred feet high, and extend on the north side from Weber Valley twenty miles up the cañon, or nearly to *Cache Cave*—on the south side the hills recede at an angle of 45°.

From Cache Cave to the summit the hills are more rounded, and slope back at a greater angle, numerous short tributaries come in on both sides, cutting the country into a succession of deep ravines and sharp ridges.

From the point where we leave the Weber Valley Line, up the cañon to Cache Cave, 21½ miles; the work is light, material good, and grades not as objectionable as in Chalk Creek Valley.

The alignment is much better than the same distance up the valley of Chalk Creek.

The summit is reached with 3.22 miles of maximum grade, where a tunnel will have to be made 4,000 feet through soft sand rock.

The altitude of this summit is 6,879 feet above the sea. The average ascent per mile from the mouth of the cañon to the foot of the maximum grade, near Cache Cave, 21.60 miles, is 44.90 feet.

From the summit, the line was run down the valley of a small tributary of Bear River, to the same; thence up Bear River Valley and the valley of Sulphur Creek to its connection with the Chalk Creek line, 24.45 miles or 49.20 miles from the mouth of Echo Cañon. The work on this last part of the line will be light. Rock for masonry convenient, and the alignment good.

By referring to the map and profile the relative merits of these two lines will be apparent.

The altitude of the summit on Echo Cañon line is 955 feet below the summit on Chalk Creek line.

The total ascending and descending grades, 1,020 feet in favor of Echo line. The alignment, excavation, and embankment is also largely in favor of this line.

Coal was seen on the Echo line in Bear River Valley, which it is believed will prove good for locomotive fuel. [p. 7]

The advantages of the Chalk Creek line are its proximity to large bodies of timber; its convenience to coal mines that are being worked in Chalk Creek Valley, and the difference in the length of the tunnels at the summit, which is 1,300 feet in favor of Chalk Creek line.

EAST BRANCH OF SULPHUR CREEK TO GREEN RIVER.

From this place to the summit, between the waters of the Great Salt Lake Basin and the Gulf of California, the line follows up a small tributary of Sulphur Creek two miles; thence over a low divide into the Valley of Quakingasp Creek—an affluent of Bear River,—and up that to its source on the divide, 124.87 miles from Great Salt Lake City.

From the summit we reach the Valley of the Muddy, an affluent of Black's Fork, in 7.70 miles; 2.4 miles of this is maximum grade. The altitude of the summit is 7,570 feet above tide.

The line was run down the Valley of the Muddy nearly to its junction with Black's Fork; thence 21 miles down the Valley of Black's Fork; thence over the divide, between Black's Fork and Green River, to that stream, which is 200.32 miles from Great Salt Lake City. From the rim on the Great Salt Lake Basin to Green river the work is generally light, and the material good. Very little rock excavation will be encountered on this portion of the line.

Immediately after crossing the summit there is a marked change in the topography of the country. Instead of the disturbed and upheaved rocks which characterize the region of the Great Salt Lake Basin; flat tables or terraces of horizontal strata now form the distinguishing feature of the country; sometimes standing alone, like islands, in the barren plains, or forming bold escarpments along the streams. The hills are fast wearing away under the influences of wind and rain.

In Green River Valley I made thorough exploration to the mouth of Bitter Creek, a distance of twenty miles. The valley is narrow, with bold escarpments on both sides of the river, rising in many places hundreds of feet, almost vertical from the water's edge. [p. 8]

To follow down the valley of Green River to Bitter Creek will require sixteen bridges over the river; otherwise the work would be light.

This involved an expense which I was anxious to avoid, if possible.

The only way that seemed practicable, was to cross the high table land between Green River and the north branch of Bitter Creek.

I traversed this country, but not as thoroughly as I wanted to do, on account of the hostility of the Indians, who were committing depredations on the whites in that vicinity while we were there. I recommend that a more thorough exploration be made from Green River to Bitter Creek before a final location is made.

From Green River to the north branch of Bitter Creek the grading will be expensive. Some rock excavation will be encountered, as shown on the profile.

This is over a desert country. No fresh water was found, and but very little grass for our animals.

From the place where we descend to the valley of the North Branch of Bitter Creek to Rock Springs, the point of connection with Mr. Evans' line, the grading and bridging is light.

It will be seen by an examination of the profile that to follow this line over the high table land the altitude to be overcome is very much increased.

From Great Salt Lake City, *via.* Echo Canon line, to our connection with Mr. Evans' line in Bitter Creek Valley, is 233.46 miles. The altitude at that point is 6,315 above the sea.

It will be observed that the profile shows a great preponderance of light work; there is a portion that is very heavy, but I think the work will compare favorably with the Baltimore and Ohio or Pennsylvania Central Railroads.

TIMPANOGOS VALLEY LINE.

This second line through the Wahsatch Mountains was commenced at a point in the Weber Valley line, near the mouth of Chalk Creek, and continued up the valley of Weber River, to and across Kamas Prairie, 26 38/100 miles, to the Timpanogos Val-[p. 9] ley. The work over this portion of the line will be very light, grades easy, and aligment good. Stone, for all the bridge structures required, convenient and abundant.

In order to conform as near as practicable to instructions, I made an extended reconnoissance of the valley of Weber River to its source, to satisfy myself beyond a doubt about the practicability of a line crossing the divide between Weber and Bear Rivers south of Chalk Creek.

My route was up the narrow valley of Weber River, in a northeasterly direction, 20 miles from Kamas Prairie, where the river is doubled back upon itself, and heads five miles east of Kamas Prairie. The high mountain range which forms the divide, is from 1,800 feet in the lowest pass, to 4,000 feet above Weber River. The summit appears to be not more than two miles from the river and is like a continuous solid wall. The water-shed to the river is narrow and steep. The altitude of the lowest point on this divide is 9,162 feet above tide. I crossed over the divide to the west branch of Bear River, and followed up that stream in a southwesterly direction, fifteen miles, to its source. From a high point, the sides of which were covered with snow, I could trace the valleys of the various rivers that take their rise in the Uinta Mountains. On my return, I followed the crest of this divide a distance of twenty miles, to the place where I crossed it on my outward trip.

I am satisfied there is no possibility of getting a line over this divide without a tunnel at least three miles long, and at a much greater altitude than the Chalk Creek line.

In the mountains I saw an abundance of white and Norway pine timber, suitable for railroad purposes. That growing on the Bear River slope is of easy access, and can be rafted down the river to the line.

On my return, we continued the line down the valley of Timpanogos River to the valley of Utah Lake.

Heavy work and 2 27/100 miles of maximum grade is encountered to get from Kamas Prairie down to the valley of the river. From thence, down the valley of the stream, 8 61/100 miles, the valley is narrow, and the grading and bridging will be expensive. From thence across Round Prairie, 11 36/100 miles, good grades, easy curves, and light work, are obtained. [p. 10]

From the west end of Round Prairie to the mouth of the cañon in Utah Lake Valley, 11 83/100 miles, the most difficult part of this line is encountered. The cañon is narrow, and, unlike Weber, is very crooked. The points, from opposite sides of the river, project past each other, making frequent crossings of the river necessary, and a constant succession of heavy rock excavations unavoidable.

The prevailing rocks are granite, lime and sand. No indications of coal were seen in this valley.

Thirty-four bridges will be required across the Timpanogos River.

The grade from the mouth of the cañon, to the foot of the maximum grade near Kamas Prairie, 31 80/100 miles, averages 47 feet per mile.

From the point where the Timpanogos River enters Utah Lake Valley, there is a wide table land or terrace extending from the mountains to the lake. We ascended from the Timpanogos Valley to this terrace, and run in a northwesterly direction through the thriving towns of Battle Creek, American Fork, and Lehi; crossed the *Jordan River* at the narrows; from thence over the extensive stock range on the west side of *Jordan* to the point of the *West Mountain*, which is 12 miles west of Great Salt Lake City. From thence westerly between the base of the *West Mountains*, and the Great Salt Lake to the end of our line in Tuilla Valley, 106 23/100 miles from the Weber Valley line, near the mouth of Chalk Creek.

An examination of the profile will show the work in Utah Lake Valley, and the valley of Great Salt Lake, with the exception of crossing the *Jordan River*, to be light. The grades and alignment are unobjectionable.

EXPLORATIONS.

During the summer, and after the above surveys were completed, I made extensive explorations of the Wahsatch, Uinta and Bear River Mountains.

The Wahsatch range was crossed at every place where there seemed to be a possibility of finding a line through the mountains between Timpanogos and Weber Rivers. [p. 11]

Between Weber and Bear rivers I traversed the summit of the mountains from the head waters of the Timpanogos River, in the Uintas, north to the source of Lost Creek (known on Stanbury's map as Pumbar Creek.) Echo Cañon Line crosses this divide in the lowest place on the range.

Between Bear River and Muddy, I followed the rim of the Great Salt Lake Basin, from the head of Sulphur Creek, in the Uinta Mountains, to the head waters of Ham's Fork, crossing with my line at the lowest place on this summit, which divides the waters of Great Salt Lake Basin from those of the Gulf of California.

From these explorations I am satisfied that I have shown the best line that can

UNION PACIFIC RAIL ROAD
SURVEY OF 1864.
MOUTH OF TIMPANOGOS CAÑON.

S.B.REED DIV. ENG.R.A./ C.L.MATHER SON, DEL.

LITH. OF MAJOR & KNAPP, 449 BROADWAY, N.Y.

be found through the Wahsatch range, north of the Uintas, unless a line should be run down the valley of Bear River. This, if practicable, will increase the distance to Salt Lake Valley about 80 miles.

You will observe that I have confined myself to the maximum grade. When I could not overcome the various difficult summits that I encountered, I abandoned the survey and sought a new line.

TIMBER AND FUEL.

This is an important subject, and it was with great interest that I observed the various places from which a partial supply of timber can be obtained. Before exploring the Uinta Mountains, I looked upon the scarcity of timber as the most serious obstacle to be overcome in building the road through the mountains.

On the head waters of Bear River, contiguous to the various tributaries of that stream, there are large tracts of white and Norway pine, suitable for railroad purposes, that can be rafted down Bear River to the line.

I was informed by Mr. Granger, who lives on Ham's Fork, that there is a large tract of pine timber on Green River, 40 miles north of the crossing of that stream. If this information is correct, of which I have no doubt, cross-ties can be obtained from there, and rafted down Green River to the line, to build the road between Green and Bear Rivers. [p. 12]

In the Wahsatch Mountains a limited number of cross-ties and some bridge timber can be obtained.

Coal is abundant on Bitter Creek, Ham's Fork, Sulphur Creek, Chalk Creek, Weber and Bear Rivers.

Indications of coal were seen on the Muddy, Yellow Creek, and in Echo Cañon.

There are Petroleum springs in the valley of Sulphur Creek, and in Pioneer Cañon, about three miles north of the place where the line crosses the divide between Bear River and Muddy.

We closed our work and started for Omaha on the 28th day of October. We encountered severe storms in the mountains and on the plains, which prevented our reaching Omaha until the 18th day of November.

In conclusion, I wish to acknowledge my obligation to Governor Brigham Young for the courteous and gentlemanly treatment I received from him. To his cheerful and prompt compliance with all my requisitions for men, means of transportation, and subsistence, the company are in a great measure indebted for my success.

To Mr. Granger, for supplies loaned us, and for his valuable assistance in exploring the country in the vicinity of Black's Fork and Green River without charge.

To Mr. A.J. Mathewson, F.J. Paris, J.F. Smith, assistants, and all other members of the party I am obliged for valuable assistance rendered during the survey.
All of which is respectfully submitted,

SAMUEL B. REED,
Division Engineer.

To T.C. DURANT, Esq.,
  Vice-Pres't U.P.R.R. Co.,
    No. 13 William st., New York. [p. 13]

TABLE OF ALTITUDES.

		Feet above the sea.
The end of the line in Great Salt Lake City		4285.8
"	mouth of Weber Cañon	4654.7
"	Devil's Gate, in Weber Cañon	4894.0
"	Weber Valley, at the mouth of Echo Cañon	5535.0
"	" " " " Chalk Creek	5645.0
"	summit at the head of Chalk Creek	7834.0
"	summit at the head of Echo Cañon	6879.4
"	surface of water in Bear River, on Chalk Creek line	7503.0
"	" " " " Echo Cañon line	7045.0
"	summit between Bear River and Muddy, the rim of Great Salt lake Basin	7567.0
In the valley of Muddy, near the Overland Stage Station		7067.0
The surface of water in Black's Fork, two miles below the mouth of Muddy		6375.0
"	surface of water in Black's Fork, twenty miles below the above	6257.0
"	summit between Black's Fork and Green River	6464.0
"	surface of water in Green River	6245.0
"	summit between Green River and north branch of Bitter Creek	7175.0
"	Bitter Creek Valley, at the junction of Mr. Evan's line	6315.0

TIMPANOGOS LINE.

	Lineal feet.
The end of the line in Tuilla Valley	4243.0
At the point of the West Mountain	4267.0

The surface of water in the Jordan River, at the Narrows	4522.0
In the Timpanogos Valley, at the mouth of the Cañon	4892.0
In the Timpanogos Valley, at Kamas Prairie	6391.0
On Kamas Prairie	6667.0
The surface of water in Weber River, at the north end of Kamas Prairie	6340.0
The mouth of Chalk Creek, in Weber Valley	5645.0

The principal bridges on the line, from the Great Salt Lake City to Bitter Creek, *via* Echo Cañon line, are— [p. 14]

16 Truss bridges over Weber River, of 250 feet each	4,000
5 " " small stream in Weber Valley of 100 ft. each	500
30 Bridges over Echo Creek, 40 feet each	1,200
6 " " Yellow Creek and branches, 40 ft. each	240
Truss bridge over Bear River	600
30 Bridges over Muddy 60 ft. each	1,800
3 Truss bridges over Black's Fork 300 "	900
1 " " " Green River	800
10 Bridges between Green River and Bitter Creek	400
[10,440]	10,400

TIMPANOGOS LINE.

	Lineal feet.
1 Truss bridge over Jordan River	300
1 " " " American Fork	150
1 Bridge over Battle Creek	50
34 Truss bridges over Timpanogos, 300 feet each	10,200
3 " " " Weber River, 250 feet each	750
3 Bridges over Beaver Creek, 40 feet each	120
	11,570

In addition to the above, there will be numerous irrigating ditches and small streams to cross.

TABLE OF GRADES.

Route	Level. Distance, Miles.	0 to 20 Ft. per Mile. Distance, Miles.	Total Ascent.	Distance, Miles.	Total Descent.	20 to 40 Ft. per Mile. Distance, Miles.	Total Ascent.	Distance, Miles.	Total Descent.	40 to 60 Ft. per Mile. Distance Miles.	Total Ascent.	Distance, Miles.	Total Descent.	60 to 80 Ft. per Mile. Distance, Miles.	Total Ascent.	Distance Mile.	Total Discent.	80 to 100 Ft. per Mile. Distance, Miles.	Total Ascent.	Mile, Descent.	Total Descent.	100 to 110 Ft. per Mile. Miles. Distance	Total Ascent.	Distance, Miles.	Total Descent.
From Great Salt Lake City, via Weber Canon & Chalk Creek to Bitter Creek....	25.84	24.21	898.8	'28.	832.5	89.27	917.9	28.81	683.4	16.99	871.1	18.71	792.6	16.89	1194.5	11.65	848.5	11.86	1060.4	2.00	190.0	15.78	179.02	11.87	1957.6
From Great Salt Lake City, via Echo Canon to Bitter Creek....	29.20	24.77	886.4	81.50	485.5	40.17	1202.6	24.17	680.4	20.57	1072.0	11.15	592.4	11.49	584.8	8.49	598.5	9.09	814.1	2.08	190.0	11.9	1279.4	10.16	1118.6
From Tullia Valley via Point of West Mountain, Jordan River, Timpanogos Valley and Kamas Prairie to Weber Valley near mouth of Chalk Creek	9.39	4.63	88.0	8.43	124.0	12.97	382.0	12.06	848.0	13.69	702.0	11.57	618.0	5.19	868.0	12.33	884.2	21.5	203.0	5.80	517.0	0.72	76.0	7.10	779.

Appendix

Travel Rates

The average miles covered per day by the gold rushers and railroad explorers of volume six, as compared to Mormon handcart companies, from estimates of distances and times, usually including 10-20 percent of the total days for necessary layovers (excepting the railroad schedules), are:

4-5	Roadbuilding, railroad surveying, 1858, 1860, 1864; L8, L12
5-8	Fremont afoot in snow, 1848-49; L6
9-16	Explorations for Pacific railroad, 1853-54; L1, L3
11	1848 opening of Carson road; 1850 inept gold rushers; K3, K7
11-12	Mormon handcart companies in 1856 winter disaster, and in 1857-60 summers; Appendix
12	Fremont with pack animals in winter of 1853-54; L6
13-14	Road improvements, 1859-60; L8
14-15	1849, 1853 gold rushers with wagons, K1, K5
15-16	Mormon handcart companies, 1856-57; Appendix
16-17	1850, 1852 gold rushers with wagons, K3, K4
18-21	Fremont with pack animals, 1848-49; L6 Lander, Berthoud with pack animals, 1854, 1861; L7, L13
19-20	Fast wagon travel on good roads, 1858, 1862, 1864; L8, L11, L12
21	Elite Mormon Elder handcart pullers; Appendix
21-24	1849-50 gold rushers with pack animals, K1, K3
31	Very fast wagon travel on good roads, 1857, 1859; L8
355	Normal Union-Central Pacific Railroad schedule, 1869
948	Special fast excursion, Union-Central Pacific Railroad, 1876

Mormon Handcart Companies

Mormon pullers and pushers of handcarts traveled just about as fast as the gold rushers with wagons. Even the two companies that met disaster in the snow traveled almost as fast as Fremont did in his wintry expeditions with pack trains.

Brigham Young instituted the use of handcarts to bring European Mormon converts cheaply from the railhead in Iowa to Salt Lake City in the summer of 1856 (Hafen 1960; Carter 1995; Bigler 1998). The first three companies (see table) left Florence (Omaha), Nebraska, before the end of July; they all safely reached their destination by October 2. But the next two companies, led by captains Willie and Martin, did not leave Omaha until August 17 and 27. With this late start, the early vicious winter storms caught them on the North Platte and Sweetwater in Wyoming without provisions or adequate clothing. Many of the more than one thousand inexperienced emigrants were either infants or the aged. Women struggled with the carts and looked after their children as well. Men sank under the incessant toil and privation. Brigham Young had learned of their plight and moved quickly to send out a heroic rescue team that brought in all the survivors before the end of November (Bartholomew and Arrington 1992). Hafen in 1960 estimated that from 200 to 225 emigrants perished in this "worst disaster in the history of Western migration." Others were maimed for life.

Brigham Young blamed the Church's immigration officials for delays all along the journey: "If they had sent our immigrants in the season that they should have done, you and I could have kept our [rescue] teams at home…This people are this day deprived of thousands of acres of wheat that would have been sowed by this time, had it not been for the misconduct of our immigration affairs this year" (Bartholomew and Arrington 1992). Perhaps the leaders of the overland trek were too anxious to get home to their families for the winter. Perhaps they had too much faith that all would be well. Young also said, "if even a bird had chirped it in the ears…[the leaders] would have known better than to rush men, women and children on to the prairie in the autumn months…to travel over a thousand miles" (Bigler 1998).

The first three handcart companies of 1856, and one of 1857, averaged 15 to 16 miles per day. Even the Willie and Martin companies averaged 11 to 12 miles per day overall, and the other 1857, 1859, and 1860 ones made 12 to 13. One elite group of 70 Elders went east in early 1857 from Salt Lake City to Omaha in 49 days at 21 miles per day. The Willie and Martin companies averaged about 4 persons per cart, whereas all others had about 5. Each company also had along from 1 to 7 wagons (Hafen 1960). In spite of many breakdowns and repairs, layovers enroute were rare. Nearly 3,000 people started for Utah with handcarts between 1856 and 1860.

See Volume 3 for other Mormon travel.

REFERENCES

Bartholomew, Rebecca, and Leonard J. Arrington, 1992 (1993 revised ed.), Rescue of the 1856 handcart companies: Provo, 63 p.; quote 44.

Bigler, David L., 1998, Forgotten Kingdom, the Mormon theocracy in the American West 1847-96: Spokane, p. 103-19, quote 119.

Carter, Lyndia McDowell, 1995, The Mormon handcart companies: Independence, Overland Journal 13/1:2-18.

Hafen, LeRoy R., and Ann W., 1960, Handcarts to Zion: Glendale, 328 p., quote 140, table 193.

TRAVEL TIMES OF ALL HANDCART COMPANIES IN DAYS
(Showing Captains, number of persons, and number of deaths, after Hafen 1960. Days include 0-13 percent stopovers, where known. In brackets are the mean travel rates in miles per day)

OMAHA TO SALT LAKE CITY, 1031 mi.

1st Co.	1856	Ellsworth, Edmund L., 274 souls, (13 deaths)	69	[15]
2nd Co.	1856	McArthur, Daniel D., 221, (7)	65	[16]
3rd Co.	1856	Bunker, Edward, 320, (less than 7)	65	[16]
4th Co.	1856	Willie, James G., 500, (67-77)	85	[12]
5th Co.	1856	Martin, Edward, 576, (135-150)	96	[11]
6th Co.	1857	Evans, Israel, 149, (?)	84	[12]
7th Co.	1857	Christiansen, Christian, 330, (6?)	69	[15]
8th Co.	1859	Rowley, George, 235, (5?)	88	[12]
9th Co.	1860	Robinson, Daniel, 233, (1)	83	[12]
10th Co.	1860	Stoddard, Oscar O., 124, (0)	81	[13]
Elders	1857	Herriman, H., 70, (0), S.L.C. to Omaha	49	[21]

News of the Plains and Rockies
A Guide to the Series

D5. Samuel Medary (Citizens of Columbus), 1843, Report on Oregon
D6. John M. Shively, 1846, Route and distances to Oregon and California
D7. Thomas H. Jefferson, 1849, Accompaniment to map, Missouri to California
D8. Samuel R. Thurston, 1850, Geographical statistics, Oregon
D9. Thomas H. Webb and George S. Park, 1854, Emigrant Aid Co.
D10. Isaac I. Stevens, 1858, Circular to emigrants, Washington Territory
D11. Medorem Crawford, 1863, Emigrant escort to Oregon
D12. James L. Fisk, 1865, Northwestern expedition, colony for Yellowstone

VOLUME 3

E. MISSIONARIES, MORMONS, 1821-1864
E1. William D. Robinson, 1821, North West coast
E2. John Dunbar, 1835, Extracts from the journal
E3. Samuel Parker, 1836, Rocky Mountain Indians
E4. Henry H. Spalding and William H. Gray, 1837, Indians west of Rocky Mts.
E5. Cornelius Rogers, 1838, Journey to the Rocky Mountains
E6. Brigham Young, 1848, General epistle from the council
E7. Brigham Young, 1849, First general epistle
E8. Brigham Young, 1849, Second general epistle
E9. Modeste Demers, 1849, Mission de Vancouver
E10. John B. Franklin, 1858, Horrors of Mormonism
E11. Anonymous, 1864, Abridged Mormon guide

F. INDIAN AGENTS, CAPTIVES, 1832-1865
F1. Isaac McCoy, 1832, Country for Indians
F2. Rachel Plummer, 1838, Rachael Plummer's servitude
F3. Caroline Harris, 1838, Captivity of Caroline Harris
F4. Clarissa Plummer, 1838, Captivity of Clarissa Plummer
F5. Thomas Fitzpatrick, 1847, Agent's letter, Bent's Fort
F6. Thomas Fitzpatrick, 1848, Report of agent, Upper Arkansas
F7. Louis Smith, 1853, Jane Adeline Wilson captivity
F8. Alfred Cumming, 1856, Indians on the Upper Missouri
F9. Edward R. Geary, 1861, Depredations by Snakes
F10. Charles D. Poston, 1865, Speech on Indian affairs

VOLUME 4

G. WARRIORS, 1834-1865
G1. Thompson B. Wheelock, 1834, Col. Dodge's expedition
G2. Joel R. Poinsett, 1838, Protection of Western frontier
G3. Anonymous, 1839, S. W. Kearny's Dragoon expedition
G4. Joel R. Poinsett, 1840, Defence of Western frontier
G5. Stephen W. Kearny, 1845, Summer campaign to the Rocky Mts.
G6. Thomas Swords, 1848, Ft. Leavenworth to California
G7. James H. Carleton, 1855, Excursion to the ruins of Abo
G8. Randolph B. Marcy, 1858, Camp Scott to New Mexico
G9. James H. Carleton, 1860, Massacre at Mt. Meadows
G10. Alfred Sully, 1864, Indian expedition
G11. John M. Chivington, 1865, To the people of Colorado...Sand Creek
G12. John Evans, 1865, Reply re massacre of Cheyennes
G13. John W. Wright, 1865, Chivington massacre of Cheyennes

H. SCIENTISTS, ARTISTS, 1835-1859
H1. John Ball, 1835, Geology west of Rocky Mountains